Architect's Illustrated Pocket Dictionary

Architect's Illustrated Pocket Dictionary

Nikolas Davies and Erkki Jokiniemi

ELSEVIER

AMSTERDAM • BOSTON • HEIDELBERG • LONDON
NEW YORK • OXFORD • PARIS • SAN DIEGO
SAN FRANCISCO • SINGAPORE • SYDNEY • TOKYO

Architectural Press is an imprint of Elsevier

Architectural
Press

Architectural Press is an imprint of Elsevier
The Boulevard, Langford Lane, Kidlington, Oxford, OX5 1GB, UK
30 Corporate Drive, Suite 400, Burlington, MA 01803, USA

First edition 2011

British Library Cataloguing-in-Publication Data
A catalogue record for this book is available from the British Library

Library of Congress Cataloging-in-Publication Data
A catalog record for this book is available from the Library of Congress

ISBN: 978-0-08-096537-6

For information on all Architectural Press publications
visit our website at www.elsevierdirect.com

Printed and bound in Great Britain

11 12   10 9 8 7 6 5 4 3 2 1

Preface

This book is a pocket edition of the *Dictionary of Architecture and Building Construction*, compiled by the authors over 15 years, and published in 2008 by the Architectural Press. It differs in format from its predecessor in that terms pertaining particularly to architecture and related professions have been selected from the original manuscript, and illustrations have been located with their subject words, as opposed to in a separate section. Many definitions have been updated, and new terms included. A full bibliography of reference works can be found in the original book.

For this edition, thanks are due to those competent and helpful staff at Elsevier — Renata Corbani, Rhys Griffiths, Soo Hamilton, Amy Laurens and Liz Burton — who worked on the book in its various stages and gave us free rein with the layout concept and cover designs. A special mention should also be given to Hannah Shakespeare for her undiluted enthusiasm and efficacy, without which this book would not have seen the light of day. As always, thanks also to the members of our extended family — Paula, Liisa, Eeva-Maija, Pauli, Maria, Sara, Robin and Samuel — for their support and patience throughout.

Nikolas Davies, Erkki Jokiniemi
Helsinki, October 2010

A

abaciscus Lat.; diminutive form of the word abacus; a patterned tile or rectangular area in a mosaic.

abacus Lat.; a flat squared slab at the very top of a classical column, the upper part of a capital above an echinus and below an entablature; see abaciscus.

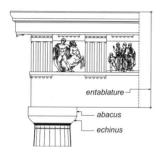

entablature
abacus
echinus

abele see poplar.

Abies spp. see fir.

above ground see surface.

abraded finish see ground, honed, rubbed finish.

abrasion the act of being rubbed or worn down.

abrasion resistance the resistance of a surface, coating, etc. to marking or scratching.

ABS acrylonitrile butadiene styrene.

absolute humidity the moisture content of air measured as the weight of water vapour per unit volume of air; SI units are kg/m^3.

absorber in acoustics, any component, unit or surface treatment for absorbing sound in a space; see also resonator.

absorbing glass see tinted solar control glass.

absorption a physical phenomenon, the soaking up of a liquid by a porous solid, a gas by a liquid, or energy in the form of sound, heat or light by matter; see sound absorption, attenuation.

absorption coefficient in room acoustics, a measure of the capacity of a material or construction to absorb sound of a given frequency incident upon it; see sound absorption coefficient.

absorptivity a material property, the ability of a solid to absorb a liquid, radiation, energy, etc.; see thermal absorptivity, light absorptivity.

abutment 1 the meeting place, joint or lap of two adjacent components, parts of construction, etc.
2 the planar joint formed by two surfaces or edges placed adjacent to or touching one another.
3 the meeting of the upper edge or verge of a pitched roof and a balustrade, parapet or upper wall surface; especially the vertical surface or structure which rises from this.
4 the part of a loadbearing system or member from which loads are supported.
5 walling or support on either side of the impost of an arch to prevent it from splaying outwards.
6 see end abutment.

abutment flashing in roof construction, a vertical sheetmetal flashing used with profiled sheet or interlocking tile roofing at an abutment.

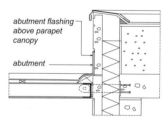

abutment flashing above parapet canopy

abutment

abutting tenon joint, butt tenon joint; a timber joint in which the grain ends of two tenons inserted in a common mortise from opposite sides abut each other.

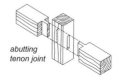

abutting tenon joint

AC see alternating current.

acacia [*Acacia spp.*] a genus of bushes and hardwood trees from warm climates, whose wood is used for outdoor furniture; specimens are often planted as ornamentals in countries with suitable conditons of warmth; *Acacia melanoxylon*, see Australian blackwood.

acanthus Lat.; carved and decorative ornament found especially adorning classical Corinthian capitals, based on stylized leaves of the Mediterranean acanthus plant, Bear's breech or brank-ursine [*Acanthus molla, Acanthus spinosus*]; akanthos in Greek.

Greek acanthus motif

accelerated curing see heat treatment.

accelerated set in concretework, an increase in the rate of stiffening during the setting of concrete.

accelerating admixture, accelerator see set accelerating admixture, strength accelerating admixture.

accent lighting interior lighting designed to illuminate or accentuate features in a room, such as artwork, architectural details and furnishings.

accepted risk, excepted risk; in project administration, known risks in construction such as uncertain ground conditions, etc., referred to in the building contract, for which the client accepts liability.

acceptor a metal or extruded plastics product attached at the edge of a wall opening, to which a door or window frame can be easily attached.

access, passage; internal or external circulation space leading to a building, opening or technical installation, or used as a route; the point at which a building or site can be entered; see site access.

access control any of a number of security systems using locks, surveillance equipment and card readers within buildings or restricted areas to allow the circulation of authorized persons but inhibit the passage of intruders.

access cover a covering hatch, plate or construction attached over an access opening in a drainage pipe, duct or vessel, removed to allow for cleaning and maintenance.

access door, access window, trapdoor; a removable panel in formwork which allows for internal inspection, cleaning, etc.

access floor, cavity floor, raised floor; flooring supported above a main floor structure to allow for the passage of electric and computer cables, ducts and other services beneath; see also platform floor.

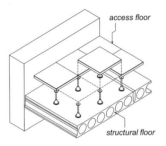

access floor

structural floor

access gully a drainage gully with a rodding eye for cleaning.

access pipe a drainage pipe with an opening for cleaning.

access stair, service stair; a secondary stairway providing access to plant or other installations.

access window see access door.

accessibility 1 the regulative requirement that buildings should be designed and constructed to allow easy access for the elderly, infirm, disabled, those with prams, etc., with the inclusion of appropriate ramps, handrails, widths of circulation spaces, lifts, etc.
2 in town and traffic planning, a measure of how easily and by which mode of transport a particular area can be reached.
3 the ability of a component or construction to be easily accessed for maintenance, repair, replacement, etc.

accessory any small components used to affix or supplement a construction, or fixings and trim supplied with a product, component or system.

accidental air see entrapped air.

accordion door a folding door with a number of hinged vertical panels which fold together when the door is open.

accordion door

accoupled in classical architecture, a description of columns or pilasters arranged in pairs, twinned or joined together.

knotted accoupled columns in St Mark's, Venice

Accrington brick a hard, dark red brick made of shale from East Lancashire in England, used for engineering and industrial purposes.

Acer spp. see maple.

acetal see polyoximethylene.

acetate a salt or ester of acetic acid, used for many plastic household products, as cellulose acetate for record discs and clear plastic sheet, etc.; acetate compounds included as separate entries are listed below:
*amyl acetate; *cellulose acetate, CA; *lead acetate; *polyacetate, see polyoximethylene, POM; *polyvinyl acetate, PVA.

acetone a colourless, strong-smelling, volatile and flammable liquid distilled from organic compounds and used as a solvent.

acid cleaning a cleaning treatment for metals using sulphuric, phosphoric or citric acids in combination with surfactants to remove contaminants, rust and scale from the surface.

acid-curing referring to two-pack lacquers and paints used on interior timber surfaces, based on urea or melamine formaldehyde resins, with good surface hardness and long pot-life and which harden by blending with an acid.

acidity, degree of acidity; the acid level of a soil, solution, etc., as measured by obtaining its pH level; see pH.

acid wash a cleaning treatment for concrete and stonework by sponging with a solution of acid salts.

ACM see polyacrylate rubber.

acorn an ovoid finial resembling the fruiting body of an oak tree; used as an ornamental terminating element for a balustrade or pier, etc., often unembellished; see pineapple, pine cone.

acorn

acorn nut see cap nut.

acoustics 1 the study of sound and hearing; the discipline of space design with regard to sound.
2 the properties of a room pertaining to sound; see room acoustics.

acoustic, acoustical; dealing with or based on sound, or the treatment of sound.

acoustic absorber see absorber, muffler.

acoustic absorption see sound absorption.

acoustic absorption coefficient see sound absorption coefficient.

acoustical analysis a study of the sound insulating, absorbing and reflecting characteristics of a building or space, or a project at design stage.

acoustical design the design of a building or space with respect to absorption, insulation or enhancement of sound.

acoustical glass see sound control glass.

acoustical treatment see acoustic treatment.

acoustic attenuation see attenuation.

acoustic attenuator see muffler.

acoustic board softboard whose surface is shaped, perforated or machined to improve its properties of sound absorption.

perforated acoustic board panel with mineral wool backing

acoustic ceiling a ceiling designed to provide sound insulation or absorption for a space.

acoustic consultant see acoustician.

acoustic control glass see sound control glass.

acoustic engineer see acoustician.

acoustic glass see sound control glass.

acoustician, acoustic engineer; an expert who provides professional consultancy on acoustic matters.

acoustic insulation see sound insulation.

acoustic intensity, acoustic intensity level see sound intensity.

acoustic isolation see sound insulation.

acoustic level, acoustic level meter see sound level.

acoustic mortar see acoustic plaster.

acoustic panel a panel designed to absorb sound and thus regulate the acoustic quality of a space.

acoustic plaster plaster containing lightweight or other porous aggregates, used for its acoustic properties, especially sound absorption; also called acoustic mortar.

acoustic plasterwork plasterwork containing aggregate which has acoustic properties; finished work in acoustic plaster.

acoustic power, acoustic power level see sound power.

acoustic pressure, acoustic pressure level see sound pressure.

acoustic propagation see sound propagation.

acoustic spectrum see audio spectrum.

acoustic treatment, acoustics; physical or spatial measures, materials or components added to affect the acoustic perception and performance in a space with respect to sound insulation, absorption and reflection.

acroterion, acroter; in classical architecture, a plinth or pedestal for statues, set at the apex or eaves of a temple; also often the statues or ornaments themselves; plural acroteria; Latin form is acroterium, Greek is akroterion.

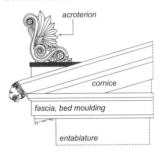

acroterion

cornice

fascia, bed moulding

entablature

acrylate adhesive acrylic-based polymer adhesive used for soft plastic seams and adhesive tapes.

acrylic a synthetic polymer resin used in plastics, paints, adhesives and textiles.

acrylic baking enamel see acrylic stoving enamel.

acrylic cellular sheet, cellular acrylic sheet; cellular sheet glazing or cladding manufactured from transparent acrylic resin.

acrylic finish, acrylic coating; any surface covering or coating, such as tiling, boarding and paints, whose finish is acrylic.

acrylic flooring compound a hardwearing flooring for sports halls, corridors, etc. laid over concrete floor slabs as a mixture of liquid acrylic, powdered hardener and fine aggregate.

acrylic paint emulsion paint based on a dispersion of acrylic in water.

acrylic polymer flooring see acrylic flooring compound.

acrylic powder coating, stoved acrylic; a hardwearing decorative coating whose binder is acrylic resin, applied to metal components as a powder and baked on.

acrylic primer acrylic paint used as a primer or undercoat.

acrylic rubber see polyacrylate rubber.

acrylic sealant an acrylic-based flexible sealant used for dry applications.

acrylic sheet strong translucent or opaque lightweight sheet of polymethyl methacrylate plastics used for glazing and cladding; marketed as Perspex and Plexiglas.

acrylic stoving enamel, acrylic baking enamel; a hardwearing paint coating used in the automotive industry, based on acrylic resin applied to metal surfaces as a liquid spray and baked on.

acrylonitrile butadiene styrene, ABS; a tough, strong thermoplastic used for waste pipes, garage doors, small vehicles and taxi-cab roofs.

act of God see force majeure.

active earth pressure the pressure of earth acting against the side of a retaining wall and against which it provides resistance.

active fire protection mechanical or electronic control systems such as sprinklers, fire alarms, etc. for indicating the presence of or extinguishing hazardous fires in buildings.

active leaf the door leaf in a double door usually used for throughfare.

doorset with active leaf closed and inactive leaf open to show fire exit bolt

acute arch see lancet arch.

Adam style a style in interior decoration in England from 1760—1770 named after the Adam brothers, John, Robert and James, and characterized by classical motifs and bold colours.

addendum a separate explanatory statement intended to clarify, amend or supplement a document, drawing, etc.

additional work see extra work.

additive a substance added to a material or process to modify its chemical or physical properties.

addressable system, intelligent fire alarm; an electronic installation for indicating the location and severity of an outbreak of hazardous fire in a building.

adhering knot see tight knot.

adhesion, bond; the action of sticking together; the strength of the attractive or fastening force evolved between a surface material or coating and its backing, or between two components which have been glued or bonded together.

adhesive a sticky solid or liquid bonding substance used for the firm sticking, surface-joining and holding together of materials and components as the adhesive dries or sets; the words adhesive and glue are generally synonymous, although adhesive is often applied to more technologically advanced products, whilst glues are often of plant or animal origin; a cement is an inorganic adhesive which sets in hard, brittle form; types of adhesive included as separate entries are listed below:
*aerosol glue, see spray adhesive; *albumen glue; *anaerobic adhesive; *animal glue; *aqueous adhesive, see water-based; bituminous adhesive; *bone glue; *brushing adhesive; *casein glue; *cassava; *cellulose adhesive; *cold curing adhesive; *cold glue, see cold setting adhesive, cold curing adhesive; *cold setting adhesive; *collagen glue, see animal glue; *contact adhesive; *cyanoacrylate adhesive; *elastomeric adhesive; *emulsion glue, emulsion adhesive; *epoxide resin adhesive, epoxy adhesive, epoxy glue, see epoxy resin adhesive; *film adhesive, see film glue; *fish glue; *gluten glue; *gunnable adhesive, see gun applied adhesive; *hide glue; *hot-melt adhesive, hot-melt glue, see thermoplastic adhesive; *hot setting adhesive, hot setting glue, see thermosetting adhesive; *interior adhesive; *isinglass, see fish glue; *melamine formaldehyde glue; *moisture curing adhesive; *moisture resistant adhesive; *one-way stick adhesive; *phenol formaldehyde glue; *polymer adhesive, polymer glue,

*see polymerizing adhesive; *polyvinyl acetate glue; protein glue; *PVA glue, polyvinyl acetate glue; *resin adhesive, resin glue, see synthetic resin adhesive; *resorcinol formaldehyde glue; *rubber adhesive, rubber glue, see elastomeric adhesive; *rubber solution; *Scotch glue; *single spread adhesive, see one-way stick adhesive; *solvent adhesive; *solvent-based adhesive, see solvent borne adhesive; *soya glue; *spray adhesive; *starch adhesive; *structural adhesive; *super glue, see cyanoacrylate adhesive; *synthetic resin adhesive; *synthetic rubber glue, see elastomeric adhesive; *thermoplastic glue, see thermoplastic adhesive; *thermosetting adhesive; *two pack adhesive, two component adhesive, two part adhesive; *two-way stick adhesive; urea formaldehyde glue; *vegetable glue; *water-borne adhesive, see water-based; *waterproof glue, waterproof adhesive, see water-resistant adhesive; *water-based adhesive, see water-based; *wood glue, see wood adhesive.*

adhesive failure, bond failure; the failure of a glued joint due to a reduction in bonding between a glue or binder and glued parts.

adiabatic referring to a thermodynamics process which occurs without the transfer of heat.

adjustable item an item in a bill of quantities for which provided information is insufficient and whose quantities are subject to reassessment.

adjustable prop see telescopic prop.

adjustable set square in technical drawing, a set square in which the angle of the hypotenuse can be adjusted by a sliding mechanism.

adjustable spanner a spanner with screw-adjustable jaws to suit a range of widths.

adjustable wrench see adjustable spanner.

adjustment see formula price adjustment.

admiralty brass an alloy of copper and zinc with additional tin to improve corrosion resistance and increase strength.

admixture a material added in small quantities to affect the properties of a concrete or mortar mix; types of admixture included as separate entries are listed below; see also agent.
*accelerating admixture, see set accelerating admixture, strength accelerating admixture; *air-detraining admixture; *air-entraining admixture; *anti-foaming admixture; *antifreezing admixture; *bonding admixture; *colouring admixture; *corrosion inhibiting admixture; *expansion producing admixture; *flocculating admixture; *foam forming admixture; *fungicidal admixture; *gas forming admixture; *high-range water-reducing admixture, see superplasticizing admixture; *mortar admixture; *permeability-reducing admixture, see pore filler; *plasticizing admixture; *set accelerating admixture; *set retarding admixture; *strength accelerating admixture; *superplasticizing admixture; *thickening admixture; *water reducing admixture; *waterproofing admixture, see water-resisting admixture.*

adobe clay and unfired brick which has been baked in the sun; forms of construction making use of this; see mud brick.

adsorption 1 the intake of a liquid or gas by a solid.
2 a water purification treatment in which water is percolated through solid granular material, to which impurities adhere.

adularia a transparent variety of the mineral orthoclase or potash feldspar found in the Alps; a milky variety of this is known as moonstone.

advance, advance payment, prepayment; a payment made prior to receipt of goods or services, such as that paid by a client to a contractor after the contract is signed but before the start of work.

adze eye hammer a hammer whose head is fixed to the shaft by means of a sleeve at the base of the head.

aedicule, aedicula (Lat.); in classical architecture, a niche, recess or pedimented structure, especially one housing a statue, surrounded by columns, pilasters or colonnettes.

aedicule

Aeolic capital in classical architecture, a forerunner of the Ionic capital with a rectangular upper section supported by volutes divided by palmette decoration.

Aeolic capital   *Ionic capital*

aerated concrete, cellular concrete, porous concrete; various types of lightweight concrete for in-situ work and precast products with good thermal insulation, produced by the introduction of bubbles of gas into the mix, either by a foaming agent, by adding foam, by mechanical foaming or by adding a chemical which reacts with the concrete to produce gas bubbles; see also gas concrete, foamed concrete.

aeration the introduction of air into a material such as soil, water, concrete, etc.; especially the introduction of oxygen into raw sewage to reduce the quantity of other dissolved gases.

aerator see tap aerator.

aerial, antenna, (pl. antennae); a telecommunications receiver for airborne electromagnetic transmissions; see also satellite link aerial.
aerial amplifier an electronic device for increasing the strength of signals picked up by an antenna or aerial.

aerial view a presentation drawing, graphic visualization or photograph in which the subject or scene is viewed from above.

aerosol a suspension of fine particles of solid or liquid in a gas, usually air.
aerosol glue see spray adhesive.
aerosol spraying the spraying of a paint, varnish, glue or other liquid from a pressurized airtight container to form an aerosol, a suspension of fine particles of paint in a gas.

Aesculapian column see serpent column.

Aesculus spp. see horse chestnut; *Aesculus hippocastanum*, see European horse chestnut.

aetoma see aetos.

aetos, aetoma; Gk.; in classical Greek architecture, the tympanum of a pediment, usually ornamented with figures.

A-frame a simple triangulated framework of two leaning beams meeting at a ridge, connected by a stiffening collar.

A-frame crucks in traditional timber-framed building

afara see limba.

African cherry see makore.

African ebony [*Diospyros crassiflora, Diospyros piscatoria*], see ebony.

African mahogany, khaya; [*Khaya ivorensis, Khaya spp.*] a group of West African hardwoods with relatively strong and durable orange-brown timber; used for interior joinery, furniture and boatbuilding; true mahogany comes from the South and Central American trees *Swietenia spp.*

African walnut, alona, Congo wood; [*Lovoa trichilioides, Lovoa klaineana*] a West African hardwood with plain golden-brown timber; used for furniture, panelling and veneers.

African whitewood see obeche.

afrormosia, kokrodua; [*Pericopsis elata*] a West African hardwood with rich yellow-brown timber used for internal and external joinery, furniture and as a substitute for teak.

afzelia, doussie; [*Afzelia spp.*] a group of African hardwoods with durable reddish-brown timber; used for interior and external joinery and cladding.

agent 1 a material or substance used for its effect on another material or process; in concreting it is often called an admixture; types of agent included as separate entries are listed below:
*air-detraining agent, see air-detraining admixture; *air-entraining agent, see air-entraining admixture; *alkaline cleaning agent; *binding agent, see binder; *bonding agent; *cleaning agent; *colouring agent, see colourant; *emulsifying agent, see emulsifier; *flocculating agent, see flocculating admixture; *foaming agent; *polishing agent, see polish; *release agent; *retarding agent, see retarder; *surface-acting agent; *suspension agent, thickening agent, see thickening admixture.*
2 one employed to organize matters on behalf of another.
3 see also site agent.

agglomerated cork a light, porous, buoyant material manufactured by reconstituting granulated cork to form slabs and other products.

aggregate inert granular material such as sand, gravel, crushed rock and clinker used as a main solid constituent in concrete, plaster, tarmacadam and asphalt; types of aggregate listed as separate entries are listed below:
*angular aggregate; *blended aggregate; *coarse aggregate; *continuously-graded aggregate; *crushed aggregate; *crusher-run aggregate; *cubical aggregate; *elongated aggregate; *expanded clay aggregate, expanded shale aggregate, see expanded aggregate; *fine aggregate; *flaky aggregate; *flaky and elongated aggregate; *gap graded aggregate; *graded aggregate; *light expanded clay aggregate, see expanded aggregate;* *lightweight aggregate; *manufactured aggregate; *natural aggregate; *rounded aggregate; *single sized aggregate; *sintered aggregate; *wood particle aggregate.*

aggregate block same as aggregate concrete block.

aggregate/cement ratio the ratio of the mass of aggregate to that of cement in concrete or mortar.

aggregate concrete block see concrete block, usually refers to a lightweight aggregate concrete block.

aggregate exposure a finish treatment for a concrete surface in which water, or in some cases acid, is sprayed to wash away the surface layer of cement, revealing the coarse aggregate; the result is called exposed aggregate concrete.

agreement a binding decision made between two parties, a contract; see articles of agreement.

agricultural drain see field drain.

A-hinge a hinge whose leaves are elongated and triangular, forming a lozenge shape when opened out; used for hanging wide or heavy doors.

A-hinge

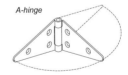

aid any substance added to a process to make it function more efficiently rather than affect the properties of the resulting product.

aileron in church architecture and similar structures, a gable with one vertical edge closing the end of an aisle; a half-gable.

aileron

facade of Il Gesú, Rome, architect Giacomo Della Porta, 1568–1584

air admittance valve a valve in a drainage system to permit the entrance of ventilating fresh air and to even out pressure differences.

airborne sound sound conveyed as pressure waves in air.

air brick, ventilating brick; a brick with regular round perforations from stretcher face to stretcher face, used to reduce the weight of walling construction and for ventilating cavity walls, basement spaces, etc.

air-change rate, ventilation rate; the specified number of times per hour that ventilating air in a room is completely renewed and old air extracted, expressed as the hourly volume of air provided to a space divided by the volume of the space.

air conditioning a mechanical installation system providing warmed, cooled, clean and otherwise treated air into the habitable spaces of a building; see also central air conditioning.
air-conditioning duct an air duct used in an air-conditioning installation.
air-conditioning unit, air-handling unit; a piece of mechanical services equipment for treating air and conveying clean air into a space or building.

air content the total amount of air in a substance, expressed as a percentage by volume; in concreting, it is the total volume of air voids per unit volume in vibrated concrete, expressed as a percentage.

air-detraining admixture, air-detraining agent; in concretework, an admixture included in the concrete mix to inhibit the inclusion of air.

air diffuser in air conditioning, an inlet grille which gives direction to supply air passing through it.

air-distribution system in air conditioning, an installation consisting of ducting and pumping plant for distributing treated air to outlets.

air dried, air seasoned; timber having reached equilibrium with outdoor atmospheric humidity, specified as 12% moisture content.

air duct in air conditioning and mechanical ventilation, a long closed pipe or vessel of sheetmetal for conveying air to its points of use; see also ventilation duct.

air-entrained concrete a form of concrete with increased workability and resistance to weathering and frost, into which minute bubbles of air have been introduced using an air-entraining admixture.
air-entraining admixture, air-entraining agent; an admixture included in the concrete mix to promote the inclusion of air to improve its workability and frost resistance.

air filter in air conditioning, a porous barrier to collect impurities and particles from intake air.

air gap 1 in piped water supply, the vertical height between the outlet of a tap and rim of a sink, or ballvalve and overflow, a measure of the precaution against backsiphonage.
2 a narrow space between adjacent building components or materials allowed for in construction for the circulation of ventilating air, or for insulating purposes.

air-gap membrane a resilient membrane of high density polyethylene or similar polymer preformed with a grid of dimples or raised pattern, laid against foundation walls as tanking, also providing a small ventilating gap to allow moisture a passage out of the substructure; also called a cavity drainage membrane or tanking membrane.

air-handling luminaire a light fitting so designed that exhaust air from an air-conditioning or ventilation system is extracted through it.

air-handling plant room see ventilation plant room.

air-handling unit see air-conditioning unit, fan unit.

air inlet see fresh-air inlet, fresh-air vent.

air intake see return-air terminal unit.

air jet, airstream; the directed flow of ventilation and air-conditioning air produced by a supply air inlet.

airless spraying, hydraulic spraying; an industrial painting process employing a high-pressure pistol with a fine nozzle to apply even coatings to building components and furniture.

air lock 1 an intermediate enclosed space or lobby between spaces with different environments or air conditions, affording access from one space to the other with minimal movement of air between the two.

2 an unwanted bubble of air trapped in pipework, inhibiting the flow of water or other fluids.

air outlet see supply air terminal unit.

air pocket see air void.

air release valve, bleed valve, pet-cock; a valve for releasing unwanted air or other gases from a system of pipes, cisterns, etc.

air resistance the property of a pigment in paint to remain stable both in colour and structure when exposed to the effects of air and airborne pollutants.

air seasoned see air dried.

airstream see air jet.

air-supported structure, pneumatic structure; any structure inflated with air as a means of structural support.

air terminal unit in air conditioning and ventilation, any device, grille, diffuser, etc. through which air is supplied to or extracted from a space; see also supply air terminal unit.

air termination a component or system of vertical or horizontal metal rods located on a roof to intercept lightning strikes; part of a lightning protection installation for a building.

air test, pneumatic test; a test to inspect and locate leaks in pipework using compressed air which is introduced into the closed system and its pressure monitored over a period of time.

air-to-air heat transmission coefficient see U-value.

air treatment in air conditioning, the heating, cooling, purifying, filtering and humidifying or dehumidifying of air from the outside prior to distribution.

air vent a terminal device designed to allow the passage of fresh air to a space from the outside, or for release of stale air.

air void, air pocket; in concretework, small spaces or voids in hardened concrete containing air and formed by air bubbles either intentionally introduced as entrained air or unintentionally as entrapped air.

aisle an open passageway in a building, auditorium, etc. for circulation; especially the longitudinal corridor flanking the nave of a church, basilica, etc., bounded by an arcade or row of columns.

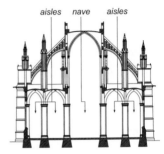

aisles   nave   aisles

alabaster a compact, fine-grained form of pure gypsum (calcium sulphate) with similar rocks such as calcareous sinter or onyx marble; easily worked, and used for interior decoration and sculptured ornament.

alarm any security or safety device which produces a signal in the form of a noise or light once triggered by a detector; see also fire alarm.

alarm bell a metal percussive device which produces a noise as an alarm sound.

alarm glass laminated glass whose inter-layer is inlaid with fine electric wires connected to a circuit, which activate an alarm if broken.

alarm system a system of warning bells, lights and other means which react to the presence of hazards in buildings such as fire, toxic gases and unauthorized entrants; see also intruder alarm system.

albumen glue glue manufactured from egg protein.

alcove any recess formed in the thickness of, or bounded by, the wall of a room.

alder [*Alnus spp.*] a group of hardwoods with light, soft, fine-textured, non-durable, pinkish timber; alders are hardy trees which can survive on poorly drained soils, available in a number of varieties and planted occasionally as waterside or street trees.

*common alder,
Alnus glutinosa*

common alder, black alder; [*Alnus glutinosa*] a European hardwood with light, soft, pale brown timber; used for joinery and plywood.

grey alder, white alder (Am); [*Alnus incana*] a European hardwood with light, soft, dull brown timber; used for plywood.

red alder [*Alnus rubra*] a North American hardwood with rich reddish timber, stronger than common alder, used for furniture and as a substitute for mahogany.

Alexandrian blue see Egyptian blue.

alidade, diopter; a sighting device for a surveying level.

alignment 1 the compositional lining up of a series of building masses or adjacent constructional surfaces, points and patterns.
2 a prehistoric straight row of standing stones, laid out for ceremonial, astronomical or symbolic purposes.

alizarin 1 a red dye used by the ancients and produced by grinding the root of the common madder plant [*Rubia tinctorum*], also known as madder red; see purpurin. After 1868 it has been manufactured artificially from anthraquinone, a coal tar derivative, and is known variously as alizarin crimson, alizarin lake, alizarin red, alizarin scarlet, or in brown form as madder brown, brown madder or alizarin brown.
2 a range of dyestuffs manufactured in this way, with the addition of metal oxides to impart different shades of colour, as alizarin blue, alizarin violet, alizarin yellow, etc.

alkali-aggregate reaction, concrete cancer; an undesirable chemical reaction in concrete between alkalis contained in the Portland cement binder and some aggregates, causing internal swelling, rupture and scaling of the surface.

alkali feldspar a mineral, potassium feldspar or sodium-enriched plagioclase rock.

alkaline cleaning agent any highly effective metal cleaning product based on a solution of sodium hydroxide (caustic soda) or potassium hydroxide (NaOH, KOH), silicates, or phosphates, with a balanced amount of surfactants in water.

alkali-resistant paint acrylic or resin paint with good resistance to alkali attack, suitable for use on concrete surfaces.

alkali-resistant primer primer used on concrete surfaces beneath other paints to protect them against alkali attack from the concrete.

alkali wash a treatment to remove grease and other impurities from metal surfaces with an alkaline solution containing a detergent and a surfactant before coating or painting.

alkyd a synthetic polyester resin used in the manufacture of paints and coatings, formed by combining an alcohol with an acid.

alkyd baking enamel see alkyd stoving enamel.

alkyd paint an oil paint which contains alkyd resins, used externally as a coating and wood preservative; it is easy to brush, durable and quick drying.

alkyd putty a sealing and glazing compound with an alkyd resin binder.

alkyd stoving enamel, alkyd baking enamel; a hardwearing paint coating used for metal components, based on a melamine or carbamine and alkyd resin binder, applied as a liquid spray and baked on.

alkyd varnish a varnish with alkyd resin as a binder, used as a protective coating for furniture, joinery and timber floors.

allen head screw a screw with hexagonal recess in its head, turned using an allen key.

all-glass a description of components such as doors, cabinets, balustrades, partitions, etc. which are made from sheets of unframed toughened glass through-bolted with steel fixings; when used for facades, this type of construction is known as structural glazing.

all-glass balustrade a simple balustrade which is a sheet of toughened and/or laminated glass, secured at its lower edge.

all-glass door a door whose leaf is an unframed sheet of structural glass, often tempered or laminated, to which hinges and door furniture are fixed.

all-glass door

alligatoring see crocodiling.

allowance, clearance, installation allowance; spaces left between adjacent components in design such as the space between a hinged door leaf or window casement and its frame, to allow for fitting, installation, manufacturing tolerances, expansion, workmanship and movement.

alloy a composition of two or more chemical elements, one of which is always a metal, combined together to form a metal substance which benefits from their combined properties to provide improved strength, ductility, corrosion resistance, etc.

alloy steel steel which contains over 5% carbon and other metals to improve its basic properties of strength, hardness and resistance to corrosion.

Alnus spp. see alder.

alona see African walnut.

alteration a minor change to a building, requiring construction work.

alternate bay construction; see chequerboard construction, alternate lane construction.

alternate lane construction, alternate bay construction; a method of casting large areas of concrete floors, etc. in which adjacent parallel areas are cast first and harden prior to casting of the remaining voids; see chequerboard construction.

alternating current, AC; electric current which reverses its direction of flow at a regular frequency.

alternating tread stair a stair with wedge-shaped steps arranged so that their wider edges alternate from side to side as the stair is ascended, used for steep stairs where space is limited.

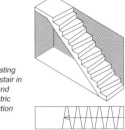
alternating tread stair in plan and isometric projection

alto rilievo, high relief; sculptured relief ornament in which figures or elements are carved to such a depth as to appear separate from their background.

alum gypsum, marble gypsum; a mixture of plaster of Paris soaked with alum solution (a sulphate salt of aluminium and potassium), burnt and finely ground, used as a high-strength, hard plaster for tiles, boards, render and in-situ work.

alumina, aluminium oxide; a chemical compound, Al_2O_3, used in the manufacture of some types of brick, as an abrasive, and as a fireproof lining for ovens; see also corundum.

alumina hydrate an artificial form of aluminium hydroxide used as an inert base in oil paints.

aluminium, aluminum (Am); a pale, lightweight, ductile, common metal, **Al**, an important building material used for lightweight construction, cladding and extrusions.

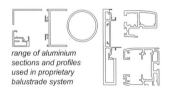
range of aluminium sections and profiles used in proprietary balustrade system

aluminium alloy aluminium which contains other metals such as manganese, magnesium and silicon to improve strength.

aluminium brass an alloy of brass with added aluminium to improve strength, hardness and corrosion resistance.

aluminium bronze a bright golden-yellow alloy of copper and aluminium which is strong and corrosion resistant.

aluminium-faced timber window see composite window.

aluminium foil aluminium produced in the form of very thin sheets.

aluminium-framed window see aluminium window.

aluminium hydroxide a non-toxic chemical alliance of aluminium with oxygen and hydrogen, **AlOH**, used as a white pigment.

aluminium paint a metallic paint consisting of powdered aluminium and a vehicle such as oil.

aluminium plate aluminium or aluminium alloy supplied in the form of metal plate.

aluminium profile often synonymous with aluminium section, but usually more complex, thin-walled or hollow; used for patent glazing, door frames, etc.

aluminium roofing see aluminium sheet.

aluminium section any thin length of aluminium steel which has been preformed by a process of welding, extrusion, etc. into a uniform cross-section of certain shape and dimensions.

aluminium sheet aluminium rolled into sheets not more than 3 mm thick; used for exterior cladding, etc.

aluminium sheet roofing profiled roofing of corrosion-free coated aluminium sheet used largely for industrial and low-cost buildings.

aluminium window a window whose frame is made primarily from coated aluminium; an aluminium-framed window; for aluminium-faced timber window, see composite window.

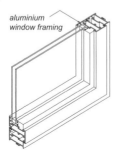

aluminium window framing

aluminium-zinc coating a protective galvanized surface coating for steel sheeting of hot-dip zinc with 55% aluminium and a small amount of silicon.

alumino-thermic welding see thermit welding.

aluminum North American spelling of aluminium.

amber, succinite; the fossilized resin from pine trees, a yellowish-brown organic mineral; used as a gemstone, for decoration and as a raw material in some paints.

ambient sound see background noise.

ambrosia beetle [*Scolytidae, Platypodidae*] a number of species of insect which cause damage to unseasoned hardwood and softwood by burrowing.

ambulatory a place for walking in a cathedral or abbey church, a cloister, apse aisle, etc.; particularly a semicircular extension of side aisles of a church to form a walk behind the high altar and round the apse; any similar processional way in a church; Latin form is ambulatorium.

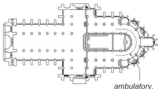

ambulatory,
Cathedral of Notre Dame, Amiens,
France, c.1220–69

amendment see revision.
  amendment arrow see arrowhead.
  amendment block see revision panel.
  amendment cloud see revision cloud.

American ash [*Fraxinus spp.*], see ash.

American beech [*Fagus grandifolia*], see beech.

American bond see English garden-wall bond.

American caisson see box caisson.

American cherry, black cherry (Am); [*Prunus serotina*], see cherry.

American elm [*Ulmus americana*], see elm.

American lime basswood see lime.

American mahogany see mahogany.

American plane, buttonwood, sycamore; [*Platanus occidentalis*], see plane.

American walnut, black walnut; [*Juglans nigra*], see walnut.

American white oak [*Quercus alba*], see oak.

American whitewood see tulipwood.

American with Flemish bond see Flemish stretcher bond.

aminobenzene see aniline.

amino-plastic a group of thermosetting resins formed by copolymerizing urea or melamine with an aldehyde, used for pressings, adhesives, coatings and laminates.

ammonia a colourless, water-soluble, gaseous, chemical compound, NH_3, which is strongly alkaline in solution and is corrosive to alloys of copper; used as a refrigerant and as a cleaning agent.

ammonium chloride, sal ammoniac; a white, crystalline, water-soluble, chemical compound, NH_4Cl, used in soldering flux, dry cells and in iron cement.

ammonium nitrate a white, crystalline, water-soluble, chemical compound, NH_4NO_3, used in explosives, fertilizers and freezing mixtures.

ammonium phosphate a chemical compound, $N_2H_9PO_4$, used as a fire-retardant and in fertilizers.

amoretto, amorino see cupid.

amorphous referring to a material whose molecules and atoms do not form a crystalline structure, or one with no determinate shape or structure.

ampere, amp; abb. **A**; SI unit of electrical current equal to a flow of one coulomb per second.

amphibole a black, dark green or brown rock-forming mineral with a double chain silicate structure, which increases the strength and toughness of the rocks in which it is found.

amphibolite a durable grey-green metamorphic rock formed from gabbro or basalt.

amphitheatre, 1 amphitheater (Am.); a classical arena for gladiatorial contests and spectacles consisting of an oval or round space surrounded by tiered seating for spectators; amphitheatron in Greek.
2 any curved or tiered structure, such as a natural hollow in the landscape used as theatre seating, a large housing mass, etc.

amplifier see aerial amplifier.

amyl acetate an organic chemical compound used as a solvent for nitrocellulose lacquers.

anaerobic adhesive an adhesive which sets by polymerization in the absence of oxygen.

anaerobic sealant a sealant which sets by polymerization in the absence of oxygen.

anaglyph referring to ornament which has been embossed or sculpted in low relief.

analogue detector an electronic fire detector which sends warning signals to a central computer in the event of fire.

anastylosis in building conservation, the process of reconstructing a historic building in such a way that new and added parts and materials are clearly differentiated from the original.

anathyrosis Gk.; the dressing of stone joints at the surface of stonework to provide a neat fit, leaving concealed areas unworked or slightly rebated.

anchor a metal fixing for connecting a structural member or secondary component firmly to a main structure or to fix something firmly in place; often called an anchorage; types of anchor included as separate entries are listed below:
*anchor bolt; *concrete screw anchor; *door-frame anchor; *ground anchor; *hollow-wall anchor; *jamb anchor; *rock anchor; *sleeve anchor, see wedge anchor.

anchorage a system of steel rods, guys, braces, bolts, etc. for fixing a structure firmly to its base or to the ground; the process thus involved; often synonymous with anchor, although anchorage is usually a construction, anchor a component; see anchor, end abutment, ground anchor, rock anchor. See illustration on facing page.

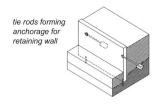

tie rods forming anchorage for retaining wall

anchor beam 1 in traditional timber frame construction, a beam whose end is anchored to a post by means of a tenon joint.

2 a timber tie beam fixed to the upper ends of parallel side walls of a building to prevent them from buckling outwards.

anchor bolt, foundation bolt, ragbolt; a bolt cast into concrete, whose threads are left protruding from the surface so that subsequent components can be attached.

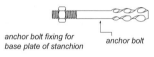

anchor bolt fixing for base plate of stanchion   *anchor bolt*

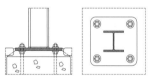

anchor bracket a fixing for attaching a pipe to a wall surface so that linear movement of the pipe is restricted.

anchor pile see piled anchorage, tension pile.

anchor strap a perforated galvanized steel strip product used for tying adjacent components such as timber framing members, brick leafs, etc. together.

anchor strap

ancient monument any ancient man-made structure such as a building or earthwork, which is of historical or cultural value and as such is protected by legislation.

ancone, ancon; in classical architecture, a curved ornamental bracket or cornice for supporting a ledge, shelf, balcony, pediment or sculpture.

ancone supporting balcony

andalusite a hard, yellowish, greenish or brownish aluminium silicate mineral used as gemstones and for decoration.

anechoic chamber an acoustic room with highly absorbing surfaces to reduce reverberation times, echoes and sound reflections to a minimum, used for testing and recording sound.

angel light in Gothic church architecture, especially of the Perpendicular period, a small triangular light between the tracery of a window, panel, or between adjacent lancets.

angle 1 the spacing or rotational dimension between two lines that diverge.

2 any profiled strip or section, L-shaped in cross-section; see angle profile, edge strip (angle bead), steel angle.

3 a component of angled guttering used at the eaves of a hipped roof to convey water around a corner.

angle bar see steel angle.

angle bead, corner bead; a strip of planed timber or other material used as trim to cover the corner joints between walls, floors, ceilings, etc.; see edge strip, plasterwork angle bead.

range of angle beads

hockey stick

cove   *quadrant*

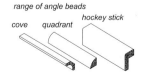

angle bevelled halved joint, lateral bevelled halved joint; a timber angled halved joint in which the laps are bevelled for increased strength.

angle brace see angle tie.

angle branch a pipe fitting for connecting a subsidiary pipe to a main pipe at an acute angle to the direction of flow.

angle brick any special brick whose end is formed at an angle other than 90° to its stretcher face, used at a change of direction at corners and curves in brick walling; see cant brick, squint brick.

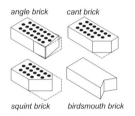

angle brick   cant brick

squint brick   birdsmouth brick

angle fillet, 1 arris fillet, cant strip; a horizontal timber strip, triangular in cross-section, laid at internal junctions in construction to round off sharp corners before the laying of membrane roofing, waterproofing, etc.

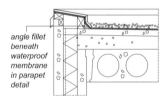

angle fillet beneath waterproof membrane in parapet detail

2 a similar triangular strip of material included in formwork to provide a chamfer in cast concrete construction.

angle grinder a hand-held power tool with a rapidly rotating thin abrasive mineral disc, used for cutting metal sections and grinding stone and metals.

angle iron see steel angle.

angle joint, corner joint; a joint formed by members which are connected but do not lie in the same line, forming an angle with one another.

angle luminaire a luminaire which provides illumination whose light distribution is noticeably directional.

angle of reflectance the angle made by a ray of light or other waveform with a reflecting surface.

angle of refraction the angle through which a ray of light bends on passing through a different medium.

angle parking, echelon parking; the layout of individual parking spaces in a sawtooth formation diagonal to a carriageway or pavement.

angle plane see corner scraper.

angle profile, angle; any metal section whose uniform cross-section resembles the letter L; in aluminium these are formed by extrusion and in steel by bending or by cold or hot rolling; also called an L-profile or L-section; see also equal angle, unequal angle, steel angle.

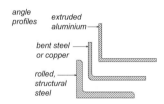

angle profiles

extruded aluminium

bent steel or copper

rolled, structural steel

angle rafter in timber roof construction, a diagonal rafter at the join of two sloping roof planes which meet at an angle; a hip rafter or valley rafter.

angle ridge see hip rafter.

angle stair see quarter turn stair.

angle tie, angle brace, diagonal brace, diagonal tie, dragon tie; in traditional timber frame construction, a diagonal member in the horizontal plane used to brace and tie together a corner joint; a similar brace in contemporary construction.

angle tile 1 in floor and wall tiling, a special L-shaped ceramic tile for covering an internal or external corner.
2 a similarly shaped exterior clay or concrete tile for tile hanging, covering the ridges and hips of tiled roofs, etc.

angle trowel, corner trowel; a plasterer's L-shaped trowel for smoothing inside and outside corners in plasterwork; see twitcher trowel (internal angle trowel), external angle trowel.

angular aggregate coarse aggregate whose particles have sharp edges.

angular guilloche see meander.

angular hip tile a special L-shaped roof tile for covering the ridge formed by a hip.

angular ridge tile an L-shaped ridge capping tile for covering the ridge of a roof.

anhydrite, anhydrous calcium sulphate; natural mineral calcium sulphate, **CaSO₄**; used as a form of plaster and often produced by burning gypsum at high temperatures; see synthetic anhydrite.

anhydrous lacking water, especially that for crystallization.

anhydrous calcium sulphate see anhydrite.

anhydrous lime see quicklime.

aniline, aminobenzene; a colourless oily liquid, originally produced by the distillation of the indigo plant [*Indigofera anil, Indigofera suffruticosa, Indigofera tinctoria*], now manufactured from nitrobenzene and used as a base in the production of dyes, drugs, plastics and rubber products; aniline colours are a group of synthetic organic pigments in use prior to the introduction of more permanent pigments.

animal capital see protome capital, bull capital, eagle capital, lion capital.

animal column, beast column; a decorative Romanesque stone column-type richly sculpted with intertwined animal figures.

animal column, abbey church of St. Pierre Moissac, France, c. 1115–20

animal-fibre reinforced referring to composites of animal hair in a binder,

traditionally used for cast and in-situ plasterwork, insulation, building boards and panels.

animal glue glue made from collagen, a protein released by boiling the bones, hides, sinews and muscles of animals; see bone glue, hide glue.

animal interlace, lacertine; any ornament which consists of stylized animal motifs.

anionic bitumen emulsion a dispersion of bitumen in water, with an emulsifying additive which coats the particles of bitumen with a negative ion, causing them to repel one another and to remain as separate droplets.

anisotropic referring to a material, object or construction which does not display the same properties in all directions; see also isotropic.

annealing a heat treatment to soften steel and relieve internal stresses caused by work hardening or welding; the temperature is raised by heating right through to a certain level and then lowered slowly and evenly.

annealed glass ordinary untoughened glass that has been heated in an oven then cooled slowly to relieve internal stresses that would otherwise arise; cf. toughened glass.

annealed wire see binding wire.

annosus root rot, butt rot; [*Fomes annosus, Heterobasidion annosum*] a fungus which decays the roots of living trees of all ages, especially conifers, spreading into the lower part of the trunk and causing death of the tree.

annotation written text or references which provide supplementary clarification about drawn objects in design drawings and documentation.

annual in landscaping, any non-woody, shallow-rooted plant grown from seed and which flowers, seeds and dies the same year.

annual ring, growth ring; one of the ringed markings in the cross-section of a tree trunk, laid down annually as a new layer of timber is formed, appearing as grain figure in converted timber.

annular bit see hole saw.

annular nail, improved nail, jagged-shank nail, ring-shanked nail; a nail, usually 19—75 mm in length, with a series of ringed protrusions around its shaft to increase its fixing strength when driven into timber; see also plasterboard nail.

types of annular nail for various applications

annular vault a barrel vault in the form of a ring or a hollow doughnut halved horizontally.

annulated column a Romanesque column-type with a number of rings or annulets carved at intervals around its shaft; also called a banded or ringed column.

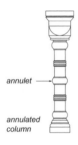

annulet →

annulated column

annulet, annulus (Lat.), shaft ring; a small semicircular or angular moulding carved round the shaft of a Doric column beneath the capital.

annunciator see indicator panel.

Anobiidae see furniture beetle; *Anobium punctatum* see common furniture beetle.

anodic dip painting see electro-dip painting.

anodizing, anodic oxide coating, anodization; the electrochemical application of a layer of coloured aluminium oxide as a corrosion-resistant and hard-wearing protective surface coating for aluminium products and components.

anorthosite a variety of dark gabbro made up of spectral plagioclase or labradorite; see also Spectrolite.

anse de panier see three-centred arch.

antechamber see anteroom.

antefixa, antefix, plural antefixae; Lat.; in classical architecture, one of a number of decorative blocks placed at the eaves of a temple to cover the ends of roofing slabs or tiles.

antefixae at eaves of Italian tiling

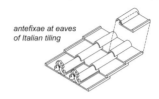

antenna plural antennae; see aerial, satellite link aerial.

antenna amplifier see aerial amplifier.

anteroom a vestibule or transitional space leading to a main room or hall; often a lobby, porch, etc.

anthemion an ornamental motif found in classical architecture consisting of stylized honeysuckle foliage; the word derives from the Greek for flower, anthos; see also lotus anthemion.

Mesopotamian hom-anthemion decorative moulding

anthemion and palmette an ornamental band motif found in the architecture of antiquity consisting of stylized honeysuckle leaves alternating with a palmette design.

anthraquinone an organic compound derived from anthracene, a blue fluorescent crystalline material obtained from coal tar; used in the manufacture of a small group of synthetic dyestuffs.

anthraquinoid red a transparent red organic pigment suitable for use in oil paints.

anthropometric design the design of buildings, rooms, etc. according to the relative proportions of measurements taken from the ideal human body, a practice originating during the Renaissance period.

anti-bandit laminated glass a class of security glass designed to resist breakage for a short length of time; 10 mm laminated glass is often used.

anti-capillary groove see capillary groove.

anti-fading glass laminated glass containing a special interlayer to absorb 99% of ultraviolet light, used in display cases, shop windows, etc. to protect coloured objects from fading.

anti-flooding a description of drainage and sanitary components designed to prevent the return passage of water, foul air, etc. into spaces and systems.
anti-flooding gully a drainage gully containing a valve to prevent the backflow of water or other liquids.
anti-flooding intercepting trap a drainage trap containing a check valve, which prevents the passage of foul air from a sewer to a drain.
anti-flooding valve a valve which prevents a drain or sewer from flooding.

anti-foaming admixture in concretework, an admixture included in a concrete mix to inhibit the formation of air bubbles.

antifreezing admixture, antifreeze; in concretework, an admixture included in the concrete mix to raise its temperature and prevent it from freezing.

antimony a brittle, metallic chemical element, **Sb**, used in a number of alloys; traditionally known as stibium.
antimony orange see antimony vermilion.
antimony vermilion, antimony orange; a range of bright poisonous red pigments based on antimony trisulphide; introduced in 1848, they have now largely been replaced by cadmium pigments.
antimony white a white pigment consisting of antimony oxide mixed with blanc fixe; used as titanium white and usually marketed under the name 'Timonox'.
antimony yellow see Naples yellow.

antique glass glass with an uneven surface, hand blown in the traditional way or manufactured to appear that way.

antistatic referring to any device, product or surface treatment which counteracts the effects of static electricity.

anti-sun glass see solar control glass.

anti-thrust action a latch mechanism in a mechanical lock whose latch bolt cannot be retracted manually.

anti-vacuum valve, vacuum breaker; a valve in a system of pipework which can be opened to admit air as compensation for loss of pressure.

anti-vandal glass a class of special laminated glasses which are relatively resistant to vandalism.

Antrodia serialis see white spongy rot.

Antwerp blue, Haarlem blue; a pale blue pigment, Prussian blue reduced with 75% inert pigment, usually alumina hydrate.

apartment formwork, room formwork, tunnel formwork; proprietary formwork used for casting two concrete side walls and a horizontal slab spanning between them in one operation.

apex the highest point of a geometrical form such as a triangle or cone, or of a pitched or ridge roof.
apex stone see saddle stone.

apophyge, apothesis; Gk.; a slight curvature of the top of the shaft of a classical column where it meets the capital, and bottom where it meets the base.

apparatus see equipment.

apple [*Malus spp.*] a genus of European hardwoods with fine-textured timber valued for its decorative grain; used for veneers and furniture.

appliance any mechanical device such as a shower, heater, fan, etc. used for a specific task in a building or technical installation.
appliance flexible connection, flexible rubber hose in gas installations, a length of resilient rubber hose for connecting the outlet of a gas pipe or riser to an appliance.
appliance governor in gas installations, a device which regulates the pressure and flow of gas to a particular appliance.

application 1 in computing, a series of interrelated software routines designed to perform a specific function.
2 a formal written request for an action to be undertaken, to order official services or permits, or for employment; see planning application, interim application.

applied column see engaged column.

applied sash glazing see secondary glazing.

approval the acceptance of a design or proposal by a client or local authority; generally an announcement to the effect that certain criteria have been satisfied.

apron 1 any protective flat vertical component or construction designed to provide a transition between adjacent areas of wall, such as a wall panel under a window opening, an upstand flashing at the junction of a lean-to roof and upper wall abutment or a flashing to direct water away from an eaves; see window apron, drop apron.
2 that part of a theatre stage in front of the curtain.

apron eaves piece in sheet roofing, a T-shaped member used to support the eaves and provide a drip.

apron flashing a roofing flashing laid at the junction of the upper end of a pitched or flat roof and abutting wall or parapet; it is tucked into the wall with an upstand, and laid over the roofing.

apse a semicircular or polygonal terminating space at or behind the high altar of a church or basilica, often roofed with a half-dome; Latin form is apsis.

apse aisle an aisle within the apse of a church; a deambulatory.

apsidal of a building form, relating to or in the form of an apse, semicircular or half-domed.

aquatic plant any species of landscaping plant which usually grows in or under water.

aqueduct a bridge or other structure designed to convey fresh water, usually a canal or river supported by piers and arches, or a tunnel; from the Latin, aquae ductus, 'conveyance of water'.

aqueous see water-based.

arabesque
intricate decoration based on Moorish and Arabic antecedents, combining a complexity of flowing lines with geometrical and symmetrical patterns.

arabesque (Alhambra)

Arabic arch see horseshoe arch.

aramid fibre a group of very strong, tough and stiff synthetic fibres used in the manufacture of radial tyres, fibre-reinforced composites, heat-resistant fabrics and bulletproof vests; one of these is commercially marketed as Kevlar.

Araucaria angustifolia see Parana pine.

arbitration an accepted procedure for settling disputes, outside the courts but with legal force, using independent persons acceptable to both parties in dispute.

arborvitae see thuja.

arcade 1 a passage or open walk, often lined with columns carrying arches, and roofed with a vaulted ceiling.

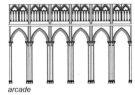
arcade

2 a row of columns surmounted by a series of arches.
3 a roofed entertainment or commercial facility, such as a shopping arcade or amusement arcade.

arcade plate in traditional timber frame construction, a horizontal member joining the tops of aisle posts and supporting rafters.

arc doubleau see transverse rib.

arch a two-dimensionally curved beam construction for supporting loads between two points of support over an opening; traditional masonry arches were constructed from wedge-shaped stones locked together by loading from above; a pattern or motif consisting of this; types of arch included as separate entries are listed below:

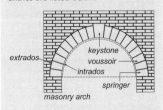
masonry arch

*acute arch, see lancet arch; *Arabic arch, see horseshoe arch; *arcuated lintel, see Syrian arch; *basket arch, see three-centred arch; *bell arch; *blind arch; *cambered arch; *chancel arch; *cinquefoil arch; *cinquefoliated arch; *circular arch; *corbelled arch, corbel arch; *corbelled lintel; *crossette, see joggled arch; *depressed arch, see drop arch; *depressed ogee arch, see two-centred ogee arch; *depressed three-centred arch; *discharging arch, see relieving arch; *draped arch; *drop arch; *Dutch arch; *elliptical arch; *equilateral arch; *false arch; *fan arch; *five-centred arch; *flat arch; *Florentine arch; *foliated arch, see cinquefoliated, multifoliated, trifoliated arches; *four-centred arch, four-centred pointed arch, see Tudor arch; *French arch, see Dutch arch; *gauged arch; *Gothic arch, see pointed arch; *horseshoe arch; *inflected arch, see ogee arch; *inverted arch; *Italian arch; *Italian pointed arch; *Italian round arch, see Florentine arch; *jack arch, see flat arch; *joggled arch; *keel arch; *lancet arch; *Moorish arch, see horseshoe arch; *multifoil arch; *multifoliated arch; *Norman arch; *ogee arch; *parabolic arch; *pointed arch; *pointed cinquefoil arch; *pointed cinquefoliated arch; *pointed equilateral arch, see equilateral arch; *pointed horseshoe arch; *pointed multifoliated arch; *pointed Saracenic arch, see stilted arch; *pointed segmental arch; *pointed trefoil arch; *pointed trifoliated arch; *principal arch; *pseudo four-centred arch; *pseudo three-centred arch; *quatrefoil arch; *Queen Anne arch; *raking arch, see rampant arch; *relieving arch; *reverse ogee arch; *Roman arch; *rood arch; *rough brick arch, rough arch; *round arch, see circular arch; *round cinquefoliated arch; *round horseshoe arch, see horseshoe arch; *round multifoliated arch; *round trefoil arch; *round trifoliated arch; *Saracenic pointed arch, see stilted arch; *segmental arch, segmented arch; *semi-arch; *semicircular arch; *skew arch; *squinch arch, see squinch; *stilted pointed arch, stilted semicircular arch, see stilted arch; *straight arch, see flat arch; *strainer arch; *straining arch; *Syrian arch; *tented arch, see draped arch; *three-centred arch; *three-pointed arch, see equilateral arch; *three-hinged arch, three-pinned arch; *transverse arch; *trefoil arch; *triangular arch; *tribunal arch; trifoliated arch; *triumphal arch; *Tudor arch; *two-centred ogee arch; *Venetian arch.

arch beam see cambered beam.

arch brace, concave brace; in traditional timber frame construction, a naturally curved timber member for bracing the junction between a post and beam, trussed rafters, etc.; also modern equivalents.
arch braced roof truss a simple traditional timber roof truss with sloping rafters braced at the eaves with arch braces.

arch brick see radial brick.

arched beam see cambered beam.

arched head, arcuated head; the curved uppermost member of an arched window.

arched truss see trussed arch.

architect a qualified professional or organization who designs buildings and supervises their construction.
architect's office, architectural practice a private company, owned or run by one or a number of architects for the professional practising of architecture.

architectonic having the spatial qualities, properties and language special to architecture.

architectural pertaining to architecture; relating to, involving, in the manner of architecture.
architectural design that part of the design of a building produced by an architect, which encompasses technical, structural, aesthetic and financial aspects.
architectural drawing a drawing produced by an architect as part of design documentation for a building project.
architectural language, vocabulary the sum of architectural elements, form, detailing, technical and functional solutions of a building, the expression, symbolism and meaning contained therein.
architectural practice see architect's office.

architecture 1 the art and science of producing built form, the product and study of this.
2 in computing, the specification of the contents and functioning of a particular computer system or network.

architrave 1 a strip or moulding used around a door frame to cover the joint between the door and the surrounding construction.
2 epistyle; in classical architecture, the lower horizontal band of an entablature, supported by columns.
3 a beam dividing aisles in a basilica.

archivolt arcus volutus (Lat.); a decorated band above or on the soffit of the intrados in an arch.

arch truss see trussed arch.

archway an arched construction, often an open door or gateway, with a path, corridor or throughfare passing through it.

arch window a window whose upper edge is in the form of an arch.

arc pattern a paving pattern of small stones or cobbles laid in a series of parallel curved rows.

arc pattern

arc welding a method of fusion welding in which the metals to be joined are melted together by an electric arc.

arcuated of a construction or pattern which features arches as a main structural device or motif, or is bowed in shape.
arcuated head see arched head.
arcuated lintel a beam over an opening, whose underside is concave to form an arch; often used as a decorative motif, see Syrian arch.

area a contained or defined part of the earth's or some other surface, often with a specific function, characteristic or ownership; a district, sector or zone; see also surface area, basement area.

area lighting, floodlighting; the illumination of large external areas such as sports venues, industrial sites, airports, storage depots, etc.

area of historical interest see historic site.

arena 1 the main central space of a Roman amphitheatre or circus, or of a bullring, often sanded, from whence the name derives (arena is Latin for 'sand').
2 a modern sports or entertainment venue, often along the lines of the above, a stadium.

arenaceous pertaining to types of soil, rock or landscape composed of or containing a large proportion of sand; arenite is a generic name for arenaceous rocks such as sandstone or other sedimentary rock composed of sandy grains.

arenite see arenaceous.

argillaceous rock, claystone; rock which contains an abundance of clay materials.

argon a gaseous chemical element, **Ar**, used in fluorescent and incandescent lamps.

arkose a form of reddish sandstone with a high content of feldspar.

armour see pitching.

armouring metal covering for an electric cable to afford protection against external forces, abrasion, etc.

armour-plated glass see bullet-resistant laminated glass.

aromatic cedar [*Juniperus virginiana*], see eastern red cedar.

arrangement drawing see general arrangement drawing.

arriccio, arricciato; in fresco painting, the coarse middle coat of three coats of plasterwork, between the trullisatio and intonaco, on which the design is sketched out.

arris 1 a corner or meeting of two planar sides of an object such as a piece of timber, masonry unit, etc.; the sharp corner line formed by this.
2 eased arris, see pencil round.
arris fillet see angle fillet.
arris gutter in roof construction, a V-shaped gutter, often constructed as a

raised strip of roofing protruding directly from the roof plane.

arris knot a knot in seasoned timber which appears on the longitudinal corner of a sawn plank.

arris knot

arrissed edge see pencil round.

arrowhead 1 in the dimensioning and annotation of drawings, etc., a notation for indicating where a dimension begins and terminates.
2 a similar triangular marking for drawing attention to recent revisions made to a drawing.

arsenic a grey, poisonous, chemical element, **As**, used in the preservation of wood and as an insecticide.
arsenic trioxide a poisonous, white, chemical compound, As_2O_3, used in the manufacture of pigments, glass and insecticides.
arsenic trisulphide a yellow or red chemical compound, As_2S_3, used as the pigment king's yellow; see also orpiment.
arsenic yellow see king's yellow.

Art Deco, Style Moderne; a style in architecture and interiors (originating from the Exposition de Arts Décoratif in Paris in 1925) in Europe and America in the 1920s and 1930s, characterized by Art Nouveau and Modernist influences, playful forms and abstract decoration.

artesando in Spanish architecture, an intricately carved wooden ceiling of Moorish influence.

articles of agreement in project administration, the document in which parties to a contract undersign as confirmation of their agreement.

artificial cementing, grouting, injection; a method of strengthening, stabilizing and waterproofing weak or porous soils or rock by injecting concrete into the voids therein.

artificial fibre, synthetic fibre; any fibre of polymer, carbon, glass, ceramic or metal which is man-made; see also natural fibre.

artificial light light produced by means other than by the sun.
artificial lighting, illumination; lighting for a space provided by lamps, luminaires or means other than by daylighting; see also permanent artificial lighting.

artificial stone see cast stone.

artificial ultramarine, French blue, French ultramarine, Gmellin's blue; an artificial blue pigment made by heating clay, soda, sulphur and coal, with the same colour and chemical properties as genuine ultramarine produced from lapis lazuli.

Art Nouveau a movement in art and architecture in Europe from 1890–1910 characterized by the use of flowing naturalistic ornament and informal compositions of plan and elevation; regional variations include Jugendstil or jugend in northern Europe, Stile Liberty (Liberty Style) in Italy, and Secessionist (Sezessionstil) in Vienna, Austria.

Art Nouveau doorway, Tampere, Finland, 1899–1900; architects Lars Sonck & Birger Federley

Arts and Crafts a movement in architecture and design from England, initiated by William Morris in 1867 to counteract industrialism; it is characterized by an interest in the handcrafted, and uses motifs from nature and the Gothic Revival.

arylide yellow, Hansa yellow; a range of slightly poisonous synthetic organic transparent yellow pigments which have good weatherability, light, acid and alkali resistance.

asbestos a mineral, magnesium silicate, occurring naturally as a glassy rock which can be split into small fibres; formerly used as reinforcement and fireproofing, it is hazardous to health and rarely used nowadays in new construction.

asbestos-free slate a roofing tile resembling a roofing slate, consisting of fibres of a material other than asbestos, and cement.

asbestos removal, asbestos work; the specialist work involving the dismantling of hazardous asbestos construction and its transport, safely packed, to a place of disposal.

Asclepian column see serpent column.

ash 1 [*Fraxinus spp.*] a pale hardwood valued for its toughness and flexibility; ash trees are occasionally planted in parks and gardens for their large size and many-stemmed exotic leaf structure; see below for the species of ash included in this work.

Fraxinus spp. - ash

American ash [*Fraxinus spp.*], a common name for the green ash, *Fraxinus pennsylvanica*, and the white ash, *Fraxinus americana*, North American hardwoods with tough and flexible grey-brown timber used for furniture, interiors and tool handles.

European ash, English ash; [*Fraxinus excelsior*] a European hardwood with flexible white to light brown timber; used for making tool handles, furniture and trim.

2 a deposit or residue that remains after the combustion of organic material.

ashlar, ashlar masonry; masonry blocks or facing stone which has been dimensioned, squarely dressed and laid in bonded courses with narrow joints; a single block of such squared and dressed stone used in masonry; types of ashlar included as separate entries are listed below:

*coursed ashlar; *dimension stone; *dry ashlar walling; *natural stone block; *range work; *rusticated ashlar, rustic ashlar; *uncoursed ashlar, random ashlar.

ashlar facing stone facing for rough or rubble masonry or concrete which consists of thin dimensioned and dressed stones; used to provide a fine finish at a lower cost than ashlar masonry.

ashlar masonry see ashlar.

ashlaring, ashlering; in traditional timber pitched roof construction, short vertical timber members for concealing the internal triangular gap between external joists, wall plate and rafters and to brace the eaves, often lined with board or infilled with blockwork.

ashlar post in traditional timber roof construction, a short post running from a wall plate to a principal rafter as part of ashlaring.

ash pan a vessel or pit inside a fireplace or solid-fuel appliance, located beneath the grate to collect ash and other debris from burnt material.

ash pan door a hatch in the front of a fireplace or solid-fuel appliance from which the ash can be removed.

Asiatic base, Ephesian base; a classical Ionic column base which evolved in Asia Minor, consisting of a drum with scotia mouldings surmounted by a reeded torus moulding.

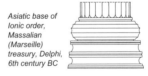

Asiatic base of Ionic order, Massalian (Marseille) treasury, Delphi, 6th century BC

aspen [*Populus tremula, Populus tremuloides*] see poplar.

asphalt a mixture of bitumen and an aggregate such as sand used as a hard-wearing surface in road construction and external paved areas.

asphaltic concrete a mixture of asphalt and concrete used in road production to provide a strong, stiff, structural surface.

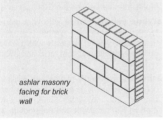

ashlar masonry facing for brick wall

asphalt oil see road oil.

asphalt roofing roofing of molten asphalt laid in successive layers.

asphalt shingles see strip slates.

asphalt topping, asphalt surfacing; asphalt laid as a final durable and flexible surface for roads, pavements, etc.

assembly 1 the putting together of pre-fabricated parts of a component, construction or installation on site.

2 a range of components which functions together to form a whole, as in a doorset.

assembly drawing a detail drawing which shows how a component, joint or construction is assembled or put together on site; a construction drawing.

assistant one who lends aid, gives advice and generally helps out in various tasks, especially in a design office.

astragal 1 'knuckle-bone' (astragalos, Gk.); in classical architecture, a small circular moulding between the shaft and capital of a column or pilaster, in the Doric order typically between the trachelion and hypotrachelion.

2 baguette moulding; an ornamental moulding consisting of a small semicircular projection in cross-section, often incorporating other motifs such as bead and reel.

3 a small dividing glazing bar in a window.

4 a vertical strip attached to the edge of a door leaf or window frame to close the gap between it and the frame.

astroturf see synthetic grass.

astwerk see branch tracery.

astylar referring to architecture, usually classical, which does not contain columns or pilasters.

asymmetrical glazing unit, asymmetrical hermetically sealed double-glazing unit; a glazed unit with two panes of glass of unequal thickness or consistency sealed around an edging strip with a gap usually filled with an inert gas.

atlas, telamon (Gk.); pl. atlantes; in classical architecture, a massive carved statuesque stooping male figure, often serving as a columnar support for a pediment.

atlas, telamon, Doge's Palace, Venice, 14th to 15th century

Atlas cedar [*Cedrus atlantica*], see cedar.

atmospheric burner see natural draught burner.

atmospheric pressure see barometric pressure.

atomizing oil burner a burner in an oil heating system in which oil is dispersed into small droplets and mixed with air prior to combustion.

atrium Lat.; originally an open central courtyard in a Roman dwelling, surrounded by the habitable spaces of the building; an aula in Greek architecture; in early medieval architecture, a forecourt, often colonnaded, in front of the vestibule of an Early Christian or Romanesque church, called atrium paradisus; a modern derivative is a space in a building which functions as a transition space into more important rooms, or a large central space or court with a glazed roof, and often the glazed roof itself.

atrium house originally a Roman dwelling type in which the building mass surrounds a main central space, the atrium, open to the sky; nowadays a modern dwelling type planned with rooms arranged around an open central space; sometimes constructed with similar buildings in an adjoined row, also called a patio house.

attached column see engaged column.

attached pier a pier structurally connected to or built into a wall to provide lateral stability.

attack see corrosion, fungal attack.

attenuation, absorption, loss; the reduction in strength of a signal in a telecommunications or sound system with distance from its source; see sound attenuation.

attenuator see muffler.

attic 1 an upper room or space contained within the pitched roofspace of a residential building; see also garret.

2 a blindstory raised above the eaves or entablature line of a classical building to conceal the roof, see attic storey.

Attic base the most common classical column base consisting of an upper and lower torus and scotia separated by a fillet, primarily found with the Ionic order.

Attic base of ionic order, temple by the Ilissus, Athens, Greece, 430 BC

attic storey 1 the uppermost storey beneath the pitched roof of a residential building, containing storage or habitable space.

2 a storey above the entablature or cornice of a classical building, in strict proportion with lower elements.

attic truss a roof truss designed so as to allow for the construction of habitable roof space between its structural members.

attic truss

attorney see letter of attorney.

Aucoumea klaineana see gaboon.

audio-frequency a frequency of sound within the audible range; frequencies of any oscillations within this range.

audio spectrum, acoustic spectrum, sound spectrum; in acoustics, the range of frequencies and intensities of sound emitted from a source or sources at any given time; the measurable make-up of a sound source.

auditorium that part of a theatre, concert hall, etc. in which the audience is seated; any building containing the above.

auger a corkscrew-like tool or drill bit used for boring round holes in solid material such as wood or stone.

auger bit a spiral drill bit in the shape of an auger, used for drilling long large-bore holes, circular housings, etc.

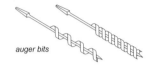

auger bits

augered pile in foundation technology, a form of bored pile in which the hole is cut with an auger.

aureolin see cobalt yellow.

auricular ornament, lobate ornament; decorative ornament, foliage and volutes, resembling parts of the human ear, found in early Baroque architecture in northern Europe in the late 1500s and early 1600s.

auricular ornament

auripigmentum see king's yellow.

aurora yellow see cadmium yellow.

aurum mussivum see mosaic gold.

austenite a solution of carbon and other materials appearing in gamma iron, formed when iron is heated over 910° C; found in some stainless steels used for cutlery.

austenitic stainless steel stainless steel which contains 16—19% chromium and 4—6% nickel.

Australian blackwood, black wattle (Aust); [*Acacia melanoxylon*] an eastern Australian hardwood with strong, flexible, golden brown timber; used for furniture, interior joinery and woodwind instruments.

autoclaving, high pressure steam curing, autoclave curing; method of curing concrete, usually lightweight concrete, by exposing it to high-pressure superheated steam in a sealed vessel (an autoclave) for a given time in order to increase dry shrinkage and speed up hardening.

autoclaved aerated concrete a form of aerated concrete often containing aluminium or zinc powder as a foaming agent, which has been steam cured in an autoclave to control the aerating process.

automatic-closing fire assembly a motorized fire door, shutter, etc., normally kept in an open position, which closes automatically in the event of fire; an automatic fire door.

automatic door a motorized door controlled by an optical or motion sensor, which operates door gear and opens and closes it automatically.

automatic door gear the range of mechanisms and equipment for controlling the opening and closing of an automatic sliding or swinging door, operated by signals from detector devices, remote controls, etc.

automatic door operator a motorized device which controls the opening and closing of a door leaf.

automatic fire door see automatic-closing fire assembly.

automatic fire extinguisher a fire extinguisher operated automatically by detectors in the event of an outbreak of fire.

automatic fire-extinguishing system, auto-suppression system; any system for detecting a building fire by means of light, heat or smoke sensors and for extinguishing it using an automated system such as a sprinkler system.

automatic fire valve see fire valve.

automatic lighting controller see photoelectric lighting controller.

automation the functioning of a process, installation or system without the use of continuous human input; door automation, see automatic door gear.

auto-suppression system see automatic fire-extinguishing system.

autoxidation the spontaneous oxidation of a material caused by the presence of oxygen; weathering and deterioration of materials due to this.

auxiliary circuit an electric circuit used as part of an installation for powering auxiliary devices such as compressors, fans, transformers, etc.

auxiliary pigment a substance used in paints as a filler, to improve opacity and to strengthen the paint film.

avenue 1 a wide, straight street in an urban context lined with broad-leaved trees.
2 a prehistoric double row of standing stones believed to form a ceremonial way to a major monument or cult centre.

award, prize; a merit, medal, sum of money, etc. awarded to successful entrants of architectural and design competitions, outstanding buildings, etc.

awl see bradawl.

awning, shade; a framed textile external shading apparatus which can be extended obliquely over and in front of windows to exclude direct sunlight from interiors.
awning window see top-hung casement window.

axe a hand tool with a handle and sharpened steel head for shaping and chopping trees and wood, bricks on site, and for treating and dressing stone surfaces by picking and scabbling; types of axe included as separate entries are listed below:
*brick axe, see bricklayer's hammer; *chop axe; *mason's axe, see masonry axe; patent axe; pickaxe, see pick; *rock axe, stone axe, stonemason's axe, trimming axe, see masonry axe.
axed finish a rough stonework finish produced by dressing with an axe, pick or bush hammer.

axial-flow fan in mechanical ventilation systems, a high-efficiency fan which pumps air through the main axis of its rotors, installed along a line of ducting.

Axminster carpet a form of carpet with a soft tufted cut pile woven into a base layer; originating in the English village of Axminster, Devon.

axonometry, parallel projection; a method of drawing in which the object is pictured in three dimensions such that all lines in each of the three major axes are parallel; especially pertaining to isometric, dimetric and trimetric projections, though usually used for all parallel projections depicting three dimensions on a flat plane.

axonometric cube see coordinate cube.

axonometric projection a form of projection drawing using axonometry, depicting three dimensions with coordinate planes inclined in relation to one another; in simplest form an oblique projection based on a true plan of a subject laid obliquely to the horizontal, usually 45° and 45° or 30° and 60° (more accurately called a military or planometric projection); verticals are drawn to the same scale as the plan and the lines in each dimension are drawn parallel; also a generic name for true isometric, dimetric and trimetric projections, in full orthographic axonometric projection.

ayous see obeche.

azo dye one of the largest classes of synthetic dyes comprising over half the commercial dyes, manufactured from various coloured organic compounds containing nitrogen and used for colouring fabrics.

azurite, azzura della magna, blue malachite, mineral blue, mountain blue; a mineral form of basic copper carbonate $Cu_3(OH)2(CO_3)_2$, used as a clear deep permanent water-based blue pigment since Roman times, and occasionally as a gemstone.

azzura della magna see azurite.

azzuro oltremarino see lapis lazuli.

B

back the reverse, inferior or secondary face of a piece, component, building, etc.; the surface of a timber board to the reverse side of the outer, usually finished surface, also called the worse face; the edge of a sawtooth adjacent to its cutting edge.

back bed in glazing, bedding compound or a proprietary product applied to a rebate in a window frame, against which a pane is fixed.

back boiler in a heating system, a boiler fitted to the rear of a solid fuel heater, which provides the thermal energy for water heating; see also high output back boiler.

back clearance in glazing, the horizontal distance between the inner face of the pane or glazing unit and its supporting frame.

back cut veneer decorative veneer formed by peeling the inner side of a half log or flitch off-centre on a lathe.

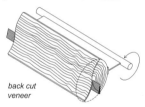

back cut veneer

backdraught, smoke explosion; a rush of smoke into a room containing smouldering contents due to the opening of a door during a hazardous building fire, causing spontaneous ignition.

backer see back-up material.

backfill, fill; in sitework, earth replaced and compacted into an excavation to cover subsoil foundations and services once they have been laid.

backflap hinge a hinge whose leaves are long rather than tall, used for applications such as furnishings and table flaps where a butt hinge is insufficient.

backflow a phenomenon in which liquid flows along a pipe or channel in the reverse direction to that intended, caused by pressure or a partial vacuum; see also backsiphonage.

backflow prevention device a device for inhibiting the backflow of water in a drainage or sanitary installation.

backflow valve, backsiphonage preventer, backwater valve, backpressure valve; a check valve in a water system which allows water in a pipeline to flow in one direction only; see pipe interrupter.

back form in concreting, formwork or formwork surfaces used in locations which remain hidden in the final structure; back formwork, in full.

background noise, ambient sound; in acoustics, general noise present in an environment.

background noise level in acoustics, the level of background noise in a space.

back gutter in roof construction, a channel or gutter formed at the junction of a pitched roof and abutment wall, or behind a parapet or chimney to convey water away.

back hearth the lowest masonry construction on which combustion takes place beneath a flue in a fireplace or fireplace recess; the floor of an open fireplace.

backing 1 a structural base such as concrete, masonry or a framework onto which cladding is fixed.
2 see back-up material.
backing coat see plaster undercoat.
backing strip see back-up material.
backings see plastering background.

backnut a nut at a threaded pipework joint which is tightened to secure the joint between two fittings; see also stop nut.

back-pressure valve see backflow valve.

back putty, bed putty; in glazing, a fillet of putty applied to a rebate in a window frame, against which a pane is bedded.

backsaw a handsaw with a rectangular blade whose back is reinforced with a metal strip to inhibit bending; used for carpenter's benchwork.

backset the horizontal distance from the face of the forend of a lock to the centre of the keyhole.

backsiphonage backflow of a liquid in pipework caused by siphonage; see also backflow.

backsiphonage preventer see backflow valve.

back sliced veneer decorative veneer sliced from the heart side of a half log or flitch.

back sliced veneer

back to wall pertaining to a soil appliance such as a bidet or WC which is connected to a wall or vertical surface, through which all pipes, drains and outlets, etc. are connected.

back-up material, backer, backing; material such as foam rubber strip placed into a construction joint to limit the depth of overlaid sealant.

backwater valve see backflow valve.

baffle a strip of material applied into construction joints between components or materials as weather or soundproofing.

bagasse board a building board manufactured from the waste fibres from sugar cane processing.

baguette moulding see astragal.

Bahia rosewood [*Dalbergia nigra*], see rosewood.

bail see shackle.

baked enamel, stoving enamel; any hardwearing protective polymeric coating for metal components, building boards, etc. which requires elevated temperatures to activate a curing process; also known as baking enamel, baking finish, stoved enamel, stoved finish; see also powder coating, stove enamelling, acrylic stoving enamel, alkyd stoving enamel.

baking see stove enamelling.

baking enamel see baked enamel, acrylic stoving enamel, alkyd stoving enamel.

baking finish see baked enamel.

bakelite see phenol formaldehyde.

balanced construction the pairing of matched layers in plywood or composite boards around either side of the central layer to form a symmetrical construction and prevent warping.

balanced door an automatic door assembly in which the counterbalanced leaf swings open around an eccentrically placed pivot.

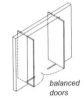

balanced doors

balanced pressure tap a mixer tap, usually of stainless steel, fitted with a regulating device which produces equal pressures of hot and cold water drawn from it.

balanced step see dancing step.

balcony an accessible outdoor or glazed and balustraded platform projecting from the external face of a building, often for recreational use.

balcony-access flats see gallery-access block.

balcony glazing a proprietary or specially designed openable glazing assembly which provides shelter from the elements by closing off the front and sides of a balcony above its balustrade.

baldachin, baldacchino, baldaquin; an ornamental canopy of or representing fabric over an altar, throne, bed or doorway; see ciborium.

baldachin

balection moulding see bolection moulding.

balk see baulk.

ball and flower, ballflower; an ovular decorative motif found in the church architecture of the early 1300s, a stylized three-petalled flower enclosing a small globule.

carved ball and flower (ballflower) ornament

ballast 1 material such as gravel, concrete slabs or cast concrete laid above an insulating layer on roofs and walkways to provide weight and prevent its removal and deterioration by the forces of weather and wind. **2** an electronic component for maintaining a constant current applied to a discharge or fluorescent lamp.

ball-bearing a construction or component consisting of a number of steel spheres arranged in a ring and cased, providing a frictionless support for a rotating attachment.
ball-bearing hinge, ball-bearing butt hinge; a hinge with a ball-bearing incorporated between adjacent knuckles to reduce friction between them.

ball-bearing butt hinges

ball catch, bullet catch; a catch which holds a door closed by means of a sprung ball in a casing, fixed into the edge of the door leaf; see also roller catch.

ball catch

ball clay a fine textured, plastic, adhesive natural clay used in the manufacture of earthenware and firebricks.

ballcock see ballvalve.

ballflower see ball and flower.

ball hinge a hinge whose pins rotate upon a ball-bearing to reduce friction in turning.

balloon see wire balloon.

balloon frame a form of timber frame construction in which vertical studs rise from sole plate to header plate through two or more stories; intermediate floors are carried on wall plates nailed to the inside face of the studs.

balloon framing

ball peen hammer a hammer whose peen is hemispherical.

ballvalve, ballcock, floatvalve, float operated valve; **1** a valve in the flushing cistern of a soil appliance which controls the level of water therein with the aid of a float; a flushing valve.
2 in plumbing pipework, a valve containing a perforated ball, which can be turned to align with ports in the casing and allow liquid to pass through.

balsam a fragrant and medicinal resinous exudation from certain conifers; see oleoresin.
balsam fir [*Abies balsamea*], see fir.
balsam poplar [*Populus balsamifera, Populus tacamahaca*], see poplar.

balsa wood [*Ochroma spp.*] a group of South American tropical hardwoods with soft and extremely light timber; used for modelmaking, floating construction and lightweight insulating coreboards.

baluster one of a series of vertical members, often ornate and carved from stone, which fill the space between the floor or ground level and handrail or coping of a balustrade; a similar slender element of timber or metal in a lightweight balustrade; also called a standard or upright.

baluster column any column whose shaft is short and thick, resembling a baluster, especially those in ancient Assyrian architecture, whose carved upper capital, lower base and cylindrical shaft form a symmetrical whole.

Assyrian baluster column,
Nineveh, Iraq, Assyrian period 850–500 BC

balustrade any waist-high barrier, open or closed, designed to provide protection from falling at the edge of a change in level; an ornate equivalent of the above, consisting of a series of ornate vertical members or balusters of stone or wood, often carved, supporting a coping; see stair balustrade.

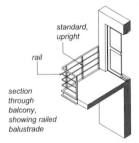

standard, upright

rail

section through balcony, showing railed balustrade

balustrade height the total height of a balustrade measured from finished floor level to top of handrail; in a stair this is measured vertically from the line of nosings.

bamboo [*Bambusa spp.*, esp. *Bambusa arundinacea*] a group of giant hollow-stemmed grasses used as a basic structural building material in tropical countries.

band 1 in acoustics and electronics, a range of frequencies between two defined limits.
2 see moulding.

band and hook hinge see hook and band hinge.

band course, string course; in masonry, a projecting course, decorative moulding, row of bricks, etc. set into an elevation, often at storey level, to throw off rainwater and as decoration.

banded column see annulated column, rusticated column.

banding 1 in decorative veneerwork and similar crafts, strips of material arranged around central panels to form a border.
2 a horizontal protrusion round the circumference of the shaft of a column.

bandsaw a mechanical saw whose blade is a toothed steel belt which revolves between two powered wheels.
bandsawn a description of timber which has been resawn with a bandsaw.

banister 1 a light balustrade for a stair comprising a handrail supported on closely spaced balusters.
2 one of the balusters in such a stair balustrade.

banker 1 a timber workbench on which traditional stonework is carried out.
2 a rough box, platform or bench in which small batches of concrete, plaster or mortar are mixed by hand.

banking a sloping mass of earth, an embankment.

baptistery, baptistry; a space, area or separate building of a church or cathedral, containing a font where baptism takes place.

bar 1 any longitudinal solid length of material with a uniform cross-section, usually metal; called a section when thin-flanged or hollow; types included as separate entries are listed below:
*angle bar, see steel angle; *crow bar; *deformed bar; *flat bar, see flat; *glazing bar; *hexagonal bar; *locking bar; *panic bar; *reinforcing bar; *round bar; *square*

bar; *T-bar, see T-section; *threaded bar, see threaded rod; *water bar.
2 the counter in a bar or restaurant, from which food and drinks may be served.

barbed moulding a decorative moulding with a series of hooked motifs joined end on end; primarily found in heraldic designs.

barbed moulding

barbed wire a steel wire product wound with a series of sharp protrusions; used for security fencing.

bar bender a manual or powered device used for bending reinforcement bars into the desired shapes for reinforced concrete; see also bending tool, bar bending machine.
bar bending machine, power bender; a powered device for bending reinforcement bars.

bar cramp see joiner's cramp.

bar cropper, bar cutter; in reinforced concretework, a machine or tool used for cutting reinforcing bars to their desired lengths.

barefaced tenon joint a mortise and tenon joint in which the tenon is cut to one side of the end of a member.

barefaced tenon joint

barefaced tongued and grooved joint a timber butt joint in which the grain end has been rebated forming a tongue which is housed in a groove in the receiving piece.

bargeboard, gableboard, timberboard, vergeboard; in timber roof construction, a board at a gable end or verge of a pitched roof which covers the joint between wall and roof.

barge couple, cantilever rafter; in timber roof construction, one of the short end rafters which projects beyond the end of a gable wall and onto which barge boards are fixed.

barge stone in masonry construction, one of a series of stones, often projecting, laid along the upper edge of a stone gable.

barite see barytes.

barium a whitish, malleable metallic chemical element, **Ba**; see compounds and products below
barium chromate a yellow chemical compound, the basic ingredient of the pigment barium yellow.
barium sulphate a white crystalline solid chemical compound, $BaSO_4$, see barytes, blanc fixe.
barium yellow, lemon yellow, permanent yellow, ultramarine yellow, yellow ultramarine; a pale yellow pigment, now obsolete, consisting of barium chromate; used formerly in oil paints.

bark the exterior protective layer of tissue on a tree.
bark beetle [*Scolytidae*] a family of insects which damage hardwood trees and their unseasoned timber by burrowing beneath the bark.
bark borer [*Ernobius mollis*] an insect whose larvae burrow under the bark of dry softwood logs.
barking chisel, peeling chisel, peeling iron; a wide-bladed chisel or similar implement for peeling or stripping bark from boles.
bark pocket see inbark.
bark-ringed knot see encased knot.

barley-sugar column see spiral column.

barometric damper see draught diverter.

barometric pressure, atmospheric pressure; the pressure of the air in the atmosphere.

Baroque an architectural style originating from southern Europe in the 1600s and 1700s, characterized by classical motifs used in a dramatic and theatrical manner, lavish ornamentation and integration of art and sculpture; the three recognized

phases of Baroque architecture are as follows:
early Baroque c.1580—1620
high Baroque c.1620—1670
late Baroque c.1670—1710

Baroque doorway, Palazzo Zuccari, Florence; Federico Zuccari, 1540–1609

Baroque window with broken top segmental pediment; Michna palace, Prague, 1640–1650

barrel bolt a simple fastener for a door or gate consisting of a round metal bar which moves in a tube or ring, fixed to the door, and engages in a hole in a jamb or gate post; see also foot bolt, flush slide.

barrel nipple, shoulder fitting (Am); in pipework, a short connecting pipe which is externally threaded at either end, and which often has a cast nut in between for tightening with a spanner.

barrel vault, cradle vault, cylindrical vault, tunnel vault, wagon vault, wagonhead vault; a masonry or concrete roof vault which is semicircular in cross-section, especially used in early churches; see pointed barrel vault.

barrel vault

barrel vaulted roof any roof structure which is semicircular in section and in the shape of an elongated semicircular arch.

barrier a physical obstacle, rail, etc. designed to prevent access or penetration; types included as separate entries are listed below:
*boom; *cavity barrier, see fire barrier; *plenum barrier; *vapour barrier.

bar schedule, bending schedule, reinforcement schedule; in the design of reinforced concrete, a document providing dimensions, bending patterns and arrangement of all reinforcement in a component.

bar stop in ornamentation, the termination of a chamfered moulding or carving with a protruding carved perpendicular bar.

bar tendon in prestressed concrete, a single reinforcing bar which acts as a prestressing tendon.

bartizan, bartisan; an overhanging corner turret in a medieval castle, palace or fortification, used for defence; often applied as ornament in later romantic revival styles

bar tracery a range of types of Gothic tracery originating in the late 1200s, formed by vertical window mullions which interlink to form intricate patterns in the pointed window head.

baryta green see manganese green.

baryta white see blanc fixe.

barytes, barite, heavy spar; a pale-coloured mineral, barium sulphate, $BaSO_4$, used as a raw material in some white paints, for increasing the specific gravity of drilling fluids and for providing protection against radiation; see Bologna stone, heavy spar.

basalt a blue-grey, brownish or black, fine-grained, dense igneous rock, often used for paving; the earth's most abundant volcanic rock type.

base 1 the lowest, thickened section of a column, pedestal, etc. beneath its shaft, often decorated, which transfers loading onto a plinth or to a foundation.
2 a substance which may chemically combine with an acid to form a salt.
3 see substrate.

baseboard see skirting board, gypsum baseboard

base coat, brown coat, browning coat, floating coat, key coat; in plastering and rendering, a roughly finished layer or layers of mortar applied to masonry to provide a key or even surface for a finish coat.

base course 1 in road construction, a surfacing layer of material directly beneath and supporting the wearing course.

2 the lowest course of stones, bricks or blocks in masonry walling, or lowest layer of logs in horizontal log construction.

base floor, bottom floor; the lowest constructed floor level of a building, adjacent to the ground; it may be at basement or ground floor level.

basement the usable area of a building that is situated partly or entirely below ground level and may contain habitable rooms; in North America it is less than halfway below ground level.

basement area, dry area, area; an unroofed narrow external space below street level to provide light, air and often access to rooms in a basement of town houses, and to separate external basement walls from the surrounding ground to prevent entry of water.

basement parking an area of parking located in the basement of a building.

base moulding a decorative moulding at the lower end of the shaft of a column.

base plate see sole plate.

base ring, base unit; in drainage, a suitably shaped precast concrete, ceramic or plastics component used as the base for an inspection chamber or well, around which it is constructed.

base rock see bedrock.

base sheet, **1** reference drawing, underlay; a drawing or graphic image whose information is used, often by tracing through, in the production of a drawing.
2 first layer felt; in built-up roofing, the lowest layer of bitumen felt, often bonded to the underlying structure and intermediate sheet above.

base unit see base unit.

basilica a Roman building type, rectangular in shape with an apse at either end, used as a court of justice and an exchange; a similar building type adopted by the Early Christian church from Greek and Roman precedents, consisting of a clerestoried nave, side aisles and terminated with a rounded apse containing an altar.

basilica church a church type based on a basilica antecedent, usually with a rectangular plan divided by colonnades into a nave and aisles, with an apse or apses at one end.

basilisk, cockatrice; in medieval ornament and depiction, a mythical reptile born of a serpent from a cock's egg, whose breath or gaze was believed to be fatal.

basilisk motif

basin an open-topped vessel, often of ceramics and built into a worktop, designed to hold water for washing and other purposes; see handrinse basin.

basin mixer a mixer tap which can be fitted for use with a basin.

basin tap any tap which can be fitted for use with a basin.

basket arch see three-centred arch.

basket capital a capital found in Byzantine architecture, consisting of a splayed upside-down pyramid or cone-shaped block with intricate carvings.

Byzantine basket capital, Hagia Sofia Istanbul, Turkey, 532–537

basketweave pattern **1** a paving pattern resembling woven strands, in which rectangular pavers are laid in twos or threes side-by-side, forming a series of squares at right angles to one another; similar patterns in tiling; see half-basketweave pattern.

basketweave paving

2 a veneering and parquetry grid pattern in which alternate squares of even size are laid with their direction of grain running perpendicular to one another, forming a chequerboard appearance.

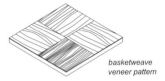

*basketweave
veneer pattern*

bas-relief see basso rilievo.

basso rilievo, bas-relief, low relief; a form of sculptured relief ornament in which figures or elements are carved so as to project half their depth from a surface or background.

basswood, American lime; [*Tilia americana*], see lime.

bastard grain grain that forms an angle of 30–60° with the face of a piece of sawn timber.

bastard sawing see through and through sawing.

bastion a polygonal structure projecting from the main fortified wall of a town or castle, with two or more long faces meeting at an angle, used for siting cannon and other weaponry to afford clear fire in a number of directions outside the main line of defence.

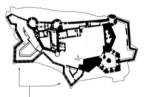

*plan showing bastions in St Olaf's
castle, Savonlinna, Finland 1475–1495
(as was in 1790)*

bat, 1 brickbat; a full brick cut down to size in order to act as a space filler in bonded brickwork; often larger than a quarter brick; types included as separate entries are listed below:
*halved three quarter bat; *half bat; *quarter bat; *three quarter bat.
2 mineral wool and other insulating products manufactured into thick slabs for ease of storage and installation.

batch a portion of material or goods mixed for use, packed for delivery, etc. at any particular time; see concrete batch, plaster batch.

batch mixer in the production of concrete, a mixer which produces a set amount of concrete at any one time; see also continuous mixer.

batch production the manufacturing or processing of a product or material in a series of predetermined quantity rather than in a continuous run.

batching see proportioning.

batching plant, batching and mixing plant; an industrial assembly for mixing concrete to be used on site.

bathroom a room for personal cleaning, containing a bath or shower and other sanitary appliances.

bathroom lock a lock designed for use principally with the doors of bathrooms, toilet cubicles, etc., containing a latch with handles, and a dead bolt operable from the inside only; the dead bolt is connected to an indicator panel to show whether the room is occupied or not.

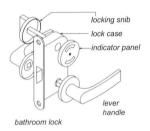

*locking snib
lock case
indicator panel
lever handle*

bathroom lock

bat's wing an arched decorative motif with lines or flutes radiating from a central point, resembling the outstretched wings of a bat.

bat's wing motif

batted finish, broad tooled finish, striated finish; a stonework finish with a series of parallel cut grooves produced by dressing with a batting tool.

batted finish

batten 1 one of a number of strips of timber laid at regular spacing as a base onto which cladding, sheet materials and tiles may be fixed; types included as separate entries are listed below: *counterbatten; *flooring batten; *tiling batten; *roof batten.
2 any sawn timber section with cross-sectional dimensions of less than 25 mm thick and 25–50 mm wide.
3 in timber classification, a sawn softwood section with cross-sectional dimensions of 44–100 mm thick and 100–200 mm wide; always considerably wider than thick.
4 parquet batten, see parquet block.
5 see screed batten.

battenboard a timber building board formed by gluing veneers on either side of a core of solid wood strips with a width greater than 30 mm; the grain of the veneers runs at 90° to that of the core.

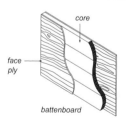

battenboard

battened stanchion a composite steel lattice column or stanchion in which vertical rolled steel sections are joined together with stiff horizontal members.

battening 1 timber strips attached to the frame of a roof or wall as a base to receive a finish such as tiling, boarding or cladding, or to support a construction, etc.
2 a series of shallow timber battens fixed to floor substructure, onto which wooden flooring or a floating floor is fixed.

3 the job of laying such battens.

batten roll joint see roll joint.

batter, rake; a slope in the face of any massive or retaining wall; in particular, the outwardly sloping base of a defensive wall in a castle or fortification, used for stability and to throw off missiles which have been dropped from the battlements; also called battering or a talus.

batter pile see raking pile.

battery, 1 cell; a portable device for producing and storing electricity via chemical reaction, used as an energy source in applications where mains supply is unavailable or impractical.
2 see heating battery.
3 see lift battery.

battery mould one of a number of formwork panels used in series for casting in-situ concrete.

batting tool, broad tool; a broad-faced masonry chisel used for dressing stone with a batted or fluted finish.

battlement, embattlement; a crenellated parapet and walkway in a castle or fortified wall, used for the purposes of defence; architectural imitation of this in decorated building frontages; see also crenellation.

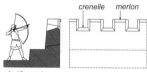

battlement

battlemented see castellated.
battlemented moulding see crenellated moulding.

baulk a piece of sawn timber with cross-sectional dimensions of 100 × 100 mm or larger; in traditional timber construction, it may be a squared log; any heavy log or timber; also variously written as bauk, balk or bawk.

bay, 1 trave; a division in a ceiling or roof marked out by adjacent vaults, beams or arches, especially in stone vaulted architecture.
2 the division of a space defined by the spacing of roof trusses, partitions or columns.

bay-leaf garland an ornamental motif found in classical and Renaissance architecture consisting of a mesh of lines which intertwine to form openings in the shape of eyes or bay leaves.

bay-leaf garland

bayonet cap a lamp cap which connects to a holder by means of transverse pins in its side.

bayonet saw see jigsaw.

bay window a window set into a protrusion from the elevational plane of a building.

beaching small stones of 70–200 mm used as revetment for embankments.

bead, 1 beading; a thin strip of planed timber or other material used for covering joints, fixing of glazing or panelling in frames and as surface decoration; see glazing bead.
2 one of a series of decorative small round (or elongated) hemispheres or half-cylinders carved or machined into a moulding, board, etc.
3 see bead moulding, beaded moulding
bead and quirk moulding see quirk bead moulding.
bead and reel, reel and bead; a decorative moulding consisting of a series of small round beads, elongated hemispheres or half-cylinders alternating with pairs of flattened discs.

bead and reel mouldings

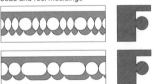

bead boarding decorative timber cladding boards whose surface is planed with a series of convex mouldings, reeds also called reeded or moulded boarding.

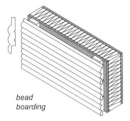

bead boarding

bead edged boarding decorative timber cladding boards whose edge has been planed with a bead.

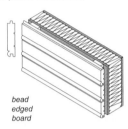

bead edged board

beaded joint a brickwork mortar joint in which the mortar is laid flush with the brick surface then scored with a special tool to form an inset convex shape or bead.
beaded moulding, paternoster, pearl moulding; an ornamental motif or moulding consisting of a row of beads or small hemispheres; also loosely known as a bead moulding; see bead and reel.

beaded moulding

beading see bead.
bead moulding, roundel; a slender decorative moulding, semicircular in cross-section; when found in classical architecture it is called an astragal; see beaded moulding, pellet moulding.
bead saw a small fine-toothed saw, 100–250 mm long, with a reinforced back and turned handle, used for fine work.
bead polystyrene see expanded polystyrene.

beakhead see beak moulding.

beak moulding, 1 beakhead; a decorative moulding of Norman origin formed with pointed projections resembling the head of a man, bird or mythical beast with a protruding beak or lip.

beak ornament

2 bird's beak moulding; a decorative quadrant moulding with a concave underside.

beak moulding

3 see cock beak moulding.

beam 1 a horizontal structural member which transfers loading from above to its bearing points; types included as separate entries are listed below.

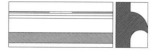

loading
span
points of
support
beam

*anchor beam; *arch beam, arched beam, see cambered beam; *architrave; *binder; *box beam; *brick beam, see reinforced brick lintel; *built-up beam, see built-up; *cambered beam; *cantilever beam; *collar beam; *composite beam; *concrete beam; *continuous beam; *corrugated ply-web beam; *cross beam; *double tee beam; *downstand beam; *dragon beam, dragging beam; *edge beam; *epistyle, see architrave; *filigree beam; *fish-bellied beam; *flanged beam; *framed beam, see trussed beam; *girder; *glued and laminated beam, glulam beam, see laminated timber beam; *ground beam, grade beam; *hammer beam; *haunched beam; *hollow

composite beam; hollow-core beam; *I-beam; *inverted beam; *joggle beam; *L-beam; *laminated timber beam; *laminated web beam; *lattice beam, see trussed beam; *lintel; *longitudinal beam; *main beam, see principal beam; *pitched beam; *plywood box beam, see box beam; *plywood web beam, ply-web beam; *precast beam; *prestressed concrete beam; *principal beam, primary beam; *ridge beam; *rood beam; *roof beam; *secondary beam; *solid timber beam; *spine beam, see mono-carriage; *steel beam; *straining beam; *strut beam, see collar beam; *summer beam, see summer; *T-beam, tee beam; *tie beam; *trabs, trabes; *transverse beam, see cross-beam; *trimmed beam; *trimmer beam, see trimmer; *trussed beam; *universal beam, see I-section; *upstand beam; *wind beam, see collar beam.
2 a narrow ray of light or other radiation.
beam block, bond-beam block see channel block.
beam box, beam form; formwork for a reinforced concrete beam.
beam brick see lintel brick.
beam form see beam box.
beam spread in artificial lighting, the angle over which a spotlight or floodlight directs the majority of its light output.
beam unit see precast beam.
beam vibrator in the compaction of fresh concrete, a surface vibrator in the shape of a beam.

bearer any device or construction for holding a component in place; a ceiling bearer, gutter bearer, soffit bearer, etc.

bearing a structural device which transfers load from a moving, moveable, slipping or rotating part to a fixed support.

bearing capacity, loadbearing capacity, loading capacity; the amount of force, pressure, weight or stress that a material, soil, foundations or a structure can safely withstand without failure.

bearing pile, foundation pile; in foundation technology, a pile which transmits vertical rather than earth-pressure loads to the ground or hard subsoil; see list of common pile types under 'pile'.

bearing surface any surface which bears the thrust of a structural component.

bearing wall see loadbearing wall.
bearing wall system see loadbearing wall construction.

beast column see animal column.

Beaux Arts an architectural style originating from France at the École de Beaux Arts in the 1800s, characterized by monumental forms and eclectic decoration.

bed 1 the lower horizontal surface of a brick or stone as laid in masonry.
2 bedding; a layer of material, often mortar, in which a brick, block or stone is laid; the horizontal joint thus formed; a bed joint.
3 floor bed, see ground supported floor.
4 the lower surface of a roofing slate.
5 stratum; in geology, a layer of sedimentary rock and the natural plane in which it lies in the ground.
6 a piece of furniture designed for sleeping in.

bedding 1 in masonry construction, the laying of a brick, block or stone into mortar or another cementitious material, and tapping it into the correct position; see bed.
2 see also edge bedding, face bedding, glazing bedding, mortar bedding, sand bedding.

bedding compound 1 a compound applied beneath materials as bedding.
2 a compound applied to joints between components.

bedding mortar 1 coarse cement consisting of a binder (lime, cement, etc.), fine aggregate and water used in masonrywork as a jointing material onto which successive courses are laid; also called masonry mortar.
2 see tiling mortar.

bedding plant in landscaping, any plant, usually flowering, seasonally planted in ornamental flower beds.

bed joint, horizontal joint; a horizontal joint between two courses of stones, bricks or blocks laid in masonry.

bed mould in classical architecture, the flat fascia course directly beneath a cornice; also called a bed; the lowest moulding in any band of mouldings.

bed moulding see bed mould.

bed putty see back putty.

bedrock, base rock; the solid layer of rock beneath loose soil, sand or silt in the earth's crust, which may be used as a firm base for bearing foundations.

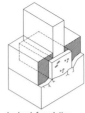
bedrock foundation

bedstone, foundation stone; a large flat boulder used as a foundation, usually for a temporary or traditional timber building.

beech [*Fagus spp.*] a group of hardwoods from Europe, Asia Minor, Japan and North America whose heavy, strong, hard, tough, pale pink timber has flecked markings; used for flooring, interiors and furniture; a large tree, often planted in parks and gardens, with many available variants; see below for list of beech species included in this work:
European beech [*Fagus sylvatica*] a European hardwood with pinkish, mottled timber; used for flooring, interiors and furniture.
American beech [*Fagus grandifolia*] a North American hardwood with whitish pink timber; used for interiors and furniture.

beeswax wax produced by bees, applied with a solvent to finished joinery and polished as a surface treatment

beetle, 1 maul; a sledgehammer with a wooden head, used for driving in pegs, wedges and staves.
2 any hard-shelled insects of the order Coleoptera, many of which cause damage to trees, timber, and timberwork in buildings; species included as separate entries are listed below:
*ambrosia beetle [Scolytidae, Platypodidae]; *bark beetle [Scolytidae]; *common furniture beetle [Anobium punctatum]; *death-watch beetle [Xestobium rufovillosum]; *furniture beetle; *house longhorn beetle [Hylotrupes bajulus]; *longhorn beetle [Cerambycidae]; *lymexylid beetle, ship timber beetle; *sawyer beetle [Monochamus]; *spruce beetle [Tetropium spp.]; *woodworm, see furniture beetle.

Belfast truss a roof truss composed of a curved upper chord and flat lower chord braced by diagonals; a bowstring truss.

Belfast truss

Belgian truss see fink truss.

bell 1 the bulging part of a hammerhead which bears the striking face, opposite the peen.

2 see socket.

3 a percussive or electronic device which produces a noise to draw attention, as in an alarm bell or door bell.

4 see calathus.

bell-and-spigot joint see spigot-and-socket joint.

bell arch a round arch supported on corbels with rounded undersides, often in a different stone; see reverse ogee arch.

bell arch

bell capital, 1 blossom capital, campaniform, open capital; an Egyptian capital carved in the form of an upside-down bell in stylized imitation of an open papyrus or lotus flower; see papyrus capital.

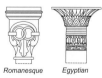

Romanesque   *Egyptian*

2 a medieval capital type with a central conical drum terminated at upper and lower edges by rings, discs or annulets.

3 see trumpet capital.

bell cast in renderwork, the thickening of the lower edge of a laid render coat to act as a drip.

bellcote, bellcot, bell gable; a small belfry which surmounts the ridge of the roof of a church or public building.

belled pile see under-reamed pile.

bell face hammer a hammer whose striking face is rounded so as to avoid damaging the surrounding surface when driving nails.

bell gable see bellcote.

bell pliers large pliers with notched jaws, side cutters and a notched depression; used for gripping and cutting wire.

belt sander a hand-held power sanding tool with a motor-driven belt of sandpaper or abrasive cloth.

bench 1 a hard seat of stone, timber, metal or plastics for a number of people, with or without a back.

2 a workman's table, see workbench.

bench chisel a traditionally wooden-handled chisel used for general woodwork.

bench grinder, grinder, grinding wheel; a benchtop power tool with a rigid rotating disc of abrasive material, used for sharpening tools and grinding metal surfaces.

benching 1 a horizontal ledge in an embankment or other earthwork.

2 the addition of concrete to support and reinforce an embankment.

3 sloping side construction in the base of a drainage manhole to control the flow of water and provide a base to stand on.

benchmark 1 in engineering, computing and technology, a predefined standard or set of operations against which to test systems under trial.

2 in surveying, a fixed point of known position and altitude, used as a datum from which other measurements can be referred.

bench plane a flat-bottomed wooden or metal plane used for reducing, levelling and smoothing wood; a generic term for all flat and wide-bottomed planes.

bench saw, joiner saw; a cross between a handsaw and a spineless backsaw.

bench vice, carpenter's vice; a vice used by a carpenter, fixed or incorporated into a workbench to hold pieces in place whilst they are being worked.

bend a curved pipe fitting to change direction of flow in a pipeline or duct;

types included as separate entries are listed below:
*bent ferrule; *branch bend; *elbow; *fire bend; *knee, see elbow; *knuckle bend; *long radius bend; *machine bend; *pulled bend; *reducing bend.

bending 1 in structures, the bowing deformation of a beam or other member under load.
2 the forming of materials or components such as metal pipes and profiles with bends.

bending moment, moment of deflection; the total bending effect at any section of a loaded beam caused by the turning effect of remote force upon a point; units are Nm.

bending radius in the bending of pipes and other metalwork, the radius of curvature of a bend.

bending schedule see bar schedule.

bending strength, flexural strength; the ability of a beam or other structural element to resist forces in bending.

bending stress in structures, the stress, usually in a beam, caused by a bending moment.

bending tool, hickey (Am), hicky (Am); a hand tool used for bending reinforcement bars, pipes, etc. into their desired shapes.

bent pertaining to pipes, glass, timber and metals which have been curved using a special tool, pressure or casting process.

bent ferrule, bend; in water and gas pipework, a pipe fitting with a 90° bend.

bent glass, curved glass; glass that has been reheated and curved in a kiln for use in special glazing applications.

bent plywood plywood which has been bent using jigs during the gluing stage of production; used for specially shaped interior panels and furniture.

bent plywood used for seat of the Paimio chair, Alvar Aalto 1933

bentonite suspension a thixotropic drilling fluid consisting of bentonite and water; betonite is a form of clay which undergoes great expansion with increase of water content; used also in rubber compounds and synthetic resins.

bent-up bar in reinforced concrete slabs and beams, a tensile reinforcing bar in a beam which has been bent to provide shear reinforcement.

benzol black see carbon black.

Berlin blue a name for the pigment Prussian blue used especially in France.

beryl a colourless or variously coloured mineral used as ornamentation and gemstones (emerald, aquamarine) and as an ore for the extraction of beryllium.

Bessemer steel high grade steel manufactured in a converter using the Bessemer process, in which hot air is blown through molten pig iron in a converter to reduce the quantities of undesirable elements such as phosphorus and silicon.

best reed, Norfolk reed; unbroken stalks of the water or common reed [*Arundo phragmites*, *Phragmites australis*], dried and used as thatched roofing, mainly in marshy areas of England, especially East Anglia.

beton brut an untreated in-situ concrete finish which bears the indentations and markings of the sawn boards into which it was cast.

better face see face side.

Betula spp. see birch.

bevel, 1 chamfer, splay; the blunting with a slanting edge of a right-angled or sharp corner.

bevel

2 see bevel moulding.
3 a slanting planar surface in a piece of glass, usually formed by grinding an edge.
4 see also grinding bevel, honing bevel, bevel square.

bevel edge chisel see bevelled-edge chisel.

bevelled joint any timber corner joint where the parts to be joined have been bevelled to fit together, see below.

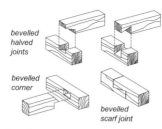

bevelled halved joints

bevelled corner

bevelled scarf joint

bevelled corner joint, splayed corner joint; a timber corner joint in which the halved ends of members are bevelled for increased strength and convenience.

bevelled halved joint, splayed halved joint; a timber halved joint whose laps are bevelled for increased strength.

bevelled housed joint in timber frame construction, a joint in which one member is received into an angled recess or housing in another.

bevelled scarf joint, longitudinal bevelled halved joint, straight bevelled halved joint; a timber lengthening joint in which the halved ends are bevelled to fit together.

bevelled-edge chisel, bevel edge chisel; a sturdy chisel whose blade is bevelled on both long edges as well as its end, used for the cleaning of edges, rebates and mortises in woodwork.

bevelled moulding see bevel moulding.

bevel moulding a decorative moulding whose cross-section is that of a fillet splayed to the vertical; also known as a chamfered or splayed moulding.

bevel square, bevel; a measuring tool with a hinged metal blade or two jointed legs used for measuring, checking and marking out angles.

bianco sangiovanni, St John's white, lime white; a white pigment consisting of a mixture of calcium hydroxide and calcium carbonate used in fresco painting.

bibcock see bib tap.

bib tap, bibcock; a simple water tap for filling or emptying vessels, etc. whose nozzle is bent downwards.

bice a variety of Bremen blue pigment.

bid, offer; an offer of a sum of money for goods or a price for the gaining of a contract, usually in competition with others for the same item; see tender.

bidet a seated sanitary appliance for washing the private parts, consisting of a bowl connected to a water supply and drain.

bidet shower a shower hose and head assembly in proximity to a WC suite and connected to a water outlet.

biennial any species of plant planted as a seed one year and which flowers, seeds and dies the following.

bi-fold door a horizontally folding door with two leaves, hinged in the middle.

bi-fold door

BIIR see bromine butyl rubber.

billet, billet moulding; a decorative moulding, found especially in Romanesque architecture, consisting of a series of recessed cylinders or rectangles arranged in a chequered pattern; see round billet, roll billet, square billet.

billet moulding

bill of quantities, bill of materials (Am); a written contract document produced by a quantity surveyor containing an itemized list of all materials, methods and workmanship for a particular construction project; see priced bill of quantities.

binder, 1 binding agent, cementitious material; any material, usually a liquid which hardens, used in mortar, concrete, paints, plaster, etc. for bonding a mass of solid particles together; see paint binder.
2 in timber frame construction, any horizontal timber member used for holding together a series of components, studs, rafters, etc. of a timber frame.
3 binding beam, binding joist, bridging joist; in traditional timber frame

construction, a heavy main beam or joist which gives intermediate support to floor or roof joists.

4 a timber tie beam for connecting the upper ends of parallel side walls to prevent them from splaying outwards.

5 see stirrup.

binding agent see binder.

binding beam see binder.

binding course in stone and brick masonry, a row of through stones or bricks laid crosswise to internally stabilize a wall, join two leaves together, etc.

binding joist see binder.

binding wire, annealed wire, iron wire, tying wire; in reinforced concrete, soft iron wire for tying reinforcing bars together before the casting of concrete.

biodegradable waste see organic waste.

biotite a form of dark brown, green or black mica, a soft potassium iron magnesium silicate mineral; see black mica, glauconite.

bi-part folding door a vertical folding door leaf of two horizontally hinged panels, which lie in a horizontal plane above the doorway when the door is fully open.

bi-part folding door

bi-parting door see centre-opening door.

birch [*Betula spp.*] a group of hardwoods from the northern hemisphere with hard, pale timber; used for furniture, interior joinery, pulp and plywood; birch plywood is plywood in which all or face plies are of birch veneer; birch trees are occasionally planted in parks and gardens for their pale

Betulus pendula – silver birch

green foliage and attractive smooth bark; see below for birch species included in this work:

European birch, silver birch, downy birch; [*Betula pendula, Betula pubescens*] a collective name for timber of the silver and downy birches, species of European hardwood with hard, strong, white to pale brown, uniform timber; used for making furniture and plywood and whose burr is often used in decorative veneers.

paper birch [*Betula papyrifera*] a North American hardwood with brown timber; used as sawn boards, in plywood, furniture and interiors.

yellow birch [*Betula alleghaniensis*] a North American hardwood with light brown to deep russet hardwearing timber; used for plywood and turnery.

bird cherry [*Prunus padus*], see cherry.

bird-pecked finish see sparrowpecked finish.

bird's beak moulding see beak moulding.

bird's eye in woodwork and joinery, pertaining to certain cuts of the sugar maple with small circular markings on the wood surface, valued for their decorative appearance.

bird's head sculpted band ornament with a row of bird heads as if hung downwards, found especially in English Norman architecture.

bird's head ornament

birdsmouth, sally; in timber frame construction, a notch cut into the end of an inclined timber to receive a horizontal timber running perpendicular to it; used for the housing of rafters; other similar notches in other components:

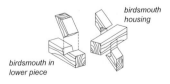

birdsmouth housing

birdsmouth in lower piece

birdsmouth brick *birdsmouth brick* a special brick manufactured with an indented end, designed for use in decorative brickwork and at an internal obtuse corner in a brick wall.

birdsmouth notched joint see birdsmouth joint.

birdsmouth joint, birdsmouthed notched joint; in timber roof construction, a joint formed by notching the extremity of a rafter with a birdsmouth and fastening it to a wall plate; any joint similar to this.

Birmingham wire gauge, Stub's wire gauge; abb. BWG; a classification of thicknesses for wire and steel sheet, based on imperial units.

biscuit referring to ceramic products which have been fired but have not undergone further treatment such as glazing.

bismuth white, Bougival white; a white pigment consisting of bismuth nitrate, used in the early 1900s and now largely replaced by zinc white.

bistre, bister, brown lampblack; a yellowish brown pigment consisting of soot containing tar from the charring of beech wood; used as a watercolour wash.

bit 1 a replaceable rotating blade or tip for use with a power tool; see cutter, drill bit, screwdriver bit.
2 a unit of information in a binary system.

bitmac see bitumen macadam.

bitter spar see magnesite, dolomite.

bitumen a solid or viscous black tarry liquid found naturally or produced from the distillation of petroleum, used as a binder, an adhesive and for waterproofing membranes.

bitumen-based coating material see bituminous paint.

bitumen-coated chipboard chipboard which has been precoated with bitumen.

bitumen emulsion a dispersion of bitumen in water with an emulsifying additive; used in construction for the bonding of overlapping membranes and general waterproofing.

bitumen felt, bituminous felt, roofing felt; a waterproofing membrane consisting of a thin fibrous mat of polyester or glass fibres saturated with bitumen or a bitumen-polymer; used for roofing, tanking, etc.

bitumen felt roofing see bituminous felt roofing, built-up roofing.

bitumen impregnated softboard a low density fibreboard impregnated with 10—30% bitumen as water resistance.

bitumen macadam, bitmac; a temporary or base surfacing for roads, coarser than asphalt, consisting of graded aggregate coated with bitumen to provide adhesion.

bitumen paint see bituminous paint.

bitumen-polymer membrane bitumen-polymer sheet used as tanking or roofing.

bitumen-polymer sheet a form of bituminous felt which contains a polymer modifier and is reinforced with a layer of fibreglass or other mesh.

bitumen primer in bituminous roofing, a bituminous liquid applied as a waterproofing coating and to glue down successive layers of roofing felt.

bitumen roofing see bitumen felt roofing, bituminous roofing.

bitumen shingles see strip slates.

bitumen solution a viscous liquid consisting of bitumen and a solvent, used for masonry tanking, waterproofing layers, coating steelwork and the underbodies of cars, etc.

bituminous pertaining to any material, product or method based on or containing bitumen or coal tar.

bituminous adhesive any adhesive based on bitumen or coal tar used for bonding sheet materials such as roofing felt and linoleum.

bituminous binder a bituminous material that has adhesive and waterproofing properties.

bituminous coating a thin layer of bitumen, applied hot by mopping, used in tanking and roofing, etc.

bituminous felt see bitumen felt.

bituminous felt roofing roofing or layers of laid bituminous felt, either glued on flat roofs using bituminous solutions or tacked on pitched roofs using clout nails; see built-up roofing, roll-jointed roofing, lap-jointed roofing, strip slates (bitumen shingles).

bituminous felt roofing with conical roll joints

bituminous membrane a general name for bitumen felt and other similar products.

bituminous paint, bitumen paint, bitumen-based coating material; paint or a thin coating consisting of asphalt or bitumen in a solvent or emulsion, used for protecting ferrous metals.

bituminous putty in glazing, a kind of putty which consists of bituminous products and elastomers.

bituminous roofing any waterproof roofing which is bitumen-based; often bituminous felt roofing; see bituminous felt roofing, built-up roofing.

black a general name for achromatic shades of colour which reflect very little light and are at the dark end of the grey scale; types of black pigment included as separate entries are listed below: *benzol black, see carbon black; *black lead, see graphite; *black oxide of cobalt; *black oxide of iron, see Mars colour; *black oxide of manganese; *blue black, see vine black; *bone black; *carbon black; *cobalt black, see black oxide of cobalt; *coke black, cork black, see vine black; *Davy's grey; *diamond black, see carbon black; *drop black; *Frankfurt black; *gas black; *German black, grape black, see vine black; graphite; *ivory black; *kernel black, see vine black; *lampblack; *manganese black; *Mars black, see Mars colour; *oil black; *Paris black; *pine soot black; *slate black; *vine black; *yeast black.

black alder [Alnus glutinosa], see alder.

black and white work traditional English and central European half-timbered wall construction in which the exposed timber frame is blackened and the wattle and daub infill is rendered white.

blackbutt [Eucalyptus pilularis], see eucalyptus.

black cherry, American cherry; see cherry.

black cottonwood [Populus trichocarpa], see poplar.

black gum see tupelo.

black iron oxide see iron oxide.

black lead see graphite.

black locust an alternative name for timber from the robinia tree.

black maple [Acer nigrum], see maple.

black mica a black or dark-coloured form of biotite mineral.

black oxide of cobalt, cobalt black; cobalt oxide, Co_3O_4, similar in properties to Mars black or black oxide of iron, used as a black pigment.

black oxide of iron see Mars colour.

black oxide of manganese natural manganese dioxide formerly used as a black pigment; see manganese black.

black poplar [Populus nigra, Populus spp.], see poplar.

blacksmith's hammer a traditional name for an engineer's hammer.

black spruce [Picea mariana], see spruce.

black spruce beetle [Tetropium castaneum], see spruce beetle.

black walnut see walnut.

black wattle see Australian blackwood.

blackwood see Australian blackwood [Acacia melanoxylon].

blade the metal cutting edge of a knife, plane, saw or any other cutting tool.

blanc fixe, baryta white, constant white, enamel white, permanent white; a form of artificial barium sulphate, $BaSO_4$, used as a base and inert pigment in paints.

blanc titane see titanium white.

blank 1 in mass-produced manufacturing, a piece of material (metal, timber or plastics), which has been roughly shaped or moulded before working into a finished state; see preform.
2 see blind.

blank cap see end cap.

blank tracery see blind tracery.

blank window a window opening which has been walled up; often the same as a false window.

blast cleaning a method of cleaning large masonry and concrete surfaces by projecting a gas (usually air), a liquid (usually water), or an abrasive through a nozzle at high velocity.

blast-furnace a large industrial vessel where iron is smelted from iron ore by mixing it with limestone and coke and heating at 1100°C.
blast-furnace cement, blast-furnace slag cement; a blended cement composed of ground blast-furnace slag mixed with a hydraulic binder such as Portland cement.
blast-furnace concrete see slag concrete.
blast-furnace slag a clinker composed mainly of calcium, magnesium and aluminosilicates, a by-product of steel production used as a binder and aggregate in concrete.
blast-furnace slag cement see blast-furnace cement.

blasting, shot firing; the removal of rock from the ground, either for commercial use or during excavation, using explosives.

blasting treatment the high-velocity projection of a gas, liquid or granular solid as a cleaning treatment and for producing a finish on stone, concrete, etc.

blast-resistant laminated glass glass specially manufactured with interlayers to have anti-bandit and bullet-resistant properties.

blast venting panel, blast wall; a panel wall designed to give way in the event of an explosion, thus absorbing some of its energy.

blast wall a structural wall designed to afford protection from an explosion; see also blast venting panel.

bleb see blow-hole.

bleeding, 1 bleed-through; a discolouring defect in a paint finish appearing where pigment or other material has diffused into the paint film from below.
2 see concrete bleeding.

bleeding Stereum [*Stereum sanguinolentum*] a fungus which attacks wood in exterior timberwork and in storage.

bleed-through see bleeding.

bleed valve see air release valve.

blemish an undesirable feature, stain, etc. that depreciates the visual appearance of a product, surface or finish, but has no effect on its quality.

blend see mixture.

blended aggregate a mix of more than one type of aggregate in concrete.

blended cement, blended hydraulic cement; a cement composed of a latent hydraulic binder such as ground blast-furnace slag, pozzolana or fuel-ash mixed with ordinary Portland cement; the mix produces a chemical reaction which improves the properties of the cement.

blended hydraulic cement see blended cement.

blending see mixing.

blind 1 a retractable shading device for a window or other glazed opening, often of textile or slatted construction; see also venetian blind, roller blind.
2 blank; referring to an opening in construction which has been walled up, or a decorative panel on a wall which imitates a window, door, tracery or some other opening.

blind arcade an arcade whose arches have been blocked up with masonry infill; a similar decorative effect formed by a series of arches on a solid masonry wall.

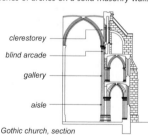

clerestorey

blind arcade

gallery

aisle

Gothic church, section

blind arch an arch which is blocked up, or appears as decoration on the surface of a solid masonry wall.
blind door see false door.
blind dovetail joint see lapped dovetail joint.
blind hinge see concealed hinge.
blind mortise see stopped mortise.
blind nailing see secret nailing.

blind tracery, blank tracery; Gothic tracery carved onto masonry wall surfaces and timber panelling as relief ornament.

blind window see false window.

blinding a layer of lean concrete 50–100 mm thick laid over soil to seal the ground and provide a clean bed for further construction work.

blinding concrete concrete suitable for use as a blinding over soil to seal it and provide a clean bed for subsequent construction work.

blinding course in construction of roads and external paving, a layer of concrete, crushed rock, gravel or sand laid to protect the surfacing from moisture rising up from the underlying ground.

blindstory 1 a portion of the external wall of a building one storey high with no openings; often a full storey parapet wall above roof level.
2 in church architecture, a triforium with a blind arcade.

blister 1 an imperfection in glass consisting of a trapped bubble of gas.
2 blistering; a defect in a plaster finish consisting of a local swelling which may cause the plaster to peel away from its base.
3 blistering; a defect in a paintwork finish consisting of trapped air bubbles caused by the evaporation of moisture or other substances beneath the paint surface.

blister figure a decorative mottled figure in veneers cut from timber with irregular grain, resembling blisters in the surface.

blistering see blister.

block, 1 building block, masonry block; a generic term for rectangular units of mineral material, solid, perforated or otherwise shaped, used in masonry construction; may be made of clay, concrete or other mineral composition and is usually larger than a brick; examples included as separate entries are listed below:
*concrete block; *hollow clay block; *glass block; *paving block, see concrete block paver.
2 any small solid piece of material such as stone, metal, wood, plastics, etc., often a squared lump used in construction used as a spacing, filling or packing piece, e.g. a location block.

3 an urban plot of densely built form bounded by three or four intersecting streets.
4 a building with a number of floors; a multistorey building.
5 see blockage.
6 see title block.

blockage, block; in pipework, trapped solid matter which inhibits the flow of a liquid or gas, or the resulting problem caused by this.

blockboard a timber building board formed by gluing veneers on either side of a core of solid wood strips with a width of between 7–30 mm; the grain of the veneers runs at 90° to that of the core.

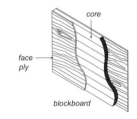

blockboard

block capital a common Romanesque capital whose roughly cubic form has a rounded undersurface; also called a cushion capital or cubic capital.

Romanesque block capital, Church of St Michael, Hildesheim, Lower Saxony, Germany, 1007–1033

block end ridge tile, ridge end; a ridge capping roof tile specially formed with one closed end to cover the end of a ridge.

block flooring see end-grain wood block flooring.

blockout see box out.

block paver see concrete block paver.

block paving see concrete block paving.

block plan, location plan; a drawing or vignette on a drawing which shows the location in plan of a site with respect to other parts of an area, or the location of part of a building with regard to the whole, usually drawn as simple outlines or blocks.

block plane a small one-handed plane for smoothing and finishing small pieces, especially useful for working the end grain of wood.

blockwork 1 walling construction in laid blocks, or the result of this process.
2 see log construction.

bloom see efflorescence.

blossom capital see bell capital.

blow see throw.

blower see fan, fan unit.

blow forming a method of forming thermoplastics moulded products by fastening a heated sheet around its edges and blowing it like a bubble; may or may not be blown against a mould.

blow-hole, bleb, bug hole; in concretework, a pitted defect in a hardened concrete surface caused by air pockets released from the concrete and becoming trapped against the formwork.

blowlamp, blowtorch; a portable burner with a hot and accurate flame produced by the forcing of liquid fuel through a nozzle, and ignition on mixing with air; used for various jobs on site such as warming, melting, cutting, etc.

blow moulding a method of forming hollow thermoplastics products by blowing air into a heated mould; sheet material is thus forced against both halves of the mould.

blown bitumen, oxidized bitumen; bitumen through which air has been blown to improve its elasticity and raise its softening temperature.

blown glass any glass traditionally produced by manual blowing; see blown sheet glass, crown glass.

blown oil, blown linseed oil; refined linseed oil which has had air blown through it to promote oxidation and thickening; used as a vehicle in paints.

blown sheet glass traditional sheet glass formed by blowing glass into cylindrical moulds, allowing it to cool, then cutting, reheating and flattening it.

blown vinyl relief wallcovering wallcovering whose face surface has been rendered with a raised pattern, formed by foaming a layer of polymer such as PVC.

blow out in concretework, the removal of unwanted material, debris, etc. from inside formwork with compressed air before casting of concrete.

blowtorch see blowlamp.

blue a general name for shades of colour in the visible spectrum with an electromagnetic wavelength in the range 440–480 μm; blue pigments included as separate entries are listed below:
*Alexandrian blue, see Egyptian blue; *alizarin blue, see alizarin; *Antwerp blue; *artificial ultramarine; *azure cobalt, see cobalt blue; *azzura della magna, see azurite; *azzuro oltremarino, see lapis lazuli; *Berlin blue; *bice; *blue ashes; *blue bice; *blue celeste, see cerulean blue; *blue malachite, see azurite; *blue verditer; *Bremen blue; *bronze blue; *Brunswick blue; *caeruleum, see cerulean blue; *celestial blue; *cerulean blue; *Chinese blue; *cobalt blue; *cobalt ultramarine; *coelin, coeruleum, see cerulean blue; *copper blue, copper green; *corruleum blue, see cerulean blue; *cyanine blue; *Egyptian blue; *French blue, French ultramarine, see artificial ultramarine; *Gahn's blue; *Gmellin's blue, see artificial ultramarine; *green ultramarine, see ultramarine, ultramarine green; *Haarlem blue, see Antwerp blue; *Indian blue, see indigo; *indanthrone blue, see indanthrene; *indigo; *intense blue, see phthalocyanine pigment; *iron blue, see Prussian blue; *Italian blue, see Egyptian blue; *king's blue; *lazuline blue, see lapis lazuli; *Leyden blue; *manganese blue; *Milori blue, see Prussian blue; *mineral blue, see azurite; *Monastral blue, see phthalocyanine pigment; *mountain blue, see azurite, Bremen blue; *Paris blue, paste blue, see Prussian blue; *phthalocyanine blue; *Pompeian blue, Pozzuoli blue, see Egyptian blue; *Prussian blue; *Saxon blue, see smalt; *soluble blue; *steel blue, see Prussian blue; *thalo blue, see phthalocyanine pigment; *Thénard's blue, see cobalt blue; *ultramarine, ultramarine blue; *Vestorian blue; *Vienna blue; *woad; *zaffer, zaffre.

blue ashes a variety of Bremen blue pigment.

blue bice a variety of Bremen blue pigment.

blue black see vine black.

blue celeste see cerulean blue.

blue fungus see blue stain.

blue malachite see azurite.

blue stain, blue fungus; an unsightly blue tinge on timber caused by fungal micro-organisms such as Ophiostoma minus, which does not affect its strength or other physical properties.

blue verditer a variety of Bremen blue pigment.

blushing a defect in a transparent lacquer or varnish finish consisting of a milkiness caused by moisture or cold.

bms see building management system.

board 1 any rigid sheet material of wood, plaster, plastics, etc. used in construction for cladding and bracing a frame; a building board.
2 in the conversion of timber, a piece of sawn timber with cross-sectional dimensions of less than 38 mm thick and greater than 75 mm wide; in general any sawn or planed section of timber of similar dimensions used in finished flooring, external cladding, linings, etc.
3 thin, stiff, wood or paper-based sheet used in drawing, painting and modelmaking.
4 a number of people chosen by shareholders to run the affairs and administration of a company or institution as its decision-making body; a board of directors.

board and batten cladding a form of board on board cladding in which the joints between laid vertical boards are covered externally with thin strips of timber.

board and batten cladding

board cladding see timber cladding, weatherboarding.

board finish plaster, board plaster; hemihydrate plaster used as a finish for even surfaces such as gypsum plasterboard and other relatively smooth building boards.

board flooring flooring composed of dressed wooden boards laid side by side, either laid over joists or on battens over a concrete slab; see wood board flooring.

board formwork formwork in which the concrete is placed against an assembly of sawn timber boards, plywood or other building boards.

boarding, 1 sheathing; the cladding of a building frame in building board as stiffening, weatherproofing, lining, etc.; the boards thus fixed.
2 sawn or planed timber boards or planks laid side by side as cladding or lining for a frame; see roof boarding, floorboards, weatherboarding, siding.

board-marked finish a finish for concrete in which the pattern of the boards used as formwork is evident in the surface.

board on board cladding, staggered siding; external timber cladding of boards laid vertically in two layers so that the outer layer covers the gaps between boards in the layer below.

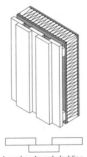
board on board cladding

board plaster see board finish plaster.

board sawn timber timber which has been converted into boards.

boaster, drover; a broad-faced masonry chisel for working stone to a relatively smooth surface. See illustration on facing page.

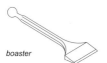

boaster

body-tinted glass glass to which a tint has been added throughout its thickness, usually for the control of solar radiation; see smoked glass, see tinted solar control glass.

bog oak see oak.

boiled linseed oil quick-drying raw linseed oil with added chemical lead or manganese-based accelerators or driers, originally cooked to induce polymerization, used as a varnish for wood finishing, or in paints and other varnishes.

boiler, furnace (Am); a water heater which heats water to below boiling point for domestic or other use; types included as separate entries are listed below:
*back boiler; *central heating boiler; *electric boiler; *electric water heater; *gravity boiler; *high output back boiler.
boiler house a building or part of a larger building complex in which the boiler plant is housed.
boiler plant, water-heating plant; mechanical plant consisting of boilers, pipework, flues, etc. to produce hot water for a building; see also heating plant.
boiler room a plant room that houses the boiler plant.

bois de rose see rosewood.

boiserie decorative timber wall panelling which is elaborately carved.

bold roll tile see double roll tile.

bole 1 the trunk of a tree especially when used for conversion into timber.
2 types of fine compact clay usually containing iron oxide, used as pigments.
3 gold size; a mixture of clay and rabbit skin or hide glue applied to the surface of an object being prepared for gilding.

bolection moulding, balection moulding, raised moulding; a moulding used to cover the joint between two flat surfaces which do not lie in the same plane, such as for the joint between a timber panel and its frame.

bollard a low sturdy cast-iron or stone post around which a rope can be tied when mooring a boat or ship, or one of concrete, steel or other construction designed to prevent the passage of vehicular traffic.

Bologna chalk calcium carbonate sulphate used as a filler in gesso for frescos.

Bologna stone the mineral heavy spar found near Bologna in Italy.

bolster,
1 headtree, saddle; in traditional timber frame construction, a horizontal timber piece

bolster, 2

fixed to the top of a post to spread the load of a beam supported by it.
2 a wide masonry chisel used for cutting bricks and blocks.
3 a thickening in the neck of a chisel and similar tools to prevent the blade being forced into the handle when it is struck with a mallet.

bolt 1 a flat-ended fastener with a helically threaded shank whose head has a hexagonal, octagonal or square projection allowing it to be tightened to a nut using a spanner; types included as separate entries are listed below:
*anchor bolt; *carriage bolt, see coach bolt; *countersunk head bolt; *cremone bolt, cremona bolt, cremorne bolt; *expanding bolt, expansion bolt; *foundation bolt, see anchor bolt; *handrail bolt, see joint bolt; *hexagonal bolt, hex-head bolt; *king bolt; *lag bolt, lag screw, see coach screw; *machine bolt; *ragbolt, see anchor bolt; *rail bolt, see joint bolt; *rock bolt; *roofing bolt; *toggle bolt.
2 any fastening or catch for a door which involves a sliding bar which engages in a housing in a jamb, the most common of which is a barrel bolt; examples included as separate entries are listed below:
*barrel bolt; *dog bolt, see hinge bolt; *fire-exit bolt, see panic bolt; *flush bolt, see flush slide; *foot bolt; *hinge

*bolt; *panic bolt; *security bolt, see hinge bolt; *slide bolt; *tower bolt.*
3 draw bolt, lock bolt; that part of a latch or lock which engages with a striking plate in the frame to hold the door in a closed position; examples included as separate entries are listed below:
*catch bolt, see return latch; *claw bolt; *dead bolt; *hook bolt; *indicating bolt; *latch bolt, see return latch; *slide bolt, snib bolt.*
4 see veneer bolt.

bolt croppers, bolt cutters; a long scissor-like tool with long handles and powerful jaws for shearing thicker metal objects such as bolts and screws.

bolted joint a joint fixed with a bolt or bolts.

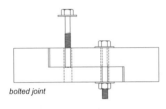

bolted joint

boltel see bowtell.

bolt-through fixing a fixing for components and fittings in which a bolt is passed through the supporting construction and fastened on the reverse side with a nut.

bond 1 the fixing or securing force provided by mortar, adhesives, coatings, etc.; see adhesion, concrete bond.
2 see brickwork bond.
3 in project management, a sum of money or securities placed by a building contractor with a client or third party as a guarantee of completion of construction work.

bond-beam block see channel block.

bond breaker see separating layer.

bonder, bondstone, bonding brick; a brick or stone laid crosswise into a wall to tie surface masonry to the rest of the wall.

bond failure see adhesive failure.

bonding admixture in concretework, a latex admixture included in the mix to improve tensile and bond strength.

bonding agent, bonding primer; a chemical substance applied in liquid form to a hardened substrate to improve the bond of subsequent layers or coatings.

bonding brick any brick which has been cut or manufactured to non-standard size or shape in order to fill space at the edges and corners of a brickwork bond; often a cut brick or bat; see also bonder.

bonding compound, hot bonding compound, hot stuff (Am); in bituminous roofing, molten oxidized bitumen applied to bond successive layers of bitumen felt together.

bonding plaster plaster used for undercoats in circumstances where the base has little key or adhesion.

bonding primer see bonding agent.

bond line see bond plane.

bond plane, bond line; the surface of adhesion or bonding in a joint.

bondstone see bonder.

bond strength 1 the strength of the adhesive bond created by glue between two glued or bonded elements, or between a coating and its substrate.
2 in reinforced concrete, the strength of the bond between reinforcing bars and the surrounding concrete, measured at the point of failure of the bond.

bond stress in reinforced concrete, stress which occurs between the surface of reinforcement and the surrounding concrete in a member under load.

bond timber, chain timber; in traditional construction, a timber laid horizontally in a solid masonry wall to provide bracing and reinforcement.

bone black a strong black pigment consisting of impure carbon obtained from burnt and ground bones; see also ivory black.

bone glue a form of animal glue, traditionally used for furniture-making, bookbinding and gums, manufactured by boiling the bones of animals.

bonnet see chimney cap.

bonnet hip tile, granny bonnet; a special roof tile formed into a convex shape to cover a hip; its open end is usually filled with mortar once laid.

bookmatching a veneering pattern in which successive sheets cut from a log are laid side by side as mirror images of one another, resembling an open book, also called book match; see also vertical butt and horizontal bookmatching.

bookmatch veneering

boom, 1 barrier; a light barrier across a road or waterway, a hinged bar or pole which can be lifted to allow traffic to pass underneath.
2 see jib.
3 see chord.

booster see booster pump, fire booster.

booster pump, booster; a pump for increasing the local pressure in a water supply pipeline.

boot lintel an L-beam supporting overhead external wall construction above a strip window.

borax sodium borate in natural form, used in soldering and as a detergent.

border 1 in landscaping, a strip of planting used at the edge of a building or pathway.
2 a decorative edging band for a panel or area of wall.
3 an inset line demarking the edge of a drawing on all four sides.
4 the dividing line between two politically or administrationally independent areas.

bored pile in foundation technology, a pile placed using excavations or boring into the ground; most often a cast-in-place pile; types included as separate entries are listed below:
*augered pile; *cast-in-place pile; *large diameter pile; *percussive bored pile.

borehole see wormhole.

boring see drilling.

Borneo camphorwood see kapur.

borocarbon see boron carbide.

boron carbide, borocarbon; a chemical compound, B_4C, used as a hard abrasive.

borosilicate glass, Pyrex; a fire-resisting glass which softens at high temperatures but does not crack.

borrowed light a glazed panel incorporated into an internal wall or partition; an internal window between two spaces.

boss 1 a decorative ovular protrusion, knob or node, found as a centrepiece in domes and ceilings, at the meeting of ribs in a vault, and as a terminating element for mouldings; see knot.
2 a protruding spout in a sanitary appliance or pipe to which a pipe fitting can be attached; see screwed boss.

bossage in stonework, projecting stones which have been left untreated either as rustication or awaiting further tooling.

bottle trap a drainage trap with a water-filled vessel divided by a baffle or interior pipe to form a lock, and a removable base to facilitate cleaning.

bottom bead the lowest glazing bead in a window, which fixes the lower edge of a pane or unit into a frame.

bottom chord see lower chord.

bottom floor see base floor.

bottomgrate, grate; a metal grille in a coal or wood fire on which the combustible material rests and under which air is free to circulate during combustion; most often a cast iron construction; see stool bottomgrate.

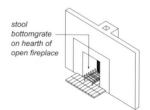

stool bottomgrate on hearth of open fireplace

bottom-hung referring to a window, casement or hatch whose opening leaf is hinged at its lower edge.

bottom-hung window

bottom rail the lowest horizontal member in a framed door leaf or window sash.

bottom raker in temporary sitework, the lowest slanting prop in a raking shore.

bottom reinforcement in reinforced concrete, longitudinal reinforcement placed near the base of a cast beam or slab to resist tensile forces.

bouchard a hand-held bush hammer; also written as boucharde.

Bougival white a form of the white pigment bismuth white.

boultine, boutell see bowtell.

bow, camber; the warping of improperly seasoned timber boards evident as longitudinal curvature along the flat faces.

bow in poorly seasoned timber board

bow handle an arched or U-shaped pull handle fixed to a door leaf by both ends.

bowstring truss a trussed beam in which the lower chord is flat and the upper chord is curved with its apex in the middle, forming a braced upside-down U-shape.

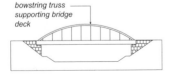

bowstring truss supporting bridge deck

bowtell, boltel, boultine, boutell, bowtel, edge roll; a decorative moulding whose cross-section is a three-quarter segment of a circle.

bowtell

bow window a bay window, curved in plan.

box beam a compound beam formed of an upper and lower chord of timber with plywood or other sheet webbing fixed to either side, thus forming a hollow box in cross-section; also similar construction in steel, when it is also known as a box girder.

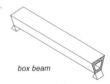

box beam

box caisson, American caisson, stranded caisson; a reinforced concrete caisson constructed in such a way that it is open at the top and closed at the base, forming a part of the final foundation construction.

box corner joint a many-tenoned corner joint used in cabinetmaking for joining boards and sheets at right angles; sometimes called a finger joint or combed joint.

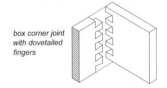

box corner joint with dovetailed fingers

box dovetail joint a many-tenoned dovetailed corner joint used in cabinetmaking for joining boards and sheets at right angles.

box frame see cased frame.

box frame construction a form of timber frame construction in which the vertical members (posts or studs), horizontal members (plates) and bracing form a rigid box; the roof structure is then placed or built on top.

box girder a box beam which consists of a welded rectangular tube of steel plate.

box girder
bridge deck

box gutter, 1 rectangular gutter; in roof construction, any rainwater gutter which is rectangular in cross-section.
2 roof channel; a large gutter set below the level of roof planes, usually rectangular in section; used for draining flat or butterfly roof forms, at valleys, behind parapets, etc.

boxing in timber construction, the casing of a timber frame with boards.

box match a veneering pattern in which four triangular pieces of straight-grained veneer are laid in a rectangular arrangement with diagonal joints, forming a series of diamond shapes by the direction of grain; see reverse box match.

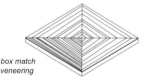

box match
veneering

box out, blockout (Am), core, former, pocket; a formwork mould for creating an opening in concrete, or the opening so formed.

box pile in foundation engineering, a pile which is a square hollow tube of welded or rolled steel; a square pipe pile.

box spreader a machine with a hopper which spreads concrete to the required thicknesses between forms to produce a concrete road surface.

box staple, keep, staple; a metal hood attached to the side of a door frame into which the latch of a rim lock engages.

box strike a metal component fitted into a mortise in a door jamb to receive a deadbolt and protect it from being tampered with when the door is closed.

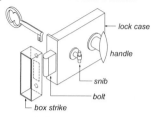

lock case

handle

snib

bolt

box strike

boxwood, box; [*Buxus sempervirens*] a hardwood from Europe, North Africa and the Middle East with pale yellow and very hard timber; used for turned work, inlay, chisel handles, chessmen and dressers.

BR butadiene rubber.

brace 1 a hand tool with a crank and handle for boring holes; a large manual drill with a kinked shaft.
2 in frame structures, any structural element which stiffens and reinforces the angle between two members, especially a diagonal structural member, strut or rod providing rigidity to a frame; see also cross brace, diagonal.

braced stanchion see lattice stanchion

brace moulding, bracket moulding, double ogee moulding; a projecting decorative moulding formed by two back to back ogees, their convex ends together; see keel moulding.

brace moulding

bracing any system of structural members designed to maintain the rigidity of a structure, frame, etc.; see brace, cross-bracing, frame bracing.

bracing panel a sheet component fixed over a frame in order to provide rigidity.

bracket 1 a secondary projecting fixing component from which other components are supported, suspended or hung from a structure.
2 a projecting construction in masonry architecture to support pediments over doorways, balconies, ornamentation, etc.
bracket fungus see conk.

bracketing in ornamental plastering, a series of timber brackets constructed to support lathing when casting a cornice.

bracket moulding see brace moulding.

bracket saw see fretsaw.

brad, 1 oval brad head nail; a slender shanked nail with a small bullet-shaped head, used for interior finishing work and locations where a concealed fixing is desirable.

brads

2 a flat L-shaped nail cut and bent from steel strip.

3 see glazing sprig.

bradawl, awl; a pointed tool used for piercing holes in thin wood or board, or for making starter holes for screws.

bradawls

bradder a small nail gun for light nails up to lengths of 75 mm; used for fixing boarding and cladding.

brad hammer see tack hammer.

brad point drill, dowel bit; a drill bit with a sharp point at the drilling end for accurate centring, used for the drilling of holes in wood.

brake in lift machinery, an electro-mechanical safety device for stopping the lift car if the electrical supply fails or is switched off.

branch 1 a secondary connection from a main to a point of use in pipework, duct-work, wiring installations, etc.; see branch fitting, branch discharge pipe.

2 one of the woody stems of a tree which spread outwards from the main trunk, from which leaves, etc. grow, and which appear as knots in sawn timber.

branch bend a curved branch fitting for changing the direction of flow in a drain-age pipeline.

branch discharge pipe a drainage pipe into which waste from one or a number of appliances on the same floor of a building is conveyed into a discharge stack.

branched knot, winged knot; a knot in seasoned timber formed by two or more branches in close proximity cut at the same point.

branched knots

branch fitting, branch; in a system of sanitary pipework, a T-shaped piece of drainage pipe, pipe fitting, etc. for making the connection of a secondary pipe to a main.

branch tracery, astwerk; the tracery found in German Gothic churches of 1400s and 1500s, with tree and branch motifs.

branch vent see branch ventilating pipe.

branch ventilating pipe, branch vent; a drainage pipe connected to a ventilation stack, providing ventilation and balancing pressure fluctuations in a branch discharge pipe.

brashy, short grained; a description of defective timber which is brittle and snaps cleanly under lateral loading, either due to fungal attack or natural causes.

brass a strong, corrosion-resistant, yellow-ish alloy containing mainly copper and zinc, often with traces of lead, tin, alumin-ium, manganese, iron and nickel; used as sheetmetal and for pipes, castings and forgings.

Brazilian rosewood [*Dalbergia sprucea-na*], see rosewood.

brazing, hard soldering; a form of sol-dering which employs alloys (often of copper, zinc and silver) which melt at a much higher temperature than normal soft solder; the joints are thus stronger.

brazing solder see hard solder.

breach of contract, violation of agreement; a situation arising when a party who has signed a contract, or made an agreement, fails to keep to the condi-tions or terms of that agreement.

break-glass unit a manual fire-indicat-ing device with an alarm switch set behind a glass panel, which must be bro-ken in order to set off the alarm.

breaking joint in masonry bonding, the overlapping of bricks in alternate courses so as to avoid continuous vertical joints.

breaking strength see ultimate strength.

breast drill a drill with an attachment which is pressed against the chest to provide additional force in drilling.

breast lining joinery panelling, boarding, etc. for the portion of the internal surface of a wall between window sill and floor.

breastsummer, bressummer, brestsummmer; in traditional timber-framed building, a timber beam which carries a load over an opening.

breather paper, building paper; in timber frame construction, thick water-resistant paper used in the thickness of wall construction, which allows for ventilation but acts as a barrier against the effects of driving rain and wind pressure.

breccia any rock consisting of angular fragments of stone solidified in a finer matrix such as limestone or clay; some marbles with this composition are used for decorative stone cladding.

breech fitting, 1 breeching; a Y-shape pipe fitting used to converge two parallel pipelines.
2 see group connector.

breeching see breech fitting.

Bremen blue, mountain blue, mountain green; a poisonous blue pigment consisting of copper hydroxide and copper carbonate, produced in various shades.

bressummer, brestsummer see breastsummer.

brick, building brick; a rectangular block made of fired clay, burnt mud, concrete or other mineral material, used for building walls, paving and other constructions; its size is usually no larger than 338 × 225 × 113 mm, so it can be held in one hand for ease of laying; types included as separate entries are listed below:

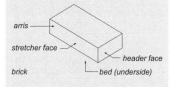

arris

stretcher face

header face

brick

bed (underside)

*Accrington brick; *air brick; *angle brick; *arch brick, see radial brick; *beam brick, see lintel brick; *birdsmouth brick; *bonder; *bonding brick; *bullhead brick, see cownose brick; *bullnose brick; *burnt brick, see fired brick; *calcium silicate brick; *cant brick; *capping brick; *cavity brick, see hollow brick; *channel brick, see lintel brick; *clay brick; *common brick; *concrete brick; *coping brick; *cored brick, see perforated brick; *cove brick; *cownose brick; *cuboid brick; *cut brick; *dogleg brick; *engineering brick; *facing brick, face brick; *firebrick; *fired brick; *fireproof brick, see flue block, firebrick; *flared brick; *flint-lime brick; *flue brick, see flue block; *glass brick, see glass block; *glazed brick; *great brick; *green brick; *handmade brick; *hollow brick; *imperial standard brick; *later; *lintel brick; *metric brick, see modular standard brick; *metric modular brick, see modular standard brick; *metric standard brick; *modular brick; *modular standard brick; *mud brick; *paving brick, paviour brick; *perforated brick; *plinth brick; *pressed brick; *purpose made brick; *radial brick; *red brick; *refractory brick, see firebrick; *rusticated brick, rustic brick; *saddleback capping brick; *saddleback coping brick; *sand-faced brick; *sand-lime brick, see calcium silicate brick; *special brick, special shape brick; *split face brick; *squint brick; *Staffordshire blue brick; *standard brick; *standard modular brick, see metric brick; *standard special brick, see special brick; *sun-baked brick, sun-dried brick, see mud brick; *tax brick; *three quarter brick, see king closer; *US standard brick; *ventilating brick, see air brick; *wirecut brick; *wooden brick, see nog.

brick-and-a-half wall, one-and-a-half brick wall; a solid bonded brick wall whose width is the sum of the length and width of one standard brick plus one intermediate joint, 13" or 327 mm.

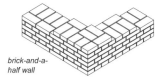

brick-and-a-half wall

brick architecture architecture in which unrendered brickwork is the principal structural, expressive or decorative material.

brick axe see bricklayer's hammer.

brickbat see bat.

brick bond see brickwork bond.

brick capping the uppermost protective course of capping bricks in a freestanding wall or parapet; see capping brick.

brick coping the uppermost protective course of coping bricks in a freestanding wall or parapet; see coping brick.

brick clay see brick earth.

brick course a single row of bricks forming a horizontal band in a wall.

brick earth, brick clay; clay suitable for use in the manufacture of bricks.

brick facing, brick veneer; a skin of non-structural brickwork attached to a structural base such as concrete, masonry or, in some cases, studwork.

brick hammer see bricklayer's hammer.

brickie a colloquial name for a bricklayer.

brick joint 1 any joint between adjacent bricks in masonry.

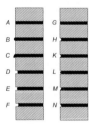

BRICK JOINTING
A flush joint, flat joint
B extruded joint, convex joint
C squeezed joint, unfinished joint
D raked joint, recessed joint
E recessed beaded joint
F recessed keyed joint, rodded joint

POINTING
G beaded joint
H concave joint, keyed joint,
  bucket-handled joint, rodded joint
K scored joint, ruled joint; V-joint
L convex V-joint
M weathered joint
N struck joint

2 the final shaped mortar in horizontal bed and vertical joints after the bricks have been laid.

bricklayer, brickie; a tradesman or skilled worker who lays bricks and blocks on a construction site.

bricklayer's hammer, brick axe, brick hammer; a light hammer used in bricklaying for shaping and chipping bricks and concrete blocks; its head has one chiselled end for cutting and one flat face or peen for tapping into place.

bricklayer's line, builder's line, stringline; a length of fine cord strung between two points on a building site to establish the line and level of prospective construction, as an aid in bricklaying and setting out, etc.

bricklayer's trowel, brick trowel, mason's trowel, masonry trowel; a steel-bladed hand tool used in bricklaying for applying and smoothing bedding and jointing mortar.

brick lintel see reinforced brick lintel.

brick nogging in traditional half-timbered construction, brick infill for the timber frame.

brick on bed see brick on flat.

brick on edge in brickwork, a brick laid on its side so as to leave either its shorter edge or its bed showing in the masonry surface; either a rowlock or

brick-on-edge paving

shiner; brick-on-edge coping is coping for a freestanding wall formed from a row of bricks laid on edge, usually across the thickness of the wall as rowlocks; brick-on-edge paving, see brick paving.

brick on end in brickwork, a brick laid on its end, either to leave the longer edge or the bed showing vertically; see soldier, sailor; brick-on-end paving, see brick paving.

brick-on-end paving

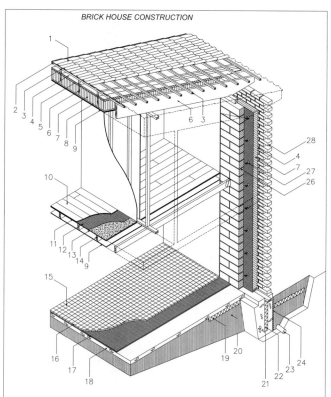

BRICK HOUSE CONSTRUCTION

ROOF CONSTRUCTION
1   tiled roofing
2   roof tile
3   tiling batten
4   ventilation gap,
5   roof sheathing
6   roof beam
7   thermal insulation
8   vapour barrier
9   ceiling boarding

UPPER FLOOR CONSTRUCTION
10   overlay flooring
11   veneered parquet,
12   impact sound isolation
13   flooring sub-base - chipboard
14   floor joist

BASE FLOOR CONSTRUCTION

15   tile flooring, floor tiling
16   ceramic tile flooring tile
17   tiling mortar
18   ground supported floor
19   thermal insulation
20   gravel fill

FOUNDATION
21   concrete strip foundation
22   cavity and thermal insulation
23   subsurface drain
24   drainage membrane,

CAVITY WALL, HOLLOW WALL
26   inner leaf - blockwork
27   wall tie, cavity tie
28   outer leaf - brickwork

brick on flat, brick on bed; a brick laid on its largest side, in the way intended; brick-on-flat paving.

brick-on-flat paving

brick paving bricks laid side by side in a horizontal plane as a hardwearing external paved surface; brick-on-edge paving is paving of bricks laid in series with sides upwards; brick-on-end paving is paving of bricks laid in series with ends upwards.

brick slip a thin cladding brick or brick-shaped tile of the same material and finish as the surrounding brick masonry, used for facing lintels, beams, etc.; often a brick cladding tile.

brick slips

brick tile a clay wall tile used as a facing for concrete and other materials in imitation of brick.

brick trowel see bricklayer's trowel.

brick veneer see brick facing.

brickwork any construction in bricks laid with a binder such as mortar; types included as separate entries are listed below:
*carved brickwork; *chequered brickwork; *coloured brickwork, see polychrome brickwork; *dogtooth brickwork; *fair-face brickwork; *gauged brickwork; *herringbone brickwork; *honeycomb brickwork; *houndstooth brickwork, see dogtooth brickwork; *loadbearing brickwork; *moulded brickwork; *mousetooth brickwork, see dogtooth brickwork; *ornamental brickwork, see decorative masonry; *patterned brickwork; *polychrome brickwork; *rendered brickwork; *rubbed brickwork, see gauged brickwork; *structural brickwork.*

brickwork bond the overlapping and interlocking of bricks laid in mortar in successive courses to provide strength and for decorative effects.

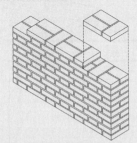

brickwork joint see brick joint.
brickwork weathering, exfoliation, flaking; the degradation and scaling of a brickwork surface over time due to exposure to the elements and chemical reaction with the cement, causing internal swelling and rupture.

brickworks an industrial plant for the production and firing of bricks.

bridging joist, binder; a main spanning beam in a timber floor, which supports floor joists.

bridled scarf joint a timber lengthening joint formed by cutting a tenon at the end of one member; this sits in a bridle (an open housing or slot) cut into the end of the other.

bridle joint a timber angle joint in which the end of one timber is cut with a groove or slot to fit into a suitably shaped cutting in the side of another; sometimes called an open tenon joint if at a corner; see double tenon joint.

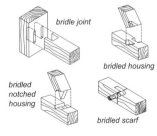
bridle joint
bridled housing
bridled notched housing
bridled scarf

brief, programme; in the commissioning of a building project, a statement of the client's requirements which includes the scope of works, usage, number and floor area of spaces and functional requirements.

bright timber commercial sawn timber with no defects in colouration or from staining.

brise soleil a window louvre.

Bristol board smooth paper-faced card available in a range of thicknesses, used in printing, drawing and modelmaking.

British Columbian cedar [*Thuja plicata*] western red cedar, see thuja.

British Columbian pine see Douglas fir.

British Standard Whitworth thread see Whitworth thread.

brittleness the property of a material or object to break suddenly under loading without appreciable deformation.

brittle point the highest temperature at which a rubber material or elastomer loses its elasticity and will fracture under sudden impact.

broach a narrow-bladed masonry chisel used for working stone surfaces.

broached hip see half hipped end.

broach stop, pyramid stop; in ornamentation, the termination of a chamfered moulding or carving with a protruding half-pyramid.

broad-leaf any non-coniferous tree, which may be deciduous or evergreen, from which hardwood is obtained; a member of the angiosperm group; see **hardwood** for list of tropical and European hardwood trees.

broad tool see batting tool.

broad tooled finish see batted finish.

broch a prehistoric Scottish fortified tower dwelling, round in plan and with a tapering profile, constructed of drystone masonry in cellular construction; alternative spellings are brough and brugh.

broken colour in paint and colour science, a base colour to which a small amount of another colour has been mixed to add subtlety.

broken pediment, broken-bed pediment, open-bed pediment; see pediment.

broken white see off-white.

bromine a dark reddish toxic chemical element, **Br**, used in the manufacture of dyes, synthetic rubbers, etc.

brominated anthranthrone a bright semi-transparent yellow pigment used in the automotive industry.

bromine butyl rubber, BIIR; a tough synthetic rubber, butyl with a halogen, used for car tyres, seals and hoses, cured more easily and readily than butyl, and thus more suitable for use with other rubbers.

bronze a hard, dark brown alloy of copper and tin which is resistant to corrosion; copper alloys with other metals, such as aluminium, magnesium and silicon are also given the name bronze; true bronze is sometimes called tin bronze.

bronze blue Prussian blue pigment which has a bronze sheen.

bronze plating see bronzing.

bronzing, 1 bronze plating; the application of a protective or decorative coating of bronze to metals.
2 the treatment of a copper surface with chemicals to alter its colour.

broomed finish see brushed finish.

brooming see brushing.

brotch, spar, spick, spike, staple; a fastener for bundles of thatched roofing made of a willow or hazel branch bent into a hook-shape and pushed into underlying construction.

plan and section of broch, Dun Troddan, Glen Elg, Scotland, c.100 BC

brown a general name for shades of darkened yellow and dusky orange colour, not evident in the visible spectrum; brown pigments included as separate entries are listed below:
*alizarin brown, see alizarin; *bister, brown lampblack, see bistre; *brown madder, see alizarin; *brown ochre; *burnt sienna; *Cologne earth, see Cassel

earth; *iron brown, see Prussian brown; *madder brown, see alizarin; *Mars brown, see Mars colour; *Prussian brown; *Rubens brown; *sepia; *sienna, siena; *umber, umbre; *Vandyke brown.

brown cement see Roman cement.

brown coat see base coat.

browning plaster plaster used for undercoats, made from gypsum and sand and used in instances where the base has a good key and adhesion; a browning coat was originally of plaster which was brown in colour, see also base coat.

brown iron ore see limonite.

brown iron oxide see burnt sienna.

brown lampblack see bistre.

brownmillerite mineral oxides of calcium, iron and aluminium oxides found in sulphate-resistant cements.

brown ochre a dull brownish yellow form of the native pigment ochre.

brown rot fungus a large group of fungi which attack the cellulose of dead wood to leave the lignin as a brown powdery residue, causing serious decay and weakening of timber construction.

bruised lath in ornamental plasterwork, timber laths which have been softened, or whose surface has been broken by striking with a hammer to provide a key for a plaster coating.

Brunswick blue a form of the blue pigment Prussian blue to which barytes has been added.

brush a sweeping, cleaning and scouring implement consisting of a number of stiff fibrous bristles fixed into a head; a similar implement with a clump of soft fibres or hairs bound to a wooden or plastic handle, used for applying paint, glue and other liquids to a surface; see paintbrushes for list of brushes.

brushed finish, broomed finish; a decorative or non-slip finish texture produced by scouring or scrubbing the surface of fresh concrete or plaster with a stiff broom.

brushing, 1 brooming; a surface treatment for fresh concrete and plaster produced by scoring with a stiff brush, either as decoration or to provide a rough finish.

2 the application of paints, coatings, adhesives, etc. manually, with a brush.

brushing adhesive types of adhesive which can be applied in liquid form with a brush.

bruzz chisel, corner chisel, dogleg chisel, parting chisel; a woodcarving chisel whose blade is V-shaped in section.

BSW thread acronym for British Standard Whitworth thread; see Whitworth thread.

bubble, bubbling; a defect in a paint finish consisting of trapped bubbles of gas in the hardened paint film, often caused by careless application or by the use of volatile solvents in the paint mix.

buck a fixing member at the side of a doorway or window opening to receive a door or window and fasten it in place; see also door lining.

bucket-handled joint see keyed joint.

buckling 1 in structures, the sudden creasing failure by crumpling of a longitudinal structural member loaded eccentrically with a compressive force.
2 the creasing of sheetmetal and other sheet products due to lateral forces, defects, impact, etc.

buckling load the compressive load at which a column or strut begins to buckle.

bucranium, bucrane; Lat.; a carved decorative motif depicting the skull of a bull, found in classical architecture; Greek form is boukranion.

bud capital, closed bud capital, closed capital; an Egyptian capital carved in stylized imitation of the closed flower of the lotus or papyrus plant; see also papyrus capital.

Egyptian papyriform bud capital

buffer 1 any device that cushions the effect of an impact or provides protection from the collision of moving objects, as installed on vehicle loading bays, trains, lifts and behind heavy doors; see door buffer, car buffer.

2 in computing, a temporary information storage area or intermediate memory used during data transfers between devices that are working at different speeds.

3 a machine tool with a rotating disc of wool or cotton fabric, used for polishing floors and other surfaces.

bug hole see blow-hole.

bugle head screw a screw with a trumpet-shaped head containing a cross, allen or Torx slot in its flat end.

builder see contractor.

builder's see building firm.

builder's lift a temporary on-site lift consisting of a moving cage, in which workmen, goods, etc. can pass rapidly between levels of a building under construction or repair.

builder's line see bricklayer's line.

building 1 any permanent structure which provides shelter, encloses space and can be occupied by people, animals, goods or services.

2 the process or product of assembly of elements, components, materials and finishes on a building site; also variously known as construction, building construction or building development to differentiate it from other forms of construction.

building automation see building management system.

building ban a local authority notice preventing the construction of a building or buildings on a particular site.

building block any mineral-based unit designed for use in construction; larger than a brick; a generic term for concrete and clay blocks and other masonry units which are often larger than bricks, usually simply called a block; see also concrete block, hollow clay block, glass block, paving block (concrete block paver).

building board any rigid sheet material of timber, mineral fibre, plastics, gypsum, etc. used in construction for cladding and lining frames as a surface for a finish, as insulation or as bracing.

building by-laws locally varying regulations controlling the construction and erection of buildings administered by local authorities on the basis of model by-laws provided by government.

building code see building regulations.

building codes of practice legal documentation setting out requirements to protect public health and safety, and outlining standards of good practice with regard to the construction and occupancy of buildings.

building component a prefabricated assemblage of parts or product such as a door or window assembly, technical utility, etc. supplied ready for installation on site after the building frame is completed.

building conservation see conservation.

building construction the discipline, process, etc. of constructing buildings; matters pertaining to this.

building contract an agreement by which a building contractor is committed to construct a building, carry out building works, etc. for a certain price within a certain time and to documented designs.

building contractor see contractor.

building control, building inspection; the process of inspection, issuing permits, granting approval, etc. pertaining to buildings under construction and repair, administered by a local authority to ensure that they are properly constructed.

building control officer, building inspector; a person, often employed by a local authority, who inspects designs and constructions to ensure they comply with standards and regulations.

building cost, construction cost; a cost incurred as a result of building development, usually plural.

building development see development.

building element any major functioning part of, or structural assembly in a building, such as roof, floor, walls, beams, slabs or foundations; sometimes made up of building components.

building envelope, external envelope the external roof and wall components and constructions of a building which protect the interior from the effects of temperature and the weather.

building firm, builder's; a private firm which provides a building service; usually a small or family business.

building floodlighting the aesthetic use of electric lighting to highlight external features of buildings and their elevations in the dark.

building frame the loadbearing elements, columns, slabs, beams, walls and foundations in a building; often simply referred to as a frame; for further information about types of frame, see the following entries: concrete frame; timber frame; steel frame.

building inspection 1 a periodic checking on site by a local authority official to ensure that parts of a building have been constructed according to regulations, by-laws, etc.; see building control.
2 the detailed surveying of a building in use to ascertain its general condition, whether it has any particular faults and and whether it is in need of remedial work.

building inspector see building control officer.

building line an agreed-upon boundary line for the area occupied by a proposed building or indicating how close to a site boundary, public land, etc. a building may be constructed, usually determined by the local authority.

building maintenance the act of looking after, servicing and cleaning property regularly.

building management system, building automation, bms; an automated computer-based system for controlling the mechanical services and security installations in a building.

building material any basic substance, raw or manufactured material, product, etc. used in the construction of buildings.

building moisture extraneous water which builds up within the construction and structure of a building due to occupation or faulty design and construction.

building paper, kraft paper; thick paper or card laminated or impregnated with a waterproofing material such as bitumen, used in the construction of roofs, floors and walls as a moisture barrier; see breather paper.

building permission see planning permission.

building permit formal approval in written form by a local authority to an application for planning permission.

building preservation an action by a planning authority to maintain a building of certain historical or cultural value in its current state, preventing alteration or demolition.

building project, development; the preliminary arrangements, administration, funding and construction work undertaken during the realization of a particular building or structure, viewed as a whole.

building regulation a statutory code which regulates the construction, alteration, maintenance, repair, and demolition of buildings and structures with regard to issues such as layout, accessibility, safety, health, materials and fire safety.

building sealant see sealant.

building site, construction site; the area of land on which excavation work, building construction, storage of materials and plant, etc. for a particular building project take place.

building stone natural stone used in building construction for walling, cladding, paving, etc.

building survey an inspection of a property, usually undertaken by a professional prior to being bought or sold, to ascertain its general condition and prospective repair work.

building surveyor a professional who inspects and reports on the condition of existing buildings and carries out building surveys.

building technology see construction technology.

built environment an urban or rural milieu, structured or produced by built form; that part of the surroundings relating to buildings, structures and civil engineering works.

built-in furnishings or other components fixed in place so as to appear or function as an integral part of a space.

built-up of beams and columns, made from more than one timber fixed together by bolts or splices to provide greater bearing capacity and improved strength. See illustration on facing page.

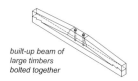

built-up beam of
large timbers
bolted together

built-up roofing, built-up felt roofing; roofing constructed from a number of layers of bitumen felt, laid in succession with overlapping joints, usually used for flat roofs.

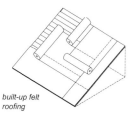

built-up felt
roofing

bulb that part of an electric lamp, usually of thin transparent or translucent glass, which contains the gas, vapour or filament from which light is emitted; see also lightbulb.

bulbous dome see onion dome.

bulk density the weight per unit volume of a loose material, measured in kg/m^3; usually used in conjunction with non-homogeneous materials such as concrete or piled timber which contain voids or water pockets.

bulk heater a device in an oil heating installation for warming oil to reduce viscosity prior to use.

bull capital an ornamental stone capital carved with a paired bull's head motif, especially found in the apadanas of ancient Persian architecture.

bulldog plate see toothed plate connector.

bullet catch see ball catch.

bullet-head nail see lost-head nail.

bullet-resistant laminated glass, armour-plated glass; glass that can withstand the penetration of gunfire, usually formed from several sheets of glass laminated together with resin.

bull-faced finish see hammer-dressed finish.

bull header see rowlock.

bullhead brick see cownose brick.

bullion, bullion glass, bull's-eye glass; a traditional form of glass with a central circular bulge, formed by rotating a clod of molten glass via its centre; the central bulge so formed.

bullnose a rounded external edge.

bullnose brick any special brick with one or more rounded edges; used for decorative brickwork, paving, etc.; see cownose brick.

bullnose brick

bullseye a small traditional round window or light glazed with crown or bullion glass; any small round window in general.

bull's-eye glass see bullion.

bull stretcher see shiner.

Bulnesia arborea see verawood.

bunch, shove; a bundle of Norfolk reed used as a basic roofing material in thatching; see also nitch.

bunched cabling electric or telecommunications cables installed together in tied groups.

bundle see bundled bars.

bundle column 1 a group of ancient Egyptian column types with shafts carved to resemble bunches of tied plant stems, named according to the plant in question; see also papyrus column.

Romanesque
bundle column,
Regensburg
Cathedral,
Germany, 1260 AD

Egyptian bundle
column, mortuary
temple of Ramses III,
Thebes, 1150 BC

2 a stone column type in Gothic, Romanesque and Renaissance architecture with a shaft carved into a number of stems, as if separate smaller columns, terminating at a capital; modern equivalents of this; see also compound pier.

bundle pier a Gothic compound pier with a large number of shafts.

bundled bars, bundle; in reinforced concretework, a group of reinforcing bars tied together in a bundle with wire, which act as one larger bar.

bundling in reinforced concrete, the placing of a number of reinforcing bars tied side by side with wire to act as a larger bar.

buon affresco see buon fresco.

buon fresco, true fresco, buon affresco; a form of mural painting in which mineral or earth pigments are applied to lime or gypsum plaster while it is still wet; see fresco secco.

buoyancy the tendency of a body immersed in a denser liquid to float; the force thus exerted, which moves the body towards the surface and causing it to float.

buprestid beetle any woodboring insect of the genus *Buprestis spp.*; see metallic wood borer.

Burgundy violet see manganese violet.

burin, graver; a small wooden-handled implement for making intricate cuts on wood or metal consisting of a metal shaft with a sharp pyramid-pointed end.

burl, burr, knur, knurl; a growth deformity in a tree which, when cut as timber, is valued for its decorative figure in veneer, furniture and turnery.

burl veneer, burr veneer; decorative veneer with mottled or wavy figure, cut from the burl of a tree.

burlap see hessian.

burner a device or chamber where the oil or gas fuel for a heating or lighting system is burned.

burnishing the polishing of a metal surface by rubbing.

burnt brick see fired brick.

burnt carmine see roasted carmine.

burnt lime see quicklime.

burnt sienna, Italian earth, natural brown iron oxide; a rich orange-brown native pigment, sienna, crushed and calcined in a furnace; one of the most used pigments.

burnt umber, jacaranda brown, mineral brown, Spanish brown; raw umber heated in a kiln to form an orange-brown native pigment; see also Vandyke brown.

burr 1 see burl.
2 see grinding burr.
burr veneer see burl veneer.

bursting see rock burst.

bush in drainage and plumbing, a short piece of pipe or pipe fitting for joining lengths of pipe with different diameters, threaded internally at one end and externally at the other; see socket reducer (reducing bush).

bush hammer a machine or hand tool for producing a textured finish on the surface of stonework and hardened concrete; a hand-held bush hammer is often called a bouchard or boucharde.

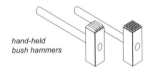

hand-held bush hammers

bush-hammered a relatively even pitted finish for concrete or stone in which the surface has been worked with a bush hammer or similar machine tool.

busk a plastering hand tool consisting of a flexible steel sheet, used for removing excess hardened plaster.

butadiene rubber, BR, polybutadiene; a synthetic resilient rubber with many uses, including car tyres, made from butadiene, a gaseous unsaturated hydrocarbon.

butane organic gas fuel, C_4H_{10}, stored and transported in compressed bottled form as liquids, used for blowtorches and other on-site burner equipment.

butt chisel, pocket chisel, sash chisel; a chisel with a short, wide blade.

buttercup yellow see zinc yellow.

butterfly damper a flue damper with paired winged flaps which are folded back in their normal open position, and spring flat to close off a duct or flue.

butterfly head screw see one-way head screw.

butterfly hinge a hinge with two decorative leaves fixed to a central knuckle, resembling a butterfly or bow-tie when opened out.

butterfly hinge

butterfly nut see wing nut.

butterfly roof, Y-form roof; a roof form in which two sloping planes rise outwards and upwards from a central gutter.

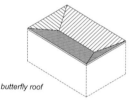

butterfly roof

butterfly tie see butterfly wall tie.

butterfly toggle see spring toggle.

butterfly wall tie a galvanized steel wire wall tie twisted into a figure '8' shape.

butterfly wall tie

buttering the smearing of mortar onto the underside and end of a brick or block before laying into masonry, especially that which forms a vertical joint or perpend in the finished wall.

butternut, white walnut; [*Juglans cinerea*], see walnut.

butt gauge see marking gauge.

butt hinge a hinge with two rectangular metal leaves and a central joining pin, usually inset into the edge of a door leaf and its frame; types included as separate entries are listed below:

butt hinge

*ball-bearing hinge, ball-bearing butt hinge; *falling-butt hinge; *lift-off butt hinge, lift-off hinge; *loose butt hinge, see lift-off butt hinge; *loose pin butt hinge, loose pin hinge; *loose-joint hinge, loose-joint butt hinge; *non-mortised hinge, non-mortised butt hinge; *pin hinge, see loose pin butt hinge; *rising hinge, rising-butt hinge.

butt joint 1 the joint or seam made by the edges of two components or sheets situated side by side without overlapping.

welded steel butt joint

2 end joint; a weak joint between two long members joined end on end without lapping or interlocking.

timber lengthening butt joint held together with dog

butt match a bookmatched veneering pattern in which adjacent sheets are mirrored vertically; see vertical butt and horizontal bookmatching.

button, turn button; a simple catch consisting of a piece of stiff material fixed with a pivot to the inside of a door or exterior door frame, and which rotates to keep the door closed; see also push button.

buttonwood see plane.

butt purlin, tenon purlin, tenoned purlin; in timber roof construction, a purlin that is tenoned into the side of principal rafters.

buttress a vertical rib or mass of masonry, concrete, etc. to provide lateral support and stability to a wall, tower, etc.; sometimes called a counterfort; see flying buttress, counterfort, pier.
buttress wall see counterfort wall.

butt rot see annosus root rot.

butt tenon joint see abutting tenon joint.

butt veneer a decorative veneer with a distorted figure, cut from the stump of a tree.

butt welding, resistance butt welding; a method of resistance welding metal bars, wire or rods end to end by pressing them together and passing a current through them.
butt weld a welded joint between abutting metal components.

butyl an isomeric form of the chemical butylene; a tough synthetic rubber used for sealing, roofing and in paints, see bromine butyl rubber.

Buxus sempervirens see boxwood.

buzzer see door transmitter.

by-law see building by-laws.

Byzantine architecture, Italian Romanesque; architecture of Byzantium or the Eastern Roman Empire originating in c. 400 AD, characterized by the round arch, the circle in plan, the dome and work in mosaic.

C

CA cellulose acetate.

CAB cellulose acetate butyrate.

cabinet hinge, furnishing hinge; traditionally any small hinge used for cupboard doors, etc., nowadays any one of a wide range of patented mechanized hinges, often with spring mechanisms and specialized fixings.

cabinet hinge

cabinet lock, furniture lock; a small lock fitted to the doors, drawers, chest lids, etc. of furnishings.

cabinet lock

cabinetmaker a craftsman who makes fine furnishings, joinery and veneerwork.

cabinetmaker's tenon joint see keyed tenon joint.

cabinet projection a form of oblique projection in which the Y and Z axes are in plan and the X axis is at 45° upward and to the right, with scaling of lines parallel to it at half that of the others; see cavalier, military projections.

cabinet saw a timber-framed bow saw like a turning saw, but with a wider blade.

cabinet scraper, spokeshave scraper; a woodworking tool used for smoothing and scraping; a scraper mounted in a spokeshave.

cabinetwork the trade of making fine furnishings, joinery and veneerwork; the furnishings thus produced.

cabin hook a large hook and eye, in which the hook and ring are attached to backplates, not screw fittings.

cable, 1 steel cable, wire rope; a structural steel product consisting of steel wire wound round a central steel core, very strong in tension and used in for guys, stays, fastening and bracing.
2 see electric cable.
3 see cable moulding.
cable balustrade, wire balustrade, wire-rope balustrade; a balustrade

with a number of parallel lengths of stainless steel wire rope strung between uprights.

cable clamp see wire-rope clamp.

cable duct, pipe duck; a pipe buried in the ground, under concrete floors, etc. to provide a protected route for electric cables.

cable ladder a series of interlinked structural brackets for supporting a group of parallel electric cables at or adjacent to a wall surface or slab soffit.

cable lift a lift system in which the car and counterweight are hung from a series of steel cables over a sheave.

cable manhole a manhole in which maintenance work can be carried out on subterranean cables; sometimes called a junction chamber.

cable moulding, cabling, rope moulding; a decorative moulding representing the twisting coils of a rope.

cable moulding

cable-stayed referring to any structure supported and braced by a system of diagonal cables or rods.

cable-stayed bridge

cable-supported referring to any structure supported by a system of cables in tension.

cable thimble see wire-rope thimble.

cable tray a pressed sheetmetal bracket for supporting a group of parallel electric cables, often at high level or in a ceiling void.

cabling see cable moulding.

CAD acronym for computer-aided design.

cadmium a soft bluish-white metal, **Cd**, whose uses in construction include the corrosion-resistant protective or rustproofing surface coating for iron and steel, called cadmium plating.

cadmium plating see above.

cadmium red, selenium red; a lightfast and alkali-resistant inorganic red pigment mixed from cadmium sulphide and cadmium selenide, in wide use since 1910, opaque, quick drying and suitable for use in all types of paint.

cadmium yellow, aurora yellow; a range of yellow pigments manufactured from cadmium sulphide with good hiding power and performance.

caeruleum see cerulean blue.

cage a three-dimensional assembly of reinforcing bars for a reinforced concrete beam or column, often prefabricated.

caisson 1 a hollow foundation system, impervious to water, which is fabricated, sunk into the ground and emptied of soil and water to allow construction work within.
2 see coffer.

calathus Lat.; the main basket-like body of a Corinthian capital, surrounded by acanthus leaves, sometimes called a bell; Greek form is kalathos.

calcareous, calcarious; pertaining to types of sedimentary rock which contain considerable amounts of calcium carbonate, $CaCO_3$, such as limestone, sinter and chalk.
calcareous tufa a form of highly porous, pure limestone or calcareous sinter, used traditionally as building stone for arches, and burnt to produce lime.

calcite, calc-spar; a crystalline, white or coloured mineral form of calcium carbonate found in limestone, marble and chalk; used in the production of Portland cement, in the chemical, glass and cellulose industry, and in the smelting of iron ores.

calcium a chemical element, **Ca**, found naturally as a carbonate in building stones such as limestone and marble, and used in compound form in the manufacture of cement; see following entries:
calcium aluminate cement see high alumina cement.
calcium carbonate a chemical compound, $CaCO_3$, the chemical form of chalk, limestone and marble; used also as a white pigment in paint; see calcite, chalk, dolomite, bitter spar (calcium magnesium carbonate), limestone, marl, quicklime, whiting.
calcium chloride a chemical compound, $CaCl_2$, used as an accelerator in concrete and mortar.

calcium hydroxide a chemical compound, $Ca(OH)_2$, calcium oxide mixed with water, used in cements and mortars as a binder; the chemical form of slaked or hydrated lime.

calcium oxide a chemical compound, **CaO**, otherwise known as quicklime, made from heating limestone or marble; forms lime putty when mixed with water.

calcium silicate one of a number of chemical salts of silicon and oxygen combined with calcium, manufactured by heating lime with silica sand and used as a binder in concrete and in the manufacture of calcium silicate boards, bricks and blocks; see entries below:
calcium silicate block a building block of similar constitution to a calcium silicate brick, but of a considerably larger size.
calcium silicate board an incombustible and chemical-resistant fibre cement board used for fireproofing applications and as a general weatherproof building board.
calcium silicate brick a light grey or white brick made by pressing a mixture of slaked lime mixed with sand (sand-lime brick) or crushed flint (flint-lime brick) and heating in a steam autoclave.

calc-spar see calcite.

Caledonian brown poor quality burnt sienna.

Caledonian white a white pigment no longer in general use, made from lead chloro-sulphite.

calendered polymeric roofing roofing membrane of compressed layers of bitumen polymer and fibre reinforcement, manufactured by controlled rolling processes, see calendering.

calendering a method of forming thin thermoplastics sheet, laminate or backed sheet by feeding molten material between hot rollers and cooling rollers in succession.

calf's-tongue moulding see calves'-tongue moulding.

caliper see calliper.

call for bids see invitation to tender.

calliper, caliper; an instrument with two hinged legs for measuring the diameter or thickness of bodies; also called callipers; calliper gauge, see vernier callipers.

call point any kind of manually operated fire alarm switch, such as a break-glass unit.

Calocedrus decurrens see incense cedar.

calorie, calory, gramme calorie; abb. **cal**; a unit of energy equal to 4.19 joules; equivalent to the amount of energy required to raise one gramme of water by 1°C, under prescribed conditions of temperature and pressure; confusingly, when written with a capital letter, a Calorie (also kilocalorie or kilogramme calorie) is 1000 calories.

calorific value, heating value; the amount of heat generated by the combustion of a unit weight of specified material; its units are kJ/kg.

calorifier, heat exchanger; a water heater used in district heating systems, etc. which heats domestic water via a heating battery containing piped hot water from a central heating plant.

calves'-tongue moulding, calf's-tongue moulding; a decorative moulding with a series of small recessed pointed arches, taking its name from the row of intermediate sharp elements which resemble the tongues of young cows or deer.

calves'-tongue moulding

camber a slight convex curvature in an otherwise horizontal line or surface as with the convex cross-sectional curvature of a road; see also hog, bow.

cambered arch a brickwork arch with a flat extrados and a curved intrados, often used to relieve the illusion of sagging.

cambered beam, arched beam; a beam with upper, lower or both surfaces curved to form an arch.

camber

cambered beam

cambered vault see segmental barrel vault.

camber piece, camber slip see turning piece.

came see lead came.

camera 1 Lat.; a vaulted roof or ceiling in Roman architecture; a chamber or space thus enclosed.

2 an optical instrument for taking photographs, either on film or as digital data; see surveillance camera and camera surveillance.

camera surveillance, video surveillance; intruder security provided by banks of cameras installed at key points in and around a building, linked to a central monitoring point.

camera survey closed circuit television survey.

campaniform 'bell-shaped'; see bell capital.

campanile an Italianate bell tower, free-standing or attached to a building.

Camponutus herculeanus see carpenter ant.

Canada balsam an oleoresin exuded from the balsam fir (*Abies balsamea*), used as a medium in paints, varnishes and adhesives.

Canadian spruce [*Picea mariana, Picea glauca*], see spruce.

canalis Lat.; in classical architecture, a fluting or hollow between volutes in an Ionic capital.

canary wood see tulipwood.

candela abb. **cd**; the SI unit of luminous intensity.

candelabrum, pl. candelabra; Lat.; a large branched candleholder which supports a number of candles or lights, often hung from the ceiling.

candelabrum column highly ornate columns in Renaissance and Baroque architecture, with decoration resembling that on candlesticks; also called a candlestick column.

Renaissance candelabrum column

candle lamp a decorative tapered light-bulb whose upper end terminates in a point, reminiscent of the flame of a candle.

candlepower distribution curve see light distribution curve.

candlestick column see candelabrum column.

canephora, canephore, canephorum, kanephoros (Gk.); 'basket-carrying' (Lat.); in classical architecture, a carved statuesque column of a draped female figure, a caryatid, carrying a basket, or with a basket on her head.

Greek canephora from the Treasury of Siphnos, Delphi, 525 BC

canker rot see red ring rot.

cannel see grinding bevel.

canopy 1 any overhanging roof, shelter or ceiling providing cover or shelter.
2 hood; the upper construction in a fireplace, which directs smoke up a chimney.
3 an open ornamental shelter or covering, especially for an altar, tomb or throne; a baldachin.

cant brick, angle brick; a special brick manufactured with one or two corners chamfered, used in decorative and angled brickwork.

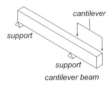

cant brick

cant chisel see framing chisel.

cantilever a horizontal structural member which is rigidly supported at one end only, forming an overhang; the structural configuration thus created.

cantilever balcony a balcony which is attached as a cantilever, without supporting tie rods or columns.

cantilever beam a beam of which part or all is a cantilever, and on which loads are supported.

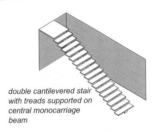

cantilever beam

cantilevered stair, flying stairs; a stair in which each step is cantilevered out from a wall or central newel; see double cantilevered stair.

double cantilevered stair with treads supported on central monocarriage beam

cantilever rafter see barge couple.
cantilever retaining wall see cantilever wall.

cantilever slab a concrete floor or roof slab which extends beyond its points of support forming a cantilever, as in a balcony.

cantilever wall a retaining wall, L-shaped in cross-section, which resists lateral pressure by the weight of earth resting on its flat protruding footing.

cantilever retaining wall

cantledge see kentledge.

cant strip see angle fillet.

caoutchouc, indiarubber; unvulcanized natural rubber, an elastic and waterproof material tapped from certain tropical trees.

cap an upper terminating fitting, strip, profile, or one designed to cover or seal an opening or joint; types included as separate entries are listed below:
*bayonet cap; *blank cap, see end cap; *chimney cap; *Edison screw cap, see screw cap; *end cap; *flue cap; *inspection cap; *lamp cap; *pile cap; *rain cap; *ridgecap, see ridge capping; *screw cap; *wall cap, see coping.

capacity 1 a measure of the internal volume of any vessel, especially the volume of liquid that a storage tank, cistern, etc. is designed to hold.
2 the ability of a system, workforce, etc. to cope with the demands of a certain task; the quantifiable ability of a machine, vehicle or other conveyor to move people, products and goods from one place to another.

capillary, capillary tube; a narrow vessel or pore narrow enough for capillary action to occur.

capillary action, capillarity; the rise of liquid in a fine bore tube or dry porous material due to surface tension.

capillary fringe an area of ground above the water table containing water held by capillary action.

capillary groove, anti-capillary groove; in window and roof construction, etc., a groove cut in a sill or overhang to prevent the backflow of water into adjacent construction.

capillary space in concretework, microscopic interlinked spaces or voids in hardened concrete containing water drawn through by capillary action; see water void.

capillary water groundwater suspended above the water table through capillary action.

capital 1 a separate block or a thickening at the top of a column or pilaster, used to spread the load of a beam, or as decoration; types included as separate entries are listed below:
*Aeolic capital; *animal capital, see protome capital; *basket capital; *bell capital; *block capital; *blossom capital, see bell capital; *bud capital; *bull capital; *closed bud capital, closed capital, see bud capital; *Composite capital; Corinthian capital; *crocket capital; *cubic capital, see block capital; *cushion capital; *double scallop capital; *eagle capital; *Egyptian capital; *figured capital; *historiated capital, see figured capital; *Ionic capital; *lily capital; *lion capital; *lotus capital, see lily capital; *moulded capital, see bell capital; *open capital, see bell capital; *palm capital; *papyrus capital, see papyrus; *plume capital, see palm capital; *protome capital; *scallop capital, scalloped cushion capital; *stalactite capital; *stiff-leaf capital; *supercapital, see dosseret; *tent-pole capital; *trumpet capital; *Tuscan capital; *vine leaf capital; *volute capital; *waterleaf capital.
2 money and property owned by a business, or money used to start a business.

cap nut, acorn nut, dome nut; a nut with a domed covering over its hexagonal base.

cap nut

capoc see kapok.

capping 1 any long timber, plastics or metal product used to cover a joint, welt or seam; see glazing capping.
2 a construction at the top of a wall or parapet to offer protection from the elements; see coping, capping brick.

capping block see coping block.

capping brick a special brick designed as the uppermost protective course in a freestanding wall or parapet; usually the same length as the width of the walling; see saddleback capping brick, coping brick.

capping tile ridge capping tile, see ridge tile.

cap sheet in built-up roofing, the uppermost layer of bitumen felt, bonded to the underlying intermediate sheet and often coated with chippings or foil and fibre reinforced.

caput mortuum a reddish-violet pigment formed from iron oxide with clays and gypsums.

carbide any of a number of chemical compounds of carbon with a metallic or semi-metallic element; see tungsten carbide, calcium carbide.

carbide hydrate see hydrated high calcium by-product lime.

carbolic acid see phenol.

carbolic oil an oily substance produced by the fractional distillation of coal tar at 170–230°C, containing naphthalene, phenols and other also alkaline compounds; used in the chemical, dye, food flavouring and cosmetic industries; also called middle oil because of its distillation sequence.

carbon a chemical element, **C**, found in many inorganic and organic compounds, and in natural form as graphite and diamond.
carbon black, benzol black, diamond black; a very fine, opaque black pigment, pure carbon, with high staining power; a shade of black which takes its name from the colour of coal.
carbon dioxide fire extinguisher a fire extinguisher used for industrial and service spaces, which functions by increasing the percentage of carbon dioxide gas in air to such a degree as to make combustion impossible.
carbon disulphide a chemical compound, CS_2, a pungent, poisonous, clear, flammable liquid used as a solvent and in the manufacture of cellophane.
carbon fibre a lightweight thread of pure carbon used for reinforcing polymers and metals.
carbon-fibre reinforced a description of plastics, mineral and metal products toughened with strengthening fibres of carbon; CRP is an acronym for carbon-fibre reinforced plastics.
carbon silicide see silicon carbide.
carbon steel steel containing carbon, which may also contain small amounts of silicon, manganese and copper according to specification; usually refers to high carbon steel; see low carbon steel, medium carbon steel, high carbon steel.

carbonation the combination of calcium oxide or calcium hydroxide with carbon dioxide, responsible for the hardening of plasters and cements.

carborundum silicon carbide used as an abrasive.
carborundum saw a circular saw whose blade is edged with carborundum.

car buffer a resilient sprung or oil-loaded construction at the base of a lift shaft to cushion the fall of the lift car in the event of failure of the lift mechanism, cabling, etc.

carburizing, cementation; a surface-hardening process for steel by heating it with charcoal and coke in a carbonaceous environment for a number of hours, during which carbon diffuses into the surface.

carcass the frame of a building excluding wall and roof cladding, services, fittings and finishes; the term usually refers to timber-framed construction; also written as carcase.

card reader in security and access control systems, an electronic device, often used in conjunction with a motor-locked door, through which an encoded card is passed to permit access.

car heating point see vehicle heating point.

carmine, Munich lake, nacarat carmine, Vienna lake; a red pigment made from cochineal.

carnauba wax a hard wax used as a vehicle in paints and varnishes, obtained from the leaves of the Brazilian palm *Copernicia cerifera* (sometimes referred to as the tree of life); often added to beeswax to provide hardness.

carnelian see cornelian.

Carolingian pertaining to the pre- and early Romanesque art and Byzantine-influenced architecture in France during the dynasty of the Frankish kings (768–843) founded by Charlemagne; often referred to as the Carolingian Renaissance or the Carolingian renovation.

carpenter a craftsman or tradesman who works on site in structural and framing timber; in North America this also includes one who works in joinery; an outdated or vernacular word for a carpenter is a wright.
carpenter and joiner a tradesman responsible for the woodwork in a building.
carpenter ant [*Camponotus herculeanus*] a species of insect which burrows and nests in dead hardwoods and softwoods.
carpenter's square see framing square.
carpenter's vice see bench vice.

carpentry construction work in timber; in North America this also includes joinery.

carpet 1 a thick floor covering woven from fibres, supplied in rolls and usually laid as fitted carpet; types included as separate entries are listed below:

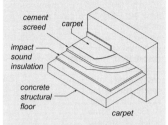

cement screed
carpet
impact sound insulation
concrete structural floor
carpet

*Axminster carpet; *cork carpet; *cut pile carpet; *fitted carpet; *flocked carpet; *looped pile carpet; *needle-punch carpet; *tufted carpet; *velvet carpet; *wall-to-wall carpet, see fitted carpet; *Wilton carpet; *woven carpet.*
2 see wearing course.

carpet strip a strip of metal, timber or plastics used to hold down the edge of a carpet or other sheet flooring.

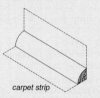

carpet strip

carpet tile a soft flooring consisting of prefabricated rectangular sheets of carpet which can be laid as tiles.

Carpinus betulus see hornbeam.

carport a covered space, canopy or shelter, open on at least one side, under which one or a number of vehicles may be parked; see also garage.

Carrara marble a high-quality, hard, white and durable form of marble, quarried in Carrara in Italy; polished and used as an external and internal finish.

carriage, centre string; a sloping beam which supports the treads of a wide stair in the middle between the strings; see mono-carriage.

carriage bolt see coach bolt.

carrier the inert liquid medium in which the adhesive material, pigment, etc. in adhesives and paints is suspended or dissolved.

carthame see safflower.

carved brickwork brickwork carved with a decorative pattern or relief after it has been laid.

carving chisel see woodcarving chisel.

carving knife a small hand tool with a short, shaped blade used for decorative woodcarving.

Carya spp. see hickory.

caryatid in classical architecture, a carved statue of a draped female figure which functions as a column.

one of six caryatids from the Erechtheum, Athens, Greece, c. 420 BC

Casali's green a form of viridian pigment.

case see casing, lock case.

cased frame, box frame; the hollow frame in a sash window, which contains the mechanisms such as a rope or cable and a counterweight.

casehardening a condition in improperly seasoned timber where the outer layers of the wood have been dried too rapidly resulting in internal tensions.

casein a phosphorous protein found in the milk of mammals; used in glues and paints.
casein glue a glue made from casein, more water-resistant than fish or animal glue.
casein paint paint supplied as a water-soluble powder, whose binder is a mixture of casein and lime; often applied as a

finish to sawn exterior timber, plaster, murals, etc.

casement an openable, framed, glazed and hinged light in a window unit.

casement door, French door, French window; a fully glazed panelled door, usually paired, which opens onto a terrace, balcony or adjacent room.

casement frame a hinged frame of metal, wood or plastics members, which holds the glass in place in a casement.

casement handle a device or fitting used for opening a casement.

casement hinge a hinge used in a side or top hung casement window.

casement stay any device for regulating and inhibiting the opening of a window casement.

casement vent a small hinged casement in a window unit, openable for ventilation.

casement window a window with one or more hinged sashes or casements; see top-hung casement window, side-hung casement window, hopper light (bottom-hinged casement window).

casement window

case mould in ornamental plastering, a flexible mould formed by pouring moulding compound into the void between the object to be modelled and a surrounding plaster case.

casework see casing.

casing, 1 casework, encasing; any material, product, boarding, etc. used as a covering for a structural member or service to conceal unsightly construction or as fireproofing; see concrete casing.
2 case, cover; a protective outer layer for an appliance, component or device.
3 see formwork, pile casing.

cassava a starch glue made from tapioca, the starch flour obtained from the tuberous root of the tropical cassava plants [*Manihot esculenta, Manihot dulcis*].

Cassel earth, Cologne earth; a form of the brown earth pigment Vandyke brown, named after the town of Cassel, Germany, where it was first obtained.

Cassel green see manganese green.

cast see fibrous plaster cast.

Castanea sativa see sweet chestnut.

castellated constructed in the form of a castle, with fortifications, turrets and battlements; describing a pattern, component, etc. which is rendered with a series of indents or rectilinear undulations, as with battlements; also called crenellated, embattled or battlemented.

castellated moulding see crenellated moulding.

castellated nut, castle nut; a nut whose outer edge is formed with a series of stepped slots to fit with a cotter pin through threaded shafts to secure the bolted joint.

castellated nut

castellation see crenellation.

cast glass, roughcast glass; traditional flat glass, often with an uneven surface, manufactured by casting on a bed of sand; see also plate glass.

casting the shaping of material such as concrete, metal or plastics by pouring it in liquid form (molten for metals) into suitably shaped moulds and allowing it to harden.

casting plaster a grade of plaster suitable for casting in moulds for ornament and mouldings.

cast-in-place same as in situ.

cast-in-place concrete see in-situ concrete.

cast-in-place pile, bored pile, cast-in-situ pile, in-situ pile; in foundation engineering, a concrete pile constructed by placing reinforcement and concrete into a preformed borehole or driven casing tube.

cast-in-situ see in situ.

cast-in-situ concrete see in-situ concrete.

cast-in-situ pile see cast-in-place pile.

cast iron a hard alloy of iron, carbon and silicon cast when molten into a mould, then often machined; written cast-iron in adjectival form.

castle nut see castellated nut.

cast steel, crucible steel; steel which has been cast from molten material, and not worked thereafter.

cast stone, artificial stone, patent stone, reconstructed stone; a reconstituted stone product used in place of natural stone, manufactured from stone fragments in a cement binder.

cast tile a tile manufactured by casting ceramic material in a mould then firing it.

catalyst, promoter; a substance, such as a hardener in some paints, which increases the rate of a chemical reaction or drying process without itself being consumed.

cataphoresis see electrophoresis.

catch any device used for the fastening of a gate, door or hatch in a certain position; see ball catch, bullet catch, magnetic catch, roller catch, turning catch.

catch

catch bolt see return latch.

cathedral a large and principal church of a diocese, the seat of a bishop.

cathedral glass a strong roughcast coloured glass, often with lead cames in imitation of stained glass.

Catherine wheel window, wheel window; a round window with a series of glazing bars radiating out from the centre, which takes its name from a decorative motif consisting of a spiked or burning wheel with radiating spokes, an instrument of torture, the symbol of Saint Catherine of Alexandria, to which she was bound.

Catherine wheel motif

Catherine wheel window, St Davids Cathedral, Wales, 1181

cathodic dip painting see electro-dip painting.

cationic bitumen emulsion a dispersion of bitumen in water, with an emulsifying additive which coats the particles of bitumen with a positive ion (a cation), causing them to repel one another and to remain as separate droplets.

cat's eye see pin knot.

cat's head, cats-head; an ornamental motif or moulding, similar to a beak-head, consisting of a series of stylized heads resembling those of cats.

cat's head ornament

catslide roof a pitched roof which continues in the same plane on one side beyond the main eaves to roof an adjacent structure, or in which the eaves are lower on one side than the other.

catslide roofs

cat's paw see nail claw.

caulicole, caulcole; the spiral stalks which carry leaves and volutes at the corners of a Corinthian capital; the Latin form is cauliculus.

caulking, 1 stopping; the filling of joints and gaps in construction with flexible material as weatherproofing and windproofing; the sealing substance or product thus used.

2 a product and process in which fibrous materials such as old rope, hemp or rags are forced into the gaps in a timber boarded structure as jointing; see oakum.

caulking chisel, caulking iron; a metal implement with a wide, blunt blade used for caulking joints.

caulking ferrule a screwed sleeve for an opening in a pipe, sealed by caulking.

caulking gun, extrusion gun, pressure gun; a simple mechanical device for applying prepacked sealant into joints, using hand pressure on a trigger.

caulking iron see caulking chisel.

causeway sett see sett.

caustic lime see quicklime.

caustic soda see sodium hydroxide.

cavalier projection in technical drawing, an oblique projection in which the Y and Z axes are in plan and the X axis is at 45° upward and to the right; all scales are the same; see cabinet, military projections.

cavetto a decorative concave moulding which is roughly a quarter of a circle in profile; when appearing in a cornice, concave side down, it may be called a cove; see also scotia.

cavetto moulding

cavitation the formation of gas bubbles in flowing liquids due to the turbulent action of a pump or propeller, which, in water supply installations, may lead to corrosive oxidation of metal parts.

cavity a void within a component to reduce weight such as in a hollow core slab, or in construction between two components for insulation, such as between the leaves of a cavity wall; see also gap.

cavity absorber, Helmholtz resonator; in acoustics, a construction consisting of bottle-like cavities containing air which absorbs sound of a narrow band of frequencies by sympathetic resonance.

cavity barrier see fire barrier.

cavity block see cellular block.

cavity bond, hollow wall bond; any true masonry bond in which bricks or blocks are stacked in such a way as to leave a cavity in the centre of the wall; see rat-trap bond, Dearne's bond.

cavity brick see hollow brick.

cavity closer in cavity wall or prefabricated concrete panel construction, a piece of timber or other rigid material placed in the cavity at an edge or opening to provide a thermal break and onto which window and door frames may be attached; also called a closure piece.

cavity drainage membrane see air-gap membrane.

cavity floor see access floor.

cavity gas the inert gas between two sheets of glass in a sealed glazing unit.

cavity membrane see air-gap membrane.

cavity tie see wall tie.

cavity wall, hollow masonry wall, hollow wall; a common exterior wall construction, often of masonry, composed of two adjacent walls or leaves tied together at intervals with an air space between, often partially or wholly filled with ventilated insulation.

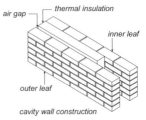

cavity wall construction

cavity wall tie see wall tie.

cavo-relievo, cavo-rilievo see sunk relief.

C-clamp see gee-clamp.

CCTV closed circuit television.

CCTV survey closed circuit television survey.

cedar [*Cedrus spp.*] a group of softwoods with strongly scented and extremely durable timber; used for joinery, fencing and interior panelling; large spreading evergreen trees which are widely planted in parks and large gardens as ornamental trees; other species such as the western red cedar, eastern red cedar, incense cedar, yellow cedar and white cedar are not true cedars; see below for list of species of true cedars included in this work:

Atlas cedar [*Cedrus atlantica*] a species of cedar native to the mountains of Algeria and Morocco in North Africa; relatively pollution resistant and widely planted in town parks and gardens.

Cedar of Lebanon [*Cedrus libani*] a softwood from the mountainous regions of the Near East and Syria with a distinctive smell, used locally for building construction; a fine ornamental tree with foliage in characteristic flattened evergreen sprays.

deodar [*Cedrus deodara*] a softwood from Afghanistan and the Himalayan mountains with pale brown timber, used for interiors; often planted as an ornamental in parks and large gardens.

Cedrus spp. see cedar.

ceiba [*Ceiba pentandra*] a tropical African and Asian hardwood with extremely light timber which is used for furniture; also a water-resistant wool product formed from the seed fibres of this tree; also called kapok.

ceiling the upper horizontal construction or surface in an interior space; usually either suspended or the soffit of the overlying construction; types included as separate entries are listed below:

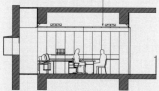

suspended mesh ceiling in section of office building

*acoustic ceiling; *coffered ceiling; *drop ceiling, false ceiling; *illuminated ceiling, luminous ceiling; *suspended ceiling.

ceiling bearer a primary profile or beam in a suspended ceiling system, from which ceiling runners are suspended.

ceiling board 1 any board products such as plasterboard, plywood, etc. fastened to a frame or soffit to make up a fixed ceiling.
2 one of a number of machined timber boards used as a ceiling.

ceiling component any component or product, a panel, hanger, runner, etc. used to form a suspended ceiling.

ceiling construction the materials, components and structure which comprise a ceiling.

ceiling fan a large-bladed rotating fan attached to a ceiling soffit to provide circulation of air within a space.

ceiling hanger, ceiling strap; one of a number of metal components attached to the soffit or frame of the floor or roof above, from which a suspended ceiling is hung.

ceiling heating radiant space heating provided by electric cables, steam or hot water pipework incorporated into ceiling panels.

ceiling height, floor-to-ceiling height, headroom, room height; the vertical height of an internal space, measured from floor level to ceiling soffit.

ceiling joist in timber roof construction, one of a number of horizontal members to which ceiling boards, panels, etc. are fixed.

ceiling linear strip see exposed runner.

ceiling luminaire a light fitting designed to be attached to a ceiling soffit.

ceiling painting see plafond.

ceiling panel a removable sheet product of gypsum board, plastics, mesh or sheetmetal, suspended on a system of rails and hangers to make up a suspended ceiling; see metal pan, metal tray.

ceiling rose see centrepiece.

ceiling runner a metal profile supported by ceiling hangers, which forms the basis of the frame into which ceiling panels are laid in a suspended ceiling.

ceiling strap see ceiling hanger.

ceiling strip a horizontal moulding or cover strip at the junction of an internal wall and ceiling; see also cornice.

ceiling surface the lower visible surface of a ceiling.

ceiling suspension system the frame of hangers and profiles by which panels in a suspended ceiling are supported.

ceiling tile a rectangular tile of plastics, laminates or ceramics used in series to form a ceiling surface.

ceiling trim see perimeter trim.

ceiling void the space between a false or suspended ceiling construction and the soffit of the overlying construction, usually taken up with services and ducts.

ceilure see celure.

celestial blue a form of the pigment Prussian blue similar to Brunswick blue.

cell 1 one of the curved vaulting panels or surfaces between the ribs in a rib vault; the curved or planar surface of a vault; also called a severy or web.

2 any small isolatory chamber or part of a building, such as a fire cell, monastic cell or prison cell; see fire compartment.

3 a normally non-rechargeable battery for a small appliance such as a radio or torch; an appliance for converting chemical or light energy into electricity; see battery, solar cell, photoelectric cell.

cella, cellae (pl) Lat.; in classical architecture, the central sanctuary space in a Roman temple containing a cult image; a naos in Greek architecture; cella is often used for all enclosed shrine-like spaces.

cellar a basement or part of a basement used for storage, heating plant and for purposes other than habitation; a cellar in a castle or palace is often called a vault.

cellar rot [*Coniophora cerebella*, *Coniophora puteana*] a fungus which attacks timber in constantly damp conditions.

cell ceiling, egg-crate ceiling, open cell ceiling; a suspended ceiling system formed from rectangular or polygonal grids of baffles, slats, etc. with openings to allow for the passage of air and light from services located in the ceiling void.

cellophane a transparent plastics material made from viscose and used for wrapping.

cellular a description of a material, construction layout or structural configuration of a number of open cells, voids, etc., such as honeycomb.

cellular acrylic sheet see acrylic cellular sheet.

cellular block a concrete building block with voids incorporated in its thickness during manufacture to reduce weight, improve thermal and sometimes acoustic performance; variously known as a cavity block or hollow concrete block.

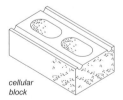

cellular block

cellular board, cellular plywood; a building board of one or more veneers glued to either side of a cellular construction.

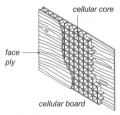

cellular core

face ply

cellular board

cellular brick a perforated brick whose cavities are large in proportion to its volume, or of particular special shape; see perforated brick (cored brick), air brick (ventilating brick), hollow brick (cavity brick).

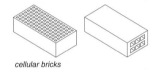

cellular bricks

cellular concrete see aerated concrete.
cellular concrete block see cellular block.
cellular glass, foam glass; a glass product manufactured by heating pulverized glass with carbon to form a strong, lightweight, fireproof and water-resistant solid foam, used as an insulating material; also known as expanded glass.
cellular glazing see cellular sheet.
cellular paver, crib paver; a concrete paving block precast with patterns of small holes, filled with earth and sown with seed compound for grass to grow; laid in series to form a hardwearing paved but grassy surface called cellular, grass or crib paving.

cellular paving

cellular plastic a generic name for both expanded plastics and foamed plastics.

cellular plywood see cellular board.

cellular polycarbonate see polycarbonate cellular sheet.

cellular raft a concrete raft foundation whose beams and crosswalls form a grid structure in plan.

cellular rubber a generic term for both foam rubber and expanded rubber.

cellular sheet, extruded cellular sheet; an insulating transparent polycarbonate or acrylic sheet product of two thin sheets around a hollow cellular core, used for lightweight glazing and roofing.

celluloid a thermoplastic made from cellulose nitrate, camphor and alcohol; traditionally used for cinema film.

cellulose a major constituent of dried wood and plant matter which, when extracted as pulp, is processed for use in the manufacture of a wide range of synthetic products including papers, fibres, plastics, paints and adhesives.

cellulose acetate, CA a tough thermoplastic used as a binder in emulsion paints, for light fittings and door furniture.

cellulose acetate butyrate, CAB; a tough thermoplastic used for coatings and illuminated signs.

cellulose adhesive any adhesive such as wallpaper paste, which contains cellulose.

cellulose lacquer, cellulose varnish; a quick drying varnish, used mainly on wooden surfaces, based on nitrocellulose compounds in a solvent-based medium, which dries by the evaporation of the solvent.

cellulose loose-fill insulation loose-fill insulation prepared from shredded waste paper, cardboard, etc., treated with water and insect repellent.

cellulose nitrate, CN; a flammable thermoplastic used for paint finishes and in the manufacture of celluloid.

cellulose paint a solvent-based paint, similar to cellulose lacquer, containing compounds of nitrocellulose and usually applied by spraying.

cellulose plastics thermoplastics such as acetate and celluloid which are manufactured from cellulose.

cellulose varnish see cellulose lacquer.

cellure see celure.

Celtic architecture the domestic, ceremonial and defensive architecture of the Celtic peoples of present-day Scotland, Wales and Brittany from 700 BC to 1100 AD, including hill forts, ceremonial Celtic crosses, standing stones and domestic dwellings; often ornamented with interlace.

celure, ceilure, cellure; in church architecture, a decorated panelled ceiling over a chancel or altar.

cembra pine see pine.

cement 1 a powdered mineral substance, usually containing lime or gypsum, mixed with water to form a paste which will set to form a hard, brittle material; used as a binder in concrete, mortars, plasters, etc.; types included as separate entries are listed below:
blast-furnace cement, blast-furnace slag cement; *blended cement, blended hydraulic cement;* *brown cement, see Roman cement;* *calcium aluminate cement, see high alumina cement;* *coloured (Portland) cement;* *composite cement, see fillerized cement;* *expanding cement;* *extra rapid-hardening Portland cement;* *Ferrari cement;* *fibre-reinforced cement, fibre cement, FRC;* *fillerized cement, filler cement, fuel-ash cement, see Portland pulverized fuel-ash cement;* *glassfibre-reinforced cement, GRC;* *high alumina cement;* *high-early-strength cement, see rapid-hardening Portland cement;* *hot cement;* *hydraulic cement;* *hydrophobic cement;* *lime cement;* *low heat cement, low heat Portland cement;* *low heat Portland blast-furnace cement;* *magnesite cement, see oxychloride cement;* *masonry cement;* *ordinary (Portland) cement;* *oxychloride cement;* *Parker's cement, see Roman cement;* *Portland blast-furnace cement;* *Portland cement;* *Portland pozzolana cement;* *Portland pulverized fuel-ash cement;* *pozzolanic cement;* *quick-setting Portland cement;* *rapid-hardening Portland cement;* *Roman cement;* *soil cement;* *sorel cement, see oxychloride cement;* *sulphate-resistant cement, see sulphate-resisting Portland cement;* *supersulphated cement;* *water-repellent cement, see hydrophobic cement;* *white (Portland) cement.*

2 any glue-like liquid substance used for sticking things together, usually an inorganic adhesive.

cementation see carburizing, grouting.

cementation process in ground engineering, a process whereby cement grout is injected into underlying soil or rock in order support and strengthen it.

cement bonded chipboard see wood cement chipboard.

cement clinker partially fused incombustible residue from a kiln created under high temperatures, ground and used as cement in concrete.

cement content in concreting, the amount of hydraulic binder per unit volume or mass of mix.

cement fillet see mortar fillet.

cement fixing see mortar fixing.

cement flooring see cement rubber latex flooring.

cement gel in concretework, the cohesive mass of microscopic calcium silicate hydrate crystals in cement.

cement gun a pipe and nozzle used with sprayed concrete and operated by compressed air.

cement grout see neat grout.

cementite a white, brittle compound, iron carbide (**Fe$_3$C**) found in white cast iron.

cementitious material see binder.

cementitious matrix in fibre-reinforced products, the medium of resin, polymer or cement into which fibres are dispersed as reinforcement.

cement lime mortar, cement lime plaster see composition mortar.

cement lime render see composition render.

cement mixer a small portable concrete mixer with a rotating ovular vessel which is pivoted in order to empty out its contents.

cement mortar, compo; mortar which contains a cement binder as well as sand and water; see also masonry cement mortar.

cement paint an absorbent water-based paint in which the binder is Portland cement, often with added pigment to provide colour.

cement paste cement powder and water mixed to form a thick smooth paste.

cement plaster see cement render, Portland cement plaster.

cement render, cement plaster; cement mortar used as render for external walls.

cement rubber latex flooring durable flooring of a mixture of cement, rubber latex and aggregates of stone, woodchips, etc., laid in situ over a concrete slab and ground to form a smooth surface.

cement screed see screed.

cement slurry a liquid mix of cement paste used in grouting and rough render for masonry wall surfaces.

cement tile see concrete tile.

cement/water ratio in mixes of concrete, mortar or grout, the ratio of the mass of cement to contained water, the reciprocal of water/cement ratio.

centering, centres; a temporary curved frame of wood or other material for supporting a masonry arch while it is being constructed.

timber centering for brick arch under construction

central air conditioning an air conditioning installation in which air treatment plant, fans, etc. are located in one place, from which conditioned air is distributed throughout a building.

Central American mahogany see Honduras mahogany.

central fan system see central plant system.

central heating a heating system for a building or group of buildings in which a centrally located boiler heats water which is then circulated as hot water or steam to radiators and storage tanks; see also district heating.

central heating boiler a boiler which provides heated water for a central heating network.

central heating installation the appliances and devices that make up a central heating system; a centralized boiler and pipework to provide heat in the form of hot water throughout a building.

centralized hot water supply, centralized boiler system; a large-scale hot water heating system for industrial premises, schools, apartment blocks, etc. in which water is heated, stored, and distributed throughout from a central location.

central locking a system by which all locks in a building or secure area can be operated from the same central lock.

centrally planned a square, circular, or polygonal building with an open space at the centre, around which other spaces are arranged.

central plant system, central fan system; an air-conditioning system in which air is treated in a centralized plant and ducted to the various spaces in a building.

central ply, core ply; the central layer or ply around which the other plies in plywood are glued.

centre bit a flat-ended drill bit with a centring spike for drilling holes or circular depressions in wood.

centre boards in the conversion of timber, boards sawn longitudinally from the middle of a log, with end grain forming a series of concentric circles.

centre gutter a flat-bottomed gutter between two inwardly sloping pitched roofs.

centre hinge see centre pivot hinge.

centre match a variation of the book-matched veneering pattern in which an even number of pieces of veneer are mirrored across the centre line of a panel to form a symmetrical image on the other half.

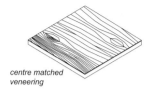

centre matched veneering

centre-opening door, bi-parting door; a double sliding door in which both leaves slide away from the middle of the opening; lift doors are a typical example.

centre-opening doors

centrepiece, rose, ceiling rose; a decorative central feature in a ceiling, from which light fittings are often suspended.

centre pivot hinge, centre hinge, centres; the pivoted fastening on which a pivot window rotates.

centre punch, punch; a tool for marking points or making starter drill holes in metal.

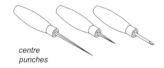

centre punches

centres, 1 centre to centre, spacing; abb. ccs; in dimensioning and general construction, a notation expressing the distance between the centres of adjacent objects such as rafters, columns, studs, beams, battens, etc. in an equally spaced series.
2 see centre pivot hinge.
3 see centering.

centre string see carriage.

centre to centre see centres.

centrifugal fan a fan used in air-conditioning installations, in which air is sucked in perpendicular to the rotor blades and blown out radially; centrifugal refers to the physical tendency of a revolving body to move away from the centre of revolution.

Cerambycidae see longhorn beetle.

ceramic pertaining to products manufactured from fired or burnt clay such as pipes, tiles, bricks, terracotta and pottery.
ceramic fibre an artificial fired clay thread used in bulk in fireproofing products.
ceramic glaze see glaze.
ceramics any products made from a mixture of mineral substance and a clay binder fired to produce a hard insoluble material; the field of practice and production in fired clay.

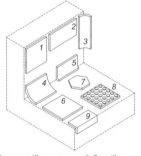

1 square tile
2 rectangular tile
3 inside corner tile
4 cove tile
5 skirting tile
6 floor tile
7 geometric tile, hexagonal tile
8 non-slip tile
9 nosing tile

ceramic tile a thin, durable clay tile, pressed and fired at a high temperature; usually used for cladding floors and walls.

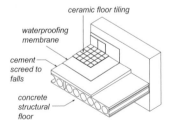

ceramic floor tiling

waterproofing membrane

cement screed to falls

concrete structural floor

ceramic tiled paving see tiled paving.

certificate a legal document issued as proof of something attained, origin of goods, standard of work, evidence of quality, etc.; see completion certificate.

cerulean blue a bright, opaque, blue pigment used in artist's paints and ceramics, consisting of cobaltous stannate, a compound of oxides of cobalt and tin; variously known as blue celeste, caeruleum, coelin, coeruleum, corruleum blue.

ceruse an old name for the pigment white lead.

cesspool, cesspit, sewage tank; in the treatment of waste water, an underground storage container, emptied at regular intervals, for sewage which cannot be piped away for treatment.

Ceylon ebony [*Diospyros ebenum*], see ebony.

Ceylon satinwood, East Indian satinwood; [*Chloroxylon swietenia*] a tropical hardwood from India and Sri Lanka with very heavy timber.

chain 1 a fastening or connecting rope-like structure formed from a number of interlocking metal loops; see door chain.
2 an ornamental motif representing the linked loops of a chain, a chain moulding.
chain link mesh wire mesh made from series of wires interwoven in a zigzag pattern to form diamond-shaped openings; most often galvanized or organically coated and used as fencing material.

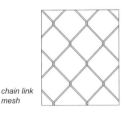

chain link mesh

chain moulding an ornamental moulding representing the linked loops of a chain.

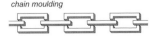

chain moulding

chain pipe wrench, chain tongs, chain vice; a tool for gripping and rotating objects such as pipes or tight bolts, consisting of a lever attached to a short length of chain which tightens around the object to be gripped.

chainsaw a hand-held motor-driven saw with a cutting chain, used for logging and rough work; see saw chain.

chain timber see bond timber.

chain tongs, chain vice see chain pipe wrench.

chair a construction of bent bars for supporting the uppermost layer of reinforcement in horizontal concrete slabs, beams, etc. while concrete is being placed.

chair rail, dado rail; an interior horizontal moulding at approximately waist height as an upper termination for wainscotting or to prevent the backs of chairs from scraping the wall surface.

chaitya a Buddhist temple or the meeting room of a monastery in India.

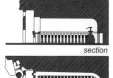

Buddhist chaitya temple, cut into rock, Karli, India, 100–125 AD

section

plan

chalcedony a blue-grey form of microcrystalline quartz, used for its decorative quality; also a general name for agate, onyx, cornelian and crysophrase.

chalk a form of soft, pale or white coloured, porous limestone used in the manufacture of drawing and writing chalks, and burnt to produce lime; artificial calcium carbonate is used as a bright white pigment in water-based paints and a ground in oil paints.

chalking a defect in an exterior paint finish consisting of the deposition of pigment in a chalky layer on the surface due to decomposition of the binder.

chalk lime quicklime produced by heating chalk.

chalk line, snap line, snapping line; a long thread covered in chalk or coloured powder, used to mark and set out long lines of proposed construction on a building site.

Chamaecyparis lawsoniana see Lawson's cypress; *Chamaecyparis nootkatensis* see yellow cedar.

chamfer, bevel; the splayed surface formed when a corner is removed from an acute or right angle, usually at 45°.

chamfered moulding a decorative moulding or trim in which any edge has been cut or formed with a chamfer.

chamfered moulding

chamfer stop in ornamentation, the terminating device for a chamfered moulding or carving.

chamotte see grog.

Champagne chalk a high-quality grade of chalk, originally found in deposits in Champagne, France.

chancel the area to the east end of the crossing of a church, containing an altar, and often a choir and an apse.

chancel aisle an aisle at the side of a chancel of a large church.

chancel arch a major transverse arch supporting the roof or tower at the intersection of the chancel and transept.

change see variation.

channel, 1 channel iron, channel section; a structural steel section formed by rolling, whose uniform cross-section resembles the letter C or U.

2 drainage channel; any open watercourse for the conveyance or drainage of water; see floor channel, box gutter (roof channel).

3 in telecommunications, a range or band of wavelengths designated for the sending of signals.

4 see canalis.

channel block a concrete block which is U-shaped in cross-section; designed for use with reinforcing bars and in-situ concrete as a beam or lintel over a

channel block

window or door opening; also called a lintel or bond-beam block.

channel brick see lintel brick.

channel glass, profile glass, glass plank; a glass product manufactured with a U-shaped section by rolling or casting; a number of these, when placed vertically together, form a glazed screen.

channel glass

channel grating a longitudinal grating over a drainage channel.

characteristic strength in structural engineering, the theoretical strength of a material gained from tests and research under normal conditions of loading, used as a base for structural calculations.

charge 1 the amount or accumulation of energy in a system, especially electricity in a battery; see electric charge.
2 debit; a sum of money demanded as payment for goods and services.

chargehand, leading hand; a tradesman who is head of a team of tradesmen and labourers on site.

chartered engineer, professional engineer; a qualified engineer who, as well as having a university degree in engineering, has met the requirements of an engineering institute.

chase 1 in general construction, a shallow channel cut into a solid wall, floor or ceiling for the location of electrical servicing or pipework, usually subsequently filled.
2 in joinery or carpentry, a long groove cut into a piece of timber to receive another piece; a housing or dado.

chattering undesirable vibration of tools which cause ripples in the finished surface of a plasterwork moulding, certain extruded products, machined timber, etc.

check 1 a split in an improperly seasoned timber piece which appears as a result of uneven shrinkage; a seasoning shake; see also heartshake (heart check), surface checks.
2 in masonry, a rebate in the face of a brick, block or stone.
3 door check, see door closer.

4 vapour check, see vapour barrier.
5 see water check.

checkered alternative spelling of chequered.
checkered pattern see square pattern.
checkerplate see chequerplate.

chequerplate

checkerwork see chequerwork.

checking a defect in a paint finish caused by a fine mesh of surface cracks caused by shrinkage or uneven drying.

check lock see snib.

check valve, clack valve, valve, non-return valve, reflux valve; a valve which allows for flow in a pipeline in one direction only; see backflow valve, pipe interrupter.

cheek 1 in timber jointing, the side of a tenon, mortise or recess.
2 the triangular side wall of a dormer window or similar construction.
3 the flat side surface of a hammerhead.

chemical cleaning the treatment of a surface or object by the application of a chemical to clean it.

chemical plating, electroless plating; the application of protective or decorative metal coatings to plastics or ceramic products by immersion into various chemical solutions, during which deposition occurs by chemical reaction without the use of electricity.

chemical reaction the chemical binding together of two or more substances to form a new substance which may have different properties from its constituents.

chemical resistance the ability of a material or finish to withstand chemical attack or reaction.

chemical shrinkage in concretework, a reduction in size caused by chemical changes during setting and final hardening.

chemically strengthened glass a toughened glass used for optical lenses and lamps, whose surface is hardened against abrasion by heating with salts to encourage replacement of ions

chequerboard construction, alternate bay construction, hit and miss construction; in concretework, a method of construction of casting large areas of deck, floor, paving, etc. to reduce cracking from drying shrinkage; diagonally adjacent areas or bays are cast then allowed to harden, after which the remaining voids are filled using the existing concrete as support.

chequerboard pattern see square pattern, basketweave pattern.

chequered brickwork decorative brickwork based on a repeated grid pattern as a result of the use of occasional coloured bricks, added stone or the arrangement of bricks of varying colour into squares or rectangles.

chequered pattern see square pattern.

chequerplate, checkerplate, raised pattern plate, tread plate; hot-rolled steel plate treated with a raised surface pattern, used as durable cladding, industrial flooring to provide grip, etc.

chequerwork, checkerwork; decoration based on the use of a squared grid in which alternate squares are rendered in a second colour, relief or manner.

cherry [*Prunus spp.*] a number of species of European hardwood tree with deep red-brown, dense and fine-grained timber; used for flooring, joinery and furniture; cherries are small trees *Prunus spp., cherry* widely planted in parks and gardens on account of their white and pink spring blooms and autumn leaf colour; see below for species included in this work; see also plum.

American cherry, black cherry (Am); [*Prunus serotina*] a North American hardwood with reddish-brown timber; used for furniture.

bird cherry [*Prunus padus*] a European hardwood with bitter scented, hard and tough timber.

sour cherry [*Prunus cerasus*] a European hardwood whose timber is used for musical instruments and for the decorative value of its grain.

sweet cherry, wild cherry; [*Prunus avium*] a European hardwood with deep red-brown timber; used for the decorative value of its grain in interiors and for musical instruments.

cherry mahogany see makore.

chert, hornstone; a dense, fine-grained sedimentary rock composed mainly of cryptocrystalline silica; difficult to work but used, like flint, for stone facing; also a general name for all horn-like rocks.

chestnut any nut-producing hardwood from the genus *Castanea*, found in temperate regions of the Northern hemisphere; see sweet chestnut; other unrelated species from other parts of the world are also known as chestnuts, see horse chestnut.

chestnut brown an alternative name for the pigment raw umber.

chevet in church or cathedral architecture, an apse with projecting radiating chapels or niches.

chevron Romanesque ornament consisting of a series of parallel zigzag lines; often called a chevron moulding.

chevron mouldings

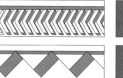

chevron match see V-match.

chicken wire a wire netting of thin galvanized wire with hexagonal openings; also known as hexagonal mesh.

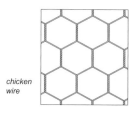

chicken wire

chickrassy, Chittagong wood; [*Chukrasia tabularis*] a southern Asian hardwood whose reddish-brown heartwood is used in furniture.

chiller see refrigeration unit.

chimney a vertical structure which contains one or more flues to extract waste gases and smoke from a building, boiler, fireplace or other apparatus; see chimney stack, flue.

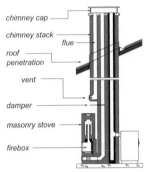

chimney cap
chimney stack
flue
roof penetration
vent
damper
masonry stove
firebox

chimney block see flue block.

chimney bond, column bond; brickwork bonds used for slender constructions such as brick chimneys, piers and columns.

chimney breast a thickening or recess in a masonry wall containing space for a fireplace and flue constructions.

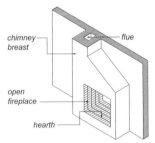

chimney breast
flue
open fireplace
hearth

chimney cap, 1 bonnet; a device attached to the outlet in the top of a flue or chimney which rotates in the wind and improves draught within the flue.
2 see flue cap, rain cap.

chimney-corner see inglenook.

chimney cricket see chimney saddle.

chimney crown the masonry or concrete construction at the top of a brick or stone chimney stack, often overhanging or weathered, to provide protection from rain, snow, etc.

chimney flashing a layer of felt or other sheet membrane laid around the base of a chimney or flue at the point at which it penetrates the roof structure, to prevent the passage of water.

chimney gutter a back gutter on the upward side of the junction between a chimney and a sloping roof to convey rainwater from behind the chimney.

chimney-nook see inglenook.

chimney saddle, chimney cricket (Am), cricket (Am); in roofing, a shaped piece of impervious sheet material, laid under roof tiles and other roofing behind a chimney to protect the junction of chimney and roof plane.

chimney shaft a large, usually industrial, freestanding chimney, containing a large flue.

chimney stack the structure or constructional surround for a chimney or flue; that part of a chimney exposed above the upper surface of a roof.

china clay, Devonshire clay; an impure variety of kaolin, hydrated aluminium silicate, a fine white mineral powder used for making chinaware and as an inert pigment in paints.

China wood oil see tung oil.

Chinese blue a form of high-quality Prussian blue pigment.

Chinese bond see rat-trap bond.

Chinese red see chrome red.

Chinese vermilion a red pigment, genuine vermilion, manufactured in China; also the name of a shade of red which takes its name from this.

Chinese white zinc white pigment prepared for use as a watercolour.

Chinese yellow a name applied to a number of yellow pigments, especially king's yellow.

chinoiserie decorative Rococo ornament and style in Europe from the 1700s which arose as a result of trade with China; it is characterized by a fascination with Chinese painting, wallpaper, vases and pagodas.

chipboard, wood chipboard; a building board formed from chipped fibrous material, usually woodchips, bonded together with resin then pressed into sheets — most often it is synonymous with particleboard, but not always; see particleboard; types of chipboard included as separate entries are listed below:
*bitumen-coated chipboard; *extruded particleboard; *graded density chipboard; *laminated chipboard; *melamine faced chipboard; *multilayer chipboard; *oriented strand board; *platen-pressed chipboard; *primed and filled chipboard; *sanded chipboard; *single layer chipboard; *tongued and grooved chipboard; *veneered chipboard; *wood cement chipboard.

chipboard flooring flooring, underflooring or decking consisting of abutted or tongued and grooved chipboard.

chipped grain a timber machining defect in which small chips are torn from the wood by blunt or worn cutting tools, leaving an undesirable pitted surface.

chipped grain in improperly converted board

Chippendale a decorative style in furniture named after the carpenter Thomas Chippendale (1718–1779), which was influenced by Rococo, Gothic, Queen Anne and chinoiserie.

chippings crushed rock aggregate between 3 mm and 20 mm used in road surfacing, roofing, render, etc.

chippy a slang term for a carpenter.

chisel a hand tool whose metal blade is sharpened at one end, used for cutting and shaping timber and stone; types included as separate entries are listed below:
*batting tool, broad tool; bench chisel; bevelled-edge chisel, bevel edge chisel; *boaster, drover; *bolster; *broach; bruzz chisel; *butt chisel; *cant chisel, see framing chisel; *carving chisel, see woodcarving chisel; *caulking chisel, caulking iron; *claw chisel, claw tool; *clourer; *cold chisel; *corner chisel, dogleg chisel, see bruzz chisel; *drawer lock chisel; *driver; *fantail tool, see fishtail chisel; *fillet chisel; *firmer chisel; *fishtail chisel, fishtail tool; *floor chisel; *framing chisel; *gouge; *hammer-headed chisel; *heading chisel, see mortise chisel; *hinge chisel; *joiner's chisel, see paring chisel; *jumper; *lock chisel; *long-cornered chisel, see skew chisel; *mallet-headed chisel; *masonry chisel, mason's chisel, see entry for full list of masonry chisels; *mortise lock chisel; *mortising chisel, mortise chisel; *nicker, see splitter; paring chisel; *parting chisel, parting tool; *patent claw chisel; *pitching tool, pincher, pitcher; *pocket chisel, see butt chisel; *point tool; *punch; *quirking tool; *registered chisel; *ripping chisel; *sash chisel, see butt chisel; *scraping tool, scraper; *sculptor's point; skew chisel; *spindle, see fillet chisel; *splitter; stonecarving chisel, stone chisel, stonemason's chisel, see masonry chisel; *swan-neck chisel, see mortise lock chisel; *tooth tool, see patent claw chisel; *tracer; *turning chisel; *turning gouge; *waster; *woodcarving chisel; *woodworking chisel, see entry for full list of woodcarving chisels.

Chittagong wood see chickrassy.

chlorinated rubber natural rubber treated with chlorine to form a hard, stable and chemically resistant compound used in paints and varnishes, and also in some adhesives and printing inks.

chlorinated rubber paint a hard, water- and chemical-resistant coating which contains a binder consisting of rubber treated with chlorine; used for anticorrosion applications and swimming pools.

chlorinated rubber varnish a varnish in which the binder is natural rubber treated with chlorine, used as a corrosion-resistant coating.

Chlorophora excelsa see iroko.

chloroprene rubber, polychloroprene; the chemical name for the synthetic rubber neoprene.

Chloroxylon swietenia see Ceylon satinwood.

choir, quire; the area in a church or cathedral where the choir sits, situated to the east of the crossing in the chancel.

choir aisle an aisle in a large church alongside the choir.

choir screen a decorative screen which separates the choir from the nave and other spaces in a church; often a rood screen.

choker ring in foundation construction, the lower, wider edge of a caisson, used for cutting its housing in the ground.

chop axe a heavy mason's axe for evening off a stone surface before dressing.

chopped strand glass reinforcement for fibreglass consisting of short lengths of glass fibre arranged in overlapping random fashion.

chord, boom; an upper or lower horizontal member in a trussed beam; see upper chord, lower chord.

chroma see colour saturation.

chromatic pertaining to the colours of the visible spectrum.

chromatic aberration an optical phenomenon, the blurring of colours at the edge of an image due to the inability of a lens to focus all colours to the same point.

chromatic colour, spectral colour; any colour contained in the spectrum of visible light.

chromatic pigment a pigment which consists of colours other than simply black, white or grey.

chromium, chrome; an extremely hard metal, **Cr**, used as an alloy in the manufacture of stainless steel, and as a corrosion-resistant coating for steel.

chrome green a range of green pigments formed by mixing blue pigments, especially Prussian blue, and chrome yellow pigments; this range includes leaf green, leek green, moss green, myrtle green, Royal green, zinnober green.

chrome orange an opaque poisonous orange pigment which consists of lead chromate; used in oil paints and glues.

chrome plating see chromium plating.

chrome red, Chinese red, Derby red; an opaque poisonous red pigment which consists of lead chromate; used in oil paints and glues.

chrome steel, chromium steel; a hard and fine-grained alloy of steel containing significant quantities of chromium.

chrome yellow, Leipzig yellow, Paris yellow; an opaque yellow pigment consisting of lead chromate, used in large quantities in cheap paints.

chroming see chromium plating.

chromium oxide green, oxide of chromium, Schnitzer's green; an opaque pale green inorganic pigment consisting of calcined chromium oxide; used in oil and watercolour paints despite its low tinting power; see also viridian.

chromium plating, chrome plating, chroming; the electrochemical application of a thin protective layer of chromium to metals; items thus treated are referred to as chrome-plated.

chrysoberyl a yellowish, greenish or brownish mineral used for ornament, as a gemstone (emerald, aquamarine) and as a raw material in the extraction of beryllium.

CHS see circular hollow section.

chuck an adjustable device for holding a drill bit in a drill, or wood on a lathe.

Chukrasia tabularis see chickrassy.

church a building or consecrated space for the practice of Christian worship.

church tower a tower often at the crossing or west end of a church, sometimes capped with a spire and containing bells.

Churrigueresque highly embellished Baroque architecture in Spain and Mexico in the 1600s and 1700s with plateresque influences, which takes its name from the Spanish architect José Churriguera (1650—1723).

chute, shaft; a vertical void or sealed hollow structure through a building through which goods, laundry and refuse are thrown, to be collected at a lower level; see concrete chute.

ciborium Lat.; in Early Christian and Byzantine churches, a canopy mounted on four posts over an altar, shrine or the tomb of a martyr; a baldachin; the original Greek form is kiborion.

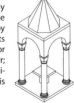

ciborium

cill see sill.

cinnabar red native mercury sulphide in ore form, used since early times to make the red pigment vermilion.

cinnamon stone hessonite.

cinquefoil a decorative and ornamental device consisting of five leaf motifs radiating out from a point; a pointed cinquefoil is one in which the foils are pointed arches.

cinquefoil motif   cinquefoil arch

cinquefoil arch a decorative arch whose extrados is composed of five lobes or foils in a cloverleaf arrangement.

cinquefoliated arch a decorative arch whose intrados is composed of five lobes or foils in a cloverleaf arrangement, and whose extrados is a round or pointed arch; especially found in Gothic architecture; see round cinquefoliated arch, pointed cinquefoliated arch.

cipollino, cipolin; a metamorphic rock originating from Italy, marble patterned with folded stripes; used in building as decorative stone.

circle-end clamp see gee-clamp.

circline lamp see circular fluorescent tube.

circlip, retaining ring, lock ring; a flat sprung steel ring with a break at one point for prising open so that it can be passed over an axle, shaft or spindle and fitted into an annular recess, providing a collar to prevent bearings and other components from moving.

circuit an arrangement of wires, electrical and electronic components for performing a function; types included as separate entries are listed below:
*auxiliary circuit; *control circuit; *electrical circuit; *final circuit; *pipe circuit; *radial circuit; *ring circuit; *short circuit.

circuit breaker, cutout, trip switch; a device which automatically stops the flow of current when an electric circuit is overloaded or otherwise in danger; once the circuit has been rectified it can be re-set.

circuit diagram a diagrammatic design drawing showing the layout and connections of the various components in an electrical circuit.

circuit efficacy, luminous efficacy, efficacy; in lighting design, the ratio of the amount of light, luminous flux, emitted by a light source compared with how much power it and its circuitry and control equipment use; its unit is the lumen/watt.

circular arch, round arch; any arch composed of a segment of a circle, usually a semicircle; see also segmental arch, horseshoe arch and semicircular arch.

circular column, round column; a column whose shaft is circular in cross-section.

circular column

circular fluorescent tube, circline lamp; a doughnut-shaped fluorescent tube.

circular hollow section, round tube, steel pipe; a circular hollow steel section formed by rolling and welding steel plate, used for structural purposes such as columns, posts, etc.

circular pattern a paving pattern of small stones or cobbles laid in a series of concentric circles with infill between; also called concentric pattern.

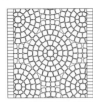

paving in circular pattern

circular plane see compass plane.

circular saw a power saw with a rotating steel cutting disc whose teeth are often shaped or tipped with abrasive; may be hand-held, mounted in a bench, or part of a larger industrial installation such as a sawmill.

circular stair any stair whose treads are arranged radially about a central newel; see spiral stair.

circulating water the heating water conveyed in sealed pipework to provide warmth to radiators, etc. in a central heating installation.

circulation in the internal planning of a building, the system of prescribed routes, including stairs, lifts and corridors used frequently by its occupants; see vertical circulation.

circulation pump, circulator; a pump used to provide pressure in the hot and cold water systems of a building.

circulation space a stair, corridor or gangway space within a building, along which people, goods, etc. can move or be moved from place to place.

circulator see circulation pump.

circus Lat.; originally a long U-shaped or enclosed arena for chariot racing; a hippodrome, in Roman architecture; in more recent times a circular open space, place, roundabout, etc. in an urban setting; a formal urban street and buildings laid out in the form of a circle or oval.

cistern 1 an open vessel for storing water at atmospheric pressure in a water supply system; a storage tank; see expansion cistern.
2 a storage tank containing water for flushing a WC or other sanitary appliance; a flushing cistern, see also dual-flush cistern.

citron yellow a form of zinc yellow pigment.

city planning see planning.

civil engineer a qualified professional who designs public utilities, roads, bridges and sewers, and supervises their construction and maintenance.

civil engineering the construction of roads, waterways, bridges, excavations, earthworks and other structures, rather than buildings.

clack valve see check valve.

cladding, facing; 1 any non-loadbearing system of boards, prefabricated components, stone, brick, sheeting, etc. attached to a building frame as weatherproofing or as an exterior or interior finish; types included as separate entries are listed below:
*external cladding; *metal cladding; *natural stone cladding; *stone cladding, see stone facing, natural stone cladding; *tile cladding; *tiling; *timber cladding; *wall cladding.
2 the action of producing the above, the work thus involved.

cladding cleat see holdfast.

cladding component see cladding unit.

cladding glass, spandrel glass; opaque float glass that has been fired on one surface with a non-transparent coloured ceramic enamel, used for external wall panels, blind windows, etc. in curtain walling.

cladding panel see cladding unit; types included as separate entries are listed below:
*ceiling panel; *cladding glass; *insulated infill panel; *precast concrete panel; *sheetmetal cladding panel.

cladding rail one of a series of lightweight metal profiles fixed at regular spacing to a structural base as a means of fixing external cladding panels, components, boards, etc.

cladding stone see stone facing.

cladding unit, cladding panel, cladding component; a prefabricated weatherproofing component of metal, concrete or composite material for cladding the exterior surface, frame, etc. of a

building; types included as separate entries are listed below:
*ceiling panel; *insulated infill panel; *precast concrete panel; *sheetmetal cladding panel.*

claim 1 in contract management, a demand by one party for additional payment to which they are entitled under the contract, or for damages for breach of contract due to faulty workmanship, failure to supply goods on time, etc.; types included as separate entries are listed below:
*contractual claim; *extra-contractual claim, ex-contractual claim; *ex-gratia claim, see ex-gratia application.*
2 an application to an insurance company for reimbursement due to damage or loss to insured goods or property.

clamp see cramp, wire-rope clamp.

clamping ring a fitting for securing the joint between a flue and the outlet pipe of a gas, oil or solid fuel appliance.

clapboarding, colonial siding; external timber wall cladding boards laid horizontally so that each board overlaps the one below.

clapboarding

class see grade.

classical 1 pertaining in general to a period in history when a culture flourishes or produces its culminating or most typifying works; especially classical Greece between the Archaic and Hellenistic periods c.480—323 BC, Rome during the time of Augustus c.63 BC—14 AD, but also Mayan architecture from 250—1000 BC, Islamic Abbasid architecture from 750—1250 AD, the Renaissance in Italy,

and France during the reigns of Henry IV and Louis XIII and XIV (1589—1715).
2 Classical; referring in particular to the architecture and art of classical Greece and Rome, or any architecture which follows the same principles and ideas, such as Renaissance, neoclassical or revival styles; see classicism, Greek architecture, Roman architecture.

classicism architecture and arts which follow the ideas and styles of classical Greek and Roman precedents, as with neoclassicism and Baroque classicism.

classification, grade, grading; the division of a mass of data, information, or products and materials into categories; the resulting scheme.

clastic sedimentary rock sedimentary rock which has formed as a result of the fusion of particles from older, weathered and broken down rocks.

claw bolt the bolt for a sliding door lock or latch, with two sprung hook-shaped pieces which grasp a striking plate attached to the door frame.

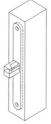

claw bolt

claw chisel a toothed hand chisel used for dressing stonework; also called a claw tool; claw chiselling refers to the final dressing of a stonework surface with such a tool.

claw chisel

claw hammer a hammer with a fork or claw opposite the striking face for extracting nails.

claw tool see claw chisel.

clay a range of fine plastic soils or rocks containing a high proportion of water;

flowing saturated clay is called mud; building work in unfired clay is called cob, adobe or pisé, depending on the method used.

clay block see hollow clay block.

clay block paving see brick paving.

clay brick the most common type of brick, made or manufactured from moulded clay, hardened by firing in a kiln or baking in the sun; see fired brick, mud brick.

clay roof tile any roof tile manufactured from fired clay.

clayslate, killas; a greenish or dark grey sedimentary rock with excellent cleavage, used as building stone for roof and wall tiles, and for insulating slabs.

claystone argillaceous rock.

clay tile any tile manufactured from fired clay; see clay roof tile.

cleaning agent any chemical substance used for removing unwanted dirt, scale and impurities from a surface.

cleaning eye, inspection eye, rodding eye; a small covered opening in a pipeline to provide access for cleaning and clearing by rodding.

cleaning hinge see easy-clean hinge.

cleanout trap, cleanout; a removable panel at lower level in formwork, from which rubbish and other unwanted material can be removed prior to casting or placing concrete.

clear, 1 colourless; a description of glass products, liquids, sealants, etc. which are uncoloured.
2 see transparent; in artificial lighting, the classification of a lamp whose bulb is of transparent rather than diffuse glass; cf. pearl, opal.
3 a description of commercial timber with no visual defects.

clearance 1 a space between two adjacent building components or constructions for fitting, access, circulation, etc.; see allowance, headroom, stair headroom.
2 the narrow gap between a hinged door leaf or window casement and its frame which allows it to open; see door clearance, back clearance, front clearance.
3 see clearing.

clear glass see clear sheet glass.
clear float glass float glass which is transparent.

clear plate glass ground cast glass or float glass.

clear sheet glass, flat drawn glass; glass formed by a process of drawing sheets of glass upwards from a reservoir of molten material to a tower where they are cut into suitable lengths.

clearing, clearance, site clearing; the removal of trees, stumps, vegetation, rubbish, stones and other unwanted debris from a building site prior to the commencement of construction.

clear span the open horizontal distance between adjacent abutments of supporting construction for a beam, truss, arch, etc.

clearstory see clerestory.

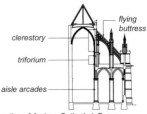

section of Amiens Cathedral, France, 13th century

clear width see stair clear width.

cleat any light secondary fixing for attaching components in place, preventing lateral movement of sheet cladding, etc.; see sheetmetal cleat, glazing cleat.

cleft stone any building stone shaped by cleaving rather than by sawing or hewing; cleaving is a neat and easy splitting along naturally weak planes in the stone.

clenching see clinching.

clerestory, clearstory; the upper part of the side walls in the main body of a Romanesque or Gothic church, often with large windows to allow light into the space. See illustration above.

clerestory lighting natural lighting for large high spaces provided by windows at high level or near the roof line.

clerestory roof see split-level roof.

clerestory window, clearstory window; a window at or near the top of an internal wall, found in basilicas,

Romanesque and Gothic churches and in some modern factory buildings, halls, gymnasia, etc. for top lighting.

clerk of works, project representative; a qualified professional employed by the client to carry out periodical inspections of a building under construction and ensure that work is carried out according to the terms of the contract.

clevis a metal fastener for chains, etc. consisting of a U-shaped metal whose ends are closed off with a threaded bolt or cotter.

clevis

client a person or organization which commissions a building or construction.

client's representative see project manager.

climbing formwork wall formwork raised and supported on previously casted concrete once this has hardened.

clinching, clenching; the hammering or bending over of the exposed ends of driven nails or bolts on the reverse side of construction to prevent the joints from working loose.

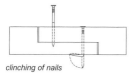

clinching of nails

clink see double welt.

clinker partially fused incombustible mineral material such as blast-furnace slag and fused ash created under high temperatures; used as a lightweight aggregate and in ground form in concrete.

---

clip 1 any small metal fastener which holds a component in place by a clamping action; examples included as separate entries are listed below:
*glazing clip; *insulation clip; *pipe clip, see saddle clip; *resilient clip; *saddle clip; *spring clip; *tile clip; *union clip; *wire-rope clip, wire-rope clamp.
2 tie, tingle; a narrow strip of metal or cleat used for securing roll joints and standing seams in sheet roofing.
circlip

---

clipped gable roof see half-hipped roof.

cloaked verge tile a special roof tile designed to cover the edge of a verge.

cloison in decorative enamelling, surface panels or cells formed by bent wire or solder fixed to the metal base to separate areas of colour in the enamelling process; a similar use of clay ridges in glazing ceramics; cloisonné refers to work carried out in this way, see also next entry.

cloisonné masonry decorative masonry in which small stone blocks or panels are framed by bricks placed vertically and horizontally in single or double courses.

cloister a covered walkway or ambulatory around an open quadrangle in a monastery, college, or monastic cathedral, previously used as a link, and for discussion and pensive thought.

cloister vault, domical vault; a domelike vault constructed over a square or polygonal base, from which curved segments rise to a central point.

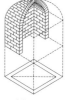

cloister vault

close boarding boarding laid side by side so that there are no gaps between adjacent boards.

close couple roof, close couple rafter roof, span roof; a couple roof tied by a ceiling joist or ties at the base of its rafters; a simple triangular roof truss.

closed assembly time the period of time during which parts of a glued joint may still be repositioned before the adhesive sets.

closed capital, closed bud capital see bud capital.

closed circuit television, CCTV; a security system of television cameras and monitors used for surveillance and observation of a building or premises.

closed circuit television camera see surveillance camera.

closed circuit television survey, camera survey, CCTV survey; the inspection of drains and sewers using remote video cameras to check for corrosion, blockages and cracks.

closed eaves overhanging eaves whose lower horizontal edge is closed with soffit boards.

closed face see tight side.

closed riser stair a stair in which the space between alternate treads is filled with a riser.

closed side see tight side.

close grained a description of slowly grown wood having densely spaced growth rings; variously known as close grown, dense grained, fine grained, fine grown, narrow grained, narrow ringed, slow grown.

close grown see close grained.

closer 1 the last brick in a brick course at a stopped end or corner, often manufactured to a non-standard large or small size to make up space in a brickwork bond.

brick closer

2 especially a brick which exposes a half-header or header in brickwork, usually used to make up space in the brick bond; see queen closer, king closer.

3 see cavity closer.

4 a device for closing a door, window or hatch automatically; see door closer.

closing face the face of a hinged door leaf, hatch or casement which closes against its frame.

closing jamb see shutting jamb.

closing stile see shutting stile.

closure a thin brick used to bond inner and outer leaves of masonry in early forms of cavity wall construction.
closure piece see cavity closer.

cloud see revision cloud.

clourer a pointed masonry chisel, used for the initial rough shaping of stone surfaces; also called a point.
cloured finish hammer-dressed finish.

clout, clout nail, felt nail; a short galvanized nail with a large flat head, used for fixing down roofing felt and thin boarding.

clout

clove oil see oil of cloves.

cloven finish see riven finish.

cloverleaf a decorative motif derived from the leaves of some plant species of the pea family which have three lobes, Trifolium spp., symbolic of the Holy Trinity.

cloverleaf motif

cloverleaf moulding see trefoil moulding.

club hammer, lump hammer, mash hammer; an iron-headed mallet or sledgehammer small enough to be held in one hand.

clustered housing housing built in close-knit groups, either detached or linked with common facilities, courtyards, foundations, etc.

clustered pier see compound pier.

clutch head screw see one-way head screw.

CN cellulose nitrate.

coach bolt, carriage bolt; a bolt with a dome-shaped head cast with a square protrusion on its underside which locks into a timber surface or shaped housing when tightened with a nut.

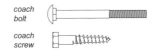
coach bolt

coach screw

coach screw, lag bolt (Am), lag screw (Am); a heavy screw whose head is hexagonal and can be turned with a spanner.

coagulation in water purification, a process of treating waste water with flocculating chemicals which adhere to impurities and encourage their removal from the water.

coal tar a dark viscous liquid formed as a result of the distillation of coal; used as a preservative and in the chemical industry.

coal-fired referring to a heating system utilizing coal as its combustible fuel.

coarse aggregate aggregate which consists largely of particles over 5 mm in diameter; types included as separate entries are listed below:
*angular aggregate; *cubical aggregate; *elongated aggregate; *flaky aggregate; *flaky and elongated aggregate; *rounded aggregate.

coarse grained, 1 granular; a description of a soil which contains a substantial proportion of sand or gravel.
2 an equivalent description for timber, see coarse textured.

coarse gravel see gravel.

coarse mortar mortar whose aggregate is coarse sand; see coarse stuff.

coarse plaster see coarse stuff.

coarse sand see sand.

coarse silt see silt.

coarse soil see granular soil.

coarse stuff 1 plaster, used for undercoats, produced from lime putty and coarse sand.
2 simple lime sand mortar used in bricklaying.

coarse textured, open grained, coarse grained; a description of wood with large pores or largely spaced growth rings.

coat a single continuous layer of material such as paint or plaster applied to a surface as protection, decoration or to provide a treatment; see plaster coat, thatch coat; see also coating for paint coating cf. film.

coated chippings, coated grit; aggregate between 3 mm and 20 mm in size range with a coating of a binder such as tar or bitumen; used in road construction.

coated felt see mineral granule surfaced bitumen felt.

coated float glass see surface coated float glass.

coated grit see coated chippings.

coated macadam see tarmacadam.

coated plywood plywood manufactured or pretreated with a thin protective or sealing surface coat of material such as polyester, urethane, epoxy, etc.

coated wallpaper a wallcovering surface-treated with a thin layer of polyvinyl acetate or similar flexible material.

coating, finish; a protective or decorative layer or coat of material such as paint, plastics, zinc, etc. applied to a surface; the surface application of one or a number of layers of protective material to provide a finish.

coating system a number of layers or coats of material applied to a surface in the correct order to provide a finish.

coaxial cable in telecommunications, a transmission cable consisting of a conductor shielded by two intertwined tubes of metal wire, designed to have low radiation losses and high resistance to external interference.

cob a traditional walling material of unburnt clay mixed with sand and straw, laid in situ and left to harden.

cobalt a silvery white metal, **Co**, used as an alloy in steel, in pigments and as an oxide in the manufacture of blue glass.

cobalt black see black oxide of cobalt.

cobalt blue a permanent, opaque, blue pigment consisting of a compound of cobalt and aluminium oxide with varying degrees of zinc, developed by the French chemist Louis Thénard in 1799; also known as azure cobalt, Thénard's blue, king's blue and Vienna blue; also a shade of blue which takes its name from this; cobalt ultramarine is a violet form of the blue pigment cobalt blue made without phosphoric acid.

cobalt green a bright green inorganic pigment consisting of a compound of cobalt zincate and zinc oxide; developed by the Swedish chemist Sven Rinman in 1780 and suitable for use in oil, watercolour and acrylic paints; variously known as Gellert green, Rinman's green, Swedish green or zinc green.

cobalt oxide see black oxide of cobalt.

cobalt violet, cobalt violet phosphate; an inorganic clear semi-opaque violet pigment originally used in fresco painting, initially made from a rare ore of cobalt and now manufactured artificially.

cobalt yellow, aureolin; a toxic bright transparent yellow pigment used in watercolour, tempera and oil paints.

cobble, 1 cobblestone; a naturally occurring lump of stone, by classification from 60–200 mm in size.
2 one of a series of small roughly squared pieces of natural stone laid in sand or mortar as road surfacing or paving; sometimes called a cube; see also pebble, sett, cube.

cobbled paving paving laid in natural stone cobbles.

cobbled paving

cobblestone see cobble.

cobblestone wall, cobble wall; a rough masonry wall constructed of rounded stones or cobbles laid in mortar.

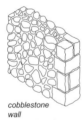
cobblestone wall

cobwork see log construction.

coccolite a white or green form of the mineral pyroxene, a silicate of lime, magnesium or manganese; used as building stone at the beginning of the 1900s.

cochineal a red dyestuff produced from the Central American insects Dactylopius coccus (a red scale insect that feeds on cacti) and the kermes insect Coccus ilicis; used in the manufacture of carmine.

cock 1 any simple tap from which piped fluid or gas can be drawn off for use, or supply cut off to particular appliances; see draw-off tap.
2 plug tap, plug cock, plug valve; in water installations, a tap or stopvalve containing a cone-shaped plug perforated with a hole, set in a housing and turned with a lever through 90° to cut off flow.

cock beak moulding a decorative moulding whose cross-section is that of a shallow convex surface with a flat underside, used in edging for boards and tables; cf. thumbnail.

cock comb see cock's comb.

cocking piece see sprocket.

cock's comb, cock comb, coxcomb; a hand-held serrated metal plate drawn across a surface to produce a grooved finish in stonework; a toothed drag.

coconut fibre see coir matting.

code of professional conduct a set of standards of integrity, ethics, guidance and procedure drawn up by a professional body, to which their members are expected to adhere.

codes of practice see building codes of practice.

coefficient a numeric factor which defines the property of a substance or process, used as a multiplier in calculations; examples included as separate entries are listed below:
*absorption coefficient; *acoustic absorption coefficient, see sound absorption coefficient; *air-to-air heat transmission coefficient, see U-value; *coefficient of diffusion, see diffusion coefficient; *coefficient of heat transfer, see U-value; *coefficient of thermal conductance, see C-value; *coefficient of thermal conductivity, see k-value; *coefficient of thermal resistance, see R-value; *coefficient of thermal transmittance, see U-value; *C-value; *external surface resistance value, see RSO-value; *heat transmission value, see k-value; *internal surface resistance value, see RSI-value; *k-value; *Los Angeles coefficient; *noise reduction coefficient; *RSI-value; *RSO-value; *R-value; *sound absorption coefficient; *surface coefficient; *U-value.*

coelin, coeruleum see cerulean blue.

coffer, caisson; one of a number of recessed polygonal panels in a decorative or structural ceiling.

coffered ceiling a decorated or structural ceiling relieved with a series of polygonal recessed panels, cassettes or coffers; see also lacunar.

coffered slab see waffle slab.

coffering the decorative relieving of a ceiling or soffit with coffers.

cog 1 in timber jointing, a square cut made into a member received by another member to prevent movement within the joint.

2 see nib.

cogged joint a timber framing joint in which the end of one member is cut with a square notch or cog to fit into another shaped member; see double cogged joint.

cogged halved joint

cogged corner joint

cogged corner joint a timber bevelled corner joint in which the halved ends of one member is cut with a cog for increased strength.

cogged halved joint a timber halving joint in which a cog or recess is cut into the halved surface to provide a lock for the joint.

cogging see notching.

cohesion the sticking together of particles of the same substance; cohesiveness is the ability of the particles in a material such as concrete, or an assembly of components, to remain united with another.

cohesion pile in foundation technology, a pile, similar in action to a friction pile, which transmits forces to surrounding ground around its circumference, through cohesive forces.

cohesive soil a soil whose particles adhere to form hard lumps due to its high content of fine particles.

coign see quoin.

coil 1 in heating and refrigeration technology, helical piping through which chilled or hot liquid is passed to alter the temperature of surrounding liquid, air, etc.

2 windings of copper wire in an electric motor, transformer, electromagnet, etc.

3 in the hot-rolling of steel, the product of a strip mill, subsequently decoiled and flattened to produce steel strip.

4 any ornament with spiral motifs; see continuous coil spiral, volute, helix.

coil coating, prepaint process; a continuous automated industrial process for coating sheetmetal before fabrication into panels and other components, in which a coil of metal is unwound and cleaned, chemically treated, primed and given a baked or painted coating and rewound ready for supply to a manufacturer.

coin see quoin.

coincidence in acoustics, a resonance-like phenomenon in which skin structures such as double glazing or panelled frames experience a loss in sound-insulating properties at certain frequencies.

coin flooring, coin-pattern flooring see studded rubber flooring.

coir matting a rough-textured floor covering woven from coir (coconut fibres), used for doormats, and for corridors, foyers, etc.

coke black see vine black.

colcothar an obsolete variety of red iron oxide pigment, formed by the distillation of sulphuric acid from iron sulphate.

cold bridge, heat bridge, thermal bridge; a conductive path in construction between interior and exterior for the easy passage of heat from inside to out, usually causing problems with heat loss, thermal discomfort and condensation.

cold chisel a heavy-duty steel-handled chisel used with a mallet for the chipping, cutting and shaping of masonry.

cold curing adhesive any adhesive that sets without the application of heat.

cold drawing, wire drawing; the production of high-strength metal wires by extruding cold material through a series of dies; cold drawn wire is used as concrete reinforcement and for nails.

cold feed pipe a pipe that conveys cold water from a cistern to a water heater.

cold forming, cold rolling; the process of forming light steel sections, profiles, etc. by bending steel plate with a series of rollers.

cold formed section a lightweight structural steel section, often formed into an open profile by bending, or rolled into various cross-sectional forms while cold.

cold galvanization the result of treating a metal surface with zinc-rich paint as corrosion protection; see zinc-rich paint.

cold glue see cold setting adhesive, cold curing adhesive.

cold oil ring main oil heating pipework in which oil is supplied to a burner unheated, and any unused fuel returned to the storage tank.

cold pressing a method of producing high-quality linseed oil, used as a vehicle in paints, by extraction under low pressure without heat.

cold rolling see cold forming.

cold roof pitched roof construction in which insulation is situated between or directly above horizontal ceiling joists, creating an uninsulated roof void or attic space above.

cold setting adhesive, cold glue; any adhesive that will set at temperatures below 23°C.

cold start lamp see instant start lamp.

cold twisted bar in reinforced concrete, a reinforcing bar, square in profile, which has been twisted to improve its strength and bonding with the concrete.

cold twisted bars

cold water pipe, cold water supply pipe; a pipe within a building which distributes cold water supply to cisterns, heaters, appliances and taps.

cold-weather bricklaying see winter bricklaying.

cold-weather concreting see winter concreting.

cold welding a welding process in which soft metals are joined together by the application of pressure through hammering.

cold working the process of working metal when cold, as in cold drawing and cold rolling, so as to increase hardness; see hot working.

cold worked deformed bar in reinforced concrete, a deformed bar which has been cold worked to improve its properties.

collagen glue see animal glue.

collapsible formwork formwork with telescopic or hinged parts that can be easily dismounted when striking.

collapsible gate, scissor gate; a side-opening shutter for goods lifts and service areas, consisting of a latticework of pivoted steel slats which enable the door to be folded to one side.

collar 1 any fixing or restraining component which fits over and is tightened to a cylindrical member.
2 see loose socket.
3 see collar beam.

collar and tie beam truss in timber frame construction, a roof truss of slanting rafters, a horizontal tie beam joining their lower edges and a collar beam situated between tie beam and ridge.

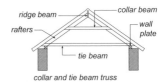

collar and tie beam truss

collar beam, collar, collar piece, strut beam, wind beam; in timber frame construction, a transverse beam between eaves level and ridge connecting two principal rafters.

collarino see trachelion.

collar piece see collar beam.

collar plate see collar purlin.

collar purlin, collar plate; in traditional timber roof construction, a longitudinal horizontal purlin carried on a crown post or by other means, and supporting the collars between pairs of rafters.

collar roof, collar rafter roof; a form of simple timber roof construction with each pair of rafters tied between eaves and ridge by a horizontal collar beam.

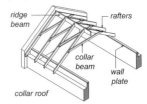

collar roof

collar screed a specially shaped screed rail used in the plastering of concrete or masonry columns.

collateral see security.

collision load a temporary dynamic load imposed on a structure by the collision of a vehicle or some other moving object.

colloid a substance consisting of ultramicroscopic solid particles suspended in a liquid or gas.

Cologne earth see Cassel earth.

colonial siding see clapboarding.

colonnade a series of columns which support a beam, roof or, in classical architecture, an entablature.

colonnette a small column often adorning windows, niches, etc. and carrying a pediment or arch.

colophony see rosin.

color see colour.

colorant see colourant, colouring admixture.

colossal order, giant order; in classical architecture, a column which extends in height through two or more storeys on the elevation of a building.

colourant, colorant (Am), colouring agent; any substance used as a physical means of adding colour to a material or surface; a stain, dye or pigment; see colouring admixture.

colour chart, 1 colour schedule; a design document containing samples to show the range of proposed colours, and often materials and finishes in a building or space.
2 printed matter reproduced as small patches indicating the range of standard colours produced by a particular paint or product manufacturer.

colour circle see colour wheel.

colour-coding any signing system which uses colour to indicate use or action of a device, escape route, etc.

coloured brickwork see polychrome brickwork.

coloured cement see coloured Portland cement.

coloured concrete concrete containing cement to which permanent, inert

pigments have been added, imparting a colour to the finished surface.

coloured mortar mortar to which a coloured pigment or aggregate has been added.

coloured opaque glass non-transparent glass body-tinted, laminated or coated with coloured material, used for work surfaces, cladding and bathroom finishes; see cladding glass, spandrel glass.

coloured Portland cement ordinary or white Portland cement to which inert pigments have been added to provide colour.

coloured rendering rendering in which coloured mortar has been used.

colour fastness the ability of a material or pigment to retain its colour over a period of time, or when exposed to the weather or treatment, etc.

colour filter see filter.

colouring admixture, colourant; in concretework, an admixture or pigment included in the mix to add colour.

colouring agent see colourant.

colouring pigment see stainer.

colour intensity in colour science and painting, the measure of purity and brightness of a hue, its saturation.

colourless, 1 clear; of a transparent material such as glass or liquids, without colour.
2 achromatic, neutral; referring to a shade of colour composed entirely of black, white and grey, without spectral colour.

colour purity in colour science, the physical equivalent of colour intensity, the property of a hue which reflects light of single wavelengths and is not mixed with black or white.

colour rendering in lighting design, the variation in appearance of colours under different lighting conditions; a colour rendering index is a measure of this, the degree to which a colour is rendered by different wavelengths of light, compared to a reference.

colour sample in design, a patch of colour or coloured material to display the final colour intended for a particular surface.

colour saturation, 1 chroma, tone; in colour science, the degree of purity of a colour, how much white, grey or black has been added to a hue.
2 the point at which the addition of pigment will no longer change the appearance of a particular colour.

colour schedule see colour chart.

colours in oil see oil paste.

colour system in colour and paint science, any system by which colours are arranged and classified in a logical manner.

colour temperature in lighting and colour science, the temperature at which a black body emits light (or radiation) of a certain colour.

colour wheel, colour circle; in colour theory, a circular diagram of the colours of the spectrum arranged around the circumference with complementary colours opposite one another.

columbarium 1 a recess left in a masonry wall as a housing for a timber joist or beam, which takes its name for the place where a dove or pigeon nests.
2 a storage place for cinerary urns, originally a Roman memorial chamber with vaulted niches containing cinerary urns of the dead.

column a structural shaft of concrete, masonry, metal or timber which transfers applied vertical loads through its length to its base; see also pillar; types included as separate entries are listed below:
*Aesculapian column, Asclepian column, see serpent column; *animal column; *annulated column; *applied column, attached column, engaged column; *baluster column; *banded column, see annulated column; *barley-sugar column, spiral column; *bundle column; *candelabrum column, candlestick column; *circular column, round column; *composite column, complex column (historical); *composite stanchion (modern); *coupled columns; *Cretan column, Minoan column; *demi-column, half-column; *detached column; *Doric column, see Doric; *edge-rolled column; *engaged column; *figured column;

*filleted column; *fluted column; *half-column, see demi-column; *Hathor column; *inserted column, see engaged column; *see Ionic column; *knotted column; *lighting column, see lighting post; *lotus column, see lotiform column; *Minoan column, Mycenaean column; *Osiris column; palm column, see palm capital; *papyrus column, papyrus-bundle column, see papyrus; *post; *proto-Doric column; *recessed column; *reverse taper column, see Minoan column; *ringed column, see annulated column; *round column, see circular column; *rusticated column; *salomonica, see spiral column; *serpent column; *spiral column, Solomonic column; *stanchion, steel column; *stone column, see vibroreplacement; *thermal column, convection column; *Tuscan column; *twinned columns, see coupled columns; *twisted column, see spiral column; *universal column, see H-section; *ventilating column; *wreathed column, see spiral column.

column and beam construction see post and beam construction.

column and slab construction a structural system in which the floors in a building are supported by a series of columns; the external walls are usually non-loadbearing.

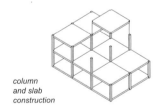

column
and slab
construction

column base see base.

column block a concrete block designed for use as a reinforced or plain concrete column or pilaster when laid in a vertical stack; also called a pilaster block.

column block

column figure carved slender figures of saints and noblemen adorning the recesses of a medieval church portal; see jamb figure, trumeau figure.

column footing, column foundation see pad foundation.

column radiator in hot water heating, a radiator with a number of interlinked vertical chambers of steel tube or cast iron, in which heating water circulates.

column reinforcement steel reinforcement for a reinforced concrete column.

column shaft see shaft.

column strip in concretework, the linear zone of a reinforced concrete slab that links the upper ends of supporting columns and oversails the column width in the spanning direction of the slab.

comb see scratcher, drag, cock's comb.

combed joint a joinery corner joint for drawers and boxes in which pieces are cut with a series of square notches to fit each other, also called a comb joint, finger joint or boxed corner joint.

combed plasterwork see comb-finish rendering.

comb-finished rendering, combed plasterwork, dragged plasterwork; rendering whose wet surface has been worked with a serrated tool to produce striations in its surface.

combination drill bit a drill bit which drills a hole and countersink for a screw head at the same time.

combination plane, universal plane; a versatile hand-held plane with adjustable and removable blades used for a variety of smoothing applications.

combination pliers see footprints.

combination sink a domestic sink with a drainer cast or pressed in one piece.

combination square see try and mitre square.

combined drainage see combined system.

combined extract and input system see mechanical input and extract ventilation.

combined sewerage see combined system.

combined system a system of drainage or sewerage in which both foul water and surface water are conveyed in the same pipelines.

comb joint see combed joint.

combustion air the air used up in combustion of fuel in a fireplace, burner, hazardous fire, etc.

combustion chamber see firebox.

combustion gas colourless and poisonous gases given off burning matter before the emission of smoke; combustion gases include carbon monoxide, carbon dioxide, hydrogen chloride and hydrogen cyanide.

combustion gas detector a fire detector which reacts to the presence of smoke and other combustion gases from hazardous building fires.

commercial timber timber of value in the construction, joinery and furniture industries, etc., often sold outside its country of origin.

commission an order from a client to an architect for the design of a building.

commissioning 1 the scope of decisions and actions by an owner or client in having a building built.
2 the testing, adjusting and running in of a technical or mechanical services installation prior to handover.

common see common brick.

common alder, black alder; [*Alnus glutinosa*], see alder.

common bond see English garden-wall bond, Flemish stretcher bond.

common brick, common; a standard general-purpose rectangular mass-produced brick with untreated faces; not generally used for special applications or visual quality.

common furniture beetle [*Anobium punctatum*] a species of insect whose larvae cause damage to furniture and other timber by burrowing.

common grounds see grounds.

common joist in timber frame construction, a basic floor or ceiling joist.

common purlin, horizontal rafter; in timber roof construction, one of a series of horizontal members parallel with a ridge or eaves, carried on principal rafters or trusses and onto which roof boarding may be nailed.

common purlin roof, horizontal rafter roof; timber roof construction in which roof trusses support a series of horizontal rafters, onto which the roof boarding or roofing material is attached.

common rafter in timber roof construction, a secondary rafter, one which does not carry purlins, supporting roof covering.

common reed [*Arundo phragmites, Phragmites australis*]; see best reed, Norfolk reed.

common wall see separating wall.

communication pipe that part of the service pipe of a water or gas supply system, outside a site boundary and thus maintained by the supplier, which connects a building to the supply main.

compact fluorescent lamp a small fluorescent lamp with good efficiency and long service life, with bayonet or screw caps and single or double U-shaped tube, often used as a replacement for incandescent lamps.

compaction see concrete compaction, ground compaction.

compartment any subdivision of a space bounded by screens, partitions or furnishing groups; a subdivision of a shelf, drawer or storage furnishing; see also fire compartment.

compartmentation see fire compartmentation.

compartment wall see fire wall.

compass plane, circular plane, roundsil (Sc.); a plane with a convex curved base for planing curved surfaces.

compass saw a small saw with a narrow tapering blade used for cutting curves or holes.

compatible referring to components, devices, computer programs and systems which will function together, fit or complement one another, or other systems, without modification.

compensation an award, usually a sum of money, paid out for injury or loss or damage to property.

competitive tendering a procedure for awarding a contract by choosing the most reasonable offer from a number of bidders.

complementary, complementary colour, complementary hue; in colour science, colours that are diametrically opposite one another on the colour circle; a colour opposite.

completion, realization; the finishing of all or parts of construction on a building site; the state of readiness for occupation of the whole works, although some minor work may be outstanding; also known as practical completion; see also partial handover (partial completion).

completion certificate in contract management, a document issued to the contractor, that certifies completion of specific areas of work, which have been approved by building control.

completion date, handover date; the date on which work on a building under construction or repair is due to be completed, as written into the building contract.

completion of defects certificate in contract management, a document issued at the end of the defects liability period certifying that all defects have been made good or repaired.

complex column see composite column.

complexity richness, variation and layering of space, form, material, colour and detail in architecture.

compo see composition mortar, cement mortar.

compo render see composition render.

component 1 one of a number of items, substances, parts, etc. which, when assembled or blended together in an appropriate way, form a different and more complex item; see building component.
2 one of a number of different semi-liquid compounds mixed together to form a substance which sets, such as an adhesive, paint or sealant.
3 in mechanics, that part of a force expressed as a vector in a particular direction.

component drawing a contract drawing showing the dimensions and construction of a component such as a door or window.

component range drawing a design or contract drawing outlining the quantity, sizes, treatments and specifications for components of a similar type in a building project.

composite any product or construction made up of a number of different materials or technologies; usually a laminated material or one of plastic, concrete or cement reinforced with fibres of glass, mineral, metals or polymers.

composite beam any beam constructed of a number of different structural materials or using a variety of loadbearing methods; see hollow composite beam, filigree beam.

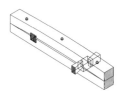

composite board a building board formed by gluing veneers on either side of a core of material other than timber, such as cardboard.

Composite capital 1 a capital at the top of a column of the classical Roman Composite order, carved both with lavish acanthus foliage and leafy volutes, surmounted by a flat abacus.

Composite capital, Triumphal Arch of Septimius Severus, Rome, 203 AD

2 composite capital; an ancient Egyptian capital combining various different motifs and styles.

composite cement see fillerized cement.

composite column, 1 complex column; an ancient Egyptian column-type combining various different motifs and styles.

Egyptian composite column with Hathor and bell capital, Kiosk of Nectanebo I (Temple of Isis), Philae c. 380–343 BC

2 Composite column; a column of the classical Roman Composite order.

3 see composite stanchion.

composite construction the acting together of two or more materials, such as steel and concrete, to form a construction with improved properties of strength, durability, etc.

composite floor slab, composite slab, steel deck floor; structural floor construction of profiled steel sheeting onto which concrete is cast; the steel acts as permanent shuttering and resists tensile forces in bending.

Composite order a classical Roman order, a hybrid of Ionian and Corinthian, with fluted columns, a capital with both volutes and acanthus leaves, a base and an entablature with dentils.

composite pile in foundation technology, any pile which makes use of a number of different methods of piling to fulfil its purpose.

composite slab see composite floor slab.

composite stanchion, composite column; a steel and concrete column consisting either of a hollow steel stanchion filled with concrete or a steel profile cased in concrete; used to minimize the amount of steel and for fire safety.

composite truss a truss in which the main spanning members or rafters are of timber and the other members, struts, infill, etc. are of steel.

composite window 1 a window assembly whose frame and casements are manufactured from different materials, often timber window frames with outer casements in aluminium; also known as a compound window. See illustration on following page.

2 two or more windows joined to fill an opening.

composition 1 the various component parts of which a substance is mixed or made up; the proportion of parts therein.
2 the deliberated arrangement of elements, forms and massing in a building, painting, sculpture, etc. to create a desired aesthetic effect.

composition mortar, compo, cement lime mortar; slow setting mortar consisting of proportioned amounts of cement, lime and sand, with good resistance to cracking, used for bricklaying and rendering.

composition render composition mortar used as exterior-grade plaster or render; usually called compo render, properly known as cement lime render.

composition shingles see strip slates.

compound pier, clustered pier, compound column; in Gothic architecture, a heavy column carved with a number of vertical cuttings to appear as if it were formed from a number of round shafts of lesser diameter; each

compound pier

shaft rises to form the various ribs of the vaulted ceiling; see also bundle pier, bundle column.

compound window see composite window.

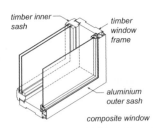
timber inner sash
timber window frame
aluminium outer sash
composite window

comprehensive development the development of a sizeable area of land with buildings or built form and associated roads, lighting and other infrastructure, usually as a phased operation.

comprehensive redevelopment, urban redevelopment; the rebuilding and modernization of a large urban area, often of derelict, redundant or unsuitable buildings, in accordance with a plan.

compressed air caisson, pneumatic caisson; a caisson whose air pressure is kept above atmospheric level to prevent the infiltration of surrounding water and allow for dry working conditions inside.

compressed straw slab see strawboard.

compression a pressing force which acts along the axis of a member or inwards on a body; the act, result and state of being pressed or squeezed with this force.

compression failure, cross break; failure of the fibres in a piece of structural timber due to excessive longitudinal compression or bending.

compression fitting a pipe fitting whose joint is secured by compressing the pipe end with a threaded nut or other clamping device.

compression moulding a method of forming thermoplastics products by placing material powder into a mould then applying heat and pressure.

compression reinforcement in reinforced concrete, reinforcement which has been designed to withstand compressive loading.

compression wood wood sawn from the undersides of branches and leaning trees with uneven growth rings and low strength; reaction wood in softwood.

compression wood

compressive strength the property of a material or component which has good resistance to forces in compression without fracture.

compressive strength test in concretework, a test to determine the compressive strength of concrete, either by cube testing or cylinder testing.

compressive washer see spring lock washer.

computer-aided design, CAD; the design and drawing of a system, building, component or object using a computer using software specially developed for that purpose.

concave joint see keyed joint.

concave moulding 1 see cavetto, congé, cove.
2 see scotia, gorge, trochilus.
3 see hollow moulding.

concealed door closer a door closer mounted within the thickness of a door leaf or threshold.

concealed dovetail joint see lapped dovetail joint.

concealed fixing see secret fixing.

concealed hinge, blind hinge; a special hinge used for high-quality joinery, visible only when the door it supports is open.

concealed nailing see secret nailing.

concealed system a suspended ceiling system whose supporting profiles are not visible in the finished ceiling surface, usually provided by slotting joints or by fixing to the rear of the ceiling panels.

concentrated load see point load.

concentric pattern see circular pattern.

concentric taper in drainage and plumbing, a short piece of conical pipe or similar fitting for joining two pipes of different diameters so that their centres lie along the same line.

concept a general abstract notion; a principal or central idea relating to a certain range of things; the underlying or generating thought, idea, philosophy, method or process for a design proposal or scheme.

concertina blind, folding blind; a pleated window blind of sheet material such as paper or cloth, which folds up or down with a concertina action.

concertina door see sliding folding door.

conch, 1 concha (Lat.); a half dome used to roof semicircular apses in some churches.
2 ornamental carving or decoration in the form of a stylized conch shell.

conch motif

concrete a mixture of sand, aggregate, cement and water, often including admixtures, which sets to form a hard, versatile building material, mainly used for its structural properties; types included as separate entries are listed below; see also precast concrete and reinforced concrete for illustrations.
*aerated concrete; *air-entrained concrete; *asphaltic concrete; *autoclaved aerated concrete; *blast-furnace concrete, see slag concrete; *blinding concrete; *cast-in-place concrete, cast-in-situ concrete, see in-situ concrete; *cellular concrete, see aerated concrete; *coloured concrete; *cyclopean concrete; *dry packed concrete; *expanded aggregate concrete; *exposed aggregate concrete; *exposed concrete; *extruded concrete; *facing concrete; *fairfaced concrete; *fat concrete, see rich concrete; *ferroconcrete, see reinforced concrete; *fibre concrete, fibrous concrete, see fibre-reinforced concrete; *flowable concrete, see self-placing concrete; *flowing concrete; *foam concrete, see foamed concrete; *fresh concrete; *gas concrete; *glass concrete; *glassfibre-reinforced polymer/concrete, glassfibre-reinforced cement; *green concrete; *grouted aggregate concrete, see grouted concrete; *hardened concrete; *heavy concrete; *high alumina cement concrete; *high-strength concrete; *high-density concrete, see heavy concrete; *in-situ concrete; *insulating lightweight concrete, see insulating concrete; *intrusion concrete, see grouted concrete; *lean concrete; *lightweight aggregate concrete; *lightweight concrete; *low heat concrete; *luminescent concrete; *mass concrete; *mixed concrete; *monolithic concrete; *no-fines concrete; *non-vibration concrete, see self-placing concrete; *no-slump concrete; *pavement concrete; *plain concrete; *plasticized concrete; *pneumatically applied concrete, see sprayed concrete; *polymer concrete; *polymer fibre reinforced concrete; *polymer impregnated concrete; *polymer modified concrete; *polymer Portland cement concrete, see polymer concrete; *porous concrete, see aerated concrete; *Portland cement concrete; *post-tensioned concrete; *precast concrete; *pre-packed concrete, see grouted concrete; *preplaced concrete, see grouted concrete;

*prestressed concrete; *pretensioned concrete; *pumpable concrete; *ready-mixed concrete, readymix concrete; *refractory concrete; *reinforced concrete; *resin concrete, see polymer concrete; *retarded concrete; *rich concrete; *roller-compacted concrete, rolled concrete; *Roman concrete; *rubble concrete; *sawdust concrete, see wood-cement concrete; *self-placing concrete, self-consolidating concrete, self-compactable concrete; *site concrete, see mixed concrete; *site mixed concrete; *slag concrete; *spaded concrete, see tamped concrete; *sprayed concrete; *steel concrete, see reinforced concrete; *steel-fibre reinforced concrete; *stiffened concrete; *structural concrete; *superplasticized concrete; *tamped concrete; *terrazzo concrete, see terrazzo; *tremie concrete; *underwater concrete; *unreinforced concrete, see plain concrete; *vacuum dewatered concrete, vacuum concrete; *vibrated concrete; *white concrete; *wood-cement concrete.

concrete admixture a substance added to a concrete mix with the aim of changing its properties of drying, setting, workability, etc.; see list of concrete admixtures under admixture.

concrete batch in concretework, an amount of concrete mixed for use at any one time.

concrete beam any beam of cast in-situ or prefabricated concrete, often prestressed or reinforced with steel; see concrete lintel, in-situ concrete beam, precast beam.

concrete bit see masonry drill.

concrete bleeding, water gain; in concretework, the seeping out of excess water not taken up by the hydration of cement.

concrete block a masonry block manufactured from precast concrete, usually of cellular or aggregate construction; types included as separate entries are listed below:

concrete block

*beam block, bond-beam block, see channel block; *capping block, see coping block; *cavity block, cellular block; *channel block; *column block; *coping block; *hollow block, see cellular block; *insulated block; *lightweight concrete block; *lintel block, see channel block; *partition block; *pilaster block, see column block; *radial block; *sill block.

concrete block paver a precast rectangular or interlocking concrete paving stone; also called a unit paver, paving block; types included as separate entries are listed below, see also next entry.
*cellular paver, crib paver; *hexagonal paver; *interlocking paver, interpaver; *interweave paver; key paver; *pattern paver; *wavy paver.

concrete block paving an external paved surface made up of evenly sized concrete units, laid on sand or a concrete bed; also called unit paving.

concrete bond in concretework, the bond caused by friction and adhesion between the concrete and steel reinforcement.

concrete brick an unfired brick made from concrete rather than clay.

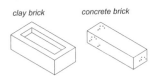

clay brick   *concrete brick*

concrete cancer see alkali-aggregate reaction.

concrete casing concrete used as a fireproof covering for structural steel.

concrete chute in the production of concrete, an inclined open steel channel along which concrete is transferred from a mixer into formwork.

concrete compaction in concreting, the manipulating of freshly placed concrete by tamping or vibration to release air voids and settle the mass.

concrete cover in reinforced concrete, the thickness of protective concrete between a reinforcing bar and the exterior surface of the concrete.

concrete cracking see cracking.

concrete curing the treatment of hardening concrete by covering, wetting, or steam treatment to maintain its temperature and moisture level, in order to provide water for hydration, prevent cracking and improve the quality of the concrete.

concrete drill see masonry drill.

concrete flag see concrete paving slab.

concrete flow test in concretework, a test to determine the workability, consistency and degree of segregation of fresh concrete by subjection to repeated jolting.

concrete formwork see formwork.

concrete frame any building frame of prefabricated or cast-in-situ concrete beams, columns, walls, slabs, etc., onto which cladding components, flooring, roofing, etc. are fixed; see precast concrete frame, in-situ concrete frame.

concrete grade see grade of concrete.

concrete lintel an in-situ or precast reinforced concrete beam component used over openings in brick and block walls.

concrete maturity in concretework, a measurement of the strength of hardening concrete as a function of time and temperature, in units of degree day or degree hour.

concrete mesh reinforcement see fabric reinforcement.

concrete mix the component parts of concrete such as sand, aggregate, cement, water and admixtures combined in an appropriate ratio.

concrete mixer in the production of concrete, a machine for mixing the various constituents to form a homogeneous concrete mix; see cement mixer.

concrete nail see masonry nail.

concrete panel see precast concrete panel.

concrete patching in concretework, the filling of surface holes and voids and repairing of defects in the cast surface with mortar after the concrete has set.

concrete pavement see concrete paving, prestressed concrete pavement, continuously reinforced concrete pavement.

concrete paver 1 a precast concrete unit or slab laid in series to form hardwearing external paved areas; see concrete block paver, concrete paving slab.
2 a machine which runs on rails and produces concrete pavement.

concrete paving 1 precast concrete units or paving slabs laid horizontally as a hardwearing external surface; see concrete block paving.
2 concrete pavement; a layer of reinforced concrete laid as a hardwearing surface on roads, pavements and pedestrian areas.

concrete paving block see concrete block paver.

concrete paving slab, precast concrete flag; a large rectangular concrete slab used for paving external surfaces such as pedestrian areas.

concrete pile in foundation technology, a reinforced concrete pile, either precast and driven in, or cast in-situ in a prebored excavation; types included as separate entries are listed below:
*augered pile; *bored pile; *cast-in-place pile, in-situ pile; *precast pile.

concrete placer see pneumatic concrete placer.

concrete placing, placement; the laying, pouring or pumping of fresh concrete into formwork, moulds, excavations, etc. to attain its final shape.

concrete plank a precast concrete flooring unit laid in series to span between beams or crosswalls and provide a floor structure; see also hollow-core beam.

concrete pump a machine for pumping concrete from a mixer or storage vehicle into formwork, excavations, etc.

concrete reinforcement 1 steel rods, deformed bars, meshes and other steel products incorporated into reinforced concrete to withstand tensile forces; types included as separate entries are listed below:
*beam reinforcement; *binder, see stirrup; *bottom reinforcement; *cage; *column reinforcement; *compression reinforcement; *concrete mesh reinforcement, see fabric; *fabric reinforcement; *foundation

reinforcement; *helical reinforcement; *lateral reinforcement; *ligature, see stirrup; *link, see stirrup; *longitudinal reinforcement; *main reinforcement; *mesh reinforcement, see fabric reinforcement; *principal reinforcement, see main reinforcement; *secondary reinforcement; *shear reinforcement; *slab reinforcement; *steel reinforcement, see concrete reinforcement; *stirrup; *tension reinforcement, tensile reinforcement; *top reinforcement; *transverse reinforcement, see lateral reinforcement; *two-way reinforcement; *web reinforcement, see shear reinforcement; *wire-mesh reinforcement, see fabric reinforcement.
2 see reinforcing bar.

concrete roof tile any roof tile manufactured from concrete.

concrete saw a large powered circular saw used for cutting openings in hardened concrete.

concrete screed see screed.

concrete screw, masonry screw; any hard-metal screw for fixing to hard porous surfaces such as concrete or masonry.

concrete screw anchor a double-helical screw for fixing components *concrete screw anchor* such as door frames, pipe hangers, etc. directly to a concrete or masonry surface into predrilled holes.

concrete segregation a defect in concreting caused by the separating out of constituent parts, especially coarse aggregate, from the mix.

concrete slab any relatively thin planar area of reinforced concrete, usually a structural floor or roof slab; types included as separate entries are listed below:
*coffered slab, see waffle slab; *column and beam construction, see post and beam construction; *column and slab construction; *concrete paving slab; *flat slab, see mushroom slab; *folded plate, folded slab; *hollow-core beam, hollow-core slab, hollow-core plank; *honeycomb slab, see waffle slab; *mushroom slab; *post and beam construction; *waffle slab.

concrete slump test a standard on-site test to ascertain the consistency of fresh concrete by measuring the degree of collapse of a poured out cone-shaped sample.

concrete spraying, spraying, pneumatic concreting, shotcreting; the application of sprayed concrete.

concrete structure see reinforced-concrete structure, concrete frame.

concrete testing various tests carries out on fresh and hardened concrete to ascertain strength, consistency, workability, etc.; see below for types included as separate entries:
*compressive strength test; *concrete flow test; *concrete slump test; *consistometer test, see VB-consistometer test; *core test; *cube test; *cylinder test; *flow test, see concrete flow test; *slump test; *strength test, see compressive strength test; *Vebe test, see VB-consistometer test; *works cube test.

concrete tile a floor or wall tile of pressed, extruded or wet-moulded concrete, usually less than 300 × 300 mm in size; also called a cement tile, depending on the aggregates used; see also concrete roof tile.

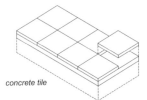

concrete tile

concrete topping a layer of concrete or mortar, usually 50 mm thick, laid as a smooth hardwearing finish for a cast concrete floor slab, deck or other construction.

concrete vibrator in the production of concrete, a mechanical device for compacting concrete by vibration.

concretework any sitework relating to the casting, erection and finishing of concrete construction; also the result of this; see also precast concretework.

concrete yield, volume yield; the volume of concrete produced by a given amount of cement aggregate and water, measured by weight.

concreting working with fresh concrete, especially concrete placing.

condensates pan, condensation pan; in an air-conditioning system, a vessel beneath a chilling coil in a condenser to collect water.

condensation the process of water vapour or steam cooling to water on contact with a surface below its dewpoint; the resulting droplets of water thus formed, surface condensation; see also flue condensation.
condensation point see dewpoint.
condensation polymerization see polycondensation.

condenser that part of an air-conditioning and refrigeration system in which refrigerant vapour is condensed, producing heat which is either reused or released to the outside.

conditional planning permission planning permission granted on the grounds that certain local authority conditions are fulfilled; see reserved matter.

conditions of contract, 1 terms of agreement; in contract administration, the terms describing the rights and obligations of the contractor to which he or she must adhere for the contract to remain valid.
2 terms of contract; a contract document outlining contractual obligations, rights of both parties and general practical matters used in a particular contract.
3 general conditions of contract; a similar standard document prepared by a professional advisory body, government department or other authority for use in all contracts.

conductance the property of a material or substance through which energy can freely flow, usually relating to heat or electricity; see thermal conductance, electrical conductance.

conductivity the measure of how well a given material will conduct heat or electricity; see thermal conductivity, electrical conductivity.

conductor any material, component or construction through which electricity or heat can pass with minimum resistance, and for which it is made use of; see electrical conductor, lightning-conductor; specifically, that part of an electric cable through which the electricity flows.

conductor header see rainwater head.

conduit a closed housing within construction to conceal or provide a passage for pipework and wiring; see electrical conduit, pipe duct.

cone penetration testing, deep penetration testing; in soil investigation, penetration testing in which a cone-shaped testing implement is pushed with a steady force into the soil to measure its bearing capacity.

congé a concave decorative moulding; a cavetto or cove surmounting a vertical surface.

conglomerate, puddingstone; rock consisting of rounded stones or pebbles embedded in a finer material such as limestone.

Congo wood see African walnut.

conical roll joint see roll joint.

conical roof a roof form in the shape of a cone.

conical vault 1 a masonry vault, or part of a vault, in the form of a segment of a cone.
2 expanding vault; a barrel vault whose diameter gradually increases along its length, used over splayed corridors and other spaces with funnel-shaped plans.

conical vault

conifer any cone-bearing evergreen tree with needle-like leaves, from which softwood is obtained; a member of the gymnosperm group which includes pines, firs, spruces, larches, etc.; see list of species of tree from which softwood is obtained under softwood.

Coniophora cerebella, Coniophora puteana see cellar rot.

conk, bracket fungus, shelf fungus, polypore; [*Polyporaceae*] a group of fungi which attack timber and produce hard fruiting bodies protruding from the trunks of trees and logs.

connecting point see connection.

connection, 1 joint; the meeting point of two components such as pipes or structural members which are fixed together; the joint thus formed.
2 connecting point; the point at which a building is connected to the mains water supply, or to a public sewer.
3 in telecommunications and networks, physical access to a phone line or network which allows for communication.

connector any accessory for fixing two components, members, pipe fittings, etc. together; examples included as separate entries are listed below:
*electrical connector; *flue connector; *group connector; *pipe fitting; *shear plate connector; *split ring connector; *toothed plate connector; *union.

consent see planning consent.

conservation the maintenance, rehabilitation and protection of old buildings and structures in their original state using traditional and authentic materials and methods; see also physical conservation.
conservation area an area or urban or rural land designated as being of special architectural or historical significance and protected by legislation to control development.

consistency the firmness or cohesiveness of thick liquid suspensions and pastes such as concrete.

consistometer an apparatus for measuring the firmness or cohesiveness of suspensions and thick liquids such as concrete, mortar, grouts and cement pastes; see VB-consistometer test.

console 1 a classical masonry bracket or corbelled stone for supporting overhangs, pediments, balconies and shelves, often ornate and decorated with volutes.
2 see monitor.
3 an operating station for electronic or automated equipment consisting of a monitor and keyboard, mouse, joystick, etc.

consolidation the compressing of soil due to the weight of overlying structures bearing down on it; see dynamic consolidation.

constant white see blanc fixe.

construction 1 an assembly of materials or components which function together to make up part of a building; examples included as separate entries are listed below:
*alternate bay construction, see chequerboard construction, alternate lane construction; *balanced construction; *box frame construction; *building construction; *ceiling construction; *chequerboard construction; *column and slab construction; *column and beam construction, see post and beam construction; *composite construction; *concrete construction; *crosswall construction; *cruck construction; *discontinuous construction; *floor construction; *half-timbered construction; *hit and miss construction, see chequerboard construction; *large-panel construction; *lift slab construction; *loadbearing wall construction; *log construction; *muntin and plank construction; *offshore construction; *panel construction; *plank construction; *post and beam construction, post and lintel construction; *precast concrete construction; *prefabricated construction, see prefabrication; *rammed earth construction, see pisé; *reconstruction; *roof construction; *shell construction; *stave construction; *steel construction; *stressed skin construction; *timber construction; *trabeated construction, see post and beam construction; *truss plate construction; *trussed construction; *window construction.
2 whole structural or building systems based on this.
3 see structure.
4 see building, building construction.
5 the setting out of technical drawings and constructing of geometrical forms such as perspectives with guide lines and other points of reference.

construction cost see building cost.

construction drawing a drawing showing how parts of a building are to be constructed on site, usually produced at a large scale (110, 120), often wall sections, junctions, etc.

construction engineering a discipline dealing with the structural frames and constructional technology of buildings and structures.

construction joint in concreting, a joint between adjacent layers or areas of concrete that have been cast at different times.

construction manager a contractor's employee responsible for managing and supervising work on a large site or several small ones; a senior site manager.

construction moisture water in laid concrete, mortar, or other wet trades, which evaporates away during the construction period.

construction sequence, sequencing of operations; in project planning, the stages in which construction proceeds, dictating the order in which materials and components arrive on site.

construction site see building site.

construction technology, building technology, building science; a branch of technology dealing with the erection and assembly of buildings, their components and structure.

construction time 1 the contract time or time for completion of a building as specified in a contract.
2 the period of time during which a building is under construction.

construction waste any material such as rubble, earth or remnants left over from construction or demolition work whose disposal is the responsibility of the contractor.

construction work any work pertaining to building construction; the various operations involved in assembling the foundations, frame, fabric and finishes for a building; types included as separate entries are listed below:
*additional work, see extra work; *asbestos work, see asbestos removal; *blockwork; *brickwork; *cabinetwork; *casework, see casing; *ceiling work; *cobwork, see log construction; *concretework; *cribwork, see cribbing; *daywork; *earthwork; *electrical work, see electrical installation work; *extra work; *facework, see fair-face brickwork; *falsework; *formwork; *framework; *groundwork; *landscape work, see landscaping; *lathwork, see lathing; *measured work; *paintwork; *panelwork, see panelling; *parquet work, see parquetry; *pipework; *plasterwork; *ragwork; *range work; *remedial work, see renovation; *repair work, see renovation; *sheetmetal work; *shift work; *specialized work; *steelwork; *stonework; *studwork; *timberwork; *veneerwork, see veneering.

construction works that body of work on a building site concerned with the actual assembling of a building, as opposed to temporary work, ground work, etc.

consultant a qualified person or professional body employed by an organization to give professional advice, liaise or produce specialist designs for various aspects of a construction project.

contact adhesive an adhesive applied in liquid form to surfaces to be joined, then allowed to partially dry before components are pressed together, resulting in instantaneous adhesion.

contact metamorphic rock a name for types of metamorphic rock which have formed under high temperatures caused by magmatic intrusion; hornfels.

containment see fire containment.

contingency sum, contingency; money set aside within a building contract to be used to cover the cost of unforeseen or unplannable items or events.

continuous beam a single beam which spans over more than two points of support, so that loading one section will affect conditions over the other spans.

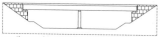

continuous beam with central pier support for deck of bridge

continuous coil spiral an ornamental motif consisting of a pattern of curving lines which meet in spirals.

continuous hinge see piano hinge.

continuously-graded aggregate in concretework, graded aggregate which contains all grain sizes within a particular range.

continuously moving form see slipform.

continuously reinforced concrete pavement, CRCP; road construction in which the main structural base is a reinforced concrete slab with no transverse movement joints.

continuous mixer in the production of concrete, a concrete mixer which produces a continuous flow of concrete.

contorta pine see pine.

contract, contractual agreement; a legally enforcing agreement between two or more parties regarding provision of goods, work or services, the scope of work included therein; see also building contract.

contract document any written, drawn or computerized document that forms part of package on which a contract is based.

contract drawing any drawing which forms part of a package on which a contract is based.

contract period a period stipulated in a contract for the execution of work, during which the contract is valid.

contract price see contract sum.

contracts manager a contractor's representative responsible for managing contractual aspects of construction projects, usually large-scale ones.

contract sum, contract price; the sum of money payable by a client to a contractor for the execution of work outlined in the building contract.

contract time, construction time, time for completion; the time specified for the prospective completion of a construction job or building, measured from an agreed starting date to handover or another specified juncture.

contraction joint, shrinkage joint; in monolithic concrete or masonry construction, a joint which allows for the shrinkage of materials on drying, often filled after the material has hardened.

contraction joint in cement screed and flooring

contractor, builder, building contractor; a person or organization which carries out building work according to a contract or agreement; types included as separate entries are listed below: *electrical works contractor; *main contractor; *management contractor; *nominated subcontractor; *specialized contractor; *subcontractor.*

contractual agreement see contract.

contractual claim a claim that can be settled within the terms of the contract without recourse to legal proceedings.

control circuit an electric circuit by which mechanical equipment is controlled.

control device, regulator; a device for operating motors, actuators, etc. to control automated and mechanical installations.

control valve, discharge valve, regulating valve; a valve for regulating the rate of flow and preventing backsiphonage of liquid in a pipeline.

convection the transfer of heat or electrical charge via thermal currents in a gas or liquid; see thermal convection, free convection.

convection column see thermal column.

convection heater see convector.

convector a space heater which provides warmth by the movement of air over a hot surface, to be conveyed into the surrounding air by convection; see also fan convector.

conventional system see low velocity system.

conversion 1 the sawing of logs into large timber sections, profiles and mouldings for use in building.

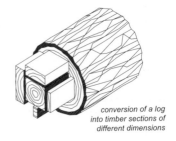
conversion of a log into timber sections of different dimensions

2 in computing, the transmutation of a computer program or file to make it usable by another computer system.

convex head roofing nail a nail for fixing corrugated roofing with an inverted cup-shaped addition beneath its *convex head roofing nail* head to cover the curved space between nail head and crest of sheeting; also variously known as a nipple head nail or springhead roofing nail.

convex joint see extruded joint.

convex plane see round plane.

conveyor belt mesh woven wire mesh with a weave permitting pivoting along its length; used for industrial conveyor belts, and as a cladding material for elevations, ceilings, etc.

conveyor belt mesh

cooler unit see unit air-conditioner.

cooling 1 the reduction in temperature of an object, gas, room, etc.
2 in air conditioning, those measures designed to produce thermal comfort by introducing cool air to a space.
3 see cooling period.

cooling coil in air conditioning, a unit containing copper tubes supplied with chilled water or other liquid to cool supply air to a desired temperature.

cooling period in the steam curing of concrete, the period during which heat is no longer applied and the concrete slowly cools.

cooling tower 1 in air conditioning, an externally mounted device for cooling warmed water from the system by spraying it over a system of ventilated baffles, causing partial evaporation and resultant cooling.
2 a wide hollow concrete chimney in which water vapour from power stations, etc. is cooled.

coordinate cube the basic volume unit or cube marked out by the three mutually perpendicular, gradated coordinate planes in an axonometric or oblique projection; sometimes called an axonometric cube.

coordinate cube

coordinator see door co-ordinator.

copaiba balsam an oleoresin exuded from some species of South American tree [*Copaifera spp.*], used with a solvent as a cleaner or isolation varnish in oil-painting.

coping, 1 capping, wall cap; a construction of brick, block, stone or sheetmetal on top of a freestanding wall or parapet to shed off and prevent infiltration of rainwater; types included as separate entries are listed below:

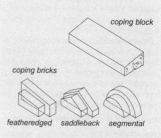
coping block

coping bricks

featheredged   saddleback   segmental

*coping brick; *featheredged coping; *pressed metal coping; *saddleback coping; *segmental coping.
2 the cutting of stone slabs by making a groove on either face with a saw and then applying blows to the groove until the stone cracks.

coping block a concrete block with a sloping upper surface, designed for use as a coping for a freestanding wall; see masonry capping.

coping brick a special capping brick designed to be wider than the freestanding wall or parapet which it protects, with throated overhangs on one or both sides; see saddleback coping brick, featheredged coping.

coping saw, scribing saw; a fine-toothed bow saw whose blade is held in tension in a deep metal frame; used for cutting out patterns and curves in board.

coping stone see masonry capping, featheredged coping.

copper a soft and malleable metal, **Cu**, which has good resistance to corrosion, is a good conductor of heat and electricity, and which can be used as an alloy with other metals; used for wires, pipework and sheetmetal cladding.

copper blue a form of the pigment Bremen blue.

copper carbonate see azurite, see malachite.

copper green a form of the pigment Bremen blue.

copper nail a round-shafted nail fabricated from copper, often for decorative use.

copper pipe, copper alloy tube; narrow-bore pipes of copper alloy used in water and gas installation pipework.

copper plate a copper mill product of flat plate over 10mm thick, usually manufactured from a copper alloy.

copper plating, coppering; the coating of an object with a thin layer of copper as corrosion resistance or decoration; the layer thus formed.

copper sheet copper rolled into sheets not more than 3 mm thick; used for patinated exterior cladding, etc.

coppering see copper plating.

coquillage Rococo decoration based on stylized shell forms.

corbel a masonry bracket projecting from the face of a building surface to provide support for an overhanging object or member.

corbelled arch, corbel arch; a false arch composed of a series of stones corbelled out from either side to meet in the middle; not a true arch.

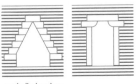

corbelled arches

corbelled lintel a lintel whose span is reduced by the use of corbel stones on either side of an opening; usually found in stone architecture.

corbelled vault a masonry vault constructed by overlapping successive courses of stone to meet at the highest point; not a true vault.

corbelling a method of constructing a masonry overhang by projecting each successive edge course slightly outward.

corbelling for dome on square base

corbel table an ornamental banded motif consisting of a series of arches which project from a wall surface; often found beneath the parapet in Romanesque architecture.

corbel table

corbie gable, corbie steps see crow steps.

cordierite, dichroite, iotite; a blue or brown magnesium aluminium silicate mineral used as a raw material in the ceramic industry and as decorative stone.

cordon 1 a masonry course, often projecting, at the foot of battlements in a wall of a castle or fortification, or along the upper surface of a ditch.
2 in walling, a projecting band course of masonry or brickwork, often rounded in cross-section.

corduroy work a surface treatment for ashlar stonework consisting of narrow vertical reeding.

core 1 the central layer of material in components such as certain forms of composite construction, building boards, composite constructions or steel cables; e.g. the internal filling of lower grade wood in a timber-based board, covered by veneers; see also door core, test core, box out.

2 the central service area in a multistorey building, where lifts, stairways, toilets and riser ducts, etc. are located; see core stiffening.

coreboard any timber building board manufactured by gluing veneers to either side of a solid timber core, to which the grain of the veneers runs at 90°; types included as separate entries are listed below:

*battenboard; *blockboard; *cellular board; *composite board; *laminboard.

cored brick see perforated brick.

core drilling in soil investigation, drilling into the ground with special apparatus to obtain core samples for testing; similar action to obtain samples of rock and cast concrete.

core form a mould introduced into the formwork for creating an opening in cast concrete.

core ply see central ply.

core plywood plywood in which the core is considerably thicker than the face plies; see coreboard.

core roll in sheet roofing, a timber fillet around which roofing material is dressed at joints and corners.

core stiffening the fixing of intermediate floors of a building to a central core, often a lift shaft, stair or services block to provide vertical stability.

core strength the compressive strength of a concrete core sample, taken from a cast or existing concrete member.

core test in concreting, a test to measure the compressive strength of a concrete core sample, drilled from a cast concrete member.

Corinthian pertaining to the Corinthian order, the youngest of the three classical Greek orders, characterized by slender fluted columns, an ornate capital lavishly carved with acanthus foliage surmounted by a flat abacus, a base and an entablature with dentils.

cork the bark of the cork oak [*Quercus suber*], used in construction for its buoyancy, lightness, insulating and resilient properties, used for thermal insulation, buoyancy aids, bottle corks, gaskets and vibration control.

cork black see vine black.

corkboard a building board made from granulated cork pressed together with a binder.

cork carpet, cork matting; a flooring product in sheet form manufactured from granulated cork, mineral fibre and a binder of resin or oil attached to a backing sheet, often with a surface coating of hard plastic.

cork linoleum a hardwearing flooring product in sheet or tile form consisting of ground cork and polymerized linseed oil on a hessian backing.

cork matting see cork carpet.

cork oak [*Quercus suber*] a Mediterranean hardwood whose outer bark, cork, is used for thermal insulation, buoyancy aids, bottle corks, gaskets, floor-coverings and vibration control.

cork tile a hardwearing rectangular floor, ceiling or wall tile which consists of granulated cork and a binder such as oil or resin attached to a backing sheet; cork ceiling tiles are made from reconstituted expanded granulated cork and often used for their acoustic properties; cork floor tiles are sheets of cork carpet laid as tiles.

cork wallpaper cork paper manufactured with a backing and used as a wallcovering.

corkscrew stair see spiral stair.

cornel see dogwood.

cornelian a reddish-brown microcrystalline variety of the mineral chalcedony, used as gemstones and for decorative ornament; alternative spelling is carnelian.

corner bead see angle bead; edge strip.

corner board in timber-clad construction, vertical boards nailed over the cladding at corners as protection.

corner chisel see bruzz chisel.

corner fillet a timber finishing strip used to cover the internal corner joint between two perpendicular surfaces.

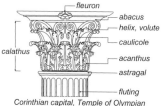

Corinthian capital, Temple of Olympian Zeus, Athens, c.170 BC – 130 AD

corner half lap joint a timber halved joint in which one member is perpendicular to another, forming the outside corner of a frame.

corner joint any joint in which the members to be connected are not in a straight line, or in the same plane; types included as separate entries are listed below:
*angle joint; *bevelled corner joint; *box corner joint; *box dovetail joint; *cogged corner joint; *corner half lap joint; *notch.

corner scraper, angle plane, French plane; a bladed hand tool used in plastering for removing excess plaster from internal corners.

cornerstone, foundation stone; a block of masonry cast or laid into foundations as a memorial of the commencement of construction of a building, usually inscribed with information about the client, contractor and the occasion at which it was laid.

corner trowel see angle trowel.

cornice, 1 ceiling strip; a decorative horizontal moulding at the meeting of internal wall and ceiling.
2 in classical architecture, the horizontal overhanging upper band of an entablature above a frieze, made up of a cymatium, corona and other mouldings.
3 in masonry, a large projecting moulding, often classical, at the top of an exterior wall.

Cornus florida see dogwood.

corona 1 Lat.; the lower moulding in a classical cornice, a projecting element with a vertical face beneath the cymatium; often called a geison in Greek temples.
2 corona moulding; any protruding horizontal moulding whose lower surface is profiled to form a drip.

corona moulding

3 a circular side chapel in a church or cathedral.

coroplastics the use of relief ornament and sculpture in terracotta work.

corridor 1 a narrow longitudinal circulation space within a building providing internal access to rooms or other spaces.
2 fire corridor, see fire break.

corrosion, attack; the wearing away, destruction or decay of a material, especially a metal, due to chemical or electrochemical reaction with its surroundings; types included as separate entries are listed below:
*crevice corrosion; *deposit corrosion; *electrochemical corrosion; *erosion corrosion; *microbiological corrosion; *pit corrosion; *stress corrosion.

corrosion fatigue fatigue in steel caused by corrosion in members subjected to repeated changing stresses in a corrosive environment.

corrosion inhibiting, rust inhibiting; the painting and other coating treatments of metal, usually steel and cast-iron components, with compounds, alloyed substances, etc. to inhibit corrosion; a surface treatment thus used is called a corrosion inhibitor.

corrosion inhibiting admixture in concretework, an admixture included in a concrete mix to inhibit the corrosion of reinforcement.

corrosion resistance the ability of a metal to withstand chemical corrosion, oxidation, weathering, etc.

corrugated a description of sheet products which have been preformed into a wavy cross-section for improved longitudinal strength longitudinal stiffening.

corrugated fastener, wiggle nail, mitre brad; a short piece of corrugated steel with sharpened edges, hammered into a timber butt joint to secure it.

corrugated fastener

corrugated glass rough cast glass sheeting manufactured with corrugations and used for glazed roofing.

corrugated iron a steel product of sheetmetal preformed in a wavy cross-section to provide longitudinal stiffening.

corrugated ply-web beam a plywood web beam whose vertical web is wavy in plan to increase transverse buckling strength. See illustration on facing page.

corrugated ply-web beam

corrugated sheeting a metal or plastics sheeting product preformed in a wavy cross-section to provide longitudinal stiffening; see also corrugated iron, corrugated sheetmetal.

corrugated sheetmetal a product of steel, zinc, aluminium, etc. sheetmetal preformed in a wavy cross-section to provide longitudinal stiffening.

corrugated sheet roofing profiled sheet roofing which has been formed with a wavy profile in cross-section.

corrugated sheet roofing

corrugated shell a tunnel, bridge, conduit, etc. structure of corrugated sheet steel.

corrugation filler in profiled sheet roofing, a component fitted beneath sheeting at eaves, ridge or other edges to block up the gaps formed beneath the corrugations.

corruleum blue see cerulean blue.

Corsican pine [*Pinus nigra*] see pine.

Cor-ten a proprietary weathering steel with a high copper content whose surface rusts evenly to form a weather-resistant orange-brown coating on exposure to the elements; used as sheeting for external cladding.

corundum a hard mineral form of aluminium oxide, Al_2O_3, used as gemstones (as ruby or sapphire) and as a grinding and polishing agent; see also emery.

Corylus avellana see hazel.

Cosmati work geometrical mosaic work in coloured marble, glass and stone, named after a group of architects, sculptors and decorative artists who worked in the same style in marble and mosaic in the 1100s to 1300s in Rome and Naples; usually religious work for choir screens, pulpits, floors and walls.

Cosmati work, Italy, 13th century

cost an amount of money outlaid or to be paid for a product, service or completed work, or spent on running a business.

cost analysis a costing technique for tendering or physical construction using estimated or costed parts of construction work distributed between cost headings, allowing for easy and efficient comparison.

cost control the task of continuous monitoring of costs incurred and available finances for a building project.

cost estimate an estimation of the cost of a construction project based on designs, often undertaken by a quantity surveyor at an early stage in design work.

cost in use a comprehensive cost estimate of a design, component or product, measured by adding together capital expenses and costs incurred subsequently by maintenance and operation.

cost index a figure expressing the change in value of products or services in relation to time.

costing the calculation of prospective costs for a development.

cost per square metre, unit cost; a measure of the potential or final relative cost of a building calculated by dividing the construction costs by built gross or net area of the building.

cost-reimbursement contract, do-and-charge work; a form of building contract in which the contractor bills for costs expended, usually taking a percentage of the total or fixed sum as payment for overheads and profit.

cotter pin a removable split wire fixing inserted into a hole in a housed component to secure it in place.

cottonseed oil, cotton oil; a semi-drying oil used as a medium in some oil paints, produced from the seeds of the cotton plant, *Gossypium spp.*

cottonwood [*Populus spp.*], see poplar.

coulomb abb. **C**; SI unit of electric charge, the quantity of energy transported by a current of 1 amp in 1 second.

coumarone indene, coumarone resin; a thermoplastic resin made from coumarone, C_8H_6O, present in coal tar, used as a medium in paints, a binder in floor tiles, in the rubber industry, etc.

council housing see public housing.

counterbatten in tiled roof construction, battens laid above the roofing membrane, onto which horizontal tiling battens are laid; see also entry below:

counterbattening in timber frame construction, secondary battening nailed across studs, rafters or primary battens to allow for ventilation and water run off within construction.

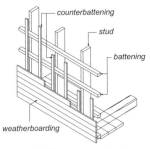

counterbattening
stud
battening
weatherboarding

counter flashing see cover flashing.

counterfort a vertical rib, projection, buttress or thickening in a wall to provide strength and stability; in retaining walls it is built into the side of the wall facing the ground and thus works in tension.
counterfort wall, buttress wall; a cantilever retaining wall ribbed with a number of spaced buttresses to reinforce the junction between wall and footing.

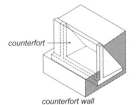

counterfort

counterfort wall

countersink a drill bit with a cutting edge for making a cone-shaped depression around the rim of a hole drilled for a countersunk screw; the widening cut thus made.

countersink

countersunk head bolt a bolt with a conical countersunk head, tightened with a screwdriver or driver bit.

countersunk head bolt

countersunk head screw

countersunk head screw, countersunk screw, flat head screw; a screw whose head is cone-shaped so that it can be housed in a sinking, flush with a finished surface.

countersunk washer see recessed screw cup.

counter top basin see vanity basin.

counterweight a weight attached with cables over a series of pulleys from a lift car to counterbalance its weight.

coupled, twinned; a description of pillars, pilasters or columns, grouped or joined together in pairs; see entries below:
coupled columns, twinned columns; a pair of columns linked or grouped together for visual effect, or used in place of a single stouter column.

medieval coupled columns in St George's Cathedral, Limburg an der Lahn, Germany, (1235 AD)

coupled door a door which has two door leaves, one behind the other, hinged on the same side and linked so that they open as one.

coupled doors

coupled light an openable component in a window consisting of two sashes, one interior and the other exterior, hinged separately but linked so they open as one.

coupled rafter roof see couple roof.

coupled rafters, couple truss; in timber roof construction, a truss consisting simply of two rafters which meet at a ridge; see couple roof.

coupled window a double-glazed window whose openable part is a coupled light.

coupler 1 a fitting for joining members in tubular scaffolding.
2 see pipe fitting.

couple roof, coupled rafter roof; the simplest form of pitched roof structure, of pairs of slanting rafters meeting at a ridge.

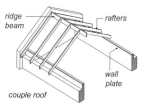

couple roof

couple truss see coupled rafters.

coupling a pipe fitting for making a connection between two pipes in a pipeline.

course a row of bricks, stones or blocks which form a horizontal band in masonry walling construction, either one brick or stone high, or of uniform height; in log construction, a single layer of logs laid as walling.

coursed ashlar ashlar masonry which has been laid in courses with horizontal joints; courses may be of equal or varying height.

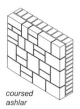

coursed ashlar

coursed rubble masonry walling of unsquared stones laid in rough courses; may be of squared or unsquared stones.

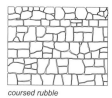

coursed rubble

coursed squared rubble masonry roughly squared pieces of stone laid as masonry in courses.

coursed squared rubble

coursed stonework any masonry laid in courses with continuous horizontal joints.

court 1 an external area bounded by walls, buildings or rooms on four sides; a courtyard.
2 an enclosed area with a flat, hard surface for playing ball games such as tennis, basketball, etc.

courtyard, court; an open area of land surrounded or enclosed by buildings or built form, often private or semi-public.

courtyard house a prehistoric dwelling from Iron Age Britain and northern Europe, with a series of chambers entered via a central area.

plan of courtyard houses, Chysauster, Cornwall, England, c.50 BC

cove 1 a curved underside or soffit.

2 coving; a concave moulding of plaster, timber or plastics, fixed as a decorative covering at the meeting of ceiling and wall; any meeting of ceiling and wall treated in this way; a cove tile; see also cavetto.

cove

3 a group of prehistoric standing stones laid out in a U-shape to form a tall unroofed box, open at the top and one side.

cove brick a special brick with a concave indentation running along one of its upper edges; used in decorative features, or at the meeting of

cove brick

a wall and brick paving, etc.

coved tile, cove tile a curved ceramic tile fitting for creating a smooth, concave join between adjacent perpendicular wall, floor or ceiling surfaces; often simply called a cove.

cove tile

coved skirting tile a cove tile used as a skirting in tiled bathrooms and wet areas; see also inside corner tile.

coved vault a masonry vault composed of four coves meeting at a central point, the reverse of a groined vault; a cloister vault.

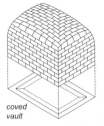

coved vault

cove lighting luminaires concealed behind a cove, directing light against a ceiling to provide indirect lighting for a space.

cover 1 the thickness of a protective layer of covering material, such as earth for a pipe, concrete over reinforcement; see concrete cover, nominal cover.

2 see casing.

cover block see spacer.

cover board in board on board cladding, one of the surface boards nailed over the base cladding to cover the vertical gaps.

cover fillet a strip of material, trim, etc. used in construction to cover a joint or seam.

cover flashing, counter flashing; in roofing, a flashing laid against an abutment to cover an upstand flashing.

cover meter a device for measuring the depth of concrete over reinforcement, or concrete cover.

cover soaker see pipe flashing.

cover strip, 1 joint strip; any strip of material, or a product, etc. used to cover a joint in construction.

2 capping; any similar product

cover strip

used to conceal unsightly construction or fixings beneath.

3 see architrave.

cover tile see capping tile.

coving see cove.

cowl a device attached to the upper outlet of a flue to improve draught and provide protection from the elements.

cownose brick, bullhead brick; any special brick with one header rounded into a semicircle, used for wall ends, decorative banding, etc.

cownose brick

cow plane see roughing plane.

coxcomb see cock's comb.

C-profile see C-section, channel.

CR chloroprene rubber.

cracking, 1 concrete cracking; a defect evident in the surface of set concrete caused by stresses induced by shrinkage, loading or chemical reaction.

2 a defect in a dry paint finish, usually caused by internal stress, poor adhesion or ageing; various types of cracking are crazing and checking.

crackle see crazing.

cradle a specially designed fitting to provide support for a length of curved plumbing and drainage pipe or any other vessel with a curving base.

cradle vault see barrel vault.

craft operative see skilled labourer

cramp, 1 clamp; a simple frame tightened with screws or wedges for holding pieces in place and applying pressure during gluing and working.
2 see dog.

crampon see dog.

crane tall freestanding mechanical plant used on site for hoisting materials and lifting components into position, allowing for movement in three dimensions.

cranked descriptive of a component, implement, etc. which is elbow shaped.
cranked brace, elbow brace; in traditional timber frame construction, a naturally bent brace at the angle between two members.
cranked handle see cranked pull handle.

cranked hinge a hinge in which one or both leaves is bent along their length, allowing movement of a door through 180°.

cranked hinge

cranked pull handle, offset handle; a pull handle for a door, whose grip is offset from its points of fixing.
cranked sheet a profiled sheeting component bent across its profile ribs, designed for use at an angle; a cranked ridge sheet is a longitudinal profiled sheet roofing component used at a ridge as capping.

crank gouge a gouge whose neck is kinked to allow for it to be driven along deep grooves.

craquelure crazing in the glaze of old pottery and ceramic tiles.

Crataegus spp. see hawthorn.

crawlway a space within floor construction or beneath a building, high enough to be crawled through, providing access to services.

crazing, 1 map cracking; fine widespread defective cracking of a surface layer of concrete, plasterwork, ceramic glazes or paint.
2 crackle, craquelure; a mesh of hairline cracks which forms on the glaze of old glazed ceramics and paintings due to shrinkage of the base.

crazy paving see ragwork.

CRCP continuously reinforced concrete pavement.

cream of lime see lime white.

creep the physical property of a material to undergo gradual permanent deformation under continual stress.

creep settlement in foundation technology, the steady downward movement of a building which occurs after immediate settlement on certain soil types due to deformation or slipping of the underlying soil without appreciable increase in loading.

Cremnitz white, Krems white; highly corroded white lead pigment made in the 1900s, using litharge instead of the metal lead.

cremone bolt, cremona bolt, cremorne bolt; a long mechanical fastener for holding double doors, with a paired bolt running the whole vertical height of the door, which, when activated by turning a handle, pushes out through the top and bottom of the door to engage in holes in the floor and frame; see espagnolette.

crenellated referring to an ornamental motif, parapet, etc. which is toothed in some way or represents a battlement; see castellated.
crenellated moulding, embattled moulding; a decorative moulding rendered with the rectilinear undulations of a battlement; see indented embattled moulding.

crenellated moulding

crenellation, crenelation; the indented upper line of a battlement parapet, with merlons providing shelter from attackers and crenelles providing openings for archers and marksmen.

crenelle, crenel, kernel; openings or indentations in the parapet of a battlement, between merlons, to allow archers and artillery to defend a fortification; an embrasure; a crenelet is a small crenelle.

creosote, creosote oil; a dark brown, strong smelling oil distilled from coal tar at 230–340°C; used as a cheap preservative for exterior woodwork and timber fencing.

crescent **1** the scythe shape which remains when one circle is cut out of the side of another one.
2 a formal urban street and buildings laid out in the form of an arc.

crest **1** the upper part of the profile of a roof tile or profiled sheet.
2 see cresting.

cresting, crest; raised and often perforated ornamentation along the ridge of a roof, or on top of a wall or screen.

Cretan column see Minoan column.

crevice corrosion a localized form of corrosion which occurs in a stagnant environment in tight spaces or crevices under gaskets, washers, insulation material, fastener heads, surface deposits, and coatings, etc., initiated by changes in local chemistry within the crevice.

crib a framework of crossed timbers or structural members used as a buttress, to line a shaft, as a container, or as steel reinforcement in a foundation.

cribbing, cribwork; a series of hollowed concrete blocks, interlocking or filled with earth, used as a banked retaining wall for earth embankments.

cribbing for earth retaining wall

crib paver, crib paving see cellular paver.

crimped mesh see crimped wire mesh.

crimped wire in pretensioned concretework, reinforcing wire which is wavy along its length for improved bonding.

crimped wire mesh a mesh product manufactured from two sets of parallel metal wires woven or welded against one another with locking crimps to maintain rigidity.

crimped wire mesh

crinkling see wrinkle.

cripple stud **1** in timber frame construction, a stud which has been trimmed for use over an opening or under a window.
2 see jamb post.

crippling load, buckling load; the load at which a column begins to buckle.

crocket Gothic ornament based on a stylized florid motif, found adorning pinnacles, capitals and spires.

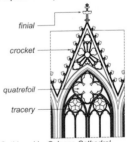

finial

crocket

quatrefoil

tracery

Gothic gable, Cologne Cathedral, Germany, c. 1250

crocket capital a capital found in Norman architecture, consisting of a block carved with a number of crockets.

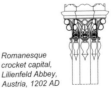

Romanesque crocket capital, Lilienfeld Abbey, Austria, 1202 AD

crocks see crucks.

crocodiling, alligatoring; a defect in a paint finish consisting of a network of cracks or splits which resemble crocodile skin, caused by shrinkage.

croft see crypt.

crook, 1 spring; a form of warp resulting in bending along the edge of an improperly seasoned timber board.

crook in improperly seasoned timber board

2 a long steel nail used in thatched roofing for fastening down reed thatch.
3 see crucks.

crooks see crucks.

cropping the removal of the unwanted projecting ends of bolts, reinforcing bars, timbers or similar components in construction; the cutting down to size of a picture, image or graphic design to enhance composition or omit unwanted elements.

cross 1 an ancient symbolic figure consisting of two bars which cross each other, often at right angles; it appears as a religious motif and ornament in many different forms.
2 a cross-shaped pipe fitting for making the connection between two secondary pipes and a main pipe at right angles.

crossbanding the laying of alternate plies in the thickness of plywood perpendicular to one another for increased strength.

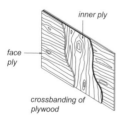

crossbanding of plywood

inner ply

face ply

cross-beam, transverse beam; a beam perpendicular to the main axis of a space, which runs between two cross walls, or is perpendicular to other beams.

cross bond any of a number of brickwork bonds with alternating courses laid so that the joints form distinct cross motifs in the surface brickwork; see English cross bond (St Andrew's cross bond), Flemish cross bond.

cross brace one of a pair of intersecting diagonal braces used to stiffen and strengthen a frame.
cross-bracing a method of stiffening a frame using diagonal tension members which cross one another.

cross break see compression failure.

cross bridging see herringbone strutting.

cross-cut saw any saw with teeth adapted for cutting across the grain of wood; see rip saw.

cross-cutting sawing across the grain of timber, perpendicular to the longitudinal axis of its fibres.

crossette see joggled arch.

crossform roof a pitched hip and valley roof for a building which is cross-shaped in plan, with four valleys and four gabled or hipped ends.

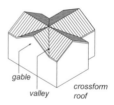

gable

valley

crossform roof

cross grain grain at an angle to the edge of a board cut from compression wood, making it difficult to work and season properly.
cross-grained float a flat-bladed wooden plastering float whose grain runs perpendicular to its length.
cross-grained plywood plywood in which the grain of the outer ply is approximately parallel to that of the lateral or shorter edge of the piece.

cross half lap joint, crosslap joint, halved crossing joint; a timber halved joint in which both face sides of crossing members are cut away to receive each other.

cross half lap joint

crossing 1 the area where the transepts, chancel and nave in a church or cathedral intersect, often surmounted by a tower.
2 a meeting and crossing of roads, pedestrian routes, railways, etc. at the same level.

crossing joint, cross joint; any joint in which two members are fixed across one another; see also cross half lap joint.

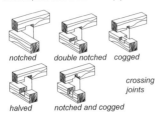

notched   double notched   cogged

halved   notched and cogged

crossing joints

cross joint, transverse joint; a construction joint perpendicular to the general plane of a surface; see perpend, crossing joint.

crosslap joint see cross half lap joint.

cross-linked polyethylene, PEX, XLPE; a tough thermosetting plastic used for electric-cable insulation, hot-water pipes, films and durable sections; cross-linking is a chemical reaction which occurs in the hardening of some thermosetting plastics and films, in which polymeric molecules form a network of links.

cross nogging see herringbone strutting.

cross peen hammer, Warrington hammer; a hammer whose peen is a sharp wedge of steel with its ridge perpendicular to the hammer shaft.

cross-section see section.

cross shakes see thunder shakes.

cross-slot screw any screw with a cross-shaped indentation in its head for turning with a special screwdriver or bit.

cross spar, pattern spar; a decorative fastener or brotch laid visible at the ridge of a thatched roof.

cross vault see groin vault.

crosswall construction a structural system in which the floors of a building are spanned across a series of transverse load-bearing walls.

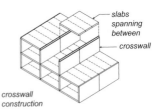

slabs spanning between

crosswall

crosswall construction

cross-welt in sheetmetal roofing, a horizontal joint in which two adjacent sheets are bent over each other then hammered down; these are usually staggered and run parallel to the eaves; see single-lock welt, double welt.

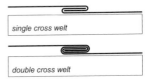

single cross welt

double cross welt

crow bar a toughened steel implement, a bar with forked ends for wrecking, prizing, wedging and extracting nails.

crown 1 the highest point or apex of an arch.
2 the highest point in the cambered cross-section of a road, usually in the centre.
3 head; in landscaping and forestry, the part of a tree above the trunk, containing branches and leaves.
4 see chimney crown.

crown course in profiled sheet roofing, a longitudinal piece used at a ridge as ridge capping.

crown glass glass made traditionally by the cutting of a hollow blown glass sphere which is spun flat into a nearly circular sheet.

crown post in traditional timber roof construction, a vertical strut between tie beam and collar beam, supporting a collar purlin.
crown post rafter roof in traditional timber roof construction, a collar roof with a purlin which runs beneath the collars and is supported on crown posts; also known as a crown post and collar purlin roof or crown post roof. See illustration on facing page.

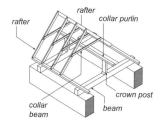

rafter

rafter   collar purlin

crown post

collar beam   beam

crown saw see hole saw.

crown silvered lamp, silvered-bowl lamp; a lightbulb whose bulbous end is internally coated with reflective material to direct light inwards and produce indirect lighting.

crow steps, corbie steps, stepped gable; in traditional masonry construction, a decorative gable parapet whose upper edge is a series of steps.

CRP carbon-fibre reinforced plastic.

crucible steel see cast steel.

cruciform in the shape of or resembling a cross, as for the ground plans of buildings, especially churches.

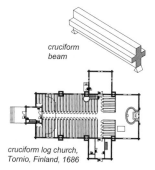

cruciform beam

cruciform log church, Tornio, Finland, 1686

crucks in traditional timber frame construction, pairs of heavy curved timbers (cruck blades) which lean together forming an inverted V-frame (a cruck truss) as the basis for a building frame; also variously known as crooks, crocks, crutches, forks or siles.

crude sewage see raw sewage.

crushed aggregate aggregate produced by crushing rocks and mineral materials.

crushed brick broken and powdered clay products used as a surface material for sports venues, as hardcore, etc.

crushed gravel fines fine aggregate produced by crushing gravel.

crushed rock coarse aggregate produced by the crushing of rocks and minerals.

crushed rock fines fine aggregate produced by crushing rock.

crusher-run aggregate an aggregate made up of ungraded crushed rock.

crypt crypta (Lat.), krypte (Gk.); a vaulted basement or undercroft in a church or cathedral, often containing a chapel and tombs or graves; sometimes called a shroud or croft.

crystal glass see lead glass.

crystalline schist a coarse-grained metamorphic rock with a structure of long sheetlike crystals.

C-section a cold-formed structural steel profile which has the cross-sectional shape of a squared letter 'C'; other metal profiles with the same shape; see channel.

Cuban mahogany see mahogany.

cube 1 a solid three-dimensional shape whose surface is composed of six squares at right angles to one another.
2 cobble; a small square sett or concrete paver, used for paving roads, driveways, etc.

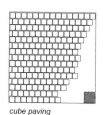

cube paving

3 see test cube.

cube strength in concretework, the compressive strength of a concrete test cube as measured in a cube test.

cube test in concretework, a compressive strength test carried out by crushing a sample cube of concrete to be used in construction.

cubical aggregate coarse aggregate whose particles are almost cubical in shape.

cubic capital see block capital.

cubicle a small area of space partitioned off to provide temporary privacy for an individual.

cuboid brick any mass-produced rectangular brick with a square cross-section, often a modular brick.

cuboid brick

cul-de-lampe a decorative console or support for a candle or light in the shape of an inverted cone.

culvert a large rigid pipe, often of plastics, concrete or metal plate which conveys water underneath a road or other obstacle.

culvert header, tapered stretcher; a special brick, wedged-shaped in section so that its long faces are not oblong, used as a header in a barrel vault.

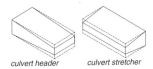

culvert header   *culvert stretcher*

culvert stretcher, tapered header; a special brick, wedged-shaped in section so that its short faces are not oblong, used as a stretcher in a barrel vault.

cup, 1 transverse warping; a form of warp resulting in cross-sectional curvature in an improperly seasoned timber board.

cup in improperly seasoned timber board

2 see screw cup.
3 see grinding cup.

cup hook a screw hook with a collar above the threaded shank to restrict its screw-in depth and cover the edges of the hole; a square cup hook is L-shaped.

cup hooks

cupid, amoretto, amorino; a classical statue, carving or depiction of the god of love, Amor or Cupid in Rome and Eros in Greece, represented as young winged boy with a bow and arrow.

cupid motif

cupola the central dome of an interior space, domed vaulting, a dome-shaped recess in a ceiling or a small dome adorning a roof.

Cupressus spp. see cypress; *Cupressus nootkatensis*; see yellow cedar.

cupro-solvency the dissolving of copper in copper and brass pipework caused by high flow rates, turbulent flow and air or particles in the water.

cup shake a shake or cracking occurring between the annual rings of a piece of timber; also known as ring failure, ring shake, shell shake; see also wind shake.

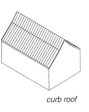

cup shake

curb see kerb.

curb roof, double pitched roof, knee roof; any pitched roof that slopes away from the main ridge in two successive planes at different angles with a ridge between; see gambrel roof, mansard roof.

curb roof

curbstone see kerbstone.

Curculionidae see weevil.

Curing the hardening and gaining strength of a paint, glue, concrete or other similar material after it has set; see also concrete curing.

curing compound in concretework, any material placed over fresh concrete to inhibit evaporation of water.

curing cycle the time taken for the complete process of steam curing of concrete, including heating and cooling periods.

curl 1 see wavy grain.
2 see knuckle.

current see electric current.

curtain 1 a domestic textile furnishing hung above a window on a sliding track to provide shade and privacy; see also blind, fire curtain, shower curtain.
2 see sag.
3 see curtain wall.

curtaining see sag.

curtain rail a rail above a window which supports a curtain, usually attached to it by means of sliding fixings.

curtain rod a rod above a window which supports a curtain, usually attached to it by means of curtain rings.

curtain wall 1 in modern construction, a lightweight exterior walling system of metal framing members and infill panels of glass, ceramics and sheetmetal for a building structure or frame; the processes involved in this; curtainwalling is an area of curtain wall, or the construction therein.

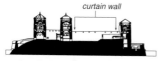

curtain wall

section showing curtain wall joining towers in St Olaf's castle, Savonlinna, Finland 1475–1495

2 curtain; the surrounding outer wall of a castle or fortification between towers, battlements and bastions; also called a curtain, cortina, bail or bailey wall in a medieval castle.

curtilage the land between a building and the boundary of the plot land on which it stands; the plot on which a building is situated.

curved glass see bent glass.

curved triangle see reuleaux triangle.

Curvilinear style a late development of the Decorated style of English Gothic architecture in the late 1300s, characterized by a flamboyance and richness of motif not encountered in the Geometric style.

curvilinear tracery see flowing tracery.

curving stair a stair which is curved in plan.

axo

plan

curving stair

cushion capital a capital found in Norman architecture, consisting of a squared block with its four lower corners rounded off; also called a block or cubic capital; any other wide capitals, especially one surmounting Minoan or other Aegean column types.

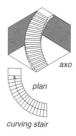

Mycenaean cushion capital, Treasury of Atreus, Mycenae, Greece, c.1325–1250 BC

cushioning see padding.

cusp in Gothic tracery and vaulting, the decorated intersection of two arcs, forming an ornamented point.

customized section a non-standard metal profile which has been specially formed to a design specification.

cut a physical division made by the action of cutting a material, product or surface; see also section.

cut back bitumen bitumen to which a volatile oil is added to reduce its viscosity.

cut brick a brick shaped by cutting, sawing or breaking on site, most often used for making up space in brickwork bonds.

cut length in steel manufacture, steel strip that has been cut to predetermined lengths from decoiled and flattened coil.

cut nail a nail whose shaft is rectangular in cross-section, manufactured by slicing from heated steel strip. See illustration on following page.

cut nails

cutout see circuit breaker, fuse.

cut pile carpet a carpet manufactured by cutting woven loops to form a surface layer of upright strands.

cut stone see dimension stone.

cutter, bit; the hard revolving cutting blade or knife of a planer, router or milling machine for planing and cutting profiles in wood, metal and plastics; the cutter of a router or milling machine is also called a machine bit.

cutting the process of splitting, sawing, or dividing parts of an object using a machine or hand tool, flame, axe, laser, etc.; see also veneer cutting.

cutting edge the sharpened edge or tip of a sawtooth, chisel blade or plane iron, honed for cutting.

cutting gauge a device used for cutting parallel to an edge of wood; a marking gauge with a blade instead of a spike.

C-value, coefficient of thermal conductance; a theoretical measure of how well a given construction will conduct heat, whose units are $W/m^2{}^\circ C$; used in heat loss calculations and taken as the amount of energy passing through a unit area of construction for unit temperature difference on either side of the construction; equal to k-value divided by thickness of construction; see also U-value.

cyanine blue a blue pigment formed by mixing the pigments cobalt blue and Prussian blue.

cyanoacrylate adhesive, super glue; an adhesive containing a compound which polymerizes instantaneously when in contact with atmospheric moisture to form strong bonding without the need for heating and clamping.

cyclopean concrete a form of concrete which contains large pieces of broken stone and boulders as a filler.

cyclopean masonry masonry construction for massive walls, originally that from ancient Mycenae, consisting of large roughly hewn irregular blocks of stone packed with clay and small stones; also

called Pelasgic masonry; generally known nowadays as polygonal masonry.

cyclopean masonry

cylinder 1 a solid shape whose surface is composed of a circle extruded through a straight line perpendicular to its plane; anything with this shape, see storage cylinder, test cylinder, concrete cylinder. **2** that component part of a cylinder lock, including tumblers and a cylinder plug, into which the key is inserted, which transmits its turning motion to operate a bolt.

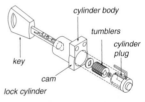

lock cylinder

cylinder body the external casing of a lock cylinder.

cylinder caisson see open caisson.

cylinder guard, cylinder collar; a metal ring-shaped component which is fitted around the keyhole of a cylinder lock to protect it and prevent forcing.

cylinder hinge a form of invisible hinge consisting of two jointed cylinders recessed into hinged components, commonly used for kitchen unit doors.

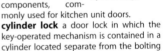

cylinder hinge

cylinder lock a door lock in which the key-operated mechanism is contained in a cylinder located separate from the bolting mechanism.

cylinder strength in concretework, the compressive strength of a concrete cylinder tested to ascertain its suitability as structural concrete.

cylinder test in concretework, a test to determine the compressive strength of a sample cylinder of concrete to be used in construction.

cylindrical vault see barrel vault.

cyma Lat. (Gk. kuma); a doubly curved S-shaped moulding composed of alternating concave and convex segments in profile, as found in classical architecture; an ogee moulding, see cyma recta, cyma reversa, Lesbian cyma, Doric cyma, Ionic cyma.

cyma recta Lat.; a doubly curved cyma or S-shaped moulding with its concave part uppermost; see Doric cyma.

cyma reversa Lat.; a doubly curved cyma or S-shaped moulding with a convex part uppermost; a reverse ogee moulding; Lesbian cyma.

cymatium, sima; the uppermost member of a classical cornice, convex in cross-section; Greek form is kymation.

cypress [*Cupressus spp., Chamaecyparis spp.*] a group of softwoods found in temperate regions, whose timber is pale pink, durable and used for external construction and joinery; see below for species of cypress included in this work.

Lawson's cypress, Port Orford cedar; [*Chamaecyparis lawsoniana*] a softwood from North America and the British Isles with pale yellow-brown timber, used in general construction work, for interiors and boat-building.

yellow cedar [*Chamaecyparis nootkatensis, Cupressus nootkatensis*] a softwood from Alaska and the west coast of North America; used in interiors, furniture and boat-building; not a true cedar, see cedar.

D

dabbed finish, dabbled finish; an even stonework finish produced by dressing with a point; a fine sparrowpecked finish.

dabs see plaster dots.

dacite a grey volcanic rock, rich in silica, used in building construction for aggregates, chippings and as decorative stone.

Dacron see polyethylene terephthalate.

dado 1 in joinery, a long groove machined into a board to house another board; a chase or housing.
2 die, tympanum; the unadorned rectangular or cylindrical central portion of a classical pedestal, on which a column is supported.
3 the portion of an internal wall up to waist height when faced or painted differently to the upper part.
dado joint see housed joint.
dado plane a plane for cutting a groove across the grain in wood.
dado rail see chair rail.

dais see podium.

Dalbergia spp. see rosewood.

damar, damar resin; a soft natural resin gathered from the forest trees of Malaya, Borneo, Java and Sumatra; mixed with a solvent such as turpentine and used as a varnish.

damp course see damp proof course.

damper see smoke damper, flue damper, fire damper, muffler, vibration insulator.
damper opening see throat.

dampness, damp; undesirable moisture within layers of construction, rooms, etc. from the ground, rainwater or as a result of poor ventilation.

damp proof, moisture resistant; a description of a material, product or construction designed to withstand or inhibit the presence of moisture.
damp proof course, damp course, dpc; a horizontal layer of impervious material laid in a masonry or concrete wall above ground level to prevent the vertical passage of moisture.

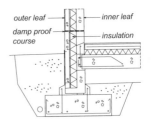

outer leaf — inner leaf
damp proof course — insulation

damp proofing the treatment of a surface or construction to inhibit the passage of moisture; also the result of this process.
damp proof membrane, dpm; 1 any impervious layer included in construction to prevent the passage of moisture.
2 a layer of plastics sheet material or mastic asphalt laid in base floor construction to prevent the passage of ground moisture upwards.

damp resisting plaster plaster or render containing an admixture which inhibits the penetration of water, sometimes called waterproof plaster or render.

dancetty banded ornament consisting of a zigzag line, a chevron or zigzag; primarily in heraldic motifs.

dancetty moulding

dancing step one of a series of tapered steps in a curving or spiral stair which do not radiate from the same point; also known as a balanced step or French flier.

darby, Darby float, derby; a long metal rule or board with handles, used for levelling fresh plasterwork on walls and ceilings.

darby, Darby float or derby

dart a decorative motif in the form of a sharp triangle, arrowhead or wedge-shaped design; see egg and dart, leaf and dart.

dash a masonry or concrete finish in which a render coat is thrown on; this may then be left as a final coat or rendered (wet dash), or coated with aggregate (dry dash), see also spatterdash.

dashed finish see wet dash.

datum in measuring and setting out, a reference point or level from which all subsequent measurements or levels are taken; a datum level is a horizontal reference plane (also known as a datum height or datum plane); a datum line is such a line marking out a datum level or a starting line for measurements.

daubing, rendering; the rough application of mortar to a wall as a rendered finish, either by hand with a trowel or with an applicator.

Davy's grey powdered slate used as a pigment; see slate black.

day joint see stop end form.

daylight in lighting design, all solar radiation, direct and indirect, that reaches the ground.

daylight lamp see neodymium oxide lamp.

daylight size see sight size.

daywork in contract management, a method of payment for additional construction work on the basis of hourly rates of labour, materials and plant.

DC direct current.

dead in room acoustics, referring to a space which has poor reverberance and little reflected sound.

dead bolt a rectangular lock bolt operable by the turning of a key only.

dead knot a knot in seasoned timber which can be easily knocked out, not intergrown with the surrounding wood.

dead leg in pipework for domestic water supply, a length of pipe extending from a circuit, whose end is fitted with a tap or appliance.

deadlight see fixed light.

dead load, permanent load; the structural load in a building due to the weight of the structure and other unchanging factors; see live load.

deadlock a lock which can be operated with a key only, but from both sides of a door.

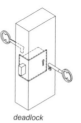

deadlock

deadman a buried concrete slab attached with ties to the rear of a retaining wall to provide a restraining anchorage.

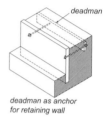

deadman as anchor for retaining wall

dead shore, vertical shore; a heavy timber post used as support for the underside of construction under repair, during underpinning, excavation work, etc.

dead-soft temper one of the annealed conditions and states of hardness in which copper is supplied; others are hard and half hard.

deal 1 commercial timber from the Scots pine tree, *Pinus sylvestris*.
2 a piece of sawn softwood with cross-sectional dimensions of 47−100 mm thick and 225−275 mm wide.

deal yard blue see yard blue.

Dearne's bond, Dearne's hollow wall; a brickwork bond in which courses of headers are laid with alternate courses of stretchers on edge to form a 9″ brick wall with cavities.

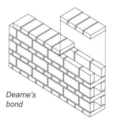

Dearne's bond

death-watch beetle [*Xestobium rufovillo-sum*] a beetle whose larvae cause damage to old wood and hardwood furniture by burrowing; it makes a ticking sound when moving, which was popularly believed to be an omen of imminent death.

deburring the removal of unwanted sharp edges from a treated or milled metal or plastics surface.

decay 1 fungal decay, see rot.
2 see dote.
decayed knot see unsound knot.
decay rate in acoustics, the rate of decrease in sound pressure level of a sound with respect to time; the slower the decay rate, the longer the reverberation time.

decibel abb. **dB**; the basic unit of sound pressure level; the decibel scale is logarithmic, where 0 dB is the threshold of hearing, and approximately 130 dB is the threshold of pain.

deciduous pertaining to species of tree which lose their leaves annually, often (but not always) one from which hardwood is obtained; see hardwood for list of tropical and European hardwood trees.

deck a loadbearing raised slab or horizontal composite construction supporting a floor, roof or external area.

decking 1 prefabricated components, boarding or other sheet material used to provide the structure of a floor, roof or deck as a base for surface materials.
2 spaced boarding laid as flooring for a veranda, or as a platform, duckboards, etc.
3 see roof decking.
4 see soffit formwork.

deck parking an area of parking on one of a number of concrete decks, usually the lower floors of a building, a multistorey car park, etc.

declination in surveying, the angle that any given plane makes with true vertical; see also solar declination.

decor see interior design.

Decorated style an architectural style in England from 1289 to 1400, the second of three phases of English Gothic architecture, characterized by rich decoration and tracery, lavish rib vaults and ogee arches; see also Geometric, Curvilinear.

decorated tracery tracery of the Decorated style; see flowing tracery.

decoration, ornament, embellishment; adornment, pattern, carvings, sculpture, etc. for a surface or space.
2 surface patterning or removable objects of art for walls, ceilings, theatre sets, etc.
3 see decorative work.

decorative art 1 art and design in the form of decorative prints, sculpture, furniture, etc. intended to enhance the interior decoration of a space.
2 enrichment; applied decoration for parts and surfaces of buildings and objects.
3 see decorative work.

decorative brickwork brickwork designed and constructed to be aesthetically pleasing, making use of bricks of various colours and textures, laid in patterned arrangements, etc.; types included as separate entries are listed below:
*carved brickwork; *chequered brickwork; *decorative masonry; *diaper; *gauged brickwork; *herringbone brickwork; *lacing course; *moulded brickwork; *patterned brickwork; *polychrome brickwork; *rubbed brickwork, see gauged brickwork.

decorative masonry, decorative brickwork; masonry which makes use of differently coloured and glazed bricks, carved stones, etc. laid in patterns and banding as decoration for wall surfaces.

decorative motif see ornamental motif.

decorative painting ornamental painting, murals, etc. applied to the surfaces of a building.

decorative tile see ornamental tile.

decorative veneer a thin sheet of high-quality wood used for its decorative value, quality of grain figure, etc. as a facing for lower quality timber, board or plywood.

decorative work the preparation of any decoration, ornamentation, painting, carving, printing, etc. for a building; variations included as separate entries are listed below:

*black and white work; *checkerwork, see chequerwork; *corduroy work; *Cosmati work; *diamond work; *fanwork, see fan tracery; *fretwork, see fret; *honeycomb work, see stalactite work; *knotwork; *leafwork, see foliated; *long and short work; *poker-work; *stalactite work; *strapwork.

deep compaction, sand piling; a method of ground stabilization in which pits or holes are made into soft ground, then filled with compacted sand or gravel to increase the bearing capacity of the ground; see also dynamic consolidation, vibrocompaction.

deep foundation any foundation which requires a deep excavation for reasons of ground, groundwater or frost conditions.

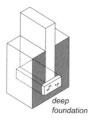

deep foundation

deep penetration testing see cone penetration testing.

deep seated rock see plutonic rock.

defect, fault; an imperfection which lowers the quality of a material, product or construction and may spoil it both physically and visually; see structural defect, seasoning defect, sawing defect.
defective referring to a material or object which is of a lower standard than required by a specification, is unserviceable or does not function properly.
defects liability period, maintenance period; the agreed period from completion of a building during which the contractor has an obligation to repair any faults and shortcomings in the construction work, performance of components and materials covered by the contract.
defects schedule see schedule of defects.

deflection, deflexion; elastic deformation of a member under load, often the downward movement of the mid-span of a loaded beam.
deflection curve, elastic curve in structural design, the curve of the main axis of a beam or other laterally stressed member under loading.

deformation in structures, the change in shape of a member or other component under loading; see also elastic deformation, plastic deformation.

deformed bar in reinforced concrete, a reinforcing bar whose surface is textured with a series of transverse parallel ridges to provide better bonding with the concrete; sometimes called a ribbed bar.

deformed bars

deformed wire steel wire, used as concrete reinforcement, which has a textured surface to improve its bonding with the concrete matrix.

degreasing the removal of grease or oily material from a surface, product or component prior to further treatment or use.

degree day in concreting, a measure of the curing time, and thus strength or maturity of cast concrete based on local statistical coldness conditions.

degree hour in concreting, a measure of the strength or maturity of concrete.

dehumidifier an appliance which decreases the relative humidity of air, making conditions more comfortable in spaces whose air contains too much moisture.

delamination in plywood or a veneered surface, adhesive failure resulting in the separation of adjacent plies; similar separation of adjacent layers in laminated construction due to poor bonding.

delay penalty see liquidated damages.

Delrin see polyoximethylene.

delta connection an electric point with three holes designed to receive a plug from a three-phase power supply.

demi-column, half-column; a decorative semicircular protrusion in a wall resembling a column which has been sunk into the wall surface, found in classical architecture.

demi-column

demirelief see mezzo rilievo.

demolition the destruction or dismantling and removal of old and unserviceable buildings or dysfunctional parts of construction, often prior to redevelopment or further construction work.
demolition ban a local authority notice preventing the demolition of a building or parts of a building.
demolition order a local authority notice requiring the demolition of a building or parts of a building.
demolition permit a permit issued in certain circumstances by a local authority prior to the demolition of a building or parts of a building, especially one which is the subject of protective legislation.

dense grained see close grained.

densifier see plasticizing admixture.

dentil an ornamental motif consisting of a series of square plates in relief.
dentil moulding, dentil frieze 1 an ornamental moulding consisting of a row of spaced rectangular recesses or projections; called a dentil frieze if below a cornice.

dentil moulding

2 see Venetian dentil moulding.
dentilation 1 masonry walling decoration consisting of a horizontal protruding toothed course of bricks or dressed stone.

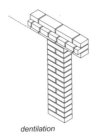

dentilation

2 dentil moulding.

deodar [*Cedrus deodara*], see cedar.

deoxidized copper a grade of copper which can be easily soldered or brazed; used, amongst other things, for domestic plumbing.

deposit corrosion, under-deposit corrosion, poultice corrosion; a form of crevice corrosion occurring under or around a hole, crack or break in a protective deposited coating on a metallic surface.

depressed arch see drop arch.
depressed ogee arch see two-centred ogee arch.
depressed three-centred arch a flat three-centred arch.

derby see darby.

Derby red see chrome red.

descriptive specification a concise specification outlining the characteristics of a product, process or design, usually including design and constructional details with sizes, basic technical data and colour and material composition.

desiccant a substance incorporated into some products, processes or sealed components to absorb unwanted moisture.

design 1 the process of formulating, creating and planning a functional, graphic or mass produced object such as a building, furnishing or fitting.
2 scheme; the representation, usually as a series of sketches, documents, drawings, models or computer generations, of a building, built area, structure or object.
3 see interior design.
4 see motif.

design and construct contract, design and build contract, package deal, turnkey contract; a form of building contract based on a brief provided by the client in which a developer organization has full responsibility for the design and construction of a project.

designated fabric in reinforced concrete, fabric reinforcement which can be defined by a coded fabric reference, negating the need for a design drawing or schedule.

design guideline information providing a specialist designer with assistance concerning design matters from the point of view of regulations, good practice, user and client requirements, etc.

design life the minimum length of time for which a component has been designed to correctly carry out its specified function.

design load in structural design, the maximum load for which a particular structure or structural member is designed.

design project, design scheme; a particular building or development at design stage.

design stage the pre-contract stage of a building project, from initiation up to tendering, when most or all of the design work is being carried out.

destructive testing the physical and chemical testing of samples of materials and components in such a way that they are damaged, crushed or changed during testing.

desulpho gypsum the mineral gypsum produced as a by-product of the purification of sulphurous flue gases produced during the combustion of fossil fuels.

detached column a column adjacent to a wall, but not physically attached to it, often a decorative column on a pedestal or plinth.

detached column

detail in design and construction, a solution to a small-scale issue such as a construction joint or the meeting of adjacent components in such a manner as to be both functional and aesthetically pleasing.

detail drawing a drawing showing a constructional detail at small scale, usually drawn as a section through the part.

detailed fabric in reinforced concrete, fabric reinforcement whose arrangement is such that it requires a detailed drawing.

detection device, detector, sensor; a device which produces a signal in the presence of smoke, heat, water or movement and triggers an alarm; see heat detector, combustion gas detector, smoke detector, flame detector, radiation detector.

detector see detection device.

detensioning, transfer; in the making of prestressed concrete, the transfer of stresses from the tendons and prestressing bed to the concrete.

determination in contract administration, bringing a building contract to an end before completion, under conditions specified in the contract or at common law.

develop and construct contract a form of building contract based on a scheme design prepared by the client, for which a contractor produces production drawings and carries out construction works.

developer a building firm which develops urban or greenfield sites with buildings, housing estates, etc.; often a speculative builder.

development, 1 the process of construction buildings or other structures.
2 project; a new building under design or construction.
3 see urban development.
4 see building project.
5 see fire development.
development control see planning control.
development with deemed consent in building control, building development that does not require formal planning permission.

devil see scraper.

devil float see nail float.

Devonshire clay see china clay.

dewatering, 1 groundwater lowering; the artificial lowering of groundwater in a particular location or construction site using excavations and other means.
2 measures such as pumping and drainage to reduce the amount of water around foundations below the water table.
3 drying; reducing the water level in a subterranean structure or the water content of a saturated material.

dewpoint, condensation point, saturation point; the lowest temperature at which the contained water vapour in air of a given humidity condenses; relative humidity at this point is 100%.

dezincification the slow disappearance or seepage of the zinc in brass due to electrolytic action when in contact with water; brass pipes are corroded as porous copper is laid down.

diabase, traprock; a dark igneous rock used as building stone, similar to basalt but with a larger grain structure.

diagonal 1 in geometry, a line which is not parallel or perpendicular to a main axis, usually from corner to corner of a rectangle.
2 see oblique.
3 a diagonal strut or tie in a trussed beam or space frame.
4 see brace, diagonal brace.

diagonal boarding, diagonal sheathing; boarding nailed diagonally to clad a building frame as bracing and for decorative effect.

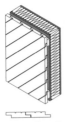

diagonal boarding

diagonal bond 1 see Flemish diagonal bond.
2 see diagonal pattern.
3 diagonal Flemish double stretcher bond; see Flemish double stretcher bond.

diagonal brace any member set diagonally from corner to corner of a frame to stiffen it; see also angle tie.

diagonal grain see sloping grain.

diagonal pattern a paving pattern in which rows of pavers are laid with joints oblique to a main axis, often forming a lozenge pattern; also called diagonal bond; similar patterns in parquetry, tiling and veneering.

diagonal paving

diagonal rib, ogive, groin rib; a rib in a rib vault which runs diagonally from corner to corner of the bay.

diagonal sheathing see diagonal boarding.

diagonal tie see angle tie.

dial gauge an instrument for measuring very small dimensions, consisting of a needle plunger configured to a dial or meter.

diamond black see carbon black.

diamond fret, lozenge fret; an ornamental motif consisting of fillets which join together forming a series of diamond shapes.

diamond fret

diamonding a form of warp which results in improperly seasoned square timber sections becoming diamond-shaped.

diamonding in improperly seasoned timber board

diamond match a veneering pattern in which four rectangular pieces of straight-grained veneer are laid together with each individual grain at an angle to one another, forming a series of diamond shapes; see also reverse diamond match.

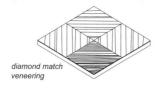

diamond match veneering

diamond moulding see diamond fret.

diamond saw a power saw whose blade is tipped with industrial diamonds, used for cutting masonry or concrete.

diamond work decorative masonrywork formed with a repeated lozenge motif.

diaper decoration consisting of a grid of elaborated or ornamented squares or lozenges; a diamond pattern in brickwork created with the use of bricks in various colours and surface textures, coloured mortar, etc.

dichroic mirror lamp a halogen lamp whose rear mirror reflector, often honeycombed, reflects light but not infrared energy, producing a cool beam; dichroism is an optical phenomenon in which an object appears to be coloured differently under different circumstances.

dichroite see cordierite.

die 1 a hard metal implement formed with an inside-threaded hole of a certain gauge, used for cutting threads into round metal rods by rotation.
2 see dado.

differential detector see thermo-differential detector.

diffraction the bending of light or sound waves when they come in close proximity to an opaque edge; effects of light or sound caused by this phenomenon.
diffracted sound in acoustics, sound which reaches the listener as a result of being bent round obstacles by diffraction.

diffused glass see diffuse reflection glass; obscured glass.

diffused illumination see diffused lighting.

diffused lighting space lighting which does not have a directional quality and provides a uniform degree of illuminance.

diffuse light light or illumination without noticeable direction, such as that from a cloudy sky.

diffuse porous wood hardwood with evenly sized and distributed pores.

diffuser 1 in an air-conditioning or mechanical ventilation system, an outlet or air terminal unit which directs supply air in the desired manner.
2 the translucent or slatted construction in a luminaire designed to scatter light and prevent glare.

diffuse reflection glass translucent glass one face of which is textured to diffuse light passing through; see also obscured glass.

diffusion bonding a method of welding specialized metal parts by pressing together under high temperatures, during which adjacent surfaces are fused together by atomic bonding caused by diffusion.

diffusion coefficient, coefficient of diffusion; a measure of the movement of water vapour through the thickness of wall, floor and roof construction when the vapour pressure is higher on one side than the other.

diffusion resistance a physical property, with units of measurement m^2sPa/kg, which determines how well a material can inhibit the transmission of water vapour.

digger see excavator.

diglyph in Renaissance architectural ornamentation, a decorative projecting element with two vertical grooves or glyphs.

diluent see thinner.

dilution 1 the thinning of a concentrated liquid such as a paint by a solvent or diluent liquid.
2 the ratio of concentrate to thinner.

dimension 1 a mode of linear extension in measurable space; length, breadth and height; see below.
2 the measurement of a distance between two points to indicate size, as

marked on drawings, etc.; types included as separate entries are listed below:
*daylight size, see sight size; *dressed size, dressed dimension; *external dimension; *finished size; *full size, see tight size; *glass size, glazing size, see pane size; measurement; *modular size, modular dimension; *neat size, see dressed size; *nominal dimension, nominal size; *overall dimension, overall size; *pane size; *span dimension;*sight size; *tight size.

dimensional coordination the dimensioning of prefabricated components and fittings such that they will comply with a modular building system.

dimensional stability the ability to retain shape and size under conditions of changing moisture and temperature.

dimensioned drawing a drawing to scale, usually of a floor plan, annotated with dimensions.

dimensioning 1 in design, the adding of annotated dimensions to a drawing.
2 the dimensions themselves.

dimension line a straight line along which incremental dimensions are added in a dimensioned drawing.

dimension stock a piece of accurately sawn timber with non-standard cross-sectional dimensions for a particular purpose.

dimension stone, natural stone block, cut stone; a piece of natural stone which has been cut into rectangular blocks for use in ashlar masonry.

dimension stone

dimetric projection 'two measurements'; any axonometric or oblique projection drawing in which lines parallel to two of the three main axes are drawn to the same relative scale, with lines on the third at a different scale; scales and angles are chosen to produce the most realistic depictions; in particular, an axonometric projection in which the projection of the X axis is 40° 31' above the horizontal, the Y axis is 7° above the horizontal, Z is vertical, and the X-axis is foreshortened using a different scale; many standardized variations of this orthographic dimetric projection are in use.

dimmer, dimmer switch; in lighting, a device to vary the amount of illumination given out by a luminaire.

Dingler's green a variety of chromium oxide green pigment.

diopside a usually greenish glassy mineral, polished for decorative inlay and as gemstones.

dioptase a glossy transparent emerald-green silicate mineral used in ornament and as a gemstone.

diopter 1 see alidade.
2 an ancient instrument for measuring angles and altitudes.

diorite a dark grey or greenish even-grained igneous rock, similar in appearance to granite; used as building stone; see also quartz diorite.

Diospyros spp. see ebony.

dioxazine purple a transparent bluish-purple organic pigment used in oil, water-colour and acrylic paints.

dip painting, dipping; a method of applying paint to objects by immersing them in a vessel of paint; see also electro-dip painting.

dipping 1 see dip painting.
2 see hot-dipping.

direct current, DC; electricity which flows in one direction only.

direct glare in lighting design, glare caused by light from a direct source.

direct glazed light fixed glazing fitted directly to the main frame of a window.

direct heating 1 any heating system in which thermal comfort is produced directly from the combustion of fuels or electricity as with stoves, bar-heaters, etc.
2 any heating system in which heating energy is produced within the building in which it is distributed.

direct hot water supply system a system of pipes and heating vessels to provide a hot water supply, heated by a direct source of energy.

direct–indirect lighting artificial lighting in which luminaires distribute an approximately equal amount of the emitted light upwards and downwards, and in which there is minimal horizontal illumination.

directional lighting space or task lighting designed to be beamed predominantly onto a certain area or feature.

direct lighting lighting for a space or task provided by a visible source of illumination; see also indirect lighting.

direct solar radiation see sunlight.

direct sound in acoustics, sound which reaches the listener directly from a source, without reflection.

disability glare in lighting design, glare which makes seeing difficult without causing physical discomfort.

disappearing stair, loft ladder; a retractable stepladder providing access to a roof space, either sprung-hinged or telescopic to fold away when not in use.

disc grinder see angle grinder.

discharge 1 see emission.
2 fluid waste from a cooling or manufacturing process, drainage system, etc.
3 flow rate; the rate of flow of a liquid in a pipeline, channel or waterway, measured in litres per second.
discharge lamp an electric lamp consisting of a glass tube containing an inert gas or metal vapour; light is produced by electrical discharge which excites the gas and vapour.
discharge pipe, drain, drainline, drain run, drain pipe; a succession of pipes joined end to end to convey waste water away from its point of use.
discharge stack in drainage, a vertical pipe into which a number of sanitary appliances, branch pipes, etc. on successive storeys of a building may discharge waste material.
discharge valve see control valve.

discharging arch see relieving arch.

discoloration a material defect, the loss or change in original colour, staining or an undesired colour phenomenon; also spelled discolouration.

discomfort glare in lighting design, glare which causes physical discomfort without making it difficult to see.

discontinuous construction in acoustics, types of construction for walls and floors, etc. in which no direct path is provided for structure-borne transmission of sound.

disc tumbler one of a number of pivoted discs in a lock mechanism which serve to hold the bolt fast until activated with a suitable key.

disc vent a round outlet device attached to a wall or ceiling surface, through which stale air passes out of a space.

dish aerial, dish antenna, satellite dish; in communications, a concave, dish-shaped aerial for receiving satellite transmissions; see satellite antenna.

dispersal 1 the encouragement of smoke flow to the outside along predesigned routes or ducts during a building fire.
2 in town planning, the migration of population and industry outwards from the inner areas and centres of cities to smaller towns, suburbs and outlying areas.

dispersion paint a paint containing droplets of pigment or latex in a non-dissolving liquid such as water; a dispersion is a mixture of one substance in another in the form of fine droplets.

dispersivity see light dispersivity.

displacer see plum.

disruption in contract administration, events or stoppages outside the contractor's control that slow down the progress of the work on site and may justify additional payments.

dissolvent see solvent.

distemper a traditional water-based paint consisting of pigment and chalk or clay bound together with glue.
distemper brush, flat brush; a large brush traditionally used for painting and decorating large internal surfaces such as ceilings or walls.

disthene see kyanite.

distributed load a structural load which acts evenly along the length of a beam, or over the surface area of a slab.

distributing pipe, distribution pipe; a pipe that conveys water, fuel, etc. from a cistern, tank or main to an appliance.

distribution bars secondary reinforcement at right angles to the main reinforcement in a reinforced concrete slab or wall, designed to spread a concentrated load, and as support during concreting.

distribution pattern in air conditioning and ventilation, a graphic representation of the spread of air from a supply air inlet, part of its technical specification.

distribution pipe see distributing pipe.

district heating a system of heating for an area or district, usually a number of residential buildings or estate, in which heated water is piped from a central heating plant; a district heating pipeline or heating main is a supply pipeline consisting of insulated pipe-in-pipe, valves and other control devices.

disturbed sample see remoulded sample.

diversity factor in pipework and electrical installations, a design factor to determine the maximum rate of flow of water or electricity in a system, based on the various appliances connected to the system and their requirements.

dividers a pair of compasses with points at the end of each leg; used for measuring, transferring dimensions and scribing arcs; see wing dividers, wing compass.

dividing strip 1 in floor construction, a strip of flexible material used to divide a monolithic floor into discrete areas to allow for movement.
2 verge, margin, median; in traffic planning, a strip of planted land to provide separation between a pedestrian path and a carriageway.

division bar see glazing bar.

division wall see fire wall.

do-and-charge work see cost-reimbursement contract.

document an official or unofficial written text, computer file, drawing, etc. produced for a particular purpose of information, intent, instruction or evidence.

documentation 1 the preparation of working drawings, specifications and other documents to form the basis of a building contract.
2 the collection of photographic and other documentary evidence of buildings for an inquiry, building survey, conservation project, etc.

dog, cramp, crampon, dog iron; a large steel or iron U-shaped fastener hammered into a timber joint to strengthen it and hold it together.

dog bolt see hinge bolt.

dog iron see dog.

dogleg descriptive of an implement or component which is elbow or L-shaped.

dogleg brick a kinked brick used at the join of two wall planes meeting at an obtuse angle.

dogleg chisel see bruzz chisel.

dogleg stair, dog-legged stair, return stair; a stair with two parallel flights side-by-side, joined by a single intermediate landing at half-storey height.

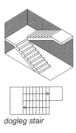

dogleg stair

dogtooth, tooth ornament; a decorative moulding found in Norman architecture, consisting of a series of raised lozenge-shapes with a carving resembling the imprint of a tooth set into each.

dogtooth ornament

dogtooth brickwork, houndstooth brickwork, mousetooth brickwork (Am); decorative brickwork in which a course or courses of bricks are laid diagonally so as to expose a horizontal sawtooth edge in a wall surface.

dogtooth brickwork

dogtooth moulding, houndstooth moulding, mousetooth moulding; a decorative sculptured band with a series of protruding notched carvings, resembling fluting in which the arcs are made into V-shapes.

dogtooth moulding

dogwood, cornel (Am); [*Cornus florida*] a hardwood from North America with pinkish non-splintering timber, traditionally used for small objects such as spindles for the textile industry.

dolerite a coarse-grained igneous rock, a form of young basalt.

dolly in piledriving, relatively soft material such as a piece of hardwood or log placed over the top of the pile as protection from impact damage during driving.

dolomite, 1 bitter spar; crystalline calcium magnesium carbonate, $CaMg(CO_3)_2$, in mineral form found in some limestones; used for its fire-resistant properties.
2 dolostone; limestone containing a high proportion of the above.
dolomitic lime, high magnesium lime; quicklime made from dolomite high in magnesium oxide, a mixture of calcium oxide and magnesium oxide in the ratio 1:1.
dolomitic limestone limestone with a high content of the mineral dolomite.
dolostone see dolomite.

dome 1 a hollow, flattened or raised hemispherical roof structure, often of masonry, which rests on a circular, square or polygonal base; types included as separate entries are listed below:

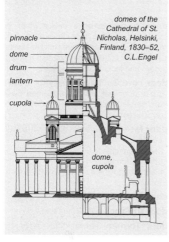

domes of the Cathedral of St. Nicholas, Helsinki, Finland, 1830–52, C.L.Engel

pinnacle
dome
drum
lantern
cupola

dome, cupola

*bulbous dome, see onion dome; *drum dome; *half dome; *melon dome, see umbrella dome; *onion dome; *parachute dome, see umbrella dome; *pendentive dome; *pumpkin dome, see umbrella dome; *sail dome, sail vault; *saucer dome; *semi-dome, see half dome; *umbrella dome.*
2 see domelight.
domed roof, 1 domical roof; a roof in the form of a dome.
3 one made up of a number of domes.
dome head screw, round head screw; a screw with a hemispherical head which protrudes above the surface into which it is fixed.

domehead screw

domelight, dome rooflight; a rooflight of moulded polycarbonate plastics or shaped glass, usually dome-shaped but often square, monopitched, barrel vaulted or a pyramid, and often functioning as a smoke vent.
dome nut see cap nut.
dome rooflight see domelight.

domestic solid fuel appliance see room heater.

domestic water heater a water heater intended for a small central heating system, for one household or a small building.

domical grating in drainage installations, a removable dome-shaped grating to protect the outlet of a drain from blockage by leaves, gravel, etc.

domical roof see domed roof.

domical vault see cloister vault.

donkey saw see mill saw.

door 1 an opening in a wall with a hinged or sliding partition to allow access from one space to another.
2 the partition itself, see door leaf.
3 the partition and its associated frame, see doorset.
4 see doorway.

see below for list of types of door included as separate entries:
*access door; *accordion door; *all-glass door; *aluminium door; *ash pan door; *automatic door; *automatic fire door, see automatic-closing fire assembly; *balanced door; *bi-fold door; *bi-part folding door; *bi-parting door, see centre-opening door; *blind door, see false door; *casement door; *centre-opening door; *concertina door, see sliding folding door; *coupled door; *double door; *double sliding door; *exit door; *external door; *false door; *fire door; *firebox door; *firebreak door, see fire door; *fireplace door; *flush door; *folding door; *framed and ledged door; *framed, ledged and braced door; *frameless glass door, see all-glass door; *French door, see casement door; *front door, see main entrance; *glass door, all-glass door; *glazed door; *hinged door; *hollow-core door; *inspection door; *internal door; *landing door; *ledged and braced door; *ledged door; *lift car door; *louvred door; *matchboard door; *metal door; *multi-folding door; *overhead door; *panelled door, panel door; *pass door, see wicket door; *plastics door; *rebated door; *revolving door; *roller door, see roller shutter; *sectional overhead door; *side-hung door; *side-opening door; *single door; *sliding door; *sliding folding door; *smoke door, smoke control door; *soot door; *stable door; *steel door; *swing door; *timber door; *timber glazed door, see glazed timber door; *trapdoor; *unframed door; *unglazed door; *up-and-over door; *vertical folding door; *wicket door; *wooden door, see timber door.

door acceptor see acceptor.

door assembly see doorset.

door automation see automatic door gear.

doorbell a sounding device attached to or near a door to attract the attention of occupants.

door buck see door lining.
see buck.

door buffer 1 a piece or strip of resilient material set in the rebate of a door jamb to reduce noise from the door leaf slamming.

2 see door stop.

door bumper see door stop.

door buzzer see door transmitter.

door casing see door lining.

door chain, door limiter; a security door fitting for inhibiting the opening of an entry door to its full extent, consisting of a short length of chain attached to the inside face of a door leaf and the locking jamb.

door check see door closer.

door clearance 1 the horizontal or vertical open dimension between the members of a door frame.
2 the small gap between door leaf and its frame, which allows it freedom of movement in opening and closing.
3 the installation gap between a doorframe and surrounding fabric to allow for manufacturing tolerances and workmanship.

door closer, door check; a sprung or hydraulic device for closing a door automatically and keeping it closed until manually opened; used for fire doors and external doors; see below for types of door closer included as separate entries.
*concealed door closer; *door spring; *jamb-mounted door closer; *overhead door closer; *surface-mounted door closer.

door co-ordinator a device fitted in conjunction with a door closer in a set of double fire doors to ensure that the leaves close in the correct order and that rebated edges and locks function properly.

door core the filling material for a composite door leaf, usually of foamed plastics, timber-based material or honeycomb construction.

door face 1 the external planar surface of a door leaf.
2 see opening face.
3 see closing face.
4 door facing; the surface covering for a door leaf.

door facing see door face.

door fittings see door furniture.

door former formwork to create an opening for a door in a concrete wall.

door frame the structural surround for a door leaf, in which it is hung.

door-frame anchor a short length of metal strip for fixing a door frame to surrounding construction.

door furniture, door ironmongery, door hardware; any fittings such as hinges, door handles and closers for the operation and functioning of a door.

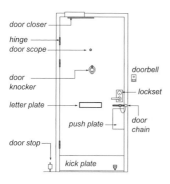

door gear 1 see automatic door gear.
2 see sliding door gear.
3 see swing-door operator.

door handle a device or fitting used for manually opening a door by grasping with the hand and pulling; types included as separate entries are listed below:
*flush handle; *lever handle; *pull handle; *sliding door handle; *trapdoor handle.

door hardware see door furniture.

door head, 1 door soffit; the horizontal flat underside of a door opening.
2 the upper horizontal member in a door frame or door lining.

door hinge a hinge designed for hanging a door leaf.

door holder a door fitting designed to hold a door in an open position, usually a hook or catch attached to a floor or adjacent wall.

door ironmongery see door furniture.

door jamb 1 one of the vertical members of a door frame.
2 see door reveal.

door knob a rounded or oval door handle.

door knocker a hinged device attached to a door leaf for tapping against the door leaf to attract the attention of the occupants of a building from outside.

door leaf the openable part of a door, usually a hinged or sliding planar construction; for double doors see active leaf, inactive leaf.

door leaf

door limiter see door chain.

door lining, door casing, door buck; boarding, etc. to cover the joint between a door frame and surrounding construction at a door reveal.

door lock any lock specially designed for securing a door, operated with a removable key.

door opening see doorway.

door operator 1 see automatic door operator.
2 see swing-door operator.

door panel one of the non-structural infills in a panelled door.

door phone see telephone entry system.

door plate 1 see kicking plate.
2 see push plate.

door post in timber-framed construction, a vertical member at the edge of a door opening onto which the door frame is fixed.

door reveal, door jamb; the vertical flat side of a doorway, perpendicular or skew to the main wall surface.

door schedule a contract document listing types of door, their ironmongery, fire-rating and other specifications for a project.

door scope, door viewer, peephole; a security door-fitting with a wide-angle lens, through which occupants can view visitors, etc. before opening the door.

door seal, door strip; a draught excluder for a door.

doorset, door assembly, door unit, door; a manufactured unit consisting of door frame, door leaf, door trim and associated ironmongery.

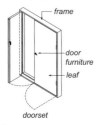

doorset

door sill 1 the lowest horizontal member in a door frame; a threshold.
2 the framing member at the base of a door opening of a traditional timber-framed building.

door soffit see door head.

door spring a simple door-closing mechanism consisting of a steel spring attached to the door leaf and frame on the hinged side.

door stay see door stop.

doorstep the small platform or short stair in front of the external door to a building, making the transition between floor level and external ground level.

door stile 1 one of the vertical framing members in a panelled door leaf.
2 see shutting stile, closing stile, lock stile.

door stop, 1 a rebate or abutment in a door frame against which the door leaf closes.
2 door stay, door buffer, door bumper; a fitting set into a wall or floor beside a door to prevent the door leaf or handle from striking the adjacent wall on opening; often a rubber stud or a metal pin with a rubber surround.

door strip see door seal.

door swing the curve traced by the edge of a door leaf as it opens, as marked on plan drawings.

door swing

door transmitter, door buzzer; an electronic doorbell device for an apartment block, often with microphones for inhabitants to communicate with visitors outside the main door.

doortree a door post, or vertical member of a door frame.

door trim a strip of rigid material fixed around a door to cover the joint between door frame and the surrounding construction; an architrave.

door unit see doorset.

door viewer see door scope.

doorway, 1 door opening; the opening formed by a door in a wall, into which the door frame is fitted.
2 door opening; the open space between the jambs of a doorframe and the threshold and door head, in which the door leaf is fitted.

Doppler effect in acoustics, an apparent change in pitch of sound as the listener moves towards or away from the source.

Doric pertaining to the architecture of the Doric order, the oldest classical Greek order, originating in Dorian Greece, characterized by the following: fluted columns, considerably sturdier than those of other classical orders, with pronounced entasis; a simple capital consisting simply of a swelling or echinus surmounted by a rectangular abacus, no column base and an entablature with triglyphs and metopes; see also proto-Doric column, Roman Doric.

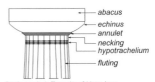

Doric capital, Temple of Hera I or 'Basilica', Paestum, Italy, 550 BC

Doric cyma an ornamental cyma recta moulding double curved in cross-section, concave at its outer edge and convex at its inner edge; in classical architecture originally rendered with a rectangular version of egg and dart embellishment.

Doric cyma moulding, leaf scroll

Doric Roman see Roman Doric.

dormant, dormant tree, dorment; in traditional timber frame construction, an old term for a timber beam or purlin which carries secondary beams.

dormer see dormer window.

dormer vault a secondary transverse vault in the side of a larger vault to make an opening for a semicircular or arched window.

dormer vault

dormer window a projecting vertical window and surrounding construction located on a pitched roof, usually to afford light to an attic or upper storey space.

dosseret an additional block of stone sometimes placed above the capital of Byzantine and Romanesque columns; also called a pulvin, impost block or supercapital.

Byzantine basket capital and dosseret at San Vitale Ravenna, Italia, 526 AD

dote, incipient decay, hardrot; fungal decay which attacks the heartwood of living trees.

dots see plaster dots.

double-acting hinge, swing door hinge; a hinge containing a mechanism which allows a swing door to open in either direction; see also next entry; a double-acting spring hinge is a double-acting hinge containing a spring mechanism to automatically return the door leaf to its closed position.

double cantilevered stair a stair in which each step is supported only at its midpoint by a sloping beam, and thus cantilevers out sideways in both directions; a double cantilevered spiral stair is a spiral stair with treads supported from their midpoints on a helical beam.

double-coated adhesive tape see double-sided adhesive tape.

double cogged joint a timber crossing joint in which a small notch is cut into one member to receive a sunken cog in the other.

double cogged joint

double cone moulding an ornamental moulding with a series of raised cone motifs joined together, apex to apex, and base to base.

double cone moulding

double C-scroll a decorative motif composed of two C-shaped scrolls joined at their tails, in mirror image of one another.

double door 1 a door with a pair of leaves meeting in the middle, hung on either jamb of the same frame. See illustration on following page.

double C-scroll

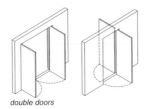

double doors

2 a door with a pair of leaves hung on the same jamb, opening successively; used for applications with demanding acoustic and thermal requirements.
see also coupled door, stable door, double sliding door.

double face hammer a small sledge-hammer with a face on both ends of the head.

double Flemish bond a brickwork bond laid with Flemish bond showing on both inner and outer faces of a solid brick wall more than 9″ thick.

double gable roof see M-roof.

double glazing glazing in which two parallel layers of glass, with a gap between them, separate the inside and outside of a building; a double-glazed unit or double-glazing component is a glazed unit with two panes of glass sealed around an edging strip with a gap between; the gap is usually filled with an inert gas; more fully known as a hermetically sealed double-glazed unit; a double-glazed window is a window with two parallel panes of glass with an air space between, either in separate frames or as a sealed unit.

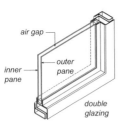

air gap
outer pane
inner pane
double glazing

double hammer beam truss in traditional timber roof construction, a roof truss with two pairs of hammer beams, one resting on the other.

double headed nail a nail with two heads on the same shank, one above the other; used in temporary

double headed nail

fixings and easily withdrawn with the claw of a hammer; also known as a duplex nail, scaffold nail or form nail.

double header bond see Flemish double header bond.

double hipped roof a roof form consisting of two hipped roofs, side by side with a gutter in between, and common eaves.

double-hung sash window see sash window.

double lap joint a timber joint in which two members in the same direction form a lap joint on either side of another timber; used in truss construction.

double lean-to roof a V-shaped roof formed by two lean-to roofs which slope towards each other with a gutter in between.

double-lock welt see double welt.

double notched joint see notched joint.

double notched joint

double ogee moulding see brace moulding.

double pantile, double S-tile; a wide pantile which has two troughs instead of one.

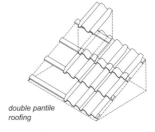

double pantile roofing

double pipe ring in pipework, a tight-enable bracket for fixing two parallel pipes to a wall surface or ceiling soffit.

double pitched roof see curb roof.

double-quirked bead moulding see flush bead moulding.

double return stair an ornamental staircase with one flight leading to an intermediate landing, and two flights leading in the return direction from that landing.

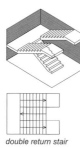

double return stair

double roll tile, bold roll tile; a double pantile or double Roman tile.

double Roman tile a wide single-lap roof tile with two waterways or channels interspersed with convex projections.

double Roman tiling

double roof see purlin roof.

double sash window a window composed of two single glazed windows hung in the same window frame, forming a kind of double glazing; if the two sashes act as one, it is called a coupled window.

double scallop capital a Romanesque scallop capital with only two convex undulations at the underside of each face.

Anglo-Norman (Romanesque) scallop capital in the church of St Michael, Bockleton, Worcestershire, England, 12th century

double-sided adhesive tape, double-coated adhesive tape, double-side tape; adhesive tape which has an adhesive coating on both sides.

double-skin facade modern facade construction methods making use of an extra cladding of glass attached separately from the external wall surface to utilize effects of cooling and warming of air within the cavity space.

double-skin roof covering roofing construction with waterproofing provided both by profiled sheeting and an underlying weatherproof membrane.

double sliding door a sliding door with two leaves, either a centre-opening or side-opening door.

double spiral screwdriver see spiral ratchet screwdriver.

double S-tile see double pantile.

double stretcher bond see monk bond.

double tee beam, double tee slab, double T plank; a precast reinforced or prestressed concrete beam component laid in series to form long-span concrete slabs; it is shaped like two adjoining tees in cross-section with an upper flat slab or table and two parallel protrusions or stalks.

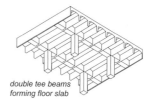

double tee beams forming floor slab

double tenon joint a strong timber joint in which the end of one member is cut with two tenons to fit into a housing or

double tenon joint

mortise in another; sometimes called a twin tenon joint or, in varied form, a bridle joint.

double T plank see double tee beam.

double triangle tie a galvanized steel wire wall tie in which wire is bent back on itself and twisted to form a pair of triangular shapes, also called a twin triangle wall tie.

double triangle tie

double welt, clink, double-lock welt; in sheetmetal roofing, a joint in which two adjacent sheets are doubly bent over each other then hammered down.

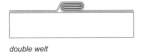

double welt

double window a window which has two lights side by side, separated by a mullion, in the same frame; see also coupled window, double-glazed window, double-hung sash window, sash window.

doubling piece, tilting fillet, eaves board; in timber roof construction, a timber strip, wedge-shaped in cross-section, used to raise the outer edge or the row of tiles or slates at the eaves.

Douglas fir, Oregon pine, British Columbian pine; [*Pseudotsuga menziesii*] a North American softwood with strong reddish timber; the most important structural timber in North America.

doussie see afzelia.

dovetail pertaining to a rhomboid or wedge-shaped form.

dovetail joint any timber joint in which a tenon or lap is splayed to form a wedge-shaped dovetail to fit into a reciprocal housing; also called a dovetailed joint; types included as separate entries are listed below:

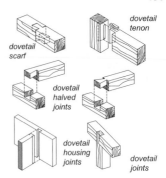

dovetail scarf

dovetail tenon

dovetail halved joints

dovetail housing joints

dovetail joints

dovetail corner joint a many-tenoned dovetailed corner joint used in cabinet-making for joining boards and sheets at right angles; also called a box dovetail joint.

dovetail halved joint, dovetail lap joint; a timber tee half-lap joint in which one halved timber is cut into a dovetail on one or both sides.

dovetail housed joint in timber frame construction, a joint in which the member to be housed is dovetailed into a recess; also called a dovetail or dovetailed housing.

dovetail lap joint see dovetail halved joint.

dovetail scarf joint a timber lengthening joint in which the halved ends of both timbers are cut with a dovetailed tenon to fit into a corresponding slot.

dovetail tenon joint in joinery, a mortise and tenon joint in which the tenon is dovetailed; a wedge or key is driven in to tighten the joint.

dovetail marker see dovetailing template.

dovetail moulding a decorative moulding carved or rendered with a series of rhomboids.

dovetail moulding

dovetail nailing see skew nailing.

dovetail saw a medium-sized backsaw or small bow saw whose blade is

200—250 mm long, used for fine work and cutting dovetails and tenons.

dovetailing template, dovetail marker; a tool or stencil for marking out dovetail joints.

dowel 1 a piece of joinery timber milled so that it is round in cross-section.

dowel, round

2 a small round wooden pin or peg used for fastening joints in timber.

dowels for fastening timber joint

dowel bar, dowel; in reinforced concrete, a short reinforcing bar which protrudes from the surface of cast concrete, extends across a joint, or onto which a fixing may be attached.

dowel bit see brad point drill.

dowel joint any timber joint in which wooden dowels are glued into receiving holes in the members to be connected.

dowel nail a wire nail with points at either ends, used for fastening secret joints.

dowel nail

dowel screw a screw fixing with threads at either end and no head, used for fastening concealed joints in timber.

dowel screw

dowel sharpener a sharpened hollow drill bit for chamfering the rims of dowels used in fastening wood joints.

down conductor in lightning protection for a building, a conductive path to convey current from a lightning strike safely to earth.

down-draught cold, downwardly moving air from the outside, inside a flue or flue system, which prevents hot combustion gases from rising and restricts it from functioning efficiently.

downlight, downlighter; a luminaire which produces a concentrated downward beam of light, used for illuminating high spaces from a ceiling to avoid glare.

downpipe a vertical water pipe directing rainwater from a roof or roof guttering to the ground or to a drain.

downstand beam a beam which protrudes from the lower surface of a concrete slab.

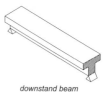

downstand beam

downy birch [*Betula pubescens*], see birch.

dpc see damp proof course.

dpm see damp proof membrane.

draft 1 the North American spelling of draught; see also words beginning with draught.
2 see preliminary.
3 see drafted margin.

draft damper see draught diverter.

drafted margin, marginal draft; in the cutting and dressing of stone, an area around the edge of a block of stone dressed initially to facilitate its further squaring and smoothing.

drafted margin

draft excluder see draught excluder.

draft flue system see natural draught flue system.

draft lobby see draught lobby.

draft stabilizer see draught diverter.

draft stop a fire-resistant partition in an attic or above a suspended ceiling to prevent the spread of a building fire within ceiling and roof voids.

draft strip see weatherstrip.

drag, 1 comb; an implement with a serrated steel blade used in plastering for spreading and evening out plaster surfaces, for removing excess plaster, spreading tiling mortar, etc.

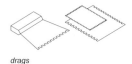

drags

2 see scratcher.

3 comb; a hand-held metal toothed or serrated plate drawn across the surface of masonrywork to produce a striated finish.

dragged plasterwork see comb-finish rendering.

dragger see flogger.

dragging beam see dragon beam.

dragline excavator a crane-like vehicle with a large bucket used for excavating soil and rock below the level at which it is stationed.

dragon beam, dragging beam; in traditional timber frame construction, a horizontal strengthening roof beam which projects outwards from a corner at 45° and receives the thrust of a hip rafter; also a similar beam in timber floor structures.

dragon tie see angle tie.

drain a channel, pipe or system of pipework to convey foul water, surface water, rainwater, etc. from buildings within a private boundary; types included as separate entries are listed below:
*agricultural drain, see field drain; *discharge pipe; *filter drain, see field drain; *floor drain; *foul water drain, foul drain; *French drain, see field drain; *gravity drain; *gully; *irrigation drain, see subsoil drain; *land drain, see field drain, ditch; *outlet; *rainwater outlet; *sand drain; *sewer; *soil water drain, soil drain;*

*storm drain; *subsoil drain, subsurface drain; *vertical sand drain, see sand drain.*

drain cock in water supply, hot water heating, air conditioning, etc., a tap at the lower end of a system of pipework for emptying the installation of liquid, condensation, etc.

drainline see discharge pipe.

drain pipe 1 a length of pipe, usually a proprietary component with suitably formed ends, joined in series to form a drain.

2 see discharge pipe.

3 perforated pipe; a proprietary product consisting of a length of plastic pipe with regular holes or slots, used in a field drain.

drain plug in heating, air conditioning and other piped systems, a plug which can be extracted for removal of excess condensation and other liquids.

drain run see discharge pipe.

drain valve a valve used to drain water or other liquid from a pipework installation, cistern, etc.

drainage 1 the removal of excess water from a building or construction.

2 the runoff of surface and rainwater from a building or built area into a system of drains.

3 see surface-water drainage.

4 the use of drain systems to remove excess water from building surfaces and use; see drainage system.

drainage channel 1 any large open watercourse for the conveyance, irrigation or drainage of water.

2 a small concave component or recess in a floor or paving, etc. for conveying surface water into a gulley or drain.

drainage gully see gully.

drainage layer layer of inert granular material in landscaped planting, green roofs, etc. beneath the growing medium, which allows water to drain away.

drainage membrane see air-gap membrane.

drainage pipe a drain pipe or discharge pipe.

drainage system a system of drains to convey waste and surface water away from a building to a soakaway, sewer or septic tank.

Dralon a proprietary name for synthetic fibres of polyacronitrile.

draped arch, tented arch; an ornamental arch whose intrados has convex haunches, as if draped with hanging fabric.

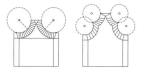

draped arches

drapery see linenfold, lambrequin.

draught, draft (Am); **1** an upward current of warm air in a flue or chimney which carries smoke and other products of combustion out of a building.
2 the feeling of discomfort arising from the movement of cool air in a space, often from gaps in construction or excess ventilation.
3 a slope given to surfaces of a concrete, plaster, etc. mould to aid the release of a cast from it; also called draw.
4 draft, see preliminary.

draught diverter, barometric damper (Am), draught stabilizer; a mechanism for reducing excessive draught in a flue by automatically introducing cold air from the outside into the flue.

draughted margin see drafted margin.

draught excluder, seal, wind stop, weatherstrip; a strip of flexible material applied into joints between a door or window casement and its frame to prevent the passage of air.

draught flue system see natural draught flue system.

draughting the profession of producing accurate line drawings of a product, component, building, etc., showing various standard annotated views by which it can be presented or constructed; written as drafting in North America.

draught lobby a small enclosed space immediately after an external door whose purpose is to prevent the movement of cold air, rain or snow into the building.

draughtsman, draftsman; a person employed in a design office to carry out technical drawing and draughting; draughtsmanship is the skill and art of this.

draught stabilizer see draught diverter.

draught strip see weatherstrip.

draw, draught; in concretework, a slight inclination of the face of formwork to make striking easier.

draw bolt see bolt.

drawboring in traditional timber pegged jointing, the practice of drilling holes slightly offset from one another so that when pegs are hammered in, the pieces are pulled together and the joint thus tightened.

drawer lock chisel a chisel with an L-shaped blade for cutting hidden mortises for locks.

drawing 1 a two-dimensional representation of an area, building, technical installation, component or detail; usually annotated and set out on a sheet of paper, card or film, or produced from a computer file; a drawing containing information for construction is often called a plan; typical types of drawing included as separate entries are listed below:
*architectural drawing; *arrangement drawing, see general arrangement drawing; *assembly drawing; *block plan; *component drawing; *component range drawing; *construction drawing; *contract drawing; *detail drawing; *dimensioned drawing; *earthworks plan; *elevation; floor plan; *foundation drawing; *general arrangement drawing, general location drawing; *layout drawing; *layout plan, see site layout plan; *location drawing; *location plan, see block plan; *measured drawing; *outline drawing, see sketch drawing; *perspective; *plan; *preliminary drawing, see sketch drawing; *production drawing;*

*projection; *record drawing; *reference drawing, see base sheet; *revised drawing, see revision; *sectional drawing, see section; *site plan; *sketch drawing; *structural drawing; *survey drawing, see record drawing; *working drawing.
2 the act of producing the above.
3 see draughting.
4 see drawing-in.

drawing file in computer-aided design, a computer file containing a design or drawings.

drawing-in, drawing; the installation of electrical cables and wiring into protective conduit by pulling them through.

drawing knife, draw knife, draw shave, shaving knife; a two-handled, bladed tool used for the removal of excess wood and bark from timber.

drawing pin, thumbtack; a pin with a large flat head which can be pushed in by hand to fix paper on board.

drawings schedule, schedule of drawings; a written tabulated document with a list of project drawings, their content and dates of amendment.

drawing up in drawing and draughting, the making of a final drawing from sketches, underlays and reference drawings; modern equivalents using computer-generated methods.

draw knife see drawing knife.

drawn glass see sheet glass.

drawn sheet glass see sheet glass.

draw-off pipe in pipework, a length of pipe to which a tap, valve or appliance is fitted.

draw-off tap, cock; a tap fitted to a piped water supply from which water can be drawn off for use.

draw shave see drawing knife.

dredging excavation work carried out from below a body of water such as a lake, river or the sea, by a special rig mounted on a floating deck.

drench shower a shower device designed to provide a rapid soaking for contents and surfaces in a building in the event of fire.

dressed, surfaced, wrot, planed; referring to sawn timber which has been smoothed with a plane or planer on one or more surfaces.

dressed dimension see dressed size.

dressed finish any kind of worked finish to a stonework surface.

dressed size, dressed dimension, neat size; in milled timber, the finished dimension after planing converted timber, slightly smaller than the sawn size.

dressed timber a range of readily available timber sections whose surfaces have been machined smoothed with a plane.

dressing, 1 planing, surfacing; the smoothing or finishing of a timber surface with a plane or planer.
2 the surface smoothing of rough timbers with an adze.
3 the working of stone with tools to provide a finished surface.
4 see top dressing.

dressing compound see levelling compound.

dressing up in ornamental plasterwork, the fixing of plaster castings in place, and the associated finishing work.

drier, 1 an agent or compound designed to speed up the drying process of paints and varnishes by oxidation of oils.
2 siccative; metallic salts (oxides of manganese, lead or cobalt), combined with oils, resins and solvents and mixed with paints and varnishes to accelerate drying.
3 see hardener.
4 see drying fan.

drill 1 a tool or machine for drilling or boring a hole; types included as separate entries are listed below:
*breast drill; *concrete drill, see masonry drill; *electric drill, see power drill; *hammer drill; *hand drill.
2 see drill bit.

drill bit a sharpened metal blade for boring holes, often helically shaped, attached to and rotated by the chuck of a brace or drill; types included as separate entries are listed below:

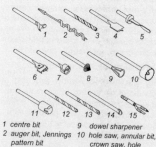

1 centre bit
2 auger bit, Jennings pattern bit
3 brad point drill
4 flat spade drill
5 combination drill bit
6 expansive bit, expansion bit
7 Forstner bit
8 countersink
9 dowel sharpener
10 hole saw, annular bit, crown saw, hole cutter, tubular saw
11 plug cutter
12 twist drill, metal drill
13 masonry drill concrete drill
14 glass drill
15 screwdriver bit

*auger bit; *brad point drill, dowel bit; *centre bit; *combination drill bit; *countersink; *dowel sharpener; *expansive bit, expansion bit; *flat spade drill; *Forstner bit; *glass drill; *grinding burr; *hole saw, tubular saw, hole cutter, annular bit, crown saw; *Jennings pattern bit; *masonry drill, concrete drill; *metal drill; *plug cutter; *reamer; *twist drill; *wood drill.

drilling, boring; the making of a hole in a material, component or the ground, using a rotating blade or similar device.

drilling hammer a heavy hammer or maul used for striking with cold chisels to drill or punch holes in stone and metal.

drill press a power drill vertically mounted in a rigid frame, used for heavy-duty drilling and accurate work.

drill stop a circular ring attached to a drill bit to regulate depth of drilling.

drip, throat, throating; in building construction, a slot in the undersurface of a protruding external component such as a sill to prevent water running back to the surface of the building.

drip edge see drop apron.

dripstone see hood-mould.

driven pile in foundation technology, any type of pile placed by driving it into the ground.

driver 1 a flat-bladed masonry chisel for dressing stone to a smooth surface.
2 device driver; in computing, software or programming which operates a device such as a disk drive or printer.

drive screw see screw nail.

driving in foundation construction, the repeated hammering of certain types of pile into the ground using a pile driver or similar apparatus; also called piledriving.

driving shoe in foundation construction, a pointed component attached to the lower end of a pile to enable it to be driven more easily into the ground.

drop see drop panel, gutta.

drop apron, drip edge; in sheet roofing, a flashing laid vertically at eaves or a verge to provide a drip and protect the edge.

drop arch, depressed arch; a form of pointed arch composed of segments whose radii are less than the span of the arch.

drop arch

drop black a variety of vine black pigment.

drop ceiling see false ceiling.

drop chute, rubble chute; a temporary chute with a number of interlocking plastic conical pieces, assembled on site and used for the removal of builder's waste from an upper level in a building during refurbishment or demolition work.

drop hammer, ram; in piledriving or drop-forging, a rig consisting of a heavy steel cylindrical weight known as a monkey, which is hoisted up and then repeatedly dropped from a controlled height to apply percussive force.

droplight see pendant luminaire.

drop panel a thickening in a flat slab or mushroom slab floor at a column head to spread the load from the slab and reinforce the joint; also called a drop.

drover see boaster.

drum see tambour.

drum dome a dome which sits atop a cylindrical wall structure or tambour.

drunken saw, wobble saw; a circular saw set so that it does not rotate in one plane; used to cut a groove or kerf.

dry see shake.

dry ashlar walling ashlar masonry which has been laid without mortar to bond the joints.

dry dash a hardwearing finish for concrete or masonry in which the surface has been treated with a coating of mortar, to which aggregate is then applied; see also pebbledash, shingle dash, spar dash.

dry fresco see fresco secco.

dry glazing glazing in which preformed polymeric seals and gaskets are used for fixing the glass in its frames rather than liquid sealants, putty, etc.

dry hydrate a white powder, calcium hydroxide, $Ca(OH)_2$, manufactured by the controlled addition of water to quicklime, calcium oxide, CaO; see also slaked lime, hydrated lime.

drying 1 the evaporation of water from a material.
2 the transformation of a coat of paint, coating, etc. from liquid to solid state.
3 see forced drying.
4 see seasoning.
5 see dewatering.

drying fan, drier; any fan which blows out a stream of warm air, used for drying of work on site, laundry, etc.

drying oil any oil used in paints as a vehicle, which then dries by oxidation or absorption of air to form a tough adhesive film.

drying shrinkage see dry shrinkage.

dry joint a masonry joint without mortar.

dry kiln a large oven for seasoning converted timber.

drylining see plasterboard drylining.

dry main see dry standpipe.

dry mix referring to cements and mortars in which all component parts are present except water, which is added on site, prior to use.

dry mix concrete dry cement powder with aggregate added, delivered to site where water is added to form concrete.

dry mix mortar see preblended mortar.

dry mix plaster see preblended plaster.

dry-mix process a sprayed concrete process in which damp aggregate and dry cement are mixed with water in the nozzle of a pump prior to being projected at high velocity; see wet-mix process.

Dryobalanops spp. see kapur.

dry packing, dry-tamp process; the placing of damp and stiff concrete with a low water content into existing hollows and joints where it is tamped with a suitable tool or compacted by ramming; dry packed concrete is concrete thus laid.

dry-pipe system a sprinkler installation used for subzero applications, whose pipes are connected to a permanent supply of water, but under normal conditions are full of air under pressure; in the event of a fire the air draws water from a main into the system.

dry powder non-conducting, non-toxic, water-repellent fine powder used in some fire extinguishers to smother flames and cool outbreaks of fire.

dry-powder extinguisher a fire extinguisher used for putting out fires caused by electrical faults and burning liquids; it is operated by exuding dry inflammable powder, see above.

dry pressing, semi-dry pressing; a method of producing clay bricks and other ceramic products by the mechanical compressing of clay powder with a water content of 6−10% into suitable shapes.

dry ridge tile a special roof tile formed to cover a ridge, fixed with a clip without mortar bedding.

dry rot, tear fungus; [*Serpula lacrymans*], [*Merulius lacrymans*] a fungal decay which attacks damp timber in unventilated spaces; also a general name for similar fungi.

dry shrinkage, drying shrinkage; in concretework, a reduction in physical size on hardening due to the evaporation of water.

dry standpipe, dry main; an empty vertical water pipe running the full height of a building, to which a fire hydrant or pumper vehicle can be connected to provide water for firefighting at each floor of the building.

dry-stone walling the technique of constructing freestanding masonry walls using unworked or roughly tooled stones stacked without the use of mortar; dry-stone walls are often used for boundary fencing.

dry-tamp process see dry packing.

dry to handle a stage in the drying of paint at which paintwork will not be damaged by handling.

dry to touch see touch dry.

dry walling any masonry walling laid without the use of bonding mortar.

drywall see plasterboard drylining.

drywall screw, plasterboard screw; a self-tapping screw with a thin shank, fine threads and flat wide head, used for fixing plasterboard to studwork.

drywall screw

dual duct system an air-conditioning system in which hot and cold air are provided in separate ducts and mixed locally according to a thermostat.

dual duct terminal unit, mixing box; a component in a dual duct air-conditioning system in which hot and cold air are blended according to strictly controlled conditions before being released to a space.

dual-flush cistern a water-saving WC-flushing cistern which provides the user with the alternative of flushing with two different amounts of water.

dubbing the application of a first layer of plaster to level off recesses and gaps in a plastering background such as lathing, masonry, etc.; also called dubbing out.

duckstone see pebble.

duct any sealed channel in a building for the passage of air, waste gases, electric cables and other services; see air duct, cable duct.

ducted flue a flue system in which intake and outlets are in the same duct or flue.

ductility the property of a material, particularly a metal, to be able to undergo plastic deformation without fracturing.

dumb scraper see scraper.

dummy a hammer whose head is of a soft metal such as zinc or lead, used for striking wooden headed chisels.

dummy furniture any fittings for a door or window which have no function other than decoration.

dummy joint, groove joint; in concrete-work, a longitudinal groove cast in the surface of concrete designed to provide a natural line for inevitable cracking during drying and expansion.

dump bucket concreting a method of placing concrete by lowering batches by crane in a closed container, from where it is discharged via a hatch into formwork or excavations.

dumper a small steerable motor vehicle with four rubber-tyred wheels and a tip-pable hopper or skip for moving earth and other materials on site.

dumpling a mass of unexcavated soil left over as excavation work is carried out initially at the edges, removed from the site as the work nears its end.

duofaced hardboard hardboard which is smooth on both surfaces.

duopitch roof see saddleback roof.

duplex nail see double headed nail.

duplex stainless steel a chemically resistant, strong and hardwearing stainless steel developed in the 1950s, containing 25% chromium and small percentages of nickel, copper and molybdenum.

durability the property of a material or component to be longlasting, especially in terms of repeated use under force, other changing circumstances, the weathering of the elements, etc.

duramen see heartwood.

durmast oak, sessile oak; [*Quercus petraea*], see oak.

dust dry, dust free; a stage in the drying of paint at which airborne dust will no longer stick to the surface.

dust-pressed tile a tile manufactured by pressing into shape from semi-dry granulated clay then fired.

dustproof relating to a construction or mechanism which is protected by casing, etc. so that the accumulation of dust does not affect its performance.

dust-tight referring to a component or construction which is sealed so as to prevent the entry of dust.

Dutch arch, French arch; a brick or stone arch formed of leaning rectangular-shaped pieces whose intrados is horizontal and nearly straight.

Dutch arch

Dutch bond, 1 staggered Flemish bond (Am); a brickwork bond in which each course consists of alternating headers and stretchers, with headers in alternate header courses laid with a half-header overlap.

Dutch bond

2 see Dutch paving.

Dutch paving paving in different sized square pavers and slabs, laid in a diagonal interlocking pattern, a type of herringbone pattern.

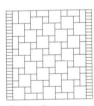

Dutch paving

Dutch white a form of the pigment white lead made by an old Dutch process.

dwarf gallery a low arcade with small arches supported on colonnettes with a passage behind, often a feature in the exterior wall of a tower, cathedral, etc., and bound by string courses.

dwarf wall a low masonry or brick wall.

dwelling a permanent residential unit usually containing sleeping, cooking and sanitary facilities; the collective name for a house, flat, home, etc.

dwelling unit a single fully functioning unit of accommodation in a larger building or complex; a flat or house.

dye-stuff see dye.

dyke rock see hypabyssal rock.

dynamic compaction a method of consolidating granular soils prior to construction by the repeated dropping of a heavy weight over areas of the soil.

dynamic consolidation, ground bashing, heavy tamping; in groundwork, the strengthening of poor soils by repeatedly dropping a heavy ram at intervals to form pits which are then filled with sand and compacted; also known as ground compaction or ground compression.

dynamic load any structural load which includes a moving element or impact such as the loads on a floor caused by the walking of occupants.

dynamic penetration testing in soil investigation, penetration testing in which the testing implement is hammered with percussive force into the soil.

E

eagle capital a Romanesque column carved with four eagle motifs.

ear see sheetmetal cleat.

early stiffening see false set; an outdated term.

earlywood, springwood; the portion of the annual ring of a tree which forms first and has large, low density cells.

earth 1 material excavated from the upper layers of the ground, fine mineral material or topsoil.
2 ground (Am); the mass of conductive earth whose potential is zero, to which cables in a low voltage electrical system are also connected; see earth electrode.

earth colour, earth pigment, natural pigment; any of a number of natural pigments such as ochre, umber and chalk made from coloured mineral earth; see below for list of earth colours and mineral pigments included as separate entries:
*bole; *brown ochre; *brown iron oxide, see burnt sienna; *burnt umber; *Caledonian brown, see burnt sienna; *caput mortuum; *chestnut brown, raw umber; *colcothar; *glauconite, see green earth; *gold ochre; *green earth; *Indian red, see oxide red; *Italian earth, see burnt sienna; *iron yellow, see Mars colour; *jacaranda brown, see burnt umber; *Mars yellow, Mars orange, see Mars colour; *mineral brown, see burnt umber; *natural brown iron oxide, see burnt sienna; *ochre, ocher; *oxide red; *Persian red, see oxide red; *raw sienna, see sienna; *raw umber; *red ochre, see red oxide paint; *red oxide paint; *reddle, see red oxide paint; *Roman ochre, yellow ochre; *ruddle, see red oxide paint; *Sicilian brown, see raw umber; *Siena, see sienna; *sil, yellow ochre; *Spanish brown, see burnt umber; *terra alba; *terra di Siena, see sienna; *terra ombre, see raw umber; *terra rossa, see red oxide paint; *Terra Sienna, see sienna; *terra verde, see green earth; *umber, umbre; *Venetian red, see oxide red; *yellow ochre; *yellow oxide of iron, see Mars colour.

earth electrode an electrical conductor such as a cable or metal pipe buried in the ground, making an earth connection for a building's electrical installation with it.

earthenware a ceramic material which contains a relatively high proportion of limestone and is used for wall tiles and ordinary quality china crockery.

earthing the connection of an electrical supply to the ground, or the result of this.

earth-moving in building construction, any operation such as excavation or backfilling prior to laying foundations which involves movement of earth.

earthquake load structural loads on a building imposed by the sporadic occurrence of an earthquake, taken account of in structural calculations in regions where one is liable to occur.

earth pigment see earth colour.

earth pressure in geotechnical engineering, the pressure exerted by a mass of ground on a retaining wall or similar construction (see active earth pressure) or the exertion required to deform a mass of earth (see passive earth pressure).

earth termination the lowest component in a lightning protection installation, any metal constructions providing a low resistance path to earth for surges of electrical current from lightning strikes.

earthwork 1 any work on a construction site involving digging, moving, filling and levelling earth; sometimes called groundwork.
2 see groundwork.
3 any artificial mound of earth, ditch or embankment used as a defensive fortification, also called a rampart.

earthworks plan a drawing to show the scope of excavations, ground levels, areas of fill for a construction project.

eased arris, eased edge see pencil round.

easement a legal right of use of part of a private area of land, such as a path, drain or waterway running through it, by a party which does not own the land.

eastern hemlock, hemlock spruce (Am); [*Tsuga canadensis*] see hemlock.

eastern larch see larch.

eastern red cedar, aromatic cedar; [*Juniperus virginiana*] a North American softwood with white streaked, red and highly aromatic timber; used for fence posts, shingles and mothproof closet linings.

East Indian rosewood see Indian rosewood.

East Indian satinwood see Ceylon satinwood.

easy-clean hinge, cleaning hinge; a hinge for a side or top hung casement window, whose pin is projected outward from the plane of the leaves, thus making it easier to clean the windows.

eaves the junction of the roof and wall of a building.

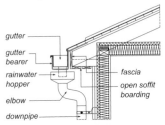

eaves board 1 a timber board laid across rafters at the eaves to raise the lower edge of the bottom row of tiles in a tiled roof to the same angle as the other tiles; same as a doubling piece.
2 see fascia board.

eaves closure piece a component fitted beneath the sheeting at the eaves to block up the corrugations in profiled sheet roofing.

eaves course the lowest course of roof tiles laid as roofing; if a double course is used, the upper of the two.

eaves flashing, pressed metal flashing, sheetmetal flashing; preformed sheetmetal or other sheeting product to convey rainwater away from adjacent eaves construction, or to rainproof the eaves.

eaves gutter a channel at eaves level to collect rainwater from the roof of a building and convey it to a downpipe.

eaves soffit see soffit board.

eaves tile a special roof tile which is shorter than other tiles, used for the lowest or eaves course in roofing.

eaves ventilator a device or component for providing an unobstructed ventilation path into roof space or roof construction at an eaves.

ebonite, vulcanite; a form of fully vulcanized hard rubber.

ebony [*Diospyros spp.*] hardwoods from South and Central America, Africa, South-East Asia and Australia with black, hard, strong and durable timber; its density is such that it does not float in water, and is chiefly used for carving and ornamental cabinetwork; see below for full list of related species included in this work.
African ebony [*Diospyros crassiflora, Diospyros piscatoria*] a tropical African hardwood with especially heavy, dark timber; widely used locally for construction timber and props.
Ceylon ebony [*Diospyros ebenum*] the original ebony, a hardwood from tropical India and Sri Lanka with very heavy and dark brown or black timber; uses included carved ornamention and parts of musical instruments.
Macassar ebony [*Diospyros celebica*] a hardwood from tropical Indonesia whose timber is very heavy and dark brown or black; used for decorative panelling, veneer, cabinetmaking and musical instruments.

eccentric referring to something which is off-centre; eccentric motion occurs when a circle is rotated about a point other than its centre.

echelon parking see angle parking.

echinus 1 in classical architecture, a ring-shaped moulding carved around the lower part of a Doric capital or above the head of a caryatid, making the transition from the abacus to the column shaft; ekhinos in Greek.
2 a decorated moulding beneath the cushion of an Ionic capital.
echinus and astragal see egg and dart.

Eclecticism a name given to a style of European and American architecture from the 1800s, characterized by the use of decorative motifs from a range of different styles.

eclogite a mottled metamorphic rock which contains a large proportion of a red variety of the mineral garnet; used locally for aggregates and decorative slabs.

The image labels: gutter, gutter bearer, rainwater hopper, elbow, downpipe, fascia, open soffit boarding.

e-coating see electro-dip painting.

ecological architecture architecture and construction whose philosophy is based on the use of energy-saving materials, methods and systems and makes use of sustainability and ecological methodology.

economiser a subsidiary water heater for preheating water conveyed to a boiler by passing it over tubes containing hot combustion gases.

edge 1 the extremity, side, boundary or arris of an object, surface or area.
2 the sharp boundary line between two perpendicular planes, as with adjacent sides of a block, etc.; an arris.
3 radial surface; the narrower side of a piece of sawn timber, which, if converted in the traditional manner, has growth rings running approximately radially in relation to the original log from which it was cut.

edge bead see edge strip.

edge beam in structures, a beam which bears the outer edge of a slab, floor or roof construction, from which exterior non-loadbearing walling or cladding is often supported.

edge bedding the laying of a brick or stone in masonrywork with its natural bedding plane vertical and perpendicular to the plane of the wall rather than the usual horizontal; used with stones laid in arches, soldier courses and copings.

edged, squared; a description of sawn timber in which the wane has been trimmed off to produce a rectangular section.

edge form, side form; formwork used for casting the edge of a concrete slab.

edge grain the surface of a piece of sawn timber which has been roughly radial in the original log.
edge grained see quartersawn.

edge-halved tenon joint a mortise and tenon joint in which the tenon is cut to one edge of the end of a member.

edge-halved tenon joint

edge knot a knot at the edge of a piece of timber.

edge panel in concretework, a precast concrete wall panel designed for use at an external corner.

edge roll see bowtell.

edge-rolled column a square column whose arrises are embellished with round mouldings.

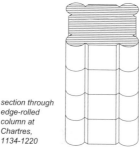

section through edge-rolled column at Chartres, 1134-1220

edge straightness the specification of timber boards, tiles, etc. to be supplied with edges straight and true.

edge strip, edging, edge bead; **1** a length of timber, plastics or metal trim to cover the edge of a panel, component or joint.
2 angle bead, corner bead, L-profile; a milled timber profile which is L-shaped in cross-section; see above.

edging 1 in the primary conversion of timber, the removal of one or two curved edges from a log to provide a flat edge prior to through and through sawing.

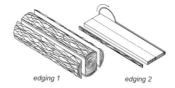

edging 1　　　*edging 2*

2 the removal of wane from sawn boards.
3 see edge strip.
4 in landscape design, a border strip for a carriageway, path, area of planting, etc.

Edison screw cap see screw cap.

efficacy see circuit efficacy.

efflorescence, 1 bloom; an often temporary defect in clay brickwork caused by soluble salts which are leached from new bricks and deposited as white crystals on the surface.
2 a defect in paintwork caused by condensation, resulting in a surface deposition of crystals of soluble salts which have migrated to the surface of the dry paint film.

effluent the liquid component of pretreated or untreated sewage conveyed to a waste water treatment plant.

effusion the passage of water vapour in circumstances when the size of pores in building construction is smaller than the average distance between adjacent water molecules.

effusive rock see volcanic rock.

egg and dart, egg and anchor, egg and arrow, egg and tongue, echinus and astragal; a classical Ionic decorative motif consisting of a series of carved ovular protrusions alternating with sharp dart-shaped infill; see also Ionic cyma.

Greek Ionic cyma moulding with egg and dart, and bead and reel ornament

egg and tongue see egg and dart.

egg-crate ceiling see cell ceiling.

eggshell a general word to describe a grade of glossiness in a dry paint surface — that between gloss and flat; in the USA, the second of four grades of glossiness, slightly more reflective than flat.
eggshell flat, low sheen, silk; the second of five grades of glossiness in a dry paint surface, characterized by little sheen from oblique angles.
eggshell gloss, low gloss, satin; the middle of five grades of glossiness in a dry paint surface, midway between gloss and matt.

Egyptian architecture architecture in ancient Egypt from c. 2850 BC to the Roman conquest in 30 BC; characterized by stone burial tombs, pyramids, massive pylons and geometrical structures, the use of beam and post construction, and elegantly carved and coloured religious and mythical motifs with characteristic two-dimensional depictions; see also full page article on Egypt, see p. 164.

Egyptian capital capitals adorning ancient Egyptian columns, often richly carved with plant motifs such as lotus and papyrus, or with the heads of deities such as Osiris and Hathor.

Egyptian column stone columns in ancient Egyptian architecture, often carved in the form of stems of plants (papyrus, lotus) or deities (Osiris, Hathor).

Egyptian pyramid great burial structures erected by the Pharaohs of Egypt, notably at Giza; usually, but not always, consisting of four sloping triangular sides culminating at an apex.

Egyptian blue, Alexandrian blue, Italian blue, Pompeian blue, Pozzuoli blue; a blue pigment consisting of a mixture of copper silicates used by the ancients in ceramics and fresco painting; one of the earliest artificial pigments.

Egyptian green a green variety of Egyptian blue pigment.

elastic compression see immediate settlement.

elastic curve see deflection curve.

elastic deformation, elastic strain; in structures, the change in dimension of a member under load within a range over which it will resume its original form when the load is released.

elastic glazing compound an elastic sealant used as a glazing compound.

elasticity the ability of a material or structural member to recover its original form after loading forces on it are released.

elastic limit the point at which a material under continuously increasing loading begins to undergo plastic deformation and will not return to its original shape.

elastic modulus see modulus of elasticity.

elastic sealant a flexible sealant which responds to movement between jointed components or materials by stretching or compressing accordingly.

elastic strain see elastic deformation.

elastomer an elastic material containing modified natural or synthetic rubber, which can be stretched and will return to its original form once stresses on it are released.

elastomeric adhesive, synthetic rubber glue; a rubber-like glue manufactured by a chemical process from polymers such as acrylic; used for gluing and sealing a wide range of materials.

elastomeric sealant a sealant applied as liquid or paste which cures to form a flexible solid.

elbow, knee; a piece of curved pipe or pipe fitting to form a sharp acute bend in a pipeline; see bend.

elbow board see window board.

elbow brace see cranked brace.

electrical appliance any device or appliance which is powered by electricity.

electrical cabinet, electrical cupboard; a built-in cupboard or proprietary storage unit containing control equipment and meters serving the electrical installation of a building.

electrical circuit an arrangement of wires and electronic components around which electricity flows to perform a function.

electrical conductance the ability of a given object to transmit or conduct electricity, the inverse of resistance, measured as current divided by voltage; its unit is the siemen.

electrical conductivity the measure of how well a given material will conduct electrical current, the inverse of resistivity, measured as conductance per unit volume.

electrical conduit small diameter plastic or metal piping laid in construction to contain a building's electrical installation wiring; sometimes known as pipe duct.

electrical connector an electric point with holes or protrusions designed to connect two parts of an installation circuit together.

electrical contact that part of an electric circuit or device by which a connection can be made.

electrical contract see electrical works contract.

electrical contractor see electrical works contractor.

electrical cupboard see electrical cabinet.

electrical engineer a qualified consultant who designs the electrical installations for a building, oversees their installation, etc.

electrical engineering a discipline which deals with the technology of electricity and its use for servicing buildings and installations.

electrical installation 1 the circuitry, wiring, control gear and fixed appliances for providing and maintaining an electricity supply within a building.
2 the job of work involved in attaching and connecting the above; also called electrical installation work.

electrical installation contract see electrical works contract.

electrical installation contractor see electrical works contractor.

electrical insulation in electrical installations, non-conductive coatings for components and conductors.

electrical lock see electric lock.

electrically wired hinge see electric hinge.

electrical resistance, resistance; the opposition to flow of electricity in a conductor, measured as amps per volt, whose basic unit is the Ω; a resistor is a device for inhibiting the flow of electricity in a circuit and converting it into heat.

electrical work see electrical installation work.

electrical works contract, electrical installation contract, electrical contract; a contract for the electrical installation work in a building project.

electrical works contractor, electrical installation contractor, electrical contractor; a specialized contractor, reputable firm, etc. which carries out electrical installation work in a building project.

electric boiler a domestic water heater powered by electricity.

electric cable an insulated metal wire or bundle of wires, part of an electrical installation for conveying electricity.

EGYPT

The timespan of Egyptian monumental architecture is the longest in the history of mankind, commencing with the **Old Kingdom** in the 27th century BC, and effectively ending in the **Late Period** in the 6th century BC, although the culture lived on for another 1000 years under foreign rule. Most Egyptian monuments predate the earliest Greek stone temples, erected in the 7th century BC, and much of Egyptian civilization centred around a belief in a material afterlife; the deceased, mummified to preserve their bodies, were required to have with them supplies sufficient for an eternal afterlife, and Egyptians spent much of their assets in preparing for this event.

Above, depictions of the naturalistic deities ANUBIS, the jackal annointer, who embalmed the deceased and led them on their journey to the afterlife, and THOTH, the ibis scribe who took stock of their souls

During the **Old Kingdom**, the **pyramid complex** of Djoser in Saqqara, designed by the architect Imhotep around 2650 BC, saw the first known **pyramid**; although based on earlier **mastaba** tombs, it seems that this 62 metre-high monument and adjoining burial complex with ceremonial **colonnades**, halls and enclosed false temples was the first to be constructed in ashlar masonry, and did not have any predecessor. **Columns** were **engaged** to walls, not freestanding, and they imitate plant stems or bundles of reeds in appearance, foreseeing the freestanding columns and **capitals** of future buldings. The 4th pharoahic dynasty, from around 2500 BC, erected the greatest genuine pyramids in Dashur and Giza, and there are more than 90 royal Egyptian pyramids, some now in ruins, built over the next thousand years.

Right,
1 Hathor fruit capital and composite column from the Kiosk of Nectanebo I (Temple of Isis, Philae) c. 380-343BC
2 closed bud papyrus capital and bundle column from the mortuary temple of Ramses II , Thebes, Egppt, 1179-1213 BC

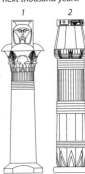

Above, plan and section of the step pyramid complex at Saqqara, 2650 BC, architect Imhotep, scale 1:6500.

The revolutionary feature of bronze-age Egyptian architecture is the use of **hewn stone** as a building material, and **trabeated construction** in burial and cult monuments, at a time when royal palaces, fortresses, walls of cities, temples and domestic buildings were constructed of **mud brick** and **rammed earth** construction, and have long since vanished. In all Egyptian pyramid and temple construction, stone blocks weighing more than 200 tons were transported and installed without iron tools and fixings, or wheels, winches and tackles, using only wedges, levers, ramps and skids.

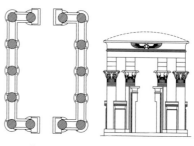

Above, plan and elevation of the Kiosk of Trajan, Philae, 100 AD, late Egyptian architecture from the Roman period, scale 1:500

During the **Middle Kingdom**, from the 21st century BC, pyramids – if erected at all – remain overshadowed by **burial temples**. For his eternal 'apartment' Pharaoh Mentuhotep II had a **rock temple** built at Deir el-Bahari, Thebes in about 2000 BC, locating it opposite the temple of Karnak on the other side of the Nile. Karnak was to grow over the next 2000 years into the most impressive temple complex in the world. Flanking Mentuhotep's rock temple is the terraced **funerary temple** for the pharaoh queen Hatshepsut, which architect Senenmut designed 550 years later, and which is still one of the most important architectural monuments in the world.

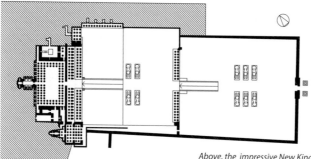

For roughly the last thousand years before Christ, the rulers of Egypt were foreigners – Nubian, Ethiopian and Persian. In the 4th century BC, Egypt was conquered by Alexander the Great and thereon its rulers were the descendants of his general Ptolemy. In 30 BC the emperor Augustus made Egypt a province of the Roman empire. All the Greek and unbaptised Roman emperors allowed themselves to be worshipped as god pharaohs, and during their rule the massive, typically Egyptian **pylon temple** complexes of Edfu, Dendera and Philae were erected. The Egyptians continued worshipping their old gods up until the Christian Late Antiquity in 500 AD.

Above, the impressive New Kingdom mortuary temple of Queen Hapshetsut and Shrine of Anubis, Deir el-Bahari, Thebes; c. 1470 BC, architect Senenmut, scale 1:3000

Below, the great pylon of the Temple of Horus, Edfu; 237-57 BC. Ptolomaic period, scale 1:2000

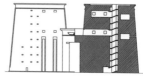

electric charge the amount of electrical energy in a body, component, system, etc.

electric current the rate of flow of electric charge whose SI-unit is the ampere (A).

electric drill see power drill.

electric fan heater see fan heater.

electric heater a heating device which converts electrical energy into useful heat; for electric fan heater, see fan heater, see also electric water heater.
electric heating space and other heating for a building for which the energy source is electricity.

electric hinge, electrically wired hinge; a hinge which allows for the passage of electrical wires from electric fittings and locks in a door leaf to a door frame.

electrician a tradesman or skilled worker who is responsible for the installation and repair of electrical services.

electricity a form of energy resulting from the existence of charged subatomic particles such as the electron and proton.
electricity meter, electric meter; a meter for measuring and recording the flow and consumption of electricity.
electricity supply 1 the supply of electricity by a generation or distribution company to buildings.
2 the provision and continuous distribution of electricity to an area or building.

electric lamp a device for converting electrical energy into useful light.

electric lead a cable with a plug for connecting an electric appliance to an electricity supply.

electric light 1 light produced by electrical means.
2 a light, lamp or luminaire powered by electricity.
electric light fitting a light fitting powered by electricity.

electric lighting artificial lighting powered by electricity.

electric load the power required by an electric appliance.

electric lock, electrical lock; a lock which is fastened or whose bolt is operated by electrical power; see electromagnetic lock, solenoid lock, electromechanical lock.

electric lock control the provision of building security with electric locks operated by timers, remote or access control, etc. to control the latches of doors.

electric meter see electricity meter.

electric point, power point; in electric installations, a point from which electricity can be drawn for appliances.

electric power see electrical energy.

electric water heater, boiler, immersion heater; a domestic water-heating appliance containing heating electrodes or elements powered by electricity.

electro-acoustics the process of converting sound energy into electrical form or electrical energy into sound.

electrochemical coating, electroplating, electrodeposition; the application of thin, corrosion-resistant and protective coatings of oxides, zinc, etc. on metals by electron transfer using electrical current.

electrochemical corrosion, galvanic corrosion; corrosion which takes place when two dissimilar metals are in direct contact in the presence of an electrolyte, setting off an electrochemical reaction which corrodes one of the metals.

electrocoating see electro-dip painting.

electrodeposition see electrochemical coating.

electro-dip painting, cathodic dip painting, anodic dip painting, e-coating; an industrial painting process developed originally for the automotive industry, in which aluminum, zinc, brass, steel, etc. parts to be coated are dipped into acrylic paint and an electrical field applied between them and an electrode, depositing an extremely uniform paint film; also known as electrocoating, electronic coating, electronic painting, electrophoretic coating.

electroless plating see chemical plating.

electrolysis chemical decomposition produced by passing an electric current through a liquid, called an electrolyte, usually a solution of salts; used for the electrolytic deposition of metal coatings and responsible for some forms of corrosion.
electrolytic zinc coating, zinc electroplating; the application of a

protective layer of zinc to steel components by electrolysis.

electromagnetic lock, magnetic lock; an electric lock which holds a door in the closed position by means of a powerful electromagnet; electromagnetism is magnetism caused by, or a product of, electrical current; see also electromechanical lock.

electromechanical lock, motor lock; a versatile electric lock used for security and access controlled applications, whose bolt is operated by a remotely controlled electric motor; see electromagnetic lock.

electromechanical lock control the provision of building security with electromechanical locks operated by timers, remote or access control, etc. to control the action of doors such that, when activated, they may be pushed open, otherwise a key must be used.

electron-beam welding a form of accurate welding making use of a dense stream of electrons converted to heat upon impact, usually carried out in a vacuum.

electronic coating, electronic painting see electro-dip painting.

electronic shielding glass glass designed to reduce the transmission of electromagnetic radiation, used for the protection of computer and other electronically or magnetically sensitive systems.

electro-osmosis in geotechnical engineering, a method of lowering the amount of groundwater in silty soils by passing a current through the ground to induce electrolytic movement, and pumping away excess water which gathers at the cathodes.

electrophoretic coating see electro-dip painting.

electroplating 1 a process whereby a layer of metal is deposited on a surface in a solution of metal salts through electrochemical action; electrochemical coating.
2 see electrolytic zinc coating.

electroslag welding a method of fusion welding for thick steel plates using a consumable electrode immersed in molten slag.

electrostatic deposition, elpo priming; the process of applying liquid or

powder coatings by charging them so that they are attracted to and deposited on the surface to be coated.

electrum 1 see German silver.
2 an alloy of gold and silver used as a decorative coating in ancient times.
3 gold found naturally which contains some silver.

element see building element.

elevation 1 one of the exterior vertical planar surfaces of a building; its facades.

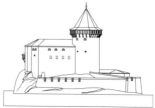

elevation of reconstruction of Raseborg castle, Tammisaari, Finland, 1374–1550; architect M. Schjerfbäck, 1887 (not realized)

2 a drawing or planar projection showing a representation of the outside face or facade of a building, viewed theoretically from infinite and at right angles to the face.
3 the height of a particular point in a building or landscape above sea level.

elevator North American word for lift.

Elizabethan architecture architecture in England during the reign of Elizabeth I (1558—1603), principally evident in secular palaces and country houses, and characterized by the use of Renaissance elements.

elliptical arch an arch composed of half an ellipse; see also five-centred arch.

elm [*Ulmus spp.*] a group of hardwoods found in temperate climates in the northern hemisphere, whose timber is hard and tough and used *Ulmus spp. elm* for interior joinery and furniture; see below.
American elm [*Ulmus americana*] a North American hardwood with strong, tough and flexible pale reddish-brown timber; used for interior joinery, furniture and coffins.

English elm [*Ulmus procera*] a European hardwood with tough, strong, dull brown timber; used for cladding, furniture and panelling.
wych elm [*Ulmus glabra*], a European hardwood, see elm for further information.

elongated aggregate coarse aggregate with longish particles.

elpo priming see electrostatic deposition.

embankment, bank; a sloping earthwork at the side of a river, road, cutting or change of level to restrain water, retain earth pressure, support a road, etc.

embattled see castellated.
embattled moulding see crenellated moulding, indented embattled moulding.

embellishment see decoration.

embrasure the recess of a window in a wall, between the reveals; originally a splayed opening in the parapet of a fortified wall, through which a gun could be fired at a range of angles, whilst giving cover to the marksman; also written as embrazure.

emerald a green variety of the mineral beryl, used as a gemstone.
emerald chromium oxide see viridian.
emerald green, Imperial green, Schweinfurt green; a very poisonous, brilliant green pigment consisting of copper aceto-arsenate now used only in artist's colours.
emeraulde green see viridian.

emergency gas control a valve in a gas-heating system designed to automatically close off supply in the event of an emergency.

emergency handset a remote telephone handset for alerting a central exchange of a building in the event of an emergency; also known as an emergency telephone.

emergency lighting see safety lighting.

emergency stair see escape stair.

emergency telephone see emergency handset.

emery cloth stiff cloth used for sanding by virtue of an abrasive coating of powdered mineral such as emery or hard metal; emery is a naturally occurring mixture of corundum and iron oxide ground.
emery paper see sandpaper.

emissivity the property of a surface to emit heat, measured as the rate at which it does so compared to that of a black body of the same temperature.

Empire style an architectural style in France from 1804 to 1815, coinciding with Napoleon's First French Empire, characterized by the use of neoclassical elements; also Russian neoclassical architecture of the same epoch.

emulsifier, emulsifying agent; a chemical agent used to promote the formation of an emulsion in liquids such as paint.

emulsion the suspension of one liquid in another as a dispersion of tiny droplets.
emulsion adhesive, emulsion glue; a cold setting adhesive consisting of an emulsion of synthetic polymer in a liquid carrier, which dries by evaporation so that the droplets coalesce together.
emulsion cleaning the precleaning of a surface using an organic solvent suspended in water to remove oils and other contaminants prior to painting.
emulsion glue see emulsion adhesive.
emulsion paint, plastic paint; a range of paints in which a dispersion of small drops of polymer such as acrylic are suspended in water; the paint dries by the evaporation of the water.

enamel, vitreous enamel; a hardwearing opaque glassy material fused at high temperatures as a protective coating for ceramics, metal and other hard materials.
enamelling, 1 enameling; (Am) the process of applying an enamel glaze to a ceramic or metal surface.
2 see stove enamelling.
enamel white see blanc fixe.

encased knot, bark-ringed knot; a knot surrounded by bark in the face of a timber board.

encased knot

encasing 1 in building construction, cladding to cover or encase unsightly structure or services, as fireproofing, etc.
2 see casing.

encaustic in ceramics, the use of inlaid clay decoration of a different colour to that of the base.

end abutment, anchorage; that part of a pre-tensioning rig to which the ends of the tendons are anchored during prestressing.

end-bearing pile, point-bearing pile; in foundation construction, a pile which transmits forces to solid ground at its base, through compression.

end cap, blank cap; in plumbing and pipework, a cup-shaped fitting which is threaded internally and attached to a pipe to close off an open end.

end grain grain whose fibres run perpendicular to the surface of a piece of timber, showing as growth rings in a log or timber section cut across its length.
end-grain wood block flooring, wood block flooring; hardwearing timber flooring, used in workshops and laboratories, in which the end grain of inlaid blocks of wood form the floor surface.

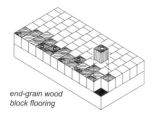

end-grain wood block flooring

end joint a butt joint formed by two timbers or long members fixed end on end.

endoscope an optical device with a rigid or flexible shaft, used for remote surveys of the interior cavities of closed bodies such as pipework, pumps or valves, or for inspecting cavities in building construction for damp problems, etc.; see also fibrescope, videoscope.

endurance limit in the fatigue testing of materials and components, the maximum stress which will not cause damage despite repeated loading and unloading.

energy-saving measures taken in the design of devices, appliances or systems to reduce the amount of energy they consume.

enfilade the vista caused through aligned doorways in a succession of rooms.

enforcement notice in building control, a notice served by a planning authority that requires a contravention of planning control to be remedied before it can be approved.

engaged column, attached column, engaged pier, applied column, inserted column; a column built into, adjacent or physically attached to a wall, either for structural stability or for decorative effect.

edge column

Engelmann spruce [*Picea engelmannii*], see spruce.

engineer a qualified professional who designs structures, technical services or public utilities and supervises their construction and maintenance; see also chartered engineer.

engineered log see milled log.

engineering a branch of science which deals largely with producing designs and structures through the use of technology; see below for list of engineering disciplines included as separate entries: *civil engineering; *construction engineering; *electrical engineering; *fire engineering; *geotechnical engineering; *ground engineering, see geotechnical engineering; *mechanical services engineering; *precision engineering; *structural engineering; *water engineering.

engineering brick a dense, evenly sized, high-quality brick with high crushing strength and low porosity used for foundation and basement walls, civil engineering projects, etc.

engineer's hammer a small cross peen sledgehammer used for striking implements and work in a metalwork shop.

engineer's sledge a large two-handed engineer's hammer, also called a peen sledge.

English ash see ash.

English bond a brickwork bond consisting of alternating courses of headers and stretchers; see variations and illustrations below.

American bond, common bond, Liverpool bond, see English garden-wall bond; St. Andrew's cross bond, see English cross bond.

English cross bond, St Andrew's cross bond; a brickwork bond with alternating courses of headers and stretchers, laid with a half-brick overlap between alternating stretcher courses to produce an interlocking cross pattern in the wall surface.

English garden-wall bond, American bond (Am), common bond (Am), Liverpool bond (Am); a brickwork bond with one course of headers alternating with three or five courses of stretchers.

English elm [*Ulmus procera*], see elm.

English Gothic an architectural style in England from 1150–1550, comprising of three phases: Early English, Decorated and Perpendicular; characterized by use of the pointed arch and medieval decoration.

English oak see oak.

English vermilion genuine vermilion pigment made in England.

English walnut see walnut.

English white see whiting.

engobe, slip; in coloured plasterwork and pottery, a cream-coloured clay dilution applied to cover the original colour of the surface.

engrailed moulding a decorative moulding consisting of a row of arched forms joined at sharp points.

engrailed moulding

enlarged base pile a foundation pile with a widening at its base to spread its loading over a wider area.

enrichment, ornamentation; decoration, pattern or artwork which embellishes a surface or space; see also plasterwork enrichment.

entablature in classical architecture, a thick horizontal band or beam member supported by columns in a portico, consisting typically of three sections: the architrave, frieze and cornice. See illustration on facing page.

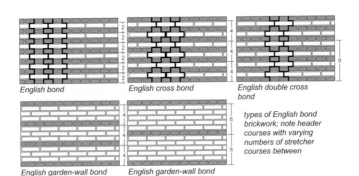

English bond

English cross bond

English double cross bond

English garden-wall bond

English garden-wall bond

types of English bond brickwork; note header courses with varying numbers of stretcher courses between

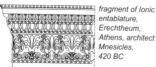

fragment of Ionic entablature, Erechtheum, Athens, architect Mnesicles, 420 BC

Entandrophragma angolense see Gedu nohor.

Entandrophragma candollei see omu; *Entandrophragma cylindricum* see sapele; *Entandrophragma utile* see utile.

entasis Gk.; in classical architecture, the slight vertical convex curvature in the length of a column shaft to give it the appearance of straightness under load.

entersole see mezzanine.

entrained air in concretework, microscopic spherical bubbles of air which have been deliberately introduced into the mix, usually by an air-entraining admixture, to improve workability and frost-resistance.

entrance a door, gate, portal, etc. by which a building or area can be entered; the area or space in its immediate vicinity.

entrance hall, 1 hall; interior circulation space adjacent to the front door of a dwelling or main entrance of a building, giving access to other spaces.
2 the main circulation space at the entrance of a prolific, large or public building, a foyer or lobby.
3 see vestibule.
4 see porch.

entranceway, passageway; an open entrance passage through a building, linking a courtyard with the street.

entrapped air, accidental air; in concretework, small unintentional air pockets in hardened concrete which occur during mixing and remain after compaction.

entrelace see interlace, knotwork.

entresol see mezzanine.

entry-phone system a door control system for flats, etc. by which communication via intercom is possible and the door can be opened by a remote switch; see also door transmitter.

envelope see building envelope.

environmental impact assessment a detailed evaluation of the potential environmental and social effects of a major development project.

EP epoxide resin.

EPDM ethylene propylene diene rubber; used in proprietary dry window and door glazing systems for preformed seals and gaskets.

Ephesian base see Asiatic base.

epistyle see architrave.

epithedes Gk.; the upper decorated moulding or cymatium, along the upper edge of a classical entablature or cornice.

epoxide resin, epoxy resin, EP; a tough, stable thermosetting resin, usually supplied in two mixable component parts, used for in-situ flooring, paints, adhesives and varnishes.

epoxy see epoxide resin.

epoxy adhesive, epoxy glue see epoxy resin adhesive.

epoxy coating a two-component epoxy resin finish for metal structures such as bridges and pipes in contact with water and subject to corrosion.

epoxy ester paint special epoxy paint used for its properties of water, acid or alkali resistance; usually a gloss paint.

epoxy paint a tough, chemical- and solvent-resistant paint containing a two-component epoxy resin binder which, on hardening, forms a thermosetting plastic coating, used for floors and hardwearing interior surfaces.

epoxy powder coating a tough, corrosion- and chemical-resistant polymeric powder coating whose binder is epoxy resin.

epoxy resin adhesive, epoxide resin adhesive, epoxy glue; an adhesive, usually supplied in two components, consisting of a synthetic thermosetting resin which produces a tough, hard chemical bond.

EPS expanded polystyrene.

equilateral arch, pointed equilateral arch, three-pointed arch; a pointed arch-form whose two radii of curvature are identical, and equal to the distance between the imposts.

equilateral arch

equilibrium moisture content in the natural seasoning of timber, the point at which the moisture content of the dried timber is the same as that of its surroundings, and drying ceases.

equipment, apparatus, plant, gear; the functioning collection of machinery or devices in a building services installation for performing a mechanical, electrical or communications task.

erection 1 the construction or assembly of a building frame or similar component, usually prefabricated, on site.
2 see formwork erection.

eremotes weevil [*Eremotes spp.*] a group of species of long-snouted insects which infest dead softwood.

Ernobius mollis see bark borer.

erosion corrosion an accelerated rate of corrosive attack in metal pipework due to the relative motion of a flowing corrosive fluid.

eruptive rock see igneous rock.

escalator, moving staircase, moving stairway; a motorized staircase used as a means of automated vertical circulation, in which treads fixed to a circulating belt move up or down in the plane of the stair.

escallop see scallop.

escape see means of egress.

escape lighting safety lighting required by law to illuminate an escape route and its signs in the event of a building fire or other emergency.
escape route 1 a designated route along which occupants can get to a safe place in the event of a fire or other emergency in a building.
2 see means of egress.
escape stair, fire escape, fire stair, emergency stair; a protected or outdoor stair which is part of an escape route for use in the event of a fire or other emergency in a building.

esconson see scuntion.

escutcheon, scutcheon; **1** escutcheon plate; any metal protective plate for a door or window, often ornate.
2 key plate, scutcheon; a metal plate which surrounds a keyhole and protects a door surface when a key is inserted.

3 an inscribed or decorated plate, especially one in the shape of a shield bearing arms.
4 a warrior's shield, the symbolic base of heraldic designs and coats of arms, much used as a decorative motif in architectural ornament.

escutcheon pin a short pin, usually brass, used for attaching ironmongery to joinery; it may be decorative.

escutcheon pin

escutcheon plate see escutcheon.

espagnolette a fastener for holding double windows or shutters closed, consisting of a long mechanism which runs the whole vertical height of the window, and, when activated, pushes hooks out through the sides of or ends of the casement to engage in holes in an adjacent window frame; see cremone bolt.

essential oil, volatile oil; an oil extracted from plants and seeds, used as a vehicle for some paints, varnishes and other substances, based on alcohol, which evaporates away on drying of the substance.

estate clerk of works a qualified professional employed on a large public property to ensure it is maintained.

estates management see property management.

etching, 1 frosting; the treatment of a glass or metallic surface with an acid or electrochemical means to roughen it or produce a matt finish.
2 a form of printmaking in which acid is used to corrode a design or pattern into the surface of a metal plate, from which prints are taken; the resulting print thus produced.

ethylene propylene diene rubber, EPDM; a tough, durable, weather- and acid-resistant synthetic rubber used for flexible seals and gaskets, cable insulation, hoses and roofing membranes.

Etruscan architecture the architecture of pre-Roman central Italy from c. 700 BC to around the beginning of the first century.

eucalyptus [*Eucalyptus spp.*] a wide-ranging genus of Australian evergreen hardwood trees, some species of which are used in the construction and timber industries; often tough and resistant to termites and insect attack; used in framing, as building timber, in joinery and as wood fibres; see species of eucalyptus below:

blackbutt [*Eucalyptus pilularis*] a southeast Australian hardwood with brown, heavy timber; used in construction for sheathing, flooring and for furniture.

jarrah [*Eucalyptus marginata*] a durable and resistant southern Western Australian hardwood with pink to dark red timber, used for heavy constructional work, flooring, panelling and veneers.

karri [*Eucalyptus diversicolor*] a durable and resistant south-west Western Australian hardwood with reddish-brown timber, used for heavy constructional work.

tallow-wood [*Eucalyptus microcorys*] an eastern Australian hardwood with heavy, yellow-brown timber, used for all kinds of construction work.

eurhythmy, eurythmy; harmonious proportions, regularity and symmetry in architecture and built form.

European ash, English ash; [*Fraxinus excelsior*], see ash.

European beech [*Fagus sylvatica*], see beech.

European birch [*Betula pendula, Betula pubescens*], see birch.

European hop-hornbeam [*Ostrya carpinifolia*] a southern European and southwest Asian hardwood with very heavy timber.

European horse chestnut [*Aesculus hippocastanum*] a European hardwood with soft whitish timber; a large round-topped tree with characteristic pinnate leaves, it is often planted alone in parks and gardens as an ornamental, and to provide shade.

European lime, linden; [*Tilia europaea, Tilia vulgaris*], see lime.

European oak, English oak; [*Quercus robur, Quercus petraea*], see oak.

European plane [*Platanus hybrida, P. acerifolia*], see plane.

European redwood the Scots pine tree, see pine.

European walnut, English walnut, Persian walnut; [*Juglans regia*], see walnut.

evaporation point in the heating of a solid or liquid, the temperature at which it will turn into a vapour.

evaporator, expansion coil; that part of an air-conditioning or refrigeration system in which coolant or refrigerant is vaporized, binding latent heat and thus producing a cooling effect.

even grained, even textured; a description of timber which has a uniform structure throughout the growth ring.

evergreen any species of tree or shrub which maintains its leaves, needles, etc. throughout the year; includes most conifers (softwoods).

excavation 1 any work on a construction site involving digging, blasting and removing material from the ground; the result of this.

2 pit; a hole, trench, etc. dug into the ground on a building site for the location of foundations, drainage services and other subterranean constructions.

excavation depth the depth to which an excavation is to be made; the lowest point in the construction of a building.

excavation shoring temporary construction works to give support for the sides of an excavation.

excavator, digger; a motor vehicle used on a construction site for making excavations, often a tractor, crane or bulldozer; see also dragline excavator.

excepted risk see accepted risk.

ex-contractual claim see extra-contractual claim.

exedra, exhedra; **1** Gk.; a semicircular recess or apse, often with a structural function and containing a raised seat. **2** in Greek and Roman architecture, a recess or room, often in the thickness of a wall, used for relaxation, contemplation and conversation.

exfoliation the natural and chemical scaling of a masonry surface due to the action of the elements; see also brickwork weathering.

ex-gratia application, ex-gratia claim; in contract management, a request by a contractor for payment in circumstances where he has no legal right to reimbursement.

exhaust in heating and ventilation, the removal of used air from a space, gases up a flue, etc. to the outside.

exhaust air in mechanical ventilation and air-conditioning systems, stale air which has been extracted from spaces and released to the outside.

exhaust duct see return-air duct.

exhaust gas waste gases produced by combustion or similar processes.

exhaust outlet an opening through which exhaust air from an air-conditioning system is conveyed to the outside.

exhaust vent in ventilation, a grille or other device to allow the passage of stale air from a room to the outside; see also exhaust outlet.

exhedra see exedra.

exit that portion of a fire escape route which is surrounded by fire-resistant construction and leads to the outside.

exit corridor in fire safety, a passageway surrounded by fire-resistant construction, part of an escape route.

exit door, final exit; in fire safety, an external door leading from an escape route to the outside.

exit lighting in fire safety, an electric lighted sign which draws attention to the presence of a fire exit.

exit stairway in fire safety, a fire-resistant stairway leading to the outdoors.

expanded aggregate, expanded shale aggregate, expanded clay aggregate, light expanded clay aggregate, Leca; a lightweight aggregate used in concrete, blocks, etc., consisting of clay, shale or other minerals, which has been heated so that it expands to form a porous structure; used also as thermal insulation for floors and flat roofs.

expanded aggregate concrete lightweight concrete whose coarse aggregate is expanded clay or shale, or perlite.

expanded clay aggregate see expanded aggregate.

expanded glass see foam glass, cellular glass.

expanded granulated cork in the manufacture of cork products, granulated cork which has been expanded by heating.

expanded metal a metal mesh product manufactured from slitted metal plate or sheet which is stretched to form lozenge-shaped perforations; expanded metal flooring is metal flooring for walkways, service gangways, access platforms, etc. fabricated from heavy-gauge expanded metal sheet in a steel frame; expanded metal lathing is a base for renderwork manufactured from metal sheet which has been perforated; see also ribbed expanded metal lathing, rib lathing.

expanded metal

expanded plastics any lightweight plastics material which has been chemically changed by the introduction of an additive which evolves gas; a cellular plastic.

expanded polystyrene, EPS, foamed polystyrene, bead polystyrene; a lightweight plastics material consisting of a foamed structure of beads, used as boards for insulation, packing, etc.; see also extruded polystyrene.

expanded rubber cellular rubber containing a network of gas bubbles which are closed and not interconnected; used for seals.

expanded shale aggregate see expanded aggregate.

expanding bolt, expansion bolt; a fastener used for anchoring components to concrete or masonry, consisting of a bolt which mechanically expands when its head is turned tight against the sides of the hole in which it is fixed.

expanding cement cement which expands on setting.

expanding vault see conical vault.

expansion bit see expansive bit.

expansion bolt see expanding bolt, wedge anchor.

expansion cistern a cistern for a hot water supply system which accommodates expansion in the heated water.

expansion coil see evaporator.

expansion joint a joint in monolithic concrete, masonry or other forms of mass construction which allows for the expansion of materials during an increase in temperature.

expansion producing admixture in concretework, an admixture included in the mix to produce a controlled expansion.

expansion tank, 1 expansion vessel, sealed expansion vessel; a reservoir to compensate for variations in volume and to contain excess liquid on expansion in a system of closed pipework with pressure and temperature differences.
2 an open vessel which allows for an increase in volume of water on heating in a hot water heating system.

expansive bit, expansion bit; a drill bit with a blade which can be adjusted to a range of diameters for the drilling of different sized holes.

explosive 1 the ability of a substance to produce an explosion; its volatility with respect to this.
2 any highly unstable substance which will cause an explosion when activated or ignited, used in blast excavating.

explosive welding the welding of metal plates by bringing them together at high velocity using a controlled explosion which fuses the pieces together at the join.

exposed aggregate finish a hardwearing, decorative concrete surface finish or thin finish facing for precast units in which coarse aggregate in the concrete is exposed by brushing or spraying with water; concrete finished in this way is known as exposed aggregate concrete.

exposed aggregate plaster a mineral plaster or render with a facing quality aggregate, which is exposed in the surface by washing, scouring or sandblasting, producing a finish not unlike dry dash.

exposed concrete concrete whose exterior surface as cast is its finished state, unfaced in the final structure; special care is usually taken with its components, surface texture, etc.

exposed runner, ceiling linear strip; in a suspended ceiling system, a profiled section which remains visible in the finished ceiling surface.

exposed system a suspended ceiling system whose supporting profiles are visible in the finished ceiling surface, usually of hung inverted T-shaped profiles which support ceiling panels.

extender, 1 filler, inert pigment; a white mineral pigment added to paints to increase volume, reduce cost or to modify the finished paint surface.
2 any of a number of fine inert granular substances added to glues to increase volume and spreading capacity.

extending the diluting of paints, glues, etc. with fillers, usually translucent white pigments for paints, to increase their volume.

extension, 1 lengthening piece; an addition to any member to increase its length.
2 addition; a building or part of a building constructed as an enlargement, annexe, etc. for an existing building.
3 see extension of time.
4 see prolongation.

extension line, leader line; in measured drawing, one of a number of straight lines projected out from the key points on a dimensioned object, at right angles to a dimension line, defining the extremities of dimensions thereon.

extension of time in contract administration, the allowance of extra time for completion due to delays outside a contractor's control.

extent of contract see scope of contract.

exterior 1 space which is outside and open to the elements, usually in close proximity to a building; the surface of a building, component, etc. facing outwards; see outer surface.
2 referring to a product which is used on the outside of a building, exposed to the elements.

exterior boarding see weatherboarding.

exterior cladding see external cladding.

exterior exit a fire exit door leading to the outside at ground level.

exterior facing see external cladding.

exterior luminaire a weatherproof luminaire designed for use outside.

exterior paint, external paint; any paint suitable for use outside and which can withstand moisture and frost.

exterior plywood plywood for external use glued with adhesives which are moisture and frost resistant.

exterior woodstain woodstain used for external applications.

external pertaining to the outside, visible on an outside surface.

external angle trowel, outside corner trowel; a plasterer's hand tool for smoothing external corners in plasterwork with a handled blade of bent steel sheet.

external boarding see weatherboarding.

external cladding, facing; any non-loadbearing material such as boards, tiles, sheetmetal pans, concrete panels, etc. for covering the wall surfaces of a building and forming their external finished surface; see also weatherboarding.

external dimension, overall dimension; in dimensioning and setting out, the dimension of the external outline of a building in plan, measured along one of its main axes.

external envelope see building envelope.

external facing see external cladding.

external glazing glazing in which at least one glass surface is exposed to the outside of a building; the outermost panes of glass in a double-glazed unit.

external leaf, outer leaf; the leaf of a cavity wall which is exposed to the elements.

external paint see exterior paint.

external surface the surface of a wall or building component facing towards the outside; see also outer surface.

external surface resistance value see RSO-value.

external tooth washer a tooth washer with serrations along its outer edge.

external vibrating, form vibrating; a method of compacting in-situ concrete using a vibrator attached to the external surface of formwork; a machine which does this is called an external or form vibrator.

external works the scope of works for a building project which lie outside a building; the landscaping, hardstanding, drainage, fences and walls, etc.; see also landscaping.

extinguishing, fire-fighting; the putting out of fire, especially actions by occupants of a building or a fire brigade to put out or contain hazardous and dangerous fires and limit their damage to a minimum using specialized equipment.

extinguishant see extinguishing medium.

extinguisher see fire extinguisher.

extinguishing foam a fire-extinguishing medium consisting of small bubbles of non-combustible material which smother, wet and cool down a fire.

extinguishing medium, extinguishant; any non-combustible material used to extinguish a fire in a building: water, inert gas, vaporizing liquid, dry powder, foam.

extra see extra work.

extra-contractual claim, ex-contractual claim; in contract administration, a claim for damages not covering matters included under terms of the contract.

extract the removal of stale air from spaces within a building via ducting or vents using a fan, see also mechanical extract.

extract air see return air.

extract duct see return-air duct.

extract fan see smoke extract fan.

extract unit see return-air terminal unit.

extract ventilation, negative pressure ventilation; a system of mechanical ventilation which functions by extraction of the air in spaces, thus causing negative pressure which sucks in fresh air.

extractor see roof extractor.

extractor hood a metal appliance with grease filters and a fan, suspended above a stove or similar appliance to convey steam and other unwanted fumes away into an air duct.

extrados the upper line of the voussoirs in an arch.

extra-low voltage electrical supply of less than 50 V.

extra rapid-hardening Portland cement Portland cement which hardens more quickly than rapid-hardening Portland cement.

extra work, extra, additional work; in contract administration, construction work ordered by the client after the contract has been awarded, not included in the contract and for which the contractor is paid separately.

extrusion a method of forming thermo-plastic, aluminium and ceramic products such as pipes, profiles, bricks, etc. by forcing hot or cold material through a die into the required cross-sectional shape.

extruded cellular sheet see cellular sheet.

extruded chipboard see extruded particleboard.

extruded chipboard

extruded concrete concrete preformed into profiled or cellular slabs by a process of extrusion.

extruded joint, convex joint; a brick-work mortar joint with mortar shaped with a tool to form a longitudinal convex bulge protruding beyond the brickwork plane.

extruded particleboard, extruded chipboard; chipboard manufactured by a process of extrusion, with particles arranged perpendicular to the plane of the board.

extruded polycarbonate sheet see polycarbonate cellular sheet.

extruded polystyrene, XPS, styro-foam, polystyrene foam board; expanded polystyrene whose structure contains small closed bubbles of gas rather than a mass of lightweight beads, used for thermal insulation.

extruded tile a tile formed by a process of extrusion.

extrusion gun see caulking gun.

extrusive rock see volcanic rock.

eyelet see oeillet, roundel.

F

fabric, 1 cloth; a textile material woven or otherwise fused from natural, mineral or synthetic fibres.
2 see welded mesh, fabric reinforcement.
3 the main constructional mass of a building; its frame, structure, walling, roofing and floors.

fabric reference in the design of reinforced concrete, a standard defining the size and spacing of bars used in fabric reinforcement.

fabric reinforcement, mesh reinforcement, wire-mesh reinforcement, welded fabric; reinforcement for concrete slabs or walls of steel bars or wires welded or woven into a preformed mesh or grid.

facade, façade; a grand or imposing elevation or outside face of a building; see elevation.

face 1 the external or visible planar surface of an object such as a door; see door face.
2 the wider side of a piece of sawn timber, whose growth rings run approximately tangentially in relation to the original log from which it was cut.
3 the exposed vertical surface of a brick, block or stone in masonry; see side, stretcher face, header face.
4 the striking surface of a hammer, axe, etc.; also called the striking face.
5 the front cutting surface of a sawtooth.

face bedding the laying of a stone or brick in masonry with its natural bedding plane upright rather than the usual horizontal; used with cladding, voussoirs, etc.

face brick see facing brick.

face coat see final plaster coat.

face contact material in concreting, any material included in the formwork, usually sheeting or boarding in direct contact with the cast concrete, providing its surface with support and shape.

face grain the surface of a piece of sawn timber which has been roughly tangential in the original log.

face joint a mortar joint visible in the surface of brickwork masonry, often finished by pointing.

face knot a knot in the face of a piece of timber.

faceplate see forend.

face ply the outer layer of veneer in plywood, often of a higher grade or quality timber than the inner plies.

face putty see putty fronting.

face side, better face, work face; the face of a piece of sawn timber which is regarded as superior in quality and to which a finish is applied.

face veneer a decorative veneer used for the surfacing of furniture, joinery and interior work.

face width in tongued and grooved or rebated boarding, the width of a board exposed on laying.

facework see fair-faced.

facing 1 the covering of a product, surface or frame with a decorative or protective finish material.
2 a layer of stone, brick, timber boarding, tiling, etc. applied to the face of a wall as cladding; see facing brick, cladding.
3 the surface application of one or a number of layers of protective material to provide a finish; see coating.
see also *ashlar facing; *brick facing, brick veneer; *door facing, see door face; *exterior facing, see external cladding; *natural stone facing; *rubble facing; *timber facing, see timber cladding.

facing brick, face brick (Am) any fairly durable brick used for its appearance in external walls.

facing concrete a layer of concrete placed over cast concrete as a finish.

facing stone high-quality dressed natural stone or similar products used for facing the external wall of a building.

factor of safety, safety factor; in structural engineering, a design coefficient utilized to ensure that structural members are never overloaded; calculated as the maximum stress that an element can withstand divided by the calculated design stress.

factory finish a finish coating applied to a component at manufacturing stage.

factory glazed window a window whose glazing is installed at the manufacturing stage, prior to its arrival on site.

factory-made see prefabricated.

fading a minor defect, the paling of surface colour in a paint, plastic or other coloured finish exposed to sunlight or chemical attack.

Fagus spp. see beech.

faience a tin-glazed or decorated form of terracotta originating in the village of Faenza, Italy.

failure the breakdown in performance of a material or component due to overloading, wear, defect, deterioration or corrosion.

fair-faced 1 referring to brickwork or blockwork of sufficient quality laid in a neat fashion without need for further covering or applied finish; fair-face brickwork is also called facework.
2 describing a fine finish in cast concrete which requires no further treatment, coating, tooling or facing; the method involved is called fair-face casting, the product fairfaced concrete.

fall the angle of a slope, line, road or river to the horizontal, measured as a difference in height per length or as a percentage.

falling-butt hinge a hinge whose cylindrical pin housings or knuckle are cut with a helix so that the door leaf drops slightly when opened and swings open under the force of gravity.

falling-butt hinge

false acacia see robinia.

false arch types of arch such as triangular or corbelled arches which do not utilize masonry voussoirs to provide support over an opening.

false bond in brickwork, the laying of bricks without overlap on successive courses such that there is no structural bonding between adjacent bricks other than that provided by the mortar.

false ceiling, drop ceiling; a ceiling which is lower than the soffit of the floor slab above to make a hidden space for services and ductwork, or to cover up unsightly overhead construction; it may be a suspended ceiling or simply attached to the underside of ceiling joists.

false door, blind door; a decorative element in a building elevation, which mimics a door, but does not function as such.

false front see screen facade.

false hammer beam in traditional timber roof construction, a hammer beam with no hammer post.

false set in concreting, the unusually rapid setting of cement which can be unhardened by further mixing; also referred to as early stiffening, hesitation set, premature stiffening, rubber set.

false tinder fungus [*Phellinus ignarius, Fomes ignarius*] fungal decay found in living hardwoods, especially aspen.

false window, blind window; a decorative element in a building elevation which mimics a window, but does not function as such.

falsework in construction work, any temporary structure for supporting unfinished structures, construction, masonry, etc.

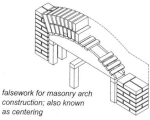
falsework for masonry arch construction; also known as centering

fan 1 blower; a device for propelling a stream of air through an air-conditioning or ventilation system; see flue fan.
2 any mechanical device, often portable, for bringing about air circulation within a space; see ceiling fan.

fan arch a decorative design with a fan motif under an arch, often with a figure at the centre.

fan circulated flue system see fanned draught flue system.

fan coil unit a localized air-conditioning unit in which air is blown into a room over coils to heat or cool it, using an in-built fan; a localized air-conditioning system consisting of a series of such units is called a fan coil system.

fan convector an electric room heater which sucks in cold air, passes it over a heating element and blows it out using a fan.

fan heater, electric fan heater; a portable heater containing a fan which blows out a stream of warm air over a heated coil; see warm-air heater.

fan heating see warm-air heating.

fanlight, transom light, transom window; any window or glazed panel above a door, often fitted in the same frame; originally a fan-shaped window with radiating glazing bars.

fanned draught flue system, fan circulated flue system; a flue system in which draught is provided by a fan.

fan pattern see fantail pattern.

fantail pattern a traditional paving pattern of small stones or cobbles forming radiating areas resembling a fan or the tail feathers of a bird; originating from the area that could be paved by hand by one man without moving from his place; also called peacock tail or fan pattern.

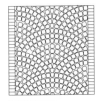

fantail paving

fantail tool see fishtail chisel.

fan tracery, fanwork; Gothic blind tracery found on the surface of fan vaulting.

fan truss a triangular roof truss whose diagonals fan out from a single point, usually the ridge.

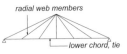

radial web members

lower chord, tie

fan unit, air-handling unit, blower; that part of a mechanical ventilation or air-conditioning system which blows air along ductwork.

fan vault intricate Gothic vaulting from the late 1400s and early 1500s with stone ribs fanning out from each column and a flat diamond-shaped area at the apex of each vaulted bay.

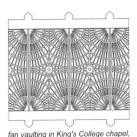

fan vaulting in King's College chapel, Cambridge, 1505–1518

fanwork see fan tracery.

fascia 1 fascia board in roof construction, a horizontal board attached vertically to the ends of joists or rafters at eaves level; other similar boards in construction see.
2 one of a number of undecorated flat horizontal bands in a classical architrave; a fascia moulding or fillet.
fascia board see fascia.
fascia bracket in roofing, a support for fixing the eaves gutter to a fascia board.
fascia gutter in roofing, a gutter fixed to the fascia board of the eaves.
fascia moulding an ornamental moulding consisting of a slightly projecting flat band, wider than a fillet; also simply called a fascia.

fastener any device or construction for fixing or holding a component in place; may be a fixing, fastening or latch, see corrugated fastener, push-pull fastener, toothed plate fastener (nail plate).

fastening see fixing.

fast-pin hinge, tight-pin hinge; a hinge whose pin is fixed in place and cannot be withdrawn, or one whose pin is integral with the lower hinge leaf.

fat concrete see rich concrete.

fatigue the permanent weakening or depreciation of the strength of a material or component, often a moving part, due to its repeated loading and unloading.
fatigue failure the physical failing of a material or component due to fatigue.

fat lime, rich lime; high-quality hydrated lime produced from pure limestone, which in lime putty can be spread evenly and has good properties of plasticity and setting.

fat mix see rich mix.

fatness see plasticity.

fatty oil, fixed oil; neutral organic hydrocarbon liquid compounds from animal or vegetable sources; oils which are viscous at normal temperatures and become fluid on heating, traditionally used in paints, varnishes and other finishes; see also mineral oil, essential oil.

faucet see water tap.

fault see defect.

faux blanc see off-white.

feasibility the analysis of costs, scheduling, funding, planning, ground conditions and resources in the planning stages of a construction project to ascertain its practicability.

feather see spline, see plug and feathers.

featherboarding see featheredged board.

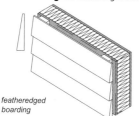

featheredged boarding

feather crotch, feather curl see feather grain.

featheredged board a timber exterior cladding board, wedge-shaped in cross-section, laid horizontally with the thicker edge of one board laid downwards and overlapping the thinner edge of the one below; featheredged boarding or featherboarding is exterior timber wall cladding in such boards; see also rebated featheredged board.

featheredged coping a coping stone or special brick which is wedge-shaped in cross-section to encourage rainwater to run off to one side.

featheredged coping

feather grain, feather curl, feather crotch; a decorative timber figure in the form of a sweeping curve, found in curl veneer.

feather joint, feather-jointed boarding see spline joint.

feed, input; the supply of a liquid to a source, water to a boiler or gas or oil to a burner.
feed pipe see cold feed pipe.
feed-roller marks defective indentations along the edge of sawn timber boards caused by mechanical feed rollers during automated conversion.

feed-roller marks along edge of improperly converted timber board

feeler gauge a simple device with a number of calibrated thin blades used for measuring a narrow gap between two components.

fee scale a scale of standard charges for services of professional consultants, local authorities.

feint, set; the slight bend along the edges of sheetmetal cappings and flashings to provide rigidity and strength.

feldspar, felspar; a common white or reddish, structurally brittle, alumino-silicate mineral; see alkali feldspar, Labrador feldspar (labradorite), potash feldspar.

felt an unwoven fabric of fibres matted together using heat, pressure or mechanical action; see roofing felt and bitumen felt.
felt nail see clout.
felt roofing see bituminous felt roofing, built-up roofing, roll-jointed roofing, lap-jointed roofing.
felt shingles, felt tiles see strip slates.
felt underlay bitumen felt used beneath tiled, slate or sheet roofing; often reinforced felt.

fencing the material or components from which a fence is made; a length of fence; the construction of fences.

fenestration 1 the multitude and arrangement of windows, glazed panels, etc. in a building elevation.
2 the arrangement of glazing bars in a single window or glazed panel.

Ferrari cement an alternative name for sulphate-resistant cement, named after its inventor.

ferric oxide see iron oxide.

ferrite a sintered ceramic material with magnetic properties, consisting of a mixture of iron and other metal oxides.
ferritic stainless steel a form of stainless steel containing 17% chromium.

ferroconcrete see reinforced concrete.

ferrous pertaining to a substance containing iron, especially an alloy or ore with a significant quantity of it; a ferrous metal is any metal whose major constituent is iron.

ferrous ferric oxide, ferrous oxide see iron oxide.

ferrule, sleeve; a metal sleeve which attaches the head to the handle or shaft of a brush, chisel or similar implement; especially a small metal ring fitted around one or both ends of the handle of a chisel or other hand tool to prevent splitting when struck with a mallet.

festoon, garland, swag; a decorative motif consisting of a hanging representation of flowers, foliage, fruit or fabric carved as if suspended between two points.

festoon ornamentation

FFL see finished floor level.

fibre, fiber (Am); a very thin filament or thread of material.

fibreboard, fibre building board; a building board manufactured from wood fibres mixed with water and compressed; see hardboard, MDF (medium density fibreboard), softboard (insulation board).

fibre cement see fibre-reinforced cement.
fibre cement sheet, fibre cement board; a non-toxic, durable, fireproof and resilient sheet material consisting of cement, cellulose and mineral filling; a replacement for asbestos products used for cladding and encasing.
fibre cement slate a rectangular or shaped roofing tile manufactured from Portland cement pressed together with natural or synthetic fibres.

fibre concrete see fibre-reinforced concrete.

fibred plaster see fibrous plaster.

fibreglass a strong lightweight material consisting of fine filaments of glass woven into a mat or matrix and embedded in a plastic or resin.

fibre optics a branch of telecommunications using a carrier beam of light to transmit signals along fine fibres of glass.

fibre-reinforced referring to any composite material which is strengthened by internal reinforcing fibres.
fibre-reinforced cement, fibre cement; a fibre-reinforced composite consisting of fibres in a Portland cement matrix, used for building boards and wall panels; often abbreviated to FRC.
fibre-reinforced composite any composite material which consists of a dispersal of reinforcing fibres in cement, concrete, plastics, etc.; often abbreviated to FRC.
fibre-reinforced concrete, fibre concrete, fibrous concrete; concrete containing fibres of glass, steel, etc. to reduce weight and increase tensile strength; often abbreviated to FRC.
fibre-reinforced plaster see fibrous plaster.
fibre-reinforced plastic, reinforced plastic; a light composite material consisting of reinforcing fibres of glass, steel or plastics in a synthetic resin matrix, usually polyester; used for structural applications, car bodies, mouldings, sheets, roofing slates and drainage fittings; often abbreviated to FRP.
fibre-reinforced render special render with added polymer fibres, which mesh together in the applied product to form a flexible and impact-resistant surface.
fibre reinforcement natural, artificial or glass fibres used as reinforcement in composite materials such as concrete, plaster, resins, plastics, etc.

fibre saturation point, saturation point; in the seasoning of timber, the point at which all free moisture has evaporated, leaving only the water in the cell walls of the wood.

fibrescope an endoscope with a long flexible tube, illuminated by fibre-optics.

fibrous concrete see fibre-reinforced concrete.

fibrous plaster, fibred plaster; gypsum plaster used for casting ornaments and mouldings, often strengthened with glass fibres, lathing or textile; fibrous plastering is the process of working in fibrous plaster.

fibrous plasterwork, ornamental plasterwork; any finishing work done in fibrous plaster.

fiddleback grain, fiddleback mottle; a decorative grain pattern found in certain hardwoods with curly figure; traditionally used for the backs of violins.

field drain, agricultural drain, filter drain, French drain, land drain; a drain for drying out damp or saturated ground consisting of a backfilled trench containing a length of perforated pipe; in building construction most often referred to as a land drain.

field drainage see land drainage.

field surveying see land surveying.

figure the pattern caused by the natural grain of wood, evident in a timber surface.

figured of ornament, decorated with depictions of animals and people, usually in carved form.

figured capital, historiated capital; a Romanesque capital decorated with figures of animals, birds, humans, etc. with or without foliage, often symbolic or part of a narrative sequence.

Romanesque figured capital at the Benedictine monastery in Alpirsbach, Germany, 1125

figured column any decorative column carved or shaped in the form of a human figure; a caryatid, canephora, atlas, etc.

filament a thin wire of tungsten inside an incandescent lamp, which glows white hot when electricity is passed through it, giving off light.

file 1 a hand tool whose steel blade is roughened with a series of serrations, used for sharpening cutting tools and shaping metal.
2 in computing, a set of related data, a document, etc. stored, used or edited as a discrete entity.

filigree beam a composite beam whose steel formwork shell is filled with concrete and acts as tension reinforcement once the concrete has set.

fill 1 in sitework, earth or other material, such as hardcore, used to raise or level the existing ground or to make an embankment; earthmoving and similar operations for this.
2 see backfill.
3 material used to fill a void in construction, as packing, etc.

filler 1 a substance added to plastics, paints and some adhesives to improve their properties and reduce cost by bulking; also known as an extender.
2 surface filler; in finishing walls and ceilings, a paste applied over a surface to fill in any irregularities and, when hard, provide a smooth surface for painting; also called stopping or spackling.
3 a fine material such as fine aggregate used to stiffen a bituminous binder.
see also corrugation filler, jamb filler, joint filler, lintel filler, pore filler.

fillerized cement, filler cement, composite cement; ordinary Portland cement to which an inert material or filler of finely ground limestone has been added to increase its volume.

fillet, 1 list; a thin straight raised or sunk horizontal decorative moulding; see raised fillet, square fillet, sunk fillet.

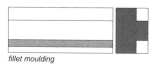

fillet moulding

2 see moulding.
3 see fascia, fascia moulding.
4 a thin strip of material, see angle fillet, mortar fillet, tile fillet.

fillet chisel, spindle; a narrow-bladed masonry chisel used for carving details and ornament in stonework.

filleted column, filleted pier; a Gothic column carved in such a way as to appear to be formed from small round columns joined together.

fillet raised moulding a decorative moulding consisting of a small rectangular projection in cross-section.

fillet saw a fine saw for cutting fillets and other details in stonework, or one for cutting mouldings in joinery.

fillet sunk moulding a decorative moulding consisting of a groove, rectangular in cross-section.

fillet weld a V-shaped butt weld in which abutting metal components have been chamfered; stronger than a normal butt weld.

fillister head screw a screw with a raised cylindrical head whose upper surface is convex.

film 1 the thin layer formed from one or a number of coats of hardened paint or varnish.
2 any thin flexible plastic sheet product, often transparent and used for packing.
3 a thin sheet of plastic with a light-sensitive coating, on which photographic and cinematic images are reproduced.

film adhesive see film glue.

film-faced plywood plywood which has been faced with resin impregnated film; has good resistance to moisture and is thus used for shuttering.

film glue solid phenol formaldehyde resin used in thin layers for gluing expensive veneers to a backing by hot pressing.

filter 1 a cleaning or purifying apparatus for the separation of unwanted particles of solid material, gas, liquid, radiation or sound from a medium.
2 colour filter, light filter; a piece of coloured translucent material placed in front of a light source to change its colour and composition.
3 a device for eliminating electromagnetic output of selected wavelengths.
4 see strainer.

filter cloth see filter fabric.

filter drain see field drain.

filter fabric strong fibrous sheet used in concrete pavement construction, paving, planted areas, etc. to prevent layers of construction mixing with one another, to provide stability and to prevent the penetration of roots, while allowing drainage through; also called filter cloth.

filter mat a sheeting component included as a layer in landscaping, green roofs, etc. to prevent fine material being drained away, whilst allowing for water to pass through; see also filter fabric.

filtration the cleansing of a liquid or gas of impurities by passing it through a filter or other screening device.

fin see flash, flash line.

final account in contract management, a document stating the cost of all work undertaken and the total payment to be paid, as accepted by all parties involved.

final certificate in contract management, a document that authorizes payment to the contractor of the final account, an approval that the terms of the contract have been met.

final circuit an electric circuit between an electric point and an appliance.

final coat, finish coat, finishing coat; in painting and plastering, the uppermost coat applied to a surface as a finish.

final exit see exit door.

final inspection a building inspection held after all work by the contractor has been completed to a reasonable degree, prior to handover and concurrent with official approval; see also period of final inspection.

final plaster coat in plastering, any coat of plaster laid as a finished surface; also called a face coat, finishing coat, setting coat or skimming coat.

final set the later period of setting of cement or concrete, as measured by standard tests.

fine see penalty.

fine aggregate aggregate consisting largely of particles with a size range of $75 \, \mu m - 5 \, mm$
fine-aggregate asphalt rolled asphalt road surfacing with a high proportion of sand or other fine aggregate.

fine grained 1 referring to very cohesive types of clay or silty soil which contain little or no coarse materials larger than 0.02 mm and are highly compressible and impermeable.
2 see close grained.

fine gravel see gravel.

fine grown see close grained.

fine mortar mortar whose aggregate is coarse sand; see coarse stuff; see also finish stuff.

fineness modulus in aggregate grading, a measure of the fineness of an aggregate obtained by passing a sample through a standard set of sieves and dividing the sum of percentages of each size by 100.

fines in soil classification, material whose particles will pass through a 0.06 mm sieve.

fine sand see sand.

fine silt see silt.

fine stuff see finish plaster.

finger joint a timber lengthening joint formed by cutting or machining deep zig-zags into the ends of two timbers to be joined, then gluing them together; used especially in laminated timber products and factory-made assemblies; see box corner joint, combed joint.

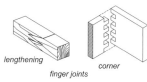

lengthening   *corner*
          finger joints

finger-jointed plywood plywood which has been increased in dimension using finger joints.

finger plate see push plate.

finial florid Gothic decoration for the top of a gable, spire or pinnacle.

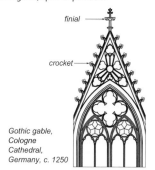

finial ———

crocket ———

Gothic gable, Cologne Cathedral, Germany, c. 1250

finish the final surface treatment or covering for an object, surface or component produced by the application of a coating or facing, by machining, or by a mechanical or chemical processes; see coating, surface treatment, finishing, stonework finish.

finish carpentry see joinery.

finish coat see final coat.

finished floor level, FFL; the floor level of flooring, screeds, etc. above the structural floor, usually excluding thin floor coverings, from which all vertical measurements and levels are taken in a room or storey.

finished size the size of a piece of machined timber, subject to machining tolerances.

finishing, finish; a final treatment, layer of material or coating for a surface or component; the act of producing a finish.

finishing coat see final coat, final plaster coat.

finishing nail see lost-head nail.

finishings the final coverings, facings, treatments or coatings for surfaces and components; see paint finishing.

finishing trowel, smoothing trowel; a plasterer's trowel used for the application and smoothing of a final coat of plaster.

finish plaster 1 fine grade plaster used as a coating for undercoat plaster, providing a finish.

2 fine stuff hard lightweight plaster used as a finish.

finish washer see screw cup.

Fink truss, Belgian truss, French truss; a diagonally braced pitched roof truss without vertical strutting, whose diagonals form a W-shaped pattern; developed by the German engineer Albert Fink in America in the 1800s.

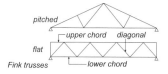

pitched

upper chord   diagonal

flat

Fink trusses   *lower chord*

fir [*Abies spp.*] a group of common softwoods from the northern hemisphere with pale, lightweight, straight-grained timber which is prone to fungal attack; used in construction work, packaging and for pulp; firs are often planted as single ornamentals in parks and gardens on account of their rich evergreen spruce-like foliage; see also Douglas fir and detailed list below:

balsam fir [Abies balsamea] a Canadian softwood whose cream-coloured timber is used for construction work and packaging, often planted as an ornamental.

Siberian fir [Abies sibirica] a Siberian softwood used principally for pulp and fibres, and planted in parks as an ornamental tree.

silver fir [Abies alba] the largest European softwood with light brown timber; used in all kinds of construction work and joinery.

white fir [Abies concolor] a North American softwood used for sawn boards, widely planted as an ornamental on account of its pale grey-green foliage and large needles.

fire 1 any heater or other appliance in which material is burned and has a live flame.
2 the destructive burning of a building or part of a building.

fire alarm a device which emits a sound on detection of the presence or outbreak of fire in a building to draw attention to a possible fire hazard; also the sound made by this device.

fire alarm indicator an electronic control panel which indicates the location of fire alarms which have been triggered by a fire.

fire alarm system a fire safety system which will sound an alarm or alarms in the presence of a building fire, triggered by a fire-detection system.

fire area in planning for fire safety, a discrete area, rooms or spaces, etc. of a building bounded by fire-resistant construction to prevent the spread of fire; the area within a fire compartment.

fire assembly any assembly of materials, construction or component which has fire-resistant properties; usually refers to a rated fire door, window or hatch with fittings.

fireback a shaped unit, laid masonry or refractory brick, etc. forming the rear and side walls of a fireplace.

fire barrier in fire protection, an area of non-combustible sheet material attached to components, across cavities within construction, etc. to inhibit the spread of fire.

fire behaviour see fire performance.

fire bend a bend in metal pipework made by softening the pipe with a blow-torch and bending; see also pulled bend.

fire block a fire barrier for preventing the spread of fire through or within timber elements such as walls or floors.

fire booster an automatic water pump used during fire-fighting to increase the pressure of water in a main for drenching water and sprinkler installations.

firebox, combustion chamber; the closed compartment of a solid fuel appliance, gas stove, burner or fireplace in which combustion takes place.
firebox door a small hinged front-opening hatch to close off the firebox of a fireplace, stove, etc.

fire break construction in a building to inhibit the spread of fire from one compartment to another.
2 open space left between rows of housing or adjacent buildings to curtail the spread of fire in a built-up area.
3 fire corridor; a linear zone of agricultural or forest land cleared to soil level of trees, plants, crops, etc. to prevent the spread of fire.
firebreak door see fire door.
firebreak floor see fire floor.
firebreak wall see fire wall.

firebrick, refractory brick; a brick of special composition capable of withstanding high temperatures without melting or fusion, used for masonry chimneys, flue linings, kilns and fireboxes.

fire cell see fire compartment.

fire certificate in planning for fire, a document, issued by the fire brigade following an inspection, specifying means of escape, alarms, extinguishers, signage and other fire precautions.

fireclay a simple ceramic material with high kaolin content used for firebricks.

fire compartment, fire cell; a subdivision of a building into an isolated unit surrounded by fire walls and floors to inhibit the spread of fire.
fire compartmentation in planning for fire safety, the division of a building or part of a building into discrete fire compartments.

fire containment 1 measures in building design to restrict the spread of fire by

inclusion of fire compartments, non-combustible construction, extinguishing systems and procedures, and smoke venting routes.
2 the restriction of smoke flow and spread of flame by firefighters during a hazardous building fire.

fire corridor see fire break.

fire curtain, safety curtain; in theatre design, a fireproof curtain which can be lowered to isolate the stage area from the main body of the auditorium in the event of a fire.

fire damper, fire shutter; a shut-off valve in an air-handling system for preventing the flow of smoke and combustion gases through a duct.

fired brick, burnt brick; any clay brick which has been fired in a kiln; cf. mud brick.

fire detector in planning for fire safety, an electric sensor which reacts to the presence of excess heat, smoke and flame; it may trigger alarms, sprinklers, alert the fire brigade and set off other methods of inhibiting the spread of fire.
fire-detection system a system of fire safety sensors which react to the presence of heat, smoke or flame and set off fire prevention measures.

fire door, firebreak door; a specially designed and approved door assembly rated to contain the spread of a building fire for a specified time.

fire escape see escape stair.

fire-exit bolt see panic bolt.

fire exit sign any sign in a building designed to indicate the location of fire escape routes and emergency exits.

---

fire extinguishing system, fire suppression system; an integrated system of piped extinguishant such as a non-combustible liquid, gas, vapour or foam released in the event of a fire; types included as separate entries are listed below:
*automatic fire extinguisher; *carbon dioxide fire extinguisher; *dry-powder extinguisher; *foam extinguisher; *halon fire-extinguishing system; *sprinkler system.*
fire extinguisher a portable apparatus for putting out a small fire.

---

fire-fighting equipment fire hoses, blankets, portable extinguishers, fixed systems and other apparatus used in the event of a fire breaking out.

fire floor, firebreak floor, party floor; the upper or lower protective construction of a fire compartment, a floor or ceiling slab which forms its fireproof boundary.

firefront, fret; the front of an open fire.

fire glass see fire-resisting glass.

fire grading see fire-resistance grading.

fire hazard any combustible material, assembly or situation which poses a threat to fire safety in a building and increases the risk of spread of fire.

fire hose a hose of approved and tested material, construction and dimension used in fire-fighting.
fire-hose reel, hose reel; a fire hose coiled and placed in a designated cabinet at a fire point with a connection to a main, used by occupants of the building in the event of a fire.

fire hydrant an outlet from a fire main from which a supply of extinguishant water can be used for fire-fighting in the event of a building fire.

fire inspection an official inspection of a building by a fire-prevention officer prior to the issue of a fire certificate.

fire insulation see fireproofing, firespraying.

fire load a measure of the combustibility of the contents of a space in a building, given as the total energy in megajoules given out when its entire contents burn, used to calculate fire severity.
fire-load density a measure of the potential relative severity of fire within a space, given as fire load per unit floor area, measured in units of MJ/m^2.
fire loading see fire load.

fire main in fire-fighting, a mains water pipe used by firemen to extinguish a fire.

fire officer, fire-prevention officer; a person, often in the employ of the local fire brigade, who inspects designs, constructions and site procedures to ensure they comply with safety standards and regulations with regard to fire.

fire performance, fire behaviour; a description of the combustibility, smoke release, toxicity, etc. of a particular material or component with regard to fire and fire safety.

fire-performance plasterboard plasterboard graded according to its properties of fire-resistance.

fireplace a domestic masonry construction, recess or proprietary metal appliance, usually open or with glazed doors at the front and fitted to a flue, in which solid fuel is burnt to provide heating and atmosphere to a room.

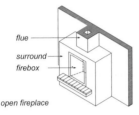

flue

surround
firebox

open fireplace

fire point a clearly marked designated place within a building where fire-extinguishing equipment is located for use in the event of a fire.

fire prevention measures taken in a building to reduce the risk of outbreak of fire.

fire-prevention officer see fire officer.

fireproof, fire-resistant; a general term for a material or component with good fire-resistance; in North America a material or component which can safely withstand the burning of the whole building.

fireproof brick see firebrick, flue block.

fireproof lining, refractory lining; non-combustible material added to a surface as fireproofing.

fireproof mortar see refractory mortar.

fireproof plaster see fire-retardant plaster.

fireproofing, fire protection; material or treatment added to construction to increase its resistance to fire; see also firespraying.

fireproofing paint see intumescent paint.

fire protection see fireproofing, active fire protection, passive fire protection.

fire pump a water pump which maintains pressure in sprinkler systems in the event of a fire.

fire rating see fire-resistance grading.

fire reserve water for use in fire-fighting stored in tanks in the basements and roof spaces of buildings.

fire resistance the relative non-combustibility of a material or component which restricts the spread of fire or maintains its structural properties in the event of a fire.

fire-resistance grading, fire grading, fire rating, fire-resistance rating; a system of grading materials and components according to the results of laboratory tests carried out to ascertain their fire-resisting properties.

fire-resistance rating see fire-resistance grading.

fire resistant see fireproof.

fire-resistant gasket in glazing, a strip of fire-resistant material fixed around the external edges of a pane of glass to provide a seal.

fire-resisting glass, fire glass, fire-resistant glass; glass of special construction or constituency, used where a certain degree of fire protection is required; see also laminated intumescent glass.

fire retardant a chemical treatment applied to materials and components, fabrics, etc. designed to inhibit their combustion; especially one applied by impregnation as protection for timber.

fire retardant board a grade of chipboard or other wood-based panel product whose surface is faced or treated with fire retardant material; suitable for use as a lining and cladding in situations such as fire escapes where the spread of fire is to be avoided.

fire retardant plaster types of plaster used to increase the level of fire protection; see also perlite plaster, vermiculite plaster; sometimes called fireproof plaster.

fire safety measures taken to reduce the risk of fire and to inhibit damage to the occupants, property and construction of a building in the event of a fire.

fire safety sign any sign in a building designed to provide information about the location of fire escape routes, emergency exits, fire-fighting equipment, smoke vents, etc.; see also fire exit sign.

fire separation fire-resistant construction such as a bounding wall, floor or roof with the appropriate properties to contain a fire within a compartment for a specified amount of time.

fire severity a measure of the combustibility of the contents and surface finishes in a fire compartment used in design for fire safety.

fire shutter 1 a large sliding, folding or rolling door to prevent the spread of fire in a building, often operated automatically.
2 see fire damper.

firespraying, sprayed mineral insulation; the sprayed application of mineral-based covering to improve the fire resistance and insulating properties of a structure or component.

fire stair see escape stair.

fire stop, fire stopping; a thin strip of non-combustible material inserted into joints to prevent the spread of fire through gaps such as joints between components, and where pipes and cables pass through construction.
fire stop sleeve, pipe closer; a pipe fitting used as fire protection for plastic pipe crossing from one fire compartment to another; if this melts during a building fire it expands to fill the gap, preventing the spread of fire.
fire stopping see fire stop.

fire suppression system see fire extinguishing system.

fire test the controlled burning of a material, construction or component under laboratory conditions to ascertain its fire rating.

fire valve a valve to automatically close off the supply of gas or oil in the event of a building fire.

fire vent, smoke outlet, smoke vent; an openable or fusible vent, window or hatch opened automatically, manually or by melting in the event of a building fire to allow the release of combustion fumes and smoke to the outside.

fire venting, smoke venting; in fire control, the expelling of combustion gases and smoke from a building through specially designed ducts and hatches.
fire venting installation 1 measures such as shafts, mechanical apparatus, vents, etc. within a building to facilitate the extraction of smoke in the event of a fire.
2 **mechanical smoke extraction system;** mechanical plant for removing smoke in the event of a fire.

fire wall, compartment wall, fire-break wall, division wall; 1 a wall or partition in a building designed to prevent the spread of fire between compartments.
2 a continuous fire-rated wall running from foundation to roof level to provide subdivision of a building or fire separation from adjoining buildings.
3 see separating wall.

fire window a window assembly which has a specified fire resistance and approved construction for its use.

firmer chisel a sturdy chisel whose blade is rectangular in section, used with a mallet for general rough work, removing of wood and initial smoothing.

firmer gouge a gouge whose blade is sharpened on its convex edge, used for cutting shallow depressions in wood; see also scribing gouge.

firm price contract a form of building contract in which the price cannot be amended regardless of changes in economic conditions.

firring, furring; thin strips or pieces of timber or other material laid or fixed to a structure or frame to raise the level of a surface cladding or to make it even, to provide falls, etc.; a firring piece, or furring piece, is a piece of timber nailed to the upper surface of roof joists to provide a slope for a flat roof.

first coat see first plaster undercoat.

first floor the storey above the ground floor in the UK; in continental Europe and USA this is the second floor.

first layer felt see base sheet.

first moment of area see static moment.

first plaster undercoat 1 in plastering, the first coat of plaster, applied directly to lathing or onto another background; see two coat, three coat plastering; also called a floating coat, pricking-up coat, render coat, scratch coat, straightening coat.
2 see base coat.

fish-bellied a description of a component whose underside is convex, bulging downwards in the middle.

fish-bellied beam a concrete or steel beam whose underside is curved downwards towards the middle, forming a U-shape.

fish-bellied beam

fish-bellied truss a trussed beam in which the upper chord is flat and the lower chord is curved, forming a braced U-shape.

fish-bellied truss

fish glue, isinglass; glue made by boiling up the swim bladders and skins of fish.

fish joint see spliced joint.

fish plate, fish piece, splice plate; a plate fixed to either side of a lengthening joint to fix two members rigidly together.
fish plate joint see spliced joint.

fishtail chisel, fishtail tool, fantail tool; a chisel with a wedge-shaped blade splayed outwards towards its cutting edge.

fishtail wall tie, fishtail tie; a wall tie formed from metal strip with split and forked ends to provide a better bond with masonry.

fishtail wall tie

fish tenon joint see free tenon joint.

fitment, fitting; a fixed component such as a hook, door handle, etc. that is not part of the building fabric.

fitted a description of a fixed furnishing which is made to measure for a particular space or situation.
fitted carpet, wall-to-wall carpet; a carpet fixed in place at its extremities and extending over the whole floor area of a space.

fitted cupboard a cupboard unit such as a kitchen unit fitted permanently in a space against a wall.

fitter a skilled workman who installs and assembles system products such as suspended ceilings, fixed furnishings and technical installations on a building site.

fitting 1 a piece of hardware for a door, window or hatch.
2 any fixed accessory such as a kitchen cupboard or basin which can be removed without damage to the building fabric.
3 the fastening in place of fixed furnishings, technical appliances and installations.
4 see installation.
5 see mounting.
6 see fitment.
see also: door fittings, door furniture; light fitting, luminaire; pipe fitting; water fitting.

fitting-out the installation of fixed furnishings, fitted cupboards and joinery, finishings and carpets, etc. for a building project.

fittings see fixed furnishings, rainwater goods, door fittings (see door furniture).

five-centred arch an arch whose intrados is constructed from five centres of curvature, an approximation of a true elliptical arch.

five-centred arch

five pound maul a heavy one-handed hammer with a steel head; used for striking chisels and other implements.

fixed furnishings, fittings; any built-in furnishings for a project, included in the contract documents.

fixed light, deadlight, fixed sash; a glazed area of window which is not openable, or a window whose glass is fixed directly to the frame.

fixed luminaire a luminaire fixed permanently to a wall, floor or other surface.

fixed oil see fatty oil.

fixed price contract a contract in which the contract sum is given in a tender or is based on a schedule of rates; this sum may be exceptionally amended due to a change in economic conditions.

fixed sash see fixed light.

fixing, 1 fastening; the connecting of two components together or the attachment of one to another.
2 any hardware such as nails, screws, bolts, etc. used to attach components in place or connect them together; also called a fastener.
3 the laying of tiles, fine stone, ashlar, etc. into mortar with fine joints; see bedding.
4 see pipe fixing.
5 see holdfast.

fixing block see nog.

fixing mortar 1 fine mortar, lime putty, stone dust or cement used for bedding stonework with fine joints.
2 see tiling mortar.

fixture any fitting, furnishing, appliance or installation built in or firmly attached to the fabric of a building; for light fixture, see luminaire.

flag see slab, natural stone paver, concrete paving slab.

flagstone a heavy paving stone, see natural stone paver.

flakeboard
particleboard manufactured from flat chips or flakes of wood bonded together with resin and pressed into sheets.

flakeboard

flake white, Flemish white, French white; white lead pigment in flake form.

flaking 1 a defect in a paint, plaster or other finish involving the separation in flakes of a coat from its underlying surface.
2 wattle, withe braiding; in thatched roofing and similar traditional construction, a layer of woven reed or thin twigs of hazel or willow laid as a base for thatch, daub, etc.
3 see brickwork weathering.

flaky aggregate coarse aggregate with flattish particles.

flaky and elongated aggregate coarse aggregate whose particles are long and flat.

Flamboyant style the later phase of French Gothic architecture from the late 1400s, characterized by flowing and flame-like tracery.
flamboyant style tracery tracery of the Flamboyant style; see flowing tracery.

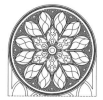
Flamboyant style rose window at Beauvais Cathedral, France, 1225–1272

flame cutting the cutting of metals by local melting using an intense flame of gas such as oxy-acetylene.

flame detector, radiation detector; a fire detector which reacts to the presence of flickering ultraviolet or infra-red light, present in many types of flame.

flamed finish, thermal finish; a rough-textured non-slip stone surface treatment produced by using high intensity flamers to crack surface crystals in the stone; often used for granite flooring and facing.

flame-retardant paint see intumescent paint.

flame-spread rating a fire safety classification which determines the surface spread of flame across an interior finish.

flammable a description of a material which will readily burn with a flame; also used for volatile liquids such as liquid fuels and thinners, and materials such as plastics and fabrics, which will burn with ease; flammability is the measure of this.

flange any flat protruding part of a component, such as the flattened end which encircles a pipe as a fixing or the upper and lower flat protrusions in an I-beam.

flanged beam a beam whose upper or compression surface is increased by widening; in a steel beam this may be the upper or lower flange, in concrete it may be a floor slab.

flanged beam

flange joint a pipework joint made by bolting the flanges at the ends of consecutive pipes together.

flanking path in acoustics, an unwelcome route for the transmission of sound from one space to another via voids, cavities, ducting, pipework, etc.

flanking transmission, flanking sound; in acoustics, the transmission of sound from one space to another through openings in partitions, usually ductwork or piping.

flanking window, wing light; a full-length window beside an external door.

flap hinge see strap hinge.

flared brick a brick which, after firing, is darker at one end, and is used as a header in patterned brickwork; similar decorative bricks with a darker or discoloured surface.

flash see flash line.

flash butt welding see flash welding.

flashing 1 a strip of impervious sheet material or preformed profile laid in construction to protect a joint from the passage of rainwater; types included as separate entries are listed below:
*abutment flashing; *apron flashing; *chimney flashing; *cover flashing; *eaves flashing; *head flashing; *pipe flashing; *pressed metal flashing; *raking flashing; *sheetmetal flashing; *stepped flashing; *upstand flashing.
2 a defect in painting consisting of glossier patches in the paintwork caused by paint drying whilst the surface is being painted.

flash line, fin, mould mark; a visible raised line evident in the surface of casted products such as fibrous plaster, concrete or plastics, caused by the seepage of cast material into joints between adjacent parts of a mould; similar linear protrusions occurring in a finished concrete surface due to slightly open joints in adjacent formwork boards.

flash welding, flash butt welding, resistance flash welding; a method of resistance welding rails end to end by passing a large current between to form

an arc and thus melt the ends before pressing together.

flat 1 a rectangular metal bar formed by rolling, whose uniform cross-sectional is wider than thick, but whose thickness exceeds one tenth of its width; uses in construction include braces, brackets, frames, base plates, ornamental work, etc.
2 matt, matte; the lowest of five grades of glossiness in a dry paint surface, characterized by little or no sheen, even from oblique angles.
3 apartment; a single (or double) storey dwelling within a multistorey residential building.

flat arch, jack arch, straight arch; a masonry arch formed of wedge-shaped pieces, whose intrados is horizontal and nearly straight.

flat arch

flat bar see flat.

flat brush 1 any paintbrush with bristles held in a flattened ferrule, forming a rectangular bristle-head; the most basic form of paintbrush, available in a range of widths and bristle-types; also called a flat wall brush, or flat varnish brush, depending on use.
2 see distemper brush.

flat cutting, flatting, ripping, ripsawing; the resawing of converted timber into planks or timber sections along the grain.

flat cut veneer a decorative veneer produced by the through slicing of a log or flitch; also variously known as flat sliced, plain cut, straight cut.

flat cut veneer

flat drawn glass see clear sheet glass.

flat glass any glass manufactured in flat sheets.

flat grain see plain sawn.

flat head screw any screw in which the upper surface of the head is flat; often a countersunk head screw.

flat joint see flush joint.

flat nose pliers pliers which have flat, wide jaws.

flat plate synonymous with metal plate, especially that made from steel.

flat roof, platform roof (Scot.); a roof which has a slope of less than 10.

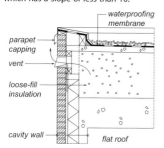

flat roof

waterproofing membrane

parapet capping

vent

loose-fill insulation

cavity wall

flatsawing see through and through sawing.

flat sawn see plain sawn.

flat slab see mushroom slab.

flat sliced veneer see flat cut veneer.

flat spade drill a drill bit with a flat, sharpened cutting edge and centre spur for drilling holes in non-metallic materials such as wood.

flat stop in ornamentation, the termination of a chamfered moulding or carving with a perpendicular triangle.

flatting see flat cutting.

flatting down, rubbing; the scouring of a primed surface with a fine abrasive to remove irregularities prior to painting.

flat top truss a steel or timber long-span lattice girder whose upper chord is parallel or nearly parallel to the lower chord; also simply called a flat truss.

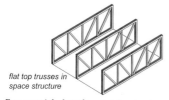

flat top trusses in space structure

flat varnish brush a flat brush whose bristles are designed for the application of varnish.

flat wall brush see flat brush.

flat washer, plain washer; an ordinary flat circular washer with a hole in the centre; if the hole is small compared with the washer's surface area, it is called a penny washer.

flat washer

flax a blue-flowered plant, *Linum usitatissimum*, whose dried stem fibres are woven into linen (in use as early as 2500 BC by the Egyptians for wrapping their mummies), pressed into flaxboard, etc., and whose seeds are pressed for linseed oil.

flaxboard particleboard manufactured from the stem fibres of the flax plant, or other similar plants, bonded together with resin then pressed into sheets.

flaxboard

fleak a rough hewn timber used in scaffolding.

Flemish bond a brickwork bond in which each course consists of alternating headers and stretchers, laid so that each header is centred over a joint in the course below; any of a number of brickwork bonds based on this pattern; see raking Flemish bond, Dutch bond and list below. See also illustrations on the following page.

Flemish cross bond a brickwork bond in which courses of alternating headers and stretchers are interspersed with courses of stretchers, laid so that joints form distinct cross motifs; a form of Flemish stretcher bond.

Flemish diagonal bond variations of Flemish stretcher and Flemish double stretcher bond in which brickwork joints create a pattern of interlocking diamond shapes.

Flemish double header bond a brickwork bond in which each course consists of stretchers alternating with two headers.

Flemish double stretcher bond a brickwork bond in which each course consists of a repeated series of one header and two stretchers; see also monk bond; see following variations:

staggered Flemish double stretcher bond; diagonal Flemish double stretcher bond; raking Flemish double stretcher bond.

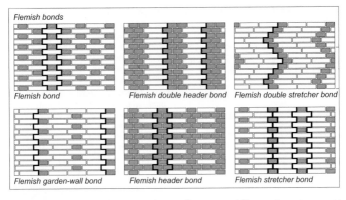

Flemish bonds

Flemish bond

Flemish double header bond

Flemish double stretcher bond

Flemish garden-wall bond

Flemish header bond

Flemish stretcher bond

Flemish garden-wall bond, Sussex bond, Silesian bond; a brickwork bond in which each course consists of a repeated series of one header and three stretchers; alternate courses are laid symmetrical about the header.

Flemish header bond 1 a brickwork bond in which courses of alternating headers and stretchers are interspersed with courses of headers, and in which the stretchers are always laid in the same vertical line.
2 see Flemish double header bond.

Flemish stretcher bond, 1 American with Flemish bond (Am), common bond; a brickwork bond in which one course of alternating headers and stretchers alternates with between one and six courses of stretchers.
2 Flemish double stretcher bond, see monk bond.

Flemish white see flake white.

fleur-de-lis, French lily; a decorative motif of three stylized lily petals tied near their base, especially used in ornament and heraldry by the French.

fleur-de-lis

fleuron decoration consisting of a carved flower or leaf motif.

fleuron

fleury moulding a decorative moulding with a series of fleur-de-lis motifs joined end on end; primarily found in heraldic designs; also called flory moulding.

fleury moulding

flexible metal roofing see supported sheetmetal roofing.

flexible mould a mould of a non-rigid material for taking ornamental plaster casts from difficult or intricate situations.

flexible pavement paved or road construction made up of a base layer of aggregate surfaced with bituminous material.

flexible pipe, hose; metal or plastics pipe which can be deformed by hand or with pipe benders, etc. without fracturing.

flexible rubber hose see appliance flexible connection.

flexible saw see saw chain.

flexible steel tape measure, tape measure; a device consisting of a scaled sprung roll of steel tape used for measuring distance.

flexible tube any tube, conduit, pipe, etc., often spiral wound or segmented, which can easily be bent by hand.

flexural strength see bending strength.

flier, 1 flyer, parallel tread; a flat rectangular step in a normal staircase.
2 see flying shore.

flight, stair flight; a number of steps in continuous series between two landings or levels; a straight section of a stair between two landings.

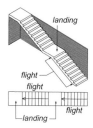

flint a dense, siliceous rock type found as distinct round lumps in chalky ground; it is difficult to work but traditionally used in England for stone facing and paving.

flint-lime brick a light, weak brick made from a mix of lime and crushed flint as opposed to clay; see calcium silicate brick.

flint nogging in traditional timber frame construction, flint infill for a timber stud frame.

flitch 1 a large rough timber sawn from a log or the trunk of a tree.
2 a log or piece of timber from which veneer is peeled or sliced; see also veneer bolt.

flitch sawing in the primary conversion of timber, the through and through sawing of a log into timber pieces of even dimension after two opposite curved edges have been removed.

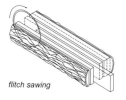

flitch sawing

float, 1 floater (Am); a hand tool for compacting and smoothing plaster surfaces, a flat steel blade with a handle on its reverse; similar hand and power tools used for smoothing concrete; types included as separate entries are listed below:

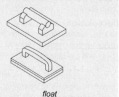

float

*cross-grained float; *darby, Darby float, derby; *devil float, see nail float; *plastering float, plasterer's float; *power float, rotary float; *skimming float; *sponge float; *straight-grained float; *wood float.
2 any material or component designed to provide buoyancy; a pontoon.

floated coat see float-finished rendering.

floated finish a smooth finish for concrete or plaster formed with a wooden or steel float.

floater see float.

float-finishing the smoothing of a concrete or plaster finish with a float in a circular action; also called floating or scouring.

float-finished rendering, floated coat; rendering whose wet surface has been worked with a hand-held float, producing a smooth but rather uneven finish.

float glass transparent sheet glass with an exceptionally smooth and even surface, manufactured by pouring molten glass onto a bed of molten tin on which it floats; see also clear float glass.

floating 1 see flooding.
2 see float-finishing.

floating coat see first plaster undercoat, second plaster undercoat, base coat.

floating floor the upper layer of floor construction supported on battens, mountings or a resilient sheet membrane of damping material such as expanded polystyrene or mineral wool to provide acoustic isolation.

floating rule a rule used in plastering for levelling a plaster surface.

floating screed concrete floor construction separated by layers of resilient material from its base and side walls to provide acoustic isolation.

float operated valve, floatvalve see ballvalve.

flocculation 1 a process of treating waste water with chemicals to form flaky solids which adhere to impurities and encourage removal from the water.
2 the tendency of the particles in some paints in storage to combine, gel or settle into distinct clumps.
flocculating admixture, flocculating agent; in concretework, an admixture included in the mix to increase cohesion.

flocked carpet carpet manufactured by electrostatic projection of polymer fibres against an adhesive-coated or surface-melted backing.

flocked wallcovering a wallcovering treated with a layer of textile fibres standing perpendicular to its surface.

flogger a paintbrush with a long head of bristles, dragged or slapped over wet paint or glaze to apply surface texture or pattern, especially used to mimic the background grain figure of woods such as mahogany, walnut, rosewood and cedar; sometimes also called a dragger.

flooding, floating; the separating out of pigments in a paint film such that one comes to the surface; may be a defect or deliberately caused for effect.

floodlight a powerful external luminaire used for area and building lighting.
floodlighting see area lighting, building floodlighting.

floor 1 the horizontal lower surface of a room or interior space and its supporting construction; see also flooring, floor covering, floor construction; types included as separate entries are listed below:

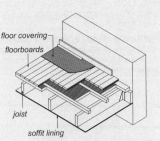

floor covering
floorboards
joist
soffit lining

timber floor construction

*access floor; *base floor, bottom floor; *cavity floor, see access floor; *fire floor, firebreak floor; *floating floor; *glazed floor, glass floor; *ground supported floor; *honeycomb floor, see waffle floor; *in-situ concrete floor; *modular floor, palette floor, see platform floor; *plate floor; *platform floor, raised access floor; *raised floor; *ramped floor; *rectangular grid floor, see waffle floor; *steel deck floor, see composite floor slab; *structural floor; *subfloor; *suspended base floor; *suspended floor; *timber floor; *waffle floor.
2 any level in a building, between two successive floors constructions; see storey.

floor base material which supports a flooring sub-base or flooring.

floor bed see ground supported floor.

floorboards, floorboarding; flooring of timber boards laid side by side over joists, battens, etc.; a floorboard is a single timber board used as flooring.

floor channel a long recess in the floor of wet spaces, garages, etc. for conveying waste and surface liquids into a drain.

floor chisel a long sturdy chisel used for prising up floorboards.

floor construction the component parts or layers of the horizontal levels in a building, including structure, insulation and floor covering.

floor covering thin sheet material such as linoleum, carpet or plastics matting used for providing a finish to a floor; see also matting and flooring for lists of types of floorcovering.

floor drain, floor gully; a trapped outlet fitting for the floor of a wet area, garage, etc., through which waste water and other fluids are conveyed into a drain.

floor finish, floor finishing; material laid above a concrete or timber floor structure or subfloor to provide a hard-wearing walking surface.

floor framing the timber frame of joists, trimming pieces and strutting, etc. which supports a boarded floor.

floor grating a framework of metal slats immediately outside external doors, often in a mat well, to collect dirt from footwear.

floor gully see floor drain.

floor heating see underfloor heating.

floor height, floor-to-floor height, storey height; the height between successive storeys of a multistorey building, as measured from floor level to adjacent floor level.

flooring any material used for surfacing a floor or providing a floor finish; types included as separate entries are listed below:
*acrylic polymer flooring, see acrylic flooring compound; *block flooring, see end-grain wood block flooring; *board flooring; *cement rubber latex flooring, cement flooring; *chipboard flooring; *coin flooring, coin-pattern flooring, see studded rubber flooring; *end-grain wood block flooring; *expanded metal flooring; *floor covering; *latex cement flooring, see cement rubber latex flooring; *metal flooring, see open metal flooring; *natural stone flooring, see stone flooring; *open bar metal flooring; *open metal flooring; *overlay flooring; *parquet flooring; *pattern flooring, see studded rubber flooring; *plank flooring, see wide plank flooring; *plywood flooring; *puncheon flooring; *raised-pattern flooring, see studded rubber flooring; *rubber flooring; *rubber latex cement flooring, see cement rubber latex flooring; *sheet flooring; *solid timber flooring; *stone flooring; *strip flooring, see wood strip flooring; *studded rubber flooring; *tiled flooring, see tile flooring; *timber flooring; *wide plank flooring; *wide strip flooring, see wide plank flooring; *wood block flooring, see end-grain wood block flooring; *wood board flooring; *wood flooring; *wood strip flooring.*

flooring batten one of a series of timber strips fixed to a structural floor as a base for decking or floorboards.

flooring bead a strip of planed timber or other material for concealing the edge of laid flooring.

flooring board see floorboard.

flooring component a prefabricated component used to form a base on which a floor surface is laid.

flooring compound see acrylic flooring compound.

flooring saw, inside start saw; a handsaw with teeth on both sides of the blade and a rounded end, enabling cuts to be started in the middle of a piece of wood; used for cutting holes in boards.

flooring strip see flooring bead.

flooring sub-base that part of floor construction which provides a base for the flooring material.

flooring tile see floor tile.

flooring underlay a sheet product designed for use as resilient underlay for matting, parquet, etc.; see underlay.

floor joist in frame construction, one of a series of beams or joists which carry flooring.

floor lamp, standard lamp; a freestanding movable lamp consisting of a light source at the top of a pole which is fixed to a base.

floor-mounted closer see floor spring.

floor outlet see floor drain.

floor paint tough paint based on epoxy or acrylic resin, used as a sealant or decoration for concrete or timber floors.

floor plan a schematic drawing showing the entire spatial layout, structure and components of a building in horizontal projection.

floor quarry see quarry tile.

floor sander a machine tool containing a dust bag and revolving sanding head used for smoothing and sanding a timber floor.

floor saw a machine tool for cutting openings in concrete floors with a diamond-tipped circular saw.

floor sealant a polyurethane-based treatment for a timber floor to increase durability and seal the pores in the wood.

floor slab a horizontal suspended construction of concrete or similar material which provides the structure for a floor; see composite floor slab.

floor space standard, floor space factor; a standard measure of the floor space per person required for buildings of different functions, used in space planning and fire safety calculations.

floor spring, floor-mounted closer; a door closer incorporated into a pivot mechanism recessed into floor construction, on which the leaf of a pivot door turns.

floor square see parquet floor square.

floor strip a thin strip of material such as plastics, timber or metal, used to cover the join between floor and wall, or adjacent areas of floor; see flooring bead, carpet strip, skirting.

floor structure loadbearing construction which supports a floor surface, often a concrete slab or a timber, steel or composite frame.

floor surface the upper surface of a floor, in contact with the occupants of a building.

floor tile, flooring tile; one of a number of tiles of ceramic, concrete, cork, stone or plastics material, laid as a durable floor surface.
floor tiling the laying of floor tiles; the product of this process.

floor-to-ceiling height see ceiling height.

floor-to-floor height see floor height.

Florentine arch, Italian round arch; a round arch whose extrados and intrados do not spring from the same point, and which is fatter at the apex than at the sides.

Florentine arch

floriated carved or rendered with decorative flower motifs; see also foliated.

flory moulding see fleury moulding.

flowable concrete see self-placing concrete.

flowing concrete concrete whose consistency is such that it flows easily when wet, achieved by adding a small percentage of superplasticizer; see also self-placing concrete.

flowing tracery, curvilinear tracery, undulating tracery; tracery found in churches of the late 1200s and 1300s (Decorated and Flamboyant styles), characterized by free-flowing patterns and ogees.

Gothic flowing tracery at the Minoritenkirche, Vienna, Austria

flow main in a district heating system, a pipeline which conveys water to a place of use from its heating plant.

flow pipe in hot water heating and similar installations, a pipe from a boiler or hot water storage vessel to radiators, outlets, etc.; cf. return pipe.

flow rate see discharge.

flow rock see igneous rock.

flow test see concrete flow test.

flow water hot water distributed for use in a central or district heating system.

fluctuation in contract management, an increase or decrease in the prices of labour, materials or plant from those specified in the tender, allowed for in the building contract.

flue, 1 smoke pipe, chimney; a vertical pipe or duct to remove smoke, combustion gases and other gaseous products from a fireplace, boiler or other heating device to the outside of a building; a chimney.
2 any vertical sealed channel for conveying ventilation air, usually out of a building.
see also insulated flue, ducted flue.

flue adaptor a fitting for connecting a solid-fuel stove or other appliance to a flue.

flue block, chimney block, flue brick;
1 a specially formed solid or hollow brick or block which is of modular size to enable it to be laid uncut for flues and chimneys.

2 a fireproof brick or block used to line a flue.

flue brick see flue block.

flue cap a flue terminal or rain cap, fitted to the upper outlet of a flue to prevent the passage of rainwater and improve draught.

flue condensation condensation which occurs in a flue as a result of flue gases being too cool.

flue connector that part of a fireplace, stove or other flued appliance, or a separate component, by which it is connected to a flue.

flue damper an adjustable pivoting sheetmetal plate for controlling the flow of air in an air-conditioning or mechanical ventilation system.

flue fan a fan connected to a flue to aid and improve natural draught.

flue gas any gas produced as a result of combustion within an appliance or installation, including soot and particles in suspension, which passes up through a flue.

flue lining fire-resistant surface material of plaster, refractory brick, etc. for the inside of a flue or chimney.

flue pipe a flue or part of a flue constructed or assembled from metal tube.

flue system an assembly of fittings for a working flue or group of flues, the means by which waste gases from a building are discharged.

flue terminal a protective device fitted to the upper outlet of a flue to prevent the passage of rainwater and snow, and to reduce or utilize the effects of wind.

flueway the inner open space of a flue, through which combustion gases are conveyed to the outside.

fluorescent pertaining to a component containing a substance such as phospor which emits light when subjected to incident radiation (ultraviolet light or X-rays) from a source such as mercury vapour.

fluorescent lamp, fluorescent tube;
an electric discharge lamp with a phosphor-coated glass tube containing argon and a mercury vapour, producing light by excitation of the layers of phosphor.

fluorescent luminaire a luminaire containing fluorescent lamps and associated starting and control devices.

fluorescent reflector lamp a fluorescent lamp with an internally silvered inner surface to reflect light outwards in a certain direction.

fluorescent tube see fluorescent lamp.

fluorite, fluorspar; a coloured, crystalline mineral used as a flux in the metal industry and in the production of hydrochloric acid.

fluorspar see fluorite.

flush a description of a surface, joint or other construction which is smooth and in a continuous plane, or of a component or fitting assembled with its outer surface at the same level as adjacent surfaces in which it is housed.

flush bead moulding, double-quirked bead moulding, recessed bead moulding; a decorative moulding cut with two parallel quirks or notches on either side to form a bead which is flush with the surface; a variety of quirk bead moulding.

flush bead muolding

flush bolt see flush slide.

flush eaves eaves in which the roof terminates at or close to the outer wall.

flush grated waste a plug-hole fitting for a basin or sink connected to a discharge pipe, which contains a grating to collect solid waste.

flush handle a handle for a door, window or hatch which is flush with the surface into which it is housed.

flushing rinsing in a sudden rush of moving water.

flushing cistern a cistern containing stored water for flushing a soil appliance.

flushing mechanism a device for producing a specified amount of flushing water for a WC in a specified time, usually by manual operation of a ballvalve.

flushing valve, flush valve, flushometer valve (Am); a valve for delivering a regulated amount of flushing water to a soil appliance.

flush joint, flat joint, plain cut joint; a brickwork mortar joint in which the mortar is laid at the level of the brickwork surface, or set slightly behind it.

flush mounting, recessed fixing; a description of a fitting such as a luminaire or electrical point installed so that its visible parts are flush with the surface in which it has been fitted.

flushometer valve see flushing valve.

flush pipe a pipe which conveys flushing water from a cistern or tank to a soil appliance.

flush pointing in brickwork, pointing in the same plane as the brick surface, forming a smooth surface.

flush pull a metal or plastics fitting housed in the leaf of a sliding door, which provides a finger recess by which the door can be opened or closed.

flush rodded joint a masonry flush joint tooled with a longitudinal concave depression when the masonry is wet.

flush slide, flush bolt; a small mechanical door bolt, often incorporated into the thickness of the door, to engage with the floor.

flush valve see flushing valve.

flute in classical architecture, one of a series of shallow concave grooves cut along the length of a column, pilaster or moulding.
Fluted referring to a surface that has been cut or formed with a series of parallel concave grooves; see also reeded.

fluted column one inscribed with flutes along the length of its shaft, originating in the masonry columns of the Greek Doric order and those of the Egyptian Old Kingdom (proto-Doric).

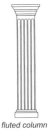

fluted column

fluted moulding any horizontal flat or torus moulding scored with a series of parallel concave indentations.

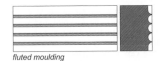

fluted moulding

fluted torus moulding a semicircular decorative moulding carved with flutes or parallel concave indentations; especially found on some classical column bases.
fluting surface decoration of flutes for classical columns and other objects.

flutter echo, flutter; in acoustics, a series of echoes in rapid succession resulting from reflection between two parallel surfaces such as walls in a corridor.

flux 1 in ceramics, a chemical applied to fired clay to aid the fusing of a subsequent glaze.
2 see luminous flux.

fly-ash see pulverized fuel-ash.

flyer see flier.

flying bond see monk bond.

flying buttress in Gothic church architecture, a stone buttress designed to take the lateral thrust of a roof, vault, or wall; it consists of a slender bar of masonry which transmits loading to a heavy pier on an outer wall.

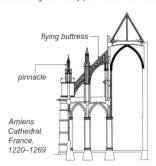

flying buttress

pinnacle

Amiens Cathedral, France, 1220–1269

flying shore, flier, horizontal shore; horizontal props to provide temporary support for the external wall of a building, sides of an excavation, etc. from an adjacent vertical structure or abutment.

flying stairs see cantilevered stair.

fly wire see insect screen.

foam any lightweight solid or liquid with considerable quantities of small entrained bubbles of gas; see also extinguishing foam.

foam compound see foaming agent.

foamed concrete, foam concrete; aerated concrete made by the addition of a foaming agent.

foamed glass see foam glass.

foamed plastics any lightweight plastics material which has been aerated to introduce gas bubbles; a cellular plastic.

foamed polystyrene see expanded polystyrene.

foamed polyurethane polyurethane to which a foaming agent has been added; used for injected cavity insulation and as a sealant.

foam extinguisher a fire extinguisher containing liquid which, on release, expands into a foam which is sprayed onto a fire.

foam forming admixture in concretework, an admixture included in the mix to promote the formation of air bubbles.

foam glass, 1 foamed glass, expanded glass; low density glass with entrained bubbles of gas used for thermal and acoustic applications.
2 see cellular glass.

foaming agent, 1 foam compound; a liquid used in fire-fighting and as fireproofing which becomes a non-combustible foam when released or activated.
2 various substances added to some plastics, rubbers or concrete to promote the formation of tiny gas bubbles within the material and improve properties of thermal insulation, fireproofing and to reduce weight.

foam rubber, sponge rubber, latex foam; a form of cellular rubber containing a network of gas bubbles which are open and interconnected; used for packing and padding.

focusing effect in acoustics, the usually undesirable effect of concave walls, domes, vaults, etc. in a space to locally reinforce sound levels by focusing reflected sound to a point.

foil 1 any metal produced in very thin sheets less than 0.15−0.25 mm thick; actual thickness varies with national specification and type of metal; see aluminium foil, gold foil (gold leaf).
2 a decorative motif representing a stylized leaf.
see trefoil, quatrefoil, cinquefoil, sexfoil, multifoil.

foil moulding a decorative moulding with a series of pointed leaf motifs joined end on end; primarily found in heraldic designs.

foil moulding

foil wallcovering see metal foil wallcovering.

folded plate, folded slab; a reinforced concrete shell structure used for long span roofs, consisting of a number of thin cast slabs at a vertical angle to one another, forming a zigzag pattern in cross-section; also called a polygonal shell.

reinforced concrete folded plate roof construction

folding blind see concertina blind.

folding casements a pair of hinged window casements, hung in either side of a frame, which do not have a mullion or frame member between them.

folding door a door hinged at one edge which folds with a concertina action along the line of a threshold; see sliding folding door, bi-part folding door, bi-fold door.

folding rule a traditional measuring stick, a rule jointed at fixed intervals for convenience in carrying.

folding wedges in timber jointing, paired timber wedges driven into a joint during or after assembly to tighten it.

folding window see sliding folding window.

foliated carved or rendered with decorative leaf motifs; foliate ornament is often called leafwork or leaf ornament; see also floriated.

foliated arch see cinquefoliated arch, multifoliated arch, trifoliated arch.

foliated gneiss see gneissose micaschist.

Foliated style a form of English Geometric Gothic architecture characterized by the use of carved leaf motifs.

foliate head, green man; a traditional decorative round semi-human face motif of plant and foliage forms representing the force of nature merging with humanity.

foliate head, green man

folium a traditional dark violet pigment made from the seeds of turnsole plant (*Chrozophora tinctoria*), used originally for inscriptions.

folly a purely decorative building or structure, often a fake ruin, tower or statue, located in parkland.

Fomes spp. a number of fungi which cause decay in wood and trees, see below for species:

Fomes annosus see annosus root rot.

Fomes ignarius see false tinder fungus.

Fomes pini see red ring rot.

foot bolt a barrel bolt set vertically at the foot of a door to hold it shut by engaging with a housing in floor construction.

footing 1 a foundation slab beneath a column or wall.

foot bolt

2 strip footing, see strip foundation.

3 column or isolated footing, see pad foundation.

footprints, combination pliers, pipe tongs; long-handled pliers or tongs with adjustable pivoted and serrated jaws, used by a pipe fitter for gripping pipes and other cylindrical objects.

forced draught burner in gas heating, a gas burning appliance whose burner is provided with air under pressure.

forced drying a mild form of baking in air at temperatures of 30–60°C for coatings and paints to greatly reduce their drying time.

forced ventilation see mechanical ventilation.

force majeure, act of God; in contract law, an unforeseeable event such as an earthquake or the outbreak of war that is outside the influence of parties to a contract and prevents a contractor from fulfilling his obligations either in part or in full.

forecourt an external courtyard, area of hardstanding or driveway in front of a building.

foreman the contractor's representative responsible for supervising work on a building site; see general foreman, section foreman, trades foreman.

forend, lock faceplate, lock front; the outer plate of a mortise lock, visible in the narrow edge of a door, which has holes for screws, a bolt, and any secondary bolts or latches.

foreshortening in perspective and axonometric drawing, the shortening of oblique or converging lines perpendicular or skew to the picture plane, to produce the illusion of three-dimensionality; in dimetric and trimetric projections this is often constructed by convention; a foreshortening factor is the ratio by which dimensions along one or two of the oblique axes are arithmetically reduced.

forging the shaping of metal by hammering, either manually or with heavy machinery, whilst red hot.

forged nail a traditional nail which has been fashioned by heating and hammering into shape; also called a wrought nail.

forged nail

forge welding, smith welding; the simple joining of metals by hammering them together when red hot.

forks see crucks.

forkstaff plane a plane for carving out and smoothing convex surfaces in wood.

form see formwork.

form lining see formwork lining.

form nail see double headed nail.

form oil see mould oil.

formply plywood used as shuttering, usually waterproofed with film or resin impregnated paper.

form stop see stop end form.

form tie see formwork tie.

form vibrating see external vibrating.

form vibrator see external vibrator.

formaldehyde, methanal; a poisonous, colourless, pungent gas, **HCHO**, used in the production of resins, adhesives, etc.; see melamine formaldehyde (melamine, MF), phenol formaldehyde (phenolic resin, PF), urea formaldehyde (UF).

formalin a solution of formaldehyde in water; used as a disinfectant and preservative.

formation see foundation.

Former see box out.

forming, shaping; in manufacturing, the pressing, extruding or moulding of a plastic material into a predesigned shape; see thermo-forming, vacuum forming.

formula price adjustment in contract management, a method of calculating the amount to be added to or deducted from a contract sum due to changes in the costs of labour, plant and materials during construction using a price variation formula.

formula variation of price contract a variation of price contract in which prices are amended according to previously agreed terms.

formwork, 1 casing, mould, shuttering; concreting moulds of boarding, sheet material or specialized construction to give temporary support for in-situ concrete while it hardens; types included as separate entries are listed below:

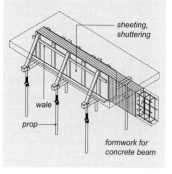

sheeting, shuttering

wale

prop

formwork for concrete beam

*apartment formwork; *board formwork; *climbing formwork; *collapsible formwork; *lost formwork; *permanent formwork; *quick strip formwork; *reusable formwork; *room formwork, see apartment formwork; *soffit formwork; *table formwork; *tilt-up formwork; *top formwork; *tunnel formwork, see apartment formwork.*

2 the on-site work involved in building and installing these; formwork erection.

formwork erection the construction or assembling of formwork prior to casting in-situ concrete.

formwork lining, form lining; sheet material included in formwork to give a particular surface texture to the concrete.

formwork nail see double headed nail.

formwork panel reusable framed sheet material against which concrete is cast in formwork; see shuttering.

formwork sheeting see sheeting.

formwork striking see striking.

formwork tie, form tie; one of a number of small steel tension members used to hold formwork accurately in place once concrete is placed.

Forstner bit a patent drill bit for drilling flat-bottomed holes or round sinkings in wood.

fortification a structure consisting of walls and battlements constructed for defence; part of a defensive structure, a fortifying component such as a battlement or tower, a work.

foul drain see foul water drain.

foul water in drainage and waste water treatment, a mixture of soil water and waste water conveyed to a sewer.

foul water drain, foul drain; in drainage and waste water treatment, a horizontal pipe, most often buried beneath the ground, for leading soil and waste water from a building to a private or public sewer.

foundation 1 a subterranean structure designed to transmit the structural loading of building to the ground; see spread foundation, piled foundation, footing. See illustration on following page.

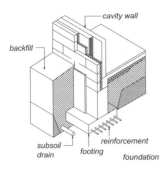

subsoil
drain   footing   reinforcement
              foundation   footing   foundation

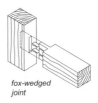

fox-wedged
joint

2 formation, subgrade, subsoil, ground; the bearing layer of soil or rock below the substructure of a building or other construction.

3 an organization which maintains and distributes funding for the arts, research, scholarships, etc.

foundation bolt see anchor bolt.

foundation depth the distance between ground level and the lowest point of foundation construction.

foundation drawing, foundation plan; a drawing produced by a structural engineer showing the layout and type of foundations for a building or structure.

foundation pile see bearing pile; see also list of common pile types under 'pile'.

foundation plan see foundation drawing.

foundation stone see bedstone, cornerstone.

foundation wall that part of the external wall of a basement which is below ground level and transmits loading to the foundations or ground below.

four-centred arch see Tudor arch, pseudo four-centred arch.

four-centred pointed arch see Tudor arch.

fox wedge, secret wedge; in timber mortise and tenon jointing, one of two wedges placed into cuts made in the base of the tenon to tighten the joint on assembly.

fox-wedged joint one which has been fastened and tightened with a fox wedge. See illustration opposite.

foyer, 1 lobby, entrance hall; a main entrance hall at ground level in a public building, hotel or large office building.

2 lobby; a main open space in a theatre or concert hall, in which the audience may gather before a performance or during the intervals.

fracture line a line along which a structural member or surface treatment has cracked or failed structurally.

frame, 1 framework; a rigid structure of slender loadbearing members joined together, for attaching and supporting cladding, infill and other components; examples included as separate entries are listed below:

*box frame, see cased frame; *casement frame; *hyperstatic frame, see statically indeterminate frame; *isostatic frame, see statically determinate frame; *loadbearing frame, structural frame; *mat well frame; *perfect frame, see statically determinate frame; *piling frame, see pile driver; *plane frame; *portal frame, rigid frame; *redundant frame, see statically indeterminate frame; *statically determinate frame; *statically indeterminate frame; *space frame; *subframe.*

2 skeleton; the loadbearing elements of a building, erected first, onto which cladding and other components are fixed.

3 see building frame (types of building frame listed there).

4 the surrounding construction of members onto which a door leaf or window casement is hinged.

5 framing; the peripheral members which form the structure of a window sash or casement, or a panelled or glazed door leaf; see window frame, door frame.

0

frame anchor see door-frame anchor.

frame bracing, frame stiffening; any elements such as crosswalls, diagonals, etc. to provide stiffening to a building frame.

framed and ledged door a door in which the leaf is formed of a rigid frame with a middle rail or ledge as stiffening; boarding is then attached to this.

framed beam see trussed beam.

framed door any door whose leaf is supported by a frame; may be a glazed door or panelled door.

framed door

framed, ledged and braced door a framed and ledged door with diagonal bracing between the horizontal members.

frameless glass door see all-glass door.

frameless glazing 1 glazing for facades, partitions, balustrades, etc. of glass panels with primarily sealed butt joints, drilled proprietary fixings, not installed in fixed framing.

2 see structural glazing.

frame member, glazing bar; part of a window frame between two openable sashes or casements; see mullion, transom.

frame saw see gang saw, mill saw.

frame stiffening see frame bracing.

framework 1 any basic secondary structural rails, battens or other structure fixed to a building frame as a base for cladding.

2 a surrounding, supporting or loadbearing structure of members for a construction; see frame.

framing see frame.

framing chisel, cant chisel; a heavy chisel with a reinforced, rounded or canted back for heavy carpentry and framing.

framing gun a robust nail gun for nails up to 100mm long, used for fixing timber flooring and in framing work; sometimes called a stud gun; see also nail gun.

framing hammer a large nail hammer used by construction workers.

framing joint any joint between two timbers used in timber frame construction, fashioned by a carpenter on site.

framing square, carpenter's square; a large steel try square with many scales and gradations used for marking and measuring 90° angles in building work; see square.

Frankfurt black a brownish-black pigment made by grinding up burnt grapevines and other waste products of the wine industry.

Franki pile in foundation technology, a patented driven cast-in-place pile consisting of a metal pipe driven into the ground and then filled with concrete.

Fraxinus spp. see ash.

FRC see fibre-reinforced concrete, fibre-reinforced cement, fibre-reinforced composite.

free convection, natural convection, self convection; the transfer of heat within a fluid or gas by movement induced by temperature and density differences within it.

free match in decorative wallpapering, a description of patterned wallpaper which does not have to be hung in a specific sequence for the overall pattern to be evident.

freestanding 1 describing a column which does not carry structure, essentially for decorative or monumental purposes, or a wall which has no support at its upper edge.

freestanding column

2 describing a dwelling surrounded by space on all sides, in a detached house.

free tenon joint, fish tenon joint, slip tenon joint; a timber mortise and tenon joint in which a mortise is cut into both members and the tenon is a separate piece.

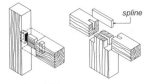

free tenon joints

French arch see Dutch arch.

French blue see artificial ultramarine.

French chalk, steatite, soapstone; ground magnesium silicate used as a dusting powder, in dry cleaning, etc.; another name for talc as sold in North America and Great Britain.

French door see casement door.

French drain see field drain.

French flier see dancing step.

French lily see fleur-de-lis.

French nail see round wire nail.

French plane see corner scraper.

French polish a mixture of shellac and a solvent such as methylated spirit rubbed with a rotary motion into smooth untreated joinery surface as a fine but non-resistant finish; French polishing is the art and craft of applying French polish to wooden artifacts, fine joinery, etc.

French truss see Fink truss.

French ultramarine see artificial ultramarine.

French white see flake white.

French window see casement door.

fresco mural painting in mineral or earth pigments applied to lime or gypsum plaster while it is still wet; otherwise known as true fresco or buon fresco.
fresco secco, dry fresco, secco; decorating painting on dry plaster or subsequent touching up for true fresco, undertaken once the plaster surface has dried.

fresh air air from the outside, drawn into a ventilation or air-conditioning system to replace stale air in a building; see supply air.

fresh-air inlet 1 an opening in an outside wall to allow the passage of fresh ventilation air into a space.
2 an opening to allow the entrance of fresh air to a drainage system.

fresh-air vent in natural and mechanical ventilation systems, a component containing a grille and filter, installed in an opening in an external wall, through which fresh air is introduced; often referred to simply as an inlet or vent.

fresh concrete concrete that has not yet begun to set and is still in a workable condition.

fret 1 banded running ornament of lines or fillets linked or interlinked to form a continuous motif; often called a key pattern, it always has orthogonal geometry; see also diamond fret, Greek key, guilloche, key pattern, labyrinth fret, meander, potenty moulding, Vitruvian scroll.

fret

2 see firefront.
fretsaw, bracket saw, jigsaw, scroll saw; a fine-toothed saw whose narrow blade is held in tension in a very deep frame, used for cutting small openings and curves in boards.
fretwork see fret.

friction joint any joint or connection which remains fast due to the action of friction.

friction pile in foundation technology, any pile which transmits forces to surrounding ground around its circumference, through friction.

friction welding a specialized method of welding in which heat is generated by the high-speed rotation of one component while pressed to the other.

frieze 1 a decorated horizontal band adorning the elevation or interior wall of a building below a cornice, eaves or ceiling line.
2 in classical architecture, the middle band of an entablature, often decorated with sculpture.

frit a blue ceramic glaze known to the Egyptians, made by melting siliceous materials with copper, lead and other metallic salts, then cooling and grinding.

fritting a protective or decorative treatment for a ceramic or glass surface consisting of granular mineral material, often powdered glass or sand, which is baked on.

frog an indentation in the upper, lower or both large surfaces of a brick, made in order to reduce weight.

frog
stretcher face   header face

front bent gouge see spoon gouge.

front clearance in glazing, the horizontal distance between the outer face of the pane or glazing unit and its glazing bead.

fronting in glazing, a fillet of soft material, putty, etc., triangular in section, applied to the external edges of a window pane to hold it in place in its frame.

frontispiece the main or monumental elevation, bay or entrance of a building.

fronton see pediment.

front putty see putty fronting.

frost action detrimental effects caused by the build-up of ice in and around construction, beneath foundations, etc. due to contained water freezing in very cold weather.

frost attack see frost damage.

frost boil in soil engineering, the softening of soil after it has thawed after a period of frost or being in a frozen state.

frost damage 1 damage which occurs to building fabric because of sub-zero weather, often due to the expansion of trapped water on freezing.
2 frost attack; the pitting and spalling of a hardened concrete surface due to the expansion of water held in pores during freezing weather.

frosted see pearl.

frost heave the rising up of the surface of ground during freezing weather due to trapped groundwater expanding as it freezes.

frosting 1 a defect in a gloss paint finish consisting of a matt or textured surface.
2 see etching.

frost protection construction measures taken in cold countries — the use of insulation in foundations, careful detailing, etc. — to prevent damage caused by freezing.

FRP see fibre-reinforced plastic.

fuel-ash see pulverized fuel-ash.

fuel-ash cement see Portland pulverized fuel-ash cement.

fugitive referring to a pigment which will not retain its colour in the prolonged presence of light.

full gloss, high gloss; the highest of five grades of glossiness in a dry paint surface, characterized by a smooth mirror-like finish.

full size see tight size.

full-spectrum lamp see neodymium oxide lamp.

full-turn stairs see one-turn stairs.

functionalism a Modernist architectural and design movement in Europe and America from the 1920s and 1930s, characterized by a concentration on the functional aspect of buildings and objects and an interest in structure and material rather than decoration.

fungi simple forms of microscopic plant whose parasitic attack of wood may cause surface staining, mould or decay; plural form of fungus; species included as separate entries are listed below:
*annosus root rot [Fomes annosus, Heterobasidion annosum]; *bleeding Stereum [Stereum sanguinolentum]; *blue stain, blue fungus, deal yard blue, log blue, sap-stain; *blue stain fungus [Ophiostoma minus]; *bracket fungus, see conk; *brown rot fungus; *canker rot, see red ring rot; *cellar rot [Coniophora cerebella, Coniophora puteana]; *conk [Polyporaceae]; *dote; *dry rot [Serpula lacrymans, Merulius lacrymans]; *false tinder fungus [Phellinus ignarius, Fomes ignarius]; *hardrot, see dote; *heartwood rot; *honeycomb rot, see red ring rot; *incipient decay, see dote; *mould; *pith flecks [Agromyza]; *pocket rot; *polypore, see conk; *red ring rot [Phellinus pini, Fomes pini, Trametes pini]; *ring scale fungus, see red ring rot; *roll-rim [Paxillus panuoides]; *root rot, see annosus root rot; *sap-stain; *sapwood rot; *scaly cap fungus [Lentinus lepideus]; *shelf fungus, see conk; *slash conk [Gloephyllum separium, Lenzites separia]; *spalt; *tear fungus, see dry rot; *white pitted rot, white pocket rot, see red ring rot; *white rot; *white spongy rot [Antrodia serialis].

fungal attack, fungal decay see rot; see list of wood-attacking fungi under fungi.

fungicidal admixture in concrete-work, an admixture included in the mix to inhibit attack from fungi.

fungicide, preservative; a substance, usually in liquid form, used for the treatment of timber against fungal attack; see also fungicidal admixture.

fungistat a substance which prevents the growth of mould and fungi, used in wood preservative and foodstuffs.

funicular polygon the polygonal shape assumed by a chord suspended at both ends which has a number of loads hung from it at intervals.

furan any of a number of colourless organic compounds with a chemical ring structure, used in plastic form for chemical-resistant adhesives, varnishes, etc.

furfuraldehyde, furfural; a colourless liquid, originally obtained from distilling bran or corn cobs, used to produce polycondensate plastics for use in laminates.

furnace see boiler.

furnishing the design and process of assembling, mounting and arranging furniture, furnishings and loose fittings in a space.

furnishing hinge see cabinet hinge.

furnishings the non-fixed items of furniture and fabrics in a building; these when regarded as a whole.

furnishing textile a general name for curtains, drapery, carpets, mats, upholstery and other fabric products used in interior decoration.

furniture 1 any non-fixed fittings in a building, such as chairs, tables, curtains, etc.
2 see door furniture.

furniture beetle, woodworm; [*Anobiidae*] a family of insects whose larvae cause damage to furniture and timber by burrowing; see also common furniture beetle [*Anobium punctatum*].

furniture designer a specialist designer of pieces of furniture, often an interior designer who also produces furnishing layouts.

furniture lock see cabinet lock.

furring see scale, firring.

fuse, cutout; an electric component which melts in the event of a flow of excess current, breaking the circuit.

fused silica glass, quartz glass; glass produced from 99% silica or quartz, expensive to manufacture and used for special applications such as laboratory equipment.

fusible link a jointing component for holding a damper or fire door open, which melts at a relatively low temperature (68°C) to release the mechanism in the event of fire.

fusion rock see igneous rock.

fusion welding a method of welding in which the metals to be joined are melted together as in gas or arc welding, often with a filler rod to provide additional material.

fuzzy grain, woolly grain; in the conversion or manufacture of timber, a machining defect resulting in wood fibres frayed loose at the surface after cutting.

G

gabbro a very dark, coarse-grained plutonic rock composed of pyroxene and plagioclase, used as a building stone.

gabion, rubble basket; a stackable component of loose stones or boulders in a rectangular cage of galvanized mesh or welded reinforcing bars, used for road embankments, retaining walls, erosion control, etc.; a gabion wall is a retaining wall of loosely stacked or tied gabions, used to restrain earth embankments at roadsides or in landscaping.

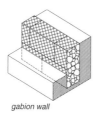

gabion wall

gable the triangular upper portion of wall at the end of a double pitched roof; called a pignon in traditional timber-framed construction.

brick gable of medieval church of St Mary, Turku, Finland, 1300s

gableboard see bargeboard.

gabled mansard roof, gambrel roof (Am); a doubly pitched roof with a gable at either end.

gable dormer a dormer window with a pitched roof and gablet over the glazed area.

gabled roof see gable roof.

gable roof

gable end an exterior elevation or end of a building containing a gable.

gable roof, gabled roof; a roof with two sloping planes which meet at a central ridge and a gable at one or both ends.

gable wall any wall which contains a gable.

gablet a small gable, as found in a dormer window.

gablet roof see gambrel roof.

gaboon, okoume; [*Aucoumea klaineana*] a West African hardwood with brown, featureless timber; used for interiors and plywood, rarely as solid wood.

gadroon, godroon, knulled ornament, lobe ornament, nulled ornament, thumb moulding; ornament made up of a number of protruding parallel convex mouldings, lumps or carvings; gadrooned means decorated with a series of longitudinal convex protrusions.

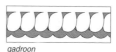

gadroon

gage see gauge.

Gahn's blue a variety of cobalt ultramarine pigment.

Galfan a high-quality zinc coating consisting of zinc with 5% aluminium and 1% misch metal.

gallery 1 an upper space, bounded by a balustrade, opening out to a larger space;

an upper storey of a church, cathedral or other large hall, which opens out into the main space, often for seating.

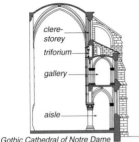

Gothic Cathedral of Notre Dame in Laon, France, c.1157–1205

2 a boutique or museum for exhibitions or for the sale of art.

gallery-access block, balcony-access flats; a multistorey residential building type in which entry to all flats is via long external walkways at storey level, each joined to a central stairway; also called gallery flats.

galvanic corrosion see electrochemical corrosion.

galvanic couple, voltaic couple; the phenomenon of electricity produced by chemical reaction between two dissimilar conductors in contact with one another, often leading to accelerated corrosion of exposed metal components in buildings; see electrochemical corrosion.

galvanization the deposition of a metal coating onto a material by electrolysis or hot dipping; in construction usually the coating of steel with a layer of zinc as corrosion resistance.

galvanized referring to a steel product which has been coated with a protective layer of zinc; see also above and following entry.

galvanized steel, galvanized iron, zinc coated steel; steel treated with a thin protective coating of zinc either by electrolysis or by dipping in baths of molten zinc.

gamboge a natural yellow gum from Thailand used as a transparent pigment.

gambrel roof, 1 gablet roof; a roof having a gablet near the ridge and the lower part hipped.

gambrel roof

2 see gabled mansard roof.

gamma iron see austenite.

ganged form, gang form; a number of prefabricated formwork panels attached together in situ for casting large concrete elements.

ganger a workman who is in charge of, and works with, a number of labourers on site.

gang form see ganged form.

gang nail see nail plate.

gang saw, 1 frame saw; a group of parallel saws which cut a log lengthways into boards simultaneously.
2 see mill saw.

gangway a narrow interior circulation space between furnishings, rows of seats, machinery or other equipment to provide access.

gap see air gap, cavity, ventilation gap, allowance (installation gap).

gap graded aggregate graded aggregate without particles of a certain size.

gapped boarding see spaced boarding.

garage gully a deep gully containing a sediment bucket to collect small amounts of waste oil and petrol in places where motor vehicles are stored or maintained.

garance a reddish dyestuff produced by treating the madder root with sulphuric acid.

garbage solid waste material from food preparation; see also domestic refuse.

garden black ant [*Lasius niger*] a species of insect which infests cladding boards, logs and wood-based insulation by burrowing and building its nest within the wood.

garden bond see mixed garden bond, English garden-wall bond, Flemish garden-wall bond.

garden furniture, outdoor furniture; any furniture, benches, tables, seats and sunshades intended for external use, usually of weatherproof materials such as treated wood, plastics and metal.

gargoyle a projecting stone water spout at the eaves or parapet of a building which has been carved into the form of a grotesque animal or head; see rainwater spout.

gargoyle at the basilica of St Nazaire, Carcassonne, France, 11th to 14th century

garland see festoon.

garnet a silicate mineral which occurs in many different types of rock and is evident in a number of colours, especially deep red; used as a grinding agent and as gemstones.

garret, loft; a habitable room, dwelling or apartment in the attic space of a building; see also attic.

gas appliance an appliance such as an oven, fire or lamp which runs on natural or bottled gas.

gas black a black pigment, carbon formed as soot from the chemical industry.

gas concrete aerated concrete made by the addition of a foaming agent.

gas detector see combustion gas detector.

gas-fired referring to a heating system which uses gas as its combustible fuel.
gas-fired central heating, gas heating; central heating in which water, etc. is heated by the combustion of gas in boilers.

gas fitter a tradesman skilled in the fitting of gas pipework and appliances.

gas forming admixture in concretework, an admixture included in the mix to promote the formation of bubbles of gas.

gas governor in gas heating, a device for regulating the flow of gas in a pipeline and for converting mains pressure to that suitable for domestic use.

gas heating see gas-fired central heating.

gas installation pipework any pipework, meters and associated apparatus which convey gas fuel to its outlets and appliances for use.
gas installation riser see installation riser.

gasket, seal; a preformed strip of flexible sheet material of variable cross-section included to form a compression seal at a butt joint or convey water out of construction joints; see also glazing gasket.

gas main a principal gas supply pipe to which individual users or buildings can be connected.

gas metal-arc welding see GMA welding.

gas meter a meter for measuring and recording the flow and consumption of gas supplied to an installation.

gas oil distilled oil which is thicker and with a higher boiling point than kerosene, used as a fuel in atomizing burners.

gas pipe any sealed tube through which gas is conveyed from a place of storage or manufacture to a point of use.

gas point a point in a gas installation from which gas can be extracted or to which an appliance can be connected.

gas service riser a length of supply and distribution pipe installed vertically in a gas installation.

gas-shielded welding one of a number of welding processes in which an inert gas is used to protect the metal being welded from reaction with the surrounding air.
gas-shielded metal-arc welding see GMA welding.

gas soundness test in gas heating, a test for leakage of gas pipework and appliances.

gas supply the supply of gas for a building from a main.

gas tungsten arc welding see TIG welding.

gas welding a skilled method of fusion welding in which the metals to be joined are melted together using a blowtorch burning oxy-acetylene, propane or oxy-hydrogen.

gate a hinged barrier, door or hatch in a wall or fence which can be opened to allow thoroughfare; see also shutter, roller shutter.

gateway the structural or ornate surround for an entrance opening in a wall or building; a portal.

the Lion Gate, Mycenae, Greece, c.1250 BC

gather, gathering; the narrowing of the top of a fireplace to meet a flue.

gauge, gage; 1 meter; any instrument designed to measure a varying dimension or quantity, displaying the measured value numerically.
2 an instrument, tool or apparatus used for measuring whether a component or material conforms to a standard or designed measurement.
3 a measure of the thickness of thin sheet objects.
4 a mason's tool used for marking out parallel lines when setting out a piece of work.
5 see honing guide.
types of gauge included as separate entries are listed below:
*Birmingham wire gauge; *cutting gauge; *dial gauge; *feeler gauge; *marking gauge; *mortise gauge; *micrometer; *plug gauge; *pressure gauge; *thread gauge; *vernier callipers; *wire gauge.

gauge board a board on which mixed plaster stands while awaiting use.

gauged arch a brick arch in which all the voussoirs are wedge-shaped.

gauged arch

gauged brickwork, rubbed brickwork; decorative and relief effects produced in facing brickwork by laying soft bricks rubbed to exact dimensions in thin mortar joints.

gauged coarse stuff plaster used for undercoats, produced from lime putty and sand mixed with Portland cement or gypsum plaster; see coarse stuff.

gauged lime plaster see gauged stuff.

gauged setting stuff finishing plaster produced from lime putty and sand mixed with gypsum plaster; cf. setting stuff.

gauged stuff, gauged lime plaster; traditional plaster consisting of lime putty mixed with either gypsum plaster or cement to reduce setting time.

gauge rod, storey rod; a vertical timber batten used in the setting out of brickwork, onto which the levels of brick courses, sill heights, etc. are marked.

gauging trowel a plasterer's trowel with a triangular metal blade used for applying small amounts of plaster.

G-clamp see gee-clamp.

gear in building installations, the mechanical apparatus for operating doors, shutters and other automated systems.

Gedu nohor [*Entandophragma angolense*] a tropical West African hardwood sold as mahogany; it has pale reddish-brown timber and is used for plywood, veneered furniture and interiors.

gee-clamp, G-clamp, C-clamp, circle-end clamp; a cramp consisting of a U-shaped piece of cast metal with a screw for clamping objects.

geison Gk.; a corona in a classical Greek cornice; see corona.

general arrangement drawing, general location drawing; a type of design drawing, usually a plan, showing the layout of construction works, how they are located in relation to one another, door and furnishing codes, and other references to detail and assembly drawings.

general conditions of contract see conditions of contract.

general contractor see main contractor.

general diffuse lighting artificial lighting in which luminaires distribute 40–60% of the emitted light downwards or to the area to be illuminated.

general foreman, foreman; the contractor's employee responsible for supervising all work on site.

general lighting lighting of a space whose task is to provide a uniform light level, as opposed to highlighting certain areas.

general lighting service lamp, GLS lamp; a standard incandescent 25–2000 W lamp running off 220–240 V, with a clear opal or pearl bulb and a screw or bayonet lamp cap.

general location drawing see general arrangement drawing.

general purpose mortar common and versatile mortars which can be used for masonry bedding, tile fixing, cement render patching, etc.

general purpose screw a steel or brass screw for fixing to wood, timber-based boards, plastic, etc.

general purpose screw

general surround lighting lighting designed to provide a general lighting level in a space, without regard to the illumination of special features or exits, etc.

generator any device for producing electrical energy from motion or mechanical energy.

geodesy see land surveying.
geodisist see land surveyor.

geogrid a synthetic sheet product with large perforations, incorporated into groundworks as soil stabilization.

geological map a map which presents distribution of underlying rock, mineral and soil types for a district, with different types usually shown in different colours.

geomembrane in geotechnical engineering, an impermeable membrane, often of sheet plastics, incorporated in the ground to inhibit penetrations of liquids and gases.

geometrical acoustics, ray acoustics; a method of analysing acoustical effects as lines of disturbance and wavefronts, used for large spaces where the wavelengths of sound are small compared with the dimensions of the space.

geometrical stair a stair cantilevered out from a wall.

geometrical tracery see geometric tracery.

Geometric style 1 a decorative style from Archaic Greece (900–750 BC) with regular geometrical patterns such as keys and frets, especially used for vase painting.
2 an early development of the Decorated style of English Gothic architecture in England in the early 1300s, characterized by geometrical patterns and forms in tracery and other decorated elements.

geometric tracery tracery found in Gothic churches of the late 1200s, with slender vertical bars supporting a pattern of foils and circles; also called geometrical tracery.

Gothic geometric tracery in Cologne Cathedral, Germany, 1248–1880

geometric tile specially shaped ceramic tiles designed to be laid with other similar tiles and form a geometric pattern on the tiled surface; see hexagonal tile.

geometric tile

Georgian wired glass wired glass with a 13 mm steel mesh.

geosynthetic referring to any synthetic product, including geomembranes and geotextiles, incorporated into the ground for soil drainage, sealing or reinforcing.

geotechnical engineering, ground engineering; a branch of engineering whose task is to investigate and improve the ground on which a building or structure is to be constructed.

geotechnical survey, geotechnical investigation, ground investigation; in geotechnical engineering, investigation of the soil and foundation conditions of a particular site.

geotextile a durable woven plastics mat incorporated into the ground to inhibit erosion and as stabilization against shear or slip.

geothermal energy heat stored naturally in underground rock formations, utilized as a heating source for buildings by drilling deep boreholes.

German black see vine black.

German silver, electrum, nickel brass; a silverish alloy of brass, containing zinc, nickel and copper.

gesso a mixture of gypsum, a glue and linseed oil used as a base in painting and for cast plaster decoration.

giant arborvitae, giant cedar [*Thuja plicata*] western red cedar, see thuja.

giant order see colossal order.

Gibbs surround an ornamental masonry surround for a doorway or window with alternately projecting blocks.

gilded, gilt; coated with a layer of gold leaf or painted with gold paint.

gilder's liquor a mixture of water and alcohol used in gilding to activate the dried glue present on the surface onto which gold leaf is applied.

gilding the art and craft of providing a decorative surface coating with a thin layer of gold leaf.

gilding size see gold size.

gilding primer in gilding, a compound or filler used to smooth and seal a surface prior to sticking down gold leaf.

gilt see gilded.

gimlet, twist gimlet, wimble; a pointed hand tool for making starter holes in wood for nails or screws.

gimlets

gimp pin a small brass panel pin for upholstery, whose shaft is 10—19 mm in length.

girder a large main steel beam with upper and lower chords separated by a web; a lattice beam, truss or universal beam.

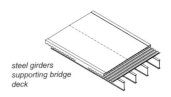

steel girders supporting bridge deck

glare in lighting design, a condition of poor light distribution in which the ability of the human eye to see is impaired due to excessive contrasts.

glass a hard, impermeable, transparent material formed from sand, soda ash, limestone and dolomite; used for many applications especially window glazing; types included as separate entries are listed below:
*absorbing glass, see tinted solar control glass; *acoustical glass, acoustic control glass, see sound control glass; *alarm glass; annealed glass; *anti-bandit laminated glass; *anti-fading glass; *anti-sun glass, see solar control glass; *anti-vandal glass; *antique glass; *armour-plated glass, see bullet-resistant laminated glass; *bent glass; *blast-resistant laminated glass; *blown glass; *blown sheet glass; *body-tinted glass; *borosilicate glass; *bull's-eye glass, see bullion; *bullet-resistant laminated glass; *bullion, bullion glass; *cast glass; *cathedral glass; *cellular glass; *channel glass; *chemically strengthened glass; *cladding glass; *clear float glass; *clear plate glass; *clear sheet glass; *coated float glass, see surface coated float glass; *coloured opaque glass; *corrugated glass; *crown glass; *crystal glass, see lead glass; *curved glass, see bent glass; *cut glass, see crystal; *diffuse reflection glass, diffused glass; *drawn sheet glass, drawn glass, see sheet glass; *electronic shielding glass; *expanded glass, see foam glass, cellular glass; *fibreglass, fiberglass; *filigree glass; *fire resisting glass, fire-resistant glass, fire glass; *flat drawn glass, see clear sheet

*glass; *flat glass; *float glass; *foam glass, foamed glass; *fused silica glass; *Georgian wired glass; *heat-absorbing glass, see tinted solar control glass; *heat resisting glass; *heat-soaked glass; *insulation glass, see sealed glazed unit; *intumescent glass, see laminated intumescent glass; *laminated glass; *laminated intumescent glass; *laminated safety glass; *laminated solar control glass; *laminated sound control glass; *laminated ultraviolet light control glass; *lead glass; *lead X-ray glass; *leaded glass, see leaded light; *low emissivity glass; *milk glass; *mirror glass, mirrored glass; *noise control glass, noise reduction glass, see sound control glass; *obscured glass; *one-way glass; *opal glass, opalescent glass; *opaque glass; *patterned glass; *plate glass, polished plate glass; *potash water glass; *profile glass, see channel glass; *Pyrex, see borosilicate glass; *quartz glass, see fused silica glass; *radiation-shielding glass; *reeded glass; *reflective float glass, see surface coated float glass; *reflective glass; *rolled glass; *roughcast glass; *safety glass; *security glass; *sheet glass; *shielding glass, see radiation-shielding glass; *silica glass, see fused silica glass; *silk-screened glass, silk-screen glass; *smoked glass; *soda-lime glass; *solar control glass; *sound control glass, sound insulation glass, sound reduction glass; *spandrel glass, see cladding glass; *special glass; *surface coated float glass; *surface-modified tinted float glass; *tempered glass, see toughened glass; *tessera; *tinted glass; *tinted solar control glass; *toughened glass; *translucent glass, see diffuse reflection glass; *transparent mirror glass; *ultraviolet control glass, see laminated ultraviolet light control glass; *Venetian mirror glass; *volcanic glass; *water glass, see sodium silicate; *window glass; *wired glass, wired cast glass; *X-ray resistant glass, see lead X-ray glass.*

glass balustrade see all-glass balustrade, glazed balustrade.

glass bit see glass drill.

glass block, glass brick, hollow glass block; a rectangular hollow block made from two moulded glass units fused together, whose surfaces may be clear,

coloured or textured; used to form glass screens and external translucent glazing.

types of glass block

glass concrete solid glass blocks bonded with reinforced concrete, used to form a wall, screen or surface.

glass cutter a small tool with a longitudinal handle and sharpened rotating wheel used by a glazier for cutting glass; a scored line is made on the glass surface, along which it will naturally snap.

glass door see glazed door, all-glass door, casement door, French door.

glass drill, glass bit; a drill bit for boring holes in sheets of glass, usually tipped with a cutting plate of hard metal.

glassfibre-base bitumen felt bitumen felt whose supporting fibrous mat is mainly of glass fibres.

glassfibre cloth, woven roving; reinforcement for fibreglass and composite materials consisting of rovings which have been woven into a mesh.

glassfibre mat a reinforcing mat of chopped strand used in fibreglass and other composite materials.

glassfibre reinforced referring to composite products and materials which consist of glass fibres in a matrix of cement, concrete, plastics, etc., also called glass reinforced.

glassfibre-reinforced cement, glassfibre-reinforced concrete, GRC; a fibre-reinforced composite consisting of glass fibres containing zirconium in a Portland cement matrix; used for thin-walled panels and street furniture.

glassfibre-reinforced concrete see glassfibre-reinforced polymer/concrete, glassfibre-reinforced cement.

glassfibre-reinforced gypsum, glass-reinforced gypsum, GRG; a tough, non-combustible composite consisting of glass fibres in a gypsum matrix; used for making fire-resisting building boards and panels.

glassfibre-reinforced plaster see glass-reinforced plaster.

glassfibre-reinforced plastics any products consisting of glass fibres which have been impregnated with synthetic resin, usually polyester; used for mouldings, sheets, roofing slates and drainage fittings.

glassfibre-reinforced polymer/concrete, glassfibre-reinforced concrete, GRPC; a polyester resin-bound concrete which contains glass fibres; less dense than ordinary concrete and with a higher tensile strength.

glass lens see lens.

glass mosaic one of a number of small, flat pieces or blocks of glass supplied on a paper backing, used as tiled floor and wall covering and for decorative effects.

glasspaper fine sanding paper whose abrasive is powdered glass, used for smoothing and polishing.

glasspaper block, sandpaper block; a small pad to which a number of sheets of abrasive paper have been attached; used for sharpening lead pencils and charcoals.

glass partition see glazed partition.

glass plank see channel glass.

glass/polyester base bitumen felt bitumen felt whose reinforcing fibrous mat is mainly of glass and polyester fibres.

glass reinforced see glassfibre reinforced.

glass-reinforced gypsum glassfibre-reinforced gypsum.

glass-reinforced plaster plaster which contains glass fibres for added reinforcement; used for ornamental pillars, pilasters, cornices, etc.; abb. GRP; often glassfibre-reinforced gypsum.

glass-reinforced polyester, GRP; a product consisting of glass fibres which have been impregnated with polyester resin; used for mouldings, sheets, roofing slates and drainage fittings.

glass silk see glass wool.

glass size see pane size.

glass tile, glass slate; a roofing tile made of glass, used to allow light into a roofspace and laid with normal roofing tiles.

glass unit see sealed glazed unit.

glass wool, glass silk; an insulating material produced from fine glass fibres which have been sprayed with a binder and formed into random masses.

Glauber salt hydrated sodium sulphate used in the manufacture of dyes and in some heat storage systems.

glauconite 1 a dark green form of the mineral biotite, an iron silicate mineral found in the sea bed.
2 see green earth.

glaze, glazing; a hardwearing glossy impenetrable finish for tiles and other ceramic products achieved by vitrification of the surface and of a surface coating such as ash, enamel, etc.

glazed 1 referring to an opening, frame or partition into which glazing has been fitted.
2 referring to ceramic products which have been fired with a glaze.

glazed balustrade a balustrade with an infill of glass in a timber, steel or aluminium frame.

glazed brick a brick of which at least one end and one face have been glazed during firing.

glazed door a door whose leaf is glazed, particularly one with glazed panels in a frame; see all-glass door, casement door, French door.

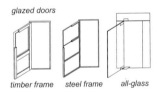

glazed doors

timber frame   *steel frame*   *all-glass*

glazed floor, glass floor; a transparent or translucent floor of specially strengthened glass panels held in frames.

glazed metal door, metal glazed door; a steel or aluminium framed door with one or more glazed panels.

glazed partition, glass partition; an interior dividing screen which consists of framed or structural glass.

glazed roof, glass roof; a roof or part of a roof constructed of glass panels in a timber, steel or aluminium frame.

glazed tile a ceramic tile which has been treated with an earthenware or enamel glaze before firing to provide a shiny impenetrable surface.

glazed timber door, timber glazed door; a timber-framed door with one or more glazed panels.

glazed unit see sealed glazed unit, double-glazed unit, triple-glazed unit.

glazed wall see window wall.

glazier a tradesman or skilled worker responsible for the installation and replacement of windows and glazing.

glazier's hammer a hammer with an angled oblong head used in framing and the pinning of glazing beads; also any small hammers used for this purpose.

glazier's point see glazing sprig.

glazier's putty see putty.

glazing 1 the installation of glass, glass panels or products into frames or other supporting systems.

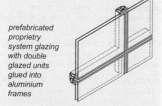

prefabricated proprietry system glazing with double glazed units glued into aluminium frames

2 the resulting glass panels and windows thus installed; see below for types included as separate entries:
*applied sash glazing, see secondary glazing; *balcony glazing; *cellular glazing, see cellular sheet; *double glazing; *dry glazing; *external glazing; *frameless glazing; *inside glazing; *internal glazing, interior glazing; *intruder glazing; *lead glazing, see leaded light; *outer glazing, see external glazing; *outside glazing; *patent glazing; *planar glazing, see structural glazing; *polycarbonate cellular glazing, see polycarbonate cellular sheet; *roof glazing, see glazed roof, rooflight; *safety glazing; *secondary glazing;

*security glazing; *single glazing; *structural glazing; *subsidiary glazing; *system glazing, see patent glazing; *triple glazing; *upper glazing, see top light.*
3 the application of a glaze to ceramic products.
see salt glazing.

glazing bar, division bar, window bar; a framing member to which glazing is fixed; part of a timber window frame or metal patent glazing, etc.; see frame member.

glazing bead, glazing fillet; a strip of timber, metal or other material used to fasten glazing in a frame.

glazing bead

glazing bedding in glazing, a bedding compound such as putty applied around the rebate in a window frame prior to the fitting of a pane of glass.

glazing block, setting block; in glazing, a packing piece set beneath or beside the glass to keep it in position in its frame while it is being fixed with putty or beads.

glazing capping a profile fixed to the outside of glazing bars to protect and conceal the joint between it and the glazing, especially one of extruded aluminium or metal clipped on over glazing bars of a patent glazing system.

glazing cleat a small angled stainless steel or aluminium metal jointing component fixed to a frame to hold a pane in position.

glazing clip in glazing, a small non-corrodible metal jointing component inserted into a hole in a metal window frame to hold a pane in position.

glazing compound in glazing, resilient material applied in semi-liquid form, putty or sealant which sets to form a seal between a glass pane and its frame; see elastic glazing compound, non-setting glazing compound, putty.

glazing fillet see glazing bead.

glazing gasket, seal; a strip of flexible material such as neoprene fixed around the external edges of a pane of glass to provide a weathertight seal between it and its framing member.

glazing peg in metal framed glazing, one of a number of pieces holding the glass pane or panel in its frame.

glazing putty see putty.

glazing rebate a rebate in a glazing bar or frame against which glazing is fitted.

glazing sealant see glazing compound.

glazing size see pane size.

glazing sprig, brad, glazier's point; in glazing, a small headless nail used to hold a pane of glass in a *glazing sprigs* timber frame while the putty hardens, or to fasten a glazing bead.

glazing system see patent glazing.

glazing tape adhesive tape used as weatherproofing for a window.

glazing unit see sealed glazed unit.
  glazing unit spacer see spacer.

globe a spherical or ovoid translucent diffuser or shade for a luminaire.

globe valve in water supply pipework, a screwdown valve with a spherical body.

Gloephyllum separium see slash conk.

gloss 1 reflectance or shininess in a surface such as paint, varnish, ceramics or other planar material.
  2 the degree of reflection of light from a dry paint surface; in Britain graded into five degrees: flat, eggshell flat, eggshell gloss, semi-gloss, full gloss; in the USA there are only four, with eggshell covering both eggshell flat and eggshell gloss.
  3 a vague word to describe grades of glossiness in a dry paint surface, characterized by a high reflectance of light.
  gloss paint any paint such as alkyd paint which has a high gloss finish, used on wood and metal surfaces.

GLS lamp see general lighting service lamp.

glue any adhesive manufactured from boiling up animal and fish remains, or one that sets without applied heat; in general use glue is synonymous with adhesive, although adhesive is the preferred term in construction; see adhesive for types of glues; see also cement.
  glue block see angle block.

glued and laminated beam see laminated timber beam.

glued joint a joint in which glue is used as the fastening medium.

glue gun an electrically heated device for applying lines of hot melt glue to parts to be joined together, seams of vinyl matting, etc.

glue laminated timber, glulam, laminated wood; a structural wood product composed of lengths of timber glued together longitudinally in strips to form a larger piece; this reduces the effects of defects in individual strips; see laminated timber beam.

glue line the thin gap or seam between two abutting glued surfaces, filled with adhesive.

glue size 1 a weak water-based glue solution for sealing plaster and other porous surfaces onto which further decoration may be applied.
  2 a similar solution used also to stiffen paper, card and cloth and for gluing light papers and metal foils to a base.

glue spreader a simple rubber or plastic implement with a straight or serrated blade for applying glue to large surfaces.

glulam see glue laminated timber.
  glulam beam see laminated timber beam.

gluten glue starch glue made from gluten, a mixture of proteins present in wheat flour.

glyph in classical architecture, a vertical decorative groove or channel found in threes making up triglyphs in an entablature.

GMA welding, gas metal-arc welding, gas-shielded metal-arc welding; a method of welding metals in which the arc is shielded with an active gas such as carbon dioxide or oxygen, an inert gas such as argon, or a mixture of the two; a generic name for MIG, MAG and TIG welding.

Gmellin's blue see artificial ultramarine.

gneiss a dark, banded, coarse-grained metamorphic rock composed of quartz, feldspar and mica, formed under intense conditions of heat and pressure; see gneissose micaschist, foliated gneiss, granite-gneiss.

gneissose micaschist, foliated gneiss; a dark grey or black layered metamorphic rock containing a high proportion of mica; a variety of gneiss, it is cleaved for use in construction as paving and tiles.

gobelin high-quality woven decorative fabric from a state-owned French carpet factory named after its founder family which supplied to the court from Arras in Flanders in the 1400s; any tapestry of a similar type or weave.

godroon see gadroon.

going, run; the horizontal dimension of a step as measured in plan, perpendicular to its front face; see also total going.

gold a yellowish, heavy, soft and malleable metal, **Au**, which is an excellent conductor of electricity; a much sought after commodity, also used in the form of leaf as a decorative finish and in industrial products such as thin conducting coatings for glass.
gold foil see gold leaf.
gold ground a method of painting in which colours are applied to a background of gesso covered with gold leaf, used especially in medieval religious art to emphasize celestial glory.
gold leaf, gold foil; a fine sheet of gold as thin as 0.0001 mm; used for the ornamental covering of embellishment, plaster casts, and for illuminating manuscripts.
gold ochre a cleaned and crushed warm brownish variety of yellow ochre pigment.
gold size an oleoresinous varnish used for sticking down gold leaf and for making fillers; also called gilding size; see also bole.

golden section, sectio aurea (Lat.); a division of a line or value into two parts such that the ratio of the length of the longer part to the whole is equal to that of the length of the shorter part to the longer part (about 1:1.618); designs made on this basis are considered to have good composition.

Gonystylus spp. see ramin.

goods lift a large robust lift designed to carry goods and people.

gorge 1 a narrow structure or neck in a castle leading to a bastion, or the rear entrance to any other fortification.
2 see trochilus.
3 see scotia.

gorgerin see hypotrachelion.

Gothic architecture see full page entry on pp. 220–221.
Gothic arch see pointed arch.

gouache a quick-drying opaque watercolour paint with a gum binder and filler of opaque white; a method or technique of painting with gouache paints.

gouge a concave chisel used for cutting rounded grooves in wood; types included as separate entries are listed below:

gouge

spoon gouge *turning gouge*

*crank gouge; *firmer gouge; *front bent gouge, spoon gouge; *turning gouge.

governor see gas governor, appliance governor.

grade 1 see gradient.
2 the ground level of final excavations and earthworks in a building site.
3 see quality.
4 see classification.
5 class; the classification of a material, product, system or piece of work regarding quality.
6 see grade of concrete.

grade beam see ground beam.

graded aggregate aggregate which has been sorted into particles of a particular range of sizes; see also continuously graded aggregate, gap graded aggregate.

graded density chipboard chipboard manufactured with woodchips of various sizes, graded from finer on the surface to coarser towards the core.

graded density chipboard

grade of concrete, concrete grade; for concrete, the specified characteristic cube strength expressed in N/mm^2.

gradient, grade, slope; the degree of slope of an inclined plane, track or pipeline relative to the (continued on p. 222)

GOTHIC

In the 1130s Abbot Suger of Saint-Denis near Paris argued that it was necessary to rebuild his abbey church because of crowding caused by the throng of pilgrims who "spilled out of every door." The chevet and narthex of 1140–44 at St. Denis were the first to represent this new style, the *opus modernum* or "French style", which lasted from the mid-12th century to the 16th century, and which is now known by the mocking term *"stilo gotico"*, the Gothic style, given by its Italian Renaissance critics.

Right: exploded view of section of compound pier from the Basilica of St Denis, 1135-1144, showing carving of main and secondary shafts

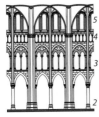 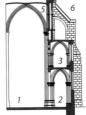

Left: internal elevation and cross section of the Gothic cathedral of Notre Dame in Noyon, France, c.1155-1205, showing 1 nave, 2 aisles, 3 gallery, 4 triforium, 5 clerestorey, and 6 flying buttress. Scale 1:800

Gothic can be described as the first "international style" because it spread rapidly from the Ile de France, Champagne and Normandy to Britain, and was thence transported via ambitious work-seeking masons around the continent, so that local variations of High and Late Gothic can be found in nearly every European country. In Britain, Gothic's different phases are divided into the **Early English** style, the **Geometric**, **Curvilinear** or **Decorated** style and the **Perpendicular** or **Rectilinear** style.

Above: High Gothic rose window at cathedral of Notre-Dame, Amiens, 1220-47

1 Moorish   *2 Early English*   *3 Decorated*   *4 Perpendicular*

Above: development of Gothic tracery from a Moorish antecent to the Perpendicular style: 1 Moorish , 2 Early Gothic, Great Abingdon church, nr. Cambridge, c.1200; 3 High Gothic, Great Haseley church, Oxfordshire, c.1300; 4 King's College Chapel, Cambridge, c.1446-1515

Gothic appears particularly in the largest and tallest **cathedrals** ever built in Europe, over a period in which Christianized Europe had extinguished paganism and the traditions of classical civilization, and in which the Catholic church had established itself as the sole spiritual power.

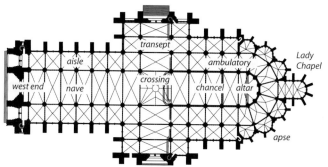

Above, High Gothic, Cathedral of Notre Dame, Amiens, France, c.1220-69, Robert of Luzarches, Thomas and Renault of Cormont (prior to addition of chapels in 16th century)

Below, tracery and other typical Gothic elements in part elevation of Kölner Dom, Cologne, 1248-1880. Scale 1:90

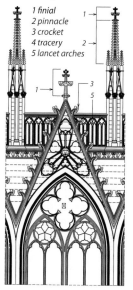

1 finial
2 pinnacle
3 crocket
4 tracery
5 lancet arches

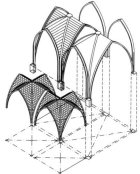

Above, system of Gothic vaulting over nave and aisles, showing quadripartite ribbed vault over nave, and groin vaults over aisles

The **pointed arch**, its most distinguished feature, is not a new invention but a loan from ancient Sassanian architecture via the Arabs and Normans from the time of the Crusades. Nevertheless, the slender high arches combined with **clustered columns** and **ribbed vaults**, the development of the exterior **flying buttress**, and the gradual reduction of walls to a system of richly decorated fenestration, refined **rose windows** and decorative designs and sculptures, including gargoyles, create the appearance of etherial skeletal structures reaching up to heaven.

horizontal, expressed as a percentage or given as a ratio of the level difference to horizontal travel.

grading 1 the breakdown of percentages by weight of different sized particles in a granular material such as soil or aggregate.
2 see sieving.
3 see classification.
4 in siteworks, the formation of masses of earth into the required contoured shape with bulldozers and other mechanical plant, into embankments, etc.
grading curve a graphical representation of the range of grain sizes of particles in a granular material such as soil or concrete.

graffiti see next entry.

graffito, pl. graffiti; **1** writing inscribed or written on a wall, especially in ancient times; nowadays unwanted writings or drawings on building surfaces in spray paints, felt pen, etc., written in plural form graffiti.
2 a marble tablet onto which carved decoration making use of shadows is inscribed.
3 see sgraffito.

graining a decorative surface treatment made by painting or otherwise imitating the figure of wood or marble.
grainer any paintbrush used for imitating the grain effects of wood and marble on wall surfaces as decoration.

grain size a property of the coarseness of a granular material, the relative size of its constituent granules.

gram, gramme; SI unit of mass, abb. **g**.

grand master key a key which fits all the locks in a number of suites of locks, each of which has a master key.

granite a very durable igneous rock type whose basic constituents are alkali feldspars and quartz, much used in construction as cladding, masonry and paving.
granite-gneiss a composite metamorphic rock – gneiss – which occurs in abundance with granite.

granny bonnet see bonnet hip tile.

granny's tooth see router plane.

granodiorite a granite-like igneous rock used in building for cobblestones, kerbstones, flooring and cladding.

granular referring to a material which is composed of discrete pellets or grains, or whose structure is such; see also coarse grained.
granular backfill, gravel fill; granular mineral material used for backfilling excavations, providing a stable and permeable covering for foundations and footings.
granular soil, coarse soil; noncohesive soil composed of particles of sand, gravel, etc. over 0.06 mm in size.

granulated blast-furnace slag blast-furnace slag, a by-product of steel making, cooled in water to form granules; it is used, ground, as a binder in cement.

granulated cork corkwood, usually off-cuts from a conversion or manufacturing process, which is ground and used as loose thermal insulation.

granulite a banded metamorphic rock which contains quartz and feldspar, similar to gneiss but without mica.

grape an ornamental motif consisting of a series of tear-shaped forms.

grape black see vine black.

graphics 1 pictorial matter produced by digital, printed or other repetitive means; computer graphics is the generation of a graphic representation, animation or drawing with a computer.
2 graphic art; art produced by a repeatable process of printmaking such as woodcut, linocut, engraving and silk screen printing; prints are limited to a certain number and each is produced by the artist himself.

graphite, plumbago; a naturally occurring form of grey carbon used as pencil lead, as a lubricant and for its properties of electrical conductivity; when used as a greyish black pigment it is known as black lead.

grass any of a large number of species of hardy plant from the family *Gramineae* or *Poaceae* used in landscaping for covering areas of parkland, fields and lawn.
grass paving see cellular paver.
grass roof see turf roof, green roof.

grate see bottomgrate, grating.

grated channel a drainage channel with a grating housed in its upper surface; used for external paved areas, garages, etc. where continuity of surface is desirable; often a rebated block channel.

grating, grate, grille; a metal barred or perforated component over an opening in construction to provide protection whilst allowing for the passage of air, water, etc.; see channel grating, domical grating, inlet grating, outlet grating.

gravel, shingle; a classification of granular mineral material, broken stone composed of particles from 2 mm to 60 mm in size; graded as fine gravel (particles size from 2 mm to 6 mm), medium gravel (particle size from 6 mm to 20 mm) and coarse gravel (particle size from 20 mm to 60 mm).

gravel fill see granular backfill.

graver see burin.

gravity boiler a heating appliance from which hot water or steam is circulated for use via convection, without the need for pumps, based on the fact that hot water in flow pipework will rise when balanced by cooler water in return pipework.

gravity door hinge see rising hinge.

gravity drain a drainpipe in which waste and soil water is conveyed by the force of gravity rather than by pumping.

gravity retaining wall a retaining wall which resists horizontal forces by virtue of its weight alone.

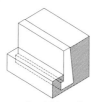
gravity retaining wall

gravity toggle a toggle bolt with a locking 'job' hinged off-centre so that it swings into a vertical position once inserted into a bored hole, and clamps against the rear of construction.

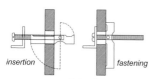
insertion   *fastening*
gravity toggle

gravity wall see gravity retaining wall.

GRC glassfibre-reinforced cement.

grease trap, grease interceptor; in the drainage of industrial kitchens and restaurants, a chamber in a drain which separates grease or oil from the waste water to prevent the clogging of pipes.

great brick a large, thin brick used in medieval England to avoid paying excessive brick tax; see also tax brick.

Grecian purple see Tyrian purple.

Greek architecture the architecture of ancient Greece from c. 3000 BC to the Roman period, characterized by temples, use of proportions and orders; roughly divided into the Geometrical, Archaic, Classic and Hellenistic periods; see also full page entry on p. 224.
see Helladic; Hellenistic; Mycenaean architecture; Minoan architecture.
Greek column see Doric column, Ionic column, Corinthian column.
Greek key classical two-tone banded ornament using a fret or meander pattern.

Greek key

Greek orders the three orders of classical Greek architecture: Doric, Ionic and Corinthian; see Greek architecture entry.

Greek pitch see rosin.

green 1 a description of timber that is freshly cut and unseasoned, with a moisture content above saturation point; see also green concrete.
2 a general name for shades of colour in the visible spectrum between blue and yellow, covering the range of electromagnetic wavelengths 480–560 µm; see below for green pigments included as separate entries:
*Arnaudon's green; *baryta green, see manganese green; *Casali's green, viridian; *Cassel green, see manganese green; *chrome green; *chromium oxide green; *cobalt green; *Dingler's green, chromium oxide green; *emerald chromium oxide,

(continued on p. 226)

GREECE

Before the first millenium BC there were two flourishing Bronze Age cultures in Greece that are usually regarded as the oldest in Europe. The older peaceful, seaborne civilization on the island of Crete is known as **Minoan** culture, and the other, mainland culture is known as **Mycenaean**, after an important archaeological site at Mycenae.

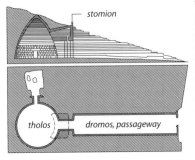

The Minoan asymmetrically-arranged palaces were constructed of stone rubble or **sun-dried brick** coated with plaster, and incorporated proper drainage systems. In their construction methods the Mycenaeans reflected Minoan influene, and they also built fortifictions with massive rough-hewn blocks of stone, each weighing several tons; the later Greeks called this technology **Cyclopean masonry**.

Left, plan and section of the Treasury of Atreus, or "Tomb of Agamemnon", Mycenae, Greece,1325-1250 BC, scale 1:1250

Around the beginning of the first millenium BC the **Dorian** Greeks arrived in the northern mainland of Greece, while the **Ionians** settled in Athens, the west coast of Asia Minor (modern Turkey) and on the Aegean islands. The first stone temples were constructed in the 7th century BC and, by this time, a standard pattern had already been adopted, which to remain unchanged over the following centuries.

The **peristyle** of columns surrounding the temple mark out the sacred and ceremonial areas. Behind them there is the **naos** – or **cella** in Latin – an otherwise empty room housing the cult image. The room behind the naos was a treasury. The temple was only a part of a much larger sacral precinct, usually including a quantity of other shrines, altars, treasuries, theatres and colonnades linked by a ceremonial road lined with statues, all accommodated naturally into the landscape.

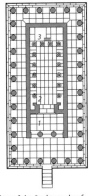

Above, plan of the 2nd temple of Zeus, Nemea, Argolis, Greece, 330 BC, 1:1000

Greek monumental architecture is based on **trabeated construction** of marble, that is, structures of **columns** and **walls** supporting horizontal **beams** over openings and rooms. The repeated combination of various architectural components according to a predefined aesthetic pattern is called an **order**.

Left, reconstructed section of the Parthenon, Athens, 447-432 BC, scale 1:1000

Greek architecture can be primarily classified by its column-types – those of the **Doric**, **Ionic** and **Corinthian** orders – whose main distinction can be found in their capitals. The order, however, is based on the combination of a larger number of architectural elements, the **entablature** or main beam above the columns, which consists of horizontal bands of **architrave**, **frieze** and **cornice**, and the column with its distinctive **capital**, **shaft** and **base**. The detailed rules of an order are defined by the details and harmony of these building parts.

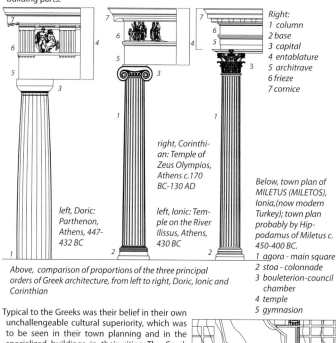

Right:
1 column
2 base
3 capital
4 entablature
5 architrave
6 frieze
7 cornice

right, Corinthian: Temple of Zeus Olympios, Athens c.170 BC-130 AD

left, Doric: Parthenon, Athens, 447-432 BC

left, Ionic: Temple on the River Ilissus, Athens, 430 BC

Above, comparison of proportions of the three principal orders of Greek architecture, from left to right, Doric, Ionic and Corinthian

Below, town plan of MILETUS (MILETOS), Ionia,(now modern Turkey); town plan probably by Hippodamus of Miletus c. 450-400 BC.
1 agora - main square
2 stoa - colonnade
3 bouleterion-council chamber
4 temple
5 gymnasion

Typical to the Greeks was their belief in their own unchallengeable cultural superiority, which was to be seen in their town planning and in the specialized buildings in their cities. The Greek traveller and geographer Pausanias wrote in his famous *Description of Greece* (2nd century AD) "From Chaeroneia it is twenty stades (2½ miles) to Panopeus, a city of the Phocians, if one can give the name of city to a habitation which possesses no government offices, no gymnasium, no theatre, no market-place, no water descending to a fountain, where the people live in bare shelters just like mountain cabins, right on a ravine. Nevertheless, they have boundaries with their neighbours, and even send delegates to the Phocian assembly." It seems that all the essential building types, with the exception of the temple, were missing in Panopeus, and the tone of the venerable author in noting this, gives an idea of the level of civilization to be expected in any typical Greek **polis** (city state).

see viridian; *emerald green; *emeraulde green, see viridian; *Gellert green, cobalt green; *green gold; *Guinet's green, see viridian; *Hungarian green, see malachite; *Imperial green; *leaf green, leek green, see chrome green; *manganese green; *mineral green, see malachite; *Mittler's green, viridian; *Monastral green, see phthalocyanine green; *moss green, see chrome green; *mountain green; *native green, chrome oxide; *nickel azo yellow, see green gold; *nitrate green, chrome green; *oil green; *oxide of chromium, see chromium oxide green; *Pannetier's green, see viridian; *phthalocyanine green; *Plessey's green, chromium oxide green; *Rinman's green, see cobalt green; *Rosenstiehl's green, see manganese green; *Royal green, see chrome green; *Schnitzer's green, see chromium oxide green; *Schweinfurt green, see emerald green; *smaragd green, see viridian; *Swedish green, see cobalt green; *thalo green, see phthalocyanine green; *transparent oxide of chromium, see viridian; *vert emeraude, see viridian; *viridian; *zinc green, see cobalt green.

green ash [*Fraxinus pennsylvanica*], see ash.

greenbelt in town planning, an area of open country, parkland, woodland, etc. within or surrounding a built-up area, left unbuilt to prevent the spread of urban development and provide amenity for the local inhabitants.

green brick a clay brick pressed into shape but not dried or fired.

green concrete a description of concrete that has set but not yet hardened.

green earth, glauconite, terra verde; a group of greenish mineral clays or earths containing iron hydroxide, used in the manufacture of earth pigments.

greenfield site a site of rural or parkland character targeted for development, often at the periphery of a built-up area, on which there are not, nor have ever been, existing buildings.

green gold, nickel azo yellow; a slightly poisonous greenish-yellow pigment used in oil paints and watercolours.

green man see foliate head.

green roof roof construction comprising growing plant material laid in soil over a drainage layer and waterproofing membrane; the soil layer provides insulation and protection from the elements; see turf roof, grass roof.

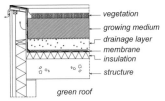

- vegetation
- growing medium
- drainage layer
- membrane
- insulation
- structure

green roof

greenstone a dark green igneous rock type, diabase, containing feldspar and hornblende.

green timber timber which is unseasoned.

grey alder, white alder (Am); [*Alnus incana*], see alder.

grey cast iron, grey iron; non-ductile cast iron which contains carbon in flake form.

grey lime quicklime produced by heating grey-coloured chalk.

grey poplar [*Populus canescens*] see poplar.

grey scale in colour theory, a scale of achromatic colours, ranging from white to black, used to define the greyness of a colour.

greywacke a grey or grey-green, fine-grained sandstone used locally for aggregates and chippings.

grey water waste water from domestic use, which does not contain soil from toilets and other soil appliances.

GRG glassfibre-reinforced gypsum.

gribble, marine crustacean; [*Limnoria spp.*] any of a number of marine organisms which cause damage to wood submerged in seawater by boring.

grid, 1 structural grid, modular grid; a regular framework of reference lines to which the dimensions of major structural components of the plan of a building are fixed.
2 in town planning, a chequerboard network of intersecting streets and avenues forming the basic layout of a city or town.

3 electricity supply grid; an area-wide distribution network of cables, substations and other equipment to provide a supply of electricity.

grid line one of the lines demarking a structural, modular or layout grid of a building, to which dimensions are coordinated.

griffe see spur.

griffin, gryphon; a decorative motif of a mythological beast with a lion's body and the head of an eagle, used especially in Romanesque times, but known from Mesopotamia, Egypt and Greece.

grill see grille.

grillage, grillage foundation; a foundation construction for a column or concentrated load consisting of a series of layered beams laid at right angles to one another.

grille, 1 grill; an open grating or screen to allow for the passage of air, as a security measure, to enclose space, etc.

2 in ventilation and air conditioning, a protective cover for an air terminal unit with openings, baffles, etc. for air to pass through.

3 see also window grille, window louvre.

grinder a machine tool with a rotating mineral disc for shaping and smoothing hard materials such as stone, concrete and metals; see also bench grinder, angle grinder.

grinding the removal of excess material on a rough stone or metal surface to produce a fine finish using an abrasive.

grinding bevel, cannel, ground bevel; the splayed end or edge surface of the blade of a chisel or other cutting tool, honed to provide a cutting edge.

grinding burr a round, conical, disc-shaped, etc. drill bit of mineral material; used in specialist stone and metalwork for smoothing and cleaning irregular surfaces.

grinding burrs

grinding cup a metal disc-attachment for a rotary stone grinder, with a raised circumferential edge coated or faced with abrasive material.

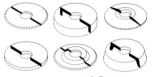

grinding cups

grinding disc a replaceable thin rotating disc of abrasive material as used in an angle grinder; used for cutting and grinding.

grinding wheel a stiff rotating disc of abrasive material used for honing tools, grinding and sanding; see also bench grinder.

grindstone an even block or spinning wheel of mineral material used for sharpening the blades of tools and grinding stone surfaces.

grinning through, grinning; a defect in a paint or plaster finish in which the colour or a pattern from an underlying layer or coat is clearly visible.

grit coarse angular aggregate used as an abrasive surface in road construction.

grog, chamotte; a ceramic material used for making firebricks and terracotta, consisting of fresh clay mixed with crushed fired clay.

groin the curved edge formed by the intersection of two masonry vaults.

groined vault see groin vault.

groin rib see diagonal rib.

groin vault, cross vault, groined vault, intersecting barrel vault; a vault formed by the perpendicular intersection of two barrel vaults, found especially in early masonry churches.

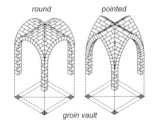

round   pointed

groin vault

groove any slot-like cutting or relief in construction, such as the recess in one side of a tongue and groove joint.

groove joint see dummy joint.

grooving saw, notching saw, stairbuilder's saw, trenching saw; a saw which resembles a plane, having a saw blade embedded in the base of the stock; used for cutting grooves in wood.

grossular a greenish variety of the mineral garnet; also known as grossular garnet or grossularite; see also hessonite, cinnamon stone.

grotesque, grottesco; a decorative artwork or carving which makes use of vines embellished with interwoven animals, plants and fruit.

ground 1 material at or under the surface of the earth or an area or plot of the earth's surface, land; see earth.
2 see foundation.
3 one of a number of timber strips fixed at regular spacing to masonry as a nailing base for finishing boards; see also grounds.
4 the treated opaque surface in painting which provides a base for the application of paint; see substrate.
5 a description of a concrete, masonry, metal, etc. finish produced by smoothing with abrasives; see honed, rubbed finish

ground anchor, ground anchorage; a system of steel rods, bolts, guys or braces for fixing a structure firmly to its base, to a foundation or to the ground.

ground bashing see dynamic consolidation.

ground beam, 1 grade beam (Am); in concrete construction, a beam which transmits the weight of walls to a foundation structure, or is itself a foundation.
2 tie beam; in piled foundation construction, a concrete beam which connects a number of piles or pile caps and transmits the loading from walls, etc. down to the piles.
3 in timber-framed construction, the lowest structural timber beam which transmits loading from walls to a foundation.

ground bevel see grinding bevel.

ground coat in paintwork, a matt base coat of pigment over which a glaze coat is applied.

ground compaction the reduction of the air and water content of the underlying soil by mechanical vibrating, rolling and by various forms of draining; see also dynamic consolidation.

ground compression see dynamic consolidation.

ground engineering see geotechnical engineering.

ground finish see ground.

ground floor a lower storey in a building that provides principal access at or near ground level; in the USA and continental Europe this is known as the first floor; see base floor.

ground improvement see soil reinforcement.

ground investigation see geotechnical survey.

ground plate, ground sill; the lowest horizontal frame member in traditional timber-framed or log construction, to which other structural components such as floor joists and posts are fixed.

ground profile see topography.

grounds, 1 groundwork; timber battens attached to a masonry or other wall surface as a base for a lining such as wallboard.
2 common grounds, rough grounds; narrow timber pieces set into or attached to masonry as nailing strips for a lining, battening or trim.
3 an area of surrounding land, gardens or an estate attached to a building.

ground sill see ground plate.

ground slab see ground supported floor.

ground supported floor, ground slab, slab-on-grade (Am), floor bed; reinforced concrete floor construction cast directly onto the underlying ground so that loads from the floor are transmitted evenly to the ground below.

groundwater lowering see dewatering.

groundwork 1 in the construction of a building, the initial stage of construction, making and filling excavations, laying drains and dealing with groundwater; also called earthwork.
2 see grounds.

group connector, breech fitting; a drain fitting with a number of inlets connected to a gully.

group heating a system of heating for a building complex or housing estate, smaller than district heating, in which heated water is piped to a number of buildings from a central heating plant.

grout 1 a liquid mixture of cement and water used for filling cracks, joints and voids in masonry and concrete construction, and for cementing components in place.
2 a soft flowing slurry of cement, sand and water injected into voids in unstable ground to provide support and reinforcement.
3 see injection mortar.
4 see tile grout.
grout concreting work in grouted concrete.
grouted aggregate concrete see grouted concrete.
grouted concrete, grouted aggregate concrete, intrusion concrete, pre-packed concrete, preplaced concrete; concrete made by placing coarse aggregate in a mould or form and then grouting or injecting with a binding mortar; used for special cases and underwater work.
grouting, cementation, injection; the strengthening and support of unstable or loose soils and rock, and in some cases old masonry, concretework, etc. by the injection of cement grout into prebored holes and small voids; see also pressure grouting, artificial cementing.
grouting concrete concrete used to fill voids and cracks in existing concrete construction.
grout rake see raker.

growing medium the uppermost layer of nutritious soil laid in landscaping and green roofs, etc. for plants to grow in; also called a growth medium.

growth ring see annual ring.

GRP glass-reinforced polyester, glass-reinforced plaster.

GRPC glassfibre-reinforced polymer/concrete.

GTA welding see TIG welding.

Guaiacum spp. see lignum vitae.

guarantee, guaranty, warranty; a written agreement covering repair or replacement of defects or faults in products or workmanship within a set period of time; see security.

guideline see design guideline.

guilloche a decorative motif consisting of interwoven curving bands surrounding a series of circles, usually applied to a moulding; a curving fret motif; angular guilloche, see meander; see also wave pattern.

guilloche

Guinet's green see viridian.

gulley see gully.

gully, drain, gulley, trapped gully; an outlet fitting for a drain, most often trapped, into which rainwater, surface water, waste water and other fluids are conveyed; see floor drain.

gum, 1 sweetgum; [*Liquidambar styraciflua*] a valuable tropical hardwood from south-east USA with pinkish-grey heartwood, used for furniture, posts and packaging; sweetgum are planted as ornamentals in North America on account of their star-shaped leaves and autumn foliage; a local name for some species of eucalyptus tree; black gum, see tupelo.
2 latex; the water-soluble resinous secretion of some tropical hardwood trees and shrubs which hardens on drying; also a corresponding synthetic product, used as a base for rubber; any sticky liquid exuded from plants which may be used as a weak adhesive, or any materials similar to this; see gutta-percha, gamboge, paste.

gum arabic, gum acacia; a water soluble gum from some species of acacia (*Acacia spp.*) in the manufacture of certain glues.

gun applied adhesive, gunnable adhesive; adhesive supplied in pre-packed tubes, suitable for application with a caulking gun.

gunite sprayed concrete containing aggregate smaller than 10 mm in size, placed by projecting it against a surface using pneumatic pressure.

gunnable adhesive see gun applied adhesive.

gunstock see jowl.

gusset, gusset plate; in timber roof construction, a piece of timber board or plywood for fastening together members in a planar truss with nails; a timber nail plate.

gutta, drop; plural guttae; Lat.; in classical architecture, one of a series of carved droplet projections beneath the regula and metopes in the Doric entablature; occasionally also called campanulae, lachrymae or trunnels.

guttae plural form of gutta.
  guttae band see regula.

gutta-percha the dried resinous sap or latex from the Malayan gutta-percha tree, *Isonandra gutta*, used as electrical insulation and in dentistry.

> **gutter** a channel to collect water and lead it away from a surface; types included as separate entries are listed below:
> *arris gutter; *box gutter; *centre gutter; *chimney gutter; *eaves gutter; *fascia gutter; *half round gutter; *hung gutter; *rainwater gutter; *secret gutter; *valley gutter.
> **gutter bearer** any device or framework for supporting or fixing a gutter in place.
> **gutter bracket** a steel strip or proprietary accessory bent into the shape of a hook; used for carrying a gutter.
> **gutter end** see stop end.
> **gutter plane** see round plane.
> **gutter stop** see stop end.

guy, guy rope, stay; a diagonal tension cable, wire or rope anchored to the ground or an abutment to stabilize a mast structure, suspension bridge or tent structure.

gymnosperm one of the two main classes of plant to which conifers or softwoods belong, with woody stems and seeds unprotected by fruit.

gypsum 1 a white or coloured mineral, hydrated calcium sulphate $CaSO_4.2H_2O$, used as a building material in plasters, etc. and as a raw material in the ceramic industry.
2 natural calcium sulphate used as an inert pigment and an adulterer in paints.
see phospho gypsum, selenite, synthetic anhydrite, terra alba, titano gypsum.

gypsum adhesive see gypsum-based adhesive.

gypsum baseboard plasterboard manufactured to receive a surface coating of plaster.

gypsum-based adhesive an adhesive whose main constituent is gypsum binder.

gypsum board see plasterboard.

gypsum-perlite plaster see perlite plaster.

gypsum plank, plasterboard plank; a plasterboard product formed in thick, narrow boards; used for ceiling panels and other cladding applications.

gypsum plaster a quick-setting plaster consisting of gypsum and water, used for plaster casts and rendering.

gypsum plasterboard see plasterboard.

gypsum plasterboard composite a laminated building board of which at least one layer is plasterboard.

gypsum rock 1 rock which contains a high proportion of gypsum.
2 see natural gypsum.

gypsum-vermiculite plaster see vermiculite plaster.

gypsum wallboard thin plasterboard, 9.5 mm thick, suitable for receiving a finish on at least one face, used for lining partitions and internal walls.

gypsum wallboard panel see prefabricated gypsum wallboard panel.

H

Haarlem blue see Antwerp blue.

habitable room any room for living in, not usually including kitchens, toilets, bathrooms and other service spaces.

hacking in concretework, the working at a hardened concrete surface with hand tool and mallet; see tooling.

hacksaw a bow saw with a fine blade held in tension in a metal frame, used for cutting metal and plastics.

haematite, hematite; a grey-black or red-brown mineral, a natural oxide of iron, Fe_2O_3, used in various forms for pigments and jewellery; also a very important iron ore; see also iron oxide.

haft the handle or shaft of a hand tool.

hag's tooth see router plane.

hagioscope see squint.

hairline crack, hair cracking; a defect in a concrete, plaster or paint finish, a very fine surface crack.

half-basketweave pattern a paving pattern resembling basketweave pattern, but with arrangements of stones forming rectangular areas; similar patterns in parquetry and tiling.

half-basketweave pattern

half bat, snap header; in brickwork bonding, the squared remains of a brick which has been cut in half, and which shows in a masonry wall as a header.

half bat

half-brick wall a solid brick wall whose thickness is that of the short side of a brick.

half-brick wall

half-column see demi-column.

half dome, semi-dome; a vaulted roof of half a hemisphere used for covering a semicircular space, as found in religious architecture over apses; see also conch.

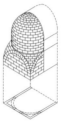
half dome

half drop see offset match.

half hipped end, broached hip; the trapezoidal sloping roof plane at one or both ends of a half-hipped roof, capped by a gable or gablet.

half-hipped roof, jerkinhead roof, hipped gable roof, shread head roof, clipped gable roof; a roof, often a mansard roof, which
half-hipped roof

is hipped from the ridge halfway down to the eaves and gabled from there down; the opposite of a gambrel roof.

half landing, half space landing; a landing between two flights of stairs parallel to one another, between two adjacent storey levels.

half lap joint see halved joint.

halfpace stair, half-space stairs; a stair which turns through 180° on its ascent, consisting of two parallel flights with a half-height landing at one end, with or without a stairwell; a halfpace stair without a well is known as a dogleg stair.

half relief see mezzo rilievo.

half round any milled joinery profile or ornamental moulding which is semicircular in cross-section.

half round profile

half round capping a half round coping brick whose length matches the width of the wall on which it is laid, without overhangs on either side.

half round channel a drainage channel which is semicircular in cross-section.

half round coping a special coping brick or block whose upper surface is semicircular, wider than the wall for which it is designed, and with throated overhangs on either side, used as an upper termination for freestanding walls and parapets.

half round gutter, rhone; a rainwater gutter which is semicircular in cross-section.

half round moulding see half round.

half round moulding

half round veneer a decorative veneer formed by peeling the outer side of a half log or flitch off-centre on a lathe.

half round veneer

half-space landing see half landing.
half-space stairs see halfpace stair.
half span roof see lean-to roof.

half tile a special roof tile which is half the width of other tiles in the same roof; used at edges and junctions.

half timber in the conversion of timber, a baulk cut longitudinally in half.

half-timbered construction a traditional form of timber frame construction in which timber cross members form a lattice of panels filled with a non-loadbearing material or nogging of brick, clay or plaster; the frame is often blackened and exposed on the outside faces of the building.

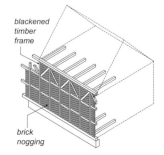

blackened timber frame

brick nogging

half truss in traditional timber frame construction, half a roof truss placed perpendicular to the other trusses at the end of a building to form a hip; also modern equivalents.

half turn stair any stair which turns through 180° on its ascent around an open well or lift shaft, with stair flights on three sides; see also halfpace stair, dogleg stair.

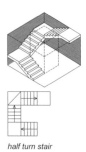

half turn stair

half turn circular stair a circular stair which occupies a semicircular shaft, turning through 180° on its ascent.

halogen a collective name for the group of gases, fluorine, chlorine, bromine, iodine and astatine, which react well with most metals and many non-metals.

halogen lamp, tungsten-halogen lamp; an electric incandescent lamp which produces light by means of a heated tungsten filament suspended in a glass tube filled with low-pressure bromine or iodine vapour.

halon any compound of carbon and bromine or fluorine with other halogens, often used in fire extinguishers but damaging to the ozone layer.

halon fire-extinguishing system a fire-extinguishing system used for technical spaces such as computer rooms and electronic archives, which operates by releasing halon gas to choke a building fire.

halved joint, half lap joint, halving joint; a timber joint in which both pieces have been cut away or halved at the joint to receive the other.

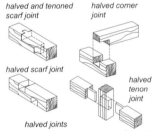

halved and tenoned scarf joint

halved corner joint

halved scarf joint

halved tenon joint

halved joints

halved and tabled scarf joint, indented scarf joint; in timber frame construction, a lengthening joint in which the ends of the timbers are cut with cogs to fit each other.

halved and tenoned scarf joint a timber lengthening joint in which the halved ends of both timbers are cut with a protruding tenon to fit into a corresponding slot.

halved crossing joint see cross half lap joint.

halved scarf joint a timber lengthening joint in which the ends of the timbers are halved to receive one another.

halved tenon joint a timber joint in which two tenons inserted in a common

mortise from opposite sides are cut in half so that they fit side-by-side.

halved three quarter bat, queen closer; a three quarter bat cut in half for use in brickwork bonding.

halved three quarter bat

halving the notching and rebating of the ends of timber members to be jointed in order to form a timber halved joint.

halving joint see halved joint.

---

hammer a hand tool with a shaft and heavy metal head for striking, breaking or driving nails; types included as separate entries are listed below (see illustration on following page):

*adze eye hammer; *ball peen hammer; *beetle; *bell face hammer; *blacksmith's hammer; *bouchard; *brad hammer, see tack hammer; *bricklayer's hammer, brick hammer, brick axe; *bush hammer; *carpenter's mallet; *claw hammer; *club hammer; *cross peen hammer; *double-clawed hammer; *double face hammer; *drilling hammer; *drop hammer, ram; *dummy; *engineer's hammer; *engineer's sledge; *five pound maul; *framing hammer; *glazier's hammer; *jack hammer; *joiner's hammer; *lump hammer, see club hammer; *machinist's hammer, peen; *mallet; *mash hammer, see club hammer; *maul, mall; *nail hammer; *peen, see machinist's hammer; *peen hammer; *peen sledge, see engineer's sledge; *pick hammer; *pin hammer, see tack hammer; *pitching hammer; *riveting hammer; *rock pick; *saddler's hammer; *scabbling hammer, scabbler; *scaling hammer; *scutch hammer, scutch; *sledgehammer, sledge; *smith's hammer, see blacksmith's hammer; *soft face hammer; *spall hammer, spalling hammer; *splitting hammer; *straight peen hammer; *striking hammer; *tack hammer; *tinner's hammer; *trimmer's hammer; *upholsterer's hammer; *veneer hammer, veneering hammer; *Warrington hammer, see cross peen hammer.
2 see water hammer.

TYPES OF HAMMER

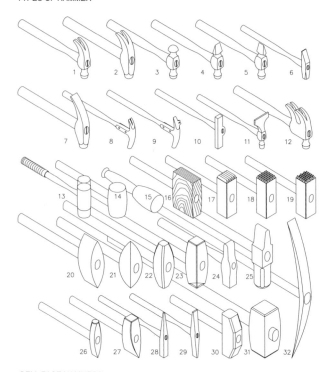

BELL FACE HAMMERS
1 claw hammer
2 framing hammer
3 ball peen hammer
4 cross peen hammer,
   Warringon hammer
5 straight peen hammer
6 joiner's hammer
7 bricklayer's hammer, scutch
8 upholsterer's hammer
9 saddler's hammer
10 glazier's hammer
11 veneer hammer, veneering
   hammer
12 double-clawed hammer

MALLETS
13 soft face hammer
14 rubber mallet
15 dummy
16 carpenter's mallet

BUSHING TOOLS
17 patent hammer, toothed axe
18 bush hammer
19 bush hammer
20 mason's axe, stone axe
21 scabbling hammer

MAULS AND SLEDGES
22 drilling hammer, maul
23 pitching hammer, striking hammer
24 machinist's hammer
25 peen sledge, engineer's sledge
26 splitting hammer, spalling hammer
27 scabbling hammer, trimming hammer
28 scaling hammer, rock pick
29 pick hammer, scutch
30 club hammer, lump hammer, maul
31 double-faced sledgehammer
32 pick, pickaxe

hammer beam in traditional timber roof construction, a short horizontal member cantilevered out from a wall top, brace or purlin, supported on an arch brace and carrying a hammer post which gives support to a primary rafter.

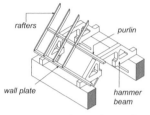

hammer beam roof

hammer beam roof a roof whose rafters are supported by hammer beams, as with many timber roofed medieval halls; see also double hammer beam truss.

hammer-beam roof truss a roof truss in which the rafters are given additional support by hammer beams, hammer posts and arch braces.

hammer-dressed finish, bull-faced finish, cloured finish, hammer-faced finish; a rough stonework finish produced with a hammer; also called a quarry finish when machined on commercial stone.

hammer drill a drill for boring a hole in masonry and concrete with a drill bit which oscillates back and forth with a chattering action.

hammer-faced finish see hammer-dressed finish.

hammer-headed chisel a solid steel masonry chisel with a flat end shaped so as to take striking with a lump hammer; cf. mallet-headed chisel.

hammer post in traditional timber roof construction, a post resting on a hammer beam and supporting a principal rafter.

handbasin see handrinse basin.

hand drill a hand tool for boring holes.

handed 1 referring to the side of a door or window casement which bears hinges; see following entry.
2 referring to hand tools, etc. supplied as mirror-image products for right-handed and left-handed users.

handing a term describing which direction a hinged door or window opens and the side on which it is hinged, affecting its hardware specification, denoted as right-handed or left-handed; there is no universal rule about which is which, and the definition of handing varies from country to country; according to the Scandinavian classification, a left-hand door which opens outwards has its hinges on the left, and so on; in Great Britain and North America this is most often called a right-hand door, but not always.

handle 1 a construction or fitting grasped by the hand for opening, closing or moving a component; see pull handle, door handle, casement handle.
2 that part of a hand tool by which it is held, its shaft or grip.

handmade brick a brick, usually uneven in shape, which has been manually moulded using a timber mould.

hand mixing the mixing of small batches of concrete using hand tools rather than mixing plant.

handover the legal process by which the contractor hands back the site and completed building to the client at the end of construction; see also partial handover.
handover date see completion date.

hand-plastering plasterwork which is carried out manually, using hand tools; sometimes called trowelled plastering.

handpull a handle, inset, etc. for opening and closing a sliding panel, door or partition.

handrail a rail for support or protection at approximately waist height above a balustrade, or fixed to a wall by a stair; see also stair rail.
handrail bolt see joint bolt.

handrinse basin, washbasin, handbasin; a small basin mounted at waist height and connected to a water supply and drain, designed for washing the hands.

handsaw any hand-held saw with a wide, tapering blade.

handset a hand-held shower head connected to a water source by a length of flexible pipe.

hand shears see tin snips.

hanger 1 in timber roof construction, a vertical timber hung from a ridge, rafter or purlin, which gives support to ceiling joists.
2 any strap or component for fixing cabling, ceilings, pipes, ducts, etc. to walls and soffits; see tie rod, pipe hanger, ceiling hanger.
3 one of a series of vertical cables or rods supported at their upper ends by a suspension bridge cable, from which the bridge deck is hung; also called a suspender.
4 see joist hanger.

hanging jamb the vertical frame member to which a window casement or door leaf is attached with hinges.

hanging sash window see sash window.

hanging stile the vertical side member of a window casement or framed door leaf from which it is attached with hinges to a frame.

Hansa yellow see arylide yellow.

hard anodizing a tin-based anodic coating for aluminium which produces shades of bronze formed during the coating process.

hardboard a dense fibreboard formed into thin sheets with a density of over 800 kg/m³; used for lining and casing, thus one side is usually smooth and the other embossed.
hardboard pin a small nail 13—38 mm in length used for fixing hardboard, softboard and thin ply, often with a square sectioned shank.

hardboard pin

hardcore small chunks of stone, broken brick, concrete and other minerals used as inorganic fill beneath foundations and roads.

hard drawn wire steel wire formed by pulling through a die at normal temperature; used as reinforcing bars.

hard dry a stage in the drying of paint at which the surface has hardened and cannot be easily marked.

hardened concrete concrete which has attained a major part of its final strength, usually at least 28 days after placing.

hardener, drier; a catalyst or other substance added to paints, varnishes, glues, concretes and plasters to increase their speed of drying.

hardening 1 the gain in strength of concrete after the initial setting of the cement.
2 a heat treatment to increase the hardness of steel by heating it to a certain temperature and then rapidly cooling in water, brine or oil.
3 see surface hardening.
hardening shrinkage autogenous shrinkage.

hard maple [*Acer saccharum, Acer nigrum*], see maple.

hardness 1 the property of a material to resist permanent change in form as a result of attempted abrasion, penetration or indentation.
2 a measure of the content of mineral salts in water, measurable with a pH test.
hardness number a value obtained by impact and compressive testing to measure the hardness, scratch resistance and resistance to deformation of a material.

hard rock, hard stone; according to a classification of hardness of rocks used by stone masons and construction technicians, rock which has a compressive strength above 1800 kg/cm²; this class includes igneous rocks, quartz and gneiss.

hardrot see dote.

hard solder, brazing solder; a form of solder which contains copper, usually an alloy of copper, zinc or silver used in brazing.
hard soldering see brazing.

hard stone see hard rock.

hard temper one of the annealed conditions of copper and states of hardness in which it is supplied; others are half hard and dead-soft.

hardware, 1 ironmongery; any of the metal fittings such as hinges, locks and latches or other equipment for a door, window or hatch; for door hardware, see door furniture.
2 a general term for computers and other associated electronic devices as opposed to software or computer programs.
hardware schedule see ironmongery schedule.

hardwood the wood from a broad-leaved tree in the botanical group angiosperm, in general denser and harder than softwood, but not necessarily so; listed below are species of

European and North American hardwood tree, followed by a list of tropical hardwoods and eucalypts; see also softwoods.

temperate climates (European and North America)

*acacia [Acacia spp.]; *alder [Alnus spp.]; *apple [Malus sylvestris]; *ash [Fraxinus spp.]; *aspen, poplars [Populus spp.]; *beech [Fagus spp.]; *basswood [Tilia spp.]; *birch [Betula spp.]; *boxwood [Buxus sempervirens]; *cherry [Prunus spp.]; *chestnut [Castanea spp., Aesculus spp.]; *dogwood [Cornus florida]; *elm [Ulmus spp.]; *hawthorn [Crataegus spp.]; *hazel [Corylus avellana]; *hickory [Carya spp.]; *hop-hornbeam [Ostrya carpinifolia]; *hornbeam [Carpinus betulus]; *horse chestnut [Aesculus spp.]; *lime [Tilia spp.]; *maples and sycamores [Acer spp.]; *oak [Quercus spp.]; *pear [Pyrus communis]; *plane [Platanus spp.]; *poplars, aspen [Populus spp.]; *robinia [Robinia pseudoacacia]; *rowan, mountain ash [Sorbus aucuparia]; *sweet chestnut [Castanea sativa]; *tulipwood [Liriodendron tulipifera]; *walnut [Juglans spp.]; *willow [Salix spp.].

tropical climates (Africa and Asia)

*African mahogany [Khaya ivorensis]; *African walnut [Lovoa trichilioides, Lovoa klaineana]; *afrormosia [Pericopsis elata]; *balsa wood [Ochroma spp.]; *ceiba [Ceiba pentandra]; *Ceylon satinwood [Chloroxylon swietenia]; *chickrassy, Chittagong wood [Chukrasia tabularis]; *ebony [Diospyros spp.]; *eucalyptus, jarrah, karri, etc. [eucalyptus spp.]; *gaboon, okoume [Aucoumea klaineana]; *Gedu nohor [Entandrophragma angolense]; *gum [Liquidambar styraciflua]; *idigbo, limba [Terminalia spp.]; *iroko [Chlorophora excelsa]; *kapur [Dryobalanops spp.]; *lignum vitae [Guaiacum spp.]; *mahogany [Swietenia spp.]; *makore [Mimusops heckelii, Tieghemella heckelii]; *obeche [Triplochiton scleroxylon]; *padauk [Pterocarpus spp.]; *ramin [Gonystylus spp.]; *rosewood, palisander [Dalbergia spp.]; *sandalwood [Santalum spp.]; *satinwood [Chloroxylon swietenia]; *teak [Tectona grandis]; *tupelo [Nyssa spp.]; *verawood, Maracaibo lignum vitae [Bulnesia arborea]; *wenge [Millettia laurentii].

hardwood board a piece of sawn hardwood with a thickness less than 50 mm.

hardwood plank a piece of sawn hardwood with a thickness greater than 50 mm.

hardwood scantling a piece of sawn hardwood with non-standard cross-sectional dimensions.

hardwood strip a piece of sawn hardwood with cross-sectional dimensions of less than 50 mm thick and 50–140 mm wide.

harewood see sycamore.

harl see wet dash.

harsh a description of a fresh concrete mix that is difficult to work and place due to its consistency.

hasp and staple a fastener for a door, gate or casket with a slotted hinged plate (a hasp) attached to the leaf, fitting over a ring attached to the jamb; the assembly is usually made fast with a padlock through the ring.

hatch a small hinged door in a roof, wall or floor; see sliding hatch, inspection hatch.

Hathor column an Egyptian column with a capital decorated with the head of the goddess Hathor on two or four sides; Hathor was the ancient Egyptian cowgoddess, giver of milk, symbolic of childbirth and caring, nursemaid to Horus, depicted as a woman with a cow's head or ears.

Hathor column at the temple of Hathor, Dendera, Egypt, 54 BC–60 AD

haunch the curved part of an arch between the crown and springing; sometimes traditionally written as hance or hanse.

haunched beam a beam with a downward thickening at its bearing points.

haunched tenon joint a joinery mortise and tenon joint with an L-shaped tenon flush with both edges of the member at its stem, then stepped back on one side towards its end.

haunched tenon joint

hawk, mortar board; a board with a straight handle fixed to its underside, for carrying plaster and mortar on site, and from which it is applied with a trowel to a surface, to bricks and block, etc.

hawthorn [*Crataegus spp.*] a hardwood tree or shrub with dense, fine-grained timber; used mainly for the decorative value of its grain in veneers and quality furniture; widely planted as hedging.

hazel [*Corylus avellana*] a deciduous hardwood from the northern hemisphere with pale red-brown or green-brown resilient timber.

HDPE, HD polythene high density polythene.

head 1 the highest or terminating part of a construction; see crown, shower head, sprinkler head, rainwater head.
2 the upper horizontal member in a door or window frame; see door head, window head.
3 the upper end of a roof tile or slate as laid.
4 the metal striking or cutting component of a hammer, axe or other similar hand tool, fixed to its shaft; see hammerhead.
5 the enlarged part of a screw, nail or other fixing, by which it is attached or driven in; see nailhead or screw head.

header 1 a brick or stone laid with its short side or end exposed in a masonry surface; see also bull header (rowlock), plinth header (header plinth), radial header, tapered header (culvert stretcher).

header

2 see head plate.
3 a heavy beam over a window in traditional timber construction.
4 rainwater header, see rainwater head.

header bond, heading bond; a brickwork bond in which each course is a series of headers; alternate courses are laid with a half header overlap; see also Flemish header bond.

header bond

header course, 1 heading course; in brickwork, a course of bricks with only their short sides showing in the wall.
2 the uppermost layer of logs in log construction.

header face the visible side of a brick when laid in masonry as a header.

header joint see perpend.

header plate see head plate.

header plinth, plinth header; a special brick whose upper arris has been chamfered along one of its short sides for use as a header in a brick coping or above a projection.

header plinth

head flashing a flashing used over an opening to direct water outwards and waterproof the lintel.

heading bond see header bond.

heading chisel see mortise chisel.

heading course see header course.

head joint see perpend.

headlap the overlap of adjacent parts of roofing material such as tiles or roof sheeting in a line parallel to the slope of the roof.

head plate, head piece; the upper horizontal framing member in a timber-framed wall or partition, or stud wall.

headroom, clearance, overhead clearance; the free height between a floor and overhead obstacle such as a door head, beam, etc.; see stair headroom, ceiling height.

headtree see bolster.

heart and dart see leaf and dart.

heart check see heartshake.

hearth the base or floor of a fireplace, on which combustion takes place.

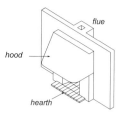

flue

hood

hearth

heart-palmette see palmette heart.

heart palmette

heartshake, heart check, rift crack, star shake; a radial crack near the centre of a tree trunk, apparent in timber cut from it.

heartshake

heartwood the central core of wood in a tree, usually darker than the outlying sapwood, made up of cells which are no longer active in transporting sap to the tree's leaves; also called duramen.

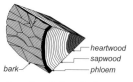

heartwood
sapwood
bark
phloem

heartwood rot fungal decay in the heartwood of timber.

heat-absorbing glass see tinted solar control glass.

heat balance the result of subtracting heat losses from heat gains for a space, building or installation; the stable temperature state

of equilibrium produced by this, known as thermodynamic equilibrium.

heat bridge see cold bridge.

heat capacity see thermal capacity.

heat detector a fire detector which reacts to the presence of heat and triggers an alarm signal at a certain temperature.

heat differential detector see thermo-differential detector.

heat distribution the distribution of heat throughout a building in the form of hot water or steam from a centralized boiler or district heating plant.

heater 1 see heating appliance; types of heater included as separate entries are listed below:
*bulk heater, outflow heater; *convection heater, see convector; *domestic water heater; *electric heater; *electric fan heater, see fan heater; *electric water heater, immersion heater; *gas heater; *outflow heater; *pressure water heater; *radiant heater; *radiator; *room heater; *sauna heater; *solid-fuel heater, see solid-fuel stove; *storage heater; *thermal storage heater, see storage heater; *warm-air heater; *water heater.*
2 that part of an air-conditioning system which transfers heat to the supply air.

heat exchanger a device which transfers thermal energy from one installation to another without the direct flowing of material between the systems.
2 in an air-conditioning system, a device for transferring heat to or from air passing over it, usually via heated or cooled liquid-filled coils, metal baffles, etc.
3 see calorifier.

heating, space heating; the provision of heat to spaces of a building by appliances and mechanical installations to provide a level of thermal comfort.

heating and ventilation see mechanical services.

heating and ventilation engineer a person who is responsible for designing technical services, and supervising their construction and maintenance.

heating appliance, heater; a device or apparatus located within a space for providing warmth, either fuelled directly by electricity, gas, oil or solid fuel, or fed with warm air or water from a centralized plant.

heating battery 1 in air-conditioning, coiled piping in which hot water is circulated; used for heating air to the desired temperature.

2 in district heating and other indirect hot water heating systems, a unit of pipework or a coil inside a cistern, through which hot water circulates to heat up water within the cistern.

heating cable an electric cable embedded in floor construction, under pavements, etc., which provides heat for underfloor heating and similar installations when electricity is passed through it.

heating installation, heating system; the means, devices and apparatus to provide warmth for a building.

heating main see district heating.

heating period, heating; in steam curing of concrete, the period for which heat is applied so that the concrete heats up slowly.

heating pipework pipework carrying hot water in a heating installation.

heating plant, boiler plant; in heating and hot water systems, the installation producing thermal energy for heating, transferred and distributed by water, steam, air, etc.

heating point see vehicle heating point.

heating season that period in the year during which the heating system of a building is required to be in use.

heating stove see room heater.

heating system see heating installation.

heating value see calorific value.

heating, ventilation and air conditioning see HEVAC.

heat insulation see thermal insulation.

heat load the amount of excess heat within a space that has to be transferred by an air-conditioning system.

heat loss the transfer of heat from a body or building to the outside, usually as waste energy.

heat of hydration a rise in temperature produced during the setting of concrete and cements due to the chemical reaction of the cement with water.

heat-proof see heat resistant.

heat pump a device, used in refrigeration, geothermal and some solar heating systems, in which a gas is compressed or expanded to raise or lower its temperature.

heat recovery in air-conditioning, a process whereby heat from exhaust air is transferred using a heat exchanger to fresh input air.

heat recovery unit, thermal wheel; in air conditioning, a heat exchanger for transferring thermal energy and sometimes moisture from the return air to the supply air.

heat resistant, heat-proof; relating to a material or surface which has the ability to withstand high temperatures.

heat resisting glass types of glass such as fire glasses or borosilicate glass which can withstand high temperatures without shattering.

heat-soaked glass toughened glass used for external wall systems and roofs, re-treated to remove imperfections and overcome the problems of spontaneous fracture.

heat transmission value see k-value.

heat-treated wood, heat-treated timber; sawn timber sections of pine, spruce, birch and aspen processed into an ecological wood product by baking at temperatures of 200°C or more to break up sugars inside the wood into a form unusable by rot fungi.

heat treatment, 1 accelerated curing; a method of curing concrete using hot water or steam to speed up hardening; it may reduce the final strength of the concrete.

2 the modification of the mechanical properties of steel by its controlled heating and cooling; heat treatments include hardening, tempering, annealing and normalizing.

heat welding a method of joining plastics components by pressing together and briefly heating by either high-frequency electric current, friction, a hot-knife or by ultrasonic means.

heavy clay a soil type that contains more than 60% clay: tough and plastic when wet, hard and uncrumbling when dry.

heavy concrete, high density concrete; concrete which contains heavy aggregate such as iron ore, scrap iron, or barium sulphate; it weighs between $2800-5000$ kg/m^3 and is used for radiative shields.

heavy plate see quarto plate.

heavy spar a naturally occurring form of the mineral barytes; see also Bologna stone.

heavy tamping see dynamic consolidation.

heel gable a gable at the outside corner of two gable roofs which meet at right angles.

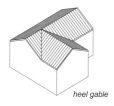

heel gable

helical reinforcement concrete column reinforcement which is spiral or helical in shape, binding the main reinforcement within the column to form a three-dimensional cage.

helical stair see spiral stair.

helicopter see power trowel.

heliotrope, bloodstone; a dark green microcrystalline variety of the mineral chalcedony speckled with red streaks of jasper; used for decorative ornament and as gemstones.

helix, 1 pl. helices; any spiral shape, especially ornament as found in a classical building.
2 Lat.; one of the spirals or volutes beneath the abacus in a classical Corinthian capital; often used in the plural, helices.

Helmholtz resonator see cavity absorber.

helm roof a hipped roof constructed diagonal to the rectilinear geometry of a building thus producing gables on all four sides; usually used for spires.

hematite see haematite.

hemihydrate plaster, hemihydrate gypsum plaster, plaster of Paris, stucco; plaster whose binder is calcium sulphate hemihydrate.

hemlock [*Tsuga spp.*] a genus of North American softwood trees with soft, light, pale brown timber; see below; often planted as a background or an evergreen ornamental on account of its feather-like fronds.
eastern hemlock, hemlock spruce (Am); [*Tsuga canadensis*] a North American softwood with soft, pale brown timber; used for interior work and fencing.
western hemlock [*Tsuga heterophylla*] a western North American softwood with white to yellowish-brown timber, one of the lightest softwood in use; used for general construction and plywood.

hempseed oil a drying oil used as a vehicle in paints, pressed from the seeds of the hemp plant [*Cannabis sativa*].

herm, herma, plural hermae; in classical architecture, a square tapered column capped with the carved head, bust or torso of a figure, often Hermes; originally used by the Greeks as a boundary marker, later as decoration.

herm

hermetically sealed glazed unit see sealed glazed unit, double-glazed unit.

herringbone a decorative pattern in which stones, bricks, tiles or lines are arranged diagonally to interlink with one another so that each successive course points in the opposite direction; see below:
herringbone brickwork, herringbone bond; decorative brickwork in which bricks are laid at a slant with alternate bricks at right angles; Roman herringbone brickwork was known as opus spicatum. See illustration on following page.

herringbone brickwork

herringbone match see herringbone pattern.

herringbone match veneering

herringbone panelling in traditional timber frame construction, the filling of the half-timbered panels in a framed wall by diagonally laid timbers or bricks.

herringbone parquet mosaic parquet flooring laid in a herringbone pattern by gluing or nailing.

herringbone pattern a veneering pattern in which veneers with slanting grain are glued side by side in mirror image along a centre line, resembling the bones of a fish attached to its spine; a similar pattern in tiling, paving and parquetry.

herringbone paving paving laid in a herringbone pattern; see also Dutch paving.

herringbone paving

herringbone strutting, cross bridging, cross nogging; short timber diagonal members used to cross brace and stiffen the joists in a timber joist floor laterally.

hertz the SI unit of frequency or cycles per second, abb. Hz.

hesitation set an outdated term meaning false set.

hessian, burlap (Am), sackcloth; a roughly woven fabric made of natural fibres such as hemp or jute; often used in construction for reinforcing plasterwork.

hessonite, cinnamon stone; a brownish-orange variety of the mineral garnet; a form of grossular.

Heterobasidion annosum see annosus root rot.

HEVAC acronym of HEating, Ventilation and Air Conditioning, also shortened to HVAC; the discipline which deals with the design and installation of heating, ventilation and air-conditioning services for a building; also called mechanical services engineering or mechanical engineering.

hexagonal bar a manufactured metal bar, hexagonal in cross-section; when of steel it is used in welded construction, for tie rods, detail work, etc.

hexagonal bolt, hex-head bolt; a bolt with a hexagonal head which can be tightened with a spanner.

hexagonal mesh see chicken wire.

hexagonal nipple a short connecting pipe fitting externally threaded at either end, whose middle section is hexagonal in section so that it can be tightened with a spanner.

hexagonal nut, hex nut; a nut which is a regular hexagon in section so that it can be tightened with a spanner.

hexagonal nut

hexagonal paver a concrete paving unit which is hexagonal, laid in a honeycomb pattern.

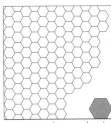

hexagonal paving

hexagonal tile a ceramic floor tile which is hexagonal, laid in a honeycomb pattern.

hexapartite vault see sexpartite vault.

hex-head bolt see hexagonal bolt.

hex nut see hexagonal nut.

H-hinge see parliament hinge.

hickey, hicky see bending tool.

hickory [*Carya spp.*] a North American hardwood with hard and strong pinkish-brown timber; used for tool handles, ladder rungs, furniture and sports equipment.

hide glue animal glue made from collagen, a protein released by boiling the hides of animals.

hiding power see opacity.

high alumina cement, calcium aluminate cement; a cement produced by grinding the clinker formed by burning calcareous and aluminous materials in a kiln; an active hydraulic binder.
high alumina cement clinker, high alumina clinker; a clinker formed by burning calcareous and aluminous materials in a kiln; composed mainly of alumina (aluminium oxide) and oxides, hydroxides or carbonates of calcium.
high alumina cement concrete concrete made with high alumina cement.

high alumina clinker see high alumina cement clinker.

high carbon steel tough steel which has a carbon content of 0.5−1.5%; used for casting and cutting tools.

high density concrete see heavy concrete.

high density polythene, HD polythene, HDPE; a hard and rigid form of polythene used for plastics sheet, containers and pipes.

high-early-strength cement see rapid-hardening Portland cement.

high gloss see full gloss.

high Gothic the middle phase of Gothic architecture in France in the 1200s (see Rayonnant) and elsewhere in Europe in the 1300s (see Decorated); see also Geometric style, Curvilinear style.

highlighting see spotlighting.

high magnesium lime see dolomitic lime.

high output back boiler a boiler fitted to the rear of a solid fuel heater which provides water for domestic use and space heating.

high performance referring to materials, products or components of reputed high quality, strength, durability or special properties; see also standard.

high-pressure sodium lamp a sodium lamp capable of producing a wider spectrum of coloured light than normal sodium lamps, used for external and garden lighting.

high pressure steam curing see autoclaving.

high pressure system see high velocity system.

high-range water-reducing admixture see superplasticizing admixture.

high relief see alto rilievo.

high-strength concrete concrete that has a cube strength at 28 days of at least 50 N/mm^2.

high-tensile brass see manganese bronze.

high-tensile steel structural steel with a carbon content of up to 3% and which may contain significant proportions of other metals.

high-tension steel cable one of a number of cables which give a post-stressed concrete member its structural strength.

high velocity system, high pressure system; an air-conditioning system in which air is forced through ductwork at 5−20 m/s using a powerful fan, enabling use of smaller duct-sizes.

high voltage a voltage greater than 1000 V in an electric circuit.

hinge a pivoting mechanism to provide a fixing and rotating action for framed door leaves, window casements, etc.; types included as separate entries are listed below:
*A-hinge; *backflap hinge; *ball-bearing hinge, ball-bearing butt hinge; *ball hinge; *band and hook hinge, see hook and band hinge; *blind hinge, see concealed hinge; *butt hinge; *butterfly hinge; *cabinet hinge; *casement hinge; *centre pivot hinge, centre hinge; *cleaning hinge, see easy-clean hinge; *concealed hinge; *continuous hinge, see

*piano hinge; *cranked hinge; *cylinder hinge; *door hinge; *double-acting hinge; *double-acting spring hinge; *easy-clean hinge; *electric hinge, electrically wired hinge; *falling-butt hinge; *fast-pin hinge; *flap hinge, see strap hinge; *furnishing hinge, see cabinet hinge; *gravity door hinge, see rising hinge; *H-hinge, see parliament hinge; *hook and band hinge; *invisible hinge; *lift-off butt hinge, lift-off hinge; *loose butt hinge, see lift-off butt hinge; *loose pin butt hinge, loose pin hinge; *loose-joint hinge, loose-joint butt hinge; *non-mortised hinge, non-mortised butt hinge; *parliament hinge; *piano hinge; *pin hinge, see loose pin butt hinge; *rising hinge, rising-butt hinge; *rule joint hinge; *screw hook and eye hinge, screw hinge; *secret hinge, see invisible hinge; *spring hinge; *strap hinge; *surface hinge; *surface-fixed hinge, see non-mortised hinge; *swing door hinge, see double-acting hinge; *tee hinge, T-hinge; *rule joint hinge, see table hinge; *tight-pin hinge, see fast-pin hinge; *weld-on hinge; *window hinge.*

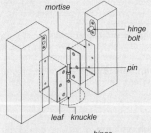

hinge

hinge bolt, dog bolt, security bolt; a metal security lug fitted to and projecting sideways from the hinge stile of a door leaf, which fits in a housing in the jamb when the door is shut and prevents it from being forced open.

hinge chisel a thin chisel with a serrated cutting edge, used for making thin mortises for concealed hinges.

hinge joint see pin joint.

hinge leaf one of the metal flaps by which a hinge is fixed to the edge of a door and its frame.

hinge mortise, hinge rebate; a shallow depression cut into a door frame and the edge of a door leaf to receive the leaves of a hinge and ensure flush installation.

hinge pin that part of a hinge around which the leaves rotate; either retractable or permanently fixed to one of the leaves; a hinge pin in a lift-off hinge is often called a pintle.

hinge rebate see hinge mortise.

hip, 1 hip end, hipped end; the sloping triangle of a roof plane at one or both ends of a hipped roof.

hip roof

2 piend; the sloping ridge formed by two pitched roofs which meet at an outside corner.

hip and valley roof a pitched roof constructed with both hips and valleys, as with an L-shaped building.

hip end, hipped end see hip.

hipped gable roof see half-hipped roof.

hipped mansard roof, mansard roof (Am); a hip roof in which all four roof surfaces are doubly pitched.

hipped mansard roof

hipped roof see hip roof.

hip rafter, angle ridge; in timber roof construction, a diagonal rafter at a junction or hip formed by two sloping roofs in different planes.

hip roof, hipped roof; a pitched roof with slopes on all four sides which meet at the corners to form hips; it may or may not have a ridge.

hip tile a roof tile which is specially formed to cover a hip; see angular hip tile, bonnet hip tile (granny bonnet).

historiated capital see figured capital.

historic site, area of historical interest; an area of land of cultural and historical value by virtue of a structure thereon, or as the site of an important historical event, often protected by legislation.

hit and miss construction see chequerboard construction.

hoarding 1 a temporary fence enclosing a construction site.

2 a large freestanding screen designed to carry adverts.

3 a covered overhanging wooden gallery built next to the parapet of a fortified wall or tower to allow defenders to drop missiles on assailants below; also known as a hoard or hourd.

hockey stick a strip of planed timber which is L-shaped or rebated in cross-section, used as trim to cover the corners or edge joints of partitions, panels, etc.; an edge strip with one limb longer than the other.

hod a three-sided wooden or plastic box supported on a short pole, used on a building site for carrying bricks, blocks or mortar to their place of use.

hog, camber, hogging; the built-in upward bowing of a prestressed or other beam, which then becomes straight on loading.

hoist apparatus for lifting and lowering components and equipment on site; see also winch.
hoisting plant see lifting equipment.
hoistway see lift well.

holdfast a metal fixing or cleat used for fastening stone cladding to a structural frame.

hole cutter see hole saw.

hole gauge see plug gauge.

hole saw, tubular saw, hole cutter, annular bit, crown saw; a drill bit for drilling large bore circular holes in board, by means of a blade which is a short length of tube with a serrated edge.

holiday see miss.

holing in slate roofing, the making of a hole in a roof slate for fixing with a nail.

hollow see hollow moulding.

hollow bedding the laying of blocks in masonry in such a way that mortar is applied only to the edges and sides to protect the blocks against cracking during movement.

hollow block see cellular block.

hollow brick, 1 cavity block; a brick manufactured with a large hole or holes through it, forming cavities within the thickness of a brick wall to reduce weight and to house wiring and pipe installations, etc.

2 a general name for all types of perforated brick.

hollow-chisel mortiser a drill or drill bit with a square casing around a helical bit, used for cutting rectangular mortises in wood.

hollow clay block a lightweight clay building block extruded with internal voids.

hollow clay block

hollow composite beam a patented hollow perforated steel beam site-grouted with concrete, used for the support of precast floor slabs and planks.

hollow concrete block see cellular block.

hollow-core beam a precast and pretensioned concrete slab unit with longitudinal voids, used as rapidly laid structural floor and roof components to span between main beams; also called a hollow-core slab or concrete plank.

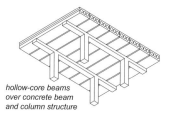

hollow-core beams over concrete beam and column structure

hollow-core door a door whose leaf is of light cellular cardboard construction with veneers or laminate sheets bonded to either side.

hollow-core door

hollow-core slab see hollow-core beam.

hollow glass block see glass block.

hollow masonry wall see cavity wall.

hollow moulding a decorative moulding composed of a curved segmental or three-quarter circular recess, used at the inner junction of perpendicular surfaces such as ceilings and walls; see also trochilus, scotia.

hollow moulding

hollow plane a woodworking plane with a concave base and blade used for cutting convex shapes; usually sold as a pair with a round plane.

hollow roll joint a bitumen sheet or sheetmetal roofing joint in which two adjacent sheets are intertwined along their edges without a core roll.

hollow roll joint

hollow section, tubular section; a round or rectangular hollow steel section formed by rolling and welding steel plate, used for structural purposes; see circular hollow section, rectangular hollow section, square hollow section.

hollow wall any wall whose construction is of two leaves, boards, etc. on either side

of a gap or lightweight frame; see cavity wall.

hollow-wall anchor, molly, toggle; a metal threaded fastener for fixing to plasterboard hollow wall surfaces, inserted into a drilled hole and secured by means of a sleeve which is retracted to clamp tight against the reverse side of construction when the screw is turned.

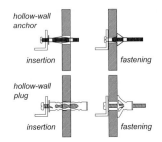

hollow-wall anchor

insertion   *fastening*

hollow-wall plug

insertion   *fastening*

hollow wall bond see cavity bond, Dearne's bond, rat-trap bond.

hollow-wall plug, molly, toggle; a nylon version of a hollow-wall anchor, used for fixing lighter objects; see also legs anchor.

homelift a lift designed for domestic use by the elderly and disabled.

homogeneous plywood plywood in which all the veneers are of the same species of wood; homogeneous refers to a material or substance which is of uniform composition.

Honduras mahogany, Central American mahogany; [*Swietenia macrophylla*] a Central American tropical hardwood with red or golden brown timber; used for interior and exterior joinery, flooring, furniture and boat-building.

hone, whetstone; a fine-grained grindstone used for sharpening the blades of tools and polishing stone surfaces.

honed a description of a smooth, lightly polished, matt finish in stonework, produced by treatment with a fine abrasive; the same as a polished finish, but without the final shine, see also rubbed finish.

honeycomb brickwork brickwork laid with staggered openings between adjacent bricks for decoration or to permit ventilation through the wall. See illustration on facing page.

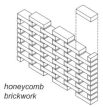

honeycomb brickwork

honeycomb floor see waffle floor.

honeycomb rot see red ring rot.

honeycomb slab see waffle slab.

honeycomb work see stalactite work.

honeycombing, rock pocket (Am); voids in faulty concrete caused by a lack of fine aggregate or insufficient compaction.

honing the sharpening of the tip of a metal blade of a hand tool or the production of a matt surface on stonework using a fine grindstone or hone.
honing bevel the very tip of the bevelled blade of a chisel or other cutting tool, ground or sharpened to provide a cutting edge.
honing guide, gauge; a device for holding the blade of a tool such as a chisel at the correct angle while it is being sharpened.

hood see extractor hood, canopy.

hood-mould, dripstone, label; a raised protruding moulding above a masonry arch or opening to throw off rainwater.

hook 1 in reinforced concrete, a reinforcing bar whose end has been bent back on itself around a thick pin in order to provide anchorage.
2 see screw hook.

hook and band hinge, band and hook hinge; a hinge consisting of a flap which fits over a pin attached to a back plate, bolt or lug; used for cupboard doors.

hook and band hinge

hook and eye a simple fastener for a window or door consisting of a pivoted hook, attached to the leaf, and a ring, attached to the frame, into which the hook fits.

hook and eye

hook bolt 1 a lock bolt which is hook-shaped or curved, used for fastening sliding doors.

hook bolt

2 a metal fastening consisting of a bolt whose end is bent over, used for fixing profiled sheet roofing to a steel frame.

hooked scarf joint see tabled scarf joint, splayed and tabled scarf joint.

hook pin in traditional timber frame construction, an iron peg hammered into a joint as a temporary fixing, replaced with a wooden peg at a later stage.

hook screw see screw hook.

hop-hornbeam see European hop-hornbeam.

hopper head see rainwater head.

hopper light a bottom-hinged window casement which opens inwards, often a small vent window beneath a larger fixed light.

horizontal boarding timber cladding boards laid horizontally on a frame as interior boarding, weatherboarding, clap-boarding or shiplap boarding.

horizontal glazing bar see lay bar.

horizontal joint any construction joint which runs horizontally; see bed joint.

horizontal pivot window, tip-up window; a window with an opening light hung centrally on pins on either side of the frame, about which it opens.

horizontal pivot window

horizontal rafter see common purlin.
horizontal rafter roof see common purlin roof.

horizontal section a drawing representing a horizontal cut through a site, building or object; a plan view.

horizontal shore see flying shore.

horizontal sliding window see sliding window.

hornbeam [*Carpinus betulus*] a European hardwood with extremely hard, heavy, dense and durable white timber which turns and machines well; used where toughness and durability are essential.

hornblende a dark brown, black or green mineral containing silicates of iron, magnesium and calcium; found in granite and many other rocks.

hornfels a collective name for types of fine-grained metamorphic rock which have formed under high temperatures, often dark grey or greenish and very weather-resistant; see contact metamorphic rock, crystalline schist.

horntail see woodwasp.

horse chestnut [*Aesculus spp.*] a genus of hardwood trees from the northern hemisphere, the most common of which is the European horse chestnut, *Aesculus hippocastanum*, a large tree (the 'conker tree') often planted in parks as a shade-giver and for its dramatic bloom spikes.

horse chestnut

horse mould see running mould.
horsed moulding see run moulding.

horseshoe arch, Arabic arch, Moorish arch, round horseshoe arch; an arch composed of a segment of a circle which subtends an angle of more than 180°, often stilted; see also pointed horseshoe arch.

horseshoe arch

hose reel see fire-hose reel.

hot-air dried see kiln dried.

hot-air stripping in painting and decorating, renovation work, etc., the softening of old paint prior to removal using an appliance which provides a blast of hot air.

hot bonding compound see bonding compound.

hot cement cement at an undesirably high temperature at its time of use, usually caused by inadequate cooling after manufacture.

hot-dipping, hot-dip zinc coating; the application of a protective layer of zinc to steel components by immersion in a bath of molten zinc; a form of galvanizing.

hot-dip zinc coating see hot-dipping.

hot forming see hot working.

hot-melt adhesive, hot-melt glue see thermoplastic adhesive.

hot pressing the production of linseed oil for paints and finishes by extraction under extreme pressure and heat.

hot rolling the most common process of forming steel sections by passing hot steel through a series of heavy rollers.
hot-rolled deformed bar a deformed bar produced by a hot rolling process; used as concrete reinforcement.
hot-rolled steel section a structural steel section formed by a process of hot rolling.

hot setting adhesive, hot setting glue see thermosetting adhesive.

hot stuff see bonding compound.

hot water water heated by gas, electricity, oil or steam to not more than 65°C for use in a domestic supply.
hot water central heating a central heating system in which piped hot water

is circulated from a boiler or storage cylinder to radiators, etc.

hot water heating a heating system in which the heating medium is circulated hot water.

hot water storage heater see storage heater.

hot water supply system, hot water system; a system of pipes and heating vessels for the provision and distribution of hot water to spaces in a building; see indirect hot water supply system and direct hot water supply system.

hot working, hot forming; the process of shaping metal when hot by forging and hot rolling, etc. to prevent brittleness in the final products; see also cold working.

houndstooth brickwork see dogtooth brickwork.

houndstooth moulding see dogtooth moulding.

hourd see hoarding.

housebuilding see housing production.

housed joint, 1 housing joint; any timber joint in which the end of one member is held in a depression or housing in another.
2 a timber joint in which the end or side of one piece is housed in a longitudinal cutting or groove in another; also called a dado joint or housing joint.

housed scarf joint, shouldered scarf joint; a timber scarf joint in which the ends of both timbers are cut with a stepped halving to interlock with one another and provide added bending strength.

housed scarf joint

house longhorn beetle [*Hylotrupes bajulus*] a large insect which causes damage to dry softwood in buildings by burrowing.

housing 1 a cutting or recess in one member to receive another.

housing

2 in joinery, a long groove machined into a board to house another member; a chase or dado; in framing construction this may be called a let-in.

3 a general term for a group of dwellings; a housing development; policies, regulations, development and other matters relating to residential buildings, when viewed as a whole; see also housing production.

housing area see residential area.

housing development, housing scheme, residential development; an area of new housing functioning as a unit, either a design scheme or as completed.

housing joint see housed joint.

housing production, housebuilding; that area of design, development and construction relating to residential buildings.

housing project see residential development, public housing.

housing scheme see housing development, residential scheme.

Howe truss a form of lattice beam or triangular truss patented by the American William Howe in 1840, in which, by virtue of the layout of its web members, all diagonals are in compression and all verticals in tension, the opposite of those in a Pratt truss; diagonals in the triangular version form a V-pattern and in flat trusses an A-pattern; see Pratt truss, Vierendeel truss, Warren truss.

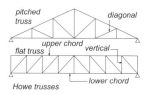

Howe trusses

H-pile any steel pile whose main shaft is an H-section.

H-section, 1 UC section, universal column; a structural steel stanchion section, formed by rolling, whose uniform cross section resembles the letter H in which the width of flanges is approximately equal to the height of the web.

2 similarly shaped non-structural sections in other metals and materials.

hue in colour science, that aspect of a colour which defines its actual colour (as opposed to brightness or saturation), caused by a specific wavelength or wavelengths of light.

human scale a concept whereby the dimensions of a built environment and its components take into account the physical and psychological well-being of its inhabitants.

humidifier an appliance which increases the relative humidity of air, making conditions more comfortable in spaces whose air is too dry; in air conditioning, the introduction of water vapour to dry air is carried out by a humidifier.

humidity **1** water vapour suspended in air.
2 a measurement of the water content of air; see relative humidity.

humus highly organic soil formed by the decomposition of vegetable matter.

hung ceiling see suspended ceiling.

hung gutter a gutter at eaves level, separate from the fascia, hung on gutter brackets.

Hungarian green see malachite.

HVAC see HEVAC.

hydrant an outlet point through which water can be drawn from a mains water supply; see fire hydrant.
hydrant box a covering construction for a hydrant, usually some sort of cupboard.

hydration **1** the chemical alliance of a substance with water.
2 the reaction of the silicates and aluminates in cement with water to form a hard mass.

hydrated high calcium by-product lime, carbide hydrate; a white powder whose main constituent is calcium hydroxide $CaOH_2$; a by-product of the manufacture of acetylene gas used as hydrated lime.

hydrated lime, lime hydrate; quicklime to which water has been added, either supplied in powdered form as dry hydrate or in liquid form as slaked lime.

hydraulics the science of fluids in motion and at rest, especially that of fluids in pipes.

hydraulic binder a cement binder which sets by chemical reaction with water, as opposed to evaporation of water, and will thus harden under water.

hydraulic cement a binder for concrete which will set under water, produced by the grinding of clinker.

hydraulic lift a lift with a lift drive powered by piped liquid under pressure to raise a piston, plunger or ram on which the lift car is located.

hydraulic lime quicklime in which the amount of silica and aluminates is sufficient for it to set in contact with water, or under water.

hydraulic lime mortar a versatile mortar made from hydraulic lime; it has good properties of elasticity, permeability and resistance to weather, fungal growth, etc., and is used for general plastering, rendering and renovation work on traditional and vernacular buildings.

hydraulic spraying see airless spraying.
hydraulic test see water test.

hydrochloric acid a corrosive solution of hydrogen chloride, **HCl**, in water; used in galvanizing, steel pickling and the electronics industry.

hydrogen the most common chemical element, **H**; a colourless, odourless gas which burns explosively in the presence of oxygen to form water.

hydrogen chloride a corrosive, gaseous chemical compound, **HCl**, which, when mixed with water, becomes hydrochloric acid.

hydrogen peroxide a chemical compound, H_2O_2; an oxidizing, antiseptic and bleaching agent.

hydrogen sulphide a poisonous, pungent, gaseous chemical compound, H_2S, used in metallurgy and in the manufacture of chemicals.

hydrophilic attracted to or having a tendency to absorb water.

hydrophobic cement, water-repellent cement; a form of Portland cement whose particles are protected with a water-repellant treatment such as wax, worn off during mixing, which prevents it from setting during storage or transport; hydrophobic means having a tendency to repel water.

hydrostatics the science of fluids at rest.

hydrostatic head, hydrostatic pressure the pressure of a liquid measured at any point; it is the depth of the liquid multiplied by its density.

hydrostatic level see water level.

hydrostatic pressure see hydrostatic head.

hygrometer, moisture meter; a device for measuring the relative humidity of air.

hygroscopic moisture the adsorbed or capillary moisture in a substance such as soil when in contact with air; hygroscopic is a description of a solid with the tendency to absorb water from air containing water vapour.

Hylotrupes bajulus see house longhorn beetle.

hypabyssal rock, dyke rock, transitional igneous rock; types of igneous rock formed from magma hardening in channels and vents in the earth's crust; their use in the building industry is minimal due to the relatively small size of deposits.

hypaethral, hypethral; in classical architecture, referring to a building which is fully or partly open to the sky.

hyperbolic paraboloid roof a shell roof shaped like a butterfly in profile, formed from the three-dimensional curvature of a hyperbolic parabola.

hyperstatic frame see statically indeterminate frame.

hypethral see hypaethral.

hypocaust in classical Roman architecture, an underfloor room heating system using voids or channels through which hot air is introduced from a central furnace; also the underfloor space itself.

hypostyle hall a hall in an Egyptian temple whose roof is supported by a dense grid of thick columns.

hypotrachelium Lat.; the upper part or groove in the shaft of a Doric column beneath the trachelion; Greek form is hypotrakhelion.

I

I-beam any steel, concrete or timber beam with an upper and lower flange connected to a central web, I-shaped in cross-section; see also I-section.

precast concrete I-beam

idigbo [*Terminalia ivorensis*] a hardwood from the West African rainforests with yellow to yellow-brown timber; used for its attractive appearance in joinery and floors.

igneous rock, magmatic rock, pyrogenic rock, fusion rock, flow rock, massive rock, eruptive rock; types of rock which have formed from the solidification of volcanic magma, including plutonic, hypabyssal and volcanic rocks; types included as separate entries are listed below:
*acidic rock, acid rock; *andesite; *basalt; *basic rock; *diabase, traprock; *diorite; *dolerite; *dyke rock, see hypabyssal rock; *effusive rock, volcanic rock; *extrusive rock, volcanic rock; *gabbro; *granite; *granodiorite; *greenstone; *hypabyssal rock, dyke rock, transitional igneous rock; *intermediate rock; *lava rock; *pegmatite; *peridotite; *plutonic rock, plutonite; *porphyry; *pyroxenite; *quartz diorite; *syenite; *transitional igneous rock, see hypabyssal rock; *ultrabasic rock; *volcanic rock, vulcanite, effusive rock, extrusive rock.

ignimbrite, welded tuff; a brown volcanic rock originally formed from fused deposits of glowing hot clouds; used locally as building stone.

illuminance in lighting design, the ratio of luminous flux per area falling on a surface, measured in lux.

illumination 1 see lighting, artificial lighting.
2 the art of decorating manuscripts with ornament, gold leaf, colours, etc.; especially those often complex and colourful designs hand-painted by monks for decorating the initial letter of a page.

illuminated ceiling see luminous ceiling.

imbrex, plural imbrices; Lat.; a U-shaped roofing tile used in conjunction with a tegula in Italian and Roman tiling, often capped with antefixae at eaves and ridge.

immediate settlement, elastic compression, initial settlement; in foundation technology, the slight downward movement of a building which occurs during and immediately after construction, caused by compression of soil grains and gas pockets in the underlying ground due to the weight of the building.

immersion heater see electric water heater.

immersion treatment the preservation of timber by immersing it in a solution of preservative for a specified time.

immersion vibration, poker vibration; the compaction of fresh concrete using an immersion vibrator.

immersion vibrator, internal vibrator, poker vibrator; a vibrating probe fully immersed in fresh concrete to provide compaction through gentle agitation, provided by means of an eccentrically rotating mechanism; see surface vibrator.

impact driver see impact screwdriver.

impact insulation class a measure of the sound caused by impacts such as walking, etc. transmitted between adjacent rooms.

impact noise see impact sound.

impact resistance see impact strength.

impact screwdriver, impact driver; a heavy-duty cast steel hand tool for opening tight screws and bolts by striking with a mallet to produce a turning action.

impact sound, impact noise; in acoustics, sound which arises as the result of an impact on building fabric, such as that of footsteps or a door closing.

impact sound isolation a thin layer of fibrous or porous sheet material laid under hard flooring to prevent vibration, walking impacts, etc. being transferred to the floor structure, and to spaces below.

impact strength the property of a material which is able to resist forces in impact without permanent deformation or rupture; impact resistance.

impedance the effective electrical resistance of a component in a circuit at a given frequency of current.

imperfection a feature that depreciates the appearance or lowers the quality of an item, product, surface or finish; a defect.

imperial standard brick a standard size of brick previously in use in Great Britain with regular dimensions of $8^5/_8" \times 4^1/_8" \times 2^5/_8"$ (219 × 104.8 × 66.8 mm).

impost a stone, block, brick or masonry from which the voussoirs of an arch are supported.

impost block 1 see dosseret.
2 a corbelled stone at the impost of a masonry arch, on which its voussoirs are supported.

impregnation a process by which timber is saturated with a wood preservative or flame retardant.
impregnated timber see pressure impregnated timber.

improved nail see annular nail.

improved wood timber whose pores are impregnated with synthetic resins, heated and subjected to pressure, used for floorings and exterior work.

inactive leaf the leaf in a double door which is usually kept locked, against which the active leaf is latched.

in-and-out screwdriver see spiral ratchet screwdriver.

in antis Lat.; in classical architecture, a description of a temple whose frontal columns are bounded at either side extensions of the side walls; see also antis temple.

inbark, bark pocket, ingrown bark; bark around branches and knots which has become embedded in wood as the tree grows.

incandescent lamp an electric lamp which produces light by means of a heated tungsten filament suspended in a glass tube in a vacuum or filled with an inert gas; incandescence is the emission of light by any heated object or body.

incense cedar [*Calocedrus decurrens*] a softwood from western USA whose close-grained timber has a fragrant resinous odour and is highly resistant to moisture; used as sawn boards.

incipient decay see dote.

inclined, sloping; of a roof, ramp, channel or other planar surface, at an angle to the horizontal; inclination is the angular measure of this slope.
inclined pile see raking pile.

indanthrene a proprietary name for a number of commercial synthetic pigments based on anthraquinone and related compounds, especially indanthrone blue (used in oil paints and acrylics for internal use) and indanthrene yellow, which has replaced traditional Indian yellow.
indanthrone pigment a group of pigments manufactured from anthraquinone; used also for dying fabrics.

indentation see indents.

indented moulding, sawtooth moulding; a decorative moulding consisting of a series of triangular indentations; see also indented embattled moulding.

indented moulding

indented embattled moulding an embattled moulding whose upper protrusions have V-shaped indentations.

indented scarf joint see halved and tabled scarf joint.

indented wire steel wire used as reinforcement, with surface indentations to improve its bonding in concrete.

indenting see indents.

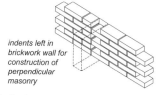

indents left in brickwork wall for construction of perpendicular masonry

indents recesses left during masonry construction into which later work, including perpendicular walls, ornament, etc. can be bonded; often called reverse toothing.

index of plasticity see plasticity index.

index of refraction see refractive index.

indiarubber see caoutchouc.

Indian blue see indigo.

Indian oak see teak.

Indian red see oxide red.

Indian rosewood, East Indian rosewood; [*Dalbergia latifolia*], see rosewood.

Indian yellow, puree, pwree; a yellow pigment used in the 1900s, originally produced in India by heating the urine of cows fed on mango leaves.

indicating bolt, snib latch; a lock for a WC or bathroom incorporating a dial indicating by colour or words whether the room is occupied.

indigo, Indian blue; a deep blue pigment originally extracted from the Indian indigo plant [*Indigofera tinctoria, Indigofera anil*] but since made synthetically from coal tar, see aniline; used mainly as a dyestuff.

indirect hot water supply system a hot water system in which hot water is provided by an indirect cylinder or calorifier rather than a boiler.

indirect lighting illumination or task lighting provided by light reflected, refracted or diffused by surfaces; see also direct lighting.

indirect solar radiation see skylight.

induced siphonage the sucking out of a water seal in a trap by siphonage caused by pressure differences in a drain, allowing foul air to escape into a room.

inductance the magnitude of electromotive force produced by a change in electrical current in a circuit or conductor.
induction convector system, induction unit system; an air-conditioning system in which the temperature of ducted air is regulated locally by hot and cold water pipes.
induction hardening a surface-hardening treatment for steel by briefly heating it with a high-frequency electrical current and then immediately quenching in water.
induction unit a localized air-conditioning unit in which ducted air is blown into a room over coils to heat or cool it; cf. fan coil unit.
induction unit system see induction convector system.

inductive loop an aerial wrapped around a building or embedded in construction, which receives electromagnetic signals from a portable transmitter; used in telecommunications and remote control doors, etc.; also called an induction loop.

industrialized building the construction of buildings using prefabrication, specialized building components and factory-made units to increase site efficiency and speed up construction.

inertia the tendency of a material or body to resist change; especially the property of a body to remain at rest or move in a straight line at a uniform velocity in the absence of external forces.
inertia block a thick layer of heavy material onto which mechanical equipment is placed to reduce its resonant frequency and absorb vibration caused by moving or oscillating parts.

inert pigment see extender.

infill, infilling; **1** material used to fill in the spaces in a building frame, such as panels of glass or sheet material held in curtainwalling profiles.
2 the part of a balustrade between the handrail and floor level which is filled with solid material, glass or obstructing wires or rods to afford protection.

infiltration 1 the seepage of fresh air into a building through open vents, cracks and construction joints around windows and doors, etc., as ventilation.
2 the undesirable leakage of air into construction and spaces; air introduced in such a way, often causing draughts and discomfort.
infiltration rate a measure of the seepage of fresh air into a building, given as m^3/h or litres per second (l/s).

inflammable same as flammable; often confused with its opposite, nonflammable.

inflected arch see ogee arch.

influence line in the theory of structures, a graph plotted to show loading at various points along a beam.

infrared radiator a heater which produces heat by the emission of infrared radiation, which is electromagnetic radiation of a longer wavelength than that of the visible spectrum.

infrasound sound with a frequency below that which can be heard by the human ear, less than about 15–30 Hz.

inglenook, chimney-corner, chimney-nook; a seat, seating place or bench integrated into a large traditional open fireplace.

ingrain wallcovering see woodchip wallpaper.

ingrown bark see inbark.

inhibitor a substance which slows down a chemical process.

initial prestress, initial stress; in prestressed concrete, the stretching force applied to prestressing tendons, which is then imparted to the concrete as compressive stress.

initial settlement see immediate settlement.

initial stress see initial prestress.

injection see artificial cementing, grouting.

injection mortar a wet mix of mortar used for grouting; grout.

injection moulding a method of forming thermoplastics and thermosetting plastics products by heating granulated material and injecting it into a mould.

inlay flush decoration made by gluing or casting material of another colour, composition or pattern into surface depressions.

inlet see fresh-air inlet, fresh-air vent.

inlet grating the perforated or slatted lid for a gully, through which surface water passes to a drain.

inner bark see phloem.

inner leaf the skin of brickwork, blockwork, stonework or concrete cavity wall construction which faces the interior of a building; in concrete construction it is usually loadbearing.

inner ply one of the layers or veneers in plywood which are not on the surface.

inner sash the sash in a coupled window which faces the interior of a room.

inorganic referring to a substance which is not found in or derived from living organisms, or one of mineral origin.
inorganic pigment, mineral pigment; a pigment which is either a synthetic metal salt such as zinc oxide, or a treated native earth such as burnt sienna; organic refers to a substance which is not found in or derived from living organisms.
inorganic polymer any polymer which does not contain carbon.

input air see supply air.

input device see supply air terminal unit.

input ventilation, pressure ventilation; mechanical ventilation by pumping fresh air into spaces, thus causing internal pressure which forces out stale air.

insanitary a description of a construction or space contaminated by biological pollutants such as bacteria and living microbes which may be a liability to the health of occupants.

insect screen, fly wire; a fine mesh of metal wire or plastics fixed to a frame to prevent insects from entering a building via windows, doors, eaves, etc.; the mesh itself is called insect mesh.

insert see patch.

inserted column see engaged column.

inserted plywood plywood in which defects in the surface plies have been repaired with patches of veneer.

inset screw cup see recessed screw cup.

inside calliper a measuring tool with a pair of curved hinged legs, used for measuring the inside diameter of pipes and other hollow objects.

inside corner tile a ceramic tile designed for use at the lowest edge of a tiled wall, where it meets the floor.

*inside corner
tile*

inside corner trowel see internal angle trowel.

inside face the face of a piece of sawn timber which is nearest the heart when cut from a log.

inside glazing glass or other glazing material that has been added to the inner side of external glazing.

inside start saw see flooring saw.

in situ, cast-in-place (Am), cast-in-situ; referring to concrete and other similar materials which have been cast fresh on site as opposed to being prefabricated; written in-situ when used as an adjective; in-situ casting is the process of doing this.

in-situ concrete, cast-in-place concrete (Am), cast-in-situ concrete; concrete placed on site in formwork rather than having been precast as units.

in-situ flooring floor surfacing laid or cast in situ.

in-situ pile see cast-in-place pile.

in-situ plasterwork, solid plasterwork; ornamental plasterwork cast or laid in its final position, as opposed to being precast and fitted; in-situ plastering or solid plastering is the process of working with in-situ plasterwork.

inspection a periodic survey or check of work at key stages in construction, undertaken on site by a qualified person such as a local authority official, clerk of works or architect to ensure that it meets with building regulations and norms and is in accordance with the designs; examples included as separate entries are listed below:
*building inspection; *final inspection; *fire inspection; *investigation; *property survey; *reinspection; *site inspection; *survey.

inspection cap an end cap for the open end of a drainage pipe, which can be removed for inspection.

inspection chamber, manhole; a subterranean chamber with a removable cover at ground level, usually located outside a building to provide open access for inspection and maintenance of a drainage or sewerage system.

inspection cover an openable cover for an inspection chamber.

inspection door an inspection hatch in a flue.

inspection eye see cleaning eye.

inspection hatch, inspection door; a door or hatch in ductwork or casing which can be opened for inspection, cleaning, maintenance, etc. of a concealed device or construction.

inspector see building control officer, fire officer.

installation 1 a fixed assembly of appliances, components and fittings which provides a mechanical or electrical service for a building or construction.

2 fitting; the fixing of prefabricated components or services in place and subsidiary work to affect their performance.

3 the fastening in place and connection to a supply of technical appliances and plant.

installation allowance, installation gap see allowance.

installation riser any vertical gas pipe within a building.

instant start lamp, cold start lamp; a fluorescent lamp which lights up immediately after being switched on.

instant tack the spontaneous sticking together of surfaces coated with wet contact adhesive as they are brought together to form a joint.

instructions to tenderers in tendering for building work, the requirements and conditions covering the preparation and submission of a tender.

insulant see insulating material.

insulated block
a lightweight concrete block with an interlayer or core of polystyrene incorporated as thermal insulation during manufacture.

insulated block

insulated flue a prefabricated flue of metal twin-wall construction with fireproof insulation between the inner steel tube and outer sheetmetal sheathing.

insulated glazing unit see sealed glazed unit.

insulated infill panel opaque infill panels for glazing and curtain walling systems, containing thermal insulation.

insulated render proprietary rendering systems in which render is applied to wire mesh lathing attached directly to a layer of thermal insulation.

insulating, non-conductive; the property of thermally, acoustically or electrically isolating with a barrier of suitable material to inhibit the flow of heat, sound or electricity.

insulating concrete, insulating lightweight concrete; concrete with a low thermal conductivity and good insulating properties.

insulating glass unit see sealed glazed unit.

insulating lightweight concrete see insulating concrete.

insulating material, insulation, insulant; any material used as thermal, electrical or sound insulation.

---

insulation the laying or installation of thermal or acoustic insulation; the insulating layer thus formed; types included as separate entries are listed below:
*acoustic insulation, see sound insulation; *electrical insulation; *fire insulation, see fireproofing; *frost insulation; *heat insulation, see thermal insulation; *insulating material; *sound insulation; *thermal insulation; *vibration insulation.*

insulation bat a preformed panel of thermal insulation such as mineral wool and wood wool slabs.

insulation board see softboard.

insulation clip a thin plastic accessory attached along the length of a wall tie to hold insulation bats in their correct position in a masonry cavity wall; also called an insulation retainer.

insulation glass see sealed glazed unit, sound insulation glass, see sound control glass.

insulation retainer see insulation clip.

INT interior adhesive.

intaglio rilevato see sunk relief.

intarsia, tarsia; decorative inlaid work in mosaic of various colours and materials, especially wooden inlay from the Italian Renaissance; see marquetry.

integrated system an air-conditioning or mechanical ventilation system using in-built ducting, air-handling luminaires, etc.

intelligent fire alarm see addressable system.

intense blue see phthalocyanine blue.

intensity level see sound intensity level.

intercepting trap, interceptor, interceptor trap; a drainage fitting or construction which inhibits the passage of unwanted gravel, silt, oil, etc. in the waste water to a drainage system; see also petrol intercepting trap, oil interceptor.

intercom see internal telephone system.

intergrown knot, live knot; 1 a knot in seasoned timber whose grain is intergrown with the surrounding wood. **2** see red knot.

intergrown knot

interim application in contract administration, a document drawn up periodically by a contractor requesting fees owed for work carried out.

interim payment in contract administration, a payment made at any given stage in construction for work carried out up to that point.

interior 1 the inside of a building, space, component, installation, etc.; that part of a building bounded by internal walls, ceilings and floors.
2 see interior design.

interior adhesive, INT; adhesive intended primarily for interior use, unresistant to prolonged damp, the weather and boiling water.

interior decoration see interior design (below).

interior glazing see internal glazing.

interior luminaire a non-weatherproof luminaire designed only for use within a building.

interior paint, internal paint; paint suitable for interior use only; often emulsion paint.

interior plaster plaster suitable for use on interior walls.

interior plywood plywood intended for interior use, glued with adhesives which have low resistance to humidity.

interior wall, partition; a wall inside a building, neither of whose faces are open to the outside.

interior design 1 the discipline and profession of designing interior spaces, including the planning of layouts, and the design and choice of surface finishes and furnishings.
2 decor, interior, interior decoration; the wall and floor finishes, surfaces materials and treatments, colour scheme, layouts and furnishing of a building or space.

interior designer a trained person or professional consultant responsible for designing and specifying decor and furnishings for the interior of a building.

interlace, entrelace; decorative ornament of complex intertwined bands or lines; see also knotwork.

interlace

interlaced arches, interlacing arches, laced arches; a series of round arches or arched shapes in which adjacent arches overlap one half-arch width.

interlaced arches

interlocked grain, interlocking grain, twisting fibres; timber grain produced in alternate groups of growth rings forming spirals in reverse directions round the tree trunk; it is generally difficult to work and used in decorative veneers.

interlocking paver, interpaver; a proprietary concrete paving product preformed in a variety of shapes and laid in groups to form patterned surfaces; sometimes called a key or interweave paver, depending on its profile.

interlocking tile a clay or concrete roof tile whose edges are moulded with a series of grooves to fit into corresponding mouldings in adjacent tiles.

interlocking tile

intermediate landing, stair landing; a horizontal platform between two flights of stairs, or at the top of a stair between two floors.

intermediate rail 1 a rail between the top and bottom rails of a panelled door to provide added stiffness.

2 a horizontal rail fixed to balusters or verticals between floor level and the handrail of a balustrade.

intermediate rock types of igneous rock whose silica content is between 52% and 66%.

intermediate sash the middle of three window sashes in a triple glazed window unit.

intermediate sheet in built-up roofing, a smooth middle layer of bitumen felt bonded to the underlying base sheet and cap sheet above.

internal angle trowel, inside corner trowel; a plasterer's trowel for smoothing internal corners in plasterwork with a handled blade of bent steel sheet.

internal door a door between two adjacent spaces in a building, neither face of which is exposed to the outside.

internal force a force occurring within, and restrained by, a structural member, material, component, etc.

internal friction see viscosity.

internal glazing glazing not exposed to the outside; a window or glass screen in an internal partition.

internal paint see interior paint.

internal plaster see interior plaster.

internal surface the surface of a wall or building component facing towards the inside.

internal surface resistance value see RSI-value.

internal telephone system, intercom; an electrical communications system for use within a building or complex.

internal tooth washer a tooth washer with serrations along its inner circumference.

internal vibrator see immersion vibrator.

internal wall see partition.

interpaver see interlocking paver.

interrupter see pipe interrupter.

intersecting barrel vault see groin vault.

intersecting tracery Gothic tracery in which parallel mullions are bent over at their upper ends to form a series of interlaced pointed arches.

Gothic intersecting tracery at Exeter Cathedral, c. 1350

intersole see mezzanine.

interspace the gas-filled cavity between adjacent sheets of glass in a sealed glazed unit.

interweave paver a specially-shaped concrete paving unit which is laid to create a regular undulating pattern.

intonaco the smooth uppermost coat of three layers of plaster, onto which a fresco is painted.

intrados the lower line, underside, soffit or face of an arch.

intruder alarm system a warning system of bells, lights and other means which react to the presence of unauthorized entrants to a building.

intruder glazing glazing designed to prevent the forced entrance of intruders to a building via its windows; types included as separate entries are listed below:
*alarm glass; *anti-bandit laminated glass; *anti-vandal glass; *armour-plated glass, see bullet-resistant laminated glass; *blast-resistant laminated glass; *security glass; *security glazing; *toughened glass.

intrusion concrete see grouted concrete.

intrusive rock see plutonic rock.

intumescent glass see laminated intumescent glass.

intumescent paint, flame-retardant paint; a surface coating for metals which changes into a fire-resisting and insulating foam in the event of excess heat from a fire.

invected moulding see scallop moulding.

invert, invert level; the level of the lowest part of the inside of a channel, pipeline or other vessel in a drainage system.

inverted arch an arch constructed upside down, usually for structural reasons.

inverted arch

inverted beam a beam which protrudes above the plane of the surface which it supports, so that its soffit is at the same level of the soffit of floor or roof construction.

inverted roof see upside down roof.

inverted siphon see sag pipe.

invert level see invert.

investigation, survey; the inspection, measuring and researching of ground conditions, condition of repair of existing structures, etc. prior to sale, construction, design, etc.; see geotechnical survey, site investigation.

invisible hinge, secret hinge; a hinge which is not visible when the door to which it is fixed is both open or closed; see also concealed hinge.

invitation to tender, call for bids (Am); in project management, an invitation to selected firms to submit tenders, or an announcement that tenders are invited to carry out certain work.

inward opening referring to a window casement or door which opens inwards with respect to the exterior of a building.

Ionic pertaining to the classical Greek Ionic order originating in Ionian Greece, characterized by fluted columns, a voluted

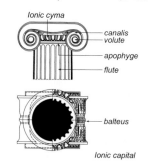

Ionic

capital, a base and an entablature with dentils.

Ionic base a column base used with the classical Ionic order, usually differentiated as an Attic base or a Samian base.

Ionic capital a capital surmounting a column of the classical Ionic order, with characteristic paired volutes over an egg and dart moulding, bound with a decorative belt known as a balteus.

Ionic column a column of the classical Greek Ionic order, with fluting, a voluted capital and Ionic base; considerably more slender than those of the Doric order.

Ionic cyma in classical ornamentation, a cyma moulding enriched with egg and dart ornament.

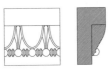

Ionic cyma, with egg and dart, and bead and reel mouldings

ionization chamber smoke detector

a smoke detector which reacts to a voltage difference between two ionization chambers, occurring in the presence of combustion gases.

iotite see cordierite.

IR isoprene rubber.

iridium a white metal, **Ir,** used in hard metal alloys.

iroko [*Chlorophora excelsa*] a tropical African hardwood whose yellow-brown to dark brown timber is strong and highly durable; used as a substitute for teak.

iron 1 a common, pale-coloured, strong metal, **Fe,** used primarily as a basic ingredient of steel, alloyed with carbon to improve its hardness and corrosion resistance.
2 the blade of a plane or similar cutting tool.

iron blue see Prussian blue.

iron brown see Prussian brown.

iron carbide see cementite.

iron disulphide see iron pyrites.

iron oxide see below.

iron pyrites, pyrite, sulphur-ore; a brassy yellow mineral, natural iron disulphide, **FeS$_2$;** an important source of sulphur, sulphuric acid and iron sulphide,

and also gold and copper, which it contains in small quantities.

iron wire see binding wire.

iron yellow see Mars colour.

ironmongery see hardware; door ironmongery, see door furniture.

ironmongery schedule, hardware schedule; a design and contract document listing and specifying metal fittings, hardware and components for doors and windows in a construction project.

iron oxide 1 ferrous oxide; a dark greenish-black chemical compound, **FeO,** used as a pigment in glasses.
2 ferric oxide, red iron oxide, haematite; a red chemical compound, **Fe$_2$O$_3$,** used as a polishing agent and as a red pigment; see limonite (brown iron ore) **Fe$_2$O$_3$.nH$_2$O** and haematite (hematite), **Fe$_2$O$_3$.**
3 ferrous ferric oxide, black iron oxide; a black chemical compound, **Fe$_3$O$_4$,** used as pigment, polishing agent and in magnetic coatings for computer disks and tapes.
see magnetite, black iron oxide, magnetic iron ore **Fe$_3$O$_4$.**
4 brown iron oxide, see burnt sienna.

irregular bond, random bond; a brickwork bond in which bricks in consecutive courses overlap, but with no regular repeating pattern.

irregular bond

irregular grain grain in a piece of timber which is not straight due to natural abnormalities in the wood.

irrigation drain see subsoil drain.

I-section 1 I-beam, UB section, universal beam, joist; a structural steel beam section formed by rolling, whose uniform cross-section resembles the letter I and whose height is over 1.2 times its width.
2 similarly shaped non-structural sections in other metals.

isinglass 1 mica, especially that found in thin sheets.
2 see fish glue.

isocyanurate see polyisocyanurate.

isodomic construction masonry laid in courses of equal height.

isolated footing see pad foundation.

isolating membrane see separating layer.

isolating varnish a general name for thin varnishes sprayed on to recently dried paint to provide a base for over-painting or correction.

isolation mount see vibration insulator.

isometric projection 1 'of equal measurement'; in general, any axonometric or oblique projection drawing in which all lines parallel to the three main axis are drawn to the same relative scale.
2 in particular a conventional axonometric drawing constructed by extending a plan drawn on axes skewed to 30° on either side of the vertical to a dimensioned height, with all lines parallel to the three main axes, which are 120° apart, drawn to the same scale; this is the most common form, properly classified as an orthographic isometric projection.

isophote, isophot; in lighting design, one of a number of theoretical lines or contours on a drawing representing points of equal light intensity.

isoprene rubber, IR; a synthetic rubber, similar to natural rubber, often found in conjunction with other polymers such as isobutene in butyl; used for inner tubes and gaskets.

Isoptera spp. see termite.

isostatic frame see statically determinate frame.

isotropic referring to a material or substance which displays the same properties in all directions.
isotropic slab a concrete floor slab construction whose inlaid reinforcement is of the same magnitude in both directions.

Italian arch a round or pointed arch whose intrados and extrados are constructed from different centres so that the

archivolt is thicker at the apex than at the base; see Italian pointed arch, Florentine arch.

Italianate referring to any architecture or ornamentation which adopts the styling and motifs of the Italian Renaissance.

Italian blue see Egyptian blue.

Italian earth see burnt sienna.

Italian pointed arch a pointed arch whose intrados and extrados are constructed from different centres so that the archivolt is thicker at the apex than at the base.

Italian round arch see Florentine arch.

Italian tiling, pan and roll tiles; roof tiling in which the gaps in a lower course of flat tiles with side lips (tegula) are covered with a course of U-shaped tiles (imbrex), laid concave side down.

Italian tiling

ivory black a strong black pigment consisting of impure carbon obtained from burnt and ground bones, originally the tusks of elephants; synonymous with bone black.

ivy leaf a Gothic decorative motif based on the leaf of the climbing plant ivy, *Hedera helix.*

ivy leaf

J

jacaranda [*Jacaranda spp.*] a group of South American tropical hardwood shrubs and trees with hard and dark timber.

jacaranda brown see burnt umber.

jack see jacking device.

jack arch see flat arch.

jacked pile in underpinning work, any pile forced into the ground in sections using the weight of the overlying building.

jack hammer a large hand-operated percussive implement powered by compressed air, used for breaking, demolishing and the digging of stone.

jacking device, jack; in concretework, a hydraulic or screw device attached to slipform to raise it at regular intervals.

jack plane a standard sized bench plane (320–360 mm long).

jack rafter in timber roof construction, a shortened rafter running between eaves and hip or valley and ridge.

jack shore a slanting member of a raking shore which supports a riding shore.

Jacobean architecture a late Renaissance architectural style in England during the reign of James I (1603–1625); found primarily in secular palaces and country houses, and characterized by the use of classical elements, Dutch gables and roof turrets.

jade a hard, green, blue or white sodium aluminium silicate mineral used principally for ornament and as jewellery; a general name for the minerals jadeite and nephrite.

jadeite a hard greenish mineral, often cut for decoration as jade.

jagged-shank nail see annular nail.

jamb 1 a vertical abutment on either side of a door or window opening; a door jamb or window jamb; see also reveal.
2 the vertical side member of a door or window frame; see closing jamb (shutting jamb), hanging jamb.

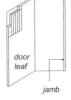

door leaf

jamb

3 a vertical timber at the edge of an opening in traditional timber construction, to which a door or window frame is fixed.

jamb anchor a metal strip used to fix a door or window frame to surrounding construction.

jamb figure a carved column figure decorating the jamb columns or recesses in the main portal of a medieval church; also called a jamb statue.

jamb filler a preformed flashing of sheetmetal; used at the side of a door or window opening to cast out water.

jamb lining a timber board used to cover the jamb of an opening.

jamb-mounted door closer a door closer mounted to the door jamb and hinged edge of the door leaf.

jamb post, cripple stud; in timber frame construction, a post which supports a lintel over an opening.

jamb statue see jamb figure.

Japanese larch [*Larix kaempferi, Larix leptolepis*], see larch.

Japanese oak [*Quercus mongolica*], see oak.

Japan scraper a set of simple steel-bladed spatulas with rounded corners and plastic or wooden handles, designed to apply and shape plaster and putty, remove paint, etc.

jarrah [*Eucalyptus marginata*], see eucalyptus.

jasper a microcrystalline variety of the mineral chalcedony, varying in colour and pattern; used as gemstones and for ornament.

jaune brilliant, jaune d'antimoine see Naples yellow.

Java cotton see kapok.

Jennings pattern bit an auger bit with a double helically shaped shank for drilling deep accurate holes in wood.

jenny leg calliper, odd leg calliper; a calliper with one leg ending in a point and the other turned in at its base; used for scribing lines parallel to a surface.

jerkinhead roof see half-hipped roof.

jet inlet, jet, nozzle; in mechanical ventilation, a small-bore terminal device which produces a stream of air in a particular direction.

jetting the cleaning of a pipeline by forcing a high pressure stream of water through it.

jib, boom; a main horizontal or slanting beam attached to the vertical mast of a crane or lifting device, from which loads are carried.

jig a device used to guide the blade of a machine tool when cutting repetitive patterns or milling; any similar implement for a specific job of work.

jigsaw, bayonet saw, sabre saw; a power operated saw with an oscillating blade for cutting curves and openings in board; a sabre saw is one in which the blade points out of the front as opposed to the rear of the saw; see also fretsaw.

Job a design or building project, the work involved therein; see also jobbing order.

jobbing order, job; small and relatively basic building works which involve simple agreements and minimal site administration and organization.

job card, production card; in stonework, a card which lists the type of masonry, scope of work, size and shape of stones, etc. for any particular job.

joggle 1 in oblique timber jointing, a shaped abutment in one piece which bears the thrust of another.
2 see joggle piece.

joggle beam a built-up timber beam in which the timbers are held in place with joggles or cogged pieces.

joggle beam

joggled arch, crossette; a masonry arch in which adjacent voussoirs are cut with rebates and interlocked.

joggled arch

joggle piece, joggle; an extra cogged piece sometimes added to tie a timber scarf joint or built-up beam together.

joggle post see king post.

joggle-spliced scarf joint a timber lengthening joint which makes use of a joggle piece to fix the pieces together.

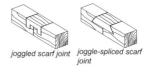

joggled scarf joint   *joggle-spliced scarf joint*

joggle tenon joint see stub tenon joint.

joggle truss a timber truss in which the chord or tie beam is above a vertical joggle post; the end of the post is triangulated with the ends of the chord by diagonal braces.

Joiner a tradesman responsible for the non-structural timberwork such as furniture, interiors and panelling in a building.

joiner saw see bench saw.

joiner's chisel see paring chisel.

joiner's cramp, bar cramp, sash cramp; a large cramp with a long bar along which adjustable stops can be placed; used for holding large objects in compression while they are being glued.

joiner's hammer a medium sized hammer with an octagonal or bell head and claw or wedge-shaped pee; used by a joiner.

joinery, finish carpentry (Am); fine woodwork such as doors, window frames, trim and panelling in a building.

joinery moulding, joinery profile see timber trim.

joint 1 the meeting of two components or materials in construction.
2 the formation and sealing material placed there.
see connection, brick joint, sand joint, construction joint, knuckle, timber joint.

joint bolt, handrail bolt, rail bolt; a threaded shaft to which nuts can be screwed; used as a concealed connector in butt jointed wooden components such as handrails.

jointer any tool for shaping and smoothing mortar jointing and pointing in brickwork.

jointer plane, trying plane; a long plane 500—750 mm in length traditionally used for dressing long timber boards.

joint filler any compound or substance applied as filling for joints between adjacent components or materials; called jointing compound if an organic sealant; see jointing strip.

jointing 1 the making or filling of construction joints.
2 the binding of bricks together using mortar; same as bedding.
3 the tidying up and smoothing of excess wet mortar from a brickwork joint, and shaping it into the desired form.
4 the result of the above actions.
jointing bead see jointing strip.
jointing compound a compound applied to joints between components or materials as bedding, weatherproofing, finishing or as an adhesive.
jointing mortar mortar used for jointing in masonrywork and tiling.
jointing strip, joint strip, jointing bead, sealant strip; preformed foam, mastic or elastic strip pushed into the gaps or open joints between adjacent components or elements to form a base for applied sealant.
jointing tape various types of adhesive tape used for joining sheet materials such as bitumen felt and carpet together and for closing seams and sealing pipe fittings, etc.
jointing tool a mason's trowel with a bent round or hemispherical steel rod which is run along mortar joints to form a keyed joint.
jointing trowel a very thin-bladed bricklayer's trowel for shaping and smoothing masonry joints.
joint method see method of joints.

joint sanding, sand jointing; the spreading or brushing of sand over freshly laid external paving to fill the joints between alternate paving stones or slabs.

joint sealant see sealant.

joint strip see cover strip, jointing strip.

joist one of a series of spaced beams used to support a floor or roof; types included as separate entries are listed below:
*binding joist, see binder; *bridging joist; *ceiling joist; *common joist; *floor joist;
*rolled steel joist (RSJ) see I-section; *roof joist; *steel joist, see I-section; *timber joist; *trimmed joist, see trimmed beam; *trimmer joist, see trimmer; *trimming joist.

joist hanger a metal fixing component for attaching the ends of joists and other horizontal timber members at right angles to other construction.
joist spacing the distance, centre to centre, between alternate joists in a floor or roof structure.

joule, newton-metre; abb. **J**; SI unit of energy or work equal to that required for a current of 1 amp to operate against a resistance of 1 ohm, or that required to move 1 metre against a force of 1 newton.

jowl, gunstock; in traditional timber frame construction, the thickening at the top of a post or column to receive another member.

juffer in traditional timber frame construction, a square timber 4—5 inches in dimension.

Juglans spp. see walnut.

jumper 1 in brick or stonework walling, a long vertical or horizontal stone which overlaps two or more smaller stones.
2 a pointed masonry chisel for making holes in stone.

junction 1 the meeting or joining place of two parts of construction such as that formed by a roof and wall.
2 a length of pipe for attaching a subsidiary pipe to a main pipeline.
junction box a casing for connections or junctions in an electrical installation.
junction chamber see cable manhole.

Juniperus spp. juniper; a genus of around 60 evergreen conifer trees and shrubs from all over the northern hemisphere, planted as ornamentals and used for their timber; Juniperus communis, the common juniper, is a softwood whose brownish-yellow aromatic timber contains numerous solid knots; Juniperus virginiana, see eastern red cedar.

jute fibres from the inner bark of the jute plant from India [Corchorus capsularis]; used for making ropes and rough fabric, canvas, sackcloth, etc.

K

kallaite see turquoise.

kaolin a form of pure clay produced from the decomposition of feldspar, hydrated aluminium silicate; used as a filler and white pigment in latex and emulsion paints; often the same as China clay.

kapok, ceiba, capoc, Java cotton, silk cotton; a water-resistant wool product formed from the seed fibres of the tropical ceiba tree [*Ceiba pentandra*]; used for stuffing mattresses and furniture.

kapur, Borneo camphorwood; [*Dryobalanops spp.*] a hardwood from Malaysia and Indonesia with coarse, heavy, reddish-brown timber; used for outdoor furniture and joinery.

karri [*Eucalyptus diversicolor*], see eucalyptus.

Kassler yellow see Turner's yellow.

keel arch a decorative pointed arch with two mirrored S-shapes which meet at the apex; a pointed reverse ogee arch.

keel arch

keel moulding an ornamental projecting moulding whose section is roughly in the shape of a pointed arch, formed by two ogees with their concave ends together.

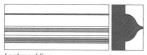

keel moulding

keep see box staple.

keeper see striking plate.

Kentish tracery Gothic tracery found in some English churches of the Perpendicular style, characterized by use of foils and barbs.

kentledge, cantledge; temporary weight added to test or provide stability to a structure.

kerb, curb (Am); in road and street construction, the raised edge of the carriageway where it adjoins a footpath, often formed by a row of cut stones or concrete units.

kerb parking see street parking.

kerbstone one of a number of cut or dressed stones or specially cast concrete units laid to form a kerb at the edge of a carriageway; written curbstone in USA.

kerf the groove made by a saw when cutting timber.

kermes a dark red dyestuff made from the bodies of adult females of the insect *Kermes ilicis*.

kernel see crenelle.

kernel black see vine black.

Kevlar see aramid fibre.

key 1 any roughness in a surface designed to encourage the bonding of a successive layer of material.

2 see keystone.

3 a small portable implement by which a lock can be operated.

4 one of the buttons on a computer keyboard which represent symbols when written.

5 see key pattern, Greek key.

6 see wood key.

key block see keystone.

key coat, primary coat; a coating or layer of material such as plaster, paint, etc. applied to a surface to promote the adhesion of further coats; see also base coat.

key drop, keyhole cover; a pivoted metal flap which covers a keyhole.

keyed alike a description and the associated programming of a number of locks within a building such that they are operable with the same key.

keyed joint 1 any timber joint tightened with a wedge or peg.

keyed splayed and tabled scarf joint

keyed tenon joint

2 bucket-handled joint, concave joint, rodded joint; in brickwork, a recessed concave mortar joint either as a key for receiving a finish or as a decorative treatment; see also raked joint.

keyed scarf joint, wedged scarf joint; a timber lengthening joint tightened by driving a pair of folded wedges into a notch cut into the splayed ends.

keyed, splayed and tabled scarf joint in timber frame construction, a splayed lengthening joint hewn so as to be tightened with a peg or pair or folding wedges after assembly; a keyed scarf joint.

keyed tenon joint, pinned tenon joint, cabinetmaker's tenon joint; any through timber mortise and tenon joint which has been fastened with a transverse wedge, peg or pin on the reverse side of the mortised piece.

keyed lock one of the locks belonging to a suite of locks.

keyhole a hole or shaped orifice which receives a key into a lock.

keyhole cover see key drop.

keyhole saw, lock saw, pad saw; a compass saw whose tapering flexible blade and handle are aligned; used for cutting the apertures for locks in doors.

keying the physical programming of locks within a suite to enable or restrict passage for various combinations of keyholders.

key pattern classical banded running ornamentation made up of horizontal and vertical lines or fillets which interlink to form a geometrical pattern; often synonymous with fret; see also angular guilloche (meander), potenty moulding, Greek key.

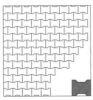

key pattern

key paver a concrete paving unit which is shaped to create a patterned paved surface of similar interlocking blocks;

key paving

also called an interlocking paver or interpaver.

key plate see escutcheon.

keystone, key, key block; the highest wedge-shaped piece in a masonry arch, often decorated, which locks the voussoirs in position.

khaya [*Khaya ivorensis*], see African mahogany.

kicker in concretework, a small raised area of a cast concrete slab which provides a location for wall or column formwork.

kicking plate, door plate, kick plate; a protective plate, usually of metal or plastics, fitted to the lower part of a door leaf to prevent wear.

killas see clayslate.

killed steel in steel processing, steel which has been well deoxidized when being poured into ingots, showing no evolution of gas as it solidifies.

kiln an oven for baking ceramics, bricks, or for the controlled drying of timber; see dry kiln.

kiln dried, hot-air dried, kiln seasoned; a description of timber which has been dried in a kiln to assure controlled seasoning and minimize warpage.

kilocalory, Calorie; abb. **Cal;** a unit of energy $= 4190$ joules; the energy required to raise one kilogram of water by $1°C$.

king block in traditional timber roof construction, a timber at which principal rafters or blades form an apex, often carrying a ridge purlin.

king bolt, king rod; in traditional timber roof construction, a vertical wrought iron rod replacing a king post in a king post roof truss.

king closer, three quarter brick; a three quarter length brick or bat with one splayed corner to give the appearance of a closer in brickwork; also misleadingly called a three quarter brick due to

king closer

the three out of four faces which can still be used as exterior edges.

king piece see king post.

king post, king piece, joggle post; in traditional timber roof construction, a central vertical strut rising from a tie beam and carrying a ridge purlin.

king post roof truss, king post truss a roof truss with a tie beam, coupled rafters and a king post.

king post roof roof construction supported by a series of king post trusses.

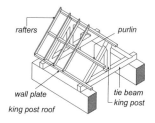

rafters

purlin

wall plate

tie beam

king post

king post roof

king rod see king bolt.

king's blue a variety of cobalt blue pigment.

king strut in traditional timber roof construction, a central vertical strut rising from a tie beam but not carrying a ridge purlin.

king strut roof truss in traditional timber roof construction, a roof truss with a tie beam, coupled rafters and a king strut.

king's yellow, arsenic yellow, auripigmentum, orpiment, Royal yellow; a very poisonous bright opaque yellow pigment consisting of artificial arsenic trisulphide; no longer in use since the introduction of cadmium yellow.

king tie, upper king post; in traditional timber roof construction, a short central vertical member rising from a collar and carrying a ridge purlin in a timber truss.

kink a localized warp in a timber board caused by the presence of a knot or other weak spot.

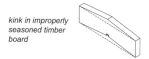

kink in improperly seasoned timber board

kit building a prefabricated building assembled from a set of standard prefabricated parts.

kite step, kite winder; a triangular or wedge-shaped step in a turning or circular stair.

knee 1 in traditional timber frame construction, a timber block fixed at the meeting of two framing members to stiffen the joint.
2 see elbow.

knee brace in traditional timber frame construction, a short up brace.

knee roof see curb roof.

knife cut veneer see sliced veneer.

knife-edge load, line load; a structural load imposed along the length of a thin line; see distributed load, point load.

knob 1 an ovoid handle for a drawer, door, etc.; see door knob.
2 a decorative carved boss, a knot.

knocker see door knocker.

knocking up see retempering.

knop a round decorative element, a boss or knot.

knosp, knot; a boss carved in the shape of a bud.

knot 1 a hard, ovoid or swirling growth evident in the surface of sawn timber; a branch stem in the original tree cut through its width.
2 boss, knosp, knop, knob; a carved decorative terminating element representing knotted twine or foliage located at the meeting of ribs in a vault or at other similar locations.

knot cluster a group of knots appearing in the surface grain pattern of seasoned timber.

knot hole a hole in a piece of machined timber left by the removal or separation of a knot.

knot hole

knot sealer see knotting.

knotted column a Romanesque stone column or coupled columns whose compound shafts are carved as if knotted together in the middle; also known as a knotted pillar.

knotted column

knotting a transparent liquid consisting of shellac dissolved in methylated spirits, used as a sealer to inhibit the bleeding through of surface resin from knots in timber before the application of paint; the application of the above.

knotwork, entrelace, interlace; in the early architecture and art of northern Europe, especially that of Christian Ireland, decorative ornamentation representing intertwined, overlapping and knotted bands.

Celtic knotwork

knuckle the joining tube of a hinge, in which the pin rotates and around which the leaves pivot; sometimes known as a loop, joint or curl.

knuckle bend a curved pipe fitting with a small radius of curvature; designed for use at a sharp change of direction in a pipeline.

knulled ornament see gadroon.

knur, knurl see burl.

kokrodua see afrormosia.

kraft paper strong brown paper made from sulphate pulp; see building paper.

Krems white see Cremnitz white.

k-value, coefficient of thermal conductivity, heat transmission value; a theoretical measure of how well a material or construction of unit thickness will conduct heat, whose units are W/m°C; calculated as the amount of energy passing through a unit area of one metre thick construction for unit temperature difference on either side of the construction; (the C-value is obtained by multiplying by thickness of construction, see also U-value)

kyanite, disthene; a hard, bluish, crystalline aluminium silicate mineral with a high melting point; used for heat-resistant materials and as jewellery.

L

label see hood-mould.

labourer a person employed on a construction site to carry out manual or unskilled work.

labour-only contract a building contract covering the supply of labour only.

Labrador a trade name for larvikite.

labradorite, Labrador feldspar; a highly coloured and specular variety of the mineral plagioclase, polished and used in ornamental masonry, or carved for decoration.

labyrinth fret see meander.

laced arches see interlaced arches.

laced stanchion a composite steel lattice column or stanchion in which vertical rolled steel sections are joined together with stiff diagonal members.

lacertine see animal interlace.

lachryma occasional name for gutta; 'tear' in Latin.

lacing see lacing course, interlaced arches (laced arches).

lacing course a course or courses of bricks or finer material used as decoration or reinforcement in a rough stone or rubble wall.

lacquer see cellulose lacquer.

lacunar Lat.; in classical architecture, a decorated ceiling relieved with a series of polygonal recessed panels or coffers; a coffered ceiling.

ladder a freestanding or fixed frame to provide temporary or permanent vertical access, consisting of two vertical side rails with horizontal rungs or steps in between; any construction resembling this.
ladder stair see open riser stair.

lag bolt see coach screw.

lagging thermal insulation of mineral wool or foamed plastics for boilers and pipes.

lag screw see coach screw.

laid on purlin see through purlin.

laissez-faire 'allow to do'; lack of government interference in economic life; in town planning the permitting of development to go ahead without planning constraint and intervention, governed solely by commercial interest.

lake any pigment formed by the addition of an organic dye to a metal oxide, hydroxide or salt to render it insoluble.
lake red a shade of red which takes its name from the colour of dye made in India from the secretion of the insect *Coccus lacca*.

lake asphalt a naturally occurring viscous liquid asphalt which, when added to distilled bitumen, increases the hardness and durability of a road surface without detracting from flexibility; see also natural rock asphalt.

lambrequin a short drapery fringe above a window, etc.; ornament representing this, especially stylized drapery hanging from the helm of a coat of arms; also called mantle or mantling.

laminate, plastics laminate; hardwearing or decorative sheet material produced by bonding thin sheets of thermosetting plastics such as melamine, urea or phenol formaldehyde resins together.

laminated referring to a material or composite product made up of thin layers of material bonded together for added strength.

laminated beam see laminated timber beam.

laminated chipboard a building board used for hardwearing interior working surfaces, cupboard doors, etc., made from chipboard with plastics laminate bonded to its surface.

laminated glass glass which has been manufactured with a core of plastic sheet to provide resistance against impact; types included as separate entries are listed below:

shattering of laminated glass: on breakage, the pane remains intact, held together by its interlayer *alarm glass; *anti-bandit laminated glass; *anti-fading glass; *coloured opaque glass; *intumescent glass, see laminated intumescent glass; *laminated safety glass; *laminated solar control glass; *laminated sound control glass; *laminated ultraviolet light control glass, ultraviolet control glass; *safety glass; *security glass.*

laminated intumescent glass a fire-resisting glass with a layer of intumescent material which expands to a foam on heating and becomes opaque and fire-resisting.

laminated safety glass safety glass whose strength is provided by laminating two or more sheets of glass around plastic interlayers.

laminated solar control glass laminated glass with a tinted interlayer between the two sheets, or in which one of the sheets is solar control glass.

laminated sound control glass laminated glass in which the plastic interlayer and thickness of the glass used make it useful for improving sound insulation.

laminated ultraviolet light control glass, ultraviolet control glass; special glass laminated with an interlayer capable of reflecting up to 98% of harmful ultraviolet radiation from the sun.

laminated log, glue-laminated log, lam-log, structural log; an industrial timber product of uniform rectangular or round cross-section and cogged ends, glue-laminated and machined from a number of strips of wood and used in the construction of system built and off-the-shelf log buildings.

laminated timber beam, glulam beam, glued and laminated beam; a beam consisting of timber strips glued one on top of the other for added strength; see also laminated web beam.

laminated timber beam

laminated timber board 1 a general term for timber boards such as plywood or blockboard made of timber strips, sheets or pieces glued together side by side.
2 a timber product used for shelves and worktops, made from strips of solid wood glued together side by side under pressure, then planed.

laminated veneered board any building board to which a surface layer of plastics laminate has been bonded for decoration or protection.

laminated web beam a laminated timber beam consisting of plywood or similar thin timber pieces glued side by side.

laminated wood see glue laminated timber.

lamination the bonding of two or more sheets of material such as paper, timber or fabric together with a polymer, resin or glue to form a composite sheet.

laminboard a timber building board manufactured by gluing veneers on either side of a core of solid wood strips with a width less than 7 mm; the grain of the veneers runs at 90° to that of the core.

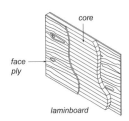

core

face ply

laminboard

lam-log see laminated log.

lamp 1 a component powered by electricity, oil, gas or other fuel to produce light.
2 the replaceable part of a luminaire from which light is emitted; a lightbulb; types included as separate entries are listed below:
*candle lamp; *circular fluorescent tube, circline lamp; *cold start lamp, see instant start lamp; *compact fluorescent lamp; *crown silvered lamp; *daylight lamp, see neodymium oxide lamp; *dichroic mirror lamp; *discharge lamp; *electric lamp; *fluorescent lamp; *fluorescent reflector lamp; *full-spectrum lamp, see neodymium*

oxide lamp; *general lighting service lamp, GLS lamp; *halogen lamp; *high-pressure sodium lamp; *incandescent lamp; *infrared lamp, mercury lamp; *metal halide lamp, metallic-additive lamp; *neodymium oxide lamp; *reflector lamp; *silvered-bowl lamp, see crown silvered lamp; *sodium lamp, sodium-vapour lamp; *spot lamp, see reflector lamp; *standard lamp, see floor lamp; *tri-phosphor lamp; *tungsten-halogen lamp, see halogen lamp; *ultraviolet lamp.

3 see luminaire.

4 a luminaire such as a table or floor lamp which can be moved while in use; a non-fixed luminaire.

lamp base see lamp cap, lamp stand.

lampblack pure carbon powder originally collected from the combustion of burning oils, used since prehistoric times as a black pigment; a form of carbon black.

lamp cap, lamp base; the metal part of an electric lamp by which it is connected to an electricity supply and fixed to a holder; see bayonet cap, (Edison) screw cap.

lampholder a device from which an electric lamp is supported, and by which a contact is made with an electricity supply.

lampshade, shade; a shading or diffusing component placed in front of or over a lamp to prevent glare and produce scattered or directional light.

lamp stand, lamp base; the base and shaft of a table or floor lamp.

lamp starter an electronic component for providing a momentary increase in voltage required to excite the gas, vapour, etc. in a discharge lamp and provide light.

lancet pertaining to Gothic windows and arches which are sharply pointed like the blade of a small lance or surgical knife; see ogival.

lancet arch, acute arch; a sharply pointed arch.

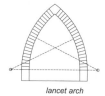

lancet arch

lancet window a slender sharp-pointed arched Gothic window.

land drainage 1 ditching, subsoil drainage, field drainage; the digging of networks of ditches to drain areas of land, usually to improve ground for agriculture, forestry and construction.

2 the control of external water around the foundations of a building or structure using a system of drains, channels and walls.

land drain see field drain.

landing a horizontal platform or level area at the top of a flight of stairs, which may have another flight leading from it; see also intermediate landing, storey landing, lift landing.

landing door the outer door of a lift, which opens out onto a landing and does not move with the lift car.

landing plate a level metal platform at either end of an escalator or similar device, from which passengers step on and off.

landing valve a water outlet located at each level in a building, connected to a fire riser, and used by firemen in the event of a fire.

land restoration work to prepare an area of land for development or other use after it has been damaged by mineral extraction or industrial processes.

landscaping, landscape work; construction work to provide a functional and amenable external environment around a building using earthworks, structures, hardy materials and planting; see also landscape design.

landscape architect, landscape designer; a qualified professional or organization responsible for designing gardens, parks and external environments.

landscape architecture the design and planning of external areas, gardens and parkland, especially those in proximity to built form, to provide a pleasing, safe and healthy environment.

landscape design 1 the discipline of planning the external areas, hard surfaces, planting and roads surrounding a new or existing building.

2 landscaping; a design or designs thus produced.

landscape designer see landscape architect.

landscape garden, English landscape garden; an informal planned garden or park surrounding a country house or mansion, fashionable in England in the 1700s.

land surveying, 1 field surveying, surveying; the physical measuring of the dimensions and topography of a particular site or area of land; a procedure of this sort is called a land survey.

2 geodesy; the science of measuring and presenting the form and size of tracts of land.

land surveyor, geodicist; a qualified professional who measures the topography of an area of land or site and produces a map or survey from the results.

land use the use of land for a specific purpose as designated by a town or area plan.

lantern the upper part of a church tower or other similar construction which is glazed to allow light in; see following entry.

lantern light, lantern; a glazed turret or other construction on the roof of a building or construction to allow daylight into a space beneath, often of ornamental nature.

lap, 1 lapping, overlap; the covering of one another by two laid adjacent materials or products such as jointed timbers, sheets, tiles, bricks, etc.; the distance, dimension or amount of this.

2 in brickwork, the surface formed by two bricks in adjacent courses which overlap to form a bond.

3 lap length; in reinforced concrete, the overlap of two longitudinal reinforcing bars to form one longer bar.

lap cement see sealing compound.

lapis albanus Lat.; see peperino.

lapis lazuli, 1 lazurite, lapis; a semi-precious blue mineral consisting of silicates of aluminium, lime and soda, found in Iran, Afghanistan, China and Chile and used for mosaics and as a pigment.

2 azzuro oltremarino, lazuline blue; a rich blue pigment formed by grinding the precious stone of the same name and refining the product; used since ancient times as ultramarine, now largely replaced with artificial ultramarine.

lap joint, lapped joint; **1** the joining of two members, components, sheets, etc. so that they overlap.

2 any timber joint in which the face sides of two members are joined together, often rebated or half lapped.

lap-jointed roofing felt roofing in which seams running parallel to the ridge and eaves are formed by overlapping the roll of felt above and nailing through.

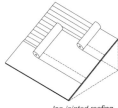

lap-jointed roofing

lap length see lap.

lapped corner joint a corner joint used in cabinetmaking for joining boards and sheets at right angles, in which the end of one piece is halved along its edge to receive the other abutting edge.

lapped corner joints

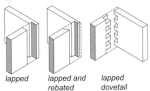

lapped   *lapped and rebated*   *lapped dovetail*

lapped dovetail joint a cabinetmaking joint in which dovetailing shows on one side of the joint only; may also be called a blind, concealed, secret or stopped dovetail joint.

lapped joint see lap joint.

lapping see lap.

lap weld a welded joint between overlapping metal components.

lap weld

larch [*Larix spp.*] a deciduous softwood of northern climates with tough, dense, durable timber which has good resistance to rot; a large tree with distinctive needled foliage, which turns golden in autumn, planted in parks and gardens as an ornamental; see below for species of larch included in this work:

Japanese larch [*Larix kaempferi, Larix leptolepis*] a hardy softwood found in Japan and the British Isles, whose timber is used for sawn boards, exterior constructions, fencing and decking.

Siberian larch [*Larix russica, Larix sibirica*] a softwood from eastern Siberia with the typical properties of larch; one of the most common source of larchwood in Europe.

tamarack, eastern larch; [*Larix laricina*] a softwood native to Canada and the north-west United States with resistant red-brown timber; used for posts and packing.

western larch [*Larix occidentalis*] a softwood native to western North America with coarse-textured reddish-brown wood; used in building construction and flooring.

large diameter pile in foundation technology, a bored pile which has a diameter of greater than 600 mm; usually a steel pile.

large-panel construction industrialized building using precast concrete panels for structural framing and cladding of buildings, involving careful design to ensure that components fit together on site, but saving time and expense at construction stage.

Larix spp. see larch.

larvikite a bluish-grey or dark green variety of syenite containing colourful feldspar, found in Larvik, Norway; used for decorative floors, as cladding and for ornamental stone, and often sold under the trade name Labrador.

laser a device which produces a narrow, powerful beam of monochromatic light.

laser cutting a method of cutting metals using a jet of gas which has been heated with a powerful laser beam.

laser welding a method of fusion welding in which heat is produced by a powerful focused laser beam.

Lasius niger see garden black ant.

latch any lock-like fastening mechanism for a door or gate, in which a handle rather than a key is pushed or turned to disengage a bolt; types included as separate entries are listed below:

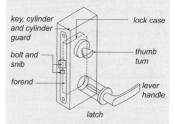

latch

*mortise latch; *panic latch; *return latch; *rim latch; *snib latch, see indicating bolt; *spring latch, see return latch; *turning latch.

latch bolt see return latch.

latchset a set of door fittings comprising a latch, two door handles, two roses, two cover plates and a spindle.

latchet see sheetmetal cleat.

late Gothic Gothic architecture in Europe from c. 1400—1500, the Flamboyant style in France and the Perpendicular in England.

lateral bevelled halved joint see angle bevelled halved joint.

lateral bracing the stiffening of a structure or building frame perpendicular to its main axis using cross walls, etc.

lateral reinforcement, transverse reinforcement; secondary concrete reinforcement linked and placed at right angles to the main reinforcement to provide stiffening and resistance against shear forces.

latewood, summerwood; the portion of the growth ring of a tree with small, dense cells, formed after earlywood during periods of slower growth.

latex the milky sap of the rubber tree or a similar synthetic liquid consisting of a polymer dispersed in a water-based vehicle; also known as gum.

latex cement flooring see cement rubber latex flooring.

latex foam see foam rubber.

latex paint an easily brushable and rapidly drying emulsion paint with a latex binder in water, which evaporates off during drying, leaving a film of latex, pigment and additives.

lath 1 a thin strip of wood, often formed by cleaving, used in basketwork, making fences and lattices.
2 a split timber batten fixed to a base in rows as a base for plaster; see lathing, bruised lath.
3 a piece of sawn timber with cross-sectional dimensions of 6–17 mm thick and 22–36 mm wide.

lathe a powered machine on which wood or metal is shaped into cylindrical or round forms by cutting blades whilst being fixed to a rapidly spinning chuck.

lathing, lathwork; any surface of timber battens, expanded metal or mesh fixed to a wall surface to provide a mechanical key for plasterwork; lathwork most often refers to timber lathing; types included as separate entries are listed below:
*bruised lath; *expanded metal lathing; *mesh lathing, see wire lathing; *metal lathing; *ribbed expanded metal lathing, rib lathing; *timber lath; *timber lathing; *wire lathing, wire-mesh lathing.

lattice any open structure or surface of long strips of material (originally laths) attached together in a crossed formation to produce an open screen-like construction; see also space lattice, and below.
lattice beam see trussed beam.
lattice stanchion, braced stanchion; a composite steel column or stanchion with a number of vertical rolled steel sections braced at intervals with diagonal or horizontal struts, or a combination of both.
lattice structure see truss.

LA unit see Los Angeles coefficient.

lava rock types of igneous rock which are ejected from the earth's crust as lava and solidify rapidly in air.

lavatory see toilet.
lavatory bowl see WC pan.

lavender oil see oil of spike.

lawn in landscaping, a mowed and tended area of grass.

Lawson's cypress, Port Orford cedar; [*Chamaecyparis lawsoniana*] see cypress.

lay bar an intermediate horizontal glazing bar in a window.

laying-on trowel see plasterer's trowel.

laylight a horizontal window set into a suspended ceiling below a rooflight.

layout the schematic arrangement of parts of a building or other designs showing how component parts fit and function together.
layout drawing a design drawing showing the spatial relationships between buildings on a site or rooms in a building.
layout plan see site layout plan.

lazuline blue see lapis lazuli.

lazurite a blue sodium aluminium silicate crystalline mineral, the main constituent of the rock lapis lazuli.

L-beam a beam which is L-shaped in cross-section, usually of concrete; see also boot lintel.

precast concrete L-beam

LDPE, LD polythene low density polythene.

lead (pronunciation: sounds like 'bed'; see next entry) a soft, malleable, heavy metal, **Pb**, with a low melting point; used in traditional paints and coatings, and as sheet-metal for roof flashings.
lead acetate a poisonous white chemical compound, $Pb(C_2H_3O_2).3H_2O$, used as a drier in paints and varnishes.
lead came a small lead glazing bar, H-shaped in cross-section, which holds panes together in leaded-light glazing.
lead carbonate a poisonous white chemical compound, $PbCO_3$, used as a pigment in exterior paints.
lead chromate a poisonous yellow chemical compound, $PbCrO_4$, used as an industrial pigment in paints.
lead drier a compound of lead used in solvent form in paints to speed up drying.
leaded brass an alloy of copper and zinc with additional lead to increase ductility and improve machinability.
leaded light, leaded glass, lead glazing; traditional glazing with small diamond-shaped or square panes of glass held in a mesh of lead glazing bars, called cames.

lead-free paint any paint which does not contain lead compounds for health reasons, according to law.

lead glass, crystal glass; a clear colourless glass containing lead oxide, used for optical devices and neon tubes.

lead glazing see leaded light.

lead in oil a traditional paint of white lead ground into linseed oil.

lead oxide, lead monoxide; a chemical compound, **PbO**, used amongst other things in the manufacture of lead glass; see red lead, massicot.

lead paint any paint which contains white lead or red lead.

lead pigment any pigment of lead salts such as lead chromate or lead carbonate, usually insoluble in water, poisonous and opaque; see also massicot (yellow), red lead, white lead.

lead plate thick rolled sheet manufactured from lead; used for soundproofing and radiation protection.

lead primer see red lead.

lead sheet rolled sheet manufactured from lead; traditionally used for flashings, roof and wall claddings and damp proof courses; see also lead plate.

lead wool lead in fibrous form, used as sealing for pipes.

lead X-ray glass, X-ray resistant glass, radiation-shielding glass; glass which contains lead oxide and is relatively resistant to X-rays.

lead (pronunciation: sounds like 'bead'; see previous entry) an insulated wire, fitted with a suitable connection at either end, which conveys electricity from a source to an appliance.

leader header see rainwater head.

leader line see extension line.

leading hand see chargehand.

leaf, 1 wythe, withe (Am); one single skin of brick, blockwork, concrete, etc. in a cavity wall, or as facing for a steel or concrete frame.
2 very thin metal sheet, see foil.
3 any flap-like component or accessory, see door leaf, hinge leaf.

leaf and dart, heart and dart, waterleaf and dart; an ornamental motif consisting of a series of stylized leaves alternating with sharp dart-shaped forms.

leaf and dart

leaf and rose scroll an ornamental motif consisting of a coiled leaf design with roses at the extremities of the coil.

leaf and tongue see leaf and dart.

leaf green see chrome green.

leaf moulding see foil moulding.

leaf ornament see foliated.

leaf scroll a classical ornamental banded motif representing coiled foliage, especially acanthus, anthemion, lotus and palmette, and in medieval architecture, vines; see also leaf and rose scroll.

leaf scroll

leafwork see foliated.

lean clay a soil type composed of 30–50% silty clays and clayey silts, generally of low to medium plasticity.

lean concrete concrete with a lower than usual percentage of cement.

lean lime low-quality hydrated lime produced from impure limestone, which, when used as lime putty, cannot be spread evenly and has poor properties of plasticity and setting.

lean mix a mix of concrete or mortar which contains little binder.

lean-to roof, half span roof; a monopitch roof whose summit is carried on a wall which extends beyond the apex of the roof; often an overhang or canopy.

lean-to roof

leathercloth a plastic-coated fabric having the appearance of leather, used in upholstery.

Leca see expanded aggregate.

ledge a horizontal structural rail in a ledged door, to which boards are fixed.
ledged and braced door a ledged door with diagonal bracing.
ledged door a simple door-type whose leaf is constructed from vertical matchboarding nailed to a series of spaced horizontal members or ledges.

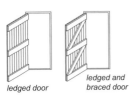

ledged door

ledged and braced door

ledger 1 a scaffolding beam running parallel to the wall of the building under construction, which carries putlogs.
2 a large flat stone which covers a tomb or grave in a church.
3 see ligger.

leek green see chrome green.

left-handed, left-hung, LH; see handing.

legget a steel-faced hammer used in thatched roofing for tapping and tightening the thatch and its fastenings.

legs anchor, hollow-wall plug; a range of nylon wall plugs for fastening to plasterboard hollow walls, with wings which spring out once pushed through a drilled hole and clamp to the reverse side.

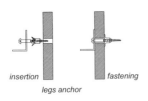

insertion

fastening

legs anchor

Leipzig yellow see chrome yellow.

lemon oil see oil of lemon.

lengthening joint any joint used to join two long pieces or members together end

on end to form one longer piece; see also scarf joint.

lengthening piece see extension.

lens 1 a transparent solid optical object shaped to bend light passing through it in a controlled way.
2 glass lens; a translucent solid glazing unit made by a pressing process; embedded in cast concrete decks, floors and footways to provide natural lighting to spaces beneath.

Lentinus lepideus see scaly cap fungus.

Lenzites separia see slash conk.

Lesbian cyma in classical ornamentation, a cyma reversa moulding enriched with leaf and dart ornament.

Lesbian cyma moulding with leaf and dart, and bead and reel mouldings

lesene, pilaster strip; an exterior pilaster without a base or capital; found primarily in Romanesque churches providing lateral support for high walls.

let-in see housing.

letter-box plate see letter plate.

lettering brush a finely pointed paintbrush used primarily for lettering on signs, plaques, etc.

lesene

letter of intent 1 a general communication from one party to another indicating a serious intention.
2 in contract administration, a formal letter from a client to the chosen tenderer stating that they propose to enter into a contract with them.

letter plate, letter-box plate, letter slot, mail slot; a slotted rectangular metal or plastics plate with covering hinged flap to allow for the conveyance of mail through a door leaf.

level 1 the height or datum of a point above sea level, as marked on drawings and maps.
2 see storey.
3 any instrument, apparatus or device for measuring true horizontal; see also levelling instrument, water level, spirit level.

level invert taper in drainage and plumbing, a short piece of conical pipe or similar fitting for joining two pipes of different diameters so that their lower internal surfaces lie along the same line.

levelling compound, dressing compound, synthetic screed; in floor construction, a material such as cement or resin mortar applied in semi-liquid form in very thin layers, which sets to provide a level surface for flooring.

levelling instrument, level; in surveying, an optical instrument used in conjunction with a levelling staff for measuring levels.

levelling staff, levelling rod; a long gradated rod used in surveying for ascertaining heights and levels from a known point.

lever handle a handle for a door or window casement, with a protruding lever, which operates a latch mechanism when turned downwards.

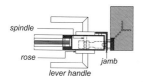
spindle
rose
jamb
lever handle

lever tap, lever-operated tap; a water tap in which water flow is controlled by a lever.

Leyden blue a form of cobalt blue pigment.

LH see handing.

lich gate see lych gate.

lierne a tertiary rib in a vault, which connects a point on a rib with a tierceron or another lierne; often for decorative rather than structural purposes.

lift, elevator (Am); a mechanical installation for lifting of passengers or goods from one level or storey in a building to another, see also lift car.

lift battery, lift group, lift bank; a number of lifts in the same area whose controls are synchronized to work together.

lift car the lowered and raised compartment for carrying passengers and goods in a lift installation.

lift car door the inner door of a lift car, which moves up and down with it; a lift gate is usually a door of open lattice construction; see also landing door.

lift drive, lift machine; the machinery, motors or apparatus for moving and halting a lift.

lift gate see lift car door.

lift group see lift battery.

lift guide, lift runner; a rail attached to the wall of a lift shaft to guide the lift car.

lift landing an area of floor in front of a lift, at which it stops.

lift machine see lift drive.

lift machine room, lift motor room, LMR; a space located adjacent to, above or below a lift shaft, with machinery to operate the movement of a lift car.

lift pit, run-by pit; a space at the base of a lift shaft to accommodate the underside of the lift car and counterweight.

lift pulley room a space located adjacent to a lift shaft, containing pulleys which operate the lift, but no machinery.

lift runner see lift guide.

lift shaft see lift well.

lift shaft module a prefabricated unit of a lift shaft, which can be lifted into place.

lift sheave, sheave; a large pulley wheel around which lift cables, lift car and counterweight are hung in a traditional overslung lift installation.

lift well, hoistway (Am), lift shaft; the duct, tube or shaft in which a lift car moves.

lift well enclosure the structure that encloses a lift shaft.

lift well module see lift shaft module.

lifting a defect in a paint finish consisting of the separation of a dry undercoat from a substrate on application of a successive coat of paint.

lifting equipment, hoisting plant; any equipment, cranes, hoists and elevators used on a building site for lifting goods, machinery and people from one level to another.

lift-off butt hinge, lift-off hinge, loose butt hinge; a hinge whose central joining pin is welded to the upper part of one hinge leaf, permitting a door to be simply lifted on or off.

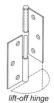
lift-off hinge

lift slab construction a method of concrete construction in which concrete floor slabs are cast one above the other then raised into position for support by columns.

ligature see stirrup.

ligger a longitudinal timber used in thatched roofing to hold down thatch.

---

light 1 electromagnetic waves which can be seen by the human eye; see also artificial light, daylight, diffuse light, natural light.
2 any device for producing illumination; a lamp or luminaire; see also droplight (pendant luminaire), electric light, floodlight, spotlight.
3 an opening in a wall for a window; a small window or glazed unit; types included as separate entries are listed below:
*angel light; *borrowed light; *coupled light; *domelight; *fanlight; *fixed light; *lantern light; *rooflight; *side light; *top light.

---

light alloy a mixture of light metals such as aluminium.

lightbulb, lamp; a device which contains a gas or metal filament enclosed in a sealed glass vessel, excited by electricity to give off light.

light dispersivity in lighting design, the property of a surface to disperse light by interference or refraction.

light distribution curve, polar curve, candlepower distribution curve; a graphical representation of the light distribution characteristics of a particular luminaire or lamp, with luminous intensities for all directions from the source plotted on polar coordinates.

light expanded clay aggregate see expanded aggregate.

lightfast, light resistant; the property of a pigment, paint film or coloured coating to resist fading or deterioration of its colours on exposure to sunlight.

light filter see filter.

light fitting, light fixture see luminaire.

lighting, illumination; the provision of light for spaces in a building by the controlled placing of lights, windows, etc.

lighting column see lighting post.

lighting controller see photoelectric lighting controller.

lighting fitting, lighting fixture see luminaire.

lighting mast, pylon; a tall freestanding structure for the high-level support of floodlighting, external area lighting, etc.

lighting point an outlet to which a light fitting can be connected to an electricity supply.

lighting post, lighting column; a freestanding column for supporting an exterior luminaire.

lighting track in artificial lighting, a surface-mounted conducting track to which movable spotlights can be attached.

light loss factor in lighting design, a measure of the aging of light sources, measured as a ratio of the illuminance after a specific period of time to the illuminance of the source as new.

lightning-conductor, lightning-rod; a simple metal rod attached to the roof of a building or the top of a mast, connected to an earthed cable and used for conveying current from lightning strikes to earth.

lightning protection the physical protection of a building from random lightning strikes using rooftop installations to lead unwanted power surges safely to earth; any system of air terminations, down conductors and earth terminations for diverting energy this way is called a lightning protective installation.

lightning-rod see lightning-conductor.

lightning shakes see thunder shakes.

light output in lighting design, the quantity of luminous flux emitted by a source of light.

light resistant see lightfast.

light sensitivity the property of a material or surface which has the tendency to react in some way to light which falls on it.

light shaft a narrow shaft either within a building or externally, but surrounded by built form to introduce natural light to internal spaces, courtyards, etc.

light transmittance in lighting design, the ratio of luminous flux transmitted through an area of material to that incident on it.

lightweight aggregate aggregate classified according to bulk density as less than 1200 kg/m³ for fine aggregate, or 1000 kg/m³ for coarse aggregate; types included as separate entries are listed below:
*expanded clay aggregate, expanded shale aggregate, light expanded clay aggregate, see expanded aggregate; *sintered aggregate; *wood particle aggregate.*
lightweight aggregate concrete lightweight concrete which makes use of a lighter than usual coarse aggregate, often vermiculite, expanded clay, blast-furnace slag or in some cases a polymer or sawdust.
lightweight aggregate concrete block a concrete block manufactured using lightweight aggregate.

lightweight block see lightweight concrete block.

lightweight concrete concrete which has a bulk density range from 400–1760 kg/m³ and is lighter than ordinary concrete, either by virtue of its lightweight aggregate (as in no-fines concrete, lightweight aggregate concrete) or entrained voids of air or gas (as in aerated concrete).
lightweight concrete block a concrete block manufactured from lightweight concrete, or one with voids; see also lightweight aggregate concrete block, cellular block.

lightweight partition an interior non-loadbearing wall for dividing a space into rooms; often of plasterboard on a studwork frame.

lightweight plaster plaster which contains lightweight aggregate.

light well a narrow external space surrounded by built form to provide light and ventilation to internal spaces, courtyards, etc.

lignin one of the organic polymeric substances which stiffens and bonds the cell structure in wood; extracted from paper pulp and used in the manufacture of plastics.

lignum vitae [*Guaiacum spp.*] a very heavy hardwood from the Caribbean and South America; its timber is greenish-black, extremely hard and durable, and has a high oil content; used for machine rollers, mallet heads and 'woods' in the game of bowls; see also verawood [*Maracaibo lignum vitae*].

lily a common motif in Egyptian architecture and art, originating from stylized depictions of species of flowering plant of the genera *Lilium*, *Nymphaea*, etc. which have bulbous blossoms on long stems; also called a lotus.

Greek lily motif

lily capital an ancient Egyptian capital carved with decoration in imitation of stylized lily blossoms; also called a lotus capital.
lily moulding see fleury moulding.

limba, afara; [*Terminalia superba*] a West African hardwood with straight-grained and coarse-textured yellowish timber, used for panelling, plywood and veneers.

lime 1 [*Tilia spp.*] a number of species of hardwood tree from Europe and North America (where it is known as basswood) with pale, soft, light, fine textured timber; used for joinery, plywood and trim; widely planted as a street tree; see below:

Tilia spp. – lime

basswood, American lime; [*Tilia americana*] a hardwood from North America; see also lime.
European lime, linden; [*Tilia europaea, Tilia vulgaris*] a European hardwood with fine-grained, light, soft, weak, pale yellowish timber; used for carving, turnery and plywood; lime trees are often planted as street trees and for lining avenues in parks.
2 chalk or limestone burnt in a kiln, used as a binder in cement and plaster; a generic name for quicklime, hydrated lime, lime putty, slaked lime, calcium oxide or calcium hydroxide.

lime cement Portland cement to which lime has been added; used as a binder in masonry cement.

lime hydrate see hydrated lime.

lime mortar brickwork mortar consisting of slaked lime and sand in the ratio of 16 or other proportions depending on usage and exposure; may occasionally also include cement; see also composition mortar (cement lime mortar), lime sand mortar, lime plaster.

lime plaster a form of crude plaster made from neat lime or a mixture of lime and sand.

lime putty soft hydrated lime in solid but plastic form; used as a binder in plaster.

lime rock rock consisting largely of limestone or partially consolidated limestone, quarried from natural limestone deposits.

lime sand mortar, coarse stuff; mortar consisting of lime and coarse sand, often delivered to site ready mixed.

limestone a sedimentary rock composed of calcium carbonate, used extensively as building stone and burnt to produce lime.

limewash see whitewash.

limewashing, whitewashing; the application of a solution of lime and water, or crushed chalk and water, to a masonry surface as a clean, white finish.

lime white, cream of lime, milk of lime; a watery or creamy emulsion of calcium hydrate or quicklime in water, traditionally used for whitewashing walls; see also bianco sangiovanni.

liming in landscaping and forestry, the addition of lime or any other calcareous material to the soil as fertilizer and to neutralize acid soils.

limiter see door chain.

Limnoria spp. see gribble.

limonite, brown iron ore; a brownish or yellowish earthy mineral, a natural oxide of iron, $Fe_2O_3.nH_2O$, used in various forms for pigments (yellow ochre); also an important iron ore.

linear strip see exposed runner.

line load see knife-edge load.

linenfold, drapery, linen scroll; carved decoration for wooden panelling, stone, etc. representing hanging cloth with loose vertical folds.

linenfold

line of draw ribbon-like variations in thickness of drawn glass caused by the manufacturing process, which give rise to visual distortion.

line of nosings, nose line, nosing line, pitch line; a theoretical line drawn between the front edge of the steps in a stair, parallel to the incline.

liner a finely pointed paintbrush with bristles shaped to produce continuous lines, used for architectural rendering, decorative edges, lettering, etc.; also called a lining brush.

lining 1 any dry covering of sheet, boarding, etc. for cladding the interior surface of a wall or wall frame.
2 a surround for a door or window reveal, covering the joint and surface between frame and adjacent construction; types included as separate entries are listed below:
*breast lining; *door lining; *formwork lining; *flue lining; *jamb lining; *plasterboard drylining; *sock lining, resin lining; *timber lining; *wall lining; *window lining.

lining brush see liner.

lining paper see wall lining.

linishing the smoothing of a surface, usually metal, using a continuously moving abrasive belt to produce a fine satin finish.

link see stirrup.

link aerial see satellite link aerial.

link house, linked dwellings; a form of low-rise residential building, similar to a terraced house, in which adjacent dwellings are connected by outhouses, car ports and pergolas; see also terraced house.

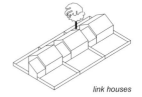

link houses

link mesh see chain link mesh.

link yoke in traditional timber frame construction, a piece joining the upper ends of principal rafters, supporting a ridge beam.

linoleum a hardwearing, soft sheet flooring consisting of fibrous mineral material such as wood, chalk, cork and flax mixed with linseed oil and calendered; shortened form is 'lino'.

linseed oil oil pressed from the ripe seeds of the flax plant (*Linum usitatissimum*), used as a vehicle and binder in paints; see also boiled linseed oil.
linseed oil putty see putty.

lintel, lintol; a beam above a window or door opening; types included as separate entries are listed below:

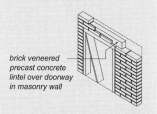

brick veneered precast concrete lintel over doorway in masonry wall

*boot lintel; *corbelled lintel; *concrete lintel; *precast concrete lintel, see concrete lintel; *pressed steel lintel; *reinforced brick lintel.*

lintel block, lintel unit; a specially formed concrete or clay block with an indentation in its upper surface for grout and reinforcing bars; used in masonry beams as the tension flange or lower soffit; see also channel block.

lintel brick, beam brick, channel brick; a clay lintel block used over an opening in brickwork, having the same outward appearance, texture and size, etc. as the other bricks.

lintel brick

lintel filler a preformed flashing, usually of sheetmetal, used over an opening.
lintel unit see lintel block.

lintol see lintel.

lion capital a capital carved with the images of two or four prostrate lions facing in opposite directions; typical of the edict columns of Indian architecture.

lion capital

liparite see rhyolite.

Liquidambar styraciflua see gum.

liquidated damages in contract administration, a predetermined amount taken from payments due to a contractor in the event of any delay on their part with regard to contractual obligation; a delay penalty.

liquid limit in soil mechanics, the maximum water content for a clay, which, when exceeded, promotes a change from the plastic to a liquid state.

Liriodendron tulipifera see tulipwood.

listed building a building of recognized historical or cultural value which has official protected status against demolition, modification and disrepair.

listel, list, tringle; a narrow flat fillet moulding.

lithopone, oleaum white; a fine white pigment consisting of zinc sulphide and barium sulphate which has good structural properties and is relatively cheap; used for exterior house paints and industrial coatings.

live referring to a device, circuit or conductor which is connected directly to an electricity supply.

live knot see intergrown knot.

live load changing structural loads in a building imposed by the use of the building, its occupants, furnishings, etc.

Liverpool bond see English garden-wall bond.

live sawing see through and through sawing.

LMR lift machine room.

load the forces imposed on a structure or structural member in use by building fabric and components, furnishings and services, internal forces and own weight, wind and snow, etc.

loadbearing brickwork brickwork which has a structural function and transfers building loads to a foundation.

loadbearing capacity see bearing capacity.

loadbearing frame, structural frame; those parts of a building which carry structural loads to the foundations.

loadbearing structure see structure.

loadbearing wall, bearing wall; any wall which transfers structural loads from above and is part of the structure or structural frame of a building.
loadbearing wall construction, bearing wall system; a structural system in which the floors in a building are supported by loadbearing external walls and partitions.

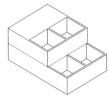

loadbearing wall construction

loading 1 the imposition of a load on a structure or structural member.
2 the variation and types of load imposed on a structure.

loading capacity see bearing capacity.

lobate ornament see auricular ornament.

local air conditioning air conditioning for a specific room or targeted area within a room.

local lighting, localized lighting; artificial lighting designed to provide a higher level of illumination in certain areas of a room or space.

local planning authority see planning authority.

local ventilation mechanical ventilation for a specific room or targeted area within a room.

location block one of a number of small pieces placed under and around a glass pane or panel to prevent it moving in its frame during installation of glazing.

location drawing a design drawing showing how or where a site, building or part of a building is situated with respect to its surroundings; see also general arrangement drawing.

location plan see block plan.

lock 1 a fastening mechanism for a door or gate, operated using an external mechanical or electronic device such as a key, push button or digital pad; types included as separate entries are listed below:
*bathroom lock; *cabinet lock; *check lock, see snib; *combination lock; *cylinder lock; *deadlock; *door lock; *electric lock; *electromagnetic lock; *furniture lock, see cabinet lock; *keyed lock; *magnetic lock, see electromagnetic lock; *mortise lock; *motor lock, see electromechanical lock; *padlock; *rim lock; *security lock; *solenoid lock; *thief-resistant lock, see security lock; *time lock; *toilet lock, WC lock, see bathroom lock; *Yale lock.

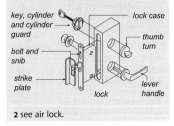

lock

2 see air lock.

lock bolt see bolt.

lock case the protective casing or covering which houses the locking mechanism of a rim or mortise lock; in a cylinder lock this may be remote from the cylinder.

lock chisel a chisel with an L-shaped blade for cutting hidden mortises for locks.

lock control the provision of security for a door or doors with the use of locks; see also electromechanical lock control, electric lock control, central locking.

lock cylinder see cylinder.

lock faceplate, lock front see forend.

locking 1 the securing of a lock with a key. **2** mechanisms and procedures associated with this.

locking bar a bar attached to a door leaf or pair of leaves to enable them to be fastened shut with a padlock.

locking snib see thumb turn, snib.

lock nut 1 a nut with a nylon friction-ring cast into its threads to prevent it from working loose once attached. **2** see stop nut.

lock nut

lock rail see middle rail.

lock ring see circlip, lock washer.

lock saw see keyhole saw.

lock stile see shutting stile.

lock suite see suite.

lock washer, lock ring; any of a number of specially shaped, toothed or sprung washers for use under bolt heads to fasten a bolted joint, especially one with a groove or projection to fit in a housing along a shaft and prevent it from rotating; see also spring lock washer.

lock washer

lodgepole pine, contorta pine, shore pine; [*Pinus contorta*], see pine.

loess in soil mechanics, fine material or silt which has been blown by the wind; also a porous, yellowish sedimentary rock formed from hardened wind-blown dust and containing the same minerals as clay.

loft an accessible space within the roof-space of a building intended for habitation and frequently used for storage; see garret.

loft ladder see disappearing stair.

log blue sap-stain in unseasoned logs.

log cabin siding decorative timber cladding boards whose outer face is rounded so as to resemble log construction.

log cabin siding

log construction, blockwork, cobwork; building frame construction using solid hewn or machined logs piled on top of one another horizontally, interlocking at the corners with joints known as notches.

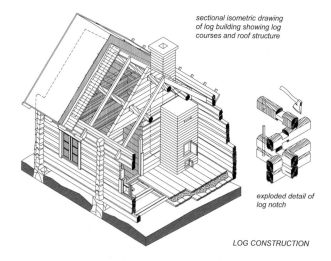

sectional isometric drawing of log building showing log courses and roof structure

exploded detail of log notch

LOG CONSTRUCTION

loggia in classical architecture, an arcaded or colonnaded porch or gallery of one or more stories attached to the ground storey of a building; also a separate colonnaded ornamental structure.

Lombardy poplar [*Populus nigra italica*], see poplar.

long and short work in stonework, a decorative quoin treatment for external masonry corners or jambs, using large stones interspersed vertically with flat stones.

long-cornered chisel see skew chisel.

long-grained plywood plywood in which the grain of the outer ply is approximately parallel to that of the longitudinal edge of the piece.

longhorn beetle, longicorn beetle; [*Cerambycidae*] a family of insects whose larvae burrow under the bark of living softwoods.

longitudinal beam a beam which lies parallel to the longer axis of a space or span.

longitudinal bevelled halved joint see bevelled scarf joint.

longitudinal reinforcement reinforcing bars which run parallel to the main axis of a reinforced concrete component, especially a beam or column.

longitudinal rib a protrusion which runs along the length of a reinforcing bar.

longitudinal ridge rib, ridge rib; a horizontal rib which runs parallel to the main axis of a space at the ridge of a rib vault.

longitudinal section, long section; a sectional drawing of a building or object cut along its long axis.

long mesh fabric fabric reinforcement for concrete, with clearly elongated rather than square openings in its mesh.

long radius bend a piece of curved drainage pipe with a large radius of curvature, designed for use at a gradual change in direction of the pipeline.

long section see longitudinal section.

long straw thatch see straw thatch.

loop see knuckle.

looped pile carpet a woven floor textile in which the weft or yarn formed in loops is left uncut at the surface.

loop tracery a form of bar tracery found in Scotland in Gothic churches constructed from 1500 to 1545, dominated by large looped forms.

Gothic looped tracery at Blackfriars chapel, St Andrews, Scotland, 1516

loose butt hinge see lift-off butt hinge.

loose-fill insulation insulation for roof spaces, wall cavities and floors consisting of lightweight granular or flaked material pumped into the void or laid in sacks; the most common forms are cellulose fibres, spun or expanded fibres or pellets of mineral material, glass, etc.; see cellulose loose-fill insulation.

loose-joint hinge, loose-joint butt hinge; a hinge which enables a door leaf to be lifted off without removing the hinge; a lift-off butt hinge.

loose leaf the leaf of a hinge which swivels around the hinge pin.

loose knot a dead knot that is loose and may become detached from a piece of timber.

loose piece mould in ornamental plastering, a mould consisting of a number of parts; used *loose knot* for taking or making casts from intricate or complex details.

loose pin butt hinge, loose pin hinge, pin hinge; a hinge with two rectangular metal leaves and a central joining pin which can be withdrawn for quick removal of a door leaf from its frame.

loose rust, loose scale; flakes of rust loosely attached to the surface of steel delivered on site, which should be removed before priming and finishing.

loose side, open face, open side, slack side; the side of a veneer sheet which has checks and markings from the cutting and is thus rougher than the face or tight side.

loose socket, collar; in plumbing and drainage pipework, a short fitting pushed over the adjacent ends of two aligned pipes to form a connection.

loose tongue see spline.

Los Angeles coefficient, LA unit; a measure of the hardness and durability of aggregates, given as the percentage of detritus forming under standard grinding tests with ball-bearings in a rotating vessel.

lost formwork in concreting, any formwork left in place once the concrete has hardened.

lost-head nail, finishing nail, bullet-head nail; a round or oval nail with a small tapered head; used in situations where the nail should remain hidden.

lost-head nail

lotiform, lotus; denoting capitals of Egyptian architecture, carved in imitation of stylized open or closed flowers of the sacred white lotus or water lily [*Nymphaea lotus*] or blue lotus [*Nymphaea caerulea*], or columns with ribbed shafts carved in imitation of tied bunches of lotus stems; similar forms in Buddhist and Hindu culture.

Egyptian lotus bud capital on bundle column, tomb of Khety, Beni Hasan, Egypt, c. 2000 BC

lotus anthemion painted ornamental banding originally from Mesopotamia, Egypt and Greece, depicting stylized lotus blooms alternating with other plant motifs such as pine cones, closed flower buds, etc.

lotus and papyrus an ornamental motif consisting of stylized lotus and papyrus leaves.

loudness in acoustics, the subjective phenomenon of sound measured in sones; one sone is equal to the perceived loudness of a 1000 Hz tone at a sound level of 40 dB.

loudness level in acoustics, the measure of loudness in phons; one phon is equal to the perceived sound level in decibels of a 1000 Hz tone above the audible sound threshold; it is thus a subjective version of the decibel, which is directly measurable.

louvre, louver (Am); one of a series of horizontal slats in a grille, venetian blind, etc.; a grille thus formed, used for shading devices, ventilation outlet covers; see window louver.

louvred blind see venetian blind.

louvred door a door with an open slatted construction to allow for the passage of air; used for the ventilation of plant rooms or for rooms in warm climates.

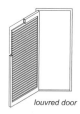

louvred door

louvred shutters see persiennes.

louvred window a window with a series of pivoted horizontal glass louvres which may be rotated open to provide ventilation; also louvre window.

Lovoa klaineana, Lovoa trichilioides see African walnut.

louvred window

low carbon steel steel with a carbon content of 0.04−0.25%, used for wire and thin sheet.

low density fibreboard see softboard.

low density polythene, LD polythene, LDPE; a tough and resilient polythene which is soft and flexible.

low emissivity glass float glass with a transparent surface treatment to reflect longer, hotter wavelengths of solar radiation outwards.

lower chord, bottom chord; the lower longitudinal horizontal member in a truss.

low gloss see eggshell gloss.

low heat cement see low heat Portland cement.

low heat concrete concrete with a slow rate of heat release from the chemical reaction which takes place during setting.

low heat Portland blast-furnace cement a blended Portland blast-furnace cement in which the heat released in setting (heat of hydration) is significantly less than that for ordinary Portland cement.

low heat Portland cement, low heat cement; a Portland cement which generates less heat on setting than ordinary Portland cement.

low-pressure hot water heating a hot water heating system in which hot water produced for circulation and use is no more than 80°C.

low-pressure sodium lamp a sodium lamp with a very efficient light source emitting strong yellow light; widely used for streetlighting.

low relief see anaglyph, basso rilievo.

low-rise pertaining to a class of residential buildings including detached houses, row and terraced houses, and multistorey residential buildings with few enough storeys (usually up to three) to negate the need for a lift.

low sheen see eggshell flat.

low velocity system, conventional system; an air-conditioning system using rectangular supply and return air ducting, in which air is conveyed at speeds of 3–8 m/s using conventional fans; cf. high velocity system.

low voltage a voltage in an electric circuit classified as less than 1000 V but greater than 50 V.

low water closet a self-contained toilet connected to a water supply, using small amounts of water for flushing waste.

lozenge fret, lozenge moulding see diamond fret.

L-profile see edge strip, angle profile.

L-roof a hip and valley roof for a building which is L-shaped in plan.

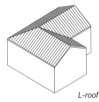

L-roof

L-section see angle profile.

L-stair see quarter turn stair.

lug sill in masonry construction, a window or door sill which extends sideways beyond the edge of the opening, and is thus built into the wall at either side.

lumber (Am) see timber.

lumen abb. **lm**; in lighting design, the SI unit of luminous flux.

luminaire, light fitting, light fixture (Am), lighting fitting; an electric fitting to provide illumination; usually a lamp contained in a base with control equipment and a diffuser or shade; types included as separate entries are listed below:
*air-handling luminaire; *angle luminaire; *ceiling luminaire; *cove lighting; *downlight, downlighter; *droplight, see pendant luminaire; *exterior luminaire; *fixed luminaire; *floodlight; *fluorescent luminaire; *inground luminaire; *interior luminaire; *non-fixed luminaire; *pendant luminaire; *recessed luminaire; *spotlight; *surface-mounted luminaire; *uplighter.

luminance in lighting design, a measure of the brightness of a surface in a given direction, measured in candelas.

luminescent having the material property of emitting small amounts of light without heat input, often as a result of phosphorescence or fluorescence.

luminescent concrete precast concrete to which luminescent material has been added; used in precast stair units to provide a low level of illumination in darkened stairways, etc.

luminescent pigment, luminescent paint; various metal sulphides used in paint to provide luminescence or fluorescence; used especially in roads signs and markings.

luminous ceiling, illuminated ceiling; a suspended ceiling whose ceiling panels are translucent glass or plastics sheets or baffles with luminaires behind, providing lighting for a space.

luminous efficacy see circuit efficacy.

luminous flux in lighting design, a measure of the flow of light energy from a light source or surface, measured in lumens.

luminous intensity in lighting design, the amount of energy in a cone of light, or solid angle from a light source; the ratio of luminous flux per solid angle, measured in candelas.

lump hammer see club hammer.

lump lime high-quality quicklime in solid lump form.

lump sum contract, stipulated sum agreement; a form of building contract in which a single agreed sum is given as payment for work done.

lunette an arched area, moulding or panel above a door, rectangular wall panel or window, especially an arched or polygonal window in a roof.

lux abb. **lx**; in lighting design, the SI unit of illuminance, given as luminous flux per unit area or lumens per square metre (lm/m^2).

lych gate, lich gate; a roofed entrance gateway to a churchyard, usually of timber, originally for the purpose of resting coffins.

lymexylid beetle, ship timber beetle; [*Lymexylidae*] a family of insects which cause damage to standing trees and unseasoned hardwoods and softwoods by burrowing.

M

macadam aggregate or crushed rock compacted for use in road construction.

Macassar ebony [*Diospyros celebica*], see ebony.

machinability, workability; the ability of a material to be shaped with ease on a lathe or other cutting machine without flaking, blunting tools, etc.

machine bend a bend in metal plumbing pipe produced with a bending machine; see pulled bend.

machine bit see cutter.

machine bolt a bolt whose shank has threads along its end portion only so a nut can be attached.

machine bolt

machine screw

machined log see milled log.

machine mixing, mechanical mixing; the mixing of concrete or mortar with a spinning or oscillating device such as a drum or pan mixer.

machine room, motor room; a plant room within a building containing equipment, motors, gear, etc. for operating mechanical installations such as lifts, fans, etc.; see lift machine room.

machine screw a screw with Whitworth or metric threads, a flat end, slotted head and a shank with an even diameter, fastened with a nut or into a predrilled hole; see also machine bolt. See machine bolt.

machine trowel see power trowel.

machining, milling; a process of shaping materials such as metal, wood and plastics using a machine tool with a swiftly rotating bit, or by rotating the material to be worked.
  machining tolerance in the machining of timber, a permissible variation in the dimensions of the machined piece.

machinist's hammer, peen; a metalwork hammer with a solid peen for shaping and bending.

madder lake, rose madder, natural madder; a red dyestuff made from the root of the madder plant [*Rubia tinctorum*], in use originally in Egypt, Greece and Rome, now mainly replaced by alizarin crimson.

madder red a red pigment traditionally produced from the root of the madder plant (see above) and the various shades of red colour thus formed.

MAG welding, metallic active-gas welding; a method of arc welding of metals in which the arc is shielded with an active gas such as carbon dioxide or oxygen.

magenta a deep purple pigment, one of the earliest dyes, named after the site of the Battle of Magenta in Italy in 1859.

magmatic rock see igneous rock.

magnesia white magnesium carbonate used as a white pigment.

magnesite, bitter spar; a mineral form of magnesium carbonate, used as a raw material in heat-resistant construction, as insulation and as a magnesium ore.
  magnesite cement see oxychloride cement.

magnesium a pale, lightweight metal, **Mg**, which is ductile and easily machined.
  magnesium carbonate a manufactured intense white chemical compound, $MgCO_3$, used as a white pigment; see also magnesite, bitter spar.
  magnesium oxychloride flooring see oxychloride cement.

magnetic catch a fastener used for furniture and other lightweight doors which holds by magnetic attraction.

magnetic flux a physical quantity whose SI unit is the weber (Wb); a measure of the strength of a magnetic field, given as the amount of magnetic field lines which pass through an area.
  magnetic flux density see magnetic induction.

magnetic iron ore see magnetite.

magnetic lock see electromagnetic lock.

magnetite, black iron oxide, magnetic iron ore; a grey-black mineral oxide of iron, Fe_3O_4, the most widespread and important iron ore; also used as a pigment, polishing agent and in magnetic tapes.

mahogany, American mahogany, Cuban mahogany; [*Swietenia spp.*] a genus of tropical Central and South American hardwoods with heavy and extremely hard and durable red or golden-brown timber; *Swietenia* is the true mahogany, although many other species are also sold as mahogany; see also *Khaya*.

mail slot see letter plate.

main a service pipe or cable which conveys electrical power, water or gas from a supplier to consumers; see also water main, gas main.

main bar one of the reinforcing bars in reinforced concrete which make up the main reinforcement.

main beam see principal beam.

main contractor, general contractor, prime contractor; a contractor who is responsible for all work on site, though they may subcontract part of it.

main entrance the principal, most important or monumental entrance door or means of entry into a building, via which most of the building users will enter.

main reinforcement, principal reinforcement; reinforcement designed to resist principal loads in reinforced concrete.

mains stopvalve, stopcock; the valve by which mains water supply to a building is controlled.

mains supply see mains voltage.

mains voltage, mains supply; the electrical potential supplied by mains electricity from generating plant, usually 220–240 V.

main switch a switch which shuts off electricity to all circuits in an electrical installation.

maintenance, servicing; the care of a building, structure, system or technical installation in order to keep it functioning.
maintenance manual a document containing the basic requirements for maintaining and servicing the finishes, appliances and other components of a building or construction works.
maintenance painting see repainting.
maintenance period see defects liability period.

maisonette, duplex apartment; a dwelling of more than one storey within a larger residential block, with its own private internal vertical circulation.

makore, African cherry, cherry mahogany; [*Tieghemella heckelii, Mimusops heckelii*] a hardwood from West Africa with pink to dark purple-red, stable and highly durable timber which has an abnormal blunting effect on tools; used for cabinets, flooring, boat-building and plywood.

malachite an opaque yellowish-green mineral, natural copper carbonate $Cu_2CO_3(OH)$, polished as a gemstone, carved for ornamental work and ground since ancient times as a bright green pigment; it is also known as Hungarian green or mineral green.
malachite green see copper green.

mall see maul.

malleable cast iron cast iron which has been heat treated to improve its toughness and strength.

mallet a hammer with a wooden, rubber or plastic head, used for striking wooden or soft objects such as chisels, pegs, etc.; see rubber mallet.

mallets with different types of head for various uses

mallet-headed chisel a masonry chisel whose handle is shaped with an ovoid end, to take striking with a wooden mallet; cf. hammer-headed chisel.

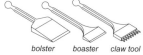

bolster   boaster   claw tool
mallet-headed chisel

Malus sylvestris see apple.

management contract a building contract in which a contractor provides consultation during the design stage and is responsible for planning and managing all post-contract activities and for the performance of the whole contract.

management contractor a person or organization, employed by the client, responsible for coordinating design and construction work in a building project.

man-day, person-day; a measure of the amount of work done by a person over the period of one day; used in estimating potential labour costs for a project.

manganese a metal, **Mn**, often used in steel alloys as a hardener.
manganese black a black pigment consisting of artificial manganese dioxide, used in cements and plasters.
manganese blue a brilliant blue pigment consisting of barium manganate.
manganese bronze, high-tensile brass; an alloy of copper and zinc which contains small amounts of manganese and other metals to increase strength and improve resistance to corrosion.
manganese dioxide MnO2, see pyrolusite.
manganese green, baryta green, Cassel green, Rosenstiehl's green; a green variety of the pigment manganese blue.
manganese spar see rhodochrosite.
manganese steel an alloy of steel with manganese and carbon, which is extremely hard, brittle and resistant to abrasion.
manganese violet, mineral violet, permanent violet, Burgundy violet; a permanent inorganic violet pigment consisting of manganese chloride, phosphoric acid and ammonium carbonate; used in oil and tempera painting.

manhole see inspection chamber.
manhole cover a removable cover for an inspection chamber, usually of concrete or cast iron.

man-hour, person-hour; a measure of the amount of work done by a person over the period of one hour; used in invoicing and estimating potential labour costs.

Manila hemp fibre from a tropical plant [*Musa textilis*], used for making rope; also written as Manilla.

mannerism 1 any architectural style or detail which incorporates classical and other motifs in a frivolous, superficial and unconventional way.
2 Mannerism a style in Italian Renaissance art and architecture which flourished from 1520; technically proficient and breaking away from classical harmony, with the emphasis on inner mysticism and external realism.

Mannerist portal of Uffizi Gallery, Florence; architect Bernardo Buontalenti, 1580

manometer see pressure gauge.

mansard an attic storey directly under a mansard or gambrel roof.
mansard roof 1 a hipped or gabled roof form in which each roof plane is doubly pitched.

gabled mansard roof

2 see hipped mansard roof.
mansard roof truss a roof truss designed to maximize the use of interior roof space by having a large open central area topped by a king post truss and sided by rafters to produce a doubly pitched roof.

mansard roof truss

mansard tile a special roof tile manufactured for use at the joint of roof planes in a mansard roof.

mantelpiece a decorative surround for an open fireplace, often forming a shelf above it; originally a beam across the face of a fireplace, supporting masonry above; also written as mantlepiece.

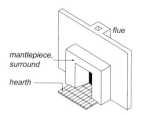

mantlepiece, surround

hearth

manual metal-arc welding, MMA welding, shielded metal-arc welding (Am), SMA welding (Am), stick welding; a manual method of arc welding using electrodes covered with material that shields the arc.

manufactured aggregate aggregate produced as the result of an industrial process.

manufacturing tolerance an acceptable range of dimensions or measurable quantities within which a manufactured item should be supplied to meet a specification.

man-year, person-year; a measure of the amount of work done by a person over the period of one year; used in estimating potential labour costs for a large project.

maple [*Acer spp.*] hardwoods of North America and Europe with fine-textured, hard, strong, tough, flexible, cream-coloured timber; used for flooring, panelling, joinery, interiors and musical instruments; with a great many species, maples are often planted as street liners and in parks and gardens for their spectacular autumn foliage; see below for full list of species of maple and sycamore included in this work:

Acer spp. – maple

black maple [*Acer nigrum*] a North American hardwood; a hard maple used for furniture and panelling.

hard maple [*Acer saccharum, Acer nigrum*] a collective name for timber of the sugar maple and black maple of North America.

red maple [*Acer rubrum*] a North American hardwood; a soft maple used for furniture and panelling.

silver maple [*Acer saccharinum*] a North American hardwood with light brown timber, marketed as soft maple; used for furniture, panelling and packaging.

soft maple [*Acer saccharinum, Acer rubrum*] a collective name for the timber of the North American silver and red maples.

sycamore, harewood; [*Acer pseudoplatanus*] a hardwood with tough, light, fairly strong perishable yellowish timber, used for flooring and veneer; in North America the tree known as sycamore is the American plane [*Platanus occidentalis*].

mapping, surveying; the making of a map or chart of an area of land on the basis of measurements and observations taken at various points.

Maracaibo lignum vitae see verawood.

marble a metamorphic rock derived from limestone or dolomite, used extensively in building for floors and walls cladding; ground and polished as sheets or used as chippings in terrazzo and other composite materials.

marble dust small chips of ground marble used as aggregate in the plaster base of fresco and mural painting.

marble flour a fine form of marble dust used in fresco painting.

marble gypsum see alum gypsum.

marble stucco high-quality polished stucco which resembles a marble surface, mixed from natural products including lime, marble dust, limestone and water.

marbling a decorative surface treatment applied by painting or other means in imitation of marble.

margin the shaped exterior edge of a rectangular object such as a stone slab, tile, wooden table top, etc.

marginal draft see drafted margin.

margin knot a knot near a corner or arris of a piece of timber.

margin strip in timber flooring, a board laid at the edge of a floor as a border.

margin trowel a narrow-bladed hand plasterer's trowel used for applying plaster to small, confined areas.

marigold window see rose window.

marine crustacean see gribble.

marine mollusc see shipworm.

marine plywood a grade of plywood manufactured from quality wood veneers bonded together with waterproof glues; used especially for applications in contact with seawater.

marking awl see scribe.

marking gauge, butt gauge; a device used in woodwork for marking out a cutting line on a piece of timber.

marking out see setting out.

marl a variety of clay containing a high proportion of calcium carbonate.

marlstone limestone with an abundance of clay material.

marquetry inlaid work of different coloured veneers as surface decoration for panelling and furniture; see intarsia.

Mars colour any of a range of coloured artificial iron oxides used as permanent pigments; Mars black (or black oxide of iron) is a dense opaque black pigment consisting of black iron oxide, suitable for use in all types of paint; Mars yellow (otherwise known as iron yellow, Mars orange, yellow oxide of iron) is a synthetic, organic, yellow iron oxide pigment which has good chemical and weather resistance; Mars brown is a form of synthetic brown iron oxide pigment.

martensitic stainless steel a variety of stainless steel which contains 13% chromium.

mascaron see mask.

mash hammer see club hammer.

mask, mascaron; carved ornamentation of a grotesque human or animal face or head, especially used for keystones and panels.

masking in painting and decorating, the temporary covering of boundary areas which are to remain free of paint with tape and paper.

masking tape pale brown adhesive paper tape used by painters and decorators for masking off boundaries of areas to be painted; also used as a general purpose tape, and often as draughting tape.

mason, stonemason; a skilled craftsman who works in stone, in building construction, producing stone walling and embellishment,

> **masonry** any construction in laid bricks, blocks or stone; types included as separate entries are listed below:
> *ashlar masonry, see ashlar; *blockwork; *brickwork; *cloisonné masonry; *coursed squared rubble masonry; *cyclopean masonry; *decorative masonry; *opus, Roman stonework; *Pelasgic masonry, see cyclopean masonry; *polygonal masonry; *random squared rubble masonry, see uncoursed squared rubble masonry; *squared rubble masonry; *stone masonry; *stonework; *thin bed masonry; *uncoursed squared rubble masonry.

masonry axe a tempered steel, double-headed axe used for dressing and smoothing stonework; variously called a stone axe, rock axe, stonemason's axe, trimming axe or chop axe.

masonry bit see masonry drill.

masonry block see block.

masonry capping, coping block, coping stone; one of a series of a bricks, blocks or stones placed along the top of a freestanding wall to protect it from the infiltration of rainwater; see also capping brick, coping brick.

masonry cement any cement used for bonding bricks, blocks or stones together in masonry walling, in particular Portland cement with finely ground lime, plasticizers or other additives.

masonry cement mortar a Portland-cement-based mortar containing a fine mineral filler and air-entraining agent; it has good workability and is used in bricklaying.

mask

masonry chisel any of a wide range of solid steel cold chisels used for shaping, carving and dressing stone; also called a stonemason's, mason's, stone or stone-carving chisel; types included as separate entries are listed below:
*batting tool, broad tool; *boaster, drover; *bolster; *broach; *claw chisel, claw tool; *clourer; *cold chisel; *driver; *fantail tool, see fishtail chisel; *fillet chisel; *fishtail chisel, fishtail tool; *hammer-headed chisel; *jumper; *mallet-headed chisel; *nicker, see splitter; *patent claw chisel; *pitching tool, pincher, pitcher; *point tool; *punch; *quirking tool; *sculptor's point; *spindle, see fillet chisel; *splitter; *tooth tool, see patent claw chisel; *tracer; *waster.

masonry drill, concrete drill, masonry bit; a drill bit for boring holes in masonry and concrete, usually tipped with a hard metal alloy such as tungsten carbide.

masonry joint any joint between adjacent stones, bricks, etc. in masonry; the final shaped mortar in bed and vertical joints.

masonry mortar see bedding mortar, masonry cement mortar.

masonry nail a smooth round hardened steel nail used for fixing materials and components to masonry and concrete.

masonry nail

masonry paint, organic rendering, plastic paint, stone paint; a thick emulsion alkali-resistant paint used for masonry surfaces.

masonry primer a primer for use on a masonry surface.

masonry saw a machine tool with a diamond-tipped circular saw, often hand-held or bolted in place, for cutting openings in masonry walling, concrete, etc.

masonry screw see concrete screw.

masonry trowel see bricklayer's trowel.

masonry unit any brick, block or stone used in the laying of a wall; a generic name for both bricks and blocks.

mason's axe see masonry axe.

mason's chisel see masonry chisel.

mason's trowel see bricklayer's trowel.

mass concrete, plain concrete; concrete containing no reinforcement, used in bulk solely for limited structural applications, fill, etc.

mass density the mass per unit volume of a solid granular material, calculated to include the spaces between the granules; its units are kg/m^3.

massicot a yellow lead oxide pigment no longer in use, occurring naturally as soft, earthy deposits.

massing the location and size of the various built volumes and forms in an architectural composition.

massive rock see igneous rock.

mass law in acoustics, an approximation according to which the acoustic insulation of a construction increases relative to its mass per unit area.

mast a tall, relatively slender vertical structure or pole, often trussed or braced with guy ropes, used for supporting antennae, lighting, flags, etc.

mastaba 1 an Arabic stone bench or seat fixed to a dwelling.
2 mastaba tomb; a large ancient Egyptian stone tomb with sloping stone sides and a flat top, built over a burial ground or chamber.

section through mastaba at Saqqara, Egypt, Old Kingdom

master key a key which fits all the locks in a suite of locks, each of which has a servant key.

mastic 1 natural resin gathered from a certain Mediterranean tree [*Pistachia lentiscus*], used with a solvent such as turpentine to form a varnish.
2 any soft non-elastic substance used as a sealant; see sealant, sealing compound.

mastic asphalt a mixture of asphalt and chippings or sand, laid hot, but which is solid at normal temperatures; used for paving, flooring and roof waterproofing.

masur birch an irregularity in birch wood which produces a speckled patterned surface; used in veneers and decorative surfaces.

mat see matting.

matchboarding, tongue and groove boarding; timber boarding which has been milled with a tongue along one edge and a corresponding groove along the other; when laid, the tongue fits into the groove of the adjacent board; a single board of this type is called a matchboard; a matchboard door is a simple ledge door faced with tongued and grooved boards.

matchboarding

matching 1 see tongue and groove jointing.
2 the alignment of adjacent sheets of patterned wallcovering so that the pattern is continuous.
3 the craft of arranging sheets of wood veneer into neat repeated or mirrored patterns for the surfaces of panels and tops or fronts of furnishings.

mate a labourer on a building site who helps a tradesman.

matrix 1 calcite, resin, Portland cement or other material which binds the grains in stone, concrete or other similar materials together; see also cementitious matrix.
2 see mould.

mat sinking see mat well.

matt, matte see flat.

matting, mat; softish floor coverings such as rubber and synthetic sheeting, linoleum and various fibrous and fabric-based sheets, usually supplied in rolls; types included as separate entries are listed below:
*carpet; *coir matting; *cork matting, see cork carpet; *filter mat; *floor covering; *glassfibre mat; *linoleum; *rubber flooring; *sisal matting; *woven matting, see woven carpet.

maturity see concrete maturity.

mat well, mat sinking; a recess in floor construction in front of an external doorway, designed to house a doormat or grill so that it is flush with the floor surface.
mat well frame a frame for the perimeter of a mat well.

maul, mall; a heavy hammer such as a sledgehammer or club hammer, used for crushing and driving; see also beetle, five pound maul, club hammer.

mauve, Perkin's violet; a synthetic organic violet pigment manufactured from coal tar intermediaries, originally discovered by Sir William Perkin in England in 1856.

maximum temperature period in the steam curing of concrete, the period over which the temperature is maintained at a constant maximum level.

Maya architecture the architecture of the Mayan Indians in Central America and Mexico from c. 400—900 characterized by ziggurats, planned gridiron towns, stone corbelled vaulting and the use of cement and concrete manufactured from burnt lime; a Mayan pyramid is known as a teocalli.

MDF medium density fibreboard.

meander, labyrinth fret; a decorative pattern of intertwining perpendicular lines forming a band; a complex or intricate fret or key pattern, sometimes called an angular guilloche; see also potenty moulding.

meander

means of access a public or private roadway, driveway or path for use of vehicles or pedestrians to enter or approach a site.

means of egress, means of escape, escape route; a term appearing in fire regulations to mean the continuous and unobstructed way of exit travel during a fire or other emergency from any point in a building or facility to a public way.

measure 1 the value or extent of a measured quantity, a unit of measurement; see also dimension.
2 an implement used in measurement, such as a graded scale or graduated glass vessel; see also measuring tape, tape measure.

measured drawing a drawing to scale produced from a survey of an existing building or structure; see also record drawing.

measured work in contract management, site work paid on the basis of measurement of its scope and quantities after it has been undertaken.

measurement 1 the measuring of magnitude of an object, site, material, physical property or building work carried out.
2 the numerical quantity which results from measuring something.
3 see system of measurement.
4 see dimension.

measurement contract a form of building contract whose final sum is based on the total amount of work done, valued according to an itemized agreed schedule of rates.

measurement preambles in contract administration, clauses that explain or clarify methods of measurement for items in a bill of quantities.

measuring tape a long steel or fibrous rolled and gradated tape up to 30 m long for measuring long distances; see also flexible steel tape measure.

measuring telescope, scope; that part of an optical surveying instrument which contains a telescope whose sight is marked with a gradated scale and cross-hairs.

mechanical adhesion the adhesion of two surfaces caused by bonding agents keying into porous or rough surfaces; cf. specific adhesion.

mechanical engineering see mechanical services engineering.

mechanical extract in ventilation, the removal of used air from a space, gases up a flue, etc. with a fan or other mechanical plant.

mechanical input and extract ventilation, combined extract and input system; a mechanical ventilation system in which both supply and extract of air through terminal devices is controlled by a fan.

mechanical joint any joint fixed without the use of glue or other bonding medium.

mechanical mixing see machine mixing.

mechanical plastering see projection plastering.

mechanical services, heating and ventilation; heating, water supply and discharge, and ventilation services for a building.
mechanical services engineering the building design and construction discipline encompassing heating, water supply, drainage and ventilation; see HEVAC.
mechanical services installation the provision, apparatus and equipment to operate the heating, water supply, and ventilation requirements of a building.

mechanical smoke extraction system see fire venting installation.

mechanical trowel see power trowel.

mechanical ventilation, forced ventilation; the ventilation of a building which relies on mechanical plant to convey, introduce and remove air.

medallion a decorative round or oval-framed wall panel, either bare, ornamented or containing a portrait.

medium see paint medium.

medium board a class of medium density fibreboards, including high density and low density medium board; density $350-800$ kg/m^3.

medium carbon steel steel with a carbon content of $0.25-0.5\%$, used for forging.

medium density fibreboard, MDF; a dense and versatile fibreboard formed through a dry process in which the fibres are bonded together with urea formaldehyde resin; its density does not exceed 600 kg/m^3.

medium gravel see gravel.

medium-hard rock according to a classification of hardness of rocks used by stone masons and construction technicians, rock which has a compressive strength between 800 kg/cm^2 and 1800 kg/cm^2.

medium sand see sand.

medium silt see silt.

medulla see pith.

medullary ray, pith ray; fine radial lines in wood extending outwards from the pith of a tree trunk.

medusa a classical decorative motif based on the only mortal of three hideous sisters or Gorgons, from Greek mythology, with live snakes for hair and a gaze that turned its onlooker to stone.

Etruscan medusa palmette, or gorgon motif

meeting, conference; a formal occasion where parties with a common aim, project, etc. gather to discuss matters and formulate decisions; see also site meeting.

meeting stile the vertical side member of the folding casement or double door leaf opposite that from which it is hung.

megalith a prehistoric structure such as a dolmen, chambered tomb or cist constructed from one or more large blocks of rough stone.

megalithic temple prehistoric temples such as those found at Tarxien, Malta, with walls constructed from shaped and placed upright blocks, or orthostats.

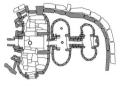

megalithic temple at Hal Tarxien, Malta, 3000–2500 BC

megaron 1 Gk.; an early Greek or Mycenaean dwelling type; a long rectangular central hall in a Mycenaean dwelling or temple, with an entrance at one end; originally evolving from the Mycenaean dwelling type.

megaron 'Phylakopi III', Mycenae, Greece 3300–1100 BC

2 a simple Greek temple type consisting of a columned pronaos (a portico or vestibule) leading to a single chamber containing a ritual hearth; also called a megaron temple.

melamine, melamine formaldehyde, MF a clear, resistant thermosetting resin used for mouldings, hardwearing surface coatings and adhesives.

melamine faced chipboard chipboard manufactured with a surface coating of melamine impregnated paper or membrane; used for hardwearing table tops and kitchen surfaces.

melamine facing the treatment of a surface by the thermal application of melamine impregnated sheet; the finish formed by this.

melamine formaldehyde the full name for melamine.

melamine formaldehyde glue a synthetic adhesive of melamine formaldehyde resin used for gluing veneers or laminated plastics.

melamine laminate any laminate whose main component is melamine formaldehyde resin; used for hardwearing surfaces of worktops and doors.

melon dome see umbrella dome.

membrane a flexible tough sheet or thin covering layer incorporated in construction to prevent the passage of moisture; types included as separate entries are listed below:
*air-gap membrane; *bitumen-polymer membrane; *bituminous membrane; *cavity drainage membrane, cavity membrane, see air-gap membrane; *damp proof membrane; *drainage membrane, see air-gap membrane; *geomembrane; *isolating membrane, see separating layer; *slip membrane; *tanking membrane, see air-gap membrane; *waterproofing membrane.

membrane absorber in acoustics, an absorbing construction consisting of a board or sheet material stretched between battens to absorb sound through sympathetic resonance.

membrane curing a method of curing concrete slabs by covering with a layer of impervious material such as polythene sheet or sprayed resin to prevent evaporation.

membrane roofing, membrane waterproofing; a general name for thin flexible sheet materials and products such as bitumen felt, plastic sheet or asphalt used to provide a waterproof upper layer in flat or pitched roof construction.

membrane waterproofing a thin layer of waterproofing material or product, usually a membrane of bitumen or other polymeric resilient sheeting, laid as the final covering for flat roof construction; see also membrane roofing.

mercury a silvery-white, highly poisonous liquid metal, **Hg**, found in the mineral cinnabar, and used in the production of thermometers and mirrors, and in alloys.

mercury vapour lamp, mercury lamp; a discharge lamp whose light emphasizes yellow and blue colours, containing mercury vapour and argon in a sealed glass tube.

merlon solid parts of a battlement parapet, alternating with openings or crenelles, which provided archers and artillery with shelter while defending a fortification; similar motifs in decoration and ornament.

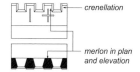

crenellation

merlon in plan and elevation

Merulius lacrymans see dry rot.

mesh 1 any product woven, welded or fused from sets of perpendicular strands to form an open sheet structure; if the openings are small it is called cloth;

types included as separate entries are listed below:
*crimped wire mesh; *conveyor belt mesh; *chain link mesh; *fabric reinforcement; *insect mesh, see insect screen; *hexagonal mesh, see chicken wire; *steel mesh; *welded mesh; *wire mesh; *woven wire mesh.
2 see mesh size.

mesh lathing see wire lathing, expanded metal lathing.

mesh reinforcement see fabric reinforcement.

mesh size the measure of fineness of a wire mesh, the distance from centre to centre of adjacent parallel wires, sometimes given as the number of openings per unit measure (inch or cm); also simply called mesh; see opening size.

Mesopotamian architecture architecture from 3000 BC to 600 BC originating in the valleys of the rivers Tigris and Euphrates in what is now Iraq; characterized by lavish palaces, tombs and ziggurats in massive masonry and mud bricks.

metal 1 one of a class of elements which are malleable, ductile, lustrous and good conductors of heat and electricity; the principal metals used in the construction of buildings, or in alloys, are listed below:
*aluminium, aluminum, **Al**; *brass; *bronze; *chromium, chrome, **Cr**; *cobalt, **Co**; *copper, **Cu**; *iron, **Fe**; *lead, **Pb**; *manganese, **Mn**; *nickel, **Ni**; *steel; *tin, **Sn**; *titanium, **Ti**; *vanadium, **V**; *zinc, **Zn**.

metal cladding any metallic surface covering for a wall, building or structure, such as sheetmetal panelling products, plate, lathing, mesh, grilles, etc.

metal component see prefabricated metal unit.

metal decking see profiled sheeting.

metal drill a hardened steel spiral-cutting drill bit for cutting round holes in metal.

metal-electrode inert-gas welding see MIG welding.

metal flooring see expanded metal flooring, open bar metal flooring, open metal flooring.

metal foil see foil.

metal foil faced bitumen felt bitumen felt which has been treated on one side with a layer of metal foil and the other with a surfacing of fine granular material.

metal foil wallcovering decorative wallcovering surface-treated with a layer of metal foil.

metal halide lamp, metallic-additive lamp; a high-pressure mercury discharge lamp containing metal halide additives to alter the colour spectrum of its light output.

metal lathing a keying base for plaster of expanded metal sheet, mesh, metal slats or laths, etc.; types included as separate entries are listed below:
*expanded metal lathing; *mesh lathing, see wire lathing; *ribbed expanded metal lathing, rib lathing; *wire lathing, wire-mesh lathing.
metal lathing plaster plaster suitable for use with metal lathing.

metallic active-gas welding see MAG welding.

metallic-additive lamp see metal halide lamp.

metallic pigment, metallic paint; inorganic paint which contains tiny flakes of metal, producing a speckled metallic sheen when applied as a surface treatment.

metallic wood borer, buprestid beetle; [*Buprestis spp.*] a group of insects with hard shiny shells whose larvae burrow beneath the bark of living trees.

metallization see zinc spraying.

metallized wallcovering decorative wallcovering with a layer of metallized plastic film applied as a shiny surface finish.

metal multi-tile roofing a form of sheetmetal roofing, often organically coated, which has been rolled into embossed sheets in imitation of slate or tiled roofing.

metal multi-tile roofing

metal pan see metal tray.

metal plate, flat plate; any metal product rolled in sheets over about 2–5 mm thick; actual thickness varies with national specification and type of metal; see also sheetmetal, foil; types included as separate entries are listed below:
*aluminium plate; *chequerplate, checkerplate; *copper plate; *lead plate; *quarto plate; *steel plate.

metal primer a priming compound for use on a metal surface.

metal roofing see sheetmetal roofing, supported sheetmetal roofing, aluminium sheet, corrugated sheetmetal, metal multi-tile roofing.

metal section any thin length of steel, aluminium, copper, brass, etc. which has been preformed by a process of rolling, extrusion, bending, etc. into a uniform cross-section of certain shape and dimensions; see section for list.

metal sheet see sheetmetal.

metal spraying see zinc spraying.

metal tray, metal pan; a pressed metal ceiling panel in a suspended ceiling.

metamerism in lighting design, a phenomenon which occurs when two colours which match under one set of lighting conditions do not match under another.

metamorphic rock rock which has been transformed from existing igneous, sedimentary and older metamorphic rock types under the influence of high pressure and temperature, causing chemical change and recrystallization to alter the structure and composition;

types included as separate entries are listed below:
*amphibolite; *cipollino, cipolin; *contact metamorphic rock; *crystalline schist; *eclogite; *foliated gneiss, see gneissose micaschist; *gneiss; *gneissose micaschist, foliated gneiss; *granite-gneiss; *granulite; *hornfels; *marble; *mica schist; *phyllite; *quartzite; *schist; *serpentine, serpentinite; *slate.

meter 1 any measuring instrument which indicates quantities by means of a graduated scale or dial; see also gauge; types included as separate entries are listed below:
*acoustic level meter, see sound level meter; *ammeter; *barometer; *consistometer; *cover meter; *electricity meter, *electric meter; *gas meter; *hydrometer; *hygrometer; *manometer, see pressure gauge; *micrometer; *moisture meter; *oil meter; *parking meter; *psychrometer; *sound level meter; *tacheometer; *water meter.
2 American spelling of metre.
meter cupboard a small space which contains an electricity or gas meter.
meter cabinet a wall-mounted unit with a hinged door, often of sheetmetal, which contains an electricity meter.

methanal see formaldehyde.

method of joints, joint method; in structural engineering, a method of calculating the forces acting on members in a truss by considering each portion of the triangulated construction as a static entity.

method of sections, sections method; in structural engineering, a method of calculating the forces acting on members in a truss by considering each joint in turn as a static entity.

metope in classical architecture, one of a series of plain or carved rectangular panels lining a Doric frieze, separated by triglyphs.

metre, meter (Am); abb. **m**; the SI basic unit of length.

metric pertaining to a system of weights and measures based on the metre and using the number 10 as a basic division.
metric brick see modular standard brick, metric standard brick.

metric modular brick see modular standard brick.
metric sabin, absorption unit; in acoustics, a unit of sound absorption equivalent to one square metre of perfect absorber.
metric standard brick a standard size of brick in use in Great Britain with regular dimensions of $215 \times 102.5 \times 65$ mm.
metric thread a standardized screw thread whose spacing is based on fractions of a metre; denser and at less of an angle than Whitworth thread.

mews a row of town dwellings converted from stables, or any modern development of a similar character; originally dwellings converted from the Royal Stables in London.

mezzanine, entersole, entresol, intersole; an intermediate storey between two adjacent floors of a building, often a gallery, balcony or partial storey.

mezzo rilievo, demirelief, half relief; sculpture in which figures and elements project half their width from the background.

MF melamine formaldehyde.

mica a shiny, soft potassium iron magnesium silicate found in mineral form as very thin flakes or small plates in granite; used in the manufacture of plastics, in electrical and thermal insulation, and as an additive in paints for its structural qualities and sparkle; see also biotite, black mica, muscovite.

mica schist a grey, fine-grained metamorphic rock containing quartz, mica and muscovite; easily cleaved and used in building as paving and tiles.

microbiological corrosion the deterioration, chemical attack, etc. of metals, concrete and other materials caused directly by, or by the acidic by-products of, microbial activity in bacteria, algae, moulds or fungi.

microcline a form of the mineral orthoclase used as a raw material in the ceramic industry and for jewellery.

micrometer, 1 micrometer gauge; an instrument with a G-frame and gradated screw for accurate measurement of fine thicknesses down to 0.001 mm.
2 see micron.

micrometre see micron.

micron, micrometre, micrometer (Am); a unit of length equal to one millionth part of a metre, 1/1000 mm.

micropascal abb. **uPa**; in acoustics, a unit of measurement of sound pressure, one millionth of a pascal.

micropile see mini-pile.

middle oil see carbolic oil.

middle rail, lock rail; the intermediate horizontal framing member between the bottom and top rails in a framed door, where the lock is often fitted.

middle raker the middle slanting prop in a raking shore.

middle strip in concrete structures, that portion of a reinforced concrete slab spanning between columns; measured as the span of the slab with the width of the column strips subtracted.

MIG welding, metal-electrode inert-gas welding; a method of arc welding light alloys and steels in which the arc is shielded with an inert gas.

migmatite a composite rock type consisting of metamorphic rock infused with bands of igneous rock when molten.

mild steel ductile steel with a carbon content of 0.15−0.25%, used for pipes, joists and bars.

military projection a form of oblique projection in which the X and Y axes are in true plan (laid at an angle) and the Y axis is drawn vertical, with scaling of lines on all axes equal; see cavalier, cabinet projections; sometimes called a planometric projection.

milk glass, opaline; ordinary glass to which ingredients are added at the molten stage to provide obscurance or translucency.

milk of lime see lime white.

milky quartz an opaque white variety of crystalline quartz, used as a gemstone and carved for ornament.

milled log, machined log, engineered log; an industrial timber product of uniform rectangular or round cross-section and cogged ends, machined from a single log and used in the construction of system built and off-the-shelf log buildings; see also laminated log.

milled sheet lead lead sheet formed by a process of rolling.

Millettia laurentii see wenge.

milling, 1 machining; the shaping of wood and other materials using a machine tool with a high-speed rotary blade.
2 the shaping of metal pieces, circular in section, on a lathe.

mill saw, donkey saw, frame saw, gang saw; an industrial saw for converting logs into timber sections with one or a series of oscillating blades held vertically in a frame.

mill scale iron oxide, Fe_3O_4, which forms on the surface of iron sections during hot rolling.

Milori blue see Prussian blue.

Mimusops heckelii see makore.

minaret a balconied tower in a mosque from which prayers and announcements are given, the faithful are called to prayer, etc.

mineral any naturally occurring solid inorganic material with definite chemical composition and usually crystalline structure obtained by mining; usually rocky material such as quartz and feldspar; see below for list of minerals included as separate entries in this work:
*adularia; *alkali feldspar; *amber, succinite; *amphibole; *andalusite; *anhydrite; *asbestos; *azurite; *barytes; *beryl; *biotite; *bitter spar, see dolomite, magnesite; *black iron oxide, see magnetite; *black mica; *Bologna stone; *brown iron ore, see limonite; *brownmillerite; *calcite; *carnelian, see cornelian; *chrysoberyl; *cinnamon stone, hessonite; *coccolite; *cordierite, dichroite, iotite; *corundum; *cornelian; *dichroite, see cordierite; *diopside; *dioptase; *disthene, see kyanite; *dolomite, bitter spar; *emerald; *feldspar, felspar; *fluorite; garnet; garnierite; *glauconite; *grossular, grossular garnet or grossularite; *gypsum; *haematite, hematite; *heavy spar; *heliotrope; *hessonite, cinnamon stone; *hornblende; *iotite, see cordierite; *iron pyrites, pyrite, sulphur-ore; *jade; *jadeite; *jasper; *kallaite, see turquoise; *kyanite, disthene; *labradorite, Labrador feldspar; *lazurite,

lapis lazuli; *limonite, brown iron ore; *magnesite, bitter spar; *magnetite, magnetic iron ore, black iron oxide; *malachite; *manganese spar, see rhodochrosite; *mica; *microcline; *muscovite; *nephrite; *opal; *orpiment; *orthoclase; *phlogopite; *plagioclase; *potash feldspar, orthoclase; *pyrites; *pyrolusite; *quartz; *rhodochrosite, manganese spar; *rhodonite; *sard; *selenite; *sillimanite; *sodalite; *succinite, see amber; *sulphur-ore, see iron pyrites; *tourmaline; *turquoise, kallaite.

mineral blue see azurite.

mineral brown see burnt umber.

mineral fibre thin filaments of man-made mineral product, rock, glass, etc. used in fireproofing and insulation; mineral fibre reinforced refers to composites consisting of man-made mineral fibres in a cellulose binder; used for fire-resistant building boards and glazing channels.

mineral granule surfaced bitumen felt, coated felt, mineral-surfaced bitumen felt; bitumen felt which has been treated on one side with coloured mineral granules and the other with a surfacing of fine granular material such as sand; used for roofing and general waterproofing.

mineral green see malachite.

mineral oil a general name for some crude petroleums after more volatile elements such as gasoline, mineral spirits and kerosene have been distilled off; viscous liquids used as lubricating oils and in some polishes and plastics.

mineral pigment a general name for natural or synthetic inorganic pigments such as umber, sienna, ochre (raw or burnt), and metal salts (chrome green, white lead); see earth colours for list of earth colours and mineral pigments; see also inorganic pigment.

mineral plaster rendering mortar containing coloured inorganic or mineral material, ground glass, etc., which may be exposed in the surface by washing, scouring or sandblasting once the coating has hardened, producing a variegated coloured surface.

mineral render see mineral plaster.

mineral spirit see white spirit.

mineral-surfaced bitumen felt see mineral granule surfaced bitumen felt.

mineral violet see manganese violet.

mineral white gypsum used as an inert pigment.

mineral wool fibrous material produced by heating and spinning rock, glass or other mineral material, formed into soft slabs (known as bats) and used as thermal insulation for walls, floors and roofs; see glass wool, rock wool.

mineral yellow see Turner's yellow.

minette a form of the pigment yellow ochre.

mini-hacksaw a small hacksaw for cutting metal, plastics and wood.

minimalism art or architecture which employs simple and often stark geometrical devices, colours, forms, etc., unadorned surfaces and pared detail.

minimum gradient, self-cleansing gradient; the smallest possible slope of a drain, etc. such that discharge will flow through and carry solid matter with it under the influence of gravity.

mini-pile, micropile, pin pile; in foundation technology, a small pile whose diameter is less than 300 mm.

minium see red lead.

Minoan architecture the architecture of bronze-age Crete from 2800–1150 BC, characterized by massive masonry in stone, elaborate building plans and planned towns.

Minoan column, Cretan column, Mycenaean column, reverse taper column; a round column type with a smooth shaft tapering down to its base, surmounted by a wide cushion capital; found originally in the Minoan architecture of Crete, and later in Mycenae on mainland Greece.

Minoan column

minor works contract a form of building contract designed for simple, low-cost projects, interior design jobs, renovations, etc., in which the freedom of the architect as client's representative is increased in the choice of subcontractors or suppliers.

mirror glass, mirrored glass; any glass coated on one side with reflective material, such as silver, from which a mirror is made; see one-way glass; transparent mirror glass, Venetian mirror glass.

mirror screw a special screw for fixing mirrors and glass fronts, which comes supplied with a domed piece to cover the slotted head and provide a neat finish.

mirror screw

mirror test an inspection for possible obstructions in pipework using a mirror or periscope.

mismatched see random match.

miss, holiday, skip; a defect in a paint finish consisting of areas which have not been painted.

mission tile see under-and-over tile.

mitre 1 mitred edge; a 45° splay cut into both ends of two corresponding frame members to form a neat right angled joint.

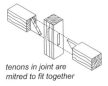

*tenons in joint are
mitred to fit together*

2 a corner joint used in picture and glazing framing, fine joinery, etc. in which two perpendicular pieces meet with joined ends splayed to 45°; also called a mitre joint.

mitre box, mitre block; a device for guiding a handsaw at a 45° or 90° angle when cutting a mitre in a piece of wood.

mitre brad see corrugated fastener.

mitre cramp see corner cramp.

mitred edge see mitre.

mitre joint, mitred joint; any framing corner joint in which members are joined with mitred edges.

mitre square an implement for measuring and marking mitres consisting of a stock with a metal blade set at 45°.

mitre stop a piece of splayed board or sheeting placed in a mould to produce a mitred termination at the external corner of an ornamental plaster or concrete moulding.

Mittler's green a variety of viridian pigment.

mix a combination of substances or ingredients which form a homogeneous whole whilst remaining chemically independent, also called a mixture or blend; concrete mix, plaster mix.

mixed concrete, site concrete; the dry constituents of concrete mixed with water ready for use on site.

mixed garden bond a brickwork bond in which a course of alternating headers and stretchers alternates with between one and six courses of stretchers in no regular pattern.

mixed plywood plywood whose core veneers or inner plies are of a different species of timber from that of the outer plies.

mixer 1 see mixer tap.
2 see concrete mixer, cement mixer.

mixer tap, mixer; a water tap in which hot and cold water are blended and released at a controlled temperature from a single nozzle; see also monobloc mixer.

mixing the mechanical stirring together, agitating, etc. of component parts of a concrete or plaster mix to form a homogeneous mass before applying; the mixing of dry powders is often called blending or preblending.

mixing box, 1 mixing unit; in certain air-conditioning systems, a chamber in which air from two supply ducts containing air with differing temperatures and humidities are blended.
2 see dual duct terminal unit.

mixing valve in plumbing and drainage, a device containing a chamber in which hot and cold water supplies can be mixed into a single stream and to a regulated temperature.

mix proportions the proportions of each of the component parts in a concrete, mortar or plaster mix.

mixture, blend, mix; a combination of substances or ingredients which form a homogeneous whole whilst remaining chemically independent.

MMA welding see manual metal-arc welding.

mobile scaffold scaffolding which can be moved from place to place without the need for dismantling; most often a framework on wheels furnished with a brake.

model 1 a construction built as an example or pattern for a component or building; see scale model.
2 computer model; a virtual three-dimensional computer representation of a design scheme, building, geographical area, etc. used to test solutions, present proposals, etc.

modelling 1 the artistic shaping of wax, clay and other plastic materials.
2 the creation, by computer, of a comprehensive three-dimensional virtual model of a building, as a design tool and for purposes of presentation.

modernism, 1 modern movement; an architectural and design movement originating in Europe in the 1920s and 1930s; it is based on the use of modern materials and methods, and disregards decoration and historical precedents.

modernist portal at the Maisterhaus, Bauhaus, Dessau, 1925–26; architect Walter Gropius

2 any architecture and art which is current and rejects traditional and classical ideologies and methods.

modification see variation.

modified binder a bituminous binder whose properties have been improved by the use of an additive.

modillion in classical architecture, one of a series of small ornate corbelled brackets which support a cornice of the Corinthian or Composite order.

modular pertaining to components, often prefabricated, which are manufactured to a standardized range of sizes; see module.
modular brick a mass-produced rectangular brick produced to metric standardized dimensions, coordinated in terms of height, length and width to a basic unit of 100 mm, varying in size from country to country and state to state; see also cuboid brick, modular standard brick, US standard brick.

modular component, module; any prefabricated building component which has been designed and dimensioned to be part of a modular building system.
modular coordination a design and construction system in which all components conform to an agreed set of sizes and are based on a single unit or module.
modular dimension see modular size.
modular floor see platform floor.
modular grid a grid of lines to which dimensions are coordinated, which marks out lines of modular coordination on a drawing.
modular size one of the basic starting dimensions used in a modular system.
modular standard brick, **modular brick, metric modular brick, metric brick, standard modular brick;** a standard size of brick in use in Great Britain with regular dimensions of $190 \times 90 \times 65$ mm; see also US standard brick.

module 1 a convenient unit of measurement used in design and construction as an aid in setting out, usually based on standard component sizes or a structural grid.
2 a prefabricated assembly of components brought to site for installation; often a whole working space such as a bathroom, staircase, serviced living accommodation, etc.; see modular component, lift shaft module.

modulus of elasticity, elastic modulus, Young's modulus the ratio of stress to strain within the elastic range of a material, whose SI units are MN/m or Gpa.

modulus of section see section modulus.

moist curing the curing of fresh concrete by covering it with a layer of damp material such as wet sand or sawdust, by ponding and by spraying with water.

moisture water in the form of surface droplets or wetness contained within the fabric of a material or construction; see also humidity, dampness, condensation; see building moisture, construction moisture.

moisture content the weight of contained or condensed water in a material expressed as a percentage of its dry weight.

moisture curing adhesive an adhesive which sets by polymerization and is cured by reaction with moisture from the air.

moisture meter an instrument used for the rapid determination of moisture content in wood by electrical means; see also hygrometer.

moisture movement the change in dimensions of a material such as timber, concrete or mortar as a result of a change in water content.

moisture resistant see damp proof, water resistant, waterproof.

moisture resistant adhesive, **MR;** a grade of adhesive which is relatively unresistant to hot water but which can withstand external exposure to weather and micro-organisms for a few years.

molding see moulding.

molly see hollow-wall plug, hollow-wall anchor.

molybdenum a pale, brittle metal, **Mo**, which, as an alloy improves the corrosion resistance of stainless steel, especially in saline conditions.

moment in mechanics, the turning effect of a force on a body around a given point, calculated by multiplying the imposed force by the perpendicular distance from its point of action.

moment of deflection see bending moment.

moment of inertia, moment of gyration, second moment of area; the sum of the products of all the elementary areas of a section multiplied by their distances from the axis squared.

moment of resistance, resistance moment; in structural engineering, the highest bending moment which a beam can withstand.

Monastral a proprietary name for certain blue and green phthalocyanine, and red and violet quinacridone pigments; see phthalocyanine.

monitor, 1 console; a long vertical strip window, part of a raised section of roof in factory buildings with sawtooth and similar roof forms.
2 screen; a television screen in a manufacturing plant, security system or control installation for surveillance of an area or process, or a television screen which displays information from a computer system; sometimes known as a VDU or visual display unit.

monitor roof a pitched roof with a raised central area, also roofed, whose vertical walls often contain glazing.

monitor roof

monk bond, flying bond, Flemish double stretcher bond, Yorkshire bond; a brickwork bond in which each course consists of a repeated series of one header and two stretchers; alternate courses are laid symmetrically about the header.

monkey, ram; in piledriving, the weighted component in a drop hammer.

monobloc mixer, single-hole tap; a mixer tap to which the flow of hot and cold water is controlled separately but mixed in a single body and released through one nozzle.

mono-carriage, spine beam; in stair construction, a single string or beam which supports the treads from their midpoints so that they cantilever out from both sides.

Monochamus see sawyer beetle.

monolithic consisting of one large block of stone, or a solid unjointed mass of material such as cement, concrete or plastics; a monolith is any large block of rough stone, prehistoric standing stone or large freestanding pillar.

monolithic concrete solid reinforced in-situ concrete construction for walls and slabs, which has no joints other than construction joints.

monopitch roof, shed roof, single pitch roof; a roof with only one sloping plane.

monopitch roof

Monterey pine see pine.

Montpelier yellow see Turner's yellow.

monument an impressive building, structure or statue, especially one erected to commemorate an event, person or group of people, or one of cultural or historical significance; see ancient monument.

monumental grand or impressive in architectural layout, size or style.

Moorish arch see horseshoe arch.

mopboard see skirting board.

mopping in bituminous roofing and tanking, the application of hot bitumen or bonding compound with a brush or mop.

Moresque stylized Spanish Islamic and Moorish geometrical and foliated surface ornament and decorative art.

Moresque column from Alhambra palace, Granada, c. 1300

mortar coarse cement consisting of a binder, fine aggregate and water used for bedding and jointing of masonrywork and tiling, and as render; types included as separate entries are listed below:
*bedding mortar; *cement mortar; *cement lime mortar, see composition mortar; *coarse stuff, see lime sand mortar; *coloured mortar; *composition mortar, compo; *fixing mortar; *jointing mortar; *lime mortar; *lime sand mortar; *masonry cement mortar; *pneumatical mortar, see sprayed concrete; *ready-mixed mortar; *refractory mortar; *tiling mortar.

mortar admixture a substance added to a mortar mix with the aim of changing its properties of drying, setting, workability, etc.

mortar bedding the layer of mortar in which a brick, block or stone is laid to secure it in place in a wall.

mortar board see hawk.

mortar fillet, cement fillet, weather fillet; a triangular strip of mortar

formed in roofing construction at the base of an upstand to lessen the angle at an inside corner, raise a layer of tiles at a verge, etc.

mortar fixing the fixing of tiles, stone facing, etc. to a wall or floor surface by bedding them in mortar; also called cement fixing.

mortar fixing of tiles to a concrete substrate

mortar mill, pug mill; a power-driven mixer for mixing mortar with blades or paddles for blending and breaking up lumps in stiff mixes.

mortise, mortice; a recess cut into a timber member to house a tenon, lock, etc.; see also hinge mortise, stopped mortise, blind mortise, slot mortise.

mortise and tenon joint, tenon joint; a strong timber framing joint in which the end of one member is cut with a tenon which fits into a housing or mortise in another; see below for list of types included as separate entries:

tenon

mortise and tenon joint

*abutting tenon joint; *barefaced tenon joint; *butt tenon joint, see abutting tenon joint; *cabinetmaker's tenon joint, see keyed tenon joint; *double tenon joint; *dovetail tenon joint; *edge-halved tenon joint; *fish tenon joint, see free tenon joint; *free tenon joint; *halved tenon joint; *haunched tenon joint; *joggle tenon joint, see stub tenon joint; *keyed tenon joint; *open tenon joint, see bridle joint; *pinned tenon joint, see keyed tenon joint; *shouldered tenon joint; *slip tenon joint, see free tenon joint; *splayed tenon joint; *stepped tenon joint, see shouldered tenon joint; *stopped tenon joint; *stub tenon joint, stub mortise and tenon joint; *stump tenon joint; *through tenon joint; *tusk tenon joint; *twin tenon joint, see double tenon joint; *undercut tenon joint.

mortise chisel, heading chisel, mortising chisel; a chisel with a narrow, thick blade for making holes and mortises in wood.

mortise gauge a device for marking out parallel lines for cutting mortises and tenons from a piece of wood, consisting of two spikes attached to a wooden body.

mortise latch a latch designed to be set into a mortise in the edge of a door leaf.

mortise lock a lock designed to be set into a mortise in the edge of a door leaf; see rim lock.

mortise lock

mortise lock chisel, swan-neck chisel; a narrow chisel with a hooked blade, used for cutting and cleaning out holes and mortises in wood.

mortiser see hollow-chisel mortiser.

mortising chisel see mortise chisel.

mosaic one of a number of small tiles or pieces of glass, stone or ceramics used as a hardwearing and waterproof surface finish for walls and floors; see also below for list of types included as separate entries; a decorative surface pattern for a wall or floor made up from the above.
*Cosmati work; *glass mosaic; *intarsia; *marquetry; *parquet mosaic, see parquet block; *sheet mosaic; *tessera; *wood mosaic, mosaic parquet.
mosaic flooring flooring of small tiles of glass, ceramics or stone, used in

Roman times for elaborately decorative flooring, and nowadays for bathrooms and external surfaces; see also wood mosaic, mosaic parquet.
mosaic gold, aurum mussivum; metallic powder consisting mainly of bisulphide of tin, formerly used as a cheap substitute for powdered gold in ornament and painting.
mosaic parquet see wood mosaic.
mosaic tile small ceramic tiles used for bathroom walls and floors; often sheet mosaic; floor or wall facing in mosaic tiles is called mosaic tiling.

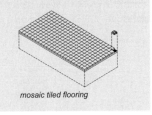

mosaic tiled flooring

motif, design, element; in architecture and ornament, a significant feature such as a component, sculpting or artwork, often repeated as part of a theme; see also ornamental motif.

motorised damper in air-conditioning and mechanical ventilation systems, a thermostatically controlled damper which automatically regulates the flow of air in ductwork.

motor lock see electromechanical lock.

motor room see machine room.

mouchette a typical pointed tracery motif formed by intersecting glazing bars in the Gothic Curvilinear style; a curved dagger motif.

mould, 1 matrix; a hollow negative or female pattern into which material to be shaped by casting or pressing is placed; types included as separate entries are listed below:
*battery mould; *bed mould; *case mould; *fibrous plastering mould; *horse mould, see running mould; *loose piece mould; *peg mould; *piece mould; *running mould, horse mould; *skin mould;

*thumb mould; *waffle mould; *waste mould.

2 see formwork.

3 a fungal growth on the surface of wood or other damp surfaces, usually visible in the form of greenish-black, blue or brown powdered residue.

moulded boarding see bead boarding.

moulded brickwork brickwork whose bricks are moulded to special shapes before firing to form a decorative relief when laid.

moulded capital see bell capital.

moulding, molding (Am); **1** a horizontal ornamental projecting band in a wall surface, often with decorative running motifs and of carved stone, timber or plasterwork.
2 band; a two-dimensional printed or rendered longitudinal decorative strip.
3 fillet; a long three-dimensional profiled strip in a wall surface.
4 strip; any long flat or profiled piece of timber or other material attached as decoration, or as an ornamental gutter, cornice or string course.
5 profile, strip; a long, narrow piece of extruded metal, machined timber or preformed plastics formed into a specific uniform cross-sectional shape; used for various applications such as for covering construction joints, as glazing bars, etc.
6 joinery moulding, see timber trim.
7 see bed mould.

moulding plane a woodworking plane with a base and blade specially shaped for working ornamental mouldings.

moulding wheel a power tool with a profile-formed rotating abrasive disc for grinding mouldings in stonework.

mould mark see flash line.

mould oil, form oil; in concretework, lubricating oil applied to the inside face of formwork sheeting to permit easy and defect-free removal from the hardened concrete surface.

mountain ash see rowan.

mountain blue see azurite, Bremen blue.

mountain green see Bremen blue; also an outdated name for the mineral and pigment malachite.

mounting, fitting; the fastening of a component, fixed furnishing, technical appliance, door leaf or services to a structural base such as a wall, floor or ceiling soffit; see surface mounting.

mounting height the height at which a component is to be fixed in place; especially used in lighting design, where it is defined as the distance at which a luminaire is or should be mounted above the working plane or floor.

mousetooth brickwork see dogtooth brickwork.

mousetooth moulding see dogtooth moulding.

movable partition a partition, often temporary, whose location within a space may be changed without alteration to the surrounding fabric.

movement joint a construction joint in a large rigid structure or monolithic concrete slab which allows for movement such as expansion or contraction to avoid the occurrence of cracks.

moving load a structural live load imposed by a moving object; see rolling load.

moving staircase, moving stairway see escalator.

moving walk see passenger conveyor.

MR moisture resistant adhesive.

M-roof, double gable roof, trough roof, valley roof; a roof formed by the junction of two simple pitched roofs with a valley between them, resembling the letter M in section.

M-roof

mud brick, sun-baked brick, sun-dried brick; an unfired clay brick which has been dried and hardened by heat from the sun, in use in various forms since ancient times; see adobe.

muffler, damper, silencer, sound attenuator; noise-reducing treatment or devices for air-handling ductwork within ceiling voids and other acoustically sensitive areas.

mullion, munnion, muntin (Am); a vertical dividing or framing member in a window, proprietary glazing systems, etc.

multifoil a decorative design consisting of a number of leaf motifs or lobes (called foils) radiating outwards from a point.

multifoil motif

multifoil arch

multifoil arch a decorative arch embellished with more than five foils.

multi-folding door a folding door with a number of side-hinged folding leaves.

multifoliated arch a decorative arch whose intrados is composed of a number of lobes or foils in a cloverleaf arrangement, and whose extrados is a round or pointed arch; especially found in Gothic architecture; see trifoliated, cinquefoliated, round multifoliated arch, pointed multifoliated arch.

multilayer chipboard chipboard manufactured in layers of chips of different sizes pressed together; the layers of finer chips on the exterior provide a denser and harder surface.

multilayer chipboard

multilayer deposit a protective finish for a metal surface formed by successive deposition of a number of layers of different metals.

multilayer parquet parquet strip flooring of matched lengths of plywood, chipboard, blockboard, etc. with a surface layer of hardwood veneer up to 5 mm thick; also called veneer parquet or veneered parquet.

multilayer parquet

multilevel development modern urban planning in which various activities such as vehicular and pedestrian circulation, commerce, dwellings, utility services, etc. are segregated and located on different vertical levels.

multi-ply plywood consisting of more than three layers or plies.

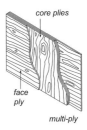

core plies

face ply

multi-ply

multipurpose plaster plaster which may be applied to a number of different backgrounds.

multistorey building, block; any building with a number of storeys, usually more than three, divided into separate flats, offices, etc. according to building usage.

multi-tile roofing see metal multi-tile roofing.

Munich lake see carmine.

munnion see mullion.

muntin 1 an upright frame member or bar, especially a subsidiary vertical frame member between the stiles of a panelled or glazed door leaf.
2 see mullion.

muntin and plank construction a form of traditional timber wall construction in which heavy horizontal planks or boards are laid between a series of slotted posts at intervals.

muntin and plank construction

mural, wall painting; a large-scale decorative painting or artwork for the wall of a building, especially that such as fresco applied directly to a wall surface.

muscovite a white variety of mica, a potassium aluminium silicate mineral.

mushroom slab, flat slab; a beamless flat concrete slab used with concrete columns which have thickenings at their upper ends, so named because the columns resemble mushrooms.

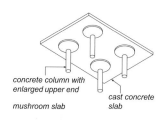

concrete column with enlarged upper end

mushroom slab

cast concrete slab

mutule in classical architecture, one of a number of projecting blocks on the underside of a corona, above a triglyph in a Doric pediment; Latin form is mutulus (plural mutuli).

N

nail **1** a slender-shafted metal fastener driven in with a hammer to fix one component to another, relying on friction as a means of attachment; types included as separate entries are listed below:

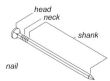

nail

*annular nail; *bullet-head nail, see lost-head nail; *clout, clout nail; *concrete nail, see masonry nail; *convex head roofing nail; *copper nail; *corrugated fastener; *cut nail; *double headed nail; *dowel nail; *duplex nail, see double headed nail; *felt nail, see clout; *finishing nail, see lost-head nail; *forged nail; *form nail, formwork nail, see double headed nail; *French nail, see round wire nail; *gang nail, see nail plate; *improved nail, see annular nail; *jagged-shank nail, see annular nail; *lost-head nail; *masonry nail; *nipple head nail, see convex head roofing nail; *oval brad head nail, see brad; *oval wire nail; *pin; *plasterboard nail; *plug nail; *ring-shanked nail, see annular nail; *roofing nail; *round nail; *round wire nail; *scaffold nail, see double headed nail; *screw nail; *sleeved nail; *springhead roofing nail, see convex head roofing nail; *square twisted shank flat head nail, see screw nail; *staple, U-pin; *trenail; *upholstery nail, see upholstery tack; *wiggle nail, see corrugated fastener; *wire nail; *wrought nail, see forged nail.
2 see gutta.

nail claw, cat's paw, nail puller; a screwdriver-like hand tool whose blade is forked and bent; used for removing nails from wood.

nailed joint a timber joint in which the members are held together with nails.

nail float, devil float; a plastering hand float whose face has a series of projecting nails or spikes; used for scraping the plaster surface to make a key for the following coat.

nail float

nail gun a power tool which fires nails into surfaces to be fixed, operated by compressed air or electricity; see framing gun, bradder.

nail hammer a hammer used for driving nails, with a round flat face and claw.

nailhead **1** the flat or bulging shaped end of a nail, by which it is driven.
2 an ornamental motif consisting of a series of pyramid-shaped protrusions, resembling the heads of hand-forged nails; a nailhead moulding is a moulding decorated with nailhead ornament.

nailhead moulding

nailing the fixing of timber and other members with nails.

nailed joint held fast by angled nails (skew nailing)

nailing block see nog.

nail plate, gang nail, toothed plate fastener, truss plate; a toothed metal plate used for joining two timbers in the same plane; especially used in the manufacture of timber roof trusses.

nail plate

nail puller see nail claw.

nail set, nail punch; a pointed metal rod used as a base for hammering nails beneath a surface, to avoid damage by the hammer face to the surface material.

naphthol carbamide a bluish-red semi-transparent pigment, invented in 1921, suitable for use in printing.

naphthol red a bright red organic pigment used in watercolours, acrylics and oil paints.

Naples yellow, antimony yellow, brilliant yellow, jaune brilliant, jaune d'antimoine; a highly poisonous heavy semi-opaque yellow pigment consisting of lead antimonite; an ancient pigment much used by painters.

narrow grained, narrow ringed see close grained.

native green natural chrome oxide, formerly used as a pigment.

natural aggregate aggregate found naturally or ground from natural minerals.

natural anhydrite the mineral anhydrite occurring in natural deposits in the earth.

natural brown iron oxide see burnt sienna.

natural convection see free convection.

natural draught burner, atmospheric burner; a gas heating appliance whose burner is provided with air at atmospheric pressure.

natural draught flue system a flue system in which draught is produced by heat from combustion.

natural exhaust in mechanical ventilation, the forced removal of stale air from a building through vents using internal pressure caused by the introduction of supply air.

natural fibre a general name for both animal and vegetable fibres.

natural gas naturally occurring gas consisting mainly of methane produced by the decay of living organisms, extracted from beneath the ground or sea bed; used for combustion, especially in gas heating.

natural gypsum, gypsum rock; the mineral gypsum which can be found in natural deposits in the earth's crust.

naturalized plant any species of plant which does not naturally grow wild in a certain habitat, but is introduced and able to thrive and reproduce there.

natural light in lighting design, light which comes through windows, rooflights or openings directly or indirectly from the sun; cf. artificial lighting.

natural pigment see earth colour.

natural resin a group of soft or hard oleoresins, hardened exudations from trees which have been refined by polymerization and other treatments.

natural rock asphalt a mixture of naturally occurring aggregate or crushed rock and bitumen, often found as sedimentary rock whose voids contain bitumen; see lake asphalt.

natural rubber rubber which has been produced from latex tapped from a rubber tree.

natural stone stone which has been quarried, cut, shaped and dressed for use in the construction industry; cf. artificial stone.

natural stone block any shaped, squared or dressed block of natural stone used in construction; nowadays usually as facing, walling, etc.; see dimension stone, ashlar.

natural stone cladding external cladding in sheets or blocks of natural stone, hung from a wall frame or structure.

natural stone cladding for concrete wall, showing fixings (holdfasts) held in rails attached to the concrete

natural stone facing external facing in natural stone, fixed to a wall frame or structure; often the same as natural stone cladding.

natural stone flooring see stone flooring.

natural stone paver, flagstone a flat rectangular paving stone made from cut or shaped natural stone; see also cobble, pebble, sett, cube.

natural stone paving see stone paving, stone block paving.

natural ventilation the ventilation of internal spaces of a building by natural convective movement of air via ducts, chimneys and openable windows without the use of mechanical plant.

nave the main longitudinal space of a church, cathedral, basilica, etc.; the body of a church between the west end and crossing.

Naxian base a classical column base which is a simple stone block without mouldings, on which the fluted column rests.

Naxian base, Delphi, Greece, c. 570 BC

NBR nitrile rubber.

neat grout, cement grout, neat cement grout; a grout consisting of a mixture of a hydraulic binder such as cement and water, without fine aggregate or sand.

neat gypsum plaster plaster produced from the mineral gypsum, with no added aggregate or sand.

neat size see dressed size.

nebule moulding an ornamental Norman moulding consisting of a raised undulating line with a sunken lower edge; also written as nebulé or nebuly.

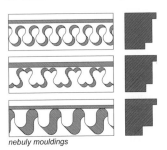

nebuly mouldings

neck 1 the thin part of a chisel blade, which separates the handle from the cutting edge.
2 the thinning behind the bell or striking face of a hammerhead.
3 the part of the shank behind the flat head of a nail.
4 shank; the square protrusion on the underside of the head of a coach bolt or other similar fastener which prevents it from turning.

neck

5 in log jointing, the notched thinning at the extremity of a log to receive another log.
6 see necking.

necking a narrow moulding at the top of the shaft of some classical columns, separating it from the capital; see also trachelion.

needle file a small, fine-toothed and thin-bladed hand tool used for the accurate filing, smoothing and grinding of metalwork.

needle-punch carpet a thin carpet made by mechanically punching an array of fibres into a supporting backing sheet.

negative pressure ventilation see extract ventilation.

negotiated contract a form of building contract between a client and a single chosen contractor in which terms and financial matters are discussed and agreed beforehand, without recourse to a tendering procedure.

neoclassicism an architectural style in Europe from the late 1700s and 1800s characterized by the use of monumental forms, strict adherence to the classical orders, and refinement of detail; see also Adam style, Empire style, Palladianism, Regency style.

neoclassical window with pediment

neodymium oxide lamp, daylight lamp, full-spectrum lamp; a standard lamp whose bulb is made of glass containing neodymium oxide, which causes the characteristic purplish hue in the glass and counteracts the adverse colour rendering of its otherwise yellow light.

neo-Gothic architecture any architecture which makes abundant use of Gothic motifs and elements, usually referring to architecture appearing in the late 1800s and 1900s.

neon tube a high-voltage fluorescent lamp which does not require a heated cathode, with a low light level meaning it is usually used for signs and advertising; usually contains neon, an inert gaseous chemical element, Ne; in general, any cold cathode lamp.

neoprene a synthetic rubber with good resistance to oils and solvents, used for seals, roofing and gaskets; a trade name for chloroprene rubber.

nephrite a hard greenish mineral, often cut for decoration as jade.

nest of saws a saw with several interchangeable saw blades which can be used at different times in the same handle.

net vault a vault whose ribs are arranged in an overlapping pattern, giving the impression of a net or mesh of rectangular or lozenge-shaped openings.

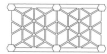

net vault of the Holy Cross Cathedral in Schwäbisch Gmünd, 1491

neutral chemically neither acid nor alkali; in colour science, without strong or marked colour.
neutral axis a line, plane or surface within a structural member in bending, which is neither in tension nor compression, nor does it undergo deformation.
neutral pressure, neutral stress see pore-water pressure.

newbuild a generic term for the design and construction of new buildings as opposed to refurbishment or amendments to existing ones.

newel a post used to support a stair balustrade at either end; the central post onto which the steps in a circular stair are fixed; also called a newel post.

newton abb. **N**; the SI basic unit of force, equal to that required to give a mass of one kilogram an acceleration of one metre per second per second; $1\,N = 1\,kg \cdot m/s^2$; at the earth's surface, the gravitational force acting on a mass of 1 kg is 9.8 N, approximated to 10 N for many purposes.
newton-metre see joule.

nib, cog; a projection at the upper end of a roof tile which, when laid, hooks over a roof batten to provide a secure fastening.

niche a recess within the thickness of a wall, usually for an ornament or artifact; see also aedicule.

nickel a whitish metal, **Ni**, used in alloys and for the protective coating of steel; it also improves the toughness of high-chrome steel.
nickel azo yellow see green gold.
nickel brass see German silver.
nickel plated referring to metals which have been treated with a thin protective coat of nickel.
nickel silver a hard and ductile alloy of copper and zinc with additional nickel to improve corrosion resistance.
nickel steel an alloy of steel containing nickel and carbon, with superior properties to those of carbon steel.

nicker see splitter.

niello a black mixture of sulphur, silver and lead or copper used to fill engravings in silver and other metals; the decorative product thus formed.

nine inch wall see one-brick wall.

niobium a grey metallic chemical element, **Nb**, used in alloys and as a superconductor; occasionally known as columbium.

nipple see hexagonal nipple.
nipple head nail see convex head roofing nail.

nit abb. **nt**; the SI basic unit of luminance equal to one candela per square metre, cd/m^2.

nitch a bundle of combed wheat reed used as a basic roofing material in thatching; see also bunch.

nitrate green a blue variety of chrome green pigment.

nitric acid a yellowish, corrosive, chemical compound, **HNO_3**, used in the manufacture of explosives and fertilizers.

nitriding in metallurgy, the hardening of a steel surface by heating it in an atmosphere of ammonia and hydrogen to produce a very hard corrosion-resistant surface layer.

nitrile rubber, NBR; a resilient oilproof synthetic polymer manufactured from acrylonitrile and butadiene; used for seals, hoses, joints and storage vessels.

nitrocellulose lacquer a highly inflammable varnish used as a transparent finish for wood, made from treating cellulose with nitric acid.

node see panel point.

nodular cast iron, spheroidal cast iron; a ductile form of cast iron produced by special heat treatment of normal cast iron.

no-fines concrete lightweight concrete consisting of coarse aggregate and cement, without sand or fine aggregate.

nog, 1 wooden brick, wooden block, fixing block, nailing block; a small piece of timber used like a brick, especially one built into brickwork as a nailing base in masonry.
2 see nogging.

nogging 1 in traditional timber frame construction, masonry infill for a timber stud frame; see brick nogging, flint nogging, stone nogging.
2 in traditional timber frame construction, short horizontal timber struts inserted between adjacent uprights, posts, studs, rafters or joists to provide lateral support; cross nogging, see herringbone strutting.

noise 1 sound in an environment which is made up of all frequencies with no regular pattern.
2 in acoustics, unwanted or disturbing sound.
3 interference; in an electronic or telecommunications system, interference caused by the obscuring action of an unwanted signal.

noise control the careful planning of buildings and measures therein taken to reduce the amount of unwanted sound in spaces, achieved by the use of isolating construction and the addition of absorbing material to surfaces.

noise control glass see sound control glass.

noise level in acoustics, the measure of undesired or overloud sound level.

noise pollution sound from external sources, such as traffic, loud music, etc., which causes a nuisance to those in nearby buildings or the immediate environment.

noise reduction in acoustics, reducing the sound pressure level or amount of unwanted noise between two adjoining spaces using careful planning, insulation and absorption.

noise reduction coefficient in acoustics, a measure of the sound absorption of a material or component, measured over a range of frequencies.

noise reduction glass see sound control glass.

nominal cover the specified thickness of concrete designed to cover reinforcing bars in reinforced concrete.

nominal dimension, nominal size; the size by which a component or material is specified; in reality it may be smaller or larger than this by an agreed tolerance.

nominated subcontractor a subcontractor who has been appointed by the client, or their representative; a nominated sub-contract is a sub-contract in which the client selects the contractor.

non-bearing wall see non-loadbearing wall.

non-combustible in fire testing, referring to a material which, under specified test conditions, can be considered not to burn.

non-conductive see insulating.

non-destructive testing the physical and chemical testing of materials and components in such a way that they are in an unaltered state after testing.

nondrying oil a range of oils extracted from vegetable products, used in paints to add flexibility and reduce the speed of drying.

non-fixed furnishing in interior design, furnishings such as tables, chairs, mats, curtains, etc. which can be moved around or easily removed.

non-fixed luminaire a light fitting such as a table lamp or lamp stand not designed to be fixed to the building fabric.

non-loadbearing partition see lightweight partition.

non-loadbearing wall, non-bearing wall; any internal or external wall in a building which supports only its own weight, including fittings and wind loads, and which does not have a structural role.

non-mortised hinge, non-mortise butt hinge, surface-fixed hinge; a hinge with one flap shaped to fit in a cut out in the other, which, when closed, has the thickness of one flap only. See illustration on facing page.

non-mortised hinge

non-plastic soil any granular soil type with a plasticity index of zero, or one for which a plasticity index cannot be determined.

non-return valve see check valve.

non-setting glazing compound a glazing compound which deforms plastically and remains in a semi-liquid state.

non-slip a treatment or fixing for floors and stairs in which the surface is roughened or profiled to provide friction on otherwise potentially slippery areas.

non-slip tile a ceramic tile manufactured with raised mouldings, grooves or a rough textured surface, designed for use at pool edges, stair nosings, etc.

non-slip tile

non-standard referring to any manufactured product or component which deviates from the usual standard form; usually requiring special manufacture.

non-vibration concrete see self-placing concrete.

Norfolk reed see best reed.

norm, standard; an officially recognized exemplary standard of measurement, quality, regulative legislation or classification.

normalizing a heat treatment to refine grain size and increase the strength of steel by heating to a certain temperature and rapidly cooling in air; normalized steel is a fine-grained, homogeneous, weldable steel which has been heat-treated by normalizing.

Norman architecture, Anglo-Norman architecture; religious architecture in England after the Norman conquest in 1066, characterized by sparing use of detail, bulky forms and the round arch; known on the continent as Romanesque architecture.

wheel window from the Norman church of St. Mary, Patrixbourne, Kent, England, 1170

Norman arch a round arch with a highly ornate archivolt, as found in Norman architecture.

northern red oak [*Quercus rubra*], see oak.

northlight roof a sawtooth roof with north facing glazed lights used for overhead illumination of industrial buildings in the northern hemisphere.

northlight shell roof a northlight roof in which the curved bands of roof between vertical lights are half barrel vaulted concrete shell structures.

Norway spruce [*Picea abies, Picea excelsa*], see spruce.

Noryl a proprietary name for polyphenylene oxide plastic.

nose see nosing.

nose line, nosing line see line of nosings.

nosing, nose; a horizontal protrusion of a stair tread beyond the riser.

nosing tile an L-shaped ceramic tile fitting designed for use at the front edge of a step.

nosing tile

no-slump concrete stiff concrete whose test sample exhibits very little slump.

notch 1 in timber frame construction and jointing, a small cutting made in the side of a framing member in order to fasten or stiffen a joint.

2 in log construction, the carefully hewn and crafted joint formed by cutting into overlaid crosswise logs so that they interlock with one another at the external corner of a log building.

notched joint 1 a timber joint in which a notch is made in one piece in order to fasten it in position; usually used for the fastening of joists on a wall plate or beam.

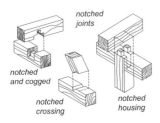

notched joints

notched and cogged

notched crossing

notched housing

2 in timber frame construction, a crossing joint in which one or both members have a recess or notch cut to receive the other.
3 see notch (log construction).
double notched joint a timber crossing joint in which the faces of both members are cut with notches to receive each other.
notched and cogged joint a timber notched joint in which a cog is cut into the receiving member to further fasten the joint.
notched housed joint in timber frame construction, a housed timber joint which has a notch cut in the end of one member for stiffening purposes.
notched lap joint a timber lap joint which has a notch in the lap and recess to strengthen the joint.
single notched joint, trenched joint; a timber crossing joint in which the face of one member is cut with a notch or groove to receive a second member.

notched trowel a plasterer's trowel whose blade has a castellated edge to provide the plaster coat with a striated texture.

notch effect in structures, a local build-up of stress at the point in a member where it turns through a sharp angle, or is notched.

notching saw see grooving saw.

notice 1 a written announcement of intent by a client, contractor or local authority informing of an action which is being undertaken, or which should be carried out.

2 the announcement by one of the parties to a contract that it is to be terminated after a specific period of time.

notice to proceed in contract administration, a written announcement by a client to a contractor informing of the duration and starting dates of construction work.

nozzle 1 the perforated outlet of a water or gas-fed appliance such as a tap or shower which controls flow and direction.
2 see spout.
3 see jet inlet.

nulled ornament see gadroon.

nut 1 a hexagonal, octagonal or square fastener with a threaded hole to receive a bolt; types of nut included as separate entries are listed below:
*acorn nut, see cap nut; *backnut; *butterfly nut, see wing nut; *cap nut; *castellated nut, castle nut; *dome nut, see cap nut; *hexagonal nut, hex nut; *lock nut; *seal nut; *square nut; *stop nut; *thumb nut; *wing nut.

hex   *lock*   *castellated*

round   *flat*   *square*

cap   *seal*   *wing*

types of nut

2 the seeds of various fruit-bearing trees, used as a source of food and pressed for oils used in some paints; these trees are often used for fine timberwork; see walnut, hazel, nut oil.
nut oil various types of drying oils used as vehicles in paints, pressed from the dried kernels of nuts such as the walnut; see hazelnut oil, walnut oil.

nylon any of a number of tough, whitish, durable polyamide thermoplastics used to produce fibres, hardware, coatings and garden furniture.

Nyssa spp. see tupelo.

O

oak [*Quercus spp.*] a group of tough, hard, heavy hardwoods of the temperate climates ranging in colour from light tan to pink or brown; used in construction and decoration, for interiors,

Quercus spp.
–oak

flooring, boat-building, plywood and raw cork (produced from bark of the cork oak, *Quercus suber*); ancient oaks are an essential part of many British and European rural landscapes; see below.

American white oak [*Quercus alba*] one of a number of similar species of North American hardwood used for flooring and other hardwearing applications.

bog oak ordinary oak which has been immersed in ponds, rivers, wet land, etc. for up to a hundred years, whose wood has a blackish hue and is valued in turnery.

durmast oak, sessile oak; [*Quercus petraea*]; a species of European oak tree with heavy, hard and strong pale brown timber marketed as European or English oak.

European oak, English oak; [*Quercus robur, Quercus petraea*] species of European hardwood with heavy, hard and strong pale brown timber; used in traditional timber construction as framing, and nowadays for joinery, flooring, veneers and furniture.

Indian oak see teak.

Japanese oak [*Quercus mongolica*] an Asian hardwood with relatively durable pale yellow timber; used in construction, for furniture and in boat-building.

pedunculate oak, common oak; [*Quercus robur*]; a European hardwood with heavy, hard and strong pale brown timber marketed as European or English oak.

red oak [*Quercus spp.*] a group of hardwoods, especially the northern red oak, *Quercus rubra*, from eastern North America with light reddish-brown timber which is relatively hard, heavy, strong, coarse-grained and used for external cladding and interiors.

white oak [*Quercus spp.*] a group of hardwoods from North America, especially the American white oak, *Quercus alba*, with heavy durable timber which is grey to reddish-brown; used for flooring, panelling and trim.

oakum a stuffing for sealing and packing horizontal joints in log buildings and wooden ships made from hemp, old rope or other fibrous material.

obeche, samba, African whitewood, wawa, ayous; [*Triplochiton scleroxylon*] a West African hardwood whose light porous timber is pale brown to white; used for interior joinery and plywood.

obelisk an Egyptian monolithic four-sided standing stone, tapering to a pyramidical cap, often inscribed with hieroglyphs and erected as a monument.

obelisk of Senuseret I, Heliopolis, Egypt, 1965–1920 BC

oblique, skew; referring to a line, plane or building orientation at an angle to a major alignment or axis.

oblique butt joint a longitudinal timber butt joint in which the ends of one or both are splayed so that the members are at an angle to one another.

oblique projection a parallel projection drawing in which the projectors are parallel but intersect the projection plane at an angle other than a right angle; one face of an object is thus drawn in true proportion, parallel to the picture plane, and the other axes are represented by extending oblique lines; see cavalier, cabinet, military projections.

oblique shake one of a series of cracks running across the grain of a timber board at an angle. See illustrations on following page *oblique shakes in improperly seasoned timber*

oblique tenon joint a mortise and tenon joint used when joining two timbers at an oblique angle to one another.

obscurance see translucency.

obscured glass translucent glass of which one face has a diffuse surface produced by sandblasting, grinding, etching or acid embossing; see also reeded glass.

observation lift, scenic lift; a glazed lift for hotel foyers, shopping centers, etc., designed to offer a view to the surrounding area.

obsidian a form of dark, compact, naturally occurring volcanic glass, traditionally used for weapons and tools, now used for ornament.

occupant one permanently resident in a dwelling, or renting space in a building.

occupant load in fire safety, a specified total number of occupants per floor area of building space.

ochre, ocher (Am); a group of earth pigments, hydrated iron oxides with added clay, which range in colour from yellow to orange-red or brown; suitable for use in all types of paint; types included as separate entries are listed below:
*brown ochre; *gold ochre; *red ochre, see red oxide paint; *Roman ochre, yellow ochre; *sil, yellow ochre.

Ochroma spp. see balsa wood.

octopartite vault a masonry vault sprung on eight points of support, octagonal or rectangular in plan and composed of eight curved roof surfaces.

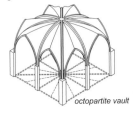

octopartite vault

oculus, plural oculi; Lat.; a circular opening or rooflight in a roof or dome, especially that in a Roman building; see roundel.

odd leg calliper see jenny leg calliper.

offer see bid.

offset handle see cranked pull handle.

offset match, half drop; a condition of patterned wallpaper which should be hung with adjacent lengths staggered vertically so that horizontal patterns match.

offset screwdriver a screwdriver whose bit and handle are not aligned; used for tightening screws in cramped positions, or for those requiring extra leverage.

off-white, broken white, faux blanc; a shade of white which has been slightly tinted with another colour, most often grey or yellow, to reduce its intensity or sterility.

ogee a continuous double curve, shaped like a shallow letter 'S'.

ogee arch, inflected arch; an arch whose intrados is composed of two mirrored ogees which meet at an apex; see depressed ogee arch (two-centred ogee arch), bell arch (reverse ogee arch).

ogee arch

ogee brace in traditional timber-framed construction, a naturally S-shaped curved timber member used to brace the junction between a post and beam.

ogee moulding a decorative moulding whose cross-section is that of an ogee or S-shaped profile, the concave part uppermost; called a cyma recta in classical architecture; see also reverse ogee moulding, cyma reversa.

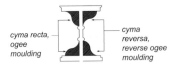

cyma recta, ogee moulding

cyma reversa, reverse ogee moulding

ogee roof an ornamental roof form which is ogee-shaped in cross-section.

ogee stop in ornamentation, the termination of a chamfered moulding or carving with a shallow S-shaped form.

ogival, lancet; a pointed arch; pertaining to Gothic architecture, as named by the French ('l'architecture ogival' or 'le style ogival').

ogive see diagonal rib.

ohm abb.; the SI unit of electrical resistance, equal to that which will produce a current of 1 amp when a potential difference of 1 volt is passed across a resistor.

oil any greasy liquid, insoluble in water, obtained from animal, vegetable and mineral sources and used for lubrication, energy production, etc.; types included as separate entries are listed below:
*anthracene oil; *asphalt oil, see road oil; *blown linseed oil; *boiled linseed oil; *carbolic oil; *China wood oil, see tung oil; *clove oil, see oil of cloves; *cottonseed oil; *creosote oil, see creosote; *crude oil, see petroleum; *diesel oil; *drying oil; *essential oil, volatile oil; *fatty oil, fixed oil; *fixed oil, see fatty oil; *form oil, see mould oil; *fuel oil; *gas oil; *hempseed oil; *lemon oil, see oil of lemon; *lavender oil, oil of spike; *linseed oil; *middle oil, see carbolic oil; *mineral oil; *mould oil, form oil; *nondrying oil; *nut oil; *oil of cloves; *oil of lemon; *oil of spike, spike lavender; *oil of turpentine, see turpentine; *paraffin oil, see paraffin; *pine oil; *poppyseed oil, poppy oil; *road oil; *soya bean oil; *stand oil; *sun-bleached oil, sun-refined oil; *sunflower seed oil; *thyme oil; *tung oil, China wood oil; *volatile oil, see essential oil; *walnut oil.

oil-based referring to a paint, sealant, etc. whose medium is oil rather than water.

oil black a black pigment manufactured from the carbon deposits from burned oil.

oil burner a device in an oil heating system for converting fuel oil into a fine spray or vapour and igniting it.

oil-fired heating, oil heating; a heating system in which the fuel used is combustible oil.

oil green a light yellow green variety of chrome green pigment.

oil heating see oil-fired heating.

oil interceptor a chamber in a drainage system where water-bound oil from drained surface water is deposited to prevent it from passing further along a drain.

oil meter a device for measuring and recording the flow and consumption of oil in an oil heating system.

oil of cloves, clove oil; an essential oil distilled from the dried buds (cloves) of the tropical myrtle plant *Eugenia caryophyllata* [*Syzygium aromaticum*], traditionally used as a slow drying solvent in paints and varnishes and as an odour-masking agent.

oil of lemon, lemon oil; oil extracted from the fresh peel of lemons, traditionally used in paints and varnishes to mask odours.

oil of spike, spike lavender; an essential oil distilled from the leaves of the broad-leaved variety of lavender, *Lavandula spica*, traditionally used as a solvent in paints and varnishes.

oil of turpentine see turpentine.

oil of vitriol see sulphuric acid.

oil paint any paint whose binder is an oil such as linseed oil, poppy oil, etc., from which the solvent evaporates to leave a tough film; used for external joinery and furniture.

oil paste, colours in oil; a concentrated colour source consisting of pigment in an oil paste, used for tinting paints.

oil ring main see cold oil ring main.

oil stain a translucent colouring agent for porous surfaces such as timber, consisting of a dye suspended in oil.

oilstone a fine-grained stone used with lubricating oil to sharpen the honed blades of tools.

oil storage tank a large vessel or similar construction for the storage of oil, especially for an oil-fired heating system or other oil-fired installation.

oil varnish a glossy varnish containing oil and resin.

okoume see gaboon.

old woman's tooth see router plane.

Olea europaea see olive.

oleoresin, balsam; a thick viscous liquid exuded from certain conifers; used as a binder in some paints and as an additive to improve brushing and flexibility.
oleoresinous paint a traditional hard gloss paint containing oleoresin.

oleum white see lithopone.

olio d'abezzo see Strasbourg turpentine.

olive [*Olea europaea*] a Mediterranean evergreen hardwood with hard and heavy greeny-brown timber; used for joinery and turnery; a shade of dark grey-green which takes its name from the colour of fruit of this tree; also known as olive green.

omu [*Entandrophragma candollei*] a tropical West African hardwood sold as mahogany; it has pale reddish-brown timber and is used for plywood, veneered furniture and interiors.

one-and-a-half brick wall see brick-and-a-half wall.

one-brick wall, nine inch wall, whole-brick wall; a solid brick wall whose width is the length of one standard brick, 9" or 215 mm.

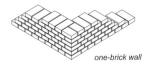
one-brick wall

one-coat plaster see single-coat plaster.

one-coat plasterwork see single-coat plasterwork.

one-component see one-pack.

one-family house a freestanding dwelling with living space for one family unit; see house.

one-pack, one-part, one-component; a description of products such as glues, sealants and paints which are supplied ready for use and do not require the addition of other components.

one-pipe system, single-pipe system; a central heating system in which each radiator is served by a circuit with one pipe, in which the heating water is piped from one to the next.

one-turn stairs, full-turn stairs; a stair which turns through 360° on its ascent, formed from straight flights which meet at corner landings.

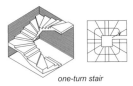
one-turn stair

one-way glass, mirror glass; glass treated on one side with a transparent reflective finish or with a laminate so as to appear see-through from one side and as a mirror on the other.

one-way head screw, clutch head screw, butterfly head screw; a screw whose head has a slot designed so that it may be tightened but not undone by a cross-slot or traditional screwdriver.

one-way slab a reinforced concrete slab whose reinforcement is designed primarily to span parallel supports in one direction.

one-way stick adhesive, single spread adhesive; an adhesive applied to only one of the surfaces to be joined.

onion dome an ogee-shaped dome resembling an onion, pointed at the top, found in Russian, Byzantine and some Baroque architecture; a common motif in Indian and other Asian architecture; also called a bulbous dome.

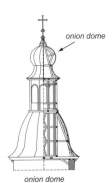
onion dome

onion dome

on-street parking see street parking.

onyx marble a pale brown or yellow banded calcareous rock used as decorative stonework in building, marketed as onyx.

oolite sedimentary rock, especially limestone, composed of spherical grains.

opacity, opaqueness, hiding power; a measure of the non-translucency of a paint; its ability to mask colours in coats beneath.

opal 1 a white or coloured mineral, an amorphous form of hydrated silica used for ornamentation, gemstones and jewellery.
2 satin; in artificial lighting, the classification of the bulb of a lamp whose inner surface is treated with a white silica coating producing stronger obscurance of the filament and better diffusion than with a pearl finish.

opal glass, opalescent glass; opaque or translucent diffuse glass with a milky coloured or white appearance, produced by laminating clear glass with an obscuring plastic sheet or by introducing fine obscuring particles into the glass itself.

opaline see milk glass.

opaque referring to a material, surface or construction which inhibits the passage of light.

opaque glass glass with a surface treatment or interlayer through which light does not penetrate, often used as cladding glass; see also coloured opaque glass, cladding glass.

opaqueness see opacity.

open balustrade a balustrade without infill between handrail and floor level; a railing.

open bar metal flooring metal flooring consisting of a grid of welded bars; used for maintenance platforms and walkways.

open bidding see open tendering.

open boarding see spaced boarding.

open caisson, cylinder caisson; a foundation caisson constructed in such a way so as to be open at both the top and bottom.

open capital see bell capital.

open ceiling 1 the underside of a timber roof or intermediated floor whose joists or beams are exposed from below.
2 a suspended ceiling of open baffles, mesh or grid, usually concealing luminaires and ventilation inlets; see cell ceiling, open mesh ceiling.

open cell ceiling see cell ceiling.

open eaves eaves which have no soffit board and are open from below.

open excavation an excavation requiring no shoring, open to the elements and often with sloping sides.

open face see loose side.

open grained see coarse textured.

open-hearth process, Siemens-martin process; a steelmaking process developed in the 1860s for producing steel on a large scale from scrap and pig iron; it utilizes hot gases to heat up the metal while removing unwanted carbon, manganese, silicon, phosphorus and sulphur.

opening a hole left or cut into a wall, floor or other component for the fitting of a door, window, hatch; if left open it is often called a void; see throat (damper opening), doorway (door opening), window opening.

opening face the side of a door leaf or window casement which opens away from the frame.

opening light a hinged or sliding part of a window unit or glazed screen which can be opened.

opening size a measure of fineness of a wire mesh, the open space between adjacent parallel wires; see mesh size.

open joint a construction joint left open between two adjacent components, without jointing compound, seals or covering.

open mesh ceiling a suspended ceiling system formed from rectangular mesh panels to allow for the passage of air and light from services located in the ceiling void.

open metal flooring metal flooring of perforated panels in or on a frame.

open mortise see slot mortise.
open mortise joint a mortise and tenon corner joint in which the mortise cut into the end of one piece is open on three

sides to receive a tenon in the other; often called a bridle joint.

open mortise joint

open piling the open stacking of timber or other wood products in layers, separated to allow for air circulation during seasoning and drying.

open plan a description of large open office space without permanent dividing walls.

open rise the open space between treads in a stair with no risers.
open riser stair, ladder stair, open rise stair, skeleton stair; a stair with no infill construction between its treads.

open riser stair

open roof, open timbered roof; pitched roof construction in which the roof structure or rafters are not concealed with a lining or ceiling and are visible from the space below.

open section a cold formed or cold pressed metal section which is not a hollow section; one bent or formed into an open shape.

open side see loose side.

open space areas between buildings or groups of buildings for recreational use; any public open urban land such as parks, gardens or squares on which no buildings have been constructed.

open stile balustrade a balustrade with a series of vertical parallel stiles between handrail and floor level to provide an intermediate barrier.

open tendering, open bidding (Am); a competitive tendering procedure in which any suitable firm or person can submit a tender for a building contract, usually as a result of a public announcement for calls to tender.

open tenon joint see bridle joint.

open timbered roof see open roof.

open time in painting and decorating, the time elapsed before a freshly painted surface has dried sufficiently for an adjacent coat to be painted next to it.

open tongue and groove boarding tongue and groove boards with rebated external edges to form longitudinal indents between adjacent laid boards.

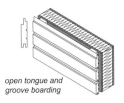

open tongue and groove boarding

operation manual a written document with specifications and a description of a particular appliance or piece of equipment, and instructions and advice for its use.

operative a skilled or semi-skilled person who carries out work on a site involving operating a machine.

Ophiostoma minus see blue stain fungus.

optical pertaining to the human eye, sight and vision, especially with regard to how it reacts to light.

optical fibre a very fine, high-quality glass tube in which light is used as a medium in telecommunications systems.

optical mixing in colour theory, the merging of small dots of colour to form different colours when viewed at a distance.

optical smoke detector, visible smoke detector; a fire detector which, using a photocell or other sensor, reacts to the disturbing effects on a light or laser beam as it passes through smoke from fire.

opus, pl. opera, work (Lat.); an artistic composition or pattern, especially as used in relation to Roman stonework.

orange vermilion a variety of cinnabar.

orangepeel, orange peeling; a defect in which a dry paint or lacquer finish has a dimpled surface resembling orange peel, caused by lack of solvent in the paint, or poor workmanship.

orant figure, orans figure; a standing figure with both arms raised in prayer, as found in Greek and Early Christian art and architectural ornamentation.

orbital sander a portable power tool with a rectangular sanding surface driven with a rapid oscillating action.

order 1 one of the predominating styles in classical architecture, a classical order; see Greek architecture, Roman architecture.
2 one of a series of projecting bands above the intrados of an arch making up an archivolt.

ordinary Portland cement, ordinary cement; a Portland cement, used in general construction, formed by mixing Portland cement clinker and calcium sulphate.

Oregon pine see Douglas fir.

organic 1 referring to a substance, a chemical compound of carbon, which is found in or derived from living organisms; with regard to plastics and polymeric products it denotes a carbon-based molecular structure in the material.
2 biogenic; of soil, some foodstuffs and other products, based on or manufactured using living organisms.
organic architecture architecture which seeks to physically, ecologically and environmentally unify buildings with their surrounding environment through careful planning, use of materials, form and technology.
organic coating see plastics coating, stove enamelling, powder coating.
organic rendering see masonry paint.
organic roof any roof whose roofing is of organic materials such as wood, bark, turf, planting, etc.
organic soil in ground engineering, soil containing decayed remnants of plants and animals, rich in organic material and with a poor bearing capacity.
organic solvent see solvent.
organic waste, biodegradable waste; waste material from industrial processes, residential establishments, etc. which is

organic and can be broken down with microbes.

organosol a dispersion of particles of a plastisol, resin or synthetic polymer in an organic solvent, which can be converted to a solid on heating; used for PVC coatings for roofing and other sheetmetal components.

oriel window, oriel; an upper storey window which protrudes from the elevational plane of a building; see bay window.

Orientalism any architectural style which borrows motifs from the Arab world, India and the Far East.

orientation, 1 direction; the angle that an object, main axis of a building or street makes with respect to due north.
2 the location of a building on its site and the arrangement of spaces therein so as to take into account the direction of sun and prevailing winds, views and disturbing factors according to the points of the compass.

oriented strand board, oriented structural board, OSB; a building board manufactured of layers of flakeboard glued together with the flakes or strands at right angles to those in adjacent layers.

oriented strand board

Orient yellow a variety of deep cadmium yellow pigment.

original a version of an architectural drawing or document, to which possible amendments are made and from which copies are taken for distribution.

Orlon a proprietary name for polyacrylonitrile plastics, used for fibres and textiles.

ornament two- or three-dimensional decoration, sculpture, carving, etc. for the surfaces or spaces of a building or other object.
ornamental bed an area of landscaped ground prepared and planted with plants and flowers as decoration.

ornamental brickwork see decorative masonry, patterned brickwork, polychrome brickwork.

ornamental motif, decorative motif; a design, pattern, sculpture, symbol, etc. used as surface decoration for the surface of a building or other object; often with specific meaning, message or symbolic value.

ornamental plaster moulding see fibrous plaster moulding.

ornamental plasterwork see fibrous plasterwork.

ornamental tile any roof, wall or floor tile with decorative profiled edges, embossing, patterns, etc.; especially a clay roof tile used for decorative eaves, verge or ridge embellishment.

ornamentation see enrichment.

orpiment a greasy, lemon yellow mineral, natural arsenic trisulphide, As_2S_3, used as the pigment king's yellow, for removing hair from animal skins and as a source of arsenic.

orthoclase see adularia, alkali feldspar, microcline, potash feldspar.

orthogonal relating to objects, axes, grids or lines which lie at right angles to one another; a line at right angles to an axis, line or plane.

orthogonal projection any projection drawing in which projectors meet the picture plane at right angles, producing a plan, elevation, side view, etc.; in practice the same as an orthographic projection.

orthographic projection a drawing which shows a surface or section drawn at scale as if from infinity, at right angles to the cutting plane or elevation; in architectural drawing the result is a plan, elevation or sectional drawing, though sometimes extended to include true axonometric projections; also called an orthogonal projection.

orthographic axonometric projection the fuller name for true isometric, dimetric and trimetric projections.

orthography the art of drawing parallel projections.

orthostat a large stone slab laid vertically in a structure or set in the ground, such as a prehistoric standing stone, a large stone in the lower part of a Greek temple or a decorated Mesopotamian monolith in the foundations or interior of a building.

orthotropic slab a reinforced concrete floor slab, such as a one-way slab, in which reinforcement in the direction of span is greater than that perpendicular to it.

OSB oriented strand board.

osier see with.

Osiris column an ancient Egyptian column carved in an image of Osiris with arms crossed; also known as an Osiris, Osirid, Osiride or Osirian pillar or column; Osiris was originally the corn god of the Nile Delta, later principal deity of the Old Kingdom; king and judge of the Underworld, depicted in mummy-dress wearing a crown of plant stems; brother of Isis, father of Horus; 'Asar' in Egyptian, 'Osiris' is Greek.

Osiris column at the Ramesseum, mortuary temple of Ramses II, Thebes, Egypt, 1279–1213 BC

ostrum see Tyrian purple.

Ostrya carpinifolia see European hop-hornbeam.

oundy moulding, swelled chamfer, undy moulding, wave moulding; an ornamental motif consisting of a series of lines representing the breaking of waves.

oundy moulding

outdoor furniture see garden furniture.

outer glazing see external glazing.

outer leaf the outer skin of masonry in a brick cavity wall or other sandwich construction; see external leaf.

outer ply in plywood, the surface layer or veneer.

outer sash the sash of a coupled window facing the exterior of a building.

outer surface, external surface, exterior; the surface of a component or construction which faces outwards, or towards the open air.

outflow heater a device for preheating oil from a storage tank to reduce its viscosity prior to use as fuel in an oil heating installation.

outlet 1 a component through which water drains off a level roof or paved surface, etc. into a drain; a gully; see below for types included as separate entries:
*floor outlet, (see floor drain); *gully; *rainwater outlet, roof outlet; *rainwater spout.
2 drain, waste; the point at which an appliance or sanitary fixing is connected to a drainage system; a drainage outlet.
3 a component through which fresh air is introduced to a space, or stale air, smoke, etc. extracted from it; see below for types included as separate entries:
*air outlet, see supply air terminal unit; *exhaust outlet; *fire vent; *smoke outlet.
4 the point at which a connection can be made to a service or public utility provided to a building; see below for types included as separate entries:
*socket outlet; *spray outlet; *telecommunications outlet; *water outlet.

outlet grating 1 see outlet strainer, wire balloon.
2 see domical grating.

outlet strainer a wire balloon, grating or other device placed over a roof gulley or rainwater outlet to prevent the passage of leaves and other detritus into the drainage system.

outline 1 the bounding line of a two-dimensional image, object or shape.
2 a preliminary sketch or initial version of a design, plan, scheme or document.

outline drawing see sketch drawing.

outline planning permission planning permission for a development granted in principle, without official status and subject to approval of further details of siting, planning or external appearance.

outline programme, tender programme; a proposed programme of work and programme chart sometimes submitted by contractors who are tendering for a project.

outside air, external air; in heating and ventilation design, the air surrounding a building, whose temperature and moisture content have an effect on the internal temperature of a building, and which is introduced as fresh air for ventilation, air-conditioning and cooling systems.

outside calliper an instrument for measuring the outside diameter of pipes and other round objects, consisting of a pair of curved hinged legs.

outside corner trowel see external angle trowel.

outside face the face of a piece of sawn timber which is furthest from the heart when cut from a log.

outside glazing glass or other glazing products which have been added to the outer surface of external glazing.

outward opening referring to a window casement or door which opens outwards with respect to the exterior of a building.

oval brad head nail see brad.

oval head screw, raised countersunk screw, oval countersunk screw; a countersunk screw with a convex head which protrudes above the surface into which it is fixed.

oval head screw

oval knot a knot in seasoned timber which has been cut at an angle to the branch and is thus oval in shape.

oval wire nail a slender nail with an oval shank 13–150 mm in length and a small bulging head.

overall dimension, overall size; the largest measurement of an object in any direction; see also external dimension.

overall programme a diagrammatic scheme produced by a main contractor indicating the various jobs of work on site pertaining to a building project, their scope, sequencing of construction, and proposed duration.

overall size see overall dimension.

overcloak the upper overlapping part of a folded sheetmetal roofing seam or welt, which covers an undercloak.

overconsolidated a description of soils, especially clays, which are in a state of compression caused by previous loading from overlying ground, buildings, etc., which are subsequently removed or demolished.

overcurrent a current in an electric circuit exceeding the rated value.

overflow 1 the escape of liquid from a vessel which is too full.
2 an opening in the side of a basin or other vessel, usually with a suitable fitting, through which water can escape into a drain if the water level rises too high; see weir overflow.
overflow pipe a drainage pipe connected to a basin or other vessel to lead water into a drain to avoid water flooding over the rim of the vessel.

overgrainer a paintbrush with groups of soft fibres tied in a row of bundles; used in decorative graining to imitate the shaped grain of hardwoods.

overhand struck joint see struck joint.

overhang see projection.

overhead clearance see headroom.

overhead door a door which runs on vertical tracks and, when open, is stored in position above the door opening; see also up and over door; sectional overhead door; roller shutter.

overhead door

overhead door closer a door closer designed to be mounted to the door head and the upper edge of the door leaf.

overhead heating downward radiant heating provided by heating panels hung high in a space.

overhead shutter a lightweight shutter designed to provide night security at open shop fronts, often of lattice construction and contained in a recess or overhead or side space when not in use.

overlaid plywood plywood whose face plies have been coated with an overlay such as paper, plastics, resins, metal, etc.

overlap 1 see lap.
2 a defect in veneering and plywood caused by the overlapping of two adjacent veneers.

overlap and double cut in wallpapering, a method of ensuring even vertical butt joints by overlapping adjacent sheets then cutting through with a knife.

overlay flooring prefabricated pre-finished panels or proprietary interlocking wood strips designed to be laid directly onto a structural floor slab; see parquet strip.

overload a structural load greater than that for which a structural system or member is designed.

overload current an electric current which exceeds the rated value without damaging an electric circuit.

overload trip, trip switch; a switch in a circuit which turns off electric current in the event of dangerously high levels or surges which may damage equipment and appliances.

overpainting see repainting.

overrun a space at the top of a lift shaft to allow for inaccuracies of control and to accommodate necessary apparatus.

ovolo moulding 1 a decorative convex moulding, semi-elliptical in cross-section.

ovolo moulding

2 a quadrant moulding found at the internal junction of perpendicular planar surfaces.

oxidation the reaction of chemical elements with oxygen; see also oxidization.
oxidation tank see aeration tank.
oxidative drying a process of drying of paints and coatings in which the evaporation of contained solvents is followed by chemical reaction between the binder and oxygen in the surrounding air.

oxide a chemical compound formed when an element reacts with oxygen; oxides included as separate entries are listed below:
*aluminium oxide, see alumina; *black iron oxide, see iron oxide; *brown iron oxide, see burnt sienna; *calcium oxide; *carbon monoxide; *cobalt oxide, see black oxide of cobalt; *chromium oxide green; *dioxide; *emerald chromium oxide, see viridian; *ferric oxide, see iron oxide; *ferrous ferric oxide, see iron oxide; *ferrous oxide, see iron oxide; *hydrogen peroxide; *hydroxide; *natural brown iron oxide, see burnt sienna; *polyphenylene oxide; *red iron oxide, see iron oxide; *trioxide; *zinc oxide; *zirconium oxide.*

oxide of chromium see chromium oxide green.

oxide red, Indian red, Persian red, Venetian red; a range of red pigments manufactured by the oxidation of ferrous salts.

oxidization a process whereby a compound, metal, etc. is brought in contact with oxygen, activating an oxidation reaction.

oxidized bitumen see blown bitumen.

oxychloride cement, magnesite cement, sorel cement; a hard, strong cement of calcined magnesite and magnesium oxychloride with an aggregate filler; used for hardwearing in-situ floor surfacing.

oxygen trim a method of controlling the air/fuel ratio fed into a gas or oil burner according to the proportion of oxygen measured in flue gases.

P

PA polyamide.

PA-system public address system.

Pacific red cedar [*Thuja plicata*] western red cedar, see thuja.

package deal see design and construct contract.

packing piece see glazing block.

padauk [*Pterocarpus spp.*] a group of hardwoods from Africa and Asia with red or purple-brown streaked timber; used in cabinetmaking and veneers.

padding, cushioning; soft or resilient material used as a base in furnishings, as protection in packing or to dissipate vibrations from heavy plant.

paddle mixer see rotating pan mixer.

pad foundation, column footing, isolated footing; a precast or in-situ rectangular block foundation of reinforced concrete which transmits vertical point loads such as those from columns to the underlying ground.

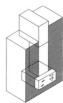

pad foundation

padlock a small detachable lock with a fastening ring, openable with a key.

*padlock and
padlock eye*

padlock eye one of a pair of perforated metal plates attached to the edge of a

hinged door and its frame, enabling it to be secured with a padlock.

pad saw a small saw with a thin tapering blade used for cutting curves or holes; see keyhole saw.

pagoda a multistorey Buddhist temple with projecting roofs at storey level, often replicated in Europe in the 1800s as an ornamental pavilion in gardens and parks.

*pagoda at the West
temple precinct,
Horyu-ji, Nara, Japan
700 AD; elevation and
section*

pain threshold see threshold of pain.

paint a liquid substance used for providing a protective or decorative surface coating, consisting of a pigment and a binder which sets or is treated to form a resistant film.

paint binder the component of paint which forms film and produces a bond to the surface being painted.

paintbrush a hand-held implement used for applying paint, consisting of fibres, bristles or hairs bound to a wooden or plastic handle, available in a range of widths, shapes and sizes; types included as separate entries are listed below:
*distemper brush; *dragger, see flogger; *dusting brush; *flat brush; *flat varnish brush; *flat wall brush, see flat brush; *flogger; lettering brush; *liner, lining brush; *overgrainer; *paint pad; *paint roller, see roller; *radiator brush; *rigger brush, rigger; round brush; *script brush; *scrubbing brush; *varnish brush, see flat varnish brush; *wall brush, see flat brush.*

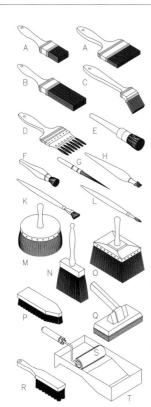

A   *flat brush, flat varnish brush*
B   *flogger, dragger*
C   *radiator brush*
D   *overgrainer, grainer*
E   *round brush*
F   *dabber, stencil brush*
G   *rigger brush*
H   *lining tool, liner*
K   *lettering brush, fitch*
L   *script brush*
M   *liming or whitewashing brush*
N   *softener, blender*
O   *distemper brush*
P   *scrubbing brush*
Q   *paint pad*
R   *dusting brush*
S   *paint roller*
T   *roller tray, paint tray*

painter a tradesman or skilled labourer who does painting work in buildings.

painter's and decorator's a commercial service which specializes in the painting and decorating of buildings and parts of buildings.

painter's putty in painting and decorating, linseed oil putty used as a filler by a painter.

paint finish a surface coating of paint, the material and process therein.

paint medium the liquid component of paint, in which pigments and fillers are suspended.

paint pad a paint applicator for delicate areas, edges, etc. consisting of a rectangular piece of soft material with a sponge back, a short nap and a handle.

paint removal, paint stripping; in painting and decorating, the removal of old paintwork before a new surface is applied.

paint remover, paint stripper; in painting, a liquid applied to soften hardened paint thus enabling it to be easily removed with a scraper, spatula or abrasive substance.

paint roller see roller.

paint scraper see scraper.

paint shop the part of a factory, works, establishment, or separate space where components are painted, usually by spraying.

paint spray gun a device with a nozzle connected to a supply of paint and powered by compressed air, used for projecting paint in a fine spray; see spray painting.

paint stripper see paint remover.
  paint stripping see paint removal.

paint system a number of layers of paint applied in the correct order to provide a durable and attractive finish.

paint tray see roller tray.

paintwork the painted surfaces in a building; the job of doing such work.

PAL permanent artificial lighting.

pale a timber post driven into the ground, freestanding or as part of a wall, fence or palisade; a timber pile; a vertical timber board or strip in a palisade fence, nailed at its upper and lower edges to rails.

palette the range or choice of colours used by an artist, interior decorator or other colour-renderer, which takes its name from the thin wooden board on which an artist mixes their paints.

palette floor see platform floor.

paling a series of pales driven into the ground to form a fence or timber wall, or a series of pales, timber boards or strips in a fence.

palisade a fence or wall made from timber posts driven into the ground; a fortified enclosure thus constructed.

palisander a name for various tropical timbers from South America, especially rosewoods [*Dalbergia spp.*]; used for high-quality work.

Palladianism an architectural style originating in Italy from the theories and practice of Andrea Palladio (1508–1580); it is characterized by close adherence to Roman orders, symmetry and proportion.

Palladian motif (otherwise known as a Serlian or Venetian motif) a Renaissance motif such as a door, window or other opening in a wall which is divided into three, and whose central portion is arched.

Palladian motif

Palladian window see Venetian window.

palm capital, palmiform; an ancient Egyptian capital carved in imitation of bunches of stylized palm fronds tied round the head of a pole, sometimes called a plume capital by virtue of its resemblance to a series of feathers bound at their base; a palm column is an ancient Egyptian column surmounted by a palm capital.

palmette a decorative motif found in the architecture of antiquity, consisting of a stylized fan-shaped palm leaf; palmette heart or heart-palmette is palmette ornament in a heart-shaped border.

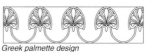
Greek palmette design

palmiform see palm capital.

pamment a thin square paving brick or tile between 9″ and 12″ long.

pan see ash pan, condensates pan, metal tray, WC pan.

PAN polyacrylonitrile.

pan and roll tiles see Italian tiles.

pane 1 a piece of glass or glazed unit fitted in a window frame or as glazing.
2 see peen.

pane size, glazing size, glass size; in glazing, the actual size of a pane of glass cut or manufactured for use in a frame.

panel 1 a distinct area of material or ornament on the surface of a wall, ceiling or vault.
2 a prefabricated cladding unit fixed to a structural frame, a cladding panel.
3 a framed decorative tablet on a wall, door or ceiling surface, or a painting or decorative motif therein.
4 in structures, the open space delineated by members or lines of force in a truss.
5 the main area of a panelled door, joinery paneling, etc., housed by framing members; a door panel.
see also ceiling panel, formwork panel, solar panel.

panel clamp a mechanism for holding formwork together during the casting of a concrete panel.

panel construction a form of construction used for panelled doors and partitions, in which main framing members have infill panels of a non-loadbearing material.

panel door, paneled door see panelled door.

panelled door

panel form a small standard-sized ply-wood unit used in series to form a larger formwork component such as one for casting a wall or floor.

paneling see panelling.

panelled door, framed door, panel door; any door whose main members (rails and stiles) are tenon jointed, forming a rigid frame for infill boarding, glazing or panelling; also written as paneled door.

panelling, paneling (Am), panelwork; internal joinery cladding for ceilings and walls; the construction of the above; see also wall paneling.

panel pin a slender small-headed nail whose shank is 13–50 mm, used in joinery, glazing, etc. where it can be nailed beneath the surface.

panel pin

panel planer see thicknessing machine.

panel point, node; the meeting point of two members in a triangulated structure such as a truss.

panel product see wood-based panel product.

panel radiator, pressed-steel radiator; a radiator manufactured from pressed sheetmetal with cavities in which hot water for space heating circulates.

panel saw a small handsaw with a long blade 250–600 mm long, used for cutting across the grain of softwood boards and sheet materials.

panel tracery see rectilinear tracery.

panel wall a wall or partition, usually of brickwork or blockwork, used as a non-structural infill within a structural frame.

panelwork see paneling.

pan form see waffle mould.

panic hardware any mechanisms for opening escape doors from the inside with a simple pushing action without a key during a building fire or other emergency.

panic bar proprietary hardware for an escape door consisting of a horizontally pivoted rod which, when pushed, opens a latch; see panic latch.

panic bolt, fire-exit bolt; a fastener fitted on the inside of a double escape door, consisting of a horizontal bar at waist height which, when pushed, will open the door.

panic latch a latch for a single escape door operated during an emergency by pushing against a panic bar or lever, or by some other simple action.

pan mixer a concrete mixer with a horizontally rotating pan in which the constituent materials are mixed.

Pannetier's green see viridian.

pantile, S-tile; a clay roof tile which is S-shaped in section to overlap with adjacent tiles in the same course; see double pantile, Roman pantile (Roman tile).

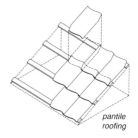

pantile roofing

paper-backed referring to a sheet product such as gypsum board, wire mesh or tiling which has been backed with paper as reinforcement.

paper birch [*Betula papyrifera*]; see birch.

paper-faced referring to a sheet product such as plywood or gypsum board which has been faced with paper.

paperhanging see wallpapering.

papyriform see papyrus.

papyrus a type of paper made originally by the Egyptians from the leaves of the rusk-like plant *Cyperus papyrus*, of the genus *Cypereae*, an aquatic sedge found in tropical and sub-tropical regions; a classical and Egyptian ornamental motif based on stylized leaves from this plant; heraldic plant of Lower Egypt (Nile Delta).

papyrus capital (also called a papyriform) an Egyptian capital carved in imitation of a tied bundle of papyrus leaves, either open, as in a bell capital, or closed, as a bud capital.

papyrus column (also called a papyrus-bundle column or papyriform) an Egyptian column type whose shaft is carved to resemble a bunch of tied papyrus stems, surmounted by a papyrus capital.

papyrus capital

parabolic arch an arch whose form traces out a parabola, a geometrical curve formed by slicing through a cone parallel to its main axis.

parabolic arch

parachute dome see umbrella dome.

paradise an open space in front of, or in the cloister or garden of, a church or monastery.

paraffin, kerosine, kerosene, paraffin oil; a product of the fractional distillation of crude oil; a volatile pleasant-smelling oil used as fuel for some vehicles, lamps and flueless heating appliances; see also paraffin wax.

paraffin wax a soft, waxy, white, solid residue from the distillation of petroleum, used as a fuel in candles and in some polishes and surface treatments.

paragone a variety of black Italian marble.

parallel connection the arrangement of appliances in an electric circuit so that each receives the same voltage.

parallel-grain plywood plywood in which the grain of each ply runs in the same direction; used for beams and other applications where loading is one-sided.

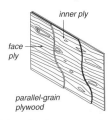

parallel-grain plywood

parallel projection a method of drawing projections in which all the projectors for a given axis or direction are parallel to one another, as if the view point is an infinite distance from the viewed object; often referred to as axonometry; cf. perspective; see axonometric projection, oblique projection, orthographic projection.

parallel tread see flier.

Parana pine [*Araucaria angustifolia*] a South American softwood with pale cream-coloured and straight grained timber; used for interior joinery, staircases and furniture.

parapet a low wall, barrier or balustrade at the edge of a roof, balcony, terrace or bridge; the junction at which an external wall and a flat roof meet, with a small upstand facing the side of the roof, against which the roofing membrane is dressed.

parapet capping a pressed metal capping to protect the upper surface of a parapet against the elements.

parapet gutter in roof construction, a gutter at the junction of a roof plane and a parapet.

parge a traditional render of cow dung, hair and lime sand mortar used as a smooth interior lining for brick chimneys; modern equivalents of this; also called parging, pargeting.

pargeting, parging; 1 a decorative, patterned or scored coat of render. **2** see parge.

paring chisel, joiner's chisel; a light, long-bladed chisel used without a mallet in joinery and cabinetwork.

Paris black an inferior grade of ivory black pigment.

Paris blue see Prussian blue.

Paris white high grade whiting.

Paris yellow see chrome yellow.

Parker's cement see Roman cement.

parking bay see parking space.

parking garage, parking hall, car park; a building or part of a building designed for the parking of motor vehicles.

parking requirement the number of parking spaces for a particular facility as required by a brief or regulatory norms.

parking space, parking bay; a marked space designated for the parking of a single vehicle.

parking standard the number of parking spaces for a development as required by statutory norms or a town plan.

parliament hinge, H-hinge, shutter hinge; a surface-mounted hinge with T-shaped leaves which open out from a central knuckle into the shape of the letter H; its pin is not in the same plane as the leaves, allowing a door or shutter to swing back against an adjacent wall.

parliament hinge

parpend, perpend stone, perpent, perpin, through stone, parpen; in masonry construction, a bonding stone or brick which is laid crosswise so that its ends are visible on both faces of a wall.

parquet, parquetry; hardwearing flooring of solid or laminated strips, blocks or staves of timber laid in rows or various rectangular arrangements; types included as separate entries are listed below:
floor square, see parquet floor square; *herringbone parquet;* *mosaic parquet;* *multilayer parquet;* *parquet batten, see parquet block;* *parquet block;* *parquet composite, see parquet strip;* *parquet floor square;* *parquet flooring;* *parquet mosaic, see parquet block;* *parquet strip;* *parquet tile, see parquet floor square;* *parquet work, see parquetry;* *solid parquet;* *strip parquet, see parquet strip;* *veneer parquet;* *veneered parquet, see multilayer parquet;* *wood mosaic, mosaic parquet.*

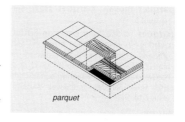
parquet

parquet batten see parquet block.

parquet block one of the small pieces of wood that make up a mosaic parquet floor; also sometimes called a stave, batten or mosaic.

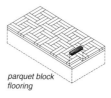
parquet block flooring

parquet composite see parquet strip.

parquet flooring floor surfacing consisting of wood blocks or thin strips, often on plywood or softwood backing, laid in a patterned or parallel arrangement; see paraquet; types included as separate entries are listed below:
multilayer parquet, veneer parquet; *solid parquet;* *wood mosaic, mosaic parquet.*

parquet floor square a square or rectangle of parquet flooring, often with battens laid in a pattern which is repeated once the squares are laid in series; a parquet tile.

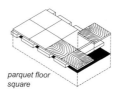
parquet floor square

parquet mosaic, parquet stave see parquet block.

parquet strip, parquet composite, overlay flooring; thin tongued and grooved boards of solid hardwood or hardwood-surfaced composite used as a hardwearing wooden flooring surface; see also solid parquet, multilayer parquet, veneer parquet.

parquet tile see parquet floor square.

parquetry parquet work; the laying of parquet flooring; the result of this; see parquet.

partial handover, partial possession; in contract administration, the process of the contractor delivering up part of the site and building works thereon to the client prior to full completion.

partially crushed gravel a coarse aggregate containing gravel, some of which has been crushed.

partial release, strain relief; in the pretensioning of concrete, the stressing of the setting concrete with part of the stresses held by the prestressing tendons.

particle analyser a device for measuring the size, quantity and consistency of particles in a gas, usually air.

> **particleboard** a range of non-structural building boards manufactured from chips or fibres of wood bonded together with resin then pressed into sheets; although the term particleboard includes products such as chipboard, flakeboard, flaxboard, and OSB, most often it is synonymous with chipboard; types included as separate entries are listed below:
> *chipboard; *fibreboard; *flakeboard; *flaxboard; *oriented strand board; *softboard; *waferboard.

parting chisel 1 see parting tool.
2 see bruzz chisel.

parting compound see release agent.

parting tool, parting chisel; a turning chisel with a flat blade pointed at its end, used for removing a piece of work from a lathe once it has been shaped.

partition a lightweight, non-loadbearing wall dividing interior space in a building; see interior wall, lightweight partition, screen.

partition block an unperforated concrete block used for constructing internal walls, providing good sound insulation between adjacent rooms.

partition block

party floor 1 see separating floor.
2 see fire floor.

party wall see separating wall.

parvis, parvise; a colonnaded entrance court in front of a church or cathedral.

pascal abb. **Pa**; the SI unit of pressure, equal to one newton per square metre ($1 N/m^2$)

pass door see wicket door.

passage a narrow exterior or subterranean circulation space intended for pedestrians, bounded on both sides and sometimes covered; also called a passageway.

passage grave, passage tomb; a stone-age chambered tomb from western Europe, with a long passage leading to a burial chamber or chambers.

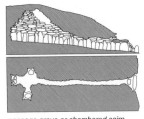
passage grave or chambered cairn, Newgrange, Ireland, c. 3250 BC

passenger conveyor, moving walk (Am); a moving horizontal or sloping belt of rubber or metal slats functioning as a means of circulation for pedestrian users of a large building such as an airport.

passenger lift a lift designed to carry people.

passivation the treatment of freshly machined metal surfaces with acids or pastes to remove contaminants and leave a very thin protective layer to improve corrosion resistance.

passive fire protection the design and planning of a building with fire safety in mind, with compartments, designated escape routes, fire-resistant materials and structure, etc.

passive solar energy solar heating based on the planning, orientation, construction techniques and mass of a building rather than solar panels and collectors.

paste, gum; a simple thick adhesive mixed from an organic material such as flour, or a polymer which swells in water; used for gluing paper and wallpaper.

paste blue see Prussian blue.

patch a piece of material used to repair damaged or defective surface construction, as with a piece of veneer used in the repair of plywood; in joinery, a small piece of wood glued into a wooden surface in order to cover a defect, loose knot, etc.; also called an insert or plug.

patch fitting hardware fittings (hinges, handles, latches) for all-glass doors and components, clamped and bolted to the glass surface; so named because they resemble patches.

patching the repair of holes, pitting and other defects in concretework, veneerwork, plasterwork and other finishings and coatings; particularly the filling of voids, cracks, etc. and repairing of defects in a plaster or cast concrete surface with mortar; see concrete patching, remedial plastering.

patent axe a metal mason's tool with raised teeth or blades, used for dressing hard stone and granite.

patent claw chisel, tooth tool; a masonry claw chisel with a replaceable blade.

patent glazing, system glazing; a dry glazing system of proprietary metal structural framing members with glazing infill, used for large glazed areas and curtain walls; also other proprietary systems with a predesigned set of accessories, gaskets and fixings, structural glass, frameless glazing, etc.

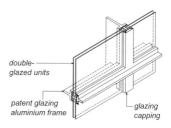

double-glazed units

patent glazing aluminium frame

glazing capping

patent stone see cast stone.

patent yellow see Turner's yellow.

patera, phiala; Lat.; a decorative ornament resembling a round dish, flat vase or flower in low relief.

patera

paternoster 1 a continuous, slow moving lift with a number of twinned cars arranged in a rotating formation so that one side moves upwards and the other downwards.
2 see beaded moulding.

pathogenic descriptive of certain substances which have the property of causing disease through contact or inhalation.

patina, patination; a coloured protective layer of oxide forming naturally on the surface of some metals such as copper and bronze (green) and lead (dark grey) on exposure to the elements.
patination the act of artificially inducing a patina on a copper or bronze surface as a hardwearing finish; also a synonym for the patina itself.

patio a paved external area directly outside a dwelling at ground floor, furnished with seats for recreation, taking outdoor meals, etc.

patio house see atrium house.

pattern an abstract design of lines, marks or forms as surface decoration; a diagram showing how something, a model or part of a design, is made; a template.

patterned brickwork decorative brickwork in different coloured and textured bricks; see polychrome brickwork.

patterned glass rolled glass treated with a patterned relief to obscure one or both surfaces.

patterned plasterwork see textured plasterwork.

pattern flooring raised pattern flooring, see studded rubber flooring.

pattern paver any specially shaped concrete paving unit which is laid to create a regular pattern; see interlocking, key, hexagonal and interweave pavers.

pattern spar see cross spar.

pavement 1 the main structural and surface construction of a road or paved area, laid in courses of concrete, stone or asphalt above a subgrade.
2 a raised path or way along the side of a road, street or carriageway for use by pedestrians.
3 see concrete paving.

pavement concrete concrete used as surfacing for external areas such as roads, pavements, etc.

pavement light a square or circular glass lens incorporated into a concrete slab to allow natural lighting to a space below.

paver any brick, concrete or natural stone product, etc. used for paving external surfaces; also called a paving stone, pavior or paviour; see also paving brick, concrete paver, concrete block paver, concrete paving slab.

pavilion a small ornamental structure or shelter set in parkland as a summer house, bandstand or to provide changing facilities and stores at a sports ground.

pavilion roof a hipped roof with a square or polygonal plan, composed of a number of triangular roof planes.

pavilion roof

paving 1 blocks, precast units or thin slabs of stone, brick, concrete or ceramic material laid horizontally as a hardwearing external surface; see stone paving, brick paving, concrete paving, tiled paving, cellular paver.

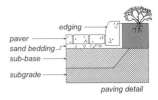

paving detail

2 the trade of laying floor slabs and paviors with butting joints as covering for external areas.

paving block see concrete block paver.

paving brick, paviour brick, paver; a brick of special dimension and durability used for paving.

paving pattern the various patterns in which stone and concrete pavers, slabs, etc. can be laid as paving.

paving slab see concrete paving slab.

paving stone, stone paver; any natural stone product used for paving.

paving unit see concrete paving slab.

pavior, paviour see paver, slab.

paviour brick see paving brick.

Paxillus panuoides see roll-rim.

PC 1 see polycarbonate.
2 acronym for personal computer.

PE polyethylene.

peacock tail pattern see fantail pattern.

pear [*Pyrus communis*] a European hardwood with rosy pink, fine-grained wood used in veneers, furniture, turned bowls and parts of musical instruments for the decorative value of its grain.

pearl, frosted; in artificial lighting, the classification of a bulb of a lamp which has a diffuse inner or outer surface produced by etching or sandblasting to obscure the filament; cf. opal lamp.

pearl moulding see beaded moulding.

pearl stone see perlite.

peat a dark and fibrous soil type formed from the decomposition of organic matter.

pebble, duckstone, cobble; naturally weathered rounded stones, larger than shingle, used in a cement or concrete base as wall facing, surface paving for driveways, etc., or laid loose around borders.

pebbledash, dry dash; a weatherproof finish for masonry and concrete with a coating of pebbles or gravel embedded into wet mortar.

pecked finish see picked finish, sparrow-pecked finish.

pedestal 1 a columnar support for an object; often used with reference to sanitary appliances, to differentiate between one which is supported by a floor on a columnar stand (pedestal), and one which is fixed to a wall (wall hung); see below.
2 a rectangular masonry block on which a classical column, statue, caryatid, etc. is supported, consisting of a plinth and dado, often surmounted with a cornice.
pedestal bidet a bidet supported by the floor on a short columnar stand.
pedestal pile see under-reamed pile.
pedestal washbasin a washbasin supported by the floor on a columnar stand rather than being attached to a wall.
pedestal WC pan a WC supported by the floor on a short columnar stand.

pediment, 1 the triangular gabled portion of a classical portico or building; forerunners of this.

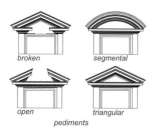

broken   *segmental*

open   *triangular*

pediments

2 fronton; in Renaissance, Baroque and Neoclassical architecture, a triangular or segmental ornamental device, panel or canopy above doorways, windows and panels; types of Renaissance, Baroque and Neoclassical pediments below:
broken pediment a pediment whose base has a central opening; also called a broken-bed pediment or open-bed pediment.
open pediment a pediment with an opening where the apex should be; also called a broken-apex pediment or open-topped pediment.

segmental pediment a pediment in which the upper chord is a segment of a circle.
triangular pediment a pediment with straight sloping upper surface meeting at a central apex.

pedunculate oak, common oak; [*Quercus robur*], see oak.

PEEK polyetheretherketone.

peelable wallcovering wallcovering which can be removed once dry so that its backing or webbing remains attached to the wall.

peeled veneer see rotary cut veneer.

peeler block a timber from which veneer is peeled.

peeling 1 a defect in a paint or plaster finish caused by separation from its underlying coat or surface.
2 see veneer peeling.

peen, 1 pein, pane; the end of the head of a hammer opposite its striking face, shaped with a point, ridge, ball, claw, etc. for a variety of uses.
2 see machinist's hammer.
peen hammer a hammer with a peen opposite its striking face; see cross peen hammer, Warrington hammer, ball peen hammer, straight peen hammer.
peen sledge see engineer's sledge.

peephole see door scope.

peg in traditional timber frame construction, a small piece of wood or dowel used for fastening or tightening joints; a timber nail; see also dowel, trenail, wood key.

peg board, perforated hardboard; hardboard manufactured with a regular grid of holes; uses include decorative and acoustic linings.

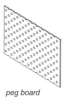

peg board

pegged joint a timber joint fastened by pegs or wooden nails.

pegmatite a very coarse-grained crystal-line igneous rock often containing rare minerals.

peg mould in ornamental plasterwork, a template drawn across a plaster surface between two pegs set apart, forming a curving moulding; a curved running mould; see run moulding.

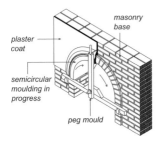

masonry base

plaster coat

semicircular moulding in progress

peg mould

pein see peen.

Pelasgic masonry see cyclopean masonry.

pellet moulding a narrow Romanesque or Gothic ornamental moulding decorated with a series of small hemispheres or raised flat discs.

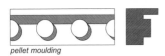

pellet moulding

pelmet a board or trim above a window opening to cover a curtain rail or blind.

penalty, fine; compensation to be paid by one who breaks an agreement or contract, or financial punishment of one who breaks the law.

penalty clause in contracts administration, a condition stating the details of the terms and amount to be paid if the contract is broken.

pencil arris see pencil round.

pencil round the blunting of the sharp edges of rectangular stone, woodwork, glass, etc. objects by slight sanding or grinding, usually with less than 3 mm chamfer; also referred to as a pencil or eased arris, or an arrised or eased edge.

pendant an elongated decorated round piece or boss hanging down at the join of ribs or other members in a vault or ornamental ceiling.

pendant luminaire, droplight; a fixed light fitting designed to be hung from a roof, structure or ceiling, and which sheds most of its light downwards.

pendentive a curved segmental surface or construction for joining the round base of a masonry dome or opening to a square structure beneath.

pendentive dome any dome constructed on pendentives; often a sail dome.

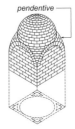

pendentive

penetration the place at which a component such as a pipe or chimney passes through a floor, wall or roof, usually requiring special measures to ensure weatherproofing and fireproofing; see roof penetration.

penetration testing in soil investigation, the testing of the stiffness of non-cohesive soils and gravel by sinking a special implement into the ground and measuring the force required to do so; see also cone penetration testing (deep penetration testing), dynamic penetration testing, static penetration testing, vane testing.

penning see pitching.

penny washer see flat washer.

Pentarthrum huttonii see wood weevil.

penthouse a separate apartment or suite of rooms at the top of a high-rise building; originally a subsidiary building with a sloping roof, attached to the exterior wall of a larger building.

penthouse roof, pent roof, shed roof; a monopitch roof which covers the top of a higher wall on which its upper end is supported; see also lean-to roof.

pentise roof a monopitch roof built against a wall as a canopy.

pent roof see penthouse roof.

peperino volcanic tuff found in the areas south-east of Rome, used as a building stone by the Romans; also called lapis albanus.

percussive bored pile in foundation technology, a bored pile in which excavation is carried out using repeated blows or vibration of the pile casing.

percussive welding, resistance percussive welding; a method of resistance welding in which a local electric current is passed concurrently with the sudden application of a high pressure.

perennial in landscaping, any species of flowering plant that lives for many years, usually dying down at winter and regrowing from shoots the following spring.

perfect frame see statically determinate frame.

perforated brick, cored brick; a clay brick which has a pattern of vertical holes through it for weight reduction, but also to save on material and improve the insulation properties of the brickwork; the maximum permitted amount of perforation is usually governed by a national standard, less than 25% in Great Britain; see also air brick (ventilating brick), hollow clay block, hollow brick.

perforated bricks

perforated hardboard see pegboard.

perforated masonry unit any brick, block or stone perforated with holes, indentations or cavities; see also perforated brick (cored brick), air brick (ventilating brick).

perforated panel absorber in acoustics, an absorbing construction consisting of a perforated board with an air gap or mineral wool behind.

perforated pipe a clay or plastics pipe with slotted perforations along its length; see drain pipe.

perforated sheetmetal a sheetmetal product manufactured with a series of regular circular or rectangular openings.

perforated sheetmetal

perforated underlay bitumen felt, vented underlay, venting layer; bitumen felt manufactured with perforations and treated with granular material on its reverse side; used in a warm flat roof as an underlay to allow for the movement of air within roof construction.

perforation the drilling, punching or forming of holes through components, sheet materials, etc.; the holes or pattern of openings thus made.

performance specification a technical specification that outlines, lists and documents the behaviour or use of a product, process, installation or service.

pergola in landscape and garden design, a passage, walkway, gateway, etc. with a canopy of trelliswork on which climbing plants are trained to grow.

Pericopsis elata see afrormosia.

peridotite a dark, coarse-grained igneous rock type used as building stone; a major constituent is olivine (also known as peridot and chrysolite) an olive green, crystalline magnesium iron silicate mineral.

perimeter surveillance the use of cameras and alarms on boundary fencing and gates to prevent the entry of intruders.

perimeter trim a profile fixed to a wall at the edges of a suspended ceiling to provide support to ceiling panels.

perinone orange a strong, clean reddish-orange organic pigment used in acrylic paints, discovered in 1924.

period of final inspection in contract administration, the time during which measurement of the completed works takes place and the final account is agreed.

peristyle, peristylium (Lat.), peristylion (Gk.); in classical architecture, a row of columns surrounding a building or open courtyard; the open courtyard or temple thus surrounded; a classical temple type which is surrounded by a colonnade on all sides is called a peristyle temple or peristylos.

Perkin's violet see mauve.

perlite, pearl stone; dark, natural volcanic glass composed of small nodules, used as a lightweight building material for filtering, filling, fireproofing and for insulation.
perlite plaster, gypsum-perlite plaster, fire-retardant plaster; plaster containing perlite aggregate in place of sand as thermal and fire resistance.

Perlon a proprietary name for a polyamide plastic; a variety of nylon produced by the polymerization of caprolactam.

permanence the property of a pigment or paint to retain the strength of its colour under prolonged exposure to light.

permanent artificial lighting, PAL; the continuous lighting with luminaires of deep office or windowless spaces in which the amount of natural light is insufficient.

permanent formwork in concreting, formwork of plywood, plastics or steel sheet, which remains in place once the concrete has hardened.

permanent load see dead load.

permanent supplementary artificial lighting of interiors, PSALI; continuous artificial lighting provided to supplement daylighting in interiors where the illumination level would otherwise be insufficient.

permanent violet see manganese violet.

permanent white see blanc fixe.

permanent yellow a loose name for barium yellow pigment.

permeability the property of a porous solid to permit the passage of liquids through, due to differential pressure.

permeability-reducing admixture see pore filler.

permissible stress, working stress; in structural design, the maximum stress which can be applied to a structure or structural member; usually set by a standard equivalent to a specified fraction of the tested failure stress of the structure.

permit an official document issuing permission to carry out a certain task or function such as construction, demolition and various types of hazardous work; examples included as separate entries are listed below:
*building permission, see planning permission; *building permit; *conditional planning permission; *demolition permit; *outline planning permission; *planning permission, planning approval, planning consent.

permitted development building work and other development that does not require planning permission.

permittivity in electronics, the ratio of electric displacement to the electric field intensity producing it.

peroxide see hydrogen peroxide.

perpend, perpend joint, cross joint, head joint, header joint; in masonry construction, a vertical joint between adjacent bricks or stones in the same course; see also parpend.

Perpendicular style, Rectilinear style; the last and longest of three phases of English Gothic architecture from 1350 to 1550, characterized by a vertical emphasis in decoration and tracery, large glazed areas and elaborate fan vaulting,
perpendicular tracery tracery of the Perpendicular style; see rectilinear tracery.

Gothic perpendicular tracery at King's College Chapel, Cambridge, England, 1446–1515

perpend joint see perpend.

perpend stone, perpent, perpin see parpend.

perron one or a number of staircases leading to a raised platform in front of a grand building; the raised platform itself.

Persian red see oxide red.

Persian walnut see walnut.

persiennes, louvred shutters; a pair of hinged external window shutters to provide shading by means of louvres held in a light frame.

person-day see man-day.

person-hour see man-hour.

person-year see man-year.

perspective 1 the optic phenomenon in which objects in the distance are perceived as smaller than objects in the foreground.
2 a technique for rendering three-dimensional objects in a realistic way on a flat surface using converging projectors; sometimes called linear perspective to distinguish it from other forms of perspective rendering.
3 the art or science of perspective drawing; see types below:
one-point perspective a method using only one vanishing point, producing a view in which verticals are seen as vertical and horizontals parallel to the picture plane seen as horizontal; also known as central, Renaissance or parallel perspective.
two-point perspective a perspective constructed from two vanishing points, producing a view in which verticals are seen as vertical and lines on other axes seen as converging; also called angular perspective and, in Great Britain, sometimes called oblique perspective.
three-point perspective a perspective drawing constructed from three vanishing points, producing a view in which lines parallel to all three major axes are converging; sometimes also known as oblique perspective in North America.
colour perspective the portrayal of apparent distance in landscape painting and architectural renderings using warmer tones in the foreground and bluer shades in the distance.
perspective grid a network of converging predrawn lines to aid in the construction of a perspective drawing; an orthogonal grid superimposed onto a three-dimensional visualization to represent the ground or datum plane.

Perspex a proprietary name for thin sheets of acrylic used as glazing, translucent roofing and for cladding; see polymethyl methacrylate.

pervious macadam a low-splash, porous and self-draining road surfacing consisting of bitumen, aggregate and a filler.

perylene, perylene red; a transparent red pigment used in watercolours and oil paints.

PET polyethylene terephthalate.

pet-cock see air release valve.

petroleum spirit see white spirit.

petrol interceptor 1 a chamber in a drainage system in which petrol and other volatile liquids are evaporated off from the surface of waste water.
2 petrol intercepting trap; an outlet construction for separating petrol and oil from waste water to inhibit its passage into the drainage system; found in garages, petrol stations and repair shops.

pewter a grey alloy of tin, antimony and copper or tin and lead used primarily for kitchen utensils and ornament.

PEX cross-linked polyethylene.

PF phenol formaldehyde.

pH or pH-value, a measure of the acidity of a solution or soils from 0−14; pH7 is neutral, under 7 is acidic, and over 7 is alkaline.

phantom in drawing and rendering, part of an object or building that has been shown transparent or in outline only so that what is behind may be shown.

phase 1 one of a number of sections of work in a large building development, often with its own contractual agreements for design, management and construction that arises from splitting up the project to make it more manageable; see stage.
2 a particular point or stage in the cycle of a wave, process, etc.; see single-phase, three-phase.

Phellinus ignarius see false tinder fungus.
Phellinus pini see red ring rot.

phenocrystal see porphyritic.

phenol, carbolic acid; any one of a group of acidic hydrocarbon compounds (especially C_6H_5OH) used in the manufacture of epoxy resins, plastics and dyes.

phenol formaldehyde, PF, bakelite; a tough, brittle, dark-coloured thermosetting resin used for moulded products and in paints and adhesives, otherwise known as phenolic resin.

phenol formaldehyde glue a thermosetting, moisture-resistant, synthetic adhesive used for gluing plywood plies, veneer, etc.; see film glue.

phenolic resin see phenol formaldehyde.

phiala see patera.

Phillips head screw a screw with a patented cross-shaped indentation in its head for turning with a special screwdriver or bit.

phloem, inner bark; the layer of living cells directly beneath the bark of a tree, which conducts synthesized food down from the leaves.

phlogopite a greyish-yellow or green-brown scaly metallic mineral, used for electrical insulation.

phon in acoustics, a unit of perceived loudness equivalent to 1 decibel at a frequency of 1000 Hz.

phosphating the pretreatment of a metal surface with hot phosphoric acid to form a corrosion-resistant layer of iron, zinc or manganese phosphate to enhance bonding of subsequent coatings; a **phosphate** is a salt of phosphoric acid, a colourless, water-soluble chemical compound, H_3PO_4.

phospho gypsum the mineral gypsum produced as a by-product of the manufacture of phosphoric acid.

photoelectric cell, photocell; a device designed to convert light into electricity; see also solar cell.

photoelectric lighting controller, automatic lighting controller; electronic control equipment for switching on electric lights and lighting systems automatically when darkness falls, operated by a signal from a photocell reacting to the level of illuminance.

photogrammetry the technique of using photographs for measurement and to make maps and drawings.

photomontage an image produced using parts of a number of photographs joined; a drawn image superimposed onto a photograph.

Phragmites australis common reed, see best reed, Norfolk reed.

phthalocyanine pigment a group of brilliant, transparent, blue and green synthetic organic pigments developed in the 1930s.

phthalocyanine blue (also called intense blue, Monastral blue, thalo blue) a deep greenish-blue opaque organic pigment, invented in 1935, consisting of copper phthalocyanine, similar in properties to Prussian blue.

phthalocyanine green (also called Monastral green, thalo green) a bright bluish-green poisonous pigment, developed in 1938, consisting of organic polychloro copper phthalocyanine and suitable for use in all kinds of paints.

phyllite a dark grey fine-grained metamorphic rock, the surface of which, when cleaved, is shiny with minute grains of mica.

physical conservation, remedial conservation; active building conservation in which direct measures are taken to prevent further deterioration of structures and properties in a state of disrepair.

physical drying the drying of paints or other coatings by simple evaporation of contained solvents.

piano hinge, continuous hinge; a long, slender butt hinge continuously formed into standard lengths which may be cut to suit the size of door or hinged surfaces; originally used for piano lids, now mainly in use for furnishings.

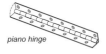

piano hinge

piano nobile the main living spaces of an Italian palazzo or townhouse, located over subsidiary rooms, above the basement or ground floor level.

piazza 1 a square or open space in an Italian town or city; a piazzetta is a small piazza.

2 a veranda or covered walkway in front of a building or square.

Picea spp. see spruce.

pick an axe whose head is sharply pointed at both ends, used for hacking stone and masonry, in demolition and excavation work, etc.; also called a pickaxe; see rock pick, pick hammer.

pickaxe see pick.

picked finish, pecked finish; a rough stonework finish produced by dressing with a pick or point.

pick hammer a small hammer with a sharp peen, used in plastering, for removing scale, raking out mortar joints, etc.

pickling the removal of oxides, scale, rust and other compounds from steel surfaces by dipping in sulphuric acid before priming or other surface treatments.

picture frame cramp see corner cramp.

picturesque referring to attractive townscape or the countryside which has the visual quality of a painting or illustration; a style in English country houses and mansions from the 1700s and early 1800s in which asymmetrical building masses and groups are set in romantic parkland.

picture window a large window which frames a particular exterior view.

piecemeal development small-scale and fragmentary urban development undertaken bit by bit without adhering to a town plan or taking into account its surroundings.

piece mould in various casting processes, a mould composed of a number of pieces which are assembled for casting and disassembled to remove the cast.

piend see hip.

pier 1 a masonry column or small section of masonry walling between two adjacent openings; see attached pier, engaged column (engaged pier).
2 a heavy stone column or pillar, especially a compound column in a Medieval religious building; see bundle pier, compound pier (clustered pier), filleted column (filleted pier).
3 a vertical protruding rib built at right angles to a wall surface to stabilize it; a buttress or counterfort.

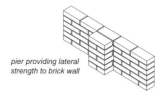

pier providing lateral strength to brick wall

4 a structure built on stilts or supported by other means, projecting over a body of water such as the sea or lake, and used as a landing stage for boats and for recreational activities; a seaside pier.

pigeonhole one of a number of open compartments in a furnishing unit in which papers, letters and memos, etc. may be stored for easy access and distribution.

pigment fine coloured powder which may be mixed with (but not dissolved into) a liquid medium such as oil or water to form paint.

pigment figure grain figure in wood with colour variation from absorbed material.

pignon, pynnion; a gable in traditional timber frame construction.

pilaster a vertical rectangular protrusion in a wall, often carved or decorated to resemble a column and usually for ornamental rather than structural purposes.

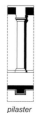

pilaster

pilaster block see column block.
pilaster strip see lesene.

pile in foundation technology, any vertical structural member of concrete steel or timber used in series as a foundation on types of soil with poor or uneven bearing capacity; it transmits building loads deep into the ground or to bedrock, or functions as an earth retaining structure; vertically loaded piles are generally called bearing or foundation piles; types included as separate entries are listed below:

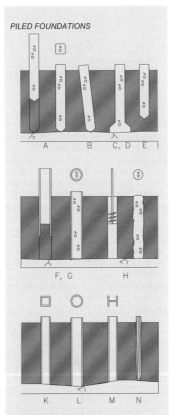

PILED FOUNDATIONS

A B C, D E

F, G H

K L M N

CONCRETE PILES
A   driven pile, precast pile
B   batter pile, raking pile, inclined pile
C   underreamed pile, belled pile,
       pedestal pile, Enlarged base pile
D   end-bearing pile, point-bearing pile
E   friction pile, cohesion pile
F   cast-in-place pile,
       in-situ pile, bored pile
G   pile casing
H   augered pile, bored pile

STEEL AND TIMBER PILES
K   box pile
L   pipe pile, tubular pile, augered steel pile
M   H-pile
N   timber pile, wooden pile

*anchor pile, see piled anchorage, see ten-
sion pile; *augered pile; *batter pile, see
raking pile; *bearing pile; *belled pile, see
under-reamed pile; *bored pile; *box pile;
*cast-in-place pile, cast-in-situ pile; *cohe-
sion pile; *composite pile; *concrete pile;
*driven pile; *end-bearing pile; *enlarged
base pile; *foundation pile; *friction pile;
*Franki pile; *friction pile; *H-pile; *in-
situ pile, see cast-in place pile; *inclined
pile, see raking pile; *jacked pile; *large
diameter pile; *micropile, see mini-pile;
*mini-pile; *pedestal pile, see under-
reamed pile; *percussive bored pile; *pin
pile, see mini-pile; *pipe pile; *point-bearing pile, see end-bearing pile; *precast
pile, prefabricated pile; *preliminary pile;
*raking pile; *screw pile; *segmental pile;
*sheet pile, see steel sheet pile; *steel pile;
*steel sheet pile; *tension pile; *test pile;
*timber pile; *trial pile; *tubular pile, see
pipe pile; *under-reamed pile; *wooden
pile, see timber pile; *working pile.

pile cap 1 a steel plate at the upper end
of a pile to provide protection during
driving.
2 a concrete footing, beam or plate to
which the upper ends of groups of piles are
attached, which transmits loading from a
building or structure to a series of piles.

pile casing a length of steel tubing sunk
into the ground as permanent or temporary formwork for a concrete pile.

**piled anchor-
age,** anchor
pile; a buried pile
or stake attached
with ties to the
rear of a retaining
wall to provide a
restraining
anchorage.

*piled anchorage for
retaining wall*

piled foundation any foundation system which makes use of piles to transmit
building loads to the underlying bedrock
or ground.

pile driver, piling frame; site plant for
hammering piles into the ground with a
repeated percussive action, usually a
winch, frame and heavy weight or drop
hammer.

piledriving, piling; the placing of concrete or timber piles into the ground by

repeated downward blows from a hammer, pile driver or similar plant.

pile-placing see piling.

pile yarn in the making of carpets, rugs and mats, yarn which forms the final wearing surface of the mat as opposed to the structure.

piling, pile-placing; the process of casting, installation or driving of foundation piles on site; see also piledriving.

piling frame see pile driver.

pillar a heavy masonry column or pier, freestanding or supporting a structure, often other than round in plan.

pillar

pillow in traditional timber frame construction, a small horizontal timber piece added to the top of a post to spread the load of a beam; a timber capital.

pin 1 a small nail or fixing with a slender shank; examples included as separate entries are listed below:
*cotter pin; *drawing pin; *escutcheon pin; *gimp pin; *hardboard pin; *hinge pin; *panel pin; *U-pin, see staple.

pin

2 in timber frame construction, a wooden peg with round cross-section driven in to the sides of a joint as a fixing.
see also dowel, hook pin, trenail.

pincers a metal scissor-like hand tool with hinged jaws used for removing nails, gripping and cutting.

pinched finish see pitched finish.

pincher see pitching tool.

pine [*Pinus spp.*] a group of common softwoods found in the northern hemisphere with pale reddish-brown timber; used for general constructional, cladding and joinery; see below for species of pure pine included in this work; see also Oregon pine, Parana pine.

pine

Corsican pine, Austrian pine; [*Pinus nigra*] a softwood with light yellowish-brown timber; used for joinery; a native to central and south-east Europe, it is widely planted for timber and as windbreaks or sand dune stabilizer in coastal areas.

lodgepole pine, contorta pine, shore pine; [*Pinus contorta*] a planted softwood from the Rockies, Scotland and Scandinavia, originating in the Pacific United States; used in the manufacture of chipboard.

pitch pine [*Pinus spp.*] a collective name for a number of pines from the east coast of North America (esp. *Pinus rigida*) with resinous timber; used occasionally for heavy construction work and in the manufacture of turpentine.

radiata pine, Monterey pine; [*Pinus radiata*] a softwood from temperate regions with pale pink timber; originating in coastal California, it is a conifer very widely planted as a shelter tree on the coast, and its wood is used for exterior cladding, flooring and joinery.

Scots pine, European redwood; [*Pinus sylvestris*] a softwood from northern Europe and north western Asia with pale reddish timber sold as red or yellow deal; used in all timber industries; one of the most common and versatile softwoods for construction.

Siberian yellow pine, cembra pine; [*Pinus cembra*] a mountainous Siberian pine with long needles and light wood, used for cabinetwork; a similar subspecies of this, the arolla pine, is found in the Alps.

western white pine, soft pine; [*Pinus monticola*] a softwood from the western USA with pale yellow-red-brown heartwood, used for interiors and plywood; the tree is widely grown locally as an ornamental.

yellow pine, Weymouth pine, white pine; [*Pinus strobus*] a softwood from eastern USA with pale yellow-brown, soft timber; used for non-structural interior work, crates and boxes, widely planted in central Europe as a timber tree.

pineapple a decorative ovoid finial carved with a web of diagonal lines or bands, resembling a pineapple; similar to pine cone.

pine cone depictions of the cone-shaped fruit of a conifer, as found in ancient banded ornament and mouldings, or sculptured as a terminating element for newel posts, pendants, balustrades, finials, etc.; similar to pineapple.

pine cone

pine oil oil extracted from the needles, wood and resin of pine trees, with characteristic odour; used as an additive in insecticides, detergents and some paints.

pine soot black a variety of Chinese lampblack pigment.

pin hammer see tack hammer.

pin hinge see loose pin butt hinge, fast-pin hinge.

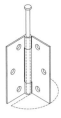

pin hinge

pinhole 1 a small round hole in wood caused by the infestation of insects.
2 see pinholing.

pinholing, pinhole; a defect in a paint finish consisting of tiny holes produced by bursting bubbles of air or gas introduced into the paint during mixing or application.

pin joint, 1 hinge joint; any joint which is free to rotate about a pivot, or can be regarded as such for purposes of structural calculation.
2 see pinned joint, dowel joint.

pin knot, cat's eye; a small knot in seasoned timber, less than 6 mm or ¼″ in diameter.

pin knot

pin leaf the leaf of a hinge to which the hinge pin is fixed.

pinnacle a small pointed or pyramidical turret in Gothic architecture, often adorning buttresses, doorways and roofs and ornamented with crockets and finials.

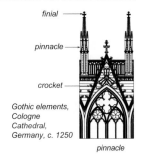

Gothic elements, Cologne Cathedral, Germany, c. 1250

finial

pinnacle

crocket

pinnacle

pinned joint a timber joint in which wooden or metal round pins are laterally driven in to fasten and tighten members together; see also dowel joint.

pinned joint

pinned tenon joint see keyed tenon joint.

pin pile see mini-pile.

pintle a hinge pin in a lift-off hinge.

pin tumbler one of a number of moving pins in a lock mechanism which holds the bolt fast until lifted with a suitable key.

Pinus spp. see pine.

pipe a rigid, hollow tubular product of plastics, ceramics, concrete or metal, usually used to convey liquids or gases; see pipeline, gas pipe, circular hollow section (steel pipe).

pipe bracket a support for fixing a pipe to the building fabric.

pipe circuit a system of pipes in which liquid or gas flows for a particular function such as heating, cold water supply, etc.

pipeclay an impure variety of kaolin.

pipe clip see saddle clip.

pipe closer see fire stop sleeve.

pipe duct, conduit; a length of usually plastic pipe built into construction to provide an unobstructed route for installation cabling and pipework; see cable duct, pipework duct.

pipe fitting, connector, coupler, coupling; a length of special pipe attached to a pipeline to alter the direction or action of the flow or to connect two pipes together; types included as separate entries are listed below:
*bend; *branch fitting; *breech fitting; *bush; *compression fitting; *connector; *coupling; *cross; *elbow; *fire stop sleeve; *gully; *hexagonal nipple; *knuckle bend; *reducing fitting, reducer; *screwed pipe; *slotted waste; *taper; *tee; *union; *waste coupling, waste; *Y branch.

pipe fixing a bracket, hanger or other means for securing a pipe to supporting construction.

pipe flashing in roof construction, a strip of impervious sheet material used to waterproof the junction where a pipe or other component penetrates roofing decking, etc.; also called a cover soaker, roof soaker or vent soaker.

pipe hanger a component for hanging a pipe from a soffit or overlying structure.

pipe-in-pipe in a district heating system, a composite tube consisting of a pipe wrapped with insulation in a hard casing, in which heated water is conveyed.

pipe interrupter a device containing apertures for the introduction of air to inhibit the backflow of water into sanitary pipework; a form of backflow valve.

pipelaying the installation of lengths of pipeline for drainage, water supply or district heating, into trenches in the ground, along the sea bed, etc.

pipeline, line; a length of pipe as part of an installation for gas, water, sewage, etc.

pipe pile, tubular pile; in foundation engineering, a pile formed from a steel pipe; see also box pile.

pipe saddle, saddle fitting, service clamp; a pipe component with a suitably shaped curved flange and socket to make a connection from a new drain to an existing sewer.

pipe shoe, rainwater shoe; a kinked fitting at the lower end of a rainwater pipe to throw water away from the surface of a building.

pipe sleeve a length of pipe built into floor or wall construction to provide an opening through which pipes or cables can later be passed.

pipe system test a test for blocks, interruptions and leaks in a system of pipework; types included as separate entries are listed below:
*air test; *gas soundness test; *hydraulic test, see water test; *mirror test; *pipe system test; *pneumatic test, see air test; *smoke test; *soundness test, see gas soundness test; *water test.

pipe tongs see footprints.

pipework the job of installing and mounting pipes for a water, drainage, heating or gas system; the pipes thus installed; see pipe circuit, plumbing, gas installation pipework.

pipework duct, pipe duct; a service duct for carrying pipework.

pipework test see pipe system test.

pipe wrench, Stillson wrench; an adjustable metal hand tool with jaws for gripping pipes and other round objects.

PIR see polyisocyanurate.

pisé, rammed earth construction, pisé de terre; a traditional walling construction of clay laid and compacted in boarded formwork, allowed to dry in the sun and often faced with stucco.

pit 1 a defect in a concrete or other finish caused by a small recess in the surface.
2 an area of ground or a room whose lowest surface is below that of its surroundings; the part of the ground floor of a theatre auditorium behind the stalls; see also excavation, lift pit.

pitch 1 the angle of a sloping plane measured as a fraction or percentage; see also slope, roof pitch.
2 the vertical distance measured from the impost to the crown of an arch; also known as rise.
3 slope; the angle of a stair from the horizontal, measured along the line of nosings.
4 the sloping of the face of a saw tooth relative to the vertical.
5 the distance between adjacent ridges in a screw thread, a measure of its fineness.
6 in acoustics, the subjective frequency of a sound as perceived by the human ear.
7 a dark resinous residue formed from the distillation of coal, crude turpentine and tar, used for caulking and waterproofing timber constructions; also any similar bituminous products; see resin.

pitch line see line of nosings.

pitch pine [*Pinus spp.*], see pine.

pitch pocket, resin pocket; a flattened round or oval separation containing resin in the grain of certain grades of softwood.

pitch streak, resin streak; a local accumulation or streak of resin in the grain of certain grades of highly resinous softwood.

pitch streak

pitched beam a concrete or steel beam whose longer upper edge is V-shaped, with a ridge in the middle, like a pitched roof.

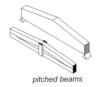
pitched beams

pitched finish, pinched finish; a stonework finish which resembles natural rock, produced by dressing with a pitching tool; the same result as a quarry finish.

pitched roof 1 a roof form of two sloping roof planes meeting at a ridge, terminating at either end with either hips or gables.

pitched roof

2 any sloping roof, usually one with a pitch of more than 20.

pitcher see pitching tool.

pitch-faced see pitched finish, quarry finish.

pitching, armour, penning, rubble revetment, soling; stones of 180—450 mm used as revetment for embankments.

pitching hammer a mason's hammer used for striking a pitching tool or punch.

pitching tool, pincher, pitcher; a chisel-like masonry tool with a blunt end, used for the initial rough dressing of stone surfaces.

pitching tool

pitchstone a form of dark, naturally occurring glass which has a resinous lustre; used as aggregate.

pit corrosion one of the most destructive forms of corrosion of metals, localized attack resulting in surface holes.

pith, medulla; the small core of soft spongy tissue at the centre of a tree trunk.
pith flecks longitudinal discolorations of wound tissue in timber caused by fly larvae of the genus *Agromyza spp.*
pith ray see medullary ray.

pit lime good quality slaked lime which has been produced and aged for a period of years in pits excavated in the ground; stored as a wet paste and used as a binder in fresco paints and a raw material in lime mortar.

pivot damper see swivel damper.

pivot window a window with an opening light hung centrally on pins attached to the frame, either vertically or horizontally, about which it opens; see vertical pivot window, horizontal pivot window (tip-up window).

pixel abb. of picture element; one of the multitude of basic square units or grains of uniform colour or illumination of which a television screen image or graphic print is composed, which defines its resolution.

placement, placing see concrete placing.

plafond a decorative painting applied to a roof or ceiling surface, or the richly decorated or ornate ceiling itself.

plagioclase one of a group of sodium-calcium mineral feldspars; see labradorite, Labrador feldspar.

plain bar a reinforcing bar whose surface is smooth with no ridges or ribs.

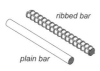

ribbed bar

plain bar

plain carbon steel any steel which contains carbon but does not contain substantial proportions of alloying element.

plain concrete, unreinforced concrete; concrete without steel reinforcement.

plain cut joint see flush joint.

plain cut veneer see flat cut veneer.

plain reinforcing bar see plain bar.

plain sawn, flat grain, flat sawn, slash grain, slash sawn, tangentially cut; a description of sawn timber which has been cut approximately tangentially from the log; plain sawing is also called through and through sawing.

plain tile a standard flat rectangular roof tile, usually of clay and with holes or nibs for fixing.

plain tiling

plain washer see flat washer.

plain weatherboard a horizontal timber cladding board, wedge-shaped in cross-section.

plan 1 a horizontal section of a building or area as if from above, drawn to scale, showing the relationships between spaces therein; a floor plan.

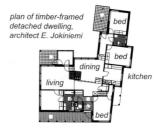

plan of timber-framed detached dwelling, architect E. Jokiniemi

2 one of the principal design drawings of a building.
3 outline; a series of decisions based on an idea, the structural formulation for realization of an idea or aim; see programme, schedule.

plan of work a document that outlines the principal stages in the design, construction and maintenance of a project and that identifies main tasks and persons; also called a work plan or work program.

planar glazing see structural glazing.

plane 1 a two-dimensional flat surface; see roof plane.
2 [Platanus spp.] a large hardwood tree from Europe, western Asia and North America with distinctive smooth mottled

bark and maple-like leaves, planted as an ornamental tree in urban squares and in parkland; see below for species:

American plane, buttonwood, sycamore; [*Platanus occidentalis*] a North American hardwood with reddish-brown timber; used for interiors and furniture.

European plane [*Platanus hybrida, P. acerifolia*] European hardwoods with warm, light-brown rayed timber; used for interiors, decorative work and veneer.

3 a powered or hand tool with a cutting edge for shaping and smoothing primarily wood, but sometimes metal and plastics; types included as separate entries are listed below:
*angle plane, see corner scraper; *bench plane; *block plane; *circular plane, see compass plane; *combination plane; *compass plane; *convex plane, see round plane; *cow plane, see roughing plane; *dado plane; *French plane, see corner scraper; *granny's tooth, see router plane; *gutter plane, see round plane; *hag's tooth, see router plane; *hollow plane; *jack plane; *jointer plane; *moulding plane; *old woman's tooth, see router plane; *rebate plane, rabbet plane; *roughing plane; *round plane; *roundsil, see compass plane; *router plane; *scrub plane, see roughing plane; *scud plane, see roughing plane; *scurfing plane, see roughing plane; *shoulder plane; *side rabbet plane; *smoothing plane; *spout plane, see round plane; *trying plane, see jointer plane; *universal plane, see combination plane.
4 see planer.

planed a description of timber which has been dressed with a plane; see dressed.

planed all round, por, surfaced four sides (Am); a description of sawn timber which has been smoothed with a plane on all four sides.

planed square-edged board, PSE; a timber board which is rectangular in cross-section and has been smoothed by a plane on all sides.

planed timber see dressed timber.

planed tongued and grooved board a timber board which has been planed and milled with a tongue and groove.

plane frame a two-dimensional framework of structural members.

plane iron the sharpened metal cutting part of a plane.

planer, 1 plane, planing machine; a machine with a wide rotating cutter mounted into a bench for smoothing or milling timber and other materials in a variety of ways; see surface planer or thicknesser.

2 rotary planer; a hand-held power tool with a narrow rotating cutting blade for planing wood.

plane truss a truss in which all members lie in the same plane.

plane wave in acoustics, a theoretical wave pattern describing a wave front in terms of a flat plane; used in modelling and calculations.

planing see dressing.

planing machine see planer.

planing mill an establishment where timber is sawn and planed.

plank a long piece of sawn softwood with cross-sectional dimensions of 38–100 mm thick and over 175 mm wide, used for flooring and walling; any wooden section of similar section, a timber board; also other types of beam-like components in other materials; types included as separate entries are listed below:
*concrete plank; *double T plank, see double tee beam; *glass plank, see channel glass; *gravel plank, see gravel board; *see gypsum plank; *hardwood plank; *plasterboard plank, see gypsum plank; *precast concrete plank, see concrete plank; *ridge plank, see ridge board; *softwood plank.

plank construction a form of traditional timber construction in which timbers are laid vertically, side by side, to form a wall; see also muntin and plank construction.

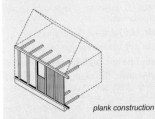

plank construction

plank flooring see wide plank flooring.

planner see town planner.

planning, 1 spatial planning; in architectural design, the creation of functional layouts or sequences of rooms or spaces as required by a brief.
2 the legislative process of land-use planning, layouts, etc. for an urban area, designed to regulate development and provide a healthy environment for its inhabitants, taking into account various socio-economic, aesthetic, industrial, and recreational factors; also called city, town or urban planning.

planning application a formal written request to a local planning authority for permission to carry out development or building work on a designated site, in the form of drawings and explanatory documentation.

planning approval see planning permission.

planning authority a local authority department which prepares plans and oversees the control of building development for a particular region through processes of planning permits and building control.

planning condition a restriction or provision imposed by a local authority as a condition of granting planning permission for a building or development.

planning consent planning permission for demolition, extension or alteration works, especially regarding listed or protected buildings, monuments, etc.

planning control, development control; in town planning, the various processes of planning applications and enforcement of planning legislation by which a planning authority controls building development; see also building control.

planning department see town planning department.

planning gain an obligation by a developer to provide associated facilities, utilities, infrastructure or amenities additional to those in a planning application, imposed by a planning authority as a condition for planning permission.

planning office see town planning department.

planning permission, planning approval, building permission, planning consent; compulsory official approval of proposed building designs or development by a local planning authority or building control department after inspection to ensure that they conform with a town plan and local bye-laws; a legally binding requirement obtained prior to commencement of building work, valid for only a limited period; see also outline planning permission, conditional planning permission.

plant 1 any heavy machinery or other mechanical devices used on a construction site; site equipment or site plant.
2 machinery which operates heating, air conditioning and other installations in a building or construction; see equipment.
3 a living vegetable organism.

planter a vessel or container of concrete, clayware, timber or plastics for decorative planting, placed on or built into hard landscaping, balconies, pedestrian areas, etc.

planting in landscape design, an area which has been planted with selected plants, groundcover, trees or shrubs.

plant room, machine room, service space; a room or space within a building containing machinery and equipment which operate technical services, air conditioning, heating, electrical and lift installations.

plan view in projection drawing, the orthographic planar projection made of an object or building on the horizontal or ground plane, as if viewed from above; also called a top view.

plasma cutting a method of cutting metals with an intense flame of ionized gas.

plasma welding arc welding in which hot plasma, an ionized gas containing electrons and free positive ions, is used as the heat source.

plaster, 1 plaster mix, plastering mix; a mixture of a hydraulic binder such as lime, gypsum or Portland cement with water and sand, used as a surface treatment for walls; the term plaster is usually used nowadays in reference to interior work — when used outside it is called render; see also render, stucco; types of plaster included as separate entries are listed below.

(empty)

2 gypsum plaster; a mixture of calcined gypsum (sulphate of lime) and water used for finishing interior walls and ceilings and moulding into ornaments.

*acoustic plaster; *base coat; *board finish plaster, board plaster; *bonding plaster; *browning plaster; *casting plaster; *cement plaster, see cement render; *see Portland cement plaster; *coarse plaster, see coarse stuff; *damp resisting plaster; *dry mix plaster, see preblended plaster; *exposed aggregate plaster; *fibrous plaster, fibre-reinforced plaster, fibred plaster; *finish plaster; *fire-retardant plaster, fireproof plaster; *gauged lime plaster, see gauged stuff; *gypsum-perlite plaster, see perlite plaster; *gypsum-vermiculite plaster, see vermiculite plaster; *gypsum plaster; *hemihydrate gypsum plaster, see hemihydrate plaster; *interior plaster, internal plaster; *lightweight plaster; *lime plaster; *metal lathing plaster; *mineral plaster; *multi-purpose plaster; *neat gypsum plaster; *one-coat plaster, see single-coat plaster; *perlite plaster; *plaster of Paris, see hemihydrate plaster; *polymer plaster, see polymer render; *Portland cement plaster; *preblended plaster; *pre-mixed plaster; *projection plaster; *Rabitz plaster; *ready-mixed plaster; *reinforced plaster; *renovation plaster; *sanded plaster; *sawdust plaster, see wood-fibred plaster; *scratch plaster; *single-coat plaster; *spray plaster, see projection plaster; *thin coat plaster; *thin wall plaster; *undercoat plaster; *vermiculite plaster, vermiculite-gypsum plaster; *waterproof plaster, see damp resisting plaster; *wood-fibred plaster; *X-ray resisting plaster.*

plaster batch in plasterwork, an amount of plaster mixed for use at any one time.

plasterboard, gypsum plasterboard; a very inert building board made from a thin layer of gypsum plaster cast between two sheets of paper; easily cut and screw-fixed to a frame and used as a drylining, internal wall cladding, etc.

plasterboard composite see gypsum plasterboard composite.

plasterboard drylining, plasterboard drywall; a lining for lightweight partitions, etc. made from gypsum wallboard, requiring no wet trades.

plasterboard joint the joint or seam formed by the butting of the edges of adjacent sheets of plasterboard, often strengthened with tape and skimmed.

plasterboard nail a galvanized nail with a large flat head and annulated shaft for greater holding power; used for fixing plasterboard to timber studs.

plasterboard screw see drywall screw.

plasterboard seamless drylining a drylining made from gypsum wallboard with seamless joints.

plasterboard seamless joint a smooth plasterboard butt joint which has been covered with tape and jointing compound.

plaster cast see fibrous plaster cast.

plaster coat a single layer of plaster laid at any one time; types included as separate entries are listed below:

*backing coat, see plaster undercoat; *brown coat, see base coat; *browning coat; *face coat, see final plaster coat; *final plaster coat; *finish coat, see final coat; *finishing coat, see final plaster coat; *first plaster undercoat, first coat; *floated coat, see float-finished rendering; *floating coat, see first plaster undercoat; *key coat; *plaster undercoat; *pricking-up coat, see first plaster undercoat; *primary coat, see key coat; *render coat; *scratch coat, see first plaster undercoat; *second plaster undercoat, second coat; *setting coat, see final plaster coat; *skimming coat, see final plaster coat; *straightening coat, see first plaster undercoat; *second plaster undercoat.*

plaster dots, plaster dabs; in plastering, a number of blobs of wet plaster thrown onto a wall at intervals and flattened as a guide to define the thickness of the plaster coat and provide a key.

plasterer a tradesman or skilled labourer who does building work on site in plaster, render and plasterboard.

plasterer's float see plastering float.

plasterer's trowel, 1 laying-on trowel; a steel-bladed hand tool for applying and smoothing plaster; see also finishing trowel.

plastering the process of applying a coat of plaster to a wall surface; types included as separate entries are listed below:
*fibrous plastering; *hand-plastering; *in-situ plasterwork; *mechanical plastering, see projection plastering; *projection plastering; *remedial plastering; *rendering; *solid plasterwork, see in-situ plasterwork; *spray plastering, see projection plastering; *trowelled plastering, see hand-plastering.

plastering background, backings; in plasterwork, any surface or structure to which plaster or plaster casts are applied.

plastering dabs, plastering dots see plaster dots.

plastering float a flat bladed hand tool used in plastering for the application and smoothing of plaster.

plastering mix see plaster.

plastering mortar mortar designed especially for use in plastering, with good adherence and resistance to cracking; also called plastering mix.

plastering screed a narrow band of plaster initially laid on a wall surface as a guide to thickness and aligning of a subsequent coat of plaster; see screed rail, collar screed.

plaster lathing see lathing.

plaster mix see plaster.

plaster mixer pump in plastering and rendering, a device for mixing plaster and pumping it to a spray gun, ready for application.

plaster of Paris see hemihydrate plaster.

plaster ornament see plasterwork enrichment

plaster pump in plastering and rendering, a device for pumping plaster to a spray gun, ready for application.

plaster spray gun a device for spraying plaster onto a surface, operated by compressed air.

plaster undercoat, backing coat; in plastering, a layer of plaster applied to a surface, which provides a base and key for the final coat.

plasterwork construction work in gypsum plaster for coating walls, rendering, ornamental mouldings, etc.; the finished work thus resulting; types included as separate entries are listed below:
*acoustic plasterwork; *combed plasterwork, see comb-finish rendering; *dragged plasterwork, see comb-finish rendering; *fibrous plasterwork; *in-situ plasterwork; *one-coat plasterwork, see single-coat plasterwork; *ornamental plasterwork, see fibrous plasterwork; *patterned plasterwork, see textured plasterwork; *rendering; *run-moulded plasterwork; *single-coat plasterwork; *solid plasterwork, see in-situ plasterwork; *stucco; *textured plasterwork; *three coat plasterwork; *two coat plasterwork.

plasterwork enrichment, plaster ornament, stucco ornament; any ornament in plaster, especially decorative plasterwork casts which are difficult to cast in situ and are added to wet plaster mouldings and surfaces.

plastic 1 relating to a material which, when deformed with a force, will not return to its original shape once the force is released.
2 a description of concrete which is easy to work.
3 sculptural; relating to the form of a building or object, free and often expressive as if moulded from clay.
4 pertaining to any product made of organic polymers; often used in the form plastics when used as an adjective; see plastics for full list of organic polymers and resins.

plastic cracking cracks caused by plastic shrinkage during the setting of fresh concrete.

plastic deformation, plastic flow, plastic yield; the change in dimension of a member under load which is permanent and will not be reversed once the load is released.

plastic-faced window a composite window in which plastic framed sashes are fixed into timber or metal frames.

plastic flow see plastic deformation.

plasticity 1 the property of a material or substance which enables it to be worked or deformed into a permanent reshapen state using mechanical force.

2 the property of how well a soil will remain whole and homogeneous under mechanical force.

3 workability, fatness; the property of how well a mortar or cement can be mixed, laid and applied.

4 an aesthetic property of architecture or sculpture, as if moulded or sculpted from clay.

plasticity index, index of plasticity; in soil analysis, a measure of the range of water contents for clay at which it remains plastic.

plasticized concrete concrete containing an admixture to increase workability when fresh.

plasticizer see plasticizing admixture, water reducing admixture.

plasticizing admixture, densifier, plasticizer; in concreting, either a water reducing admixture or a superplasticizing admixture, included in the mix to increase workability.

plastic limit in soil analysis, the lowest water content for which a clay remains in the plastic state.

plastic paint see masonry paint, emulsion paint.

plastics any of a vast range of polymeric organic materials derived from petroleum or coal which can be shaped by heat or pressure at some stage in production; types included as separate entries are listed below:
*acrylonitrile butadiene styrene, ABS; *acetal, see polyoximethylene; *acetate; *acrylic; *alkyd resin; *amino-plastic; *bakelite, see phenol formaldehyde; *cellophane; *celluloid; *cellulose acetate, CA; *cellulose acetate butyrate, CAB; *cellulose nitrate, CN; *cross-linked polyethylene, PEX, XLPE; *Dacron, see polyethylene terephthalate; *Delrin, see polyoximethylene; *Dralon, see polyacrylonitryl; *epoxide resin, epoxy resin, EP; *expanded polystyrene, EPS; *extruded polystyrene, XPS; *fibre-reinforced plastic, FRP; *foamed plastics; *foamed polystyrene, see expanded polystyrene; *foamed polyurethane; *furan; *furfuraldehyde, furfural; *gutta-percha; *high density polythene,

HDPE; *isocyanurate, see polyisocyanurate; *laminate; *low density polythene, LDPE; *melamine formaldehyde, melamine, MF; *Noryl, polyphenylene oxide; *nylon, polyamide; *Orlon, polyacrylonitrile; *Perlon, polyamide; *Perspex, polymethyl methacrylate; *phenol formaldehyde, phenolic resin, PF; *polyacetal, polyacetate, see polyoximethylene; *polyacrylonitrile, PAN; *polyamide, PA; *polycarbonate, PC; *polyester; *polyester resin, UP; *polyetheretherketone, PEEK; *polyethylene, PE; *polyethylene terephthalate, PET; *polyformaldehyde, see polyoximethylene; *polyisocyanurate, PIR; *polymethyl methacrylate, PMMA; *polyolefin; *polyoximethylene, POM; *polyphenylene oxide, PPO; *polypropylene, PP; *polystyrene, PS; *polysulphone, PSU, polysulfone (Am); *polytetrafluoroethylene, PTFE; *polyurethane, PU; *polyvinyl acetate, PVAC; *polyvinyl alcohol, PVA; *polyvinyl chloride, PVC; *polyvinyl fluoride, PVF; *polyvinylidene chloride, PVDC; *polyvinylidene fluoride, PVDF; *reinforced plastic, see fibre-reinforced plastic; *Rilsan, polyamide; *silicone, SI; *styrene-acrylonitrile, SAN; *teflon, polytetrafluoroethylene; *thermoplastics; *thermosetting plastics; *unsaturated polyester, see polyester resin; *urea formaldehyde, UF; *vinylidene chloride, see polyvinylidene chloride.

plastics coating, organic coating; the electrostatic application of a protective surface layer of polyester or other plastics to metal surfaces for resistance to corrosion.

plastic sealant flexible sealant with plastic properties, which undergoes permanent change of form as a response to movement between jointed components or materials.

plastic settlement see secondary consolidation.

plastic sheet curing see membrane curing.

plastic shrinkage the shrinkage and cracking of fresh concrete as it loses moisture due to the effects of temperature, lack of humidity and wind after placement, but before any strength development has occurred; a problem especially in hot countries.

plastics laminate see laminate.

plastic soil the classification of very cohesive soils, such as clay, which can be rolled into thin threads without crumbling.

plastics pipe stiff pipe formed from a polymer such as polythene and unplasticized polyvinyl chloride, used for a number of applications including drainage pipework.

plastics wallcovering hardwearing and water-resistant decorative wallcovering made of plastics, supplied in rolls and used for wet areas, etc.

plastics window see PVC-U window.

plastic yield see plastic deformation.

plastisol a thin coating, often polyvinyl chloride dissolved in a plasticizer, baked to provide a hardwearing and corrosion-resistant surface for steel components.

plastomer a molecule or combination of molecules that form the basis of a plastic; usually a resin or other thermosetting polymer.

Platanus spp. see plane.

plat band a flat decorative horizontal band or course slightly projecting from the surface of a masonry wall.

plate 1 any thin, rigid sheet or piece of material, structural layer, etc.; see below for examples:
*chequerplate, checkerplate; *key plate, see escutcheon; *kicking plate; *metal plate, flat plate; *name-plate; *push plate; *quarto plate.*
2 any horizontal member fixed to walling and used as a bearing for joists and other members; see wall plate, sole plate.

plate floor a solid concrete floor slab of even thickness in which bottom reinforcement compensates for the lack of supporting beams.

plate girder, welded plate girder; an I-beam welded from steel plate, used for long spans; the thickness and size of the flange and web may be varied according to loading requirements.

plate glass, polished plate glass; thick cast glass which has been ground and polished; largely replaced with float glass; see clear plate glass.

platen-pressed chipboard, pressed chipboard; chipboard manufactured by pressing between flat steel plates.

plate tracery early Gothic tracery consisting of a simply divided arched opening with a solid plate of masonry or spandrel above, into which a foil or other shape has been cut.

Gothic plate tracery, basilica of San Francesco, Assisi, Italy 1228–1253; architect Jacobus von Meruan

platform any area artificially raised higher than its surroundings, on stilts, piers or a structural base; any level area at the top of a building or construction; a long raised area used for passengers embarking or disembarking vehicles such as trains, trams and buses; see also plinth.

platform floor, modular floor, palette floor, raised access floor; floor construction supported on a series of props above the main floor structure to allow for the passage of cables and ducts.

platform frame, platform framing, western framing; a form of multistorey timber frame construction in which single-storey stud walls bear on the floor or platform constructed at the level below.

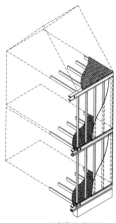

platform frame

platform roof see flat roof.

platinum a heavy, ductile silver-coloured metal, **Pt**, which is corrosion resistant and has a high melting point.

plaza originally a Spanish urban square; nowadays any large open urban space, often linked to a prestigious building.

pleat a localized defect in veneering and plywood caused by lifting and folding of plies.

plenum barrier the upper extension of a partition into a ceiling void providing an acoustic barrier to inhibit the transmission of sound to adjacent spaces.

Plessey's green a variety of chromium oxide green pigment.

Plexiglas a proprietary name for thin sheets of acrylic used as glazing, translucent roofing and for cladding.

pliable tube metal or plastics pipe which can be bent into shape with pipe benders, etc. without fracturing; pliability is the property of a solid material which is easily bent or folded.

pliers a metal scissor-like tool used for gripping objects.

plinth 1 a thickening or base at the base of a wall, column or building, on which it stands.
2 the round or square construction on which a classical column is supported; the lowest part of a classical base or pedestal.
3 see plinth brick.

plinth brick, plinth; a special brick with one upper edge splayed along its length, used in a brick coping, above a projection, etc.; see also header plinth, stretcher plinth.

plinth header see header plinth.

plinth stretcher see stretcher plinth.

plot ratio an indication of the density of building for a particular area, the ratio of built floor area to area of site on which a building stands.

plucking a defect in concretework caused by the separation of surface material from the concrete on striking of the formwork.

plug 1 a rubber, metal or plastics accessory for a sink or basin to temporary close the outlet to a discharge pipe.

2 see stopper.
3 see electric plug.
4 see patch.
5 see wall plug, hollow-wall plug.

plug and feathers an implement for cleaving stone in a quarry, consisting of two semicircular metal plates, known as feathers, inserted into a shallow hole; a wedge, known as a plug, is then driven between, causing the stone to cleave.

plug cock see cock.

plug cutter a drill bit for cutting circular wooden inserts to conceal the heads of submerged screws.

plug gauge, hole gauge; a cylindrical metal bar with stepped or cone-shaped machined ends used for the accurate measurement or checking of round holes.

plugmold see skirting trunking.

plug nail a fastener consisting of a serrated nail in a plastics wall plug; used for fixing components to concrete or masonry.

plug socket see socket outlet.

plug tap, plug valve see cock.

plum 1 [*Prunus domestica*] a hardwood with dense, fine-grained timber used mainly for the decorative value of its grain in veneers and quality furniture; planted as a small tree in gardens for its fruit and decorative flowers.
2 displacer, plum stone; in concretework, a large stone or piece of hardened concrete placed in the pour as a space filler.

plumb in surveying, setting out and construction work, measured as or installed exactly vertical.

plumbago see graphite.

plumber a tradesman who installs and repairs water pipes, drains, sanitary fittings and other water systems.

plumbing 1 the job of installing the pipework and other assemblies for a functioning water supply or drainage system; the various systems of pipes and fittings thus installed, called pipework.
2 the measuring or setting up of a construction to true vertical.

plumbing unit a prefabricated assembly of water fittings or sanitary appliances with supporting framework, which can be installed and connected as a unit.

plumb line a device used to indicate true vertical by means of a length of fine cord with a weight hung on the end.

plume capital see palm capital.

plum stone see plum.

plutonic rock, plutonite, intrusive rock, deep seated rock; types of coarse-grained igneous rock which form from slowly solidified magma in the lower part of the earth's crust; these include granite, diorite, gabbro and peridotite.

ply 1 a layer of sheet material in laminated construction, particularly a layer of veneer in plywood.
2 a common abbreviation for 'plywood'.

ply-web beam see plywood web beam, corrugated ply-web beam.

---

plywood, ply; a timber building board manufactured by gluing an odd number of thin timber veneers or plies face to face under pressure; each alternate veneer is arranged with its grain at 90° to the adjacent veneer to increase strength; also called veneer plywood; types included as separate entries are listed below:
*bent plywood; *birch plywood; *cellular plywood, cellular board; *coated plywood; *core plywood; *cross-grained plywood; *exterior plywood; *film-faced plywood; *finger-jointed plywood; *foil-faced plywood; *formply; *hardwood plywood; *homogeneous plywood; *inserted plywood; *interior plywood; *long-grained plywood; *marine plywood; *metal-faced plywood; *mixed plywood; *multi-ply; *overlaid plywood; *parallel-grain plywood; *prefinished plywood; *preformed plywood; *raw plywood; *repaired

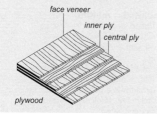

plywood; *sanded plywood; *scarf-jointed plywood; *scraped plywood; *softwood plywood; *special plywood; *treated plywood; *unsanded plywood; *wood-based core plywood.

plywood beam see corrugated ply-web beam, laminated web beam, plywood box beam (see box beam), plywood web beam (ply-web beam).

plywood beam

plywood flooring flooring consisting of plywood boards, often with matched edges.

plywood web beam, ply-web beam; a composite beam made with an upper and lower chord of a timber section with a plywood web in between; see also corrugated ply-web beam.

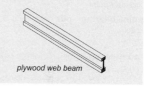

plywood web beam

PMMA polymethyl methacrylate.

pneumatically applied concrete see sprayed concrete.

pneumatical mortar see sprayed concrete.

pneumatic caisson see compressed air caisson.

pneumatic concrete placer a machine for pumping concrete into formwork, operated by compressed air.

pneumatic concreting see concrete spraying.

pneumatic document conveyor see tube conveyor.

pneumatic structure see air-supported structure.

pneumatic test see air test.

pocket see box out.

pocket chisel see butt chisel.

(caption for image 1)

face veneer

inner ply

central ply

plywood

pocket rot localized fungal decay in timber, surrounded by sound wood.

podium, 1 dais, stand; a platform, stage or raised area of floor in a hall or auditorium for a speaker, committee, dignitaries or for a presentation, etc.; a raised platform from which speeches and other performances are given.
2 Lat.; in classical architecture, a wall and raised platform surrounding the arena in an amphitheatre or theatre, reserved for the seating of high-ranked officials; the high base on which a temple, column or statue stands; also called a crepidoma.

podzol a light, grey soil type common to cold and damp climates, in which most of the soluble minerals have been leached to underlying soils by rainwater.

point, 1 point tool, clourer; a pointed masonry chisel, used for the initial rough shaping of stone surfaces or to produce a pitted finish to smooth stonework.
2 the outlet at which a device can be connected to a supply; see electric point, lighting point.

point-bearing pile see end-bearing pile.

> **pointed arch** any arch with a pointed apex; sometimes called a Gothic arch; types included as separate entries are listed below:
> *equilateral arch; *Italian pointed arch; *lancet arch; *pointed cinquefoil arch; *pointed cinquefoliated arch; *pointed horseshoe arch; pointed multifoliated arch; *pointed Saracenic arch, see stilted arch; *pointed segmental arch; *pointed trefoil arch; *pointed trifoliated arch; *Saracenic pointed arch, stilted pointed arch, see pointed Saracenic arch; *Venetian arch.

pointed architecture see Gothic architecture.

pointed barrel vault, Gothic vault; a curved masonry roof vault which is pointed in uniform cross-section, found especially in Gothic churches.

pointed barrel vault

pointed cinquefoil a decorative and ornamental device consisting of five pointed arches motifs radiating out from a point.

pointed cinquefoil   *pointed cinquefoil arch*

pointed cinquefoil arch an arch composed of five pointed lobes or foils in a cloverleaf arrangement.

pointed cinquefoliated arch a decorative arch whose intrados is composed of five pointed lobes or foils, and whose extrados is a pointed arch.

pointed cinquefoliated arch

pointed equilateral arch see equilateral arch.

pointed horseshoe arch an arch composed of two segments of a circle which meet at an apex and bow outwards.

pointed horseshoe arch

pointed multifoliated arch a decorative arch whose intrados is composed of a number of pointed lobes or foils, and whose extrados is a pointed arch; see trifoliated, cinquefoliated.

pointed multifoliated arch

pointed quatre-foil a decorative motif of four intersecting pointed arches radiating outwards from a point.

pointed quatrefoil

pointed Saracenic arch see stilted arch.

pointed segmental arch any type of pointed arch composed of two segments of a circle leaning in on one another.

pointed trefoil a decorative motif of three intersecting pointed arches radiating outwards from a point.

pointed trefoil arch an arch composed of three pointed lobes or foils in a cloverleaf arrangement.

pointed trefoil   *pointed trefoil arch*

pointed trifoliated arch a decorative arch whose intrados is composed of three pointed lobes or foils in a cloverleaf arrangement, and whose extrados is a pointed arch.

pointed trifoliated arch

pointed vault see pointed barrel vault.

pointing the filling of masonry joints with better quality mortar after the bedding mortar has hardened in order to provide a smooth, compressed and attractive surface.

pointing compound a flexible joint filler used in glazing.

pointing mortar mortar designed especially for use in pointing brickwork and masonrywork.

point load, concentrated load; a structural load imposed over a small area, in theory a point, as opposed to being spread evenly over a larger area.

point of inflection see inflection point.

points per inch see PPI.

point tool a pointed masonry chisel, see point.

point tool finish a finish for concrete produced by dressing with a point tool.

poisonous referring to a substance which has a toxic effect on human health, or may cause death, in even small amounts.

poker vibration see immersion vibration.

poker vibrator see immersion vibrator.

poker-work the burning of a design or decoration onto a wooden surface with a heated metal instrument; the product of this process.

polar curve see light distribution curve.

pole plate in traditional timber roof construction, a horizontal timber supported by the lower end of principal rafters, which carries the lower end of common rafters.

poling board in excavation work, one of a series of vertical timber boards which support the sides of a trench or excavation.

polish, polishing agent; a minutely abrasive substance rubbed into a smooth surface to provide a glossy sheen as a finish.

polished finish a description of an easily scratched glossy finish in stonework caused by the natural reflection density of the stone's crystals; created by treating with a very high diamond abrasive such as 8000 grit, polishing bricks or powders; similar glossy finishes for other materials.

polished plate glass see plate glass.

polishing the finish treatment of a smooth surface by rubbing with very fine abrasives, leather or cotton fabric until a glossy sheen is produced; see also burnishing, French polish.

polishing agent see polish.

pollution substances or phenomena, hazardous to health, which contaminate the environment; see noise pollution, air pollution.

polyacetal, **polyacetate** see polyoximethylene.

polyacrylate rubber, ACM, acrylic rubber; a synthetic rubber with good oil and heat resistance, used for seals, gaskets and hoses.

polyacrylonitrile, PAN; any of a range of acrylic plastics based on acrylonitrile, resilient and UV-resistant plastics sold as Dralon and Orlon and used as fibres.

polyaddition see addition polymerization.

polyamide, PA; any of a range of synthetic resins whose chemical units are linked together with amide molecules; proprietary names are Nylon, Perlon and Rilsan.

Polybutadiene see butadiene rubber.

polycarbonate, PC; a dense, hard, tough, transparent thermoplastic used as a glazing material.

polycarbonate cellular sheet, cellular polycarbonate; lightweight cellular sheet glazing or cladding manufactured from two sheets of transparent polycarbonate separated by an insulating cellular polycarbonate structure.

polychloroprene see chloroprene rubber.

polychrome brickwork brickwork which makes use of bricks of differing colours for decorative effect.

polychromy the use of a range of different colours in architecture and painting for decorative effect.

polycondensation polymerization in which a simple molecule such as water is condensed out; a polymer produced by this process is called a polycondensate.

polyester a group of plastics which are polymerized from ester; used for making fibres for fabrics and textiles.

polyester base felt roofing roofing felt whose fibrous mat is primarily of polyester fibres.

polyester resin, UP, unsaturated polyester; a thermosetting resin which hardens without heat or pressure; used in

glass-reinforced plastics and paints, varnishes and floor coverings.

polyetheretherketone, PEEK; a high-strength radiation-resistant engineering plastic used in electrical installations and appliances for the chemical industry.

polyethylene, polythene, PE; a chemically resistant thermoplastic; a polymer of ethylene used for drainage and water pipes, membranes and concrete curing sheets.

polyethylene terephthalate, Dacron, PET; a strong, tough, heat-resistant polymer used to make textile fibres.

polyformaldehyde see polyoximethylene.

polygonal masonry, cyclopean masonry; uncoursed masonry walling laid of large irregular stones in rough polygonal shapes to fit in with adjacent stones, often without mortar; ancient polygonal masonry was known as Pelasgic masonry, while Roman polygonal masonry was known as opus siliceum.

polygonal masonry

polygonal shell see folded plate.

polygonal truss a truss whose upper chord is made up of more than two angled segments of a polygon.

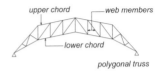

polygonal truss

polygonal wall see polygonal masonry.

polyisocyanurate, isocyanurate, PIR; a non-flammable urethane foam used as thermal insulation in composite structures.

polyisoprene a polymer of isoprene, one form of which is natural rubber.

polymer any chemical compound consisting of long chains of similar repeated molecules; most plastics are polymers; see plastics for full list of organic polymers and resins.

polymer adhesive see polymerizing adhesive.

polymer binder, polymeric binder; a synthetic resin binder for paints and glues that sets by polymerization.

polymer concrete, polymer Portland cement concrete, resin concrete; chemically resistant concrete whose binder is an organic polymer.

polymer fibre reinforced concrete concrete reinforced with polypropylene fibres, used for in-situ concrete and piles.

polymer glue see polymerizing adhesive.

polymeric binder see polymer binder.

polymeric roofing see calendered polymeric roofing.

polymer impregnated concrete concrete which, when hard, has been impregnated with a polymer.

polymerization the chemical action of forming polymers or long chain molecules from simple repeated molecules; most plastics are formed by this process.

polymerizing adhesive any adhesive which sets by polymerization.

polymer modified concrete concrete which contains an emulsion of PVC to increase strength and resistance to oil and abrasion.

polymer plaster see polymer render.

polymer Portland cement concrete see polymer concrete.

polymer render types of render or plaster designed for difficult external wall surfaces, consisting of mineral aggregate in a polymer binder; also called polymer plaster.

polymethyl methacrylate, PMMA, polymethyl methylacrylic; a clear acrylic resin used in sheets for glazing and roofing, and formed into light fittings, basins, urinals and signs; sold variously as Perspex and Plexiglas.

polymorphism the use of a repeated element, form, volume or space in a number of different ways in architectural composition, etc.

polyolefin any plastic manufactured by the additional polymerization of ethylene and propylene; used for synthetic fibres.

polyoximethylene, polyacetal, polyacetate, polyformaldehyde, POM, acetal, Delrin; a tough, strong polymer manufactured from formaldehyde and used for wearing parts of bearings, cogs, taps, pumps, zips and valves.

polyphase current a number of electric currents supplied with identical frequency but differing phases.

polyphenylene oxide, PPO, Noryl; a high-strength, temperature- and moisture-resisting plastic used for computer equipment, appliances and pipes.

polypore see conk.

polypropylene, PP; a thermoplastic used for drainage pipes and fittings, road gullies, WC seats and cavity trays.

polystyrene, PS; a brittle, flammable, low-cost thermoplastic, clear in unmodified form, used for light fittings, formwork, paints and as expanded polystyrene (bead or foamed polystyrene) and extruded polystyrene.

polystyrene foam board see extruded polystyrene.

polysulphide a synthetic rubber used in mastics and sealants.

polysulphone, PSU, polysulfone (Am); a tough, strong, stiff, heat- and chemical-resistant synthetic resin used for plumbing fixtures, automotive parts and cable insulation.

polytetrafluoroethylene, PTFE, teflon; a resistant, expensive thermoplastic used for non-stick surfaces, dirt-repellant coatings and sliding expansion joints in large structures.

polythene the more common abbreviated name for polyethylene; see high density polythene, low density polythene.

polythene sheet curing see membrane curing.

polyurethane, PU; a hardwearing, resilient, stable thermosetting plastic used for paints, varnishes, sealants, sheeting and foams.

polyurethane foam, PU foam; an expanded plastic made from polyurethane and freon gas, used for rigid thermal insulation in cavities and composite products.

polyurethane powder coating a pigmented polymeric powder coating whose binder is polyurethane.

polyurethane varnish, urethane varnish; a clear, waterproof, durable gloss varnish which contains polyurethane as a binder.

polyvinyl acetate, PVAC; a thermoplastic used in wood glues, emulsion paints, plaster, screed bonding agents and in-situ floor coverings.

polyvinyl acetate glue, PVA glue; an emulsion glue with a binder of polyvinyl acetate used for gluing paper and card.

polyvinyl alcohol, PVA; a resin formed by treating polyvinyl acetate with acids or alkalis; used in paints and adhesives, for films, and as a raw material in textile fibres.

polyvinyl chloride, PVC; a versatile, low-cost thermoplastic used for coatings, pipes and trim.

polyvinyl fluoride, PVF; a thermoplastic used as a decorative and protective surface film for metals and plywood.

polyvinylidene chloride, PVDC, vinylidene chloride; a plastic manufactured into extruded films for the packaging industry.

polyvinylidene fluoride, PVDF; a plastic used for injection-moulded products and extruded films.

POM polyoximethylene.

pomegranate the reddish fruit of the tree *Punica granatum* with many seeds and a hard rind; in classical ornament, symbolic of fertility, love, and of life and death; in the medieval Catholic church, symbolic of the blood of the Virgin Mary.

Pompeian blue see Egyptian blue.

ponding, 1 water seasoning; a process in which logs are stored under water prior to conversion, to protect them from insect and fungal attack.

2 the curing of fresh concrete by pouring a shallow layer of water on top of it.

pontoon, float; a floating support such as an air-filled barrel used to support a bridge, jetty or temporary structure on water.

poplar [*Populus spp.*] a group of large, fast growing hardwoods from Europe and North America with soft, pale timber which does not splinter; used for furniture, packaging, panelling and plywood;

Populus spp. – poplar

poplars are widely planted as a landscape, street or park tree, but should not be planted too near buildings because of root damage to foundations; see below for related species included in this work; see also tulipwood (yellow poplar, *Liriodendron tulipifera*).

aspen [*Populus tremula, Populus tremuloides*] hardwoods from Europe and North America respectively with soft, porous, straight-grained, pale-coloured timber; used as boards for cladding and for plywood and matches; *Populus tremuloides*, the American species, is called quaking aspen.

balsam poplar [*Populus balsamifera, Populus tacamahaca*] a North American hardwood with pale brown timber; used in plywood, as sawn boards and for furniture.

black cottonwood [*Populus trichocarpa*] a North American hardwood whose pale brown timber is used as sawn boards and for plywood, packing and furniture.

black poplar [*Populus nigra, Populus spp.*] a group of hardwoods, especially from Europe, with soft, pale timber; used for plywood; the Lombardy poplar [*Populus nigra italica*] is a tall slender variety of black poplar.

cottonwood [*Populus spp.*] a group of hardwoods from North America with soft, pale timber; used for furniture, panelling and plywood.

grey poplar [*Populus canescens*] a hardwood from Europe; a hybrid between the aspen and the white poplar.

white poplar, silver poplar, abele; [*Populus alba*] a hardwood from Europe and Central Asia with silver-green foliage and leaves with bright white undersides, planted in rural areas.

poppy oil, poppyseed oil; a clear, slow-drying oil pressed from the seeds of the poppy plant, used as a vehicle in some paints.

pop rivet a light, hollow aluminium rivet used to form quick and clean joints in sheetmetalwork using special pliers.

Populus spp. see poplar.

pop-up waste a pipe fitting for joining a sink or basin to a discharge pipe at a plug-hole, which incorporates a raisable plug operated by a lever.

por see planed all round.

porcelain a ceramic material similar to vitreous china but made from higher quality products under more controlled conditions; used for high class crockery and electrical insulators.

porch 1 a space immediately in front of the external door of a building, usually unheated and sometimes glazed.
2 the main entrance door and surrounding wall fabric of a temple, church or other religious building, often highly ornate; an enclosed and roofed entrance room or space in a church.

pore a cross-cut vessel in the structure of hardwood, or small void in soils, mortar and concrete, etc.
pore filler, permeability-reducing admixture; a mineral admixture included in a concrete mix to reduce the size of voids or pores by filling them.
pore-water pressure, neutral pressure, neutral stress; in soil mechanics, the pressure of water contained in voids or pores in saturated soil.

porosity a measure of the ratio of voids to total volume in a granular or porous solid.

porous concrete see aerated concrete.

porous wood wood with longitudinal cells which transport water in a living tree; these same cells in converted timber form the basic structure of hardwood.

porphrytic, phenocrystal; a description of types of rock which contain distinct crystals in a homogeneous mineral matrix.

porphyry an igneous rock with large red or white feldspar crystals set in a fine-grained mass.

portability the ability of a component, furnishing or construction to be easily carried or moved without excess difficulty, heavy transport or machinery.

portal a grand, often ornamental gateway, porch or main entrance for a castle, religious or large public building.

portal frame, rigid frame; a simple beam and column framework with rigid joints, often of welded steel girders or lattice construction.

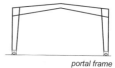

portal frame

porte cochère a doorway or porch designed to allow for the passage of a vehicle, originally one to allow the passage of carriages into a courtyard.

portico a formal ornamental gateway, porch or main covered entranceway for a classical temple, religious or public building, etc. consisting of rows of columns which support a roof, often pedimented.

porticus 1 Lat.; any open Roman building, canopy or structure whose roof is supported on one side by a row of columns; the roofed veranda around the edges of a peristyle in a Roman dwelling; a portico.
2 shallow side spaces off the nave of a Saxon church.

Portland cement an active hydraulic binder (so named because it resembles Portland stone) formed by grinding the clinker which is produced by burning clay and lime in a kiln; nowadays all cement used in concrete is Portland cement.
Portland blast-furnace cement a blended cement formed by a ground mixture of blast-furnace slag, Portland cement and calcium sulphate.
Portland cement clinker, Portland clinker; clinker composed mainly of calcium silicates made by burning clay and lime in a kiln; used in Portland cement.
Portland cement concrete concrete whose binder is Portland cement.
Portland cement plaster plaster produced with Portland cement as a binder.
Portland pozzolana cement a blended cement formed from a ground mixture of Portland cement and pozzolan.
Portland pulverized fuel-ash cement, fuel-ash cement; a blended

cement formed from a ground mixture of Portland cement and pulverized fuel-ash. see also quick-setting Portland cement, rapid-hardening Portland cement.

Port Orford cedar see cypress.

possession see possession of site, handover.

possession of site, site possession; the contractor's legal right to occupy a site after the signing of a building contract in order to carry out construction work.

post any slender column, often round in plan; either freestanding as a fixing for lighting, one supporting a fence, etc. or a structural vertical timber which acts as a column or strut to support overlying structure.

post and beam construction a structural framing system for a building in which floor and wall loads are transferred via framing beams to a grid of supporting columns down to foundations; also called post and lintel construction, column and beam construction (especially in concrete or steel construction), trabeated construction.

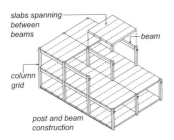

slabs spanning between beams

beam

column grid

post and beam construction

post and lintel construction see post and beam construction.

post and rail balustrade a balustrade constructed of horizontal rails supported by regularly spaced uprights, with or without an infill material of glass, mesh, boarding, etc.

post-contract stage in contract management, the range of sitework, construction and administration events commencing from the point at which a contract is signed.

postern a secondary, side or rear doorway in a fortified wall; a secondary gateway in the wall of an enclosure such as a churchyard.

post-tensioned concrete a form of prestressed concrete, usually manufactured on site, in which tendons are placed in tension once the concrete has hardened; this method is called post-tensioning; see also pretensioned concrete.

potash a crude form of potassium carbonate.

potash feldspar, orthoclase; a potassium silicate mineral used as a raw material in the ceramic and glass industries; see adularia.

potash water glass a thick alkaline liquid, potassium silicate, which dries to form a weak type of glass used as a glaze or medium in some painting.

potassium carbonate an alkaline compound used in the production of washing powders and some types of glass; potash is a crude form.

potential the electrical force at any point in a circuit caused by the presence of an electric charge.

potential difference see voltage.

potenty moulding classical fret ornament made up of a series of crutch-like forms joined end-on end.

potenty moulding

pot life, working life; the period of time after mixing during which an adhesive or varnish remains in a usable state.

potstone see soapstone.

Potter's flint any silica or quartz-based material ground to a powder as a basic material in ceramics.

poultice corrosion see deposit corrosion.

powder coating a hardwearing protective or decorative coating formed by the application of a finely divided pigmented organic polymer fused into a continuous film by the application of heat during a baking process; see acrylic powder coating.

power a measure of rate of exchange of energy in a system, a physical quantity whose SI unit is the watt (W).

power bender see bar bending machine.

power drill, electric drill; a hand-held machine tool for boring holes.

power factor the ratio of active power to apparent power in an electric circuit; the lower the power factor, the less efficient the circuit.

power float, rotary float; a machine tool for the finishing of concrete slabs after the initial set with rotating steel smoothing blades, a horizontal disc or some other smoothing mechanism; see power trowel.
power floated finish, power trowelled finish; a smooth concrete floor finish formed with a power float.

power line any main cable used for distribution of electricity.

power point see electric point.

power saw any saw or sawing device powered by electricity.

power trowel, helicopter, mechanical trowel, machine trowel, rotary trowel; a power-driven machine with a number of rotating blades in its base, used for producing a smooth finish on freshly cast concrete floors; cf. power float.
power trowelled finish see power floated finish.

Pozidriv head screw a screw whose head has a patented cross-shaped indentation similar to the Phillips, but with small oblique notches for added grip when turning.

pozzolan, pozzolana, pozzuolana; a siliceous volcanic dust occurring naturally in Pozzuoli, Italy and used by the Romans in their concretework; nowadays a finely ground manufactured product, it sets in the presence of calcium hydroxide and water to form a hardwearing cement binder.

pozzolanic cement a blended cement formed from a ground mixture of Portland cement and a pozzolan (which has to have passed a pozzolanicity test).

Pozzuoli blue see Egyptian blue.

PP polypropylene.

PPI points per inch; a measure of the fineness of a saw blade or similar implement, the number of points of sawteeth per inch.

PPO polyphenylene oxide.

practical spreading rate the rate at which a coating can be applied to a surface under normal conditions.

Pratt truss a form of lattice beam or triangular truss patented by the Americans Thomas and Caleb Pratt in 1844 in which, by virtue of the layout of the members, all diagonals are in tension and all verticals in compression, the opposite of those in a Howe truss; in the triangular truss diagonals form an A-pattern and in flat trusses a V-pattern; see Howe truss, Vierendeel truss, Warren truss.

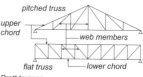

Pratt trusses

preblending the mechanical stirring together of dry or powdered component parts of a concrete, plaster, paint, etc. mix to form a homogeneous mass; packed and supplied in bags as dry mix.
preblended mortar the component parts of a mortar mix, mechanically mixed together as dry powder before supply, and mixed with clean water on site prior to use; also known as premixed mortar or dry mix mortar.
preblended plaster the component parts of a plaster mix, mixed together as dry powder before supply, and mixed with clean water on site prior to use; also known as premixed plaster or dry mix plaster.

precast concrete constructional concrete in the form of prefabricated units and manufactured products that are cast with fixings and openings, and cured under controlled conditions in a factory or plant, then transported to a building site for installation or erection; mainly used for structural components such as walls and slabs. See illustration on following page.
precast beam, beam unit; a concrete beam manufactured in a plant, brought

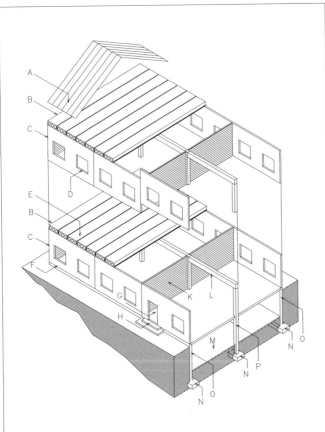

A   roof, roofing
B   roof slab – hollow-core
       slab, hollow-core beam
C   external wall –
       load bearing wall unit,
       load bearing wall panel
D   window opening
E   intermediate floor
F   base wall, wall base
G   doorway, door opening
H   doorstep

K   internal wall, partition
L   precast beam, beam unit
M   base floor, bottom floor
N   footing, foundation
O   foundation wall
P   precast column,
       column unit

to site ready made with reinforcement and fixings for erection; see also concrete plank, hollow-core beam.

precast concrete flag see concrete paving slab.

precast concrete frame a concrete building frame whose beams, columns, slabs, etc. have been cast elsewhere, and brought to site for assembly.

precast concrete panel a precast concrete unit for wall structure or cladding; types included as separate entries are listed below:
*edge panel; *sandwich panel; *wall panel; *window panel.

precast concrete paver see concrete block paver.

precast concrete ring a large-bore precast concrete pipe used for manholes, wells, soakaways, etc.

precast concrete slab unit see precast slab unit.

precast concrete unit a concrete component, usually for floor or wall construction, that is cast in a factory under controlled conditions, then assembled on site as a unit when hardened and cured; see also entries under precast concrete.

precast concrete work the casting, finishing and installing of precast concrete panels and units.

precast flag see concrete paving slab.

precast panel see precast concrete panel, precast concrete unit.

precast paver see concrete block paver.

precast pile in foundation technology, a pile consisting of a prefabricated, prestressed or reinforced concrete unit.

precast plank see concrete plank.

precast ring see precast concrete ring.

precast slab unit, slab unit; any of a number of prefabricated concrete units used as floor structure in multistorey buildings.

precipitation 1 the separation of a solid from a liquid as the result of a chemical process.
2 water falling from the atmosphere as rain, snow or hail.

precision engineering the accurate design, manufacture and maintenance of machines, devices and appliances which have small components.

precision tube relatively thin-walled manufactured steel tubing used for applications such as bicycle frames, furnishings and trim.

precompression see prestressing.

preconsolidation the process of compacting the ground upon which foundations of a building are to be laid by using a preload or other techniques prior to construction, in order to limit the amount of final settlement.

pre-contract stage in contract administration, the stage of design work, tendering, administration, etc. prior to the point at which a contract for construction work on site is placed.

predecorated, prefinished; pertaining to wallboard and other sheet or strip products which have been given a factory finish.

prefabricated, factory-made; referring to a product or component which is manufactured or assembled in a factory as opposed to on site; precast is the term used for prefabricated concrete products.

prefabricated building a building for which the majority of elements and components are prefabricated elsewhere for assembly on site; called a kit building if consisting of a set of standard prefabricated parts.

prefabricated gypsum wallboard panel a prefabricated partition panel consisting of gypsum wallboard fixed to either side of a frame or core.

prefabricated pile see precast pile.

prefabricated unit, prefabricated component, unit; any building component or set of components which have been manufactured and assembled prior to arrival on site; see also precast concrete.

prefabrication, prefabricated construction; a quick and clean method of construction in which components or groups of components are made under workshop conditions and transported to site for installation.

prefinished see predecorated.

prefinished plywood plywood whose face plies have been surface treated at the manufacturing stage.

preform, blank; the basic shape of a key or other moulded product before it has been cut for use.

preformed plywood plywood which has been bent or moulded during the gluing stage of production, using clamps, heat treatment, etc.

preformed rope, trulay rope; metal or plastics rope whose strands or wires have been bent into their final helical shape before laying to remove internal stresses and prevent fraying when cut.

preformed wire rope preformed rope manufactured from metal wires; used for tension and bracing cables.

preheater see bulk heater.

preliminaries in contract administration, that part of a bill of quantities or specification that describes not the work itself, but associated matters such as site use, facilities, security, etc.

preliminary, draft; a rough or initial version of a drawing or document, often used as a basis for further design development.

preliminary drawing see sketch drawing.

preliminary pile in foundation technology, a pile sunk prior to foundation construction to test design criteria, structural suitability and dimensions of the piling system; see also test pile, trial pile.

preload embankment, preload fill; a pile of earth placed over the location of future foundations of a building for a period of time prior to commencement of construction to compress the ground beneath and limit the amount of settlement of the building once constructed; see preconsolidation.

premature stiffening see false set.

premixed pertaining to mortar or plaster which is delivered on site as a dry powder in a ready mixed condition.

pre-packed concrete see grouted concrete.

prepaint process see coil coating.

prepayment see advance.

preplaced concrete see grouted concrete.

prepolymer in plastics technology, an intermediate product of polymerization processes used as a raw material and fully polymerized at a later stage in manufacture.

presentation model a scale model of the final design for a project or proposal, constructed for the purposes of presenting or selling a scheme to clients.

preservation 1 the treatment of timber with a preservative to protect it from fungal decay and insect attack.
2 see building preservation.

preservative, wood preservative; any substance used to protect timber from fungal decay or insect attack; see also fungicide.

pressed brick a brick made by moulding under high pressure.

pressed chipboard see platen-pressed chipboard.

pressed metal components and construction of sheetmetal or thin plate which has been preformed by bending and stamping into flashings, beams drips, upstands and cladding panels.

pressed metal capping preformed sheetmetal construction of galvanized steel, zinc or aluminium used as a weatherproof covering for an exposed abutment, parapet, upstand or upper surface of a freestanding wall; see also next entry.

pressed metal coping a sheetmetal capping for the exposed top of a freestanding wall or parapet.

pressed metal facing unit see sheetmetal cladding panel.

pressed metal flashing a pressed sheetmetal component included above openings and at junctions, etc. in construction to direct water to the outside of a building; see also eaves flashing.

pressed metal sill a sill of pressed sheetmetal beneath a window to protect the join between window frame and wall from infiltration by rainwater.

pressed steel lintel a proprietary or standard steel beam for supporting walling loads over a window or door opening.

pressed-steel radiator see panel radiator.

pressing 1 one of a number of products such as sheetmetal flashings or some solid plastic components which are formed in batches by compressing raw material in moulds or by the application of localized bending pressure to sheetmetals.
2 the mechanical processes of producing such products, natural oils, etc.

pressure the physical quantity of force per unit area, whose SI unit is the pascal, or newton per square metre, N/m^2.

pressure gauge, manometer; an instrument for measuring the pressure of fluids or gases.

pressure grouting a strengthening process in which voids and air pockets in hardened concrete and soil are filled with grout, cement or mortar injected under pressure.

pressure gun see caulking gun.

pressure impregnated timber timber which has been saturated with preservative, usually a toxic liquid compound of copper with chromium or arsenic, in a sealed vacuum or under pressure, to ensure deep penetration; this process is known as pressure impregnation or pressure treatment.

pressure reducing valve, reducing valve; a valve which maintains a constant pressure in pipework regardless of the changes in pressure of gas entering it.

pressure surge see water hammer.

pressure tank 1 any vessel for storage of gases and liquids under pressure.
2 a water tank to which pressurized gas is applied, providing the force for circulation in a high-pressure hot water heating system.

pressure treatment see pressure impregnation.

pressure ventilation see input ventilation.

pressure vessel any pipe, chamber or boiler in a heating system whose pressure is greater than that of the surrounding air.

pressure water heater a water heater in which water is heated to over boiling point under pressure.

pressure welding, solid-phase welding; a method of welding in which heated parts to be joined are held together under pressure, either by machine or by hammering.

pressurized space any space in which air pressure is maintained at a higher level than in surrounding spaces, often for purposes of industry, ventilation or research.

prestress see prestressing force.

prestressed the condition of a structural concrete component of being internally compressed by steel tendons in tension prior to use to compensate for tensile stresses when the component is under load.

prestressed concrete reinforced concrete placed in a state of permanent compression by stretched high-tensile steel wires, strands or tendons within its fabric; these enable the component to withstand higher tensile loading than normal; see also post-tensioned, pretensioned concrete.

prestressed concrete beam a concrete beam which contains tensioned cables or tendons which enable it to withstand greater loads than a simply reinforced concrete beam.

prestressed concrete pavement a structural base and surfacing of large prestressed concrete decking slabs for roads, factory floors and airstrips.

prestressing, precompression; the application of an internal force to a concrete component, usually with tensioned steel tendons, to put it in a state of compression when in a normal non-loadbearing condition, thus improving its strength under tensile loading.

prestressing force, prestress; in prestressed concrete, the tensile loading applied to prestressing tendons, which, on their release, exerts an internal compressive force on the concrete.

prestressing strand in prestressed concrete, a prestressing cable formed from a number, usually 6, 19 or 37, of cold drawn wires wound together round a central core wire.

prestressing system the proprietary assembly, fixings, anchors and tendons that are used in the prestressing of concrete members.

prestressing tendon see tendon.

prestress loss in prestressed concrete, the difference in theoretical prestressing force and that occurring after transfer, due to shrinkage of the concrete and creep of the steel tendons.

pretensioned concrete prestressed concrete, usually precast units, in which the tendons are placed in tension before the concrete is cast around them; the hardened concrete is placed in compression when the force on the tendons is released.

pretensioning a prestressing method of placing a concrete unit in continual compression to enable it to resist tensional loading, using embedded steel tendons which are placed in tension while the concrete is wet.

pretensioning tendon a steel prestressing rod, cable or strand in pretensioned concrete.

pretreatment any treatment for a product or surface, often factory-produced, which cleans or primes it to receive a finish; a similar stage in other production processes.

price adjustment see formula price adjustment.

priced bill of quantities a bill of quantities in which a contractor has entered rates and costs against items to produce a total tender sum.

price variation formula in contract administration, a standardized method of amending contract prices to reflect variation in economic conditions, cost and price fluctuations, etc.

pricking-up coat see first plaster undercoat.

primary beam see principal beam.

primary coat see key coat.

primary colour any of the three main colours from which all other colours can be mixed: red, green and blue for light, and red, yellow and blue for pigments.

primary consolidation, primary compression; the reduction in volume of soil beneath the foundations of a new building due to the gradual squeezing out of water from it.

prime coat see priming coat.

prime contractor see main contractor.

primed referring to a component or surface to which a treatment has been applied prior to a subsequent or final coating.

primed and filled chipboard smooth chipboard supplied with its surface treated with a filler, to even out irregularities,

and a primer to reduce porosity and receive a finish.

primer, priming paint; a paint or liquid compound applied to a surface to ensure that subsequent coats will adhere, to seal a porous base, etc.; see also masonry primer, metal primer, wood primer, sealant primer.

primer-sealer paint applied to a surface to reduce its absorbency and ensure that subsequent coats will adhere.

priming the treating of a surface with a primer.

priming coat, prime coat; an initial coat applied to seal a wall surface, steel component, etc. as a base onto which successive coats or a final coat may be applied; a coat of primer.

priming paint see primer.

primrose yellow a loose name for the pigments cadmium yellow, cobalt yellow and zinc yellow, after the flower of the primrose [*Primula vulgaris*]; a general name for shades of pale yellow.

princess post in traditional timber roof construction, where a queen post is used for long spans, an intermediate post between the queen post and eaves.

principal see principal beam; principal rafter.

principal arch one of a series of major arches lining the sides of the nave of a vaulted building such as a Romanesque basilica church, supported on columns; any similar or large arch in a modern structure.

principal beam, principal, main beam, primary beam; a beam which bears major structural loading or which supports other beams.

principal designer the coordinating professional or firm in a construction project responsible for the overall design of the building, usually a qualified architect.

principal post, teagle post; in traditional timber frame construction, a main post at a corner or meeting of walls responsible for the support of the building.

principal rafter, principal; in timber roof construction, a main rafter supporting purlins, which in turn support common rafters.

principal reinforcement see main reinforcement.

principal roof truss in framed roof construction, a roof truss which provides intermediate support for purlins, which in turn carry rafters.

principal shaft a large or main shaft in a bundle or clustered column, essentially found in Gothic architecture.

principal shaft of
column in Gothic
cathedral

privacy, seclusion; the provision for occupants of a space with visual isolation, physical separation, screening from noise or protection from other disturbance.

probe, sensor; a metal extension to a measuring instrument by which temperature, moisture level, etc. can be measured.

production card see job card.

production drawing, working drawing; an annotated and scaled design drawing intended for use by a contractor as a guide to the manufacture of components and construction of parts of a building.

profession a skilled occupation, usually one requiring specific education, training, knowledge or experience.

professional practice the practising of an occupation according to accepted professional procedures, ethics and guidelines.

profile 1 the outline shape of an object or form as if viewed in projection; a silhouette or sectional cut.
2 any length of material preformed into a uniform cross-section of certain shape and dimensions; often synonymous with section, but in metals usually more complex, thin-walled or hollow; used for patent glazing, door frames, etc.; types included as separate entries are listed below:

*aluminium profile; *angle profile; *C-profile, see C-section, channel; *L-profile, see edge strip; *joinery profile, see timber trim; *metal profile; *steel profile; *thermal-break profile; *U-profile, see channel.
3 see template.

profiled sheet roofing roofing of proprietary sheets of metal, plastics or fibre cement formed into a wavy or undulating profile to increase stiffness along their length; see troughed sheet, corrugated sheet.

profiled sheet roofing

profiled sheeting, 1 metal decking, tray decking; structural roofing or decking formed of sheetmetal or plate ribbed with deep corrugations to provide a load-bearing base for further construction.
2 troughed sheeting; roofing formed of sheeting (usually treated steel, plastic or aluminium) ribbed with a continuous series of shallow corrugations to give it added stiffness in one direction.
3 ribbed-sheet roofing; the same as the previous entry, but with only occasional or spaced ribs.
4 see corrugated sheeting.

profile glass see channel glass.

programme, schedule; a written or graphical statement of the sequence and timing of operations of work on a construction project; see also brief, outline programme, overall programme, plan, site preparation programme.

programme chart a graphic representation of a programme of work or overall programme, showing various stages and their timing, etc.

project 1 an undertaking, plan, commission or process intended to put into action and bring to completion a conceived idea or design; a design project is one on which an architect will work; site or completed work relates to a construction project.

2 see development.

3 see public housing.

projecting headers headers in brickwork bonds laid projecting from a wall surface for decorative effect.

projecting window a window which projects from the exterior wall plane of a building; see also oriel windowbay window.

projection 1 the technical drawing of three-dimensional objects on a two-dimensional plane by extending imaginary lines, called projectors, from a point or from infinity through the object to be visualized onto the plane; types included as separate entries are listed below:

*axonometric projection; *cabinet projection; *cavalier projection; *dimetric projection; *isometric projection; *military projection, planometric projection; *oblique projection; *orthogonal projection; *orthographic projection; *parallel projection; *perspective; *trimetric projection.

2 the drawing resulting from this method, a projection drawing.

3 overhang; part of a building such as a balcony, oriel window, moulding, upper storey, etc. which projects outwards from an external wall.

projection plastering, mechanical plastering, spray plastering; plasterwork applied by spraying and finished with tools or left as a textured surface; plaster suitable for use in projection plastering is called projection plaster or spray plaster.

projection welding, resistance projection welding; industrial resistance welding utilizing an electric current passed through a number of points of contact provided by small surface projections; similar to spot welding.

project management the profession of running construction projects on behalf of a third party.

project manager, client's representative; a professional person or body whose task is to run construction projects for a client.

project representative see clerk of works.

project signboard a large sign or plaque erected at the edge of a building site containing information pertaining to the building under construction, listing who commissioned and paid for it, its designers, engineers, consultants and contractors, and its completion date.

project specification a specification of works written for a particular construction project, rather than a standard document.

prolongation an extension to a building contract period that requires the payment of costs by the client to the contractor or vice versa.

promoter see catalyst.

prop a short timber member used in construction for temporary vertical support and shoring of groundwork, scaffolding, unfinished construction, etc.

propagation see sound propagation.

propellant the compressed inert gas in an aerosol can or similar device which provides the pressure to expel its contents.

property survey, property inspection; a detailed inspection by an official, qualified professional or specialist to assess the condition of a building.

proportion 1 an aesthetic quality relating to the massing and relative sizes of forms, lines, etc.

2 the empirical or numerical comparison of one dimension or quantity with another.

proportioning, batching; in concreting, the measuring out of the constituent parts of concrete into their correct amounts prior to mixing; see weight batching, volume batching.

proposal a design, idea, etc. presented for assessment, approval or discussion.

proprietary referring to a product made and manufactured under patent or licence.

propriety wall tie

propylaeum, propylon (Gk.); Lat.; in classical and Egyptian architecture, a monumental gateway to a sacred enclosure, fortification, town or square; often used in the plural form propylaea, as used for the gateway to the Acropolis, Athens.

protected corridor, protected lobby; part of a fireproofed escape route within the storey height of a building, which leads to an exit.

protected membrane roof see upside down roof.

protective finish, protective coating; a layer of material such as paint, anodization, zinc coating, etc. applied to the external surface of a component as protection against wear, weathering and corrosion.

protein glue glue made from vegetable or animal proteins.

proto-Doric column an Egyptian column of the Old Kingdom, polygonal or fluted in section and with a simple capital, often thought to be the forerunner of the Greek Doric column.

proto-Doric column at Beni-Hasan, Egypt, 2040–1782 BC

protome, protoma; a classical decorative or sculptural motif depicting the stylized forepart and head of an animal.

protome capital a decorative capital carved with the stylized head and upper body of an animal or animals, found especially in medieval architecture.

Romanesque protome capital at Speyer Cathedral, Germany, 1032–90

proto-Renaissance architecture regarded as being the direct forebear of Renaissance, such as the severe Tuscan Romanesque architecture with classical influences c. 1100–1200 or that from the lower reaches of the Rhone.

Prunus spp. see cherry, plum.

Prussian blue a deep intense opaque greenish-blue pigment consisting of ferric-ferrocyanide; it was simultaneously discovered by Diesbach in Berlin and Milori in Paris in the early 1700s and is used in oil and watercolour paints; variously known as Berlin blue, iron blue, Milori blue, Paris blue, paste blue, steel blue.

Prussian brown, iron brown; a permanent opaque brown pigment, natural red iron oxide, formed by burning Prussian blue pigment.

PS polystyrene.

PSALI acronym for permanent supplementary artificial lighting of interiors.

PSE planed square-edged board.

pseudo four-centred arch a triangular arch whose extremities are curved.

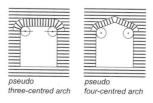

pseudo three-centred arch   *pseudo four-centred arch*

pseudo three-centred arch an arch with a flat intrados whose sides are curved downward.

Pseudotsuga menziesii see Douglas fir.

PSU polysulphone.

psychrometer a hygrometer for measuring atmospheric humidity with dry bulb and wet bulb thermometers.

Pterocarpus spp. see padauk.

PTFE polytetrafluoroethylene.

P trap a drainage trap in the shape of the letter P lying on its back, with a vertical inlet and a horizontal outlet.

PU polyurethane.

public address system, PA-system; a system of loudspeakers installed at key points in a building or complex for relating audial messages to occupants.

public building an administrative or recreational building maintained by local or national government with taxpayers' money.

public housing, council housing, housing project (Am), project (Am), social housing; affordable rented housing provided by a town council, municipality or the state for its citizens.

public sewer a system of sewers laid, run and maintained by a municipality or public water treatment company, which conveys foul water to a water treatment plant.

public space space to which the public has right of access.

puddingstone see conglomerate.

puddling furnace a small furnace in which pig iron and millscale are heated to produce wrought iron.

pugging boards, sound boarding; boards attached between or to the underside of floor or ceiling joists, traditionally used to carry sand or other material as thermal and acoustic insulation (pugging).

pug mill see mortar mill.

pulled bend in plumbing and drainage, a bend in metal pipework formed by mechanical bending with special tools.

pulley room see lift pulley room.

pull handle a handle fixed to a door, window or hatch, containing a grip by which it can be pulled open; see bow handle, cranked pull handle (offset handle), wire pull handle (wire handle).

pulpit a raised structure in a church from which a sermon is delivered.

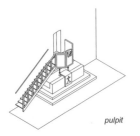

pulpit

pulverized fuel-ash, fly-ash; a fine material extracted from the combustion gases of bituminous coal; used as a binder in some cements.

pulvin 1 the baluster-shaped piece at the sides of an Ionic capital which joins the paired volutes on either face; also called pulvinus, meaning cushion in Latin.
2 see dosseret.

pumice a light, porous lava stone or volcanic glass with a high silica content; used as an abrasive and a polishing compound.

pump a mechanical device for providing the force to move mass materials in liquid, granular or gaseous form, or to compress gases; see concrete pump, site pump.

pumpable concrete concrete of a consistency that enables it to be placed with a pump when fresh.

pumped circulation the circulation of water supply, gas or other liquid in a mechanical service installation, induced by pressure from a pump.

pumped drainage, pumped sewerage; an installation in which sewage and foul water are conveyed from a building to a sewer at a higher level, requiring mechanical pumps or compressed air.

pumping aid an admixture included in a concrete mix to reduce friction while pumping it into formwork.

pumpkin dome see umbrella dome.

pump screwdriver see spiral ratchet screwdriver.

punch 1 a hard metal tool consisting of a shaft with a patterned end; used with a hammer or press for embossing designs and lettering into a metal surface.
2 a pointed steel masonry chisel used for the rough dressing of stone.
3 see centre punch.
4 see nail set.

puncheon in traditional timber frame construction, a vertical framing member or stud in a wall.
puncheon flooring timber flooring of halved logs with their flat faces upwards.

punning see tamping.

puree Indian yellow pigment in crude form.

purging the displacement of unwanted air, etc. by another gas in a gas pipeline.

purlin a horizontal roof beam running parallel to the ridge or longitudinal axis to give added intermediate support for roof joists or rafters.
purlin brace see wind brace.

purlin roof, double roof; roof construction in which secondary support is given to rafters by purlins; see also trussed purlin roof.

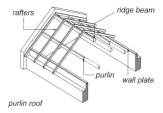

purlin roof

purple a shade of colour between crimson and violet, formed when red and blue are blended, originally obtained as a pigment from the shellfish *Murex purpurea, Murex brandaris,* or other molluscs of the genera *Nucella, Thais;* it is the complementary colour for green and does not appear in the visible spectrum; see below for list of purple and violet pigments:
*alizarin violet; *Burgundy violet, see manganese violet; *Byzantine purple, Byzantium purple; *cobalt violet; *dioxazine purple; *Grecian purple, see Tyrian purple; *magenta; *manganese violet; *mineral violet, see manganese violet; *ostrum, see Tyrian purple; *permanent violet, see manganese violet; *purple of the ancients, see Tyrian purple; *purpurin; *quinacridone violet; *Tyrian purple; *violet madder lake, see alizarin violet.

purpose made brick a non-standard clay brick specially shaped, or of unusual colour or consistency, for a particular purpose; see also special brick.

purpurin a red-coloured substance obtained from the root of the madder plant [*Rubia tinctorum*]; used as a colourant in dyeing processes.

push button a disc or button-like mechanism which operates an electrical or mechanical device when pressed with the thumb or forefinger.

push pad a protective plate attached to a door leaf but slightly apart from it, by which it can be pushed open.

push plate, finger plate; a protective metal or plastics plate attached to a door leaf, by which it can be pushed open at approximately waist height.

push-pull fastener a catch which holds a door closed but releases it on application of pressure to the door leaf.

putlog in scaffolding, horizontal members supporting a walkway.
putlog scaffolding scaffolding supported on one side by props or standards and on the other by the building itself.

putty, glazier's putty, glazing putty; a mixture of chalk and linseed oil traditionally used for the fixing of glazing into a window frame, for stopping or spackling, etc.; see also glazing compound.
putty fronting, face putty, front putty; in glazing, a triangular fillet of putty applied to the external edges of a window pane to hold it in place.
putty knife, spackling knife, stopping knife; a knife with a metal blade used by a decorator and glazier for applying filler, stopping, etc. putty.

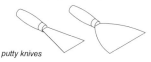

putty knives

PVA polyvinyl alcohol.
PVA glue see polyvinyl acetate glue.

PVAC polyvinyl acetate.

PVC polyvinyl chloride.

PVC-U window plastics window; a window whose frame is made primarily from PVC-U plastics.

PVDC polyvinylidene chloride.

PVDF polyvinylidene fluoride.

PVF polyvinyl fluoride.

pwree see Indian yellow.

pylon 1 in Egyptian architecture, one of a pair of gigantic tapered stone towers surrounding a monumental temple gateway.

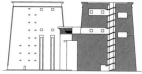

Great pylon of the Temple of Horus, Edfu, Egypt; New Kingdom, 237–57 BC

2 a large freestanding open-lattice steel structure for carrying overhead power lines.

3 a tall steel or concrete tower from which suspension or cable-stay bridge cables are strung; a bridge pylon.

4 see lighting mast.

pynnion see pignon.

pyramid 1 a three-dimensional shape in which one surface is a polygon and the others are triangles which meet at a single point.

2 a huge monumental Egyptian stone tomb, the burial place of a Pharaoh, usually consisting of four sloping triangular sides on a square base, culminating at an apex; see also ziggurat, teocalli.

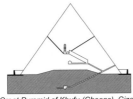

Great Pyramid of Khufu (Cheops), Giza, Egypt; Old Kingdom, 2589–2566 BC

pyramidion a small secondary pyramid such as the pyramid-shaped termination of an Egyptian obelisk.

pyramid roof a hipped roof on a square plan whose four identical triangular roof planes meet at a central point.

pyramid stop see broach stop.

Pyrex a trade name for borosilicate glass.

pyrites hard, pale-coloured crumbly mineral sulphides of metal in mineral form, especially iron disulphide; see iron pyrites.

pyroclastic rock any rock which has been ejected by volcanic action.

pyrogenic rock see igneous rock.

pyrolusite a grey metallic mineral, natural manganese dioxide, MnO_2, used for colouring glass and an important ore of manganese.

pyrolysis the decomposition or chemical alteration of a substance by the action of heat.

pyroxenite a dark-coloured igneous rock composed almost entirely of the mineral pyroxene — a dark green, black or brown mineral composed of calcium and magnesium silicates.

Pyrus communis see pear.

Q

quadrangle, 1 any planar four-sided figure with four internal angles.
2 quad; an open square or rectangular space wholly surrounded by buildings, often with a central lawn and within a college or monastery.

quadrant 1 a sector of a circle bounded by two radii at right angles to one another and the enclosed length of circumference; one quarter of a circle.
2 a decorative strip, moulding or piece of joinery trim which is a quarter circle in cross-section.

quadrant angle bead

quadriga Lat.; in classical architecture, a triumphal statue or rendering of a chariot pulled by four horses.

quadripartite vault a masonry vault sprung on four points of support; square or rectangular in plan and composed of four curved roof surfaces or compartments divided by ribs.

quadripartite vault

quadriportico an area closed off on four sides by building form or masonry, with an entrance portico on each side.

quadro riportato decorative ceiling painting which depicts scenes in normal perspective.

quaking aspen [*Populus tremuloides*] see poplar.

quality, grade; the classifiable characteristics of a material or product as demanded by use or suitability.
quality control a system whereby products or services are checked for a specified quality at each stage in processing.

quality grading the classification of sawn timber and other mass products according to visual defects.

quantity survey a central contract document itemizing materials, products and components used in building work, their amounts and costs; undertaken by a qualified quantity surveyor, and presented as a bill of quantities prior to construction.
quantity surveyor a qualified professional responsible for drawing up bills of quantities and advising the client on contractual and financial matters.

quarry 1 a place where rock is extracted from the ground for use in construction, etc.
2 a quarry tile.
quarry finish an uneven, rough-textured stone surface treatment, produced by dressing with hand or machine tools to resemble stone in its natural state; also variously called rubble or scabbled finish, or pitch or rock-faced, and hammer-dressed or pitched when produced by hand-tooling.

quarry finish

quarry tile, floor quarry; a thick unglazed clay floor tile formed by extrusion.

quarter bat, quarter; a brick which has been cut to one quarter of its length for use in brickwork bonding.

quarter bat

quarter brick wall a thin brick wall laid with bricks on edge, whose thickness is the same as the height of a brick.

quarter brick wall

quarter cut see quarter sliced veneer.

quarterpace stairs, quarter-space stair; an L-shaped stair which turns through 90° at a landing.

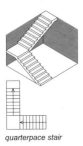

quarterpace stair

quarter round a decorative moulding which is a quarter of a circle in cross-section; a quadrant; see also cock beak moulding, thumbnail bead moulding.

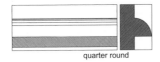

quarter round

quartersawing, radial cutting, rift sawing; a method of converting timber by sawing a log radially into quarters and then converting the segments to provide fine quality timber boards with relatively even perpendicular end grain; see also sawing round the log.

quartersawing

quartersawn, 1 edge grained, radially cut, rift sawn, vertical grained; a description of timber sawn approximately radially from a log.
2 see quarter sliced veneer.

quarter sliced veneer a decorative veneer formed by the radial slicing of a quarter log or flitch; also called quarter cut or quartersawn.

quarter sliced veneer

quarter-space stairs see quarterpace stair.

quarter turn stair, 1 angle stair, L-stair; an L-shaped stair which turns through a right angle on its ascent, either with a landing, as with a quarterpace stair, or with a series of wedge-shaped steps.

2 see quarterpace stair.

quarto plate, heavy plate; relatively thick, uncoiled and heavy steel plate rolled to individual specification regarding composition and size, manufactured on a special quarto plate mill.

quartz a very hard, transparent, whitish mineral form of silica, often found naturally in the form of hexagonal crystals; a violet form is known as amethyst; all types included as separate entries are listed below:
*amethyst; *chalcedony; *milky quartz; *quartzite; *rose quartz; *smoky quartz.
quartz diorite an igneous rock, similar to granite and diorite, containing a high proportion of quartz; its uses in building are similar to that of granite.
quartz glass see fused silica glass.
quartzite a white, grey or reddish metamorphic or sedimentary rock which consists almost wholly of quartz; it is durable and resistant to chemical and frost action, and is used for flooring tiles.
quartz porphyry see rhyolite.

quatrefoil a decorative motif consisting of four stylized leaf designs radiating out from a point; see also pointed quatrefoil.

quatrefoil

quatrefoil arch an arch composed of four lobes or foils.

Queen Anne style an architectural and interior decoration style in England during the reign of Queen Anne (1702–1714), evident principally in urban buildings and residences and characterized by the use of red brickwork in a mix of Renaissance and Baroque motifs from Holland and England.

Queen Anne arch a pointed arch over a tripartite window, with a horizontal intrados and a protruding arched portion in the centre.

Queen Anne revival a revival style in town house architecture in England from the 1800s, characterized by the use of red brick, white framed windows, bay and oriel windows and dramatic roof forms.

queen closer 1 a cut brick which shows a half-header width in a brick wall; a brick halved lengthways to fit in with a bonding pattern.

queen closer

2 a quarter bat.
3 a three quarter brick which has been cut in half lengthways.

queen post in traditional timber roof construction, one of a pair of posts carrying purlins in a queen post truss, which is a timber truss consisting of a tie beam, a pair of vertical queen posts, a collar or straining beam and principal rafters.

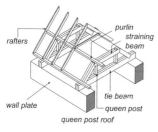

queen post roof

queen post collar rafter roof a collar roof with purlins supported on queen posts.

queen post rafter roof a rafter roof with purlins supported on queen posts, with a brace between them; also called a queen post roof.

queen strut in timber roof construction, a queen post that does not carry a purlin directly.

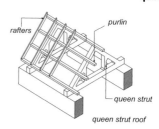

queen strut roof

queen strut roof truss a timber truss in which rafters are supported by purlins carried on queen struts.

quenching in the tempering of metals, rapid cooling of the heated metal by plunging it in water or some other liquid.

Quercus spp. see oak.

quicklime, anhydrous lime, burnt lime, caustic lime; lime which has been produced by the burning of limestone or calcium carbonate, **CaCO₃**, to form calcium oxide; mixed with water to form slaked lime.

quick-setting Portland cement a Portland cement which sets more rapidly than ordinary Portland cement.

quick strip formwork formwork used for casting and supporting the underside of a concrete slab, which can be removed without necessitating the removal of its supports.

quilted figure a decorative figure in veneers cut from irregular grained timber, especially bigleaf maple, as if the surface is quilted.

quinacridone a group of durable and light-fast dark-reddish synthetic pigments based on organic hydrocarbon polymers; used for high performance paints in the automotive industry, and for industrial coatings.

quinacridone red a synthetic lightfast organic red pigment used in many types of paint.

quinacridone violet a synthetic organic violet-red pigment used since the 1960s in oil, watercolour and acrylic paints.

quirk a narrow decorative cutting in a moulding or ornate surface to separate main elements such as beads, rolls, etc.

quirk bead moulding, bead and quirk moulding, quirked bead

moulding; a decorative moulding whose cross-section is that of a bead or ovoid formed with a quirk or notch on one or both sides; see also flush bead moulding.

quirking tool a small masonry chisel for cutting narrow grooves or quirks in decorative stonework.

quoin one of a series of staggered corner stones or bricks at an external masonry corner, often of a different material or colour to the rest of the wall, as decoration; also spelled coign or coin.

quoin

quoining when masonry blocks or bricks are added to the external corner of a building's wall as quoins.

R

rabbet see rebate.

rabbet plane see rebate plane.

Rabitz plaster special gypsum lime plaster reinforced with a mesh and animal hair, invented by Karl Rabitz in 1878; used primarily for domes and other vaulted structures.

raceway see trunking.

racking, racking back see raking.

rad and dab see wattle and daub.

radial see radial brick.

radial arm saw a circular saw suspended from and moving along a cantilevered arm, used for various cross-cuts in wood.

radial block a concrete block manufactured with curving vertical faces, designed for use in curved wall construction.

radial block

radial brick, arch brick; any special brick shaped for use in a curved or vaulted brick surface such as a well or barrel vault; see also radial stretcher, radial header, culvert stretcher (tapered header), culvert header (tapered stretcher).

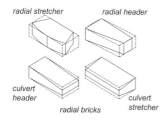

radial stretcher   *radial header*

culvert header   *culvert stretcher*

radial bricks

radial circuit an electric circuit with a number of appliances attached to a single power supply.

radial cutting see quartersawing.

radial header a special brick which is wedged-shaped in plan; used as a header in a curving brick wall, circular well or chimney stack, etc.

radial joint one of the joints between voussoirs in a masonry arch.

radially cut see quartersawn.

radial stretcher a special brick which is bow-shaped in one of its long faces and wedge-shaped in plan; used as a stretcher in a curving brick wall.

radial surface see edge.

radiant heater, radiant panel, radiator; any heating device which imparts thermal energy primarily by radiation; radiant heating is heating in which thermal comfort for a space is provided by radiant heat, as opposed to warm air, convection, etc.

radiant moulding see rayonny moulding.

radiant panel see radiant heater.

radiata pine, Monterey pine; [*Pinus radiata*], see pine.

radiation the transmission of energy in the form of electromagnetic waves; see thermal radiation, cold radiation.

radiation detector see flame detector.

radiation resistance the ability of a material or construction to resist penetration by nuclear radiation.

radiation-shielding glass any protective glass designed with interlayers and added compounds to reflect or absorb radiation and restrict its transmission; see lead X-ray glass, electronic shielding glass.

radiation-shielding mortar; see X-ray resisting plaster.

radiator 1 a space heating appliance, which may be part of a central heating system or an individual heater, in which hot liquid (water or oil) circulates in a metal chamber.
2 see radiant heater.

radiator brush a long-handled painter's and decorator's brush with either a kinked or a perpendicular handle; used for painting difficult or constrained areas such as behind radiators and crevices.

radiator heating a hot water central heating system in which heating water is circulated to radiators.

radius of gyration in mechanics, the effective distance of the centre of mass of an object from its centre of rotation or oscillation.

rafter

82

rafter one of a series of timber beams carrying roofing in a sloping roof; the upper member of a roof truss or a sloping roof joist, a roof beam; types included as separate entries are listed below:
*angle rafter; *common rafter; *hip rafter; *horizontal rafter, see common purlin; *jack rafter; *principal rafter; *trimmed rafter; *trimming rafter; *valley rafter.

rafter bracket a roofing accessory for fixing an eaves gutter to the end of a rafter.

rafter roof in timber roof construction, a roof in which rafters are the basic frame supporting the roof covering.

raft foundation a foundation consisting of a continuous reinforced concrete slab (usually the lowest floor slab of a building) which transmits overlying loads over its whole area.

raft foundation

ragbolt see anchor bolt.

raguly moulding a crenellated moulding whose castellations are slanting, resembling the stumps left when branches are sawn from a tree trunk.

raguly moulding

ragwork 1 masonry walling of rough thin stones laid horizontally; see slate walling.

ragwork paving

ragwork walling

2 crazy paving, random stone paving; stone paving of irregularly shaped and randomly sized stones.

rail 1 a horizontal frame member in a door leaf, sash, casement or other framework; see bottom rail, middle rail (lock rail), intermediate rail, top rail.

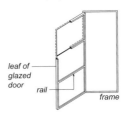

leaf of glazed door
rail
frame

2 a horizontal profile, moulding or section in a balustrade or similar framework.
3 a lightweight balustrade, open waist-height barrier, handrail, etc.; see railing, guard rail, handrail, safety rail, stair rail.
4 a shaped metal supporting bar for a moving system such as a track, sliding screen or electrical installation; see cladding rail, curtain rail, chair rail, (dado rail), towel rail (drying rail).
5 a steel product, one of a pair of formed bars of specified cross-sectional profile laid side by side to form a railway track.
6 see screed rail.

rail bolt see joint bolt.

railing a fence, balustrade or low barrier of metal bars fixed to a frame structure, supported by posts at regular intervals; often used in the plural.

rainbow roof a roof in the cross-sectional form of a pointed arch.

rain cap, flue cap; a lightweight protective construction fitted over the upper outlet of a flue to prevent the passage of rainwater and snow.

rainproof referring to a component or construction which is impervious to rain or resistant to the penetration of rainwater.

rainwater system a system of gutters, channels, outlets and pipes which collect water from roofs and other areas and convey it to a drainage system.

rainwater goods, rainwater fittings; gutters, downpipes and other metal, plastic or ceramic fittings, often part of a manufacturer's system of parts; used to convey rainwater from roofs and other surfaces into drains.

rainwater gully, surface water gully; an inlet to lead surface water and rainwater from paved external areas and downpipes to a drainage system.

rainwater gutter, roof gutter; a slightly sloping channel at an abutment, eaves, etc., to collect rainwater from a roof surface and convey it to a downpipe.

rainwater head, conductor header (Am), hopper head, leader header (Am), rainwater header, rainwater hopper; in roof construction, a funnel-shaped vessel designed to collect rainwater from a gutter and convey it to a downpipe.

rainwater header, rainwater hopper see rainwater head.

rainwater outlet, roof outlet, roof gully; a component, fitting or construction through which rainwater collecting on a flat roof surface is led out to a drain, downpipe, etc.

rainwater pipe a drainpipe conveying rainwater away from a roof or paved surface; see also downpipe.

rainwater shoe see pipe shoe.

rainwater spout, gargoyle, outlet, water spout; in roof construction, a piped fitting to cast rainwater from a gutter or roof surface away from the roof and wall surfaces of a building.

raised access floor see platform floor.

raised countersunk head screw see oval head screw.

raised fillet a plain, thin decorative moulding, protruding from a flat surface.

raised fillet

raised floor 1 any floor which has been raised as a dais, platform, stage or access floor.

2 see access floor.

raised grain in woodworking, the natural raising of wood fibres after the wet application of a finish, sanded down on drying before a final coat.

raised moulding see bolection moulding.

raised pattern flooring see studded rubber flooring.

raised pattern plate see chequerplate.

rake see batter.

raked joint, keyed joint, raked-out joint, recessed joint; a brickwork mortar joint which has been recessed to a certain depth either as a key for plaster or pointing, or for decorative effect.

raker 1 in bricklaying, a simple metal tool used for removing excess or old mortar from a joint.

2 one of the slanting support props in a raking shore; see bottom raker, middle raker, top raker.

raking 1 referring to vertical joints in adjacent courses of bonded masonry which form a regular diagonal sawtoothed pattern in a wall surface; bricks are laid with one quarter brick overlap.

2 racking back, raking back; the laying of bricks or stones in stepped layers at the end of a brick wall under construction to support a builder's line and ease the laying of the rest of the wall.

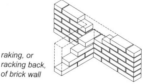

raking, or racking back, of brick wall

3 using a rake to even out a granular surface, or remove excess material from a lawn or other landscaped surface.

raking arch see rampant arch.

raking back see raking.

raking bond any brickwork pattern whose vertical joints form a regular diagonal sawtoothed pattern in the wall surface; see raking Flemish bond; raking stretcher bond.

raking flashing in roofing, a flashing at the junction of the side of a sloping roof and a parapet or wall; the upper surface of its upstand is sloping at the same pitch as the roof plane.

raking Flemish bond brickwork laid in Flemish bond with a quarter brick overlap between courses so that the vertical joints form a regular diagonal sawtoothed pattern in the wall surface.

raking Flemish bond

raking pile, batter pile; in foundation technology, any pile placed at a slant to the vertical; often a tension pile.

raking shore excavation shoring in the form of a series of slanting props to support a wall.

raking stretcher bond 1 a brickwork bond consisting entirely of courses of stretchers, in which alternate courses are laid with a quarter brick overlap.
2 the same with modular bricks in which alternating courses are laid with a one-third brick overlap.

ram see monkey.

ramin [*Gonystylus spp.*] a group of hardwoods from South-East Asia with pale, featureless, timber; it smells unpleasant when freshly cut and is used for joinery and furniture.

rammed earth construction see pisé.

ramming see tamping.

ramp a sloping planar surface providing access from one level to another.

ramp stair a gradually ascending stair with deep treads and short risers, resembling a ramp.

rampant arch, raking arch; an arch whose imposts are at different levels.

ramp stair

rampant arch

rampant vault a masonry vault which is a rampant or asymmetrical arch in uniform cross-section; used over stairs and changes in level.

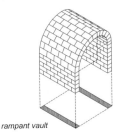

rampant vault

rampart the fortified wall or earthwork surrounding a castle, encampment or town; used as a defensive barrier, see enceinte; originally the embankment of earth excavated from a surrounding ditch.

ranch house a single storey American dwelling type built in a rustic style to imitate a house on a ranch.

random ashlar see coursed squared rubble, uncoursed ashlar.

random bond see irregular bond, random paving.

random match, mismatched; veneering using veneers which are variable in grain pattern and are glued in no strict pattern.

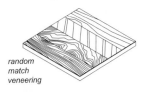

random match veneering

random paving paving in rectangular pavers of differing sizes in no particular recognizable pattern; see also ragwork.

random paving pattern

random rubble masonry construction of roughly shaped stones not laid in courses; also called uncoursed rubble.

random rubble wall

random squared rubble masonry see uncoursed squared rubble masonry.

random stone paving see ragwork.

ranger see waling.

range work stonework which is composed of coursed ashlar with small stones.

rapakivi, rapakivi granite; a reddish or brown porphyritic hornblende granite originating in Finland, characterized by roundish deposits of feldspar, prone to decay and used as building stone for cladding.

rapid-hardening Portland cement, high-early-strength cement; a Portland cement that produces concrete which hardens more rapidly in early stages than ordinary concrete.

rasp a toothed metal tool or coarse file for rough shaping and smoothing of wood and plastics.

ratan see rattan.

ratchet, ratch; a gear wheel with slanting teeth and a stopper or pawl which allows for turning in one direction only; used in some winches and handtools.

ratchet screwdriver a screwdriver with a ratchet mechanism to operate in one selected direction at a time.

rate of placing, rate of placement; the speed at which concrete is placed in formwork, regulated to prevent drying, cracking or the formation of voids.

rationalism a movement in architecture which sought to reorder the process of design and construction in a logical way.

rattan, ratan; the dried stems of a range of tropical climbing palms used for making cane furniture and fittings.

rat-trap bond, Chinese bond, rowlock bond, silverlock bond; a brickwork bond in which all bricks are laid on edge with each course consisting of alternating headers and stretchers in a similar way to Flemish bond; used for hybrid cavity wall construction.

rat-trap bond

raw plywood plywood whose face plies have undergone no treatment during manufacture other than sanding or scraping.

raw sewage, crude sewage, untreated sewage; sewage which has yet to undergo any treatment at a water treatment plant.

raw sienna see sienna.

raw umber, Sicilian brown, terra ombre; dark brown iron oxide containing manganese hydroxide; used as a pigment in a similar way to ochre.

raw water water obtained by a water board for distribution to a water supply, to which further purifying aids are sometimes added.

ray acoustics see geometrical acoustics.

ray figure, ray fleck, splash figure, storied rays, ripple marks; a decorative figure produced by the radial slicing of certain hardwoods for veneers, caused by the rays in the wood appearing as ripples in the surface.
ray figured veneer decorative veneer with ray figure.

ray fleck see ray figure.

Rayonnant style the middle phase of French Gothic architecture from the 1200s and 1300s, characterized by radiating lines in tracery.

Rayonnant rose window of the Minoritenkirche, Vienna, 1276–1350

rayonny moulding banded ornament consisting of a series of flame-like motifs; primarily found in heraldic motifs; also called radiant, rayonnant, rayonné moulding.

rayonny moulding

rays tissues in the structure of wood radiating in bands from the pith towards the bark of a tree.

r.c., r-c, rc reinforced concrete.

reaction wood wood with unevenly spaced growth rings, which is weak and prone to warping, resulting from abnormal growth of a tree.

ready-mixed referring to concretes, cements and mortars in which all component parts, including water, have been mixed together before delivery for use on site; also written as readymix; see also dry mix.

ready-mixed concrete concrete which has been mixed either in a suitable vehicle or an off-site mixing plant, and is delivered for immediate use on site.

ready-mixed mortar mortar delivered to site mixed and with water added.

ready-mixed plaster plaster delivered to site mixed and with water added.

realization see completion.

reamer a hand tool or drill bit with a straight or tapered serrated blade, used for enlarging or cleaning out drilled holes in metal, rock and other materials.

reamers

reaming the enlargement or finishing of such holes.

rebar see reinforcing bar.

rebate, 1 rabbet; a step-shaped reduction along the edge of or in the face of a piece of timber or other component, usually to receive another piece.
2 a housing in a window or door frame in which a door leaf, casement or pane of glass is fitted; see glazing rebate.

3 a hinge rebate, see hinge mortise.
4 a sum of money paid back or deducted as a result of commercial dealings.

rebated block channel a drainage channel which is rectangular in cross-section, shaped with a semicircular recess and rebates to house a grating along its upper face.

rebated corner joint a lapped corner joint used in cabinetmaking for joining boards and sheets at right angles, in which the end of one piece is grooved near its edge to receive the rebated edge of the other piece.

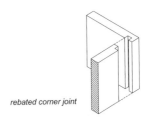

rebated corner joint

rebated door a door whose leaf has edges rebated to form a small overlap with surrounding framing members.

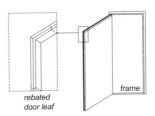

rebated door leaf

frame

rebated featheredged board a timber cladding board, wedge-shaped and rebated in cross-section.

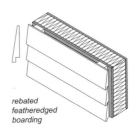

rebated featheredged boarding

rebate joint a timber joint in which one piece has been rebated to receive another; see lapped corner joint, rebated corner joint.

rebated housing joint

rebate plane, rabbet plane; a plane for cutting a groove or rebate in a piece of wood.

rebound material from spray concreting and painting processes which does not adhere to the intended surfaces and bounces off or is otherwise lost as waste.

recaulking the refilling of horizontal timber joints in log construction with caulk after the initial settlement of the building frame.

recess any setting back or a depression of a wall in plan, often to allow for servicing installations, a door or window, or ornament; see niche.

recessed bead moulding see flush bead moulding.

recessed column a column incorporated within a small recess in an adjacent wall.

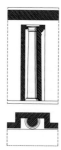

recessed column

recessed fixing see flush mounting.

recessed joint see raked joint.

recessed luminaire a light fitting designed to be flush mounted into a ceiling, or set into a suitable niche or recess.

recessed portal a main doorway in a Romanesque or Gothic church, stepped inwards with columns bearing sculpted figures.

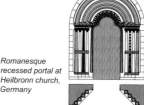

Romanesque recessed portal at Heilbronn church, Germany

recessed screw cup, countersunk washer, inset screw cup; a pressed metal recessed ring for a countersunk screw to protect the base into which it is being fixed.

recessed screw cup

recirculated air in air conditioning, return air which is reused once it has been pumped back to the plant rooms.

recirculation duct in air conditioning, a duct conveying return air back to a plant room for reuse.

reconditioning the steam treatment of improperly seasoned timber to reduce distortion and warping.

reconstituted stone, reconstituted marble; a stone product consisting of fragments of marble or other soft rock embedded in a matrix of resin, cement or marble dust, cast, cut and shaped as building stone.

reconstructed stone see cast stone.

reconstruction restoring or rebuilding a dilapidated, ruined or non-existent building, often using archive documentation; the product of this process.

record drawing, survey drawing; a drawing produced from data and measurements taken during a land or building survey; a measured drawing.

recoverable tie a formwork tie removed for reuse once formwork is struck.

rectangular grid floor see waffle floor.

rectangular gutter see box gutter.

rectangular hollow section, RHS; a rectangular hollow steel section formed by rolling and welding steel plate; used for structural purposes such as framing, columns, posts, etc.

rectangular tile
any tile whose face is rectangular in shape.

rectangular tube
a metal profile of hollow rectangular cross-section; when in steel and used for structural purposes, it is called a rectangular hollow section, RHS.

rectangular tile

Rectilinear style see Perpendicular style.

rectilinear tracery, panel tracery, perpendicular tracery; Gothic tracery found in churches of the Perpendicular style, characterized by the use of a lacework of vertical glazing bars.

rectilinear or perpendicular tracery, Winchester Cathedral, from 1079 to 16th century

red a general name for a range of wavelengths of coloured light from the visible spectrum between 640–780 m; see list of red pigments:
*alizarin; *aniline colour; *anthraquinoid red; *antimony vermilion; *cadmium red; *carmine; *carthame, see safflower; *Chinese red, see chrome red; *Chinese vermilion; *chrome red; *cinnabar; *cochineal; *Derby red, see chrome red; *English vermilion; *ferric oxide, see iron oxide; *garance; *haematite, see iron oxide; *iron oxide; *kermes; *madder lake; *mauve; *minium, see red lead; *Munich lake, see carmine; *nacarat carmine; *naphthol carbamide; *natural madder, see madder lake; *orange vermilion; *perinone orange; *Perkin's violet, see mauve; *perylene; *purpurin; *quinacridone red; *red iron oxide, see iron oxide; *red lead; *red ochre, see red oxide paint; *rose madder, see madder lake; *safflower; *saturnine red, see red lead; *scarlet vermilion, see vermilion; *selenium red, see cadmium red; *toluidine red; *vermilion; *Vienna lake, see carmine; *zinnober, see cinnabar.*

red alder [*Alnus rubra*], see alder.

red brick a very common clay brick containing iron oxide which gives it a reddish brown colour.

red cedar [*Thuja plicata*] western red cedar, see thuja.

red deal the timber from a Scots pine tree.

reddle see red oxide paint.

redevelopment the rebuilding, reshaping or improvement of a building, block or urban area; see urban renewal, comprehensive redevelopment.

red gold a metal alloy consisting of 95% gold and 5% copper.

red iron oxide see iron oxide.

red knot an intergrown knot in softwood.

red lead, lead oxide, lead primer, minium, saturnine red; a heavy poisonous lead oxide (Pb₃O₄) pigment used in paints, metal primers, glass, glazes, putties and batteries.

red maple [*Acer rubrum*], see maple.

red oak [*Quercus spp.*], see oak.

red ochre see red oxide paint.

red oxide iron oxide when used as a red pigment.

red oxide paint traditional paint used for external timber surfaces, a mixture of earth rich in iron-oxide and oil; the earth, used in differing mediums as paint is variously known as red ochre, reddle, ruddle and terra rossa.

red ring rot, red rot, canker rot, honeycomb rot, ring scale fungus, white pocket rot, white pitted rot, white speck; [*Phellinus pini, Fomes pini, Trametes pini*] a fungal decay in living conifers in Europe and North America which, in its early stages, forms a red stain in the heartwood, spreading as pockets of white filaments which weaken the timber.

reducer 1 see thinner.
2 see reducing fitting.

reducing bush see socket reducer.

reducing fitting, reducer; a pipe fitting for joining two pipes of different diameters; see also straight reducer.
  reducing bend a piece of curved reducing fitting which changes the direction of a pipeline.
  reducing cross a pipe fitting to connect two smaller bore subsidiary pipes at right angles to a main pipe.
  reducing elbow a small radius reducing bend.
  reducing socket a short length of connecting pipe which is internally threaded and shaped for joining pipes of different diameters.
  reducing tee a pipe fitting for connecting a smaller-bore subsidiary pipe at right angles to a larger-bore main pipeline.

reducing valve see pressure reducing valve.

reduction, smelting; the process of heating metal ore in order to extract useful metal.

redundant frame see statically indeterminate frame.

redwood, sequoia; [*Sequoia sempervirens*] a softwood from North America with dark red-brown heartwood and white sapwood, resistant to fungal attack; used for vats, tanks, joinery, plywood and construction work.

reed 1 a grassy plant found growing near water and on marshland, with long, hollow stems used for thatching roofs, matting, reed pens, etc.; see best reed, Norfolk reed.
2 a thin decorative band; see reeded, reeding.

reed and tie moulding a decorative moulding representing a parallel set of reeds bound intermittently with diagonal crossed ribbons.

reeded referring to a surface that has been cut or formed with a series of parallel convex ridges; see fluted.
  reeded boarding see bead boarding.
  reeded glass glass which has been obscured with a reeded pattern of parallel grooves impressed into one side.
  reeded moulding any horizontal flat or torus moulding scored with a series of parallel indentations, convex carvings or protrusions.

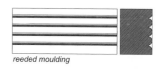
reeded moulding

reeded torus moulding a semicircular decorative moulding carved with reeds or parallel convex projections.

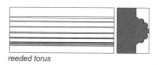
reeded torus

reeding an ornamental motif or surface treatment for masonry, glass, sheet products, etc. with a series of parallel convex carvings or protrusions.

reed thatch thatching material of dried unbroken reed stems.

reel and bead see bead and reel.

reference drawing see base sheet.

reflectance in lighting design, a measure of the reflectivity of a surface given as a fraction of the luminous flux that is reflected from it; see also value.

reflected glare in lighting design, glare caused by light from an indirect or reflected source.

reflected sound in acoustics, sound which reaches the listener after bouncing off a wall, floor or ceiling surface.

reflection the bouncing or turning back of wave motion as it strikes a smooth surface; see sound reverberation, specular reflection.

reflective glass solar control glass surface treated or coated with a layer to reflect solar radiation; see surface coated float glass.
  reflective float glass see surface coated float glass.

reflector that part of a lamp, luminaire, sign or treated surface designed to direct reflected light in a certain direction.
  reflector lamp, spot lamp; a lamp with an internally silvered lining to reflect light outwards with a directional narrow beam.

reflux valve see check valve.

refraction the change in direction of a wave such as a beam of light as it enters a medium of different density at an angle.

refractive index, index of refraction; the ratio of the speed of an electromagnetic wave in a certain material to that in a vacuum.

refractory a description of a fireproof material or construction which is non-combustible, resistant to the action of heat, or is difficult to melt fuse, or destroy by heating.

refractory brick see firebrick.

refractory concrete concrete designed to withstand high temperatures; for use in flues, fireboxes, etc.; prepared with calcium aluminate cement and refractory aggregate.

refractory lining see fireproof lining.

refractory mortar finely crushed mortar, often made from fireclay, silica sand and firebrick, able to withstand high temperatures and used for masonry flues and ovens.

refrigerant a liquid medium through which energy in air-conditioning refrigeration plant and other cooling installations is transferred.

refrigeration unit, chiller; an air-conditioning appliance for producing a cold stream of liquid used for cooling conditioned input air.

refurbishment, renovation; the action of bringing buildings, structures and their technical installations up to modern requirements, or restoring them to meet current functional standards.

refuse solid waste products from consumption, manufacture, industrial processes, etc.

refuse bin, ashcan (Am), bin, dustbin, trash can (Am), rubbish bin; in waste management, a container for the storage of household and commercial solid waste.

refuse chute see waste chute.

refuse collection, waste collection; the organized collection of waste material from buildings, and its transportation to a refuse dump.

Regency style 1 an architectural style in England from the early 1800s between the Georgian and Victorian periods when George, Prince of Wales, was regent; it is characterized by use of classical proportion and eclectic motifs.

2 a style of Rococo and late Baroque architecture in France from the early 1700s during the period when Philip, Duke of Orleans, was regent.

registered chisel a sturdy chisel used for heavy work, which has a ferrule at either end of the handle to prevent it from splitting when struck with a mallet.

regularizing the planing of seasoned softwood sections on four sides to produce an accurately measured cross-section.

regularized timber timber which has been resawn this way.

regulating valve see control valve.

regulation a rule provided by an authority indicating the way in which a matter should be undertaken; see building regulation.

regulator see control device.

rehabilitation an action of bringing buildings, structures and their servicing back to a state of functional repair.

reheating in certain air-conditioning systems, the final heating up of conditioned air, governed by a thermostat within the space, prior to release as supply air.

reinforced blockwork blockwork with reinforcing bars laid in bed joints to withstand structural loading.

reinforced brick lintel, brick beam; a laid-in-situ or prefabricated beam of bricks and reinforcing bars in bed joints; used over openings in walls.

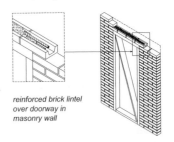

reinforced brick lintel over doorway in masonry wall

reinforced brickwork brickwork with reinforcing bars laid in bed joints to withstand structural loading.

reinforced concrete, ferroconcrete, steel concrete; structural concrete containing inlaid steel reinforcing bars or a mesh to increase strength in tension; often written as rc, r-c or r.c.

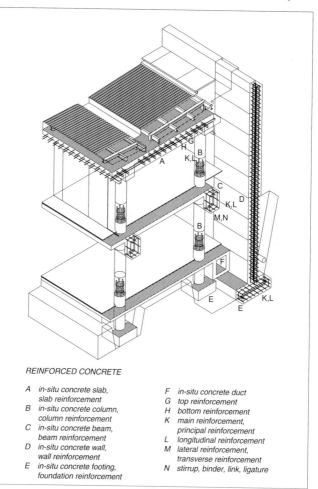

REINFORCED CONCRETE

A   in-situ concrete slab,
    slab reinforcement
B   in-situ concrete column,
    column reinforcement
C   in-situ concrete beam,
    beam reinforcement
D   in-situ concrete wall,
    wall reinforcement
E   in-situ concrete footing,
    foundation reinforcement

F   in-situ concrete duct
G   top reinforcement
H   bottom reinforcement
K   main reinforcement,
    principal reinforcement
L   longitudinal reinforcement
M   lateral reinforcement,
    transverse reinforcement
N   stirrup, binder, link, ligature

reinforced concrete pavement see continuously reinforced concrete pavement.

reinforced concrete structure any structure designed to make use of concrete and its contained steel reinforcement acting together to withstand loading.

reinforced earth earth with inlaid layers of binding reinforcement such as geotextile; used for stabilizing embankments and earthworks.

reinforced felt, sarking felt; bitumen felt reinforced with a hessian web; used beneath tiled or slate roofing.

reinforced joint a horizontal joint in which reinforcing bars have been set; used in structural brickwork over openings, etc.

reinforced plaster any plaster or render which has been strengthened with or supported by a steel mesh; see fibrous plaster, fibre-reinforced plaster (fibred plaster), metal lathing plaster, Rabitz plaster.

reinforced plastic see fibre-reinforced plastic.

reinforced render see reinforced plaster.

reinforcement 1 any rods, fibres, mesh or fabric added to a mass product (concrete, plaster or plastics) to withstand the loading against which the material itself is weak; see concrete reinforcement for list of separate types of reinforcement for concrete; see also soil reinforcement, fibre reinforcement.
2 see reinforcing bar.
3 see steel fixing.

reinforcement schedule see bar schedule.

reinforcement spacer see spacer.

reinforcing bar one of a number or configuration of deformed steel bars used in reinforced concrete to provide resistance to tensile stresses; also called a rebar.

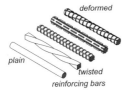

reinforcing bars

reinforcing cage see cage.

reinforcing fabric an area of plaster-soaked textile used in plaster casting as structural reinforcement.

reinforcing strip see taping strip.

reinspection a subsequent building inspection held after defects in building work have been made following an initial inspection, or where work has not been ready or the approved plans and specifications are not on site during an initial inspection.

reinstatement the restoring of public areas, infrastructure, landscaping and surroundings which have been affected by construction work to their pre-existing state after the completion of building work.

reject a material or product which is not acceptable for use in construction work due to its poor quality, imperfections or faults, or because it does not meet a specification.

relative humidity the ratio of the humidity of air to the saturation point of air at the same temperature and pressure.

relaxation in structural engineering, the loss of stress in a loaded tensile member due to creep.

relay an electromagnetic switch in an electric circuit.

release agent, parting compound; in concreting, a material or compound applied to formwork to facilitate its removal from the concrete.

relief, 1 relievo; a two-dimensional design, pattern or sculpture which is raised partly or entirely above a flat surface to appear as if in three dimensions.
2 decorative ornament carved, embossed or otherwise pressed into a surface.
see sunk relief (cavo-relievo, intaglio rilevato), anaglyph, basso rilievo (low relief, bas-relief), mezzo rilievo (half relief), alto rilievo (high relief).

relief wallcovering wallcovering with a face surface rendered or embossed with a raised pattern.

relieving arch, discharging arch; a blind arch built into masonry above a window or door opening to spread loading to side wall abutments.

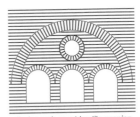

relieving arch over tripartite opening

relieving vault a simple vaulting system found above chambers in the Egyptian pyramids and other massive stone monuments, whose purpose is to redirect loads bearing directly onto the chamber roof to side abutments.

relievo see relief.

relocatable partition see demountable partition.

remedial pertaining to a process or procedure intended to return or repair something to its original state.

remedial conservation see physical conservation.

remedial plastering the repairing of pits and cracks in an existing plaster surface using small areas of fresh plaster, having first removed loose material and wetted the treatable areas; also known as patching.

remedial work see renovation.

remoulded sample, disturbed sample; a soil sample which has been manipulated on removal from the ground and has had its structure altered.

Renaissance the rebirth of classicism, a cultural movement originating in Florence, Italy in the 1400s; in architecture it is characterized by the use of classical elements for primarily secular buildings; styles of Renaissance are listed below; see also Mannerism.

early Renaissance Renaissance architecture from the early period, quattrocento in Italy, c. 1420–1490.

high Renaissance the middle phase of Renaissance architecture, cinquecento in Italy, c. 1480–1535.

late Renaissance the latter stage in Renaissance architecture, c.1530–1580.

neo-Renaissance eclectic Renaissance styles in architecture from the end of the nineteenth century.

proto-Renaissance architecture regarded as being the direct forebear of Renaissance, such as the severe Tuscan Romanesque architecture with classical influences, c. 1100–1200, or that from the lower reaches of the Rhone.

render, 1 rendering; an exterior finish for concrete, masonry and rough stonework consisting of a mixture of cement, sand and water, applied wet; commonly also known as plaster, though this usually applies to traditional methods and materials, or interior work; types included as separate entries are listed below:
*cement render; *cement lime render, see composition render; *composition render,

*compo render; *fibre-reinforced render; *insulated render; *mineral render, see mineral plaster; *polymer render; *reinforced render, see reinforced plaster; *scratch render, see scratch plaster; *thin coat render, thin section render; *waterproof render, see damp resisting plaster.
2 see rendering mortar.

render and set see two coat plasterwork.

render coat a single layer of render laid as surfacing for a wall at any one time; see first plaster undercoat.

rendered brickwork brick masonry waterproofed with a render finish.

render, float and set see three coat plasterwork.

rendering 1 the process of applying a coat of render to a wall surface; see also daubing.
2 the render thus applied; see plaster, plasterwork, render, stucco; types of rendering included as separate entries are listed below:
*coloured rendering, *comb-finished rendering, *float-finished rendering, *masonry paint (organic rendering), *trowel-finished rendering.
3 see torching.
4 in computer graphics and CAD, the application of surface colour or texture to an image or model.
5 see colour rendering.

rendering mortar mortar designed especially for use in rendering and plastering, with good adherence and resistance to cracking; also called render.

renewal see urban renewal.

renovation, remedial work, repair work; the action of repairing or remodelling a building or a space within a building to meet current requirements; see refurbishment.

renovation plaster plaster used for repairs in old buildings where the background may be damp.

reorganization, reconstruction; the rearranging of the contents or methods of operation of an existing building, organization or business to improve its performance or effectiveness.

repainting, 1 maintenance painting; in painting and decorating, the addition of a fresh coat of paint to an existing painted surface, including filling cracks, removing hardened paint which is loose, etc.
2 overpainting; the adding of subsequent coats of paint to a freshly painted surface.

repair the action of restoring an item, part of a building or component which is broken or in poor condition to its original functional state; the result of this action.

repaired plywood plywood in which defects in the face plies have been patched or filled.

repair work see renovation.

reprocessing the industrial recycling of waste material into new materials or products.

request for bids, request for tender; the stage in a contract tendering procedure during which sets of tender documents are sent to a number of potential contractors, to which they will supply a tender price or bid.

requirement in design and construction, a local authority, client or contractual condition, obligation, standard or imposition which should be fulfilled.

resawing the longitudinal sawing of converted and seasoned timber into smaller sections.

reserve water tank a tank of water from which extinguishant water is pumped in the event of a building fire.

reservoir any vessel which temporarily stores liquid used in a process, installation, etc.; a natural or man-made lake for the storage of a large volume of water.

residential pertaining to or characterized by homes and dwellings; see following entries.
residential area, housing area; an urban district consisting principally of dwellings; an area on a town plan designated for dwellings.
residential building, dwelling house; a building which contains one or a number of dwellings, or one whose sole purpose is to serve as such.
residential development, housing project; a new area of dwellings under design or construction; see housing development.
residential scheme, housing scheme; a distinct unit of new housing, usually arranged around a yard and with certain communal facilities.

resident parking an area of parking designed for the use of residents of adjacent dwellings.

residual stress internal stresses in a structural member or component caused by manufacturing processes, etc. rather than applied loading.

residue waste or unusable material deposited from a chemical or sedimentation process.

resilient a description of a compomnent or material which is elastic and will return to its original form after release of stresses; especially used with regard to acoustic products and vibration dampers.
resilient channel a metal acoustic channel fixing to prevent any vibration of fittings and wall surfaces being transmitted to the building fabric.
resilient clip a metal fixing clip used in acoustic construction to prevent any vibration of fittings, etc. being transmitted to the building fabric.
resilient mounting any flexible support or fixing designed to prevent vibration from fittings, mechanical plant, etc. being transmitted to the building fabric.

resin 1 a natural or synthetic organic polymer used in the manufacture of varnishes, adhesives, paints and plastics; types included as separate entries are listed below.
2 pitch; the viscous secretion from the resin canals of some pines, distilled to form tar, oil of turpentine and other products; see also natural resin.
*alkyd resin; *amber, succinite; *bakelite, see phenol formaldehyde; *coumarone resin, see coumarone indene; *damar resin, see damar; *epoxide resin, epoxy resin, EP; *fossil resin; *gutta-percha; *melamine formaldehyde, melamine, MF; *natural resin; *oleoresin, balsam; *phenol formaldehyde, phenolic resin, PF; *polyester resin, UP; *polysulphone, PSU, polysulfone (Am); *polyvinyl alcohol, PVA; *unsaturated polyester, see polyester resin; *urea formaldehyde, UF.

resin adhesive, resin glue see synthetic resin adhesive.
resin concrete see polymer concrete.
resin lining see sock lining.
resin pocket see pitch pocket.
resin streak see pitch streak.

resistance moment see moment of resistance.

resistance welding a range of welding processes in which metal objects to be welded are pressed together and heat for fusion is provided by electrical resistance; examples of this are spot, seam, projection and butt welding.
resistance butt welding see butt welding.
resistance flash welding see flash welding.

resistor see electrical resistor.

resonance a physical phenomenon, the lively sympathetic vibration of an object or component at certain frequencies of induced vibration.
resonant frequency a frequency at which resonance occurs.
resonator in acoustics, a construction designed to absorb sound of a narrow band of frequencies by sympathetic resonance; a type of absorber.

resorcinol formaldehyde glue a synthetic resin adhesive which is water soluble for several hours, then insoluble and chemically resistant.

restoration the action of bringing a building, piece of furniture or work of art back to its original state by repair work, cleaning, etc.; see also land restoration.

restrictor see throat restrictor.

resultant force, resultant; in mechanics, the overall force vector resulting from all the different forces acting on a body or at a joint.

retainage see retention sum.

retainer 1 see retention sum.
2 insulation retainer, see insulation clip.

retaining ring see circlip.

retaining wall a structural wall designed to withstand lateral forces from the abutting ground or a body of

water on one side of it; types included as separate entries are listed below:
*anchored retaining wall; *buttress wall, see counterfort wall; *cantilever wall, cantilever retaining wall; *counterfort wall; *cribbing, cribwork; *gabion wall; *gravity retaining wall, gravity wall; *sheet piling, trench sheeting; *wing wall.

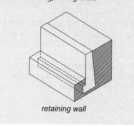

retaining wall

retarder, retarding agent; an additive for cement, plaster and glues to slow down the rate of setting.
retarded concrete concrete which contains an admixture to increase its setting time.

retempering, knocking up; the addition of water to concrete or mortar in use in order to increase its workability, which also reduces its final strength.

retention sum, retainage; in contract administration, a sum retained for a certain period by the client to offset costs that may arise from the contractor's failure to comply fully with the contract.

reticulated a description of a pattern or construction resembling a net.
reticulated finish an irregularly lined or grooved finish in stonework produced by dressing with a point tool.
reticulated tracery Gothic tracery of vertical members which are interlaced in the upper arch of a window with undulating ogee forms.

reticulated tracery, St Ouen, Rouen, France, 1318–1515

retrofit the installation of components and plant after the usual completion of a building or surrounding construction.

return 1 a short perpendicular change in direction at the end of a wall, moulding, etc. **2** see return pipe.

return air, extract air; in air conditioning and mechanical ventilation, stale air extracted from a space.
return-air duct, extract duct, exhaust duct; a mechanical ventilation or air-conditioning duct carrying stale air away from a space.
return-air terminal unit, air intake, extract unit; in air conditioning and mechanical ventilation, a grille or other device through which stale air is sucked out of a space.

return end, return wall; a short perpendicular change in direction at the end of a wall.

return latch, catch bolt, latch bolt, spring latch, tongue; the bevelled metal springloaded tongue in a latch, which engages in a plate fixed to a door jamb and retracts when a door handle is turned.

return latch

return pipe, return; a pipeline which conveys fluid from a place of use such as a radiator back to a storage or plant facility.

return stair see dogleg stair; double return stair.

return wall see return end.

return water water in a hot water heating circuit which is returned from radiators, etc. for reheating.

reuleaux triangle, curved triangle; a three-sided geometrical figure in which each equilateral side is constructed by scribing an arc around the opposite apex, and whose height measured through its centre is, like a circle, a constant; often found as a decorative motif in Byzantine, Syrian and Gothic architecture, symbolic of the manifestation of divine will.

reuleaux triangle

reusable formwork in concreting, specialized or proprietary formwork which is not destroyed on striking, and can be used over again.

reuse the use of waste materials in the manufacture of new products; the use of redundant buildings and plots for new and different purposes; see also recycling.

reveal, jamb; the vertical side surfaces of an opening in a wall, usually at right angles or splayed with respect to the main wall surface.

reverberation 1 see sound reflection, sound reverberation.
2 see water hammer.
reverberation time in acoustics, the time taken for the sound pressure level to drop below 60 dB after the initial sound has stopped.
reverberatory a description of a room with spatial conditions and reflective surfaces which produce long reverberation times.

reverse alternate lengths a method of hanging wallpaper in which every other vertical length is laid upside down.

reverse box match a veneering pattern in which four triangular pieces of straight-grained veneer are laid in a rectangular arrangement with diagonal joints in such a way that the direction of grain is from the centre point outwards.

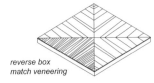

reverse box match veneering

reverse diamond match a veneering pattern in which four rectangular pieces of straight-grained veneer are laid in a group so that the grain of each is at an angle and radiating away from the centre point. See illustration on facing page.

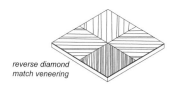

reverse diamond match veneering

reverse ogee arch, bell arch; a decorative round or pointed arch formed of two back-to-back ogees with their concave parts meeting at the apex; see also keel arch.

reverse ogee arch

reverse ogee moulding a decorative moulding whose cross-section is that of an ogee, the convex part uppermost; called a cyma reversa in classical architecture.

reverse taper column see Minoan column.

reverse toothing recesses left in the face of a brick wall under construction into which lapping courses in a perpendicular cross wall can be bonded; also called indents.

reversionary development development which returns land or buildings to their original use or state, after a period specified in planning permission.

revetment 1 a layer of binding material, concrete, stone, etc. laid over a natural embankment or sloping earthwork as stabilization.
2 a retaining wall for an earthwork or embankment.

revibration the recompaction of concrete a few hours after placing using a vibrator to reduce settlement cracks, release trapped water and increase bonding with reinforcement.

revision, 1 amendment; an annotated change to documentation due to alterations in a design.
2 revised drawing; a documentation or design drawing which has been altered because of the above.
revision arrow see arrowhead.
revision cloud a rough ring added to draw attention to recent alterations in a

design drawing, also called an amendment cloud.
revision panel tabulated information in a design drawing, listing the revisions made, dates, etc.; also called an amendment block.

revival style a general name for styles in architecture such as the Greek revival and Gothic revival which derive forms and motifs from historical precedents and bygone eras.

revolving door a door with a number of leaves which revolve around a central axis.

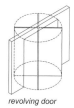

revolving door

RH see right-handed.

rhodochrosite, manganese spar; a red, brown or pinkish mineral, natural manganese carbonate, $MnCO_3$, used as a local manganese ore and polished for jewellery and ornamental stone.

rhodonite a black-veined, pink or red mineral, a silicate of manganese used as ornamental stone and occasionally as an ore of manganese.

rhone see half round gutter.

RHS see rectangular hollow section, rolled hollow section.

rhyolite, liparite, quartz porphyry; a silica-rich, fine-grained volcanic rock used as aggregates and chippings, for paving and as ornamental stone.

rib 1 in reinforced concrete construction, one of a number of projections on a deformed reinforcing bar to provide a better bond with the concrete matrix; see longitudinal rib, transverse rib.
2 the main structural member in a rib vault, or a line of stone which marks it; types included as separate entries are listed below:
*arc doubleau, see transverse rib; *diagonal rib; *groin rib, see diagonal rib; *ogive, see

diagonal rib; *lierne; *longitudinal ridge rib;
*ridge rib, see longitudinal ridge rib, trans-
verse ridge rib; *secondary rib, see tierceron; *tertiary rib, see lierne; *tierceron;
*transverse rib; *transverse ridge rib.

ribbed bar see deformed bar.

ribbed bar

ribbed board hardboard with one face
moulded with a ribbed texture.

ribbed expanded metal lathing, rib
lathing; lathing, a base for plaster, made
from expanded metal which has been
ribbed to give a better key.

ribbed-sheet roofing see profiled
sheeting.

ribbed vault see rib vault.

ribbon a narrow flat woven band often
used as a decorative motif in carved
stonework, woodwork and plasterwork.

ribbon figure, ribbon grain, stripe
figure; a decorative striped figure in sawn
timber and veneers, produced by the
radial cutting of the wood from the log.

ribbon window see window band.

rib lathing see ribbed expanded metal
lathing.

rib vault, ribbed vault; a vault constructed of structural arched stone members or ribs with an infill of masonry; often
with tiercerons or secondary ribs, and
liernes or tertiary ribs. See illustration below.

rich concrete, fat concrete; a concrete
mix whose proportion of cement is
greater than usual.

rich lime see fat lime.

rich mix, fat mix; a mix of concrete or
mortar with a high content of binder.

ridge the longitudinal apex where two
sloping planes in a pitched roof meet; the

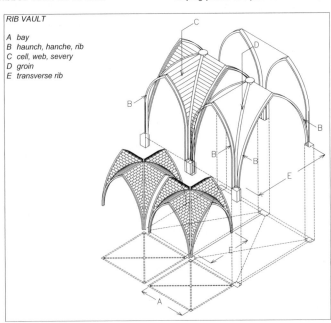

RIB VAULT

A bay
B haunch, hanche, rib
C cell, web, severy
D groin
E transverse rib

straight line running along the highest point of a sloping roof.

ridge beam, ridge purlin, rooftree; in timber roof construction, a horizontal timber which supports the ends of coupled rafters at the ridge.

ridge board, ridge plank, ridge piece; in timber roof construction, a horizontal board at ridge level onto which rafters bear.

ridge capping, ridgecap, ridge covering; a longitudinal construction or component for covering the ridge of a roof; often a channel, board, row of U-shaped tiles, etc.

ridge capping tile see ridge tile.

ridge covering see ridge capping.

ridge end in roofing, a special tile or other construction at the end of a ridge; see block end ridge tile.

ridge gusset in timber roof construction, a fish plate for connecting a pair of rafters at the ridge.

ridge piece, ridge plank see ridge board.

ridge plate in timber pitched roof construction, a piece placed at ridge level onto which the ridge capping may be fixed.

ridge pole a ridge beam in traditional and log construction.

ridge purlin see ridge beam.

ridge rib see longitudinal ridge rib, transverse ridge rib.

---

ridge tile, ridge capping tile; a special roof tile designed to cover the ridge of a roof; types included as separate entries are listed below:
*angular ridge tile; *block end ridge tile, ridge end; *ventilating ridge tile; *dry ridge tile.

---

riding shore a slanting prop or raker sprung from another raker in a raking shore.

rift crack see heartshake.

rift sawing see quartersawing.

rift sawn see quartersawn.

rift sliced veneer a decorative veneer formed by the oblique slicing of a quarter log or flitch.

rigger brush a slender paintbrush with very long fibres culminating in a point; used by artists and decorators for precision work; also simply called a rigger.

right-handed, right-hung, RH see handing.

rigid a description of a structure which will resist deformation under load due to adequate bracing and stiff joints; see also stiff; rigidity or stiffness is the property of a material, structure or body to resist bending, stretching and deformation.

rigid composite pavement road or paved construction of a structural concrete slab surfaced with layers of bituminous material.

rigid frame see portal frame.

rigid joint any joint between two members which is fixed in place and undergoes no rotation about a pivot for purposes of structural calculation.

rigid pavement road or paved construction consisting of a concrete slab providing both structure and surfacing.

rigid pipe pipes of ceramics, metal, concrete, etc. which are brittle and cannot be deformed without fracturing.

rilevato, rilievo see relief.

Rilsan proprietary name for a tough, polyamide thermoplastic used as fibres.

rim latch a latch attached to the surface of a door rather than incorporated into its thickness.

rim lock a lock attached to the surface of a door rather than incorporated into its thickness; see also mortise lock.

rinceau Gothic and Romanesque decorative ornament in low relief with representations of foliage, acanthus leaves, vines and berries.

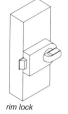
rim lock

ring see annulet, annual ring.

ring circuit a ring-shaped electric circuit connected to a power supply.

ringed column see annulated column, rusticated column.

ring failure see cup shake.

ring main 1 a pressurized pipe circuit for the continuous supply of hot water to a building.
2 see cold oil ring main.

ring porous wood hardwood with relatively large pores concentrated in early wood and small pores in latewood.

ring pull a handle consisting of a hinged ring by which a door, drawer, hatch, etc. is pulled open.

ring scale fungus see red ring rot.

ring shake see cup shake.

ring-shanked nail see annular nail.

Rinman's green see cobalt green.

ripper a tool consisting of a steel bar for removing old surface construction such as plasterwork, boarding, etc.

ripping see flat cutting.

ripping chisel a large chisel used for heavy and rough work.

ripple marks see ray figure.

rip-rap 1 rubble and loose stone used to form a foundation, ramp, bridge abutment, bank or breakwater; a construction thus built.
2 loose stones of stones of 7–70 kg used as covering for a revetment.

rip saw a saw with teeth adapted for cutting along the grain of wood; see crosscut saw.
rip-sawing also called flat cutting.

rise, 1 pitch; the vertical distance measured from the impost to the crown of an arch.
2 the vertical height of a step, or the vertical distance between adjacent treads in a stair.

riser 1 the vertical surface forming the front face of a step.
2 a vertical service pipe or duct in a building; see rising main, ventilation stack (ventilation riser).

rising hinge, gravity door hinge, rising-butt hinge; a hinge with two metal flaps and a central joining pin, whose housing is cut with a helix so that

the door rises slightly when opened, and swings shut under its own weight.

rising hinge

rising main, riser; a vertical service main to provide a water, electricity, gas telecommunications supply or service to upper floors of a multistorey building.

riveling see wrinkle.

riven finish, cloven finish; a stonework finish produced by cleaving or splitting; the finished surface is the same as the cleavage plane.

rivet a short flat-headed metal pin used for fixing metal sheet or plate by inserting it into holes in the sheets to be fastened and hammering to flatten the other end.
riveted joint a metalwork joint fastened with rivets.

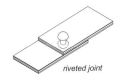

riveted joint

riveting the process of fixing metal plates together with rivets, and the result of this action.
riveting hammer a hammer with a small face and cross peen used in riveting work.

road oil, asphalt oil; a viscous oily substance distilled from crude oil; used as a surface treatment or binder in road and paved construction.

road tar a blend of coal tar and tar oil used in road construction.

robinia, false acacia, black locust (Am); [*Robinia pseudoacacia*] a hardwood of Europe and the USA with golden brown, hard and heavy timber; used for furniture, fences and posts.

rocaille, French Rococo, Louis XV style; an exuberantly decorative style of Rococo architecture in France during the reign of Louis XV (1715–1774).

rock a naturally occurring agglomeration of minerals forming a distinct and definable geological body; stone in its natural habitat within the earth's crust.
see **igneous rock** for ancient igneous rock types (granite, basalt, etc.)
see **metamorphic rock** for metamorphic rock types (marble, schist, slate, etc.)
see **sedimentary rock** for types of sedimentary rock (limestone, sandstone, etc.)

rock anchor, rock anchorage; a system of steel rods, guys or braces to fix a structure firmly to bedrock.

rock axe see masonry axe.

rock bolt a fixing which receives the forces from a rock anchorage and transmits them to the bedrock in which it is embedded.

rock burst, rock bursting; the breaking away of a larger area of rock face than intended during blasting excavation.

rock-faced see quarry finish.

rock flour rock which has been crushed into a powder with grains which are well under 1 mm in size.

rock maple see maple.

rock pick a small hammer with a bladed peen, used for careful removal of stone from surfaces, geological specimens, archeological finds, etc.

rock plant any species of landscaping plant which usually grows and thrives in rocky or dry areas.

rock pocket see honeycombing.

rock socket, rock shoe; the lower end of a foundation pile, by which it is bored into and connected to bedrock.

rock wool mineral wool produced from volcanic rock or other rock types; used for thermal insulation.

Rococo an architectural and decorative style originating from France c.

1725–1775, characterized by abundant lightweight ornament.

Rococo window   *Rococo portal*

rodded joint see keyed joint.

rodding see tamping.
rodding eye see cleaning eye.

roll billet see round billet.

rolled asphalt asphalt laid hot and compacted by rolling plant; used for wearing courses, basecourses or roadbases in road construction and external paving.

rolled concrete, roller-compacted concrete; stiff concrete compacted using a vibrating roller; used for roads and pavements.

rolled glass glass manufactured by passing molten glass between steel rollers, often shaped to provide patterned surfaces; see patterned glass.

rolled hollow section, RHS; a structural steel section formed by processes of rolling, whose uniform cross-section is most often a hollow rectangle (also RHS), but may also be a square or circle; see circular hollow section, rectangular hollow section, square hollow section.

rolled steel section a structural steel profile with a uniform cross-section produced by rolling.
rolled steel joist, rsj see I-section.

roller, paint roller; a hand-held implement consisting of a roll of absorbent material on an axle; used for the rapid application of paint to a surface.

roller bearing a structural bearing consisting of one or more cylindrical pieces which transfers loading between parallel plates.

roller blind an internal fabric window blind with a spring mechanism to enable it to be retracted by rolling up around a central rod above the window opening.

roller catch a fastening device fixed into the edge of a door leaf to hold it in a closed position by means of a sprung cylinder in a casing; see also ball catch.

roller-compacted concrete see rolled concrete.

roller compaction see rolling.

roller door see roller shutter.

roller painting the application of paint on wall surfaces with a paint roller.

roller shutter any door, gate, shutter or screen which is rolled up around an overhead horizontal axle when in an open position; especially an overhead door or shutter made up from hinged slats, cloth, etc. which roll up around a drum above the opening; usually a high-speed motorized door.

roller catch

roller shutter

roller tray a shallow plastic vessel in which paint is held while being transferred to a paint roller; also called a paint tray.

rolling, 1 roller compaction; in road construction, the compaction and evening out of a freshly laid surface or substrate with heavy rolling plant.
2 in landscaping, the evening and flattening of lawns, etc. with a manual roller.
3 the production of metal bars, plate, etc. with a uniform cross-section in a rolling mill using industrial methods; see cold forming (cold rolling), hot rolling.

rolling load a structural live load imposed by a moving vehicle; see also moving load.

roll joint, batten roll joint, conical roll joint, wood roll joint; in sheet roofing, a joint formed by dressing roofing material around a timber fillet with welted joints, or nailing the sheet material to the fillet and fixing a capping on top; see hollow roll joint.

roll joint

roll-jointed roof a sheetmetal roof whose adjacent strips of roofing are connected with roll joints.
roll-jointed roofing felt or sheetmetal roofing in which adjacent seams running from ridge to eaves are formed using roll joints.

roll moulding, round moulding; a decorative moulding which is half round (or a greater part of a circle) in cross-section; see scroll moulding, round billet (roll billet).

roll-rim [*Paxillus panuoides*] a brown rot fungus which attacks timber in damp conditions, forming brown lobed shelf-like growths.

roll tile a pantile or Roman tile.

Roman architecture the post-Etruscan classical architecture of the Romans from 750 BC—476 AD, characterized by Greek-influenced temples, theatres, baths and tenements, and by engineering ingenuity for structures such as roads, bridges and conduits; see also full page article on Roman architecture on p. 404.
Roman arch a masonry arch whose intrados describes half a circle; a semicircular arch.
Roman cement 1 a pozzolanic (hydraulic) cement used since Roman times,

made from natural pozzolan mixed with lime.

2 Parker's cement, brown cement; a proprietary form of cement produced from burnt clay and used as render in England in the 1800s.

Roman concrete Roman walling construction made from two skins of rubble with an infill of cement and small stones poured at intervals during construction.

Roman Corinthian order a variation of the Greek Corinthian order, especially favoured during the Renaissance, in which bare columns are crowned with tall Corinthian capitals, and the entablature has richer embellishment.

Roman Doric order, Doric Roman order; a Roman and Renaissance version of the Doric order comprising columns with fluted shafts, simple capitals (consisting of a decorated echinus above an annulet and surmounted by an abacus edged with a cyma moulding), bases, and an entablature with triglyphs and metopes.

Roman Doric capitals

Roman Ionic order a Roman variation of the Greek Ionic order whose volutes have greater sculpturing than the original.

Roman ochre a variety of yellow ochre pigment, either one used in ancient Rome or found naturally in Italy.

Romanesque religious architecture in Western Europe from the early eleventh century, characterized by bulky massing, massive semicircular masonry vaults for roofing the nave and aisles, sparing use of detail, and the round arch with a heavy intrados (a Romanesque arch); known in England as Norman architecture; see also Carolingian and article on Romanesque architecture on p. 406.

Romayne pertaining to decorative carving, furniture and panelling in England in the early 1500s, typically characterized by foliage and medallions and with Italian Renaissance influences.

rood a large crucifix in a church.

rood altar an altar against a rood screen, facing the nave.

rood arch the main arch in a rood screen.

rood beam a beam spanning across the chancel to support a rood screen.

rood loft a gallery running along the top of a rood screen intended to carry candles, effigies or a crucifix.

rood screen a screen which separates the nave and chancel of a church and is intended to carry a crucifix.

rood spire, rood tower a spire and tower (respectively) over the crossing of a church.

roof 1 those parts of the top of a building which provide shelter against the elements; the uppermost weatherproof level in a building. See illustration on p. 408.
2 see roofing, roof covering.
roof types according to structure, method of construction and materials are listed below; roof types according to shape are listed under roof form.
*barrel vaulted roof; *clasped purlin collar rafter roof; *close couple roof, close couple rafter roof; *cold roof; *collar roof, collar rafter roof; *common purlin roof, horizontal rafter roof; *couple roof, coupled rafter roof; *crown post rafter roof, crown post and collar purlin roof; *crown post rafter roof, crown post roof; *double roof, see purlin roof; *glazed roof, glass roof; *grass roof, see turf roof, green roof; *green roof; *hammer-beam roof; *horizontal rafter roof, see common purlin roof; *inverted roof, see upside down roof; *king post roof; *northlight shell roof; *open roof, open timbered roof; *organic roof; *protected membrane roof, see upside down roof; *purlin roof, double roof; *queen post collar rafter roof, queen post roof; *queen post rafter roof; *rafter roof; *roll-jointed roof; *Roman tiled roof illustration; *scissor roof, scissor rafter roof; *shake roof; *sheetmetal roof; *shell roof; *shingle roof; *single roof; *slate roof; *span roof, see close couple*

(continued on p. 408)

ROME

Romans were followers of the Greeks aesthetically, but their construction technology resolved numerous problems which were unknown to the Greeks. The city of Rome, *urbs Roma – caput mundi* – 'capital of the world', had about a million inhabitants during the early imperial age in the 2nd century AD. Typical to its architecture, as in any other large Roman city, were monumental squares lined with public administrative buildings and temples, broad streets, multistorey blocks of flats (***insulae***) with shops (***tabernae***), public baths (***thermae***), amphitheatres, libraries, and water distribution and sewerage systems. These represent a new urban architecture.

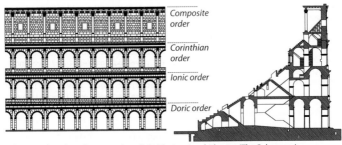

Composite order

Corinthian order

Ionic order

Doric order

elevational study and cross section of the Flavian Amphitheatre (The Colosseum), Rome, 72-80 AD, scale ~1:1400, showing superimposed orders of outer wall

Roman architects re-evaluated the meaning of the wall in a spatial sense and developed new types of interiors by using vaults, domes and apses above circular and polygonal plans. Of great importance in this was *opus caementicum* (**Roman concrete**), a mixture of water, lime, volcanic sand and crushed stone, which formed the plastic hardcore of stone or brick veneered walls. Concrete, **arches** and **vaults** were not in themselves new inventions, but by combining them, Romans created constructions on a vast scale such as had never been seen before. With the fall of the Western Roman Empire, Roman concrete technology disappeared for nearly 1500 years.

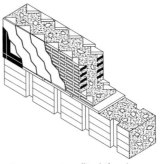

Roman concrete walling (otherwise known as opus testaceum), cutaway to show brick facing of triangular pieces around a concrete core, with plaster facing

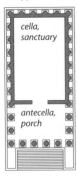

cella, sanctuary

antecella, porch

Roman pseudoperipteral temple (hexastyle), "Maison Carrée", 20-15 BC, Nîmes, France, scale 1:800

Although Romans followed Greek patterns in their temples, they were not simply imitations. They used predominantly **Ionic** and **Corinthian** orders, seldom Doric, and a temple was built on a high pedestal and entered through a staircase and a frontal portico. Temples were not surrounded by peristyle colonnades as in Greek models, exterior walls being adorned rather by half-columns.

The Romans had a highly organized society, exemplified by a system of law, large public building projects and a vast well-disciplined army, a tool which allowed them to practice aggressive expansionism. At its territorial peak in the 2nd century AD, the Roman Empire included all of modern western Europe, extending as far north as the Scottish border, and including Egypt and Lebanon in the east, and the whole of coastal North Africa. The Roman military camp (***castrum***) which was erected to a standardized format, was always arranged regularly around a main square (the ***forum***) surrounded by religious and administrative buildings at the crossing of main streets, the ***decumanus*** from east to west and the ***cardo*** from north to south. It was a layout repeated across the empire from Egypt to Britain, and formed the beginning of a number of Mediterranean and European towns. In Britain, the suffix '*chester*' at the end of town's name is indicative of its origin as the site of a Roman military camp.

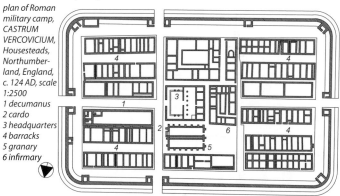

plan of Roman military camp, CASTRUM VERCOVICIUM, Housesteads, Northumberland, England, c. 124 AD, scale 1:2500
1 decumanus
2 cardo
3 headquarters
4 barracks
5 granary
6 infirmary

Perhaps the most important legacy of Roman architecture for modern times is the **basilica**, a Roman secular meeting hall or court building, that became the archetype of the Christian church in Western Europe until the beginning of the 20th century. *Basilica* originally refers to a king's tribunal chamber, and in some Christian contexts it may refer to an important church where certain ceremonial rites are held. Architecturally, a basilica is a great hall divided by colonnades into aisles which often terminate in apses at one end. Typically there are two rows of columns, and the broader central aisle or nave rises above flanking aisles to allow for the penetration of light through upper clerestory windows.

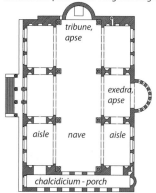

tribune, apse

exedra, apse

aisle   nave   aisle

chalcidicium - porch

Left and below, plan and section of Roman basilica (the Basilica of Maxentius (Basilica Maxentii), or Basilica of Constantine, Rome, 306-312 AD, scale ~1:2000, showing clerestoreyed nave, side aisles and end apse as a precursor to the plan of a western Christian church

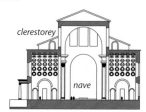

clerestorey

nave

ROMANESQUE

Romanesque describes the architecture of Europe between 950–1150. This less-than-satisfactory term – which means 'pseudo-Roman' – was coined in the early 19th century in Normandy during an era when monumental archaeology and newly re-discovered medieval art had become fashionable, and it gives an impression of medieval art as an imitation of Mediterranean Late Antiquity. In itself the term would be better suited to its predecessors, **Carolingian** and Ottonian architecture.

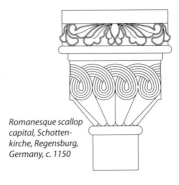

Romanesque scallop capital, Schotten-kirche, Regensburg, Germany, c. 1150

In the Carolingian era details such as **columns, bases** and **mouldings** were often introduced directly from Rome. A Carolingian invention, the **westwork** – the tower-like western end to a church, containing an entrance vestibule with a private chapel above, flanked by two stair towers – bears resemblance to a Roman imperial town gate and is a symbol of the church militant. Galleries opening onto the nave above the aisles were accessible through westwork stairs. The whole structure was later replaced with magnificent Romanesque and Gothic **west ends**, and the solarium windows of palatine chapels above the entrance gave way to **wheel and rose windows**.

Left: carolingian westwork of the Benedictine Abbey of Corvey on the Weser (New Corbie), Westphalia, Germany; 822-885 (remodelled in 1596)

Below: Anglo-Norman (English Romanesque) wheel window, St. Mary's church, Patrixbourne, Kent, 1170

During the Romanesque period new unparalleled structures take shape, ones that would become characteristic to all European architecture. Their development can be associated with monasticism, prince bishops and abbeys, feudalism and castles, pilgrimages and crusades, and with the spread of knowledge.

Romanesque architecture invented wide naves and broad transepts that afforded space for daily rituals and processions to the shrine. The **round arch** and the constructions based on this are central to Romanesque architecture. The **tunnel vault** above thick masonry walls became universal in a constructional as well as a decorative sense; its span increased, and successive arches created ever longer vaulted spaces. The most ambitious vaults on the continent were erected at the beginning of the 12th century.

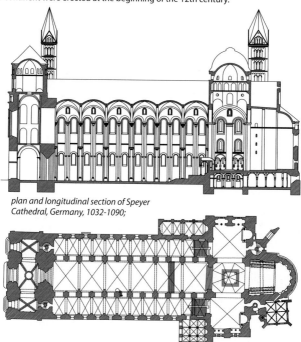

plan and longitudinal section of Speyer Cathedral, Germany, 1032-1090;

An essential feature of Romanesque church architecture is the crypt under the choir. The crypt was used for displaying the relics of a saint to pilgrims and to offer burial places near the saint's grave.

In **arcades**, pillars of laid block masonry were used instead of massive stone columns, and the **alternating system of columns and piers** were used for both constructional and spatial reasons. Groin vaults linked naves and transepts and formed a crossing between the choir and the body of the church. The richly decorated round arches and column capitals reflected old superstition, illustrating imaginary demons and creatures as well as naturalistic embellishment.

Below: diagram of Romanesque barrel-vaulted roof showing alternation of supports

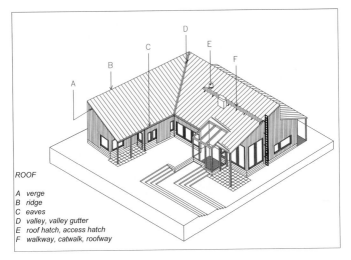

ROOF

A verge
B ridge
C eaves
D valley, valley gutter
E roof hatch, access hatch
F walkway, catwalk, roofway

*roof; *thatched roof; *tie beam roof; *tiled roof, tile roof; *timber roof; *trussed roof, triple roof; *trussed purlin roof; *trussed rafter roof; *trussed roof, triple roof; *turf roof; *unventilated roof; *upside down roof; *ventilated roof; *warm roof.*

roof batten one of a number of timber strips laid to provide a nailing base and a ventilation gap for roofing material.

roof beam one of a series of horizontal or slanting structural members for supporting roof construction; see also rafter, joist.

roof boarding, sarking; in roof construction, timber boards laid onto rafters as a base for roofing material such as felt, sheetmetal, turf, etc.

roof channel see box gutter.

roof conductor the metal components attached to a roof in a lightning protection system, for directing current from lightning strikes to a down conductor.

roof construction the component parts or layers of the uppermost level in a building, including structure, insulation and roofing material.

roof covering see roofing.

roof decking, roof sheathing; in roof construction, any stiff sheet material such as plywood, boarding etc. laid above rafters or trusses as a base for roofing material.

roof extractor in air conditioning and ventilation, a protected fan unit situated on a roof or at the top of flues, ducts, etc. to extract waste gases.

roof form the shape of the roof of a building; roof types according to shape are listed below; roof types according to structure, method of construction and materials are listed under roof.
*butterfly roof, Y-form roof; *catslide roof; *clerestory roof, see split-level roof; *clipped gable roof, see half-hipped roof; *conical roof; *crossform roof; *curb roof, double pitched roof, knee roof; *domed roof, domical roof; *double gable roof, see M-roof; *double hipped roof; *double lean-to roof; *double pitched roof, see curb roof; *duopitch roof, see saddleback roof; *flat roof, platform roof; *gable roof, gabled roof; *gabled mansard roof, gambrel roof;*

*gambrel roof, gablet roof; *half span roof, see lean-to roof; *half-hipped roof; *helm roof; *hip and valley roof; *hip roof, hipped roof; *hipped gable roof, see half-hipped roof; *hipped mansard roof; *hyperbolic paraboloid roof; *jerkinhead roof, see half-hipped roof; *knee roof, see curb roof; *lean-to roof, half span roof; *L-roof; *M-roof; *mansard roof; *monitor roof; *mono-pitch roof; *northlight roof; *ogee roof; *pavilion roof; *penthouse roof, pent roof; *pentise roof; *pitched roof; *platform roof, see flat roof; *pyramid roof; *rainbow roof; *saddleback roof, saddle roof; *saw-tooth roof; *shed roof, see monopitch roof, see penthouse roof; *shread head roof, see half-hipped roof; *single pitch roof, see monopitch roof; *skirt roof; *southlight roof; *spire roof; *split-level roof, clerestory roof; *station roof, umbrella roof; *suspended roof, suspension roof; *trough roof, see M-roof; *valley roof, see M-roof; *Y-form roof, see butterfly roof.*

roof glazing see glazed roof, rooflight.

roof gully see rainwater outlet.

roof gutter see rainwater gutter.

roofing, 1 roof covering, weather-proofing; in roof construction, the impermeable outer surface and finish material which provides waterproof and weatherproof protection for a roof; various types of roofing are listed below:
*aluminium sheet roofing, aluminium roofing; *asphalt roofing; *bitumen felt roofing, built-up roofing; *bituminous roofing; *built-up roofing, built-up felt roofing; *calendered polymeric roofing; *corrugated sheet roofing; *felt roofing, see bituminous felt roofing; *flexible metal roofing, see supported sheetmetal roofing; *lap-jointed roofing; *membrane roofing; *metal multi-tile roofing; *metal roofing, see sheetmetal roofing; *polyester base felt roofing; *polymeric roofing, see calendered polymeric roofing; *profiled sheet roofing; *ribbed-sheet roofing, see profiled sheeting; *roll-jointed roofing; *seam-welded roofing; *sheet roofing; *sheetmetal roofing; *strip slate roofing; *supported sheetmetal roofing; *tiled roofing, see roof tiling; *troughed sheet roofing.*
2 the laying of weatherproof roofing material, or the construction of a roof.

roofing bolt a metal bolt with an integrated sealing washer, used for attaching profiled or other sheet roofing onto a frame.

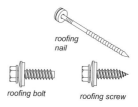

roofing nail

roofing bolt   roofing screw

roofing cleat see cleat.

roofing felt sheet roofing material composed of a thin fibrous mat soaked in a waterproofing compound such as bitumen, supplied in rolls; see bitumen felt.

roofing nail a galvanized or stainless steel nail used for fixing down tiles, slates, roofing battens or roof sheeting; often provided with a soft washer or shaped head to seal the nail hole; see clout, convex head roofing nail.

roofing screw a pointed metal screw with an integrated sealing washer, used for fastening profiled sheet roofing to a base; see sheetmetal screw.

roofing sheet see roof sheeting.

roofing slate, roof slate, slate; a piece of thin stone, usually slate, nailed to battens in overlapping rows as roofing.

roofing system proprietary roofing supplied with all relevant fixings, seals and sealant, flashings, trim and special components included.

roofing tile see roof tile.

roof tiles

roofing underlay a layer of roofing felt used as a waterproof underlay for profiled sheet, tiled or slate roofing; also called sheathing.

roofing upstand the turning up of the edges of roofing felt or sheetmetal roofing against a vertical verge, parapet or abutment.

roof insulation those layers of roof construction which provide thermal insulation.

roof joist any beam which supports a roof; see rafter.

rooflight, roof window, skylight; a window or glazed panel in a roof to provide natural lighting for the interior; may be horizontal or at an angle; see also lantern light.

rooflight sheet translucent sheet material such as glass or plastics laid alongside similarly formed opaque roof sheeting to allow light into spaces below.

roof outlet see rainwater outlet.

roof penetration the place at which a chimney, flue or other component passes through a roof, requiring particular measures to ensure weatherproofing and waterproofing.

roof pitch the slope of a roof plane, given as a percentage or ratio.

roof plane one of the flat surfaces which make up the outer surface of a roof.

roof plate in timber roof construction, a horizontal member running parallel to the ridge, which spreads the load of roof trusses onto a wall or beam.

roof screen a fire barrier within or above a roof space.

roof sheathing see roof decking.

roof sheeting, roofing sheet; rigid sheet material, such as sheetmetal, fibre cement sheet and profiled plastics sheeting, used as impervious roofing material; see also sheet roofing, sheetmetal roofing.

roof slate see roofing slate.

roof soaker see pipe flashing.

roof space, roof void; the uppermost level beneath the pitched roof of a building; often a loft or attic.

roof structure the structural elements which form a roof and support the layers of decking and waterproofing; see also roof truss.

roof surfacing a layer of chippings or other material used as a protective covering for bituminous roofing against the elements.

roof tile, roofing tile; a flat slab of burnt clay, concrete, or other rigid material fastened overlapping or interlocking in series as a roof covering; types included as separate entries are listed below:
*angular hip tile; *block end ridge tile; *bonnet hip tile; *clay roof tile; *cloaked verge tile; *concrete roof tile; *double Roman tile; *dry ridge tile; *eaves tile; *half tile; *hip tile; *interlocking tile; *mansard tile; *ornamental tile; *pantile; *plain tile; *ridge tile; *Roman tile; *shingle tile; *single Roman tile; *roofing slate; *strip slates; *top course tile; *under-and-over tile; *valley tile; *ventilating tile; *verge tile.

roof tiling, tiled roofing; a roof surface or roofing of interlocking or overlapping tiles.

rooftree see ridge beam.

roof truss in roof construction, a triangulated timber frame which supports secondary construction and roofing material; see truss for list of different types of roof trusses.

roof valley see valley.

roof vent a component for ventilating a closed roofspace or roof construction.

roof ventilation the natural circulation of outside air through roof construction and voids to remove unwanted moisture.

roof void a space in between the uppermost habitable room and the roofing in a building too small to stand up in; see also roof space.

roof window see rooflight.

room any enclosed space within a building excluding circulation space; see also habitable room.

room acoustics the characteristics of a space with respect to sound quality and audibility.

room air-conditioner see unit air-conditioner.

room formwork see apartment formwork.

room heater, domestic solid-fuel appliance, heating stove; a wood or coal fired heater, range or other closed flued appliance used in the home to provide occasional heating.

room height see ceiling height.

room index in lighting design, a design formula relating to the geometry of a space, given as follows $(l \times w)/h(l + w)$, where h is the working height.

room temperature the normal internal temperature of the habitable spaces of a building, usually between 15°C and 21°C.

root barrier a layer of resilient sheeting laid beneath landscaped planting, green roofs, etc. to prevent roots from growing plants damaging waterproofing membranes and other underlying construction.

root rot see annosus root rot.

rope a thick wound twine of fibrous material, plastics or metal consisting of a core around which at least three strands are spirally wound.

rope moulding see cable moulding.

rose 1 any round boss-like fitting to cover an outlet, often decorative; a metal plate or fitting for covering the hole in a door through which the spindle of a door handle passes; the round perforated nozzle of a shower outlet; an ornamental ceiling fitting from which a luminaire can be mounted, a centrepiece.
2 a decorative motif of a stylized rose bloom; see rosette, Tudor rose, whorl.

rose madder see madder lake.

Rosenstiehl's green see manganese green.

rose quartz a cloudy pink variety of quartz used for ornament and as a gemstone.

rosette, rose; a decorative circular ornament which represents a stylized rose or any other similar flower; see also whorl.

rose window, marigold window; in medieval religious architecture, a large round ornamental window with tracery.

rose window in Rouen Cathedral, France, 14th century

rosewood [*Dalbergia spp.*] hardwoods from South America and India with purplish brown timber and decorative grain, used for decorative panelling, furniture and cabinets; often also called palisander; other similar species are often sold as rosewood; see below for full list of related species included in this work.
Bahia rosewood [*Dalbergia nigra*] a Brazilian tropical hardwood with yellowish brown streaked timber; used in veneers and for interiors.
Brazilian rosewood [*Dalbergia sprucea-na*] a tropical hardwood from the Amazon basin with red or violet streaked timber; used for furniture and interiors.
Indian rosewood, East Indian rosewood; [*Dalbergia latifolia*] a tropical hardwood native to the Indian peninsula with reddish-violet streaked timber; used for high-class furniture.

rosin, colophony, Greek pitch; a hard transparent brittle resinous residue formed during the production of turpentine; used with a solvent as a weak adhesive and in some paints.

rostrum a platform for public speaking, a podium.

rot, decay, fungal decay; the decomposition of wood by the attack of fungi and other micro-organisms; see list of wood-attacking fungi under fungi.

rotary cut veneer, peeled veneer; veneer cut from a rotating log or flitch to produce a continuous sheet; sometimes called unrolled veneer.

rotary cut veneer

rotary float see power float.

rotary planer see planer.

rotary trowel see power trowel.

rotating damper a rotating metal flap incorporated within a flue or chimney to regulate the amount of draught for combustion, or to shut off the flueway completely.

rotating pan mixer, paddle mixer; in the production of concrete, a pan mixer which has rotating mixing baffles.

rotten knot see unsound knot.

rotunda a classical circular domed building used for ceremonial or public functions.

rough board finish a finish for concrete in which the grain and sawing pattern of the boards used as formwork are evident in the surface.

rough brick arch, rough arch; a structural arch laid with rectangular bricks in wedge-shaped joints.

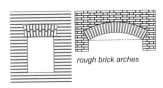

rough brick arches

roughcast, 1 trullisatio; the first undercoat or key layer of rough plaster added to a masonry surface onto which a fresco is to be painted; see intonaco, arriccio.
2 see wet dash.

roughcast glass glass with an obscuring surface on one side, traditionally produced by casting molten glass on a bed of sand; see also cast glass.

rough grounds see grounds.

roughing plane, cow plane, scrub plane, scud plane, scurfing plane; a woodworking hand tool with an uneven blade for shaping and roughing timber surfaces prior to gluing.

rough planed a classification of a timber surface which has undergone preliminary smoothing with a plane.

rough t and g board a timber cladding board which has a sawn finish, as opposed to being planed, and also has matched tongue and groove edges.

round 1 a milled joinery profile which is round in cross-section; also called a dowel.
2 see round bar.

round arch any arch whose intrados is the arc of a circle; types included as separate entries are listed below:
*circular arch; *Florentine arch; *horseshoe arch; *Italian round arch, see Florentine arch; *Norman arch; *Roman arch; *round cinquefoliated arch; round horseshoe arch, see horseshoe arch; *round multifoliated arch; *round trefoil arch; *round trifoliated arch; *segmental arch, segmented arch; *semicircular arch.

round-arris boarding see round-edged boarding.

round bar a metal bar with a circular cross-section; uses in construction include framing, brackets, tie rods, concrete reinforcement, stakes and ornamental work.

round billet, roll billet; an ornamental billet moulding consisting of a chequerwork of elongated convex forms or cylinders.

round billet

round brush any paintbrush with a round head and round handle; used primarily in decorative work and stencilling.

round cinquefoliated arch a decorative arch whose intrados is composed of five circular lobes or foils, and whose extrados is a semicircle.

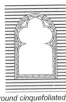

round cinquefoliated arch

round column see circular column.

rounded aggregate coarse aggregate whose particles are rounded in shape.

rounded arris see pencil round.

rounded edge see bullnose.

round-edged boarding, round-arris boarding; timber cladding boards with rectangular cross-section whose outer edges have been rounded; used for decking, outdoor furniture, etc.

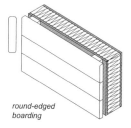

round-edged boarding

roundel, 1 oculus, round window; a window which is round in shape; see also bullseye, rose window.

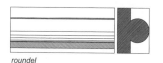

roundel

2 any decorative circular panel, tablet, relief or window; see tondo, medallion.
3 any straight decorative moulding which is half a circle or more in cross-section; an astragal, roll moulding, bead moulding, etc.

roundel

4 a round or semicircular turret in a castle or fortification.

round head screw see dome head screw.

round hollow section see circular hollow section.

round horseshoe arch see horseshoe arch.

round knot a knot in a sawn timber surface, roughly circular in shape.

round knot

round moulding see bowtell, half round moulding, roll moulding, three-quarter round, torus.

round multifoliated arch a decorative arch whose intrados is composed of a number of circular lobes or foils, and whose extrados is a semicircle; see trifoliated, cinquefoliated.

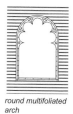

round multifoliated arch

round nail any nail whose shank is round in cross-section; see also round wire nail.

round nose pliers a pair of pliers whose jaws are smooth but rounded conical rods, used for gripping and bending wire.

round plane, convex plane, gutter plane, spout plane; a woodworking plane with a convex base and blade for cutting concave rebates; usually sold in a pair with a hollow plane.

round section see circular hollow section, round bar.

roundsil see compass plane.

round trefoil arch a decorative arch with three circular lobes or foils in a cloverleaf arrangement.

round trifoliated arch a decorative arch whose intrados is composed of three circular lobes or foils in a cloverleaf arrangement, and whose extrados is a semicircle. See illustration on following page.

round trifoliated arch

round tube a metal profile of hollow round cross-section; when in steel and used for structural purposes, it is called a circular hollow section, a CHS.

round window see roundel, Catherine wheel window, rose window (marigold window).

round wire nail, French nail; a nail with a round shank and flat chequered head, 13–150 mm in length.

router a motor-driven hand-held cutter for making a variety of cuts in wood, including grooves, rebates, housings or mouldings.

router plane, granny's tooth, hag's tooth, old woman's tooth; a two-handled woodworking plane with a narrow protruding blade for cleaning out and smoothing the base of grooves.

roving in glassfibre construction, a number of parallel glass strands wound through one full turn to form a loose bundle; used as a basic material for woven glassfibre fabric.

rowan, mountain ash; [*Sorbus aucuparia*] a relatively small European hardwood tree with hard yellow-brown timber, used for small items, tool handles and spinning wheels; it is often planted as an ornamental in parks and gardens on account of its feathery pinnate leaves, white flowers, red berries and autumn foliage.

*Sorbus aucuparia –
rowan*

row house any small dwelling constructed in a row, with common party walls or subsidiary buildings joining one to another; see terraced house, link house.

rowlock, bull header; a brick on edge with its end showing in a masonry wall.

rowlock

rowlock course, bull header course; a brickwork course made up entirely of rowlocks.

rowlock bond see rat-trap bond.

Royal green see chrome green.

Royal yellow see king's yellow.

RSI-value, internal surface resistance value; a theoretical measure of the thermal insulation properties of the internal surface of a given construction or component parts of a given construction; used in the calculation of U-values; units are m^2 C/W.

rsj rolled steel joist, see I-section.

RSO-value, external surface resistance value; a theoretical measure of the thermal insulation properties of the external surface of a given construction or component parts of a given construction; used in the calculation of U-values; units are m^2 C/W.

rubbed brickwork see gauged brickwork and following entry.

rubbed finish a smooth finish in stonework, brickwork and concreting produced by manual rubbing with abrasives; see also gauged brickwork.

rubbed joint a brickwork mortar joint flush to the brickwork surface, formed by clearing off excess mortar with a rag when wet.

rubber a synthetic organic polymer or natural product obtained as sap from certain species of plants and trees with good properties of elasticity and waterproofing; used in the construction industry for seals and waterproofing, as latex in paints, in flooring, etc.; types

included as separate entries are listed below:
*acrylic rubber, see polyacrylate rubber; *bromine butyl rubber, BIIR; *butadiene rubber; *butyl rubber; *cellular rubber; *chloroprene rubber, CR; *ethylene propylene diene rubber, EPDM; *expanded rubber; *foam rubber; *isoprene rubber, IR; *natural rubber, NR; *nitrile rubber; *polyacrylate rubber, ACM; *polyisoprene; *silicone rubber; *sponge rubber, see foam rubber; *styrene-butadiene rubber SBR; *synthetic rubber.*

rubber adhesive, rubber glue see elastomeric adhesive, rubber solution.

rubber flooring durable flooring in sheet or tile form, manufactured in rolls from natural or synthetic rubber; see also studded rubber flooring, cement rubber latex flooring.

rubber latex cement flooring see cement rubber latex flooring.

rubber mallet a mallet whose head is made of rubber; used for jobs where a steel head may cause damage to that being struck.

rubber set an outdated name for false set.

rubber solution, rubber glue; glue manufactured from natural or synthetic rubber and used for gluing rubber products.

rubber spreader see spreader.

rubbing see flatting down.

rubble 1 any broken pieces of brick, stone, concrete, etc. resulting from demolition work and building waste; used as fill and hardcore; see also hardcore.
2 roughly cut or irregular stones used in masonry walling; types included as separate entries are listed below:
*coursed rubble; *coursed squared rubble masonry; *random rubble; *squared rubble masonry; *random squared rubble masonry, see uncoursed squared rubble masonry; *uncoursed rubble, see random rubble; *uncoursed squared rubble masonry.*

rubble basket see gabion.

rubble chute see drop chute.

rubble concrete concrete containing large pieces of broken stone, masonry, concrete and building rubble as a filler.

rubble facing stone facing of a rough or rustic nature for masonry walling; used to provide a fine finish at a lower cost than rubble masonry.

rubble finish see quarry finish.

rubble revetment see pitching.

rubblestone walling masonry of rough coursed stones with varying height.

rubble wall a masonry wall constructed from roughly cut or irregular stones; sometimes also called ragstone wall; types included as separate entries are listed below:
*coursed rubble; *dry-stone wall; *gabion wall; *random rubble, uncoursed rubble; *squared rubble masonry.*

Rubens brown a form of Vandyke brown earth pigment.

Rubens madder a brownish shade of alizarin crimson pigment.

rubidium a silver-white, metallic chemical element, **Rb**, used in the manufacture of photoelectric cells.

rubstone an abrasive stone used for sharpening chisels or for producing a fine surface on stonework.

ruddle see red oxide paint.

rule see scale rule, screed board.

ruled joint see scored joint.

rule joint hinge, table hinge; a backflap hinge with one leaf wider than the other; used for hinged table tops.

rule joint hinge

run 1 a defect in a paint finish caused by drips from thickly painted areas running down the surface once setting has begun.
2 see going, total going.
3 drain run, see discharge pipe.

run-by pit see lift pit.

run cast a preformed decorative plaster cast formed of fibrous plaster by running a template known as a run mould across it when wet.

run moulding, horsed moulding; an ornamental plasterwork moulding shaped by dragging a template in the profile of the final moulding across wet plaster.

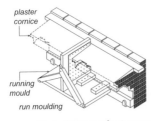

plaster cornice

running mould

run moulding

run-moulded plasterwork plasterwork shaped into a profiled moulding by this method.

runner 1 in excavation work, one of a series of timber boards driven into the earth at the side of a proposed trench, after which soil is removed from the trench side.
2 in thatched roofing, a flexible stick of hazel or willow used to tie thatch to rafters; see withe.
3 in timber frame construction, a horizontal timber member to which other members including joists are fixed.
4 see ceiling runner.
5 see lift guide.

running, 1 repeated; a description of ornament, decoration and brick bonds, etc. which are composed of the same interlinked recurring motif; see running bond, running ornament.
2 in ornamental plasterwork, the making of run mouldings such as cornices by drawing a shaped profile across the face of wet plaster.

running bond 1 a brickwork bond consisting entirely of courses of stretchers, with alternate courses laid with a half brick overlap, primarily called stretcher bond.

running bond

2 a paving pattern in which alternate rows of rectangular pavers are laid with a half-stone overlap with respect to neighbouring rows; similar patterns in parquetry and tiling.

running dimensions dimensioning for a drawing, usually a survey, in which all measurements in any one line are taken from a single reference point.

running dog classical ornament made up of a series of S-shaped curves joined end-on end, synonymous with Vitruvian scroll; sometimes rendered as a fret with squared lines or fillets.

running mould, horse mould; a metal or wooden template drawn across a plaster surface to form an ornamental moulding with a uniform cross-section; see run moulding.

running ornament any banded ornamental motif made up of a pattern of wavy lines which intermingle to form a continuous design, rather than having simple distinct repeated motifs.

running rule in making a plaster moulding, a long strip of timber used as a guide for a running mould.

running sand a soil type, sand saturated with water, which behaves in a similar fashion to a liquid.

rupture a break in a material or component which can lead to failure.

Ruskinian an architectural movement in England from the 1800s linked to the Arts and Crafts, which championed the Venetian Gothic style advocated by the writer John Ruskin and sought solutions to industrial living from medieval precedent.

rust the reddish-brown product of oxidation which forms on the surface of untreated iron and steel when in prolonged contact with water or air.

rust inhibiting see corrosion inhibiting.

rustication 1 in masonrywork, decorative rebates or sinkings around the edges of individual stones to emphasize joints and give articulation to the surface; especially prevalent in Renaissance architecture.
2 see textured finish.

rusticated masonry corner

rusticated ashlar, rustic ashlar; coursed and dressed stonework with edges and joints emphasized by rustication.

rusticated brick, rustic brick; any brick whose face has been treated or pressed with a pattern or texture.

rusticated column a column with a series of square blocks arranged vertically up its round shaft, often decorated with surface texture; found primarily in classical architecture from the late Renaissance onwards; may also be called a banded or ringed column.

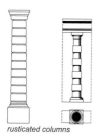

rusticated columns

rustication strip strip material attached to the inside of formwork to provide grooves and indentations in cast concrete surfaces.

rustic brick see rusticated brick.

rustic finish see textured finish.

ruthenium a light, spongy, white, durable metal, **Ru**, from the platinum group; used as a hardener in some alloys.

R-value, coefficient of thermal resistance; a theoretical measure of the thermal insulation properties of a given construction or component parts of a given construction; the reciprocal of C-value, whose units are m^2 C/W.

S

sabin see metric sabin.

sabre saw see jigsaw.

sackcloth see hessian.

saddle 1 see bolster.
  2 in thatched roofing, long straw laid over a ridge and secured with hazel or willow branches; see also brotch, ligger.
  3 see chimney saddle.
  4 see saddle junction.
  5 see pipe saddle.

saddleback see saddleback coping.

saddleback capping brick a saddleback coping brick whose length matches the width of the wall on which it is laid, without overhangs on either side.

saddleback coping, saddleback, saddle coping; a coping stone, brick or other construction with a central linear ridge and two downwardly sloping upper faces, forming a weatherproof capping for the top of a freestanding masonry wall or parapet.

saddleback coping

saddleback coping brick a special brick with a ridged upper surface and throated overhangs providing a saddleback coping.

saddleback roof, duopitch roof, saddle roof; a pitched roof of two sloping planes which meet at an upper ridge with a gable at either end.

saddle clip, pipe clip; a U-shaped metal fixing with protruding lugs, designed to attach a pipe to the building fabric with screws.

saddle coping see saddleback coping.

saddle fitting see pipe saddle.

saddle junction, saddle; in plumbing and drainage, a branch connection made by boring a hole in a main pipeline and joining a subsidiary pipe with a special fitting.

saddle notch in log construction, a simple log corner joint in which the underside of each log is cut with a transverse V-shaped notch to fit with the corresponding shaping of the upper surface of the log below.

saddle roof see saddleback roof.

saddler's hammer a tack hammer with a small claw attached perpendicular to its peen; used for pulling out tacks.

saddle stone, apex stone; the uppermost stone in a gable, pediment or other triangular or conical stone construction.

safe anchorage a fixing or cleat anchored to a roof surface for tying safety ropes and cables during maintenance.

safety the range of legislation and codes of practice for building construction pertaining to structural stability, constructional integrity, measures taken to prevent and protect against fire damage, etc.

safety curtain see fire curtain.

safety factor see factor of safety.

safety glass glass which resists breakage, or breaks in such a way as to reduce the risk of injury to a minimum; includes toughened glass, laminated glass and wired glass.

safety glazing glazing designed to withstand a specified level of physical impact without breaking; see safety glass.

safety lighting, emergency lighting; auxiliary lighting used in emergencies to provide illumination for escape during fire, power failure, etc.; see also standby lighting.

safety officer a local authority inspector who ensures that designs, constructions and site procedures comply with safety standards and regulations.

safety rail a light open balustrade or railing at the side of access stairs, gantries, platforms, etc. to afford protection during maintenance.

safety sign see fire safety sign; fire exit sign.

safety valve a valve operated automatically or manually to release excess pressure in any system of pipework and vessels containing a gas or liquid.

safflower, carthame; a red dye made from the dried petals of the flowers of the safflower plant [*Carthamus tinctorius*].

saffron a yellow pigment, used in Roman times, obtained from crushing the dried stigmas of the flower *Crocus sativus*.

sag, curtain, curtaining, sagging; a defect in a paint finish caused by an area of thickly applied paint which begins to run down the surface producing a horizontal ridge.

sag pipe, inverted siphon; in drainage, a kink in a horizontal inground drainpipe or sewer to convey its contents under an obstacle, relying on siphonage to function.

sail dome, sail vault; a round or hemispherical dome constructed on pendentives, so named because it resembles the form of a billowing sail with arched openings between its corners; see also pendentive dome.

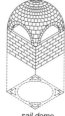

sail dome

sailor a brick on end with its bed showing in the face of a masonry wall, used in a row for string courses, fill and decorative effects; a sailor course is a brick course made up entirely of sailors.

sailor

sail vault see sail dome.

sal ammoniac see ammonium chloride.

salamander a portable heater used during cold weather for curing freshly poured concrete with a naked flame.

Salix spp. see willow; *Salix alba*, see white willow.

sallied half lap joint a timber lengthening joint in which the halved ends of both pieces are splayed with a V-shaped or sallied end termination to fit into corresponding cuttings.

sallied mortised housing

sallied half lap joint

sally see birdsmouth.

salomonica see spiral column.

salt glazing the glazing of ceramics by covering with a layer of common salt which fuses on firing to provide a protective surface.

salvage, scrap; solid metal waste which can be recycled.

samba see obeche.

Samian base a classical Ionic column base in which the lower end of the column rests on a spira, a cushion-like protrusion with horizontal fluting.

Samian base

sample 1 a section of a building or construction, interior space, component, product, material or colour which has been assembled or presented to give an indication of how it will function or appear once finished; a mock-up.
2 a part removed from a whole for testing; a soil sample, concrete test sample or component from a batch.
3 an example for demonstration or sales, as with a product sample or colour sample.

samson post in traditional timber frame construction, a freestanding post for carrying a beam, supported directly from a floor.

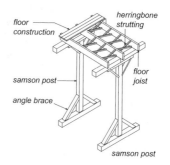

floor construction

herringbone strutting

floor joist

samson post

angle brace

samson post

SAN styrene-acrylonitrile.

sand mineral soil composed of particles between 0.06−2 mm in size; classified variously as fine sand (particles from 0.06 mm to 0.2 mm), medium sand (particles from 0.2 mm to 0.6 mm), coarse sand (particles from 0.6 mm to 2 mm); sandy soils and rocks are described as arenaceous.

sandalwood [*Santalum spp.*] a tropical evergreen hardwood from Asia and Australia whose timber is used in decorative work.

sand bedding a layer of sand spread over a structural base, in which paving stones are laid.

sand blasting a smoothing, finishing or cleaning treatment for concrete, glass or masonry surfaces in which sand or other particles are mechanically projected at high velocity by compressed air; also written as sandblasting.

sand curing a method of curing concrete by placing a layer of wet sand on top.

sand drain, vertical sand drain; in soil mechanics, a bored excavation filled with sand to drain and consolidate clay and silty soils.

sanded a description of an even, smooth and matt surface or finish for masonry and wood produced by rubbing or blasting with abrasives; a description of materials to which sand has been added.

sanded chipboard, sanded plywood chipboard and plywood respectively whose surfaces have been sanded smooth during manufacture.

sanded finish a finish for timber or masonry thus produced.

sanded plaster a plaster mix containing a high proportion of sand.

sander a machine tool used for smoothing timber surfaces; see belt sander, orbital sander.

sand-faced brick a brick, one end and one side of which have been given a coating of sand before firing.

sanding 1 the producing of an even, unpitted, smooth surface finish in timber, stone, etc. using an abrasive.
2 see joint sanding.

sanding block a small block of wood, rubber or cork around which sandpaper is wrapped during manual sanding.

sand joint a joint between adjacent laid paving stones, filled with brushed sand.

sand jointing see joint sanding.

sand-lime brick see calcium silicate brick.

sandpaper, emery paper; paper coated with an abrasive such as powdered glass, mineral, emery or hard metal for sanding by hand or machine.

sandpaper block see glasspaper block.

sand piling see deep compaction.

sandstone a brown, beige or reddish sedimentary rock formed of particles of quartz cemented together by other minerals; relatively easy to shape and used extensively as a building stone.

sandwich panel a prefabricated composite concrete wall panel consisting of an inner structural and outer cladding leaf bonded on either side of a layer of fluted insulation.

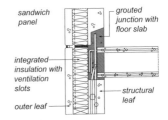

sandwich panel — grouted junction with floor slab — integrated insulation with ventilation slots — outer leaf — structural leaf

sanitary appliance any device in a building supplied with water and connected to a drain; used for drinking, cleaning or disposal of foul water.

sanitary module a prefabricated assembly of sanitary fittings with surrounding fabric and finishes, used on large projects with a high degree of prefabrication; brought to site and connected to structure and service outlets.

sanitary pipework, sanitary plumbing; the system of drain pipes which convey foul water from a building to an inground drain or sewer.

sanitary space a general term for washrooms and toilets.

sanitary ware sanitary fittings such as basins, WCs and urinals, moulded from vitreous china and glazed.

sanitation installation an installation of plumbing and appliances in a building for providing water and disposal of waste.

Santalum spp. see sandalwood.

sapele [*Entandrophragma cylindricum*] a West African hardwood with red to golden brown, strong and durable timber; used as a substitute for mahogany in furniture, panelling, flooring and veneers.

saponification a defect in paints caused by the breakdown of the oil medium to form a soft soapy mass in the presence of alkalis and moisture; especially occurring when applied to mineral-based surfaces such as masonry, new concrete, plaster and render.

sap-stain a fungus which leaves a dark tinge, usually bluish, on the surface of timber.

sapwood living wood found in the outer area of a tree trunk.

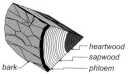

heartwood
sapwood
bark
phloem

sapwood rot fungal decay in the sapwood of timber.

Saracenic pointed arch see stilted arch.

sard a reddish-brown microcrystalline variety of the mineral chalcedony, used as a gemstone and for decoration; a form of cornelian.

sarking see roof boarding.
  sarking and sheathing grade insulating board a grade of insulating board suitable for cladding roofs and walls.
  sarking felt see reinforced felt.

sarsen a rough unhewn boulder of sandstone which occurs naturally on the surface of the land, often previously used as building stone.

sash, window sash; an openable framed part of a window opened either by sliding or on hinges; a casement is a hinged sash.

sash chisel see butt chisel.

sash cramp see joiner's cramp.

sash handle a device or fitting used for opening a window sash.

sash window, double-hung sash window, hanging sash window, vertical sliding window; a window with an openable sash or sashes which slide vertically in a frame; for sliding sash window, see sliding window.

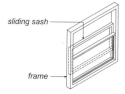

sliding sash

frame

satellite link aerial, satellite antenna; a telecommunications receiver for relaying electromagnetic signals via a satellite; a round satellite aerial is called a satellite dish.

satin see opal, eggshell gloss.

satinwood [*Chloroxylon swietenia*] see Ceylon satinwood.

saturated colour in colour theory, a colour whose outward appearance cannot be intensified by the addition of more of the same coloured pigment.

saturated soil soil whose voids are filled with water.

saturation 1 the relative amount of water filling voids in soil or other porous or absorbent substance; especially its maximum possible water content.
  2 see colour saturation.

saturation point see fibre saturation point, see dewpoint.

saturnine red see red lead.

saucer dome a dome whose height is small in relation to its diameter; a shallow dome.

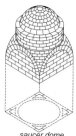

saucer dome

sauna a building, room or series of spaces with wooden benches and a stove for bathing in steam.

saw one of a wide range of hand or machine tools with toothed blades, used for cutting materials; types included as separate entries are listed below:
*backsaw; *bandsaw; *bayonet saw, see jigsaw; *bead saw; *bench saw; *bracket saw, see fretsaw; *cabinet saw; *carborundum saw; *chainsaw; *circular saw; *compass saw; *concrete saw; *coping saw; *cross-cut saw; *crown saw, see hole saw; *diamond saw; *donkey saw, see mill saw; *dovetail saw; *drunken saw; *felling saw; *fillet saw; *flexible saw, see saw chain; *floor saw; *flooring saw; *frame saw, see gang saw, mill saw; *fretsaw; *grooving saw; *hacksaw; *handsaw; *hole saw; *inside start saw, see flooring saw; *jigsaw; *joiner saw, see bench saw; *keyhole saw; *lock saw, see keyhole saw; *masonry saw; *mill saw; *mini-hacksaw; *notching saw, see grooving saw; *pad saw; *panel saw; *power saw; *radial arm saw; *rip saw; *sabre saw, see jigsaw; *scribing saw, see coping saw; *scroll saw, see fretsaw; *stairbuilder's saw, see grooving saw; *steel bow saw, see bow saw; *tenon saw; *trenching saw, see grooving saw; *tubular saw, see hole saw; *turning saw; *veneer saw; *web saw, see turning saw; *wire saw; *wobble saw, see drunken saw.

saw buck see saw horse.

saw chain, flexible saw; a saw consisting of a barbed chain pulled back and forth across wood; a manual chainsaw.

sawdust the fine powdered wood resulting from sawing, sanding and milling timber.

sawdust concrete see wood-cement concrete.

sawdust plaster see wood-fibred plaster.

saw horse, saw buck, trestle; a timber A-frame structure on which wood may be sawn.

sawing the cutting of timber, stone, etc. with a saw; variations in methods of sawing included as separate entries are listed below:
*band sawing; *flatsawing, plain sawing, through and through sawing; *flitch sawing; *live sawing, *sawing round the log; *resawing; *rift sawing, quartersawing; *rip-sawing, see flat cutting.

sawing defect a defect or blemish in sawn timber caused by blunt or poorly adjusted machining tools.

sawing round the log a method of quartersawing timber by removing four thick sectors and resawing them into relatively even-grained boards, thus leaving a square central section; often used for logs with heart rot.

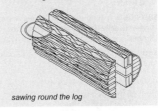
sawing round the log

sawmill an industrial plant for converting timber from logs into sawn boards.

sawn, 1 sawed; a description of a surface, object or material such as timber, board, stone or concrete that has been cut or worked with a saw.
2 one of the industrial surface finishes available for building stone, obtained by sawing blocks into slabs or cutting stones to required sizes, with cutting marks from diamond disc or gangsaw blades clearly visible on the surface.

sawn finish 1 a rough but even surface on timber boards, stone, etc. produced by conversion with a band saw or circular saw; see also previous entry.
2 an even finish produced by sawing stone; see sawn.

sawn veneer high-quality decorative veneer cut with a fine saw as opposed to peeled.

saw set a slotted tool for setting the teeth of a saw.

sawtooth each of the small cutting serrations along a saw blade.

sawtooth moulding see indented moulding.

sawtooth roof an industrial roof type having a number of parallel roof surfaces of triangular section with a profile similar to the teeth in a saw; the steeper side, usually vertical, is often glazed; see also northlight roof, southlight roof.

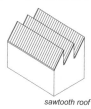

sawtooth roof

sawyer beetle a longhorned beetle of the genus [*Monochamus*], whose larvae cause damage to conifers by boring.

Saxon blue see smalt.

SBR styrene-butadiene rubber.

scabbling in concretework, the removal of a surface layer of hardened concrete to expose the aggregate; see tooling; also the rough dressing of a stone finish.
scabbled finish see quarry finish.
scabbler see scabbling hammer.
scabbling hammer a mason's hammer whose head has a sharp point at one end, used for the rough dressing of granite and other hard stone.

scaffold, scaffolding; a temporary structure erected alongside the external wall of a building under construction or repair to support workmen and materials.
scaffolding boards, scaffold boards; boards used to form a walkway or working platform in a scaffold.
scaffold nail see double headed nail.

scagliola a decorative masonry finish imitating marble, originally used in classical Rome, composed of an applied mixture of alabaster, gypsum, lime, marble and cement which is heated and polished to a very high sheen; sometimes referred to as stucco lustro, though generally regarded as its precursor.

scale 1 the proportion relative to full size at which a design drawing, model or map is produced; see also human scale.
2 a gradated measuring implement or classification; see fee scale, grey scale, vernier scale (see vernier callipers).

3 furring; in plumbing and hot water installations, an undesirable hard chalky deposit from hard water building up on the inside surface of water pipes and heating vessels; other types of unwanted sedimentary detritus; see loose rust (loose scale), mill scale.

scale model a three-dimensional realization of a design, usually to a smaller scale and to a lesser degree of complexity, for the purposes of presentation and as a design aid.

scaling the manual removal of loose rock and stones from a freshly blasted rock surface, or loose scale from a metal surface.
scaling hammer a hand-held hammer whose head has one chisel edge and a sharpened edge opposite; used for removing deposits, rust and scale from metal and stonework.

scallop ornamental carving or decoration with a stylized fan-shaped shell motif; see also scallop moulding.

scallop motif

scallop capital, scalloped cushion capital; a capital found in Norman architecture, consisting of a squared block with its lower edges cut with radiating reed ornamentation resembling a scallop shell; see also double scallop capital.

Anglo-Norman scallop capital at Fountains Abbey, Ripon, Yorkshire, England, c.1135–1147

scallop moulding, invected moulding; a Romanesque decorative moulding consisting of a series of stylized scallop shells; a series of arcs joined end on end.

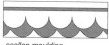

scallop moulding

scaly cap fungus, scaly lentinus; [*Lentinus lepideus*] a brown rot fungus with a scaly cap and white flesh which attacks timber in contact with damp ground.

scamillus Lat.; diminutive form of scamnum; a small unadorned plinth beneath the bases of Ionic and Corinthian columns.

scantling a piece of sawn timber with cross-sectional dimensions of 38–75 mm thick and 75–175 mm wide.

scarf joint, scarfed joint; a timber lengthening joint for connecting two timbers or boards end to end by cutting and overlapping to provide a gluing or fixing edge; see lengthening joint.
scarf-jointed plywood, or scarfed plywood plywood which has been extended or lengthened using scarf joints.

scarlet vermilion see vermilion.

scattering the spreading out or diffusing of radiation when passing through matter; in lighting design, the diffusing of sunlight when passing through the earth's atmosphere.

scenic lift see observation lift.

schedule written design documentation for doors, windows, ironmongery, etc. in the form of tables or detailed lists specifying type, finish, quantity, location and other information not found on drawings; an itemized list or programme; see below for derivative entries, and also drawings schedule, ironmongery schedule, window schedule.
schedule of defects, defects schedule; a list of defects, omissions and errors, poor workmanship, etc. in building work drawn up during the final inspection of a building nearing completion, obliging the contractor to make reparations accordingly.
schedule of drawings see drawings schedule.
schedule of fixtures and finishes a contract document specifying surfaces finishes, interior materials and fixed fittings for each space in a building.
schedule of rates a schedule in which the prices applicable to various items of work are listed.
schedule of works in contract administration, an itemized list of work to be undertaken for a construction project, often written prior to the contract stage or forming the basis of a contract without a bill of quantities.

scheduled fabric in reinforced concrete, fabric reinforcement defined by specifying the size and spacing of the wires or bars.

scheme, 1 design; designs of a building project or development presented as drawings, models or computer generations; the building produced from these designs.
2 a building group or a cluster of linked or physically attached buildings serving an associated function, as in a housing scheme.

schist a group of medium-grained metamorphic rocks in which the minerals are arranged in parallel layers similar to that of sedimentary rocks; see also crystalline schist, foliated gneiss (gneissose mica-schist), mica schist.

schistose rock rock containing schist or with a texture similar to schist.

Schnitzer's green see chromium oxide green.

Schweinfurt green see emerald green.

scissor brace in traditional timber frame construction, the cross bracing of pairs of common rafters.

scissor gate see collapsible gate.

scissor lift a steel platform raised and lowered by the hydraulic action of a hinged scissor-like structure beneath; used in loading bays, etc. for raising goods through short distances.

scissor roof, scissor rafter roof; a timber roof which has diagonal cross braces, called scissor braces, as a means of supporting and stiffening the rafters.

scissor roof

scissors truss a pitched truss whose lower chords cross to form an inverted V-shape.

scissor truss

scoinson see scuntion.

sconce 1 a bracket fixed to a wall to hold a candle or light fixture.
2 a secondary fortification to protect a castle entrance.

sconcheon, scontion see scuntion.

scoop see scorp.

scope of contract the range of tasks which a particular contractor or subcontractor has contractually agreed to undertake within a building project; the boundary thus formed between work undertaken by similarly obligated contractors; also referred to as extent of contract.

scored joint, ruled joint; a horizontal brickwork joint with lines scribed in the mortar to sharpen the appearance.

scorp, scoop; a drawing knife used for scooping out hollows in wood.

Scotch glue a variety of animal glue.

scotia, 1 gorge, trochilus; a horizontal moulding found especially in the bases and capitals of classical columns, consisting of a deep concave asymmetrical cutting in cross-section.

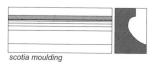

scotia moulding

2 a strip of wood, metal or plastics with a uniform cross-section shaped with a concave recess; used as trim for covering the internal join between two perpendicular surfaces.

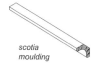

scotia moulding

Scots pine, European redwood; [*Pinus sylvestris*], see pine.

Scolytidae see bark beetle, ambrosia beetle.

scour, erosion; the gradual wearing away of a surface layer (a coastline, riverbed, pipelines) due to the effects of a flowing liquid.

scouring in plastering, compacting and smoothing of the surface of a fresh coat using a float worked in a circular motion; also called float-finishing.

scrap see salvage.

scraped plywood plywood whose face plies have been smoothed with a mechanical scraper during manufacture.

scraper, 1 devil, dumb scraper; a small piece of sharpened steel plate used for smoothing and scraping the surface of wood and other materials as a finish; see also Japan scraper.

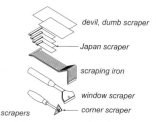

devil, dumb scraper

Japan scraper

scraping iron

window scraper

corner scraper

scrapers

2 paint scraper, scraping iron; a hand tool with a lateral metal blade fixed to a handle; used for the removal of old paint, dirt and coatings from surfaces prior to refinishing.
3 see scraping tool.

scraping iron see scraper.

scraping tool, scraper; a turning chisel used for the accurate shaping of wood, available with a number of different shaped blades.

scratch the undesirable linear marking or scoring of a surface, coating or component; a defect occurring during manufacture, handling or use.

scratch coat see first plaster undercoat.

scratcher, comb, drag; a hand tool used to provide a key for subsequent coats of plaster, or to spread tiling mortar, etc., consisting of a set of steel points or a serrated blade set in a handle.

scratch plaster patterned plaster which has been scored with a nail float after application, producing a rough striated surface; also called scratch render.

scratch resistance the ability of a surface such as a paint film or other coating to resist scratching or abrasion, measured by standardized tests.

screed 1 a layer of concrete, mortar or cement up to 75 mm thick applied to a horizontal concrete slab as a level and smooth base for a floor finish.
2 a straightedge dragged across the above surface to form an even thickness; see screed board.
3 a strip of material to regulate the thickness of the above; see screed rail.

screed batten in concretework, one of a pair of wooden strips fixed to a base to define the thickness of a screed cast in between, along which a screed board is guided.

screed board, screeding board, screed, straightedge, rule, tamper; a board dragged across the surface of fresh concrete between two screed rails; used for the production of an even and level surface, or screed; see also vibrating screed board.

screeding 1 the dragging of a board across wet plaster between guides to form a level surface and strike off unwanted material.
2 the laying of an even surface layer of concrete up to 75 mm thick on a floor or ground slab using a screed board and rails.

screeding board see screed board.

screed rail, 1 plastering screed; in plastering, a strip of wood or cast plaster used to regulate the thickness of a plaster surface.
2 a batten or rail for regulating the thickness of a horizontal concrete screed.

screen, 1 sieve; a graded wire mesh in a frame used for the sorting by size of granular material such as aggregate.
2 partition; a lightweight interior wall, often freestanding or with upper glazing, used for dividing up a larger space.

3 any vertical wall-like barrier, often with perforations, to provide visual separation, privacy and protection from the wind and sun, etc.
4 a visual interface on which films and other graphics are projected or otherwise displayed.

screen facade, false front; the non-structural grand front of a building, especially in Italian Renaissance architecture, which disguises the true interior form or size of the building.

screening 1 a method of grading aggregate by passing it through screens of a certain mesh size to separate out particles of that size.
2 in the treatment of waste water, the process of straining out some of the larger solids, paper, etc. from the incoming sewage using a coarse screen of bars; a subsequent process using fine mesh screens to remove grit, etc.

screen wall a regularly perforated wall of mesh, slats, louvres, etc. used for internal separation, visual separation and to give privacy to an area.

screw a pointed fastener with a helical threaded shank and head which has a shaped indentation, allowing it to be fixed by turning with a screwdriver or similar tool; types included as separate entries are listed below:
*adjustment screw; *allen head screw; *bugle head screw; *butterfly head screw, see one-way head screw; *clutch head screw, see one-way head screw; *coach screw; *concrete screw; *countersunk screw, countersunk head screw; *cross-slot screw; *dome head screw; *dowel screw; *drive screw, see screw nail; *drywall screw; *fillister head screw; *flat head screw; *general purpose screw; *hook screw, see screw hook; *lag screw, see coach screw; *machine screw; *masonry screw, see concrete screw; *mirror screw; *one-way head screw; *oval countersunk screw, see oval head screw; *Phillips head screw; *plasterboard screw, see drywall screw; *Pozidriv head screw; *raised countersunk head screw, see oval head screw; *roofing screw; *round head screw, see dome head screw; *self-tapping screw; *set screw; *sheetmetal screw; *tapping screw, see self-tapping screw;

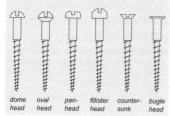

dome head | oval head | pan-head | fillister head | counter-sunk | bugle head

screw anchor see concrete screw anchor.

screwback see skewback.

screw cap, Edison screw cap; the metal part of an electric lightbulb to which an electric supply is connected, provided with a screw thread as a means of connecting it to a holder.

screw cup, finish washer; a pressed metal raised ring for a countersunk screw to protect the base material into which it is being fixed; see also recessed screw cup.

screw cup

screwdriver a hand tool with a steel blade for fixing screws with a turning action; types included as separate entries are listed below:
*impact screwdriver; *offset screwdriver; *ratchet screwdriver, spiral ratchet screwdriver.
screwdriver bit an interchangeable steel attachment for an electric drill or power screwdriver whose end is suitable for tightening screws.

screwed boss a threaded spout protruding from an appliance or pipeline to which a pipe can be fitted.

screwed pipe any cast-iron or steel pipe or pipe fitting joined via threaded ends and connectors.

screwed union a short pipe fitting threaded at both ends; used for connecting a threaded pipe to the outlet of an appliance.

screw eye a wire fixing whose end is shaped into a closed loop, with a threaded end for screwing into a wall surface.

screw eyes

screw head the enlarged slotted part of a screw, by which it is driven in with a screwdriver.

straight | Phillips | Torx | Allen

Pozidriv | Supadriv | square | one-way

screw slots

screw hinge see screw hook and eye hinge.

screw-hole a hole into which a screw is fixed, either pre-bored or made by the screw as it is tightened.

screw hook, hook screw; a wire fixing in the shape of a hook with a threaded end for screwing into a wall surface.

screw hook

screw hook and eye hinge a rudimentary hinge used for hanging gates, consisting of two threaded and pivoting shanks one of which is screwed into the gate and the other to its gatepost.

screw hook and eye hinge

screw nail, drive screw, square twisted shank flat head nail; a nail with a square spiralled shank to increase its fixing strength when driven in.

screw pile in foundation technology, a pile for soft silts and sands whose base is helically tipped to enable it to be screwed into the ground, and to provide a greater bearing area.

screw thread see thread.

scribe, marking awl, scriber; a sharp-pointed metal instrument for marking out lines on metal, timber and stone surfaces.

scribing saw see coping saw.

scrim coarse fabric or a mesh product used in plastering as reinforcement for wallboard joints and fibrous plasterwork.

script brush a finely pointed paintbrush with bristles shaped to produce fine lines; used for intricate decoration, especially flowing writing.

---

scroll an ornamental motif resembling a coiled band or line, or a scroll of paper; types included as separate entries are listed below:
*linen scroll, see linenfold; *double C-scroll; *leaf and rose scroll; *leaf scroll; *Vitruvian scroll; *volute.

scroll

scroll moulding, roll moulding; a decorative moulding which is scrolled in cross-section.

scroll ornament any ornament, medallion, etc. with spirals, coiled lines or bands; see scroll.

---

scroll saw see fretsaw.

scrubboard see skirting board.

scrub plane see roughing plane.

scud plane see roughing plane.

sculptor's point a pointed mason's chisel used for carving detail on stonework.

sculptured portal a main doorway in a medieval church, with sculptured jamb and trumeau figures of saints, prophets, nobility, etc.

scuntion, esconson, scoinson, scontion, sconchion, scuncheon; a reveal at an opening in a wall.

scupper in roof construction, an opening in a parapet from which rainwater from a gutter or roof surface may drain.

scurfing plane see roughing plane.

scutcheon see escutcheon.

scutch hammer, scutch; in bricklaying, a small pick-like tool with a blade on either end of the head; used for shaping and cutting bricks and blocks.

seal a component or product used to form a weathertight, watertight or airtight joint; draught excluder, weatherstrip, weatherseal, gasket.

sealant 1 any resilient material used to seal a joint.
2 building sealant, joint sealant, mastic, sealing compound; a soft, flexible compound applied to construction joints between components or material as weatherproofing.
3 see glazing compound.

sealant primer a priming treatment for construction joints in porous materials prior to the application of a sealant.

sealant strip see jointing strip.

sealed expansion vessel see expansion tank.

sealed glazed unit, insulating glass unit, insulated glazing unit, sealed glazing unit; an insulating glazing component with two or more panes of glass sealed around an edging strip and the gap between each pane filled with an inert gas; officially called a hermetically sealed multiple glazed unit.

sealer any material applied in liquid form to porous surfaces as waterproofing, sealing, or to reduce their absorptivity prior to painting and finishing.

sealing compound, 1 mastic; solid or semi-solid plastic material used as a sealant for joints between components or parts of construction.
2 lap cement; in built-up roofing, cold liquid bitumen used for sealing the lapped joints between layers of bitumen felt.
3 see sealant.

sealing strip a flexible strip applied to construction joints between components or material as weatherproofing.

seal nut a nut with an incorporated rubber bung, which seals any opening over which it is tightened.

seal nut

seam the joint between adjacent sheets of sheetmetal, linoleum, matting or cloth; see also standing seam.

seaming the forming of folded and rolled seams between adjacent strips in supported sheetmetal roofing using a special tool or machine.

seam welding, resistance seam welding; a method of resistance welding to produce continuous joints in overlapping metal sheets by means of an electric current passed via a pair of rollers which press the components together.

seam-welded roofing supported sheetmetal roofing whose joints are seam welded on site by machine.

seasoning, drying; the process of drying timber using natural or artificial methods to produce a product with minimal warpage and cracking; an equivalent process for stone.

seasoning defects defects and warpage in sawn timber sections which occur as a result of improper seasoning.

seasoning shake a split in the surface of a timber piece which appears as a result of uneven shrinkage during incorrect seasoning; also called a check.

secco see fresco secco.

seclusion see privacy.

secondary beam one of a number of regularly spaced beams, joists, etc. which are supported by heavier principal cross-beams.

secondary colour in colour theory, a hue formed by mixing two of the three primary colours together in equal parts.

secondary consolidation, plastic settlement; the permanent reduction in volume of soil beneath the foundations of a new building due to compression caused by the weight of the building.

secondary glazing, applied sash glazing, secondary sash glazing; a lightweight glazed sash added at a later stage to the inner face of single glazing to form a kind of double glazing; see also subsidiary glazing.

secondary reinforcement concrete reinforcement designed to distribute loads resisted by main reinforcement, and resist shear and thermal expansion.

secondary rib see tierceron.

secondary roof truss in traditional timber roof construction, a smaller roof truss supported by purlins between the principal roof trusses.

secondary sash glazing see secondary glazing.

secondary shaft a small or minor shaft in a bundle or clustered column, essentially found in Gothic architecture.

second coat see second plaster undercoat.

second moment of area see moment of inertia.

second plaster undercoat, floating coat, straightening coat; the second coat of plaster in three coat plastering, applied above the first coat to provide a smooth base for the final coat.

secret dovetail joint a cabinetmaking dovetailed joint in which the various cuts are concealed within the assembled joint.

secret fixing, concealed fixing; the fastening of timber boarding and other components so that its fixings are not visible in a finished surface.

secret gutter a roof gutter concealed from view, often included in the thickness of roof construction or behind a parapet.

secret hinge see invisible hinge.

secret joint a timber joint in which cuttings such as dovetails, notches, tables, etc. are concealed within the assembled joint.

secret nailing, blind nailing, concealed nailing; the nailing of timber boarding so that the nails remain hidden.

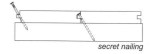

secret nailing

secret wedge see fox wedge.

sectio aurea Lat.; see golden section.

section 1 any thin length of material which has been preformed by a process of rolling, extrusion, sawing, etc. into a uniform cross-section of certain shape and dimensions; see also bar, profile; types included as separate entries are listed below:
*aluminium section; *bar; *channel, channel section; *circular hollow section; *cold formed section; *C-profile, see C-section, channel; *C-section; *customized section; *H-section; *hollow section; *hot-rolled steel section; *I-section; *L-profile, see angle profile; *open section; profile; *rectangular hollow section, RHS; *rolled hollow section, RHS; *rolled steel section; *round hollow section, round section, see circular hollow section; *square hollow section; *steel section; *structural hollow section; *T-section, T-bar, tee section; *tubular section, see hollow section; *UB section, see I-section; *UC section, see H-section; *U-section; *Z-section.
2 cross-section, cut, sectional drawing; a design drawing or view representing a theoretical cut through a site, building or object, showing objects in view from the cutting plane and often the construction of the structure which is cut.

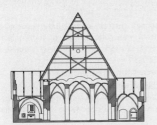

section through medieval church of St Mary, Turku, Finland, 1300s, showing timber roof structure and masonry external walls

sectional drawing see section.

sectional overhead door an overhead door whose leaf is made up of horizontal hinged segments, opened by pulling it upwards between vertical tracks on either side; the door leaf is horizontal and above the door opening once open.

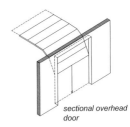

sectional overhead door

section foreman a contractor's representative responsible for supervising part of the work on site.

section modulus, modulus of section; in structural engineering, the moment of inertia of a beam section divided by the distance from the extreme fibre to the neutral axis; the extreme fibre is the point on the section furthest from the axis.

sections method see method of sections.

security 1 protective measures taken in a building to prevent unauthorized intrusion and burglary.
2 guarantee, collateral; a sum of money, assets or property agreed as a guarantee for a loan; if the loan is not repaid, this is taken instead; see bond.

security bolt see hinge bolt.

security door chain see door chain.

security glass laminated glass specially designed to resist vandalism, burglary or penetration during physical attack; see anti-bandit laminated glass, anti-vandal glass, blast-resistant laminated glass, armour-plated glass (bullet-resistant laminated glass); see also following entry.

security glazing glazing with security glass and specially approved secure glazing beads designed to withstand intrusion.

security lock, thief-resistant lock; a lock designed to prevent the inward entry of intruders but to allow outward passage in the event of an emergency.

sedge a species of grass [*Cladium mariscus*] whose cut and dried stems are particularly used for ridges in thatched roofing.

sedimentary rock forms of rock formed by the layered deposition of granular material; types included as separate entries are listed below:
*arenite; *bauxite; *calcareous rock; *chert, hornstone; *clastic sedimentary rock; *clayslate, killas; *limestone; *loess; *natural rock asphalt; *oolite; *quartzite; *sandstone; *selenite; *shale; *siliceous rock; *tufa.

sedimentation, settling; **1** the gradual sinking of granular solid insoluble particles to the bottom of a liquid in which they are suspended;.
2 the mechanical process of water purification by allowing solid matter to sink to the bottom of a sedimentation tank.

sediment, precipitate; the solid mass of sunken particles.

sediment trap a device for inhibiting the passage of granular solids suspended in surface water into a drain.

SE duct a ducted flue system in which air is drawn in at the base and released as combustion gases at the top.

segmental arch, segmented arch; an arch composed of an arc of a circle which is less than a semicircle.

segmental arch

segmental barrel vault, segmental vault, surbased vault, cambered vault; a shallow masonry barrel vault whose curvature is less than a semicircle.

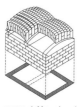
segmental barrel vault

segmental coping a coping stone or masonry unit whose upper surface is convex in cross-section; see also half round coping.

segmental coping

segmental pediment see pediment.

segmental pile in foundation technology, a pile formed from short lengths of concrete placed on top of one another.

segmental vault see segmental barrel vault.

segmented arch see segmental arch.

selective tendering competitive tendering in which a limited number of persons or firms are invited to submit a tender.

selenite gypsum in crystalline form, or a sedimentary rock based on this mineral; used in building as decorative stone.

selenium a poisonous, non-metallic chemical element, **Se**, used in the manufacture of solar cells.

selenium red see cadmium red.

self-build, do-it-yourself, DIY; building processes, usually small scale and domestic in nature, in which the owner or client is responsible for organizing labour, acquiring materials, and is often involved in the actual construction work.

self-cleansing gradient see minimum gradient.

self-compactable concrete, self-consolidating concrete see self-placing concrete.

self-contained air-conditioner see unit air-conditioner.

self convection see free convection.

self-levelling concrete self-placing concrete used for screeds and flooring, which, due to its low viscosity, will flow into a naturally horizontal surface without the need for vibration or floating.

self-placing concrete types of very workable and easily placeable concrete used for densely reinforced structures, difficult voids, intricate formwork, etc., which will settle or flow into its final position without the need for compaction or vibration; also known as self-compactable concrete, self-consolidating concrete, flowable concrete or non-vibration concrete.

self-siphonage the sucking out of a water seal from a trap by siphonage induced by the introduction of water from a sanitary appliance or a fluctuation in pressure.

self-supporting referring to a component or member capable of supporting its own weight without the need for a structure or frame.

self-tapping screw, tapping screw; a screw which makes its own hole and cuts its own threads as it is screwed in; used for fixing metals, wood, etc.

semi-aquatic plant any species of landscaping plant which usually thrives in shallow water.

semi-arch an arch with only half a curve, terminating at its crown, as with a flying buttress.

semicircular in the shape of half of a circle; also called half round.
semicircular arch an arch whose intrados describes half a circle.

semicircular arch

semicircular capping see half round capping.
semicircular channel see half round channel.
semicircular coping see half round coping.
semicircular gutter see half round gutter.
semicircular moulding see half round moulding.
semicircular stair, semi-spiral stair; a stair which is a half circle in plan, with wedge-shaped steps arranged radially around a single newel post or opening.

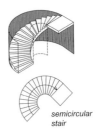

semicircular stair

semi-detached house, duplex house, two-family house; a residential building of two dwellings structurally joined but separated by a common dividing wall or intermediate floor; often simply called a semi.

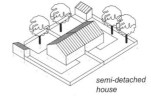

semi-detached house

semi-direct lighting artificial lighting in which luminaires distribute 60–90% of the emitted light downwards or to the area to be illuminated.

semi-dome see half dome.

semi-dry pressing see dry pressing.

semi-gloss the fourth of five grades of glossiness in a dry paint surface; slightly less glossy than full gloss.

semi-indirect lighting artificial lighting in which luminaires distribute 10–40% of the emitted light downwards, or to the area to be illuminated.

semi-skilled worker a construction worker in level of skill between a tradesman and labourer.

semi-spiral stair see semicircular stair.

sense of place, genius loci, spirit of place; a characteristic feature, identifying emotion, etc. of a particular natural or built environment.

sensitivity 1 in soil mechanics, a proportional measure of how much a sample of clay will change its strength characteristics once it has been remoulded.
2 see light sensitivity.

sensitive clay clay which loses compressive strength when moulded.

sensitivity ratio in soil mechanics, a measure of the sensitivity of clay defined as its compressive strength in the undisturbed state to that of a sample which has been reworked.

sensor see probe, detection device.

separate drainage, separate sewerage see separate system.

separate system, separate drainage; a drainage or sewerage system in which surface water and sewage are conveyed in separate pipes.

separating floor, party floor; a floor slab or structure which divides adjacent premises or dwellings within the same block, often with different ownership, and which usually has to meet certain requirements of fire resistance and sound insulation.

separating layer in floor and roof construction, a layer of impervious sheet material used to isolate layers in construction to prevent bonding; also called an isolating membrane or bond breaker.

separating wall, common wall (Am), party wall; a wall which divides adjacent premises or dwellings within the same block, often with different ownership, and usually has to meet certain requirements of fire resistance and sound insulation; see also fire wall.

sepia a dark greenish-brown pigment extracted from the ink sacs of the cuttlefish [*Sepia officinalis*]; nowadays produced synthetically for watercolour paints.

septic tank, settlement tank; in the treatment of waste water, a small-scale treatment plant for one building or complex, in which the solid matter in sewage settles and the remaining effluent is purified and released.

sequencing of operations see construction sequence.

sequoia [*Sequoia sempervirens*], see redwood.

serial contract a contract let for work of a similar nature to previous work, or following directly on from it.

series connection the arrangement of appliances in an electric circuit so that each receives the same current.

serigraphy see silkscreen printing.

Serlian motif see Palladian motif.

serpent column, Aesculapian column, Asclepian column; an ornamental freestanding Greek column constructed as part of monument commemorating victory in battle, with three spirally intertwined snakes carrying a golden cauldron on their heads; also named after Aesculapius, the Greek god of healing and medicine.

Greek serpent column, Aesculapian column, Asclepian column – Delphi, Greece

serpentine, 1 serpentinite; a soft, dark green, metamorphic rock composed of hydrated magnesium silicate, often richly patterned; easily polishable and used as decorative stone in building, for jewellery, etc.

2 a greenish or yellow mineral found in veins in metamorphic rock, especially the above.

Serpula lacrymans see dry rot.

servant key a key which operates only one or a limited number of locks in a suite of locks for which there is a master key.

service, technical installation, utility; any system, installation, etc. in a building providing water, air, gas, communications or electricity or disposing of waste; see also services.

service clamp see pipe saddle.

serviced housing see sheltered housing.

service duct a duct for cables, pipes or equipment that also allows space for working.

service illuminance in lighting design, a measure of the illuminance of a surface or space averaged over the maintenance cycle of the luminaires and the space in which they are situated; see also standard service illuminance.

service lift a lift designed to carry goods for providing a service to a building, too small to carry people.

service pipe a pipeline which conveys water or gas from a supply main to a building.

service road a road leading to a building, used by service or maintenance traffic and emergency services.

services 1 the provision of water, gas, electricity, phone lines and other basic infrastructure for a building.
2 the provision by a local authority of schools, hospitals, transport, information, maintenance, etc. for a community.

service space 1 a space within a building involved with its maintenance or servicing; see also plant room.
2 a secondary space whose function is to serve a major space; see also utility room.

service stair see access stair.

servicing see maintenance.

servicing valve a plumbing valve attached to an appliance or pipeline for switching off a water supply during maintenance.

sessile oak the durmast oak, see oak.

set 1 see setting, accelerated set.
2 the slight bending to either side of alternate teeth in a saw blade to allow for easier movement of the saw through wood.
3 see feint.

set accelerating admixture, accelerator; an admixture included in a concrete mix to increase its setting rate.

setback the recessing of the facade of a building, usually at ground floor or upper storey level.

set retarding admixture an admixture included in a concrete mix to reduce its setting rate.

set screw a threaded fastener without a head, used to secure a sleeve, collar or gear on a shaft by compression, preventing relative movement.

set square a technical drawing implement for drawing perpendicular or angled lines, a right-angled triangular piece of thin transparent plastic, wood, etc. with either two 45° angles or 30° and 60°; see also adjustable set square.

sett, cobble; a small hewn rectangular block of natural stone such as granite or sandstone used in series as paving for roads and hard areas;

sett paving

ranging in size from $50 \times 50 \times 50$ mm to $300 \times 200 \times 100$ mm; sometimes called a cobble; a small sett is known as a cube.

setting 1 in general construction, the hardening to its usable form of any material applied or cast as a liquid or paste.
2 set; the hardening of the cement in concrete from a liquid to a soft crumbly solid, occurring before the hardening or strength-gaining stage.
3 in the sharpening of a saw, the action of bending teeth over alternatively to one side and then the other so that the saw cut is greater than the thickness of the saw blade.

setting block see glazing block.

setting coat see final plaster coat.

setting out, 1 marking out, staking out; the marking of boundaries and levels on a construction site for a prospective building before construction begins.
2 the laying out of the parts of a technical or design drawing, various projections, title block, borders, etc. on the paper or drawing plane.

setting stuff plaster used for finishes, produced from lime putty and fine sand.

setting time the period of time after application over which a liquid such as glue turns into a solid; the time taken for the cement in a concrete mix to harden to the required degree, measured by a standard test.

setting up see upsetting.

settlement 1 the collection of particles suspended in a liquid at the bottom due to the action of gravity.
2 the movement of a building downwards soon after construction as ground material underneath is compressed; see immediate settlement, creep settlement.

settlement damage problems of cracking, structural damage, and doors and windows that don't open, caused by the differential settlement of a building after construction.

settlement tank see septic tank.

settling see sedimentation.

settling tank see sedimentation tank.

severy see cell.

sewage soil water and solid human waste, not surface water, conveyed in a sewer away from buildings.

sewage disposal, sewage treatment the screening, sedimentation, filtration, etc. of waste water and solids from a sewer, and the disposal of settled sludge in digestion tanks or on drying beds at a sewage treatment plant.

sewage pumping station pumping plant for raising sewage from a drainage system to a sewer located at a higher level.

sewage tank see cesspool.

sewer a large diameter pipe which conveys waste liquids and solids in suspension away from a building's soil and foul water drainage systems to a treatment plant; any pipeline or channel which conveys foul waste.

sewer pipe a length of proprietary pipe with suitably formed interconnecting ends, joined in series to form a sewer.

sewerage, sewerage system; a public drainage installation or network consisting of branch and main sewer pipes, inspection chambers, pumps, valves, etc. which convey foul water to a sewage treatment plant.

sexfoil a decorative motif found in Gothic tracery consisting of six lobes or pointed arched protrusions radiating outwards from a central point.

sexpartite vault, hexapartite vault; a vault sprung on six points of support, hexagonal or rectangular in plan, composed

sexpartite vault

of six ribbed bays with curved roof surfaces.

sgraffito, graffiti; in coloured plasterwork and pottery, a pattern scratched in surface material which allows for a backing material or colour to shine through.

shackle, bail; any looped metal bar or construction such as the fastener for a padlock; used in fixing, securing gates and scaffolding, attaching chains, etc.

shackle

shade 1 in lighting design, an area over which direct light, especially sunlight, does not fall.

2 a device placed externally over a window or around a light fitting to prevent glare or diffuse direct light; see awning, sunshade, lampshade.

3 see tint.

shadow bead a strip of planed timber or other material with a rebated or recessed edge; used as trim to form a recessed joint between adjacent components.

shadow bead

shaft 1 the straight vertical part of a column, by which loads are transmitted to a base or foundation; a column shaft.

2 one of the distinctly carved merged piers in a Gothic compound column, which continues upwards in vaulting as a rib; see principal shaft, secondary shaft.

3 the longitudinal body of an implement such as an axe, hammer, drill bit or other device, usually connecting one part to another, or that of a nail or screw (also called a shank).

4 an enclosed vertical opening, hole, etc. in a building or the ground; see well, chute, chimney shaft, lift well, light shaft, stairwell, ventilation shaft.

shaft ring see annulet.

shake 1 a crack which occurs in timber due to natural causes; see below:
*seasoning shake, check; *cup shake; *heartshake; *straight shake; *oblique shake; *wind shake.

2 dry, shakes; a fine crack or vent which occurs across the cleavage plane of rock or stone due to a natural imperfection.

3 split shingle; a thin timber cladding or roofing tile made by splitting a short log of timber along the grain.

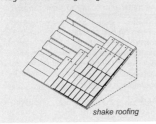

shake roofing

shale a layered, crumbly argillaceous sedimentary rock formed by the deposition of clay and silt.

shallow foundation any foundation, such as a footing, pad or raft foundation, which does not require a deep excavation.

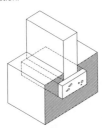

shallow foundation

shank, 1 shaft; the straight slender body of a nail, screw, bolt, etc., between its head and tip.
2 see neck.

shape code in reinforced concrete, the standard notation for the shape of a reinforcing bar.

shaping 1 see forming.
2 in the sharpening of a saw, the filing of teeth to a uniform shape after they have been topped.

shave hook a scraping tool consisting of a thin blade attached perpendicular to a handle; used by a painter for removing unwanted paint splashes from glazing and other surfaces.

shaving knife see drawing knife.

shear, shear force; an internal splitting force caused by two forces acting in opposite directions at a distance to one another on the cross-section of a structural member.

shear crack one of a number of diagonal cracks which may appear in the web of a beam or bracing wall due to shear stresses exceeding shear strength.

shear force see shear.

shearing stress load on a structural member due to shear forces exceeding shear strength.

shear plate connector in timber frame construction, a round flanged metal plate housed between two bolted timber members to strengthen the joint.

shear plate connector

shear reinforcement, web reinforcement; in reinforced concretework, reinforcement designed to resist shear forces.

shear strength the stress at which a material, component or construction will structurally fail in shear.

shear stress the force per unit area in kN/m^2 acting on the cross-section of a structural member due to external forces acting on it in opposite directions but not along the same line.

shear wall a wall designed to resist horizontal forces along its length; used to provide bracing for concrete frames.

shears see tin snips.

sheath in post-tensioned concrete, a pipe cast into the concrete into which the pre-stressing cables are placed so that they will not adhere to the concrete while it is hardening.

sheathing 1 board laid over a frame to cover a surface or construction; see sheeting, boarding, roof decking.
2 a layer of roofing felt used as underlay for profiled sheet roofing.
3 the outer insulating and protective covering for electric wires in a cable.

sheathing grade insulating board
see sarking and sheathing grade insulating board.

sheave see lift sheave.

shed roof see monopitch roof, penthouse roof.

sheen a grade of paintwork finish which appears glossy at an angle but appears matt when viewed straight on.

sheer legs a simple hoisting device consisting of a crude tripod over which a rope is slung.

sheet any material or product manufactured into planar sizes of preset length with a thickness of between 0.15 mm and 10 mm; see sheetmetal, sheet glass.

sheet curing see membrane curing.

sheet flooring flooring of sheet material, boarding, etc. with butt or housed joints.

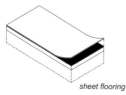

sheet flooring

sheet glass, drawn sheet glass, drawn glass; glass manufactured by vertical drawing of molten glass from a furnace in a continuous sheet, rarely used nowadays because of its uneven surfaces.

sheeting 1 any material or surface construction formed into continuous rigid or flexible sheets with a thickness of between 0.15 mm and 10 mm.
2 sheathing, shuttering; sheet material or rough boarding used in formwork to support and form the shape of cast concrete while it is hardening.

sheet laminate a durable facing product of layers of paper, wood, glass fibre or fabrics impregnated with synthetic resins and pressed into sheets.

sheetmetal, metal sheet; metal produced in sheets less than about 2—5 mm thick according to type of metal; see also metal plate, foil; types included as separate entries are listed below:

*aluminium sheet; *copper sheet; *corrugated sheetmetal; *expanded metal; *lead sheet; *perforated sheetmetal; *sheet steel.

sheetmetal capping see pressed metal capping.

sheetmetal cladding panel, pressed metal facing unit; a prefabricated exterior cladding unit made of pressed sheetmetal with turned in edges and proprietary fixings.

sheetmetal cleat, roofing cleat, latchet, ear; a small L-shaped metal fixing for attaching sheetmetal roofing to decking below, and included in standing seams and roll joints; also called a clip, tie or shingle.

sheetmetal coping see pressed metal coping.

sheetmetal duct a ventilation or air-conditioning duct made from galvanized sheetmetal, often rectangular in cross-section.

sheetmetal flashing, pressed metal flashing; a strip of sheetmetal laid over a joint to inhibit or divert the passage of water; see also eaves flashing.

sheetmetal joint see welt, standing seam.

sheetmetal roof a roof clad with thin metal sheet, either supported or profiled and usually of aluminium, lead, copper, or galvanized or coated steel.

sheetmetal roofing, roof sheeting; roofing of profiled or seamed sheets of steel, stainless steel, lead, zinc or aluminium; types included as separate entries are listed below:
*supported sheetmetal roofing; *aluminium sheet roofing; *corrugated sheetmetal; *metal multi-tile roofing.

sheetmetal screw a self-tapping screw with a flat head, used for fixing sheetmetal to a frame or base; see roofing screw.

sheetmetal screw

sheetmetal sill see pressed metal sill.
sheetmetal work any work on a construction site using sheetmetal, usually by folding and spot welding or pop-riveting.

sheet mosaic mosaic tiles or tesserae fixed to a paper or mesh-backed web to enable them to be easily laid on floors and wall surfaces.

sheet pile see steel sheet pile.

sheet piling, trench sheeting; vertical members of interlocking profiled steel plate driven into the ground to support the sides of a major excavation; see steel sheet pile.

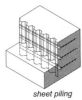
sheet piling

sheet roofing any roofing material manufactured and laid in sheets; bitumen felt, sheetmetal, ribbed polymer sheeting, etc.; types included as separate entries are listed below:
*aluminium sheet roofing; *bituminous roofing; *corrugated sheet roofing; *felt roofing, bituminous felt roofing; *membrane roofing; *profiled sheeting, ribbed-sheet roofing; *profiled sheet roofing; *sheetmetal roofing.

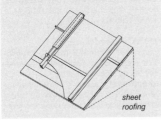
sheet roofing

sheet steel, steel sheet; steel rolled into sheets not more than 3 mm thick.

shelf fungus see conk.

shelf life, storage life; the length of time an adhesive, paint or other building material can be kept in storage without deterioration.

shell 1 a thin, hard, structural or protective outer facing for a building, construction or component; see shell construction, shell structure.

2 decoration or ornament in the form of shell motifs; see scallop, conch.

shellac a natural resin gathered from the twigs of certain Indian fig trees, mixed with a solvent such as alcohol and used as a varnish.

shell construction a thin curved load-bearing concrete, steel or plastics slab used for loadbearing roof forms; also called a shell structure; types included as separate entries are listed below:
*barrel shell; *concrete shell; *polygonal shell, see folded plate; *prismatic shell.

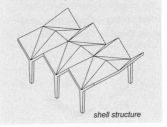
shell structure

shell roof a thin self-supporting roof construction of reinforced or prestressed concrete or other plastic material, often designed in three-dimensionally curving or polygonal forms.

shell shake see cup shake.

shell structure see shell construction.

shelterbelt a row or rows of landscaped trees or shrubs forming a shelter against wind, sun, noise, etc.

sheltered housing, serviced housing; housing or a residential block for the handicapped or elderly with communal facilities and staff on call in case of emergency.

sherardizing a rust-proofing treatment for a steel or iron surface consisting of a coating of zinc dust applied at a temperature slightly below its melting point.

shielded metal-arc welding see manual metal-arc welding.

shielding angle a measure of glare in artificial lighting design, the angle to horizontal above which a lamp in a ceiling luminaire can be seen through a diffuser.

shielding glass glass design to provide protection from radiation of various kinds; see radiation-shielding glass, electronic shielding glass, lead X-ray glass.

shim a thin strip of veneer used in the repair of veneerwork or plywood.

shiner, bull stretcher; a brick on edge laid with its bed showing in a masonry wall.

shiner

shiner course, bull stretcher course; a brickwork course made up entirely of shiners.

shingle 1 naturally rounded stones of variable size used as coarse aggregate and for surfacing flat roofs and driveways; see gravel.
2 a sawn timber tile used for cladding roofs and walls.
3 felt shingles, see strip slates.

shingle dash, dry dash; a weatherproof rendered finish for masonry and concrete with a coating of shingle embedded into wet mortar.

shingle roof a pitched roof clad in timber shingles.

shingle roofing

shingle tile a clay or concrete roof tile manufactured in imitation of a wooden shingle, often with a rustic surface and a curved or decorative tail.

shingle tile roofing

shingling the trade of laying shingles as roofing and external wall cladding.

shiplap boarding rebated and recessed timber cladding boards laid horizontally so that adjacent boards overlap one another.

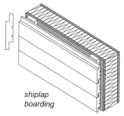

shiplap boarding

shiplap joint a timber joint used in overlapping boarding, with the edges of each board rebated to receive an adjacent board.

ship timber beetle see lymexylid beetle.

shipworm, marine mollusc; [*Teredo spp.*] a marine organism which causes damage to wood submerged in seawater by boring.

shoddy fibrous material made from old cloth, often used as caulking in log construction.

shoe see driving shoe.

shore a temporary support or prop for an excavation or work under construction; types included as separate entries are listed below:
*dead shore; *flying shore; *horizontal shore, see flying shore; *jack shore; *raking shore; *riding shore; *single flying shore; *sloping shore; *vertical shore, see dead shore.

shore pine see pine.

shoring the erection of one or a configuration of slanting timber props or shores as temporary support for a structure under construction or under repair; the construction thus formed; see excavation shoring.

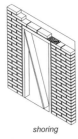

shoring

short circuit the situation occurring in an electric circuit when two points with different voltages come into direct contact with little resistance, causing a surge which may damage equipment and appliances.

short grained see brashy.

shotcrete sprayed concrete containing aggregate over 10 mm in particle size, placed by spraying it against a surface using pneumatic pressure.

shotcreting see previous entry and concrete spraying, spray concreting.

shot firing see blasting.

shothole a 2–3 mm diameter hole in the surface of wood, caused by burrowing insects.

shoulder 1 in timber tenon jointing, the timber surface at the base of a tenon which abuts the face of the mortised member.
2 the widening of the blade of a chisel or other similar tool between the neck and cutting area.

shouldered scarf joint see housed scarf joint.

shouldered tenon joint, stepped tenon joint; a framing mortise and tenon joint for the ends of joists and window and door

shouldered tenon joint

headers, in which the mortised member is cut to incorporate the side of the tenoned piece; often the same as an undercut tenon joint.

shoulder fitting see barrel nipple.

shoulder plane a narrow plane with a chamfered blade, used for cleaning up the inside corners of shoulders, grooves and rebates in wood.

shove see bunch.

shower a sanitary installation with a controllable spray or jet of water for washing and cleaning.
shower head, shower rose; the perforated part of a shower assembly through which water is ejected, usually a spray outlet.
shower tap, shower mixer, shower unit; the mechanism by which the supply of hot and cold water to a shower head is controlled.

shread head roof see half-hipped roof.

shrinkage the reduction in dimensional volume of a material due to compression, evaporation of water, or change in state or temperature; see autogenous shrinkage, chemical shrinkage, dry shrinkage plastic shrinkage.
shrinkage crack a crack occurring during the setting of concretework as a result of the evaporation of water.
shrinkage joint see contraction joint.
shrinkage preventer an admixture included in a concrete mix to inhibit shrinkage.

SHS see square hollow section.

shutter, 1 window shutter; an opaque or louvred panel, usually hinged or sliding, used to cover or shade a window; see persiennes.
2 gate; a light construction, often of light or lattice construction used to close off an opening such as a shop front or doorway.
3 see fire shutter, fire damper.

shutter hinge 1 a hinge used to hang a shutter.
2 see parliament hinge.

shuttering see formwork, sheeting.

shutting jamb, closing jamb; the vertical framing member against which a window casement or door leaf shuts and into which a lock, latch or catch engages.

shutting stile, closing stile, lock stile; the vertical side framing member of a window casement or door leaf opposite that from which it is hung, often containing a lock or fastening device.

SI 1 silicone.
2 International System of Units, an internationally accepted series of measures of basic quantities and units.

Siberian fir [*Abies sibirica*], see fir.

Siberian larch [*Larix russica, Larix sibirica*] a softwood from eastern Siberia with typical properties of the larch; one of the most common source of larchwood in Europe.

Siberian spruce [*Picea obovata*], see spruce.

Siberian yellow pine, cembra pine; [*Pinus cembra*], see pine.

siccative see drier.

Sicilian brown see raw umber.

side board in the conversion of timber, a rectangular sawn board cut tangentially from the edge of a log, with end grain forming a series of concentric arcs.

side form see edge form.

side hung referring to a window, casement, door or hatch whose opening leaf is hinged at the side.

side-hung door a term which distinguishes the most common category of doors which have hinges along one vertical edge, rather than sliding, tilting or other mechanisms.

sidelap the overlap of adjacent parts of roofing material such as tiles or roof sheeting on either side.

side light 1 a glazed panel at the side of a doorway.
2 a narrow glazed casement at the side of a window unit, hinged on one vertical edge.

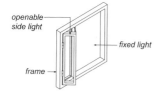

openable side light

fixed light

frame

side-opening door a double sliding door in which both leaves slide to one side of the door opening; lift doors are typical examples.

side-opening door

side plane see profile plane.

side purlin in timber roof construction, a purlin situated between ridge and eaves level for supporting common rafters.

side rabbet plane a small woodworking plane with a narrow blade for widening and shaping rebates; it may sometimes have two blades for cutting in either direction.

side rezor, side wevor, side wyver; a side purlin in traditional timber frame construction.

siding see weatherboarding (also for list of different types of weatherboarding).

Siemens-martin process see openhearth process.

Siena see sienna.

sienna, Terra Sienna, raw sienna; a form of yellowish-brown native pigment, named after earth found near the Italian city of Siena (called Sienna by the English), consisting of hydrated mineral iron oxide; used in watercolour and oil paints; see also burnt sienna.

sieve see screen, strainer.

sieving, grading; a method of sorting aggregate by passing it through successive sieves of certain mesh size to separate out grains of the required size.

sight in surveying, a device connected to an optical instrument or level to guide the eye, or to visually ascertain an alignment.

sight size, daylight size; the size of the opening in glazing or a window frame, measured from inner edge to opposite inner edge; smaller than the tight size.

sign the graphic representation of a message, instruction or advertisement; the device or board on which it is presented.

Silesian bond see Flemish garden-wall bond.

silencer see muffler.

siles see crucks.

silica, silicon dioxide; a mineral chemical compound, SiO_2, used in the manufacture of glass, porcelain and abrasives and in metallurgy; found naturally in sandstones, quartz, flint, opal and agate.

silica gel a gelatinous form of silica used as a desiccant.

silica glass see fused silica glass.

silicate a salt derived of silicic acids; also any of the largest group of minerals which includes clay, quartz, mica and feldspar.

silicate mortar types of mortar containing silicates of potassium, etc., used for their resistance to high temperatures and acidic conditions.

siliceous rock types of sedimentary rock which have a silica content of over 50%; includes chert and flint.

silicon a common chemical element, Si, found in the earth's crust in minerals and rocks; used in the production of glass, bricks and alloys, and in steelmaking; not to be confused with silicone.

silicon bronze, silicon brass; a durable copper alloy with zinc, silicon and small quantities of other metals such as manganese and beryllium; used for corrosion-resistant fixings.

silicon carbide, carbon silicide; an extremely hard crystalline chemical compound, SiC, used as an abrasive, for fireproof products and for electrical resistors in high temperature applications.

silicon dioxide see silica.

silicone, SI; a clear, flexible, waterproof thermosetting resin used as a sealant and in paints; not to be confused with silicon.

silicone paint a durable heat-resistant paint consisting of silicone solutions mixed with polymers.

silicone rubber an elastomer made from silicone, used for seals and electrical insulation.

silicone sealant a silicone-based flexible sealant with a characteristic acidic odour, applied with a caulking gun for sealing internal corners in tiling and other wet applications.

silk see eggshell flat.

silk cotton see kapok.

silk-screened glass, silkscreen glass; decorative, reduced-glare or obscured glass whose surface is silk-screen printed with a pattern of baked enamel, paint or frit during tempering.

silkscreen printing, serigraphy; a method of making graphic prints in paint or ink which is pushed through a fine mesh, originally of silk, masked off with a patterned stencil.

sill, cill; the lowest horizontal member in a door, window or other vertical framework; see window sill, door sill, ground plate.

sill block a concrete block with a sloping upper surface, designed for use as a sill below a window opening.

sill board see window board.

sill plate, cill plate; a horizontal timber base member fixed to a footing or foundation, onto which a timber frame is constructed; see also ground plate.

sillimanite a hard, greenish or brownish aluminium silicate mineral; used for gemstones and in ornament.

silt a soil type composed of particles between 0.002 and 0.06 mm in size; graded as fine (particles from 0.002 mm to 0.006 mm), medium (particles from 0.006 mm to 0.02 mm), coarse silt (particles from 0.02 mm to 0.06 mm).

silver a heavy, pale, soft and malleable metal, Ag; a good conductor of electricity used as a decorative coating on other metals and in some photographic compounds; coating colours associated with this.

silver birch [*Betula pendula*], see birch.

silvered-bowl lamp see crown silvered lamp.

silver fir [*Abies alba*], see fir.

silver leaf sheets of silver beaten or rolled as thin as 0.001 mm, used as surface decoration in a similar way to gold leaf; usually treated with varnishes to prevent the blackening effects of oxidation.

silver maple [*Acer saccharinum*], see maple.

silver poplar see poplar.

silverlock bond see rat-trap bond.

sima see cymatium.

simply supported stair a stair in which each step is supported at both ends.

simply supported stair

single-coat plaster, one-coat plaster; plaster designed to be both an undercoat and a final coat, laid over a base as a single layer.

single-coat plasterwork (one-coat plasterwork) plasterwork laid as one thin layer of final plaster.

single drainage system an outdated drainage system in which foul water and surface water from domestic premises are combined in a single drain.

single-family house see one-family house.

single Flemish bond a brickwork bond giving the appearance of a Flemish bond on the outer face of a brick wall more than 9" thick.

single flying shore a flying shore in which the supporting element is a single member.

single glazing glazing with a single uninsulated layer of glass separating the inside and outside of a building.

single-hole tap see monobloc mixer.

single layer chipboard, standard grade chipboard; chipboard manufactured from chips of an even size, or of chips of varying size evenly distributed throughout the thickness of board; see also graded density chipboard, multilayer chipboard.

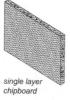

single layer chipboard

single lever tap a lever tap in which hot and cold water supplies are mixed and

their temperature and pressure controlled, operated by one lever fitted on a ball joint.

single-lock welt, single-lock crosswelt; a sheetmetal roofing joint in which the edges of two adjacent sheets are bent over each other then hammered down.

single-lock welt

single notched joint, trenched joint; a timber crossing joint in which the face of one member is cut with a notch or groove to receive a second member.

single notched joint

single orientation referring to an apartment or dwelling unit with windows on one external wall only, opening out in the same direction.

single-phase a description of alternating current at 240 volts with one phase, or with phases at an angle of 180°; used for normal applications such as residential and office buildings.

single-pipe system see one-pipe system.

single pitch roof see monopitch roof.

single Roman tile a wide single-lap roof tile with one flat waterway or channel between convex projections.

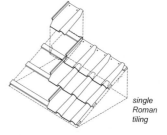

single Roman tiling

single roof a roof construction in which rafters are unsupported by purlins or primary beams.

single sized aggregate aggregate consisting of particles of relatively even size.

single spread adhesive see one-way stick adhesive.

single welt see welted edge.

sink a sanitary vessel of vitreous china or stainless steel for washing utensils, hands, etc., connected to a drainage system, fixed to a wall or furnishing at waist height and usually fitted with a plug-hole and taps; see also handbasin.

sinking a recess or groove cut into a surface, especially stone or timber.

sinter a range of yellow-brown minerals and rocks formed as a build-up of deposits from mineral-rich spring water; includes calcareous tuff and travertine.

sintering the process of heating particles of mineral matter to such a temperature that they fuse together to form a porous solid without becoming liquid.

sintered aggregate lightweight aggregate produced from particles which have fused together on heating.

sinuous grain see wavy grain.

siphon a tubular apparatus for transferring liquid over an obstacle from one level to a lower level, which operates by the pressure difference acting on columns of water within the tube; see induced siphonage.

siphonage, siphonic action; the conveyance of a liquid using a siphon, or by such principles.

siphonic WC pan a WC in which soil falls into a water-filled bowl and is removed by the siphonic action of flushing water.

sipo see utile.

Siricidae see wood wasp.

sisal the dried leaf-fibre from one of a number of Central American plants, especially *Agave sisalana*; used for making ropes and matting.

sisal matting a natural floor covering woven from sisal fibres.

sistrum ornament based on an ancient Egyptian musical instrument composed of a metal handled loop and crossbar with perforated discs threaded onto it; making a gentle rattling sound and used in sacred rituals of the cow-goddess Hathor, it features in many ornamental motifs and column capitals

sistrum ornament at top of Egyptian Hathor capital

site 1 the place at which construction work is undertaken; a building site.
2 an area of land designated by a planning application for a specific development, or one for which a proposed building is to be designed.

site access, site road; either a road which permits access from a public right of way to a private plot, a point of access for vehicles entering a building site, or a temporary road on the building site itself.

site accommodation, site hut; a temporary portable shelter with electricity and water supply used by the contractor and other site employees for on-site administration, storage and as sanitary facilities during a construction project.

site agent a contractor's representative responsible for managing and supervising work on a small site.

site assembly pertaining to components and parts of construction which are built or assembled on site rather than by a process of prefabrication.

site boundary the official boundary of ownership or right of use for a particular plot of land, often a building plot.

site concrete see mixed concrete.

site engineer a contractor's representative responsible for overviewing external and structural work, setting out and foundations, etc.

site equipment, site plant; plant, heavy tools and other machinery used in on-site building construction, rather than that installed in the building itself.

site hut see site accommodation.

site inspection the initial overviewing of a building plot or site prior to site investigation, surveys and the commencement of construction, or an inspection of building works under construction, carried out on site.

site investigation an investigation of the subterranean site conditions of a building site prior to foundation design to ascertain soil types, bearing capacity and evidence of toxic substances.

site manager a contractor's representative responsible for managing and supervising work on a large site.

site meeting a meeting held at or near a construction site in which the designers, contractors, client representatives and other associated parties meet to discuss progress and problems regarding the project, make decisions, etc.

site mixed concrete concrete mixed on site rather than delivered pre-mixed or ready-mixed.

site office a temporary office on a building site where site administration is carried out, and in which site meetings are held.

site plan a drawing showing in plan the layout of a site and buildings, roads and landscape thereon.

site plan of churchyard, showing roof plans of main buildings, boundary wall, planting and paths

site plant see site equipment.

site possession see possession of site.

site preparation programme a series of documents and drawings produced by a contractor to indicate means of access to a site, location of stores, materials, signs, any demolition work, huts and other site arrangements during construction.

site pump mobile mechanical plant for pumping rainwater and groundwater from surface areas and excavations, and for lowering the water table on a building site.

site road see site access.

Sitka spruce [*Picea sitchensis*], see spruce.

size 1 the magnitude of an object; examples of sizes used in dimensioning and construction included as separate entries are listed below:
*daylight size, see sight size; *dressed size, dressed dimension; *external dimension; *finished size; *full size, see tight size; *glass size, glazing size, see pane size; *grain size; *measurement; *mesh size; *modular size, modular dimension; *neat size, see dressed size; *nominal dimension, nominal size; *opening size; *overall dimension, overall size; *pane size; *span dimension; *sight size; *tight size.
2 sizing; a clear water-based glue or varnish used for sealing porous surfaces such as painting canvas or plaster before the application of paint, wallcovering, etc.; types included as separate entries are listed below:
*bole; *glue size; *gold size, gilding size; *varnish size.

size water a water-based solution of gelatine used for slowing down the setting rate of casting plaster.

sizing 1 the sealing of a plaster wall, painter's canvas or other absorbent surface with size before painting.
2 see size.

skeleton see frame.

skeleton stair see open riser stair.

sketch drawing, preliminary drawing, outline drawing; a drawing made at an early stage in the design of a building to show the designer's concept and initial layout of spaces and massing, etc.

skew see oblique.

skew arch a form of arch whose abutments or supporting structural elements are on different lines in plan to the face of the arch.

skewback, screwback; the wedge-shaped masonry abutment or splayed stone at the springing of an arch to transmit its thrust downward.

skew chisel, long-cornered chisel; a straight-bladed turning chisel whose cutting edge is set at an angle; used for smoothing and accurate shaping of wood on a lathe.

skew filler piece a proprietary component fitted beneath profiled roof sheeting at slanting eaves or a hip to block up the corrugations.

skew nailing the hammering of nails into a surface at an angle when attaching a timber on end or to provide a stronger fixing; also called toe nailing or dovetail nailing.

skilled labourer, craft operative, skilled operative; a construction worker whose skill is equivalent to that of a tradesman, often one skilled in a modern trade.

skimming coat see final plaster coat.

skimming float a thin-bladed hand float used for the application of finish plaster.

skin a lightweight and non-structural outer facing, cladding or layer for a wall or component.

skin mould in ornamental plastering, a membrane-like flexible mould in which decorative castings are made.

skip 1 see miss.
2 any large open steel container for collecting building rubbish, conveying material, etc.

skirting 1 an area of roofing which has been turned upwards against an abutment to provide protection at the upper edge of a roof.

skirting

2 a strip of metal, wood or plastics for covering the construction joint between floor and wall in a room.

skirting board a wooden board, strip or component funtioning as a skirting (also variously known as a baseboard, mopboard, scrubboard or washboard).

skirting tile a ceramic tile designed for use at the lowest edge of a tiled wall, where it meets the floor; see also coved skirting tile.

skirting tile

skirting trunking, plugmold, wireway (Am); an openable conduit for cables and wiring in an electric installation, which also functions as skirting.

skirt roof a false overhanging roof or canopy fixed to a wall at storey level.

skirt roof

sky factor, sky component; in daylight calculations for a room, the portion of daylight which is diffuse radiation from the sky as opposed to direct sunlight.

skylight, 1 indirect solar radiation; in lighting design, that part of solar illuminance that reaches the ground as diffuse light from the sun.
2 see rooflight.

slab 1 any thin plate-like structure, especially solid in-situ concrete or precast concrete units, which function as floor or roof structure; see floor slab.
2 flag, pavior; a hard, thick, fairly large cladding tile for floors or external areas, usually of stone, clay or a mineral-based material such as concrete; see concrete paving slab.
3 in the conversion of timber, curved-edged or waney boards cut from the edge of a log, often with attached bark.

slab

slab block an elongated multistorey residential block, most often rectangular in plan, whose dwelling units are arranged around, and accessed by, a series of vertical circulation cores with stairs and lifts.

slab-on-grade see ground supported floor.

slab reinforcement steel reinforcement for a reinforced concrete slab.

slack side see loose side.

slag a mineral by-product of steel production used in construction; see blast-furnace slag for further information.

slag concrete, blast-furnace concrete; lightweight concrete using granulated blast-furnace slag as a coarse aggregate.

slag wool a brittle fibrous material formed by the heating and spinning of blast-furnace slag; manufactured into slabs and used as thermal and acoustic insulation.

slaked lime hydrated lime or calcium hydroxide in liquid form, produced on site by slaking.

slaking the mixing of water with quick-lime (calcium oxide) to form slaked lime (carbon hydroxide); used as a binder in plaster and as an opaque white pigment in whitewash; see also wet slaking, dry hydrate.

slap dash see wet dash.

slash conk [*Gloephyllum separium, Lenzites separia*] a form of brown rot which attacks timber whose moisture content alternates between being damp and dry.

slash grain see plain sawn.

slash sawing see through and through sawing.

slash sawn see plain sawn.

slat a thin piece of wood or other material used in a shading device or grille.

slate a dark grey aluminium silicate metamorphic rock formed in thin layers; it can be easily cleft into sheets and is used for roof tiles (also called slates) and paving slabs; see roofing slate.

slate black a greyish-black pigment of powdered slate or shale used in some water-based paints.

slate fillet one of a series of pieces of slate laid in mortar as an upstand in traditional roofing construction.

slate hanging the hanging of slates on battening as cladding for external walls.

slate roof a sloping roof whose weatherproofing is provided by rows of overlapping roofing slates nailed to horizontal battens.

slate walling masonry walling of pieces of slate laid horizontally and bedded in mortar.

slating the trade of laying slates as roofing or walling; the work thus done.

slatting in timber-clad construction, battening laid with spaces between the ends of the battens to allow for the passage of ventilating air within construction.

sledgehammer, sledge; a heavy two-handed hammer with a long shaft and heavy iron or steel head, used for crushing, breaking and driving; types included as separate entries are listed below:
*beetle; blacksmith's hammer; *club hammer; *double face hammer; *drilling hammer; *engineer's hammer; *engineer's sledge; *lump hammer, mash hammer, see club hammer; *maul, mall; *peen sledge, see engineer's sledge; *smith's hammer, see blacksmith's hammer; *striking hammer.

sleeper see ground plate.

sleeper wall a low masonry wall which carries timber floor joists at intervals between side walls, usually in honeycomb bond to allow for underfloor ventilation.

sleeve see pipe sleeve, ferrule.

sleeve anchor see wedge anchor.

sleeved nail a round-shanked nail with an outer sleeve which expands as the nail is driven home.

sliced veneer, knife cut veneer; veneer produced by moving a log or flitch vertically against a fixed veneer knife; see veneer slicing.

slide bolt, 1 snib bolt; a secondary bolt incorporated in a rim latch, operable from the inside only.
2 thumb slide; a small barrel bolt.

slide damper in air conditioning and mechanical ventilation installations, a damper which functions by sliding across a duct to control the flow of air.

sliding bearing a structural bearing consisting of two surfaces which can move horizontally with respect to one another.

sliding bevel a bevel square which has a slot through the blade so that it may be extended out for added versatility.

sliding damper a sliding metal flap incorporated within a flue or chimney to regulate the amount of draught for combustion.

sliding door a door opened by sliding its leaf along an upper or lower track, with manual or motorized action, see types below:
*double sliding door; *sliding folding door; *centre-opening door, bi-parting door.*

sliding door

sliding door gear mechanisms for opening and closing an automatic sliding door, operated by signals from a detector device, remote controls, etc.

sliding door handle a device or fitting by which a sliding door may be pulled open.

sliding folding door, concertina door; a sliding door whose leaf is also hinged so that it slides along a track and folds with a concertina action.

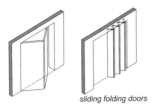

sliding folding doors

sliding folding window a sliding window whose sash is hinged so that it also folds, thus increasing the area of openable window.

sliding folding window

sliding hatch a hatch for sales, serveries, information desks, etc., which opens and shuts by sliding horizontally in tracks.

sliding sash a framed light in a window, opened by sliding.

sliding sash window see sliding window.

sliding window, horizontal sliding window, sliding sash window; a window with a sash or sashes that slide open horizontally within a frame; see sliding folding window, sash window.

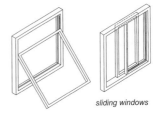

sliding windows

slip see engobe, brick slip.

slipform, continuously moving form; proprietary formwork used for large-scale and seamless concretework, consisting of a rig which moves continuously along a plane while casting is taking place.

slipform casting the in-situ casting of concrete in continuously moving formwork.

slip layer a coating applied to the shaft of a foundation pile to minimize friction between it and the surrounding ground during piledriving.

slip match a veneering pattern in which similar pieces of veneer are glued side by side to form a repeated pattern.

slip match

slip membrane one or two layers of sheet material, often polyurethane sheet, used to provide a horizontal movement joint between successive layers of floor construction.

slip sill in masonry construction, a window or door sill which does not extend beyond the edge of the opening into which it fits, and is not built into the wall at either side.

slip tenon joint see free tenon joint.

slit coil a steel product from a rolling mill; coil which has been cut lengthways into strips.

slope an area of terrain or land at an angle to the horizontal; the angle that a stair, roof, etc. makes with the horizontal; see pitch, gradient.

sloping grain, diagonal grain; grain in a piece of sawn timber which is not parallel to one of its straight edges.

sloping roof see pitched roof.

sloping shore a flying shore assembled at an angle for increased stability, etc.

slop moulding see soft-mud process.

slot 1 any long, narrow recess or gap formed into a surface.
2 the sinking in the head of a screw or other fastener, by which it is rotated with a tool.

slot mortise, open mortise; a mortise for a timber joint that is cut through the end of a piece, having three open sides.

joint with slot mortise

slot overflow a rectangular opening near the rim of a basin or sink through which water can flow into a drain if the water level rises too high.

slotted panel absorber an acoustical absorbing construction consisting of a perforated board with an air gap or mineral wool behind.

slotted waste a pipe fitting at a slot overflow, which joins a sink or basin to a discharge pipe.

slow grown see close grained.

slump test an on-site test to determine the consistency of fresh concrete by filling a metal cone-shaped mould and measuring how much it subsides when the mould is removed.

slurry a mixture of fine solid particles suspended in a liquid, having the general flow properties of a thick liquid; see cement slurry.

slurrying in stonework under construction or repair, the application of a temporary coating of lime and stone dust to provide protection during further construction, washed off on completion of works.

smalt, Saxon blue; a form of powdered blue potassium glass, with traces of cobalt, used as a pigment in paints, glass, ceramics and enamels.

smaragd green see viridian.

smart card a personalized card with a microchip or magnetized strip containing information which can be updated, used for phonecards, credit and swipe cards, etc.

smart key a range of electronic products used as keys for access control and automated access systems, in which the personal information of the carrier, and their accessibility credentials, are encoded within; see entry above.

SMA welding acronym for shielded metal-arc welding; see manual metal-arc welding.

smelting see reduction.

smith's hammer a blacksmith's hammer.

smith welding see forge welding.

smoke alarm an alarm triggered by the presence of smoke.

smoke chamber the space in a fireplace formed by a throat, gather and smoke shelf.

smoke control measures taken in design and practice to control the flow of smoke outwards from a hazardous building fire.
smoke control door see smoke door.

smoke damper a hinged or sliding metal flap in a fireplace flue for regulating the amount of draught for combustion; sometimes called a throat restrictor; see sliding damper, rotating damper.

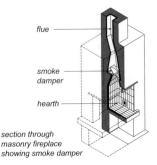

flue

smoke damper

hearth

section through masonry fireplace showing smoke damper

smoke detector a fire safety sensor or fire detector which reacts to the presence of smoke and triggers fire safety measures and warnings.

smoke developed rating a standardized classification of the amount of smoke given off by the combustion of an interior finish; sometimes also known as smoke development rating.

smoke dispersal see dispersal, fire venting.

smoked glass glass manufactured with a grey or brown body tint, achieved by the addition of nickel, iron, copper or cobalt oxide.

smoke door, smoke control door, smoke stop door; an approved door type with seals around its edges to prevent the passage of cold smoke.

smoke extract fan a fan which removes smoke from hazardous building fires by blowing it along designated routes, corridors or ducts to the outside.

smoke outlet an opening in the upper part of an external wall, shaft, etc. through which smoke from a building fire may be vented to the outside; see fire vent.

smoke pipe see flue.

smoke shelf an upwardly curving ledge in a fireplace to direct smoke up the flue.

smoke shutter an automatic door, hatch or shutter designed to close and prevent smoke spreading from one space into another during a building fire.

smoke stop door see smoke door.

smoke test a test for unwanted openings and flow in a system of plumbing pipes or ventilation ducts by introducing smoke or other coloured non-toxic gas.

smoke vent see fire vent.
  smoke venting see fire venting.
  smoke venting rooflight a rooflight which also functions as a fire vent.

smoky quartz a brownish or smoke-coloured variety of quartz used for ornament and for gemstones.

smoothing see sanding, dressing, surfacing, float-finishing.
  smoothing compound a material applied in semi-liquid form to interior floor construction, which sets to provide a smooth flooring.
  smoothing plane a small bench plane used for the final smoothing or cleaning off of work.
  smoothing trowel see finishing trowel.

smooth planed a description of sawn timber which has been smoothed with a plane to produce a finished surface.

snaked finish a smooth, lightly polished matt finish in stonework produced by rubbing with a fine abrasive or whetstone.

snap header, half bat; a half brick used in walling to appear in a wall surface as a header.

snap line, snapping line see chalk line.

sneck a small stone used in rough masonry joints as a gap filler and to stabilize walling.

snib, check lock, locking snib, thumb slide; a mechanism in a lock or latch to hold its bolt in a closed or open position, usually operated by a sliding button in the forend.

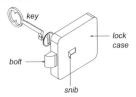

key

lock case

bolt

snib

snib bolt see slide bolt.
snib latch see indicating bolt.

snowguard a horizontal bar or rail fixed at eaves level on a pitched roof in cold climates to prevent the slippage of snow onto the ground below.

snow load a structural live load imposed by the weight of snow on a roof.

soakaway a rudimentary drain consisting of an excavated pit filled with sand, gravel or stones, into which waste water is discharged and from which it leaks away into the surrounding soil.

soaker 1 in roof construction, a small piece of metal sheet laid beneath roof tiles at a hip, valley or abutment.
2 roof soaker, see pipe flashing.
3 a strip of waterproofing material laid between courses of roof shingles in exposed areas.

soap a special brick with a square profile, usually $50 \times 50 \times 215$ mm.

soapstone, steatite, potstone; a soft, grey rock whose surface has a soapy feel; it contains a high proportion of talc and is used for baths, sinks, fireplaces and in industry; see also French chalk.

social housing see public housing.

socket, 1 bell (Am); the enlarged end of a drainage pipe which fits over the end of another pipe and forms a join.
2 a short length of connecting pipe which is internally threaded.
3 see socket outlet, telecommunications outlet.

socket outlet, plug socket; electric installation casing and switches to receive an electric plug at a power point.

socket reducer, reducing bush; a small pipe fitting attached into the socketed end of one pipe to reduce its bore for the attachment of a smaller bore pipe.

sock lining a method of repairing a leak or hole in underground pipes by inserting a resin-soaked felt "stocking" into the pipe and then expanding it against the pipe wall with compressed air or water; this provides a seal when the resin sets; also called resin lining.

soda-lime glass the most common type of glass, manufactured from sand, soda ash and limestone; used for flat glass, bottles and light bulbs.

sodalite a blue or yellowish white aluminium silicate mineral, a major constituent of lapis lazuli; used for jewellery and fashioned into ornamental objects.

sodium a soft, silver-white metallic chemical element, **Na**, found in common salt and discharge lamps.

sodium bicarbonate, sodium hydrogen carbonate; a white, water-soluble chemical compound, **NaHCO$_3$**, used in fire extinguishers and baking.

sodium borate see sodium tetraborate; see borax.

sodium chlorate a colourless, water-soluble chemical compound, **NaClO$_3$**, used in explosives, matches and as a bleaching agent.

sodium cyanide a white, poisonous chemical compound, **NaCN**, used in the surface treatment of metals and for carburizing steel alloys.

sodium hydrogen carbonate see sodium bicarbonate.

sodium hydroxide, caustic soda; a corrosive alkaline chemical compound, **NaOH**, used in the manufacture of pigments, soap, cellulose and paper.

sodium hypochlorite a pale green, crystalline chemical compound, **NaOCl**, used as a bleaching agent in the textile and paper industries, in water purification, and for domestic use.

sodium lamp, sodium-vapour lamp; a discharge lamp used primarily for street and external lighting, producing yellow light from sodium vapour; see high-pressure sodium lamp, low-pressure sodium lamp.

sodium nitrate a crystalline, water-soluble chemical compound, **NaNO$_3$**, used in explosives, fertilizers, the manufacture of glass, and as a colour stabilizer in processed meat.

sodium silicate, water glass; one of a number of chemical compounds used in the production of soaps, detergents, in the textile industry, as wood preservative, and in the manufacture of paper products and cement.

sodium sulphate a white, crystalline, water-soluble chemical compound, **Na$_2$SO$_4$**, used in the manufacture of dyes, soaps, glass and ceramic glazes.

sodium tetraborate, sodium borate; a chemical compound, **Na$_2$B$_4$O$_7$ (10H$_2$O)**, used for dissolving metal oxides, cleaning soldered surfaces, and in glazing and enamelling; found naturally as borax.

sodium-vapour lamp see sodium lamp.

soffit, 1 undersurface; the lower face of any building component or structure such as a ceiling, arch or slab; the upper undersurface of a window or door opening, also called a head; see window soffit, door head. **2** see intrados.
3 see soffit board.

soffit bearer in timber roof construction, a small horizontal timber at eaves level to which a soffit board is nailed.

soffit board, soffit; a horizontal board or boarding fixed to the underside of the ends of joists or rafters in projecting eaves.

soffit formwork, decking; formwork for casting and supporting the underside of a concrete slab.

softboard, insulation board; a lightweight timber-based sheet product with porous construction; a low density fibreboard whose density is less than 350 kg/m^3; used for sound and thermal insulation.

soft face hammer a hammer with a plastic, leather or rubber head for hammering easily breakable surfaces.

soft maple [*Acer saccharinum, Acer rubrum*], see maple.

soft-mud process, slop moulding; a process of forming bricks or other ceramic products from wet clay which contains 20–30% water.

soft pine see pine.

soft rock, soft stone; according to a hardness classification of rocks used by stone masons and construction technicians, rock which has a compressive strength below 800 kg/cm^2; includes sandstones and limestones.

soft soldering the normal method of soldering used for joining copper and brass pipes and electronic components using soft solder, an alloy of tin with a low melting point.

soft stone see soft rock.

softwood the collective name for timber from any coniferous tree, in general light-coloured with pronounced growth rings, which, despite its name, may sometimes be harder than some hardwoods; see below for list of species of conifers (softwood tree) included as separate entries in this book:

cedars, Cedrus spp.; for other trees called by the name cedar see *Calocedrus decurrens, Chamaecyparis lawsoniana, Juniperus, Thuja;* *cypresses, *Cupressus* spp.; *Lawson's cypress, *Chamaecyparis lawsoniana;* *southern cypress, *Taxodium distichum;* *firs, *Abies* spp.; *Douglas fir, see *Pseudotsuga douglasii;* *hemlocks, *Tsuga* spp.; *juniper, eastern red cedar, *Juniperus* spp.; *larches, *Larix* spp.; *pines, *Pinus* spp.; Oregon pine, *Pseudotsuga douglasii;* Parana pine, *Araucaria angustifolia;* *spruces, *Picea* spp.; *yew, *Taxus baccata.

softwood board a piece of sawn softwood with cross-sectional dimensions of less than 47 mm thick and greater than 100 mm wide.

softwood plank a piece of sawn softwood with cross-sectional dimensions of 47–100 mm thick and greater than 275 mm wide.

softwood plywood plywood whose veneers are made from softwood.

softwood scantling a piece of sawn softwood with cross-sectional dimensions of 47–100 mm thick and 50–125 mm wide.

softwood strip a piece of sawn softwood with cross-sectional dimensions of less than 50 mm thick and less than 125 mm wide.

soil 1 fragmented, granular or loose mineral or organic material within the earth's crust, consisting of weathered and crushed rock, including humus; earth above the bedrock, classified according to composition and grain size; natural granular material with appropriate nutrients, laid as a growing medium for planting; types included as separate entries are listed below:
coarse soil, see granular soil; *cohesive soil;* *fine-grained soil;* *granular soil;* *growing medium;* *non-plastic soil;* *organic soil;* *plastic soil;* *saturated soil;* *subsoil;* *topsoil;* *vegetable soil.
2 see soil water.

soil amelioration in landscaping, the improvement of the quality and drainage of soil by the addition of granular material.

soil anchorage a system of steel rods, guys or braces to fix a structure firmly to the underlying ground.

soil appliance, soil fitment; any appliance for the disposal of human waste, a toilet or urinal, connected to a soil drain.

soil binder plants and bushes planted on embankments and other sloping surfaces, whose roots provide reinforcement for the soil.

soil cement cement with soil as its aggregate, used in road construction and soil stabilization.

soil conditioning in landscaping, the improvement of the quality and drainage of soil by the addition of chemical material.

soil drain see soil water drain.

soil fitment see soil appliance.

soil mechanics the science surrounding the investigation of soils by the collection and testing of samples in order to provide information used for foundation design.

soil reinforcement, ground improvement; the strengthening of soil to be used for loadbearing earthworks, soil structures, embankments and under foundations using geotextiles and other reinforcing measures.

soil sample a sample of loose subterranean material or earth taken from a site to ascertain bearing conditions, contamination, etc.

soil stabilization the strengthening, reinforcing, supporting or compacting of weak and porous soils to prevent erosion and provide a structural base for roads and other earthworks.

soil stack a vertical drainage pipe into which soil water is discharged into a soil drain.

soil water, soil; discharge containing human solid waste from WCs.
soil water drain, soil drain; a horizontal pipe buried beneath the ground for leading soil water from a building to a private or public sewer.

solar altitude in lighting design, the height of the sun in the sky, measured in degrees above the horizon.

solar building a building heated wholly or partly by energy from the sun.

solar cell one of the photoelectric cells in a solar panel which converts light into electricity.

solar collector that part of a solar heating system designed to absorb solar energy and heat up water or other liquids.

solar constant the average amount of the sun's energy received by the earth, measured as that received over unit time by a unit area of the earth's surface at a theoretical mean perpendicular distance from the sun, taken as approximately 1.94 cal/min/cm^2.

solar control glass, anti-sun glass; glass which has been treated with a body tint or reflective coating to improve solar absorption and reflection; types included as separate entries are listed below:
*anti-fading glass; *absorbing glass, heat-absorbing glass, see tinted solar control glass; *laminated solar control glass; *low emissivity glass; *reflective glass; *surface coated float glass; *surface-modified tinted float glass; *tinted solar control glass.

solar declination in lighting design, the angular distance of the sun measured north or south of a plane traced out by the equator.

solar energy energy received as radiation direct from the sun, or electricity produced from this.

solar heating any system which makes use of the radiant energy of the sun to provide heat; see passive solar energy.

solar panel in a solar heating system, a device containing solar cells for converting radiant energy from the sun into electricity.

solar power electricity produced by a solar cell or panel.

soldering the joining of metals together by melting a soft metal alloy or solder at a join and allowing it to harden; widely used for fastening electronic components and metal plumbing connections; see also soft soldering, brazing.

solder a metal alloy used in joining metals together by soldering; usually an alloy of lead and tin for soft soldering, or copper and zinc for brazing; see soft solder, hard solder.

soldered joint a joint in plumbing or other metalwork formed and sealed by soldering.

soldering iron a tool with a thin copper blade heated electrically or by gas; used for melting solder and applying it to metal connections.

soldering torch a device consisting of a vessel containing a combustible liquid or gas attached to a nozzle, which, when ignited, produces a flame used to provide melting heat for soldering.

soldier in brickwork, a brick on end with its face showing in a masonry wall, used in a row for copings, string courses and in flat arches.

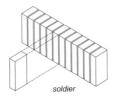

soldier

soldier course a course of bricks made up entirely of soldiers, usually for decorative bands, above openings, etc.

sole member see sole plate.

solenoid a coil of metal wire, usually copper, that becomes magnetized when a current is passed through it.

solenoid lock an electric lock whose latch is restrained or freed for use by means of a solenoid.

sole piece in traditional timber frame construction, a short horizontal lateral timber which provides the bearing for a common rafter onto a wall; see also sole plate.

sole plate, base plate, sole member, sole piece; in timber frame construction, the lower horizontal member in a stud wall, onto which vertical framing members are fixed.

solid background any solid masonry or concrete surface, as distinct from lathing or battening, to which plasterwork or plasterboard is applied.

solid fuel any solid material such as coal, wood, etc. used as fuel to provide energy when burned.

solid-fuel appliance, solid-fuel heater see solid-fuel stove.

solid-fuel heating, wood-fired heating; heating a building or space by the combustion of solid fuels such as wood, peat or coal.

solid-fuel stove, cast-iron stove; a freestanding heater which burns coal and wood as fuel; usually a patented product of metal plate or cast-iron construction connected to a flue.

solid parquet parquet strip flooring of solid matched lengths of hardwood laid in parallel arrangement.

solid-phase welding see pressure welding.

solid plasterwork see in-situ plasterwork.

solid timber, solid wood timber products or sections which are unprocessed wood throughout their thickness rather than veneered board, framed panels, facing, etc.; often includes glue-laminated timber beams and planks.

solid timber beam a beam produced either from a single piece of sawn or hewn timber, or one of glue-laminated rather than composite or built-up construction.

solid timber flooring flooring material of planed timber sections rather than parquetry or wood products.

soling see pitching.

Solomonic column see spiral column.

soluble blue a form of water-soluble Prussian blue pigment.

solute a material that is dissolved in another.

solution 1 a chemical mixture consisting of a material (called a solute) dissolved in a liquid (a solvent).
2 an answer, series of decisions or outcome to a particular problem or dilemma.

solvent, dissolvent; a liquid in which another substance will dissolve; an organic solvent is any highly volatile organic liquid used as a vehicle in paints and adhesives, and for paint and grease removal.

solvent adhesive a polymer-based adhesive for plastics, which dissolves surfaces to be joined, forming a bond as its solvent evaporates.

solvent borne adhesive, solvent-based adhesive; any adhesive whose binder is dissolved in an organic solvent which sets by evaporation.

sone in acoustics, a unit of subjective loudness equivalent to a tone of frequency 1000 Hz at a sound pressure level of 40 dB.

soot door a hatch at the base of a chimney or fireplace through which a flue can be swept.

Sorbus aucuparia see rowan.

sorel cement see oxychloride cement.

sound 1 a sensation produced in the ear by rapid waves of pressure in a body of material, often air or water.
2 a description of a construction, structure, material, etc. which is unbroken, stable, in good working order or without defects.

sound absorber see absorber, muffler.

sound absorption the ability of a material or construction to absorb sound by inhibiting or preventing reflections from its surface; also called acoustic absorption.
sound absorption coefficient the proportion of sound energy incident on a surface which is absorbed by that surface.

sound attenuation in acoustics, the prevention of echoes, reverberation and reflections of sound in a space due to scattering and absorbing of sound waves by surface treatments and careful design; also called acoustic attenuation.
sound attenuator see muffler.

sound boarding see pugging boards.

sound control glass window glass whose properties of sound insulation are improved with extra thickness, added compounds or special interlayers; also variously called acoustical glass, acoustic control glass, noise control glass, noise reduction glass, sound insulation glass and sound reduction glass; see laminated sound control glass.

sounder that part of a fire alarm, doorbell or other device designed to produce a noise by mechanical or electronic means.

sounding 1 in soil investigation, the driving of a steel rod into the ground to discern the level of underlying bedrock.
2 depth sounding; a process of determining the depth of a body of water by various methods including dropping weighted lines or echo-sounding.

sounding board see tester.

sound insulation, 1 soundproofing, sound isolation; dense material used to prevent the travel of sound from one space in a building to another; also called acoustic insulation.
2 the prevention of travel of sound from one space to another; also called acoustic isolation; see impact sound isolation.
sound insulation glass see sound control glass.

sound intensity in acoustics, the rate at which sound energy progresses through a given medium; measured in units of W/m^2; also called acoustic intensity.
sound intensity level the measure of relative sound intensity, in decibels.

sound isolation see sound insulation, impact sound isolation.

sound knot a knot in seasoned timber which is free from decay and as hard as the surrounding wood.

sound level in acoustics, the make-up and intensity of a sound source, measured by a microphone linked to a calibrated electronic sound level meter.
sound level meter an electronic instrument used in acoustics for measuring sound pressure levels.

soundness, integrity; the property of a material, structure or product which is free of defects, whole and unbroken.
soundness test see gas soundness test.

sound power in acoustics, the sound energy per time emitted by a sound source.
sound power level the measure of sound pressure.

sound pressure in acoustics, a measure of the pressure at any point in a sound wave.
sound pressure level the logarithm of the ratio of a given sound pressure to a reference sound pressure.

soundproof in acoustics, referring to a material or component which inhibits the transmission of sound through its mass, structure or envelope.

soundproofed a description of a space, duct, chamber, etc. constructed with sound insulating material and resilient joints to prevent sound from passing in or out of it.

soundproofing see sound insulation.

sound propagation in acoustics, the travel of sound via wave movement.

sound reduction in acoustics, the ability of a material or construction to inhibit the transmission of airborne and impact sound through it.
sound reduction glass see sound control glass.
sound reduction index a measure of the sound transmission through an object or material.

sound reflection, reverberation; in acoustics, the various ways in which sound is reflected within a space, dependent on its shape, surface materials and treatment.

sound resistance the ability of a given material or construction to inhibit the transmission of sound.

sound reverberation in acoustics, a number of late secondary reflections in a space which unite to form a continuous aftersound.

sound spectrum see audio spectrum.

sound timber timber which is free from fungal decay or insect attack.

sound wave a longitudinal pressure wave in air or other media which produces the sensation of sound in the ear.

sour cherry [*Prunus cerasus*], see cherry.

southern cypress, swamp cypress (Am); [*Taxodium distichum*] a deciduous softwood from the swamps of east and south USA; its timber is yellow-brown and used for interior and exterior cladding and furniture.

southlight roof a sawtooth roof with south-facing glazed lights used for industrial buildings in the southern hemisphere; see northlight roof.

soya bean oil a drying oil used as a vehicle in paints, pressed from soya beans; used widely as an industrial substitute for linseed oil.

soya glue glue made from soya bean meal after the extraction of its oil.

space 1 an area or volume bounded actually or theoretically; a continuous extension in three dimensions; a bounded area within a building.
2 the measured length from one point of a sawtooth to the next, a measure of the fineness of the cut of a saw.

spaced boarding, open boarding; sawn timber boards laid on a building frame with noticeable gaps between each, often as a base for cladding, roofing or flooring.

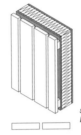

*spaced
boarding*

space frame, space structure; any three-dimensional framework, especially a deck structure for long spans, consisting of a three-dimensional lattice of triangulated members, usually steel tubes connected at their ends; see also space lattice.

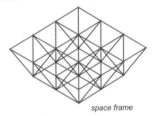

space frame

space heating see heating.

space lattice a space frame assembled from a number of parallel lattice girders connected with lateral members.

spacer, 1 cover block, reinforcement spacer; in reinforced concrete, a small piece of concrete, plastic or steel fixed over reinforcing bars to provide the appropriate amount of concrete cover between the bar and the formwork surface.
2 glazing unit spacer; a hollow metal tube sealed around the edges of adjacent panes in a sealed glazing unit to keep them apart and provide an insulating gap.

space structure see space frame.

spacial see spatial.

spacing see centers.

spacing plate a large perforated plate placed underneath a bolt-head or nut in a bolt fixing, which acts as a spacer and transfers the pressure of the fixing over a wider area.

spackling a very fine paste which sets to form a hard, smooth surface; applied in thin layers by a painter to fill small cracks, holes, joints and other blemishes in a surface prior to painting or wallcovering; also called spackling compound, stopping or filler; the job of applying this; also called stopping or filling.
spackling knife see putty knife.

spaded concrete see tamped concrete.

spading see tamping.

spall in masonry construction, flakes of stone removed during dressing with a tool, or which become detached due to frost or chemical action.
spall hammer, spalling hammer; a mason's hammer for the rough dressing of hard stone by spalling off small pieces.
spalling a defect in a stone, masonry or plaster finish caused by the separation of pieces from the surface.

spalt an early form of white rot in timber causing white areas surrounded by dark lines.

span the area or axis over which the unsupported part of a beam or arch lies, between adjacent columns or main supports; the horizontal distance measured from centre to center; also called a span dimension; see clear span.
span roof see close couple roof.

spandrel 1 an almost triangular area of wall or structure bounded by an arch and a rectangle which surrounds it, often embellished.

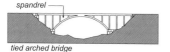

tied arched bridge

2 the area of wall between two adjacent arches in an arcade.
3 a triangular area of wall beneath a stair.

spandrel glass see cladding glass.
spandrel step one of a number of solid steps, triangular in cross-section, which form a stair with a smooth sloping soffit.

Spanish bond a paving pattern of a series of square pavers bordered with smaller stones, resembling basketweave pattern, but with arrangements of stones forming rectangular areas; similar patterns in parquetry and tiling.

Spanish bond paving

Spanish brown see burnt umber.

Spanish chestnut see sweet chestnut.

Spanish tile see under-and-over tile.

Spanish white high grade whiting in lump form.

spanner, wrench (Am); a simple steel tool with jaws fixed at a certain width for undoing or tightening nuts.

spar 1 a structural timber or mast, circular in cross-section.
2 see brotch.
3 see cross spar.

spar dash, dry dash; a rendered finish for masonry and concrete in which white spar pebbles are applied to a surface coating of mortar.

sparrowpecked finish, stugged finish; a relatively even stonework finish produced by dressing with a small pick.

spatial, special; relating to the quality and characteristics of an interior or exterior space.
spatial planning see planning.

spatterdash 1 a mix of cement and sand thrown roughly onto a masonry wall surface as a key for further rendering or plasterwork.
2 a wet mix of plaster flicked onto a masonry wall by hand or machine to provide a mottled external finish.

spatula a bladed hand tool used in painting and decorating, plastering and masonry for applying and smoothing fillers, plasterwork and mortar.

special referring to any product or component which is available in non-standard form, one which has unusual properties, or one which has been produced for a specific purpose; see following entries.

special brick, 1 special, special shape brick (Am); any brick in a manufacturer's mass-produced range which is of non-standard shape or size; sometimes also called a standard special brick; types included as separate entries are listed below:
*angle brick; *arch brick, see radial brick; *birdsmouth brick; *bullhead brick, see cownose brick; *bullnose brick; *cant brick; *capping brick; *coping brick; *cove brick; *cownose brick; *culvert header; *culvert stretcher; *featheredged coping; *header plinth; *plinth brick; *plinth header, see header plinth; *plinth stretcher, see stretcher plinth; *radial brick; *radial header; *radial stretcher; *saddleback coping brick; *soap; *stretcher plinth; *tapered header, see culvert stretcher; *tapered stretcher, see culvert header.
2 see purpose made brick.

special colour any colour which is not standard for ranges of supplied proprietary items, or is unusual because of its composition.

special glass any glass such as tempered, toughened, coated, body-tinted or laminated glass which has special properties of strength, durability or colour.

specialized contractor, speciality contractor, trade subcontractor; a building contractor employed to carry out work on site requiring specialized skills or expert knowledge.

specialized work work on a building site requiring contractors or tradesmen with skills in unusual or demanding areas of construction, modern technologies, etc.

special roof tile any roof tile in a manufacturer's mass-produced range which is of non-standard shape or size, for use at particular junctions or penetrations; types included as separate entries are listed below:
*angular hip tile; *block end ridge tile; *bonnet hip tile; *cloaked verge tile; *dry ridge tile; *eaves tile; *half tile; *hip tile; *mansard tile; *ornamental tile; *ridge tile; *top course tile; *valley tile; *ventilating tile; *verge tile.

special shape brick see special brick.

specific heat the heat required to raise the temperature of one unit of a particular material by 1°C, measured in MJ/kg°C.

specification see specification of works, descriptive specification, performance specification, project specification, technical specification.

specification of works, specification; a written contract document that describes in detail all parts of work for a construction project to be carried out by a contractor, including standards of workmanship, testing and other procedures.

specified see as specified.

spectral colour see chromatic colour.

Spectrolite the trade name for the rock anorthosite containing a high proportion of labradorite; a dark rock, iridescent with blue reflective plates when polished; used for decorative effect and exported from Finland.

spectrum the range of wavelengths of any type of wave; see visible spectrum, audio spectrum (sound spectrum, acoustic spectrum).

specular reflection the reflectance of visible light without distortion or dispersion, as if by a perfect mirror.

speculative builder a person or construction company who constructs buildings without having a buyer or occupant for them in advance, and thus bears the inherent financial risk.

speculative development the practice by a builder, developer, financier, etc. of having buildings designed and constructed with a view to selling them to previously unknown buyers, often before the completion of the buildings themselves.

spherical wave in acoustics, the spreading out of sound in all directions from a point source.

spheroidal cast iron see nodular cast iron.

sphinx an ancient Egyptian sculpted figure which has the prostrate body of a lion and the head of a human (androsphinx) or other animal such as a ram (criosphinx).

criosphinx (ram-headed sphinx), Karnak, Egypt

spick see brotch.

spigot the plain, annulated or threaded pipe-end which fits into the socket of another.

spigot-and-socket joint, bell-and-spigot joint (Am), spigot joint; a joint formed between two drainage pipes by means of a socket enlargement at the end of one pipe, which fits over the end of another and is sealed.

spike a large cut iron nail traditionally used in framing.

spike

spike knot a knot in seasoned timber formed from a branch that has been cut lengthways.

spike knot

spike lavender see oil of spike.

spike plate a small serrated metal washer clamped between two timbers in a bolted joint to provide stiffness.

spike plate

spill-over level the level of liquid in a basin, bath, sink or other vessel at which it will spill over the rim.

spindle **1** a square metal rod that fits into a handle on one or both sides of a door leaf and turns a latch mechanism.
2 see fillet chisel.

spindle moulder a woodworking machine tool with a rapidly rotating cutter for machining housings and mouldings; a router mounted upside down on a bench.

spine beam see mono-carriage.

spine wall a principal loadbearing wall parallel to the main axis or structural layout of a building.

spira Lat.; a cylindrical torus moulding in an Ionic or Corinthian column base.

spiral, volute; a curve which may be constructed mathematically, consisting of a line or lines rotating around a fixed point with a steadily decreasing distance; often used as a decorative device; see also continuous coil spiral.

spiral column a column type with a shaft carved into a helical form, appearing in Late Gothic and Baroque architecture, and found in the legendary temple of King Solomon; variously called a barley-sugar column, salomonica, Solomonic column, torso, twisted column or wreathed column.

spiral column

spiral cutter a woodworking tool for machining decorative spirals or threads onto dowel.

spiral grain, torse grain; contorted grain in a piece of sawn timber which makes it difficult to work, formed by steep spiral arrangements of fibres in the tree trunk from which it was cut.

spiral grain

spiral ratchet screwdriver, double spiral screwdriver, in-and-out screwdriver, pump screwdriver, spiral screwdriver, Yankee screwdriver; a screwdriver with a spiral mechanism to enable screws to be tightened or loosened simply by pressing down on its handle.

spiral stair, corkscrew stair, helical stair, spiral staircase; a stair which is usually circular in plan, with steps arranged radially around a single newel post or opening.

spiral stair

spire the tall pointed roof of a church tower, which may be round, polygonal or square in plan and resembles a very steep pavilion or conical roof.

spire

spire roof a very sharply pointed hipped or conical roof.

spirit level a device for indicating true horizontal, by means of an air bubble sealed in a marked, liquid-filled glass tube mounted in a frame; the tube is horizontal when the bubble is between two marks.

spirit of place see sense of place.

spirits of turpentine see turpentine.

spirit stain a translucent colouring agent consisting of a dye suspended in spirits, used for porous surfaces such as timber.

spit in manual excavation work and landscaping, a depth of soil equal to the length of the blade of a spade.

splash figure see ray figure.

splashback an area of sheetmetal or other sheet material such as plastics or coated plywood attached behind a sink as waterproof protection for an adjacent wall.

splashboard, waterboard; a strip of timber or other material attached to the base of a door or cladding to throw rainwater away from the surface or threshold.

splay 1 the surface formed when a corner is removed from a rectangle; a chamfer or bevel.
2 a splayed moulding, see bevel moulding.

splayed and tabled scarf joint, hooked scarf joint; a timber lengthening joint formed by making a slanting Z-shaped cut in the end of both timbers to fit each other.

splayed and tabled scarf joint

splayed bridle joint

splayed scarf joint

splayed corner joint see bevelled corner joint.
splayed halved joint see bevelled halved joint.
splayed moulding see chamfered moulding.
splayed scarf joint a timber lengthening joint formed by splaying the ends of both timbers; often simply called a scarf joint.

splayed tenon joint a timber joint in which two tenons inserted in a common mortise from opposite sides are splayed to abut one another.

splay knot in timber grading, an elongated oval knot formed from a branch that has been cut lengthways, which crosses an arris on a sawn board.

splay knot

splice an end-to-end joint of timbers or other components such that there is an overlapping area (called a scarf) or strengthening piece (a splicing piece, fish plate or joggle) to give added support.

spliced joint, fish joint, fish plate joint; a longitudinal timber joint in which fish plates are fixed on either side to strengthen the joint.

spliced joint

spliced scarf joint a timber lengthening joint with a splicing piece added as strengthening.

splice plate see fish plate.

splicing piece a piece fixed to or incorporated in a timber lengthening joint to strengthen or stiffen it.

spline, loose tongue, feather; a thin piece of material inserted into a longitudinal grooved joint as a strengthening piece.

spline joint, feather joint; a timber joint in which timbers are joined lengthways by cutting a groove in the edges of each and inserting a tongue or spline.

spline-jointed boarding, feather-jointed boarding timber cladding boarding with grooved edges into which a loose connecting spline is concealed to provide rigidity.

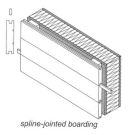

spline-jointed boarding

split face brick a facing brick whose rough texture is achieved by splitting off the surface layer.

split-level house a house-type for a sloping site, in which floor levels on the high side of the site are a half a storey higher than those on the low side, with entrances at either side on different levels.

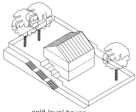

split-level house

split-level roof, clerestory roof; a pitched roof with two roof planes separated vertically by an area of walling; used for buildings with a varying number of stories or on sloping sites, either with roof planes parallel or in mirror image.

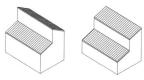

split-level roofs

split ring connector in timber-framed construction, a split metal ring housed between two bolted timbers to strengthen a joint between timbers.

split ring connector

split-ring washer see spring lock washer.

split shingle see shake.

splitter, nicker; a wide-bladed masonry chisel whose cutting edge is approximately 2 mm thick.

split tile a tile manufactured by splitting an extruded tile into two, once fired, through its thickness.

splitting hammer a mason's hammer with a sharp axe-like blade, used for splitting stone; often held by one person against the stone surface while another strikes with a sledgehammer.

spokeshave a small winged woodworking plane for planing curved surfaces.

spokeshave scraper see cabinet scraper.

sponge a soft, porous cleaning implement used for soaking up water, wiping, texturing plaster and concrete, etc.

spongeable wallcovering wallcovering that can be cleaned by wiping with a damp sponge or moist cloth without causing damage.

sponge float in concretework and plastering, a hand float whose blade is coated with a synthetic sponge; used on a wet surface to produce a specific finish.

sponge rubber see foam rubber.

spoon gouge, front bent gouge; a gouge with a hooked, spoon-shaped blade, used for carving deep recesses in wood.

spot see spotlight, reflector lamp.

spot board see hawk.

spot gluing the adhesion of one material to another using small areas of glue as opposed to a uniform glue film.

spot lamp see reflector lamp.

spotlight, spot; a luminaire which emits a narrow beam of light, used for highlighting elevational features, task lighting, ornament, displays, exhibitions, etc.

spotlighting directional lighting for the above, using spotlights.

spot welding, resistance spot welding; a method of resistance welding for sheetmetal, using electric current passed through small diameter electrodes which press the components together and cause a localized fusing at that point.

spout nozzle; the outlet pipe or assembly of a tap, from which water is discharged; see also rainwater spout.

spout plane see round plane.

spray adhesive, aerosol glue; an adhesive stored in a pressurized can and applied by spraying.

spray concreting, shotcreting; the application of concrete to a surface by firing it at high velocity through a nozzle, propelled by compressed air; used for stabilizing and sealing rock faces, tunnel walls and embankments.

sprayed concrete, pneumatically applied concrete, pneumatic mortar; concrete placed by spraying through a nozzle against a surface using pneumatic pressure; used for stabilizing rock walls and repairing reinforced concrete; see shotcrete, gunite.

sprayed mineral insulation see firespraying.

spray gun see paint spray gun, plaster spray gun.

spraying 1 the application of liquid paints, glues and other surface treatments under pressure as a spray of fine droplets; see concrete spraying, zinc spraying.
2 a method of curing concrete with a continuous spray of water to keep it moist and inhibit evaporation.

spray outlet, spray nozzle; a perforated outlet for a tap or valve designed to produce a spray or shower of droplets rather than stream of liquid.

spray paint any paint with a consistency suitable for spray painting, including aerosol paints.

spray painting an efficient form of painting using a spray gun, aerosol, etc. to apply a smooth, even film of paint.

spray plaster see projection plaster.
spray plastering see projection plastering.

spreader 1 a rubber or plastic hand-held implement with a bevelled edge, used by a painter and decorator for applying and spreading glue and filler, smoothing and shaping, etc.; see glue spreader, squeegee.
2 see box spreader.

spread foundation any foundation, as distinct from pile and special foundation systems, which transmits loading to the ground beneath by means of a widened plate or raft beneath a wall, column, etc.

spreading rate the unit area covered by unit quantity of paint or glue.

sprig see glazing sprig.

spring 1 an elastic device of coiled metal, etc., which can be wound or tensioned to store mechanical energy.
2 see crook.

3 a natural source of water from the ground.

spring clamp in joinery and cabinetmaking, a clamp whose pressing force is provided and released with a spring.

spring clip any small metal fixing for securing components in place with a push-pull action; especially used for holding infilling, glazing, etc. in frames before the application of fronting or capping.

springer, springing stone; one of the two lowest wedge-shaped pieces or voussoirs on either side of a true masonry arch.

springhead roofing nail see convex head roofing nail.

spring hinge a hinge containing a spring mechanism to return it to its folded position; used for closing a door or flap automatically; see double-acting spring hinge.

springing line see spring line.

springing stone see springer.

spring latch see return latch.

spring line, springing line; a theoretical horizontal line from which the curvature of an arch begins.

spring lock washer, split-ring washer, compressive washer; a slightly helical washer inserted beneath a screw or bolt head, which, when tightened, compresses to form a firm joint.

spring lock washer

spring toggle, butterfly toggle; a toggle bolt whose locking part is made up of paired wings which open under a spring action and clamp against the rear of construction.

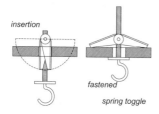

insertion

fastened

spring toggle

spring washer see spring lock washer.

springwood see earlywood.

sprinkler system a fire safety system of ceiling-mounted water outlets (sprinklers) connected to a main, which shower extinguishing water downwards into a space in the event of a building fire.

sprinkler a sprinkler system or sprinkler head.

sprinklered referring to a space protected against the spread of fire with a sprinkler system.

sprinkler head the specially shaped outlet nozzle of a sprinkler, through which water is released and dispersed in the event of a building fire.

sprinkling in landscaping, the watering of dried areas of planting, lawns, etc. using spray outlets.

sprocket, cocking piece; in timber roof construction, a piece of timber attached to a rafter at eaves level, forming a sprocketed eaves.

sprocketed eaves in timber roof construction, eaves which have a smaller fall than the common rafters.

spruce [*Picea spp.*] a common softwood found in the northern hemisphere with pale timber similar in properties to pinewood; used in general construction and for cladding and joinery; see below for species of spruce included in this work:

spruce

black spruce [*Picea mariana*] a softwood native to Canada and north-east United States, marketed as Canadian spruce; occasionally planted as an ornamental tree on account of its attractive purple cones.

Canadian spruce [*Picea mariana, Picea glauca*] a collective name for the black and white spruces; common North American softwoods with stiff, resilient, pale yellow timber; used widely in building construction and joinery.

Engelmann spruce [*Picea engelmannii*]; a softwood native to western North America, planted for timber in Europe and marketed as Canadian spruce; occasionally planted as an ornamental tree in parks and gardens.

Norway spruce [*Picea abies, Picea excelsa*] a common European softwood with soft, light, pale-coloured timber; used widely for framing, interior and exterior cladding and pulp; one of the most common European construction and structural timbers.

Siberian spruce [*Picea obovata*] a Russian softwood from the Siberian taiga with pale timber, very similar to Norway spruce, logged as construction timber.

Sitka spruce [*Picea sitchensis*] a spruce from western North America with high-quality, relatively knot-free pale pink timber; used for building construction, cladding and joinery; one of the most important forestry trees in Britain.

white spruce [*Picea glauca*]; a softwood native to Canada and north-east United States, marketed as Canadian spruce; planted as an ornamental tree in gardens on account of its grey-blue evergreen foliage.

spruce beetle a small group of longhorn beetles [*Tetropium fuscum* – brown spruce longhorn, *Tetropium castaneum* – black spruce beetle] whose larvae kill living trees by tunnelling beneath the bark and disrupting the transfer of nutrients; mainly found on spruce trees in Europe but also known to attack other conifers and occasionally hardwoods.

spur in Byzantine, Romanesque or early Gothic architecture, one of a number of decorative devices set at the corners of a square or polygonal base supporting a round column, often of leaf or grotesque ornament; also called a griffe.

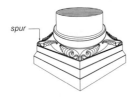

spur

square bar a manufactured steel bar, square in cross-section, used in welded steel construction, detail work, etc.

square billet an ornamental billet motif consisting of a chequerwork of squares.

square cup hook a square screw hook with a collar above the threaded shank to restrict its screw-in depth and cover the edges of the hole.

square cup hook

squared see edged.

squared rubble masonry roughly squared pieces of stone laid as a masonry wall; may be constructed in courses (coursed) or laid with no definable courses (random, uncoursed).

square-edged boarding, butt-edged boarding; timber boards with rectangular cross-section laid horizontally as cladding for a wall frame; see planed square-edged board.

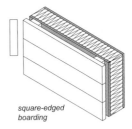

square-edged boarding

square external angle trowel a hand tool for smoothing external corners in plasterwork with a handled blade of bent steel sheet.

square fillet a thin straight decorative moulding, square in profile.

square hollow section, square tube; a hollow steel section, square in cross-section, formed by rolling and welding steel plate; used for structural purposes such as framing, columns, posts, balustrades, etc.

square hook a screw hook which is L-shaped.

square hook

square internal angle trowel a hand tool for smoothing internal corners in plasterwork with a handled blade of bent steel sheet.

square nut a nut which is square in form.

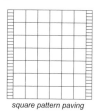

square nut

square pattern a paving pattern in which rows of square pavers or paving slabs are laid to form a simple grid pattern; when alternate stones are of different colours it may be called a checkered, chequered or checkerboard pattern; similar patterns in parquetry, tiling and veneering.

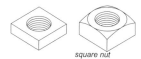

square pattern paving

square tile any ceramic tile whose exposed face is square in shape.

square tile

square tube a metal profile of hollow square cross-section; when in steel and used for structural purposes, it is called a square hollow section or SHS.

square twisted shank flat head nail see screw nail.

squeegee a hand-held implement with a wide flexible rubber blade attached to a handle; used for wiping and spreading liquids.

squinch, squinch arch; a series of adjacent masonry arches, each successive arch larger than the last; used as corner vaulting to support a polygonal structure or dome on a square base.

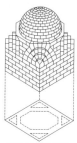

dome on squinches

squint, 1 hagioscope; a small oblique opening in the wall of a church to allow people in the side aisles and transepts to see the altar.
2 a squint brick.

squint brick a special angle brick with a shaped chamfered end, designed for use at an external obtuse corner in a brick wall; manufactured for standard corners of 30°, 45° or 60°.

squint brick

St Andrew's cross bond see English cross bond.

St John's white see bianco sangiovanni.

stability the ability of a structure to resist buckling, bending and collapse.

stabilization see soil stabilization.

stable door a door type whose leaf is composed of two parts hinged separately, one above the other.

stable door

stack a tall, narrow chimney or duct; see chimney stack, discharge stack, soil stack, ventilation stack.

stack effect a thermal phenomenon governed by the tendency of heated gases to rise causing suction beneath; an effect on which the functioning of chimneys, fire venting and natural ventilation rely.

stack vent, stench pipe, vent pipe; a length of ventilating pipe attached to the upper end of a discharge stack or pipe, to relieve pressure and through which foul air from a drain can pass into the open air.

stack bond, 1 stacked bond; a brickwork bond with courses of bricks on end and continuous vertical joints; not a true bond.

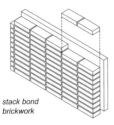

*stack bond
brickwork*

2 a paving pattern in which rows of rectangular pavers are laid with joints running in orthogonal lines, forming a chequered pattern; similar patterns in parquetry and tiling.

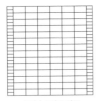

stack bond paving

stacked joint see straight joint.

Staffordshire blue brick, blue brick; a hard, dense, dark blue brick made from the shales of Staffordshire, England; used for engineering and industrial purposes.

stage 1 a raised platform in a theatre or auditorium for performance; that area of a theatre in front of the seats, from which a performance is carried out.

2 one of a series of sections of work in a construction project; also called a phase; see design stage, phase; post-contract stage; pre-contract stage.

staggered referring to a pattern of lines, construction joints or a layout in which adjacent elements are slightly overlapping and every other element is aligned, as with crenellations or masonry; particularly for brickwork in which vertical masonry joints in adjacent courses form a regular toothed pattern, achieved by laying bricks with a quarter brick overlap; cf. raking.

staggered bond any brickwork pattern whose joints form a regular vertical toothed pattern in the wall surface; see Dutch bond (staggered Flemish bond), staggered Flemish double stretcher bond.

staggered jointing in built-up roofing, the laying of successive layers of bitumen felt such that the joints between them are covered by the sheet above; the similar overlapping in other repeated construction such as brickwork and roof tiling.

staggered siding see board on board cladding.

staggered stud partition an acoustical stud wall construction in which alternate studs are placed off-centre in the thickness of the wall to prevent direct transmission of sound through them.

stain 1 a defect in a surface occurring due to the presence of unwanted colour.

2 a translucent colourant for porous surfaces consisting of a dye suspended in a clear liquid; when used on timber the liquid penetrates the surface and allows the underlying pattern or grain to show through; see oil stain, spirit stain, stainer.

stained glass coloured and patterned surface-tinted decorative glass held in lead cames, often depicting biblical scenes in ecclesiastical buildings.

stainer, colouring pigment, tinter; a translucent colouring agent for paints consisting of a pigment suspended in an oil paste.

staining 1 the colouring of a timber surface with coloured stain.

2 an unsightly defect in a finish or surface caused by uneven discoloration.

staining power see tinting strength.

stainless steel a range of types of silver-coloured alloy steel with good corrosion resistance, usually containing a high proportion of chromium (up to 18%) and nickel (up to 8%); used for structural members, cladding, furniture and fittings, hardware, tubes, windows and fixings.

stair, stairs, staircase, stairway; a means of vertical circulation consisting of a number of steps from one level to another; although usually called "stairs" in the colloquial, "stair" may be used in preference to denote a single unit of vertical circulation; types included as separate entries are listed below:
*alternating tread stair; *angle stair, see quarter turn stair; *cantilevered stair; *circular stair; *closed riser stair; *concrete stair; *corkscrew stair, see spiral stair; *curving stair; *disappearing stair; *dogleg stair, dog-legged stair; *double cantilevered spiral stair; *double cantilevered stair; *double return stair; *emergency stair, see escape stair; *escape stair; *external stair; *fire stair, see escape stair; *geometrical stair; *grand stair; *halfpace stair; *half turn circular stair; *half turn stair; *helical stair, see spiral stair; *ladder stair, see open riser stair; *L-stair, see quarter turn stair; *main stair; *open rise stair, see open riser stair; *prefabricated stair; *quarter turn stair; *ramp stair; *return stair, see dogleg stair; *semicircular stair, semi-spiral stair; *service stair, see access stair; *simply supported stair; *skeleton stair, see open riser stair; *spiral stair; *straight flight stair; *three-quarter turn stair; *turning stair, winding stair.*

flight — handrail

well

landing — stair enclosure

stair balustrade a balustrade for the sides of a stair; see also banister.

stairbuilder's saw see grooving saw.

staircase 1 originally the space occupied by a stair and its structure, nowadays the stair itself; see also stairway.
2 a grand, main or public stair.

stair clearance see stair headroom.

stair clear width the minimum unobstructed width of a stair on plan, measured at right angles to the direction of travel.

stair enclosure that part of the building fabric in which a stair is enclosed.

stair flight see flight.

stair headroom, clearance; in stair and ramp design, the minimum vertical height from a stairline, slope or landing to the lowest overhead obstruction.

stair landing see intermediate landing, storey landing.

stairlift a domestic lift designed for the disabled or elderly to operate along the line of a stair.

stair nosing see nosing.

stair rail a light balustrade for the side or sides of a stair, or a handrail often fixed to the wall of a stair enclosure, or atop a stair balustrade.

stair riser see riser.

stairs see stair.

stair shaft see stairwell.

stair spandrel in stair construction, a triangular shaped infill construction or panelling beneath a string and the floor.

stair tower a tower articulated on the outside of a medieval or later historical building containing a spiral or winding staircase; a similar element in a modern multistorey building.

stair tread see tread.

stairway, 1 staircase; an enclosed space containing a stair.
2 a stair.

stairwell 1 the space within a stair enclosure in which stair flights and landings are located; also called a stair shaft.
2 the open void between adjacent flights of a stair, or a full height shaft-like opening at the side of a stair.

stake, stave; a timber post driven into the ground as part of a foundation structure, for marking out, etc.; a timber pile; see also pale.

staking out see setting out.

stalactite work in Islamic decoration, clustered small pendant-like secondary vaults which hang down in geometrically arranged tiers from main vaulting, resembling geological formations called stalactites; also known as honeycomb work.

stalactite capital a Moorish capital carved with embellishment resembling stalactite work.

stalactite capital

stalk the downward vertical flange of a precast concrete tee beam.

stanchion a column of metal, usually steel; types included as separate entries are listed below:
*battened stanchion; *braced stanchion, lattice stanchion; *composite stanchion; *laced stanchion; *steel stanchion.*

standard 1 any product, method, process or procedure which has been established as an exemplar, is a stock or basic item or otherwise represents the norm; see norm.
2 a vertical scaffolding post.
3 upright; one of a series of spaced vertical framing members in a balustrade, to which infill, rails, a handrail, etc. are fixed.

standard brick any mass-produced rectangular brick produced to standardized dimensions, often coordinated in terms of height, length and width, varying in size from country to country and state to state; see also following entries.
*metric standard brick; *modular standard brick; *imperial standard brick; *US standard brick.*

standard colour one of number of set colours in which proprietary items of a particular range of prefinished products are usually supplied.

standard concrete cube see test cube.

standard concrete cylinder see test cylinder.

standard grade chipboard see single layer chipboard.

standard lamp see floor lamp.

standard modular brick see metric brick, US standard brick.

standard service illuminance the recommended level of illuminance for a specific space, setting or task.

standard special brick see special brick.

standby lighting building lighting with an independent power source; used in an emergency during the failure of normal lighting.

standby pump in sewage pumping and other pumped installations, a reserve pump which cuts in automatically if the main pump fails.

standing seam a sheetmetal roofing joint in which two adjacent sheets are bent over each other and left standing perpendicular to the roof plane.

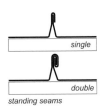

single

double

standing seams

standing wave, stationary wave; an acoustical phenomenon in corridors or narrow rooms with smooth parallel walls, in which sounds of certain frequencies are intensified, caused by waves whose positions of maximum and minimum oscillation remain stationary.

stand oil a heavy, viscous refined linseed oil which has been polymerized by heating to over 500°C for a number of hours; used as a vehicle in paints.

standpipe a vertical water pipe, usually from a water main to domestic premises, with a tap fitted to its upper end.

staple, 1 U-pin; a U-shaped nail, used to fix boards, cable, etc.

staple

2 a small U-shaped wire fastener, projected from a hand-held device to fix sheet material together, to another component, or to a frame.

3 see brotch.

staple gun, stapler, stapling machine; a tool used for fixing light board, sheet, fabric or paper to a frame or base with wire staples, either driven by compressed air or electricity, lighter versions are spring-loaded.

starch adhesive an adhesive for internal use made from vegetable starch mixed with water.

star formation the arrangement of adjacent plies in plywood with their grains at a noticeable angle to one another, not necessarily a right angle as with crossbanding.

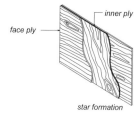

star formation

star-ribbed vault see stellar vault.

star shake see heartshake.

starter see lamp starter, starter bar.

starter bar, starter, stub bar; a reinforcing bar which protrudes from cast areas of reinforced concrete, to which reinforcement in the next batch or stage can be attached.

starting device see lamp starter.

starved joint a poorly bonded glue joint caused by lack of applied adhesive.

statically determinate frame, isostatic frame, perfect frame; a structural frame with no redundant members, in which all the forces, loads and bending moments can be determined by the laws of statics.

statically indeterminate frame, hyperstatic frame, redundant frame; a structural frame in which all the forces, loads and bending moments cannot be determined by the laws of statics, due to the presence of redundant members.

static load a structural load which is non-moving and unchanging in terms of magnitude and direction.

static moment, first moment of area; in structural statics, the sum of products obtained by multiplying the area of a structural section by its distance from an axis.

static penetration testing in soil investigation, penetration testing using a testing implement which is pushed with a steady force into the soil.

stationary wave see standing wave.

station roof, umbrella roof; a roof used for open shelters, canopies, etc., carried on a single row of stanchions or columns, cantilevered on one or both sides.

stave 1 see stake, pale, timber pile.

2 see parquet block.

stave construction a traditional form of timber construction based on a series of staves or pales driven into the ground side by side as side walls.

stay 1 a structural member such as a prop, pier, buttress or cable, which gives support to a construction; see support, guy.

2 a simple device for holding a window or door open or in a certain fixed position; see casement stay, door stop (door stay).

stayed see cable-stayed.

steam curing the curing of concrete by placing it in a chamber with steam to speed up its gain of strength and reduce dry shrinkage; see autoclaving, low pressure steam curing.

steam heating an industrial space-heating system in which the heating medium is steam, circulated from a main heating plant.

steatite see soapstone, French chalk.

steel a versatile, strong, finely crystalline alloy of iron with a carbon content of up to 2%; one of the most common building and structural materials.

steel angle, angle bar, angle iron; a structural steel section whose uniform cross-section resembles the letter L, formed by a process of rolling.

steel bar any longitudinal solid length of steel rolled into a uniform cross-section; used in construction.

steel beam 1 any beam rolled, welded or manufactured from steel.
2 see pressed steel lintel.

steel cable see cable, high-tension steel cable.

steel column a column manufactured from steel; often a standard steel section; see stanchion, H-section (universal column).

steel concrete see reinforced concrete.

steel construction building work using structural steel; the product of this; see steelwork.

steel deck floor see composite floor slab.

steel-fibre reinforced concrete sprayed or cast concrete reinforced with less than 2% steel fibres; used for road and floor surfaces, pipes and thin structural sections; the steel fibres used are thin crimped filaments of steel, betwwen 50–100 mm long and 0.5 mm thick; used in bulk.

steel fixing, reinforcement; in reinforced concretework, the cutting, bending, binding and placing of steel reinforcement prior to pouring the concrete.

steel frame any frame structure composed of steel beams, columns, bracing, etc. joined at their ends, onto which cladding components, flooring, roofing, etc. are fixed.

steel joist rolled steel joist, see I-section.

steel lintel see pressed steel lintel.

steel mesh any mesh product manufactured primarily of steel; see wire mesh for list of mesh types; see welded mesh, fabric reinforcement.

steel mesh reinforcement see fabric reinforcement.

steel nail a round nail made from tempered steel; used for nailing to concrete and masonry surfaces.

steel pile any foundation pile fabricated from steel; see box pile, H-pile, pipe pile (tubular pile).

steel pipe see circular hollow section.

steel plate flat plate manufactured from steel; see quarto plate, chequerplate (checkerplate).

steel profile any length of steel preformed into a uniform cross-section of certain shape and dimensions, often synonymous with section, but usually more complex; used for patent glazing, door frames, etc.

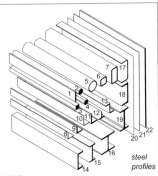

steel profiles

BARS
1 flat bar, flat
2 round bar
3 square bar
4 hexagonal bar

HOLLOW SECTIONS AND TUBES
5 round hollow section, round tube
6 square hollow section, SHS; square tube
7 rectangular hollow section, RHS

ANGLES AND OPEN SECTIONS
8, 9 equal angle
10, 11 unequal angle
12 T-bar, structural tee
13 Z-bar
14 channel, U-section, C-section
15 I-section, universal beam, UB section
16 H-section, universal column, UC section
17 cold formed or cold rolled steel beam
18 hot rolled steel beam
19 plate girder, welded plate girder

SHEET PRODUCTS
20 metal foil, foil
21 metal sheet, sheetmetal
22 metal plate

steel purlin a lightweight secondary steel beam laid in series for supporting floor or roof construction; usually a Z-, C- or I-profile.

steel reinforcement see concrete reinforcement, reinforcing bar.

steel rule a straight parallel-sided strip of steel, often gradated, used for scribing and measuring.

steel section any thin length of steel which has been preformed by a process of rolling, extrusion, bending, etc. into a uniform cross-section of certain shape and dimensions, often for structural use; see steel bar, steel profile, hollow section (structural hollow section).

steel sheet see sheet steel.

steel sheet pile, sheet pile; in excavation work, one of a series of interlocking steel profiles driven into the ground prior to excavation to retain the sides of the subsequent excavation.

steel sheet piling a number of these which form a retaining wall for an excavation; see also sheet piling.

steelwork, steel construction; framing construction work in welded or bolted steel sections, usually structural steelwork; the construction and structure resulting from this.

steeple the combined tower and spire of a church.

stela, stele (Gk.); Lat.; a slab or upright stone in antiquity with inscriptions and carvings; often a gravestone or commemorative pillar.

Greek marble stela with inscription, 207 AD, erected in fulfilment of a sacrificial vow by a husband on behalf of his ailing wife

stellar vault, star-ribbed vault, star vault; a masonry vault used for medieval church roofs, whose ribs, tiercerons and liernes form a star-shaped pattern in the interior ceiling.

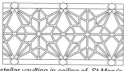

stellar vaulting in ceiling of St Mary's Church, Turku, Finland, 14th century

stellite a cobalt-chromium-tungsten metal alloy, used for hard facings for cutting tools, bearings, valves and other components prone to wear.

stench pipe see stack vent.

stencil a template used for application of lettering and painted motifs in printing, interiors design and draughting.

stencilling, stencil painting; a form of applied decoration produced by painting over sheet material with patterned perforations to leave a negative design on a surface.

step a shallow platform or construction designed to negotiate a pedestrian change in level by means of a short horizontal surface connected to a vertical riser, either on its own or as part of a stair; types included as separate entries are listed below:
*balanced step, see dancing step; *corbie steps, see crow steps; *dancing step, French flier; *doorstep; *flier; *kite step, kite winder; *parallel tread, see flier; *spandrel step; *tapered step; *tread; *wheel step, wheeling step, see winder.

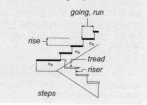

step iron one of a number of iron fastenings in series providing vertical stepped access to a shaft, manhole or up the side of a chimney stack.

step-off part of the horizontal end of an escalator made up of two stair units, from which a passenger steps to leave the escalator.

step-on part of the horizontal beginning of an escalator made up of two stair units, onto which a passenger initially steps.

stepped flashing in roof construction, an upstand flashing at the junction of the verge of a sloping roof and a masonry parapet or wall, whose upper surface is stepped and housed in horizontal joints in the masonry.

stepped gable see crow steps.

stepped tenon joint see shouldered tenon joint.

steps an external solid stair in a garden, park, yard or urban environment.

stereobate in classical architecture, a masonry base or visible foundation for a column or wall; the base or foundation on which a building is constructed; see also stylobate.

Stereum sanguinolentum see bleeding Stereum.

stick, sticker; a strip of wood for separating layers of piled timber being seasoned or stored to aid air circulation.

stick welding see manual metal-arc welding.

stiffened concrete laid or cast concrete that has hardened to a degree that it is no longer workable.

stiffening see frame bracing.

stiff-leaf carved decoration of stylized foliage motifs found in Norman architecture.
stiff-leaf capital is a Norman capital consisting of a block carved with stiff-leaf, possibly inspired by the classical Corinthian equivalent.

Romanesque stiff-leaf capital at church of St Mary the Virgin, West Walton, Norfolk, England, 1240

stiffness see rigid.

stilb abb. **sb;** a unit of luminance equal to one candela per square centimetre; cd/cm².

S-tile see pantile.

stile 1 a vertical side framing member of a door leaf or window casement; see door stile.

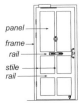

panel
frame
rail
stile
rail

2 a low external construction of steps to provide passage over a wall or fence in rural areas for people but not animals.

Stillson wrench see pipe wrench.

stilted arch an arch whose curvature begins above the impost, as if on stilts.
pointed Saracenic arch, stilted pointed arch; a stilted arch with a pointed apex.
stilted semicircular arch a stilted arch which is semicircular.

stippling the producing of a decorative mottled surface for paint or plaster by regular dabbing with a stippler.
stippler also called a stippling brush or stipple; a stiff brush, sponge, or similar hand-held implement.

stipulated sum agreement see lump sum contract.

stirrup 1 in timber frame construction, a metal strip or belt fixing for two perpendicular pieces, fastened to both sides of one piece and wrapped around the other.
2 one of a number of bent secondary reinforcing bars which bind the main reinforcement and resist shear forces in a reinforced concrete beam or pile; also called a link, binder or ligature.

stone 1 a generic name for the rigid mineral material forming the earth's crust; used in building construction as masonry, paving, cladding, concrete aggregates, decoration, etc.; see rock for references to lists of building stones, rocks and minerals; see natural stone, cast stone.
2 an imperfection in manufactured glass caused by a small solid lump or fleck of opaque mineral material.

stone axe see masonry axe.

stone block see natural stone block, dimension stone, ashlar.

stone block paving a paved surface made up of evenly sized stone units or slabs.

stone carving the carving of patterns, sculpture, ornament and lettering into stone with tempered steel tools.
stonecarving chisel, stone chisel see masonry chisel.

stone cladding see stone facing, natural stone cladding.

stone column see vibroreplacement.

stone facing any cladding in sheets or fragments of natural stone cemented or hung on a base of brick, concrete, etc.; see natural stone facing, ashlar facing, rubble facing; if in thin precut sheets it is called stone veneer.

stone flooring hardwearing or decorative flooring of natural or cast stone slabs.

stone masonry masonry in roughly hewn, cut or sawn stones laid as structural walling, arches, vaults, cladding, etc.

stonemason see mason.

stonemason's axe see masonry axe.

stonemason's chisel see masonry chisel.

stone nogging stone infill for the timber stud frame of a traditional half-timbered building.

stone paint see masonry paint.

stone paver see natural stone paver, paving stone.

stone paving, natural stone paving; shaped flat slabs of natural stone laid horizontally as a hardwearing external surface; see pebble, sett; for crazy paving, random stone paving, see ragwork.

stone slab a large solid flattish slab of natural stone, worked into shape; used for many purposes in construction; see paving stone.

stone veneer see stone facing.

stoneware a hard ceramic material containing a relatively high proportion of glass, fired at high temperatures of $1200-1300°C$ and used for unglazed drainage products, pipes, channels, etc.

stonework any part of a building, structure, cladding or paving which incorporates natural stone as a primary material; construction and detailing in stone; some types included as separate entries are listed below:
*diamond work; *long and short work; *ragwork; *range work.

stool bottomgrate a cast-iron grated podium in an open hearth fire, on which solid fuel rests during combustion so that air may be drawn up through it.

stop 1 a rebate in a door or window frame, against which the door leaf or window casement rests when closed; see door stop.
2 in stonework and carving, a decorative terminating element for horizontal mouldings.
3 a termination or closing construction for a long component or construction such as a gutter.

stopcock see stopvalve, mains stopvalve.

stop end, 1 gutter end; the closed end of an eaves gutter, or a terminating component which achieves this; see stop-end outlet.
2 see stopped end.

stop end form, day joint, form stop; formwork sheeting placed at a joint, at the edge of a component or to contain the edge of concrete being cast.

stop-end outlet a terminating drainage channel or guttering section blocked at one end, with an opening in its base to release drainage water.

stop notice a notice served by a planning authority requiring building work, demolition or other activity on site that is in contravention of planning control to be immediately stopped.

stop nut, back nut, lock nut; a nut screwed tightly against the back of another nut to prevent it from working loose.

stopped a description of a timber joint in which a mortise or recess is cut only part way into the timber receiving a tenon, rather than right through.

stopped dovetail joint see lapped dovetail joint.

stopped end the end of a laid masonry wall which terminates in a straight vertical line through the use of bonding stones; see return end.

stopped mortise, blind mortise; in timber mortise and tenon jointing, a mortise that does not fully penetrate the piece into which it is cut.

stopped tenon joint a timber mortise and tenon joint whose tenon does not fully penetrate the piece into which it is fitted; see stub tenon joint.

stopper, plug; a simple conical, wedge-shaped or threaded component for closing an opening or orifice in a tube, pipework, duct, etc.; see tap-hole stopper.

stopping the filling of cracks, holes, joints and other blemishes in a surface with filler prior to painting; the product used for this, usually a very smooth paste which sets to form a smooth finish; spackling or filler; see caulking, putty.
stopping in in plasterwork, the filling and smoothing of joints in plasterboard construction and ornamental plasterwork.
stopping knife see putty knife.

stopvalve, stopcock; a valve in a system of water or gas pipework to shut off flow.

storage cylinder a closed cylindrical pressure vessel for storing hot water for domestic use.

storage heater, 1 thermal storage heater; a unit heater consisting of electrodes embedded in a mass of material with a high thermal capacity surrounded by insulation; the electrodes heat up the mass with off-peak electricity during the night and the resultant heat is given off slowly during the day; see also next entry.
2 hot water storage heater, storage water heater; in hot water systems, a hot water storage vessel in which water is also heated.
storage heating space heating with a series of storage heaters utilizing off-peak electricity, or with massive masonry fireplaces providing slow release of heat.

storage life see shelf life.

storage tank see oil storage tank, cistern.

storage unit a piece of domestic or office furniture or in-built fitting containing a number of cupboards for storage.

storage water heater see storage heater.

store 1 a building or room within a building devoted to storage or distribution of supplies.
2 storage space; a space or part of a space within a building for the storage of equipment, supplies or goods.

storey, floor, story (Am), level; one of the horizontal floor levels in a building; the area between vertically adjacent floors of a building.

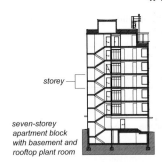

storey

seven-storey
apartment block
with basement and
rooftop plant room

storey height see floor height.
storey landing a stair landing at the same level as adjacent floor construction.
storey rod see gauge rod.

storied rays see ray figure.

stormwater, storm sewage; rainwater from heavy rainfall which has been collected as runoff from external surfaces of a building and conveyed to storm drains, often mixed with foul water to prevent overflow.
storm drain, storm sewer, stormwater sewer; a municipal or private drain for conveying water directly to a river in the event of heavy rainfall.
storm sewage see stormwater.
storm sewer see storm drain.
stormwater sewer see storm drain.

story see storey.

stove a closed appliance for heating a space, often freestanding and connected to a flue if solid-fuel, gas or oil-fired, or ventilated if operated by electricity.

stove enamelling, baking, stoving; the process of drying or fusing an applied polymeric coating by the application of artificial heat; products thus coated are variously stove enamelled, stove finished, baked or stoved; see also acrylic stoving enamel, alkyd stoving enamel.
stoved acrylic see acrylic powder coating.
stoved enamel, stove enamel, stoved finish see baked enamel.
stove finished, stoving see stove enamelling.
stoving enamel see acrylic stoving enamel, alkyd stoving enamel.

stoving lacquer lacquer dried by a sustained period of baking or application of heat.

straight arch see flat arch.

straight bands those internal plies in the thickness of plywood whose grain is in the same direction as the face plies.

straight bevelled halved joint see bevelled scarf joint.

straight cut veneer see flat cut veneer.

straightedge 1 a long straight rod used for measuring and setting out.
2 see screed board.

straightening coat see first plaster undercoat, second plaster undercoat.

straight flight stair a stair which consists of a single linear flight with no intermediate landing; see also straight stairs.

straight flight stair

straight grained a description of a piece of sawn timber whose grain is approximately parallel to an edge.
straight-grained float a flat-bladed wooden float used for smoothing plastering, whose timber grain is parallel to its length.

straight joint, stacked joint; a vertical brickwork joint which rises through more than one course and provides only a weak bond.

straight match a condition of decorative or patterned wallpaper which should be hung with horizontal patterns aligned on adjacent sheets.

straight peen hammer a hammer whose peen is aligned with its shaft.

straight reducer a pipe fitting for joining two pipes of different diameters in a straight line.

straight-run stairs see straight stairs.

straight shake a crack running along the grain of a timber board.

straight shake in improperly seasoned timber board

straight stairs, straight-run stairs; a stair which ascends in a straight line, with or without intermediate landings; see straight flight stair.

strain in structural mechanics, unit deformation of a member resulting from applied stress.
strain energy the energy stored in an elastic body under stress.
strain relief see partial release.

strainer a coarse filtering device or sieve for preventing solid matter in liquid suspension from passing a certain point in a flow system such as sewage treatment; see also outlet strainer.

strainer arch a supplementary masonry arch constructed part way down a high opening to prevent buckling of its sides.

straining arch a structural arch which functions as a brace, as in a flying buttress.

straining arch

straining beam in traditional timber roof construction, the upper beam between the tops of queen posts in a queen post truss.

straining sill in traditional timber roof construction, timbers attached to the top of a tie beam to prevent the base of queen posts from moving.

strand 1 one of the wound fibres, filaments or threads in a rope, cable or cord.

2 a bundle of many glass fibres, often hundreds, used as reinforcement in fibreglass.

3 see prestressing strand.

stranded caisson see box caisson.

S trap a drainage trap shaped in the letter "S" lying on its side, with both the inlet and outlet vertical and a water seal contained in the lower bend.

strap **1** a metal strip or belt fastened across a joint to secure a fixing in timber frame construction.

2 ceiling strap, see ceiling hanger.

3 see anchor strap.

strap hinge, flap hinge; a surface-mounted hinge with long, tapered or straight flaps; see also tee hinge.

strap hinge

strapwork surface decoration of interwoven bands rendered as if cut from a sheet material such as leather, originating in the Netherlands in the 1500s.

strapwork

Strasbourg turpentine, olio d'abezzo; a variety of turpentine exuded from the silver fir [*Abies alba*], used as a medium in paints, varnishes and adhesives.

stratification a defect in cast concrete resulting from overvibration, causing lighter constituent materials such as water and cement to rise to the surface.

strawboard, compressed straw slab; an insulating building board manufactured by compressing straw under heat between sheets of card.

straw thatch, long straw thatch; roofing thatch of unbroken, dried wheat, barley, rye or sedge stalks.

street parking, on-street parking, kerb parking, curb parking (Am); the provision of parking places in marked spaces lining the edge of a street carriageway.

strength the property of a material or component to withstand forces without fracture or failure.

strength accelerating admixture, accelerator; an admixture included in a concrete mix to increase its hardening rate.

strength test see compressive strength test.

stress the effect of an external force or forces on a structure or structural member; the force per unit area resulting from external loads on a structure, or internal forces such as drying, in units of N/m^2.

stress corrosion corrosion leading to potentially disastrous cracking and failure taking place in steel structural members under tensile stress.

stress grading the classification of sawn timber according to structural defects.

stressing the application of stress or load to a structure or structural member.

stressed skin construction a method of construction of walls, floors and panels in which boards or membranes are fixed to either side of a frame or series of structural members as bracing.

stressed skin component a prefabricated structural timber walling or flooring component with boarding fixed on either side of a timber or pressed metal frame.

stressed skin panel a rigid structural element consisting of a frame onto which boards or sheets are fixed as bracing.

stretcher a bonded brick or stone laid with its long side or face exposed in the surface of a masonry wall.

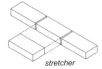

stretcher

stretcher bond **1** running bond; a brickwork bond consisting entirely of courses of stretchers, with alternate courses laid with a half brick overlap. See illustration on facing page.

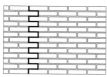

stretcher bond

2 any brickwork bond consisting of single courses of Flemish, etc. interspersed with an odd number of courses of stretchers; see Flemish stretcher bond, monk bond (Flemish double stretcher bond), raking stretcher bond.

stretcher course, stretching course; a course of bonded brickwork which consists entirely of stretchers.

stretcher face the visible side of a brick when laid in masonry as a stretcher.

stretcher plinth, plinth stretcher;
a special brick whose upper arris has been chamfered along one of its long sides; used

stretcher plinth

as a stretcher in a brick coping or above a projection.

stretching course see stretcher course.

striated finish see batted finish.

strigil ornament in Roman architecture, a decorative motif of shallow recurring S-shaped carvings for vertical surfaces; it takes its name from the curved implement used by wrestlers to scrape the oil, sweat and dust from their bodies after bouts in the arena or palaestra (wrestling area).

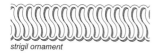

strigil ornament

strike, strike plate see striking plate.

striking, stripping; the removal of formwork from hardened concrete.

striking face see face.

striking hammer a heavy hammer or maul used for striking cold chisels and other cutting and shaping tools in stone and metalwork; see drilling hammer, mallet.

striking piece in concreting, a piece of formwork sheeting which can easily be removed to aid dismantling of the rest of the formwork.

striking plate, keeper, strike, strike plate; a metal plate with a rectangular perforation, attached to a door jamb to receive a latch or bolt when the door is closed.

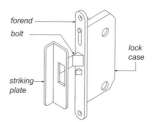

striking time, stripping time; the time from placing of cast concrete after it has reached an accepted degree of hardness so that formwork can be safely removed.

string stringer; an inclined beam which carries the treads in a stair.

string course see band course.

stringer see string.

stringline see bricklayer's line.

stripe figure see ribbon grain.

strip flooring see wood strip flooring, wide plank flooring, solid parquet, parquet strip.

strip foundation, strip footing; a wall foundation consisting of a continuous horizontal strip of concrete; see widestrip foundation.

strip foundation

strippable wallcovering wallcovering which can be removed in one piece once dry.

strip parquet see parquet strip.

strippers see wire strippers.

stripping see striking, paint removal (hot-air stripping).

stripping knife a flat-bladed spatula used for removing old paintwork and wallcoverings.

stripping time see striking time.

strip slates a roofing product of small pieces of shaped bitumen felt laid in the same manner as roof tiles; if sold in attached groups they are called strip slates or tiles, if sold as single nailable items they are variously known as asphalt, bitumen, composition or felt shingles.

strip slates

strip soaker a strip of waterproofing material laid between courses of roof shingles in exposed areas.

strip tie see strip wall tie.

strip tiles see strip slates.

strip wall tie any wall tie formed from metal strip rather than wire; see vertical twist tie, fishtail tie.

strip window see window band.

strongback a structural member used as a spreader beam, soldier or as waling in formwork.

strontium a metallic chemical element, **Sr**, compounds of which are used in pigments, optics, fireworks, flares and some armaments.

strontium white strontium sulphate ($SrSO_4$) used as a pigment in the same way as blanc fixe and barites.

strontium yellow a pale bright yellow pigment manufactured from strontium chromate, now almost obsolete.

struck joint, overhand struck joint; a horizontal brickwork mortar joint used for interior and sheltered work, which is slanting in cross-section and made by pressing the mortar in at the bottom of the joint; see weathered joint.

structural pertaining to loadbearing systems, forces or elements; referring to a material, member, etc. whose function is loadbearing.

structural adhesive a strong and durable adhesive for joining structural components.

structural board any building board used for its loadbearing properties as decking, bracing, etc.

structural brickwork brickwork which is designed to be loadbearing.

structural concrete concrete designed to carry loads or be part of the structure of a building.

structural concretework any work on site involving reinforced concrete frames, including formwork erection, casting, installation of precast panels, etc.

structural defect an imperfection affecting the strength of the structure of a building, component or material such as timber.

structural design the design, theoretical testing and calculation of structural loads, stresses and sizing of structural members undertaken by a structural engineer.

structural drawing a design drawing produced by a structural engineer to show the layout, materials and sizing of structural units of a building.

structural engineering the engineering discipline which deals with the design, calculation and testing of structures.

structural engineer a qualified professional responsible for designing structures and supervising their construction and maintenance.

structural floor those loadbearing layers of floor construction designed to support dead and imposed loading, over which flooring is laid.

structural frame see loadbearing frame.

structural glazing, frameless glazing, planar glazing; a system of glazing in which the glass itself has a structural role, usually unframed sheets of toughened glass hung on patch or spot fittings with sealed butt joints. See illustration on facing page.

structural glazing

structural grid the orthogonal layout of columns and main structural elements in a building; see also grid.

structural hollow section a structural steel section formed by rolling or welding, whose cross-section is a hollow rectangular, circular or other shaped tube.

structural member one of the component parts of a structural system designed to carry load.

structural skeleton, frame; the primary framework for a building or structure.

structural steel a general name for rolled steel sections, beams and columns used in construction for framing and other loadbearing functions; structural steel sections included as separate entries are listed below:
*bar; *channel, channel section; *circular hollow section; *C-section; *H-section; *hollow section; *hot-rolled steel section; *I-section; *L-profile, see angle profile; *rectangular hollow section, RHS; *rolled hollow section, RHS; *rolled steel section; *round hollow section, round section, see circular hollow section; *square hollow section; *structural hollow section; *T-section, T-bar, tee section; *tubular section, see hollow section; *UB section, see I-section; *UC section, see H-section; *U-section; *Z-section.

structural steelwork any structural work or loadbearing frames consisting of steel sections fixed together.

structural threshold in threshold analysis, existing built form or urban grain which presents a barrier to further urban expansion.

structural timber timber and timber products used in construction for their structural and loadbearing properties in framing, beams, trusses, etc.

structure, 1 loadbearing structure; a combination of parts joined together to form a loadbearing or rigid whole.
2 composition; the construction or make-up of an object, compound, material such as stone or timber, organism or component and the relationship of parts therein.

structure borne sound in acoustics, sound transmitted by the fabric or other components of a building.

structure borne sound transmission sound transmission through the building fabric.

strut any structural member which resists forces in compression along its length; especially a secondary vertical or oblique member which resists compressive forces, a column or diagonal; in timber roof construction, struts are secondary members carrying the thrust from purlins or otherwise adding support to a rafter.

strut beam see collar beam.

strutting see herringbone strutting.

Stuart architecture an architectural style in England during the reigns of Charles II and James II (1660–1688); it is evident principally in secular palaces and country houses, and is characterized by use of Baroque elements.

stub bar see starter bar.

stub mortise and tenon joint see stub tenon joint.

stub stack a vertical pipe, closed at its upper end, into which a number of sanitary appliances at one level may discharge.

Stub's wire gauge see Birmingham wire gauge.

stub tenon joint, joggle tenon joint, stopped tenon joint, stub mortise and tenon joint; any mortise and tenon joint in which the mortise does not penetrate right through to the other side of a receiving member.

stub tenon joint

stucco any plaster used for facing the outside of buildings, for decorative castings, etc.; stucco usually refers to textured renderwork in lime mortar, cement mortar or lime cement mortar, especially fine plasterwork for classical or Baroque decorative work, columns, rustication, etc. in imitation of stone; see hemihydrate gypsum plaster, marble stucco, plasterwork enrichment.

stucco architecture ornate architectural styles in which stonework is imitated in decorative plasterwork, much in vogue in the eclecticism of the 1800s.

stucco lustro a technique of marble-imitation plasterwork invented in the seventeenth century, in which coloured pigments, marble dust, etc. are sprinkled or painted over the plaster when wet, then the surface is polished to a sheen with a hot iron; sometimes called marmorino or, for high-quality interior finishes, Venetian stucco; see also scagliola.

stud 1 in timber frame construction, spaced vertical timber members in a wall frame, to which external cladding and internal lining are attached; a spaced vertical timber or pressed metal framing member in a lightweight partition.
2 a metal fixing consisting of a short steel rod threaded at one or both ends to take a bolt.
3 a bolt or nail attached by firing with a special pistol.

studded rubber flooring proprietary sheet or tile flooring of natural or synthetic rubber whose surface has been textured with low projections to provide friction; also known as raised-pattern, coin-pattern or coin flooring.

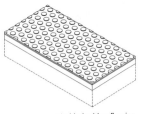

studded rubber flooring

studding see studwork, threaded rod.
stud gun a robust nail gun for firing nails or fixings into masonry and concrete.

stud partition a lightweight internal dividing wall constructed with a frame of spaced verticals lined with a building board.

stud wall in frame construction, any wall framed with spaced vertical timbers or studs.

stud welding a method of resistance welding threaded studs onto steel frames using special guns, as a fixing for claddings and other components.

studwork studding; timber or pressed metal sections laid vertically as a framework for lightweight partitions or timber sections in timber framed walls.

stugged finish see sparrowpecked finish.

stump tenon joint in timber frame construction, a joint in which the end of a post is received into a housing in a horizontal sill or head member.

stump tenon joint

stupa a dome-shaped sacred Buddhist building, often surrounded by a freestanding wall or railing and containing holy relics.

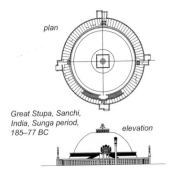

plan

Great Stupa, Sanchi, India, Sunga period, 185–77 BC

elevation

stylobate 1 in classical architecture, the upper stepped course of a crepidoma, on which a temple stands.
2 a plinth or base for a colonnade.

styrene a clear volatile liquid produced from benzene and used in the manufacture of plastics.

styrene-acrylonitrile, SAN; a thermoplastic formed by copolymerization of styrene with acrylonitrile; used in the automotive industry, for kitchenware, appliances and furniture.

styrene-butadiene rubber, SBR; a resilient synthetic rubber used for car tyres, carpet-backing and wire insulation.

styrofoam see extruded polystyrene.

sub-base in foundation, paving and road construction, a layer of material such as hardcore, cement, etc. laid beneath the substructure to spread loading evenly to underlying soil, to restrict frost heave and as drainage; see also flooring sub-base.

sub-basement a storey under the main basement of a building.

sub-contract a contract to carry out a part of a larger contract, paid for and managed by a main contractor.

sub-contracting a procedure that enables a main contractor to contract out specific parts of the building work, often of a specialist nature or trade, to another subsidiary contractor, called a subcontractor.

subfloor those layers of floor construction above a structural floor which provide a base for the flooring material; see flooring sub-base.

subframe wall framing at the edges of a door or window opening, to which a door or window frame is directly fixed.

subgrade in paving and road construction, that part of the ground or an earthwork which bears loads from the overlying road structure; see also foundation.

submerged-arc welding a method of arc welding steel plates in which an electric arc is applied across an intermediate electrode, carried out under a mass of molten flux.

submersible pump a small pump for drawing relatively clean water from wells, excavations, etc. by immersion in the water.

subsidiary glazing, secondary glazing; proprietary glazing units, usually in metal frames, attached to the front side of old or leaky windows to improve performance.

subsill the lower member of a window opening, formed into a sill onto which a window frame rests and is fixed; see timber subsill.

subsoil a layer of soil immediately above solid ground, but below topsoil; see also foundation.

subsoil drain 1 a perforated pipe laid beneath the ground in sand or gravel to dry out damp soil and lead seepage water away from the substructure of a building or road to a public drain.

2 irrigation drain; in the treatment of waste water, a perforated drain which discharges effluent from a septic tank into the surrounding soil.

subsoil drainage see land drainage.

substrate any surface to which a finish, coating or adhesive may be applied; also called a base or ground.

substructure that part of the structure of a building, particularly those constructed below ground, which transmits loading to the ground below.

subsurface drain see subsoil drain.

subtractive mixture in colour science, darker colours formed when colours are combined, each absorbing a part of the light incident on it.

succinite see amber.

sugar maple, rock maple; [*Acer saccharum*], see maple.

sui generis use 'of its own kind, unique' (Lat.); in planning control, a class of development which does not fit into any of the main defined classes.

suite, 1 lock suite, suite of locks; a group of locks within a building which can be opened by a single master key, and each has its own individual key which fits only that lock.

2 a set of furniture comprising, for example, a sofa and two armchairs of the same or similar style.

3 a group of rooms and service spaces planned for a particular use; see WC suite.

suiteing the planning and formulation of a suite of locks within a building or complex to suit the needs of user groups, but in such a way that all are openable by a master key.

sulfur see sulphur.

sulphate sulfate (Am); any of a number of water-soluble compounds formed by the reaction of minerals or metals with sulphur; used in traditional paints as fixatives and to prevent attack of timber by insects and fungi.

sulphate attack a fault in hardened concrete caused by the attack of dissolved sulphate salts.

sulphate-resisting Portland cement, sulphate-resistant cement; a Portland cement, low in tricalcium aluminate, which has a better resistance to attack by sulphates dissolved in water than ordinary Portland cement.

sulphur, sulfur (Am); a yellow chemical element, **S**, used in matches, explosives and the vulcanization of rubber.

sulphur dioxide a poisonous, gaseous, chemical compound, SO_2, used in bleaching; a major source of air pollution.

sulphuric acid, oil of vitriol; a dense, oily, corrosive chemical compound, H_2SO_4, used in the chemical industry, pickling of steel surfaces, and in dye manufacture.

sulphur-ore see iron pyrites.

summer, summer beam, summer tree; in traditional timber-framed building, a heavy main beam which carries a wall or other continuous load.

summerwood see latewood.

sun-baked brick see mud brick.

sun-bleached oil see sun-refined oil.

sunburst matching a veneering pattern for round or polygonal tabletops in which segmental slices of burl or crotch veneer are glued side by side to form a repeated star-like pattern.

sun-dried brick see mud brick.

sunflower seed oil, sunflower oil; a drying oil pressed from the seeds of the sunflower plant [*Helianthus annuus*], used as a vehicle in paints.

sunk bead a thin hollow moulding, semicircular in profile.

sunken half round a hollow moulding, semicircular in profile.

sunken half round

sunk fillet a thin hollow moulding, rectangular in profile.

sunk fillet moulding

sunk relief, cavo-relievo, cavo-rilievo, intaglio rilevato; carved ornament or decoration which does not project from the surface into which it is carved.

sunlight, direct solar radiation; in lighting design, that part of illumination reaching the ground as direct, unobscured and unreflected light from the sun.

sun-refined oil, sun-bleached oil; traditional linseed oil refined by leaving it in the sun in glass vessels for a number of weeks; used as a vehicle in paints.

sunshade, shade; any grill, set of baffles or blind fixed externally above a window or glazing to provide shade from the sun.

super abacus, supercapital see dosseret.

super glue see cyanoacrylate adhesive.

superimposed orders the stacking of classical orders as elevational devices in successive storeys of a classical building, by convention (from the bottom) Tuscan, Doric, Ionic, Corinthian and Composite.

superplasticizing admixture, superplasticizer, high-range water-reducing admixture; in concretework, a powerful admixture included in the mix to maintain workability with a reduced water content.

superplasticized concrete liquid concrete with a superplasticizer added to increase workability; used for patching structural defects in reinforced concrete.

superposition principle a structural theory for calculating forces in redundant frames by dividing them up into a number of superimposed perfect frames.

superstructure that part of the structure of a building or bridge above its substructure or foundations; parts of a building which remain above ground level.

supersulphated cement blended cement composed of blast-furnace cement mixed with calcium sulphates and lime or cement clinker.

superterranean see surface.

supplier a commercial organization which stocks, produces or delivers materials, components or products for a building project.

supply 1 goods or services which are provided or available.

2 the conveyance of electricity, gas, water or other service to a building via a main; see electricity supply, gas supply, water supply.

3 in mechanical ventilation and air conditioning, the introduction of ducted fresh air into a space using fans.

supply air, 1 input air; treated air introduced into a space by an air-conditioning system.

2 fresh air; air pumped into a space by mechanical ventilation plant to replace stale air.

supply air terminal unit, outlet, input device; in air conditioning and ventilation, any device, grille, diffuser, etc. through which air is supplied to a space.

supply pipe that part of the service pipe of a water or gas supply installation which connects the supply of a building to the communication pipe, lies inside a site boundary, and is not maintained by the supplier.

support, stay; any construction or component which keeps something in place or bears a load such as a prop, beam, bracket, cleat or column.

supported sheetmetal roofing, flexible metal roofing; roofing of thin, flat sheets of metal laid in bands with longitudinal joints, standing seams, etc. over boarding or decking; unlike profiled sheeting, it is not self-supporting; see also seam-welded roofing.

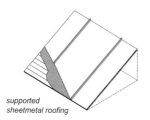

*supported
sheetmetal roofing*

surbased vault see segmental barrel vault.

surcharge the overflowing of a drain or sewer caused by an excess of pressure or capacity.

surface 1 the outermost bounding layer of an object, especially when coated or treated.

2 superterranean, above ground; referring to any construction work undertaken above ground level.

surface-acting agent, 1 surfactant; an additive which reduces the surface tension in a liquid; used in detergents and to make paint more brushable.

2 an additive for concrete which lowers the surface tension in mixing water to aid penetration of the concrete into formwork voids and dispersion and foaming of other additives.

surface area a measure of the two-dimensional space taken up by a surface, abb. **a**; in architectural design a measure of the floor area of buildings or parts of buildings.

surface box, valve box; a receptacle with a hinged lid, submerged into hard external surfaces, floors, footpaths, etc., to offer protection to a valve or pipe fitting, and from which it can be operated and serviced.

surface checks surface splitting in the face of an improperly seasoned timber board.

surface checks

surface coated float glass, reflective float glass; float glass treated with a transparent but reflective surface layer of metal oxide or other material to reduce transmission of solar radiation.

surface coefficient in calculations for thermal conductivity of a construction, the heat loss per $°C$ of temperature difference between a surface and the surrounding air; units are $W/m_2°C$; see also U-value, C-value.

surface condensation undesirable water vapour or steam which condenses on cool internal surfaces such as ceilings, window frames or walls as droplets of water.

surfaced see dressed, dressed timber.

surfaced bitumen felt see mineral granule surfaced bitumen felt.

surfaced four sides (Am) see planed all round.

surfaced sawn, surfaced two sides (Am); a description of sawn timber which has been planed on three sides only, leaving one face unplanned.

surface filler see filler.

surface-fixed hinge see non-mortised hinge.

surface hardening a process of hardening of the surface of steel for use in tools by various heat-treatment processes.

surface hinge a hinge designed to be mounted to the face of a door, gate or hatch rather than its edge.

surface-modified tinted float glass float glass treated with a layer of tinting metal ions during manufacture to reduce transmission of solar radiation.

surface mounting the fixing of electric cables and other services to the surfaces of ceiling, floors and walls, as opposed to installing them in ducts, housings or trunking.

surface-mounted door closer a door closer designed to be fixed to the face of a door leaf.

surface-mounted luminaire a luminaire designed to be fixed to and protrude from a surface, rather than being sunken into it.

surface planer, surfacer; a machine with a wide rotating cutter mounted into a bench for planing a flat, even surface on a wooden board; see thicknessing machine.

surface retarder a material applied to concrete formwork to slow down the setting of surface concrete, providing an exposed aggregate finish once the formwork is struck.

surface tension a property of the surface of a liquid to behave as if covered with a supporting film.

surface treatment, finish; the protective or decorative treatment of a surface

by mechanical or chemical means, or by the application of a coating to produce a finish.

surface vibration the compacting of fresh concrete by applying vibration to its outer surface with a type of vibrator called a surface vibrator, rather than immersing a vibrator into it; see also immersion vibrator (poker vibrator), beam vibrator.

surface water rainwater which falls on the ground, roofs of buildings, roads and paved areas, and is collected in a drain.

surface-water drainage the conveyance of rainwater from the slightly sloping surface of paving, roads, etc. into a system of drains.

surface-water erosion the erosion caused by surface water running over loose and granular soils, causing damage and subsidence and contributing sedimentation to streams and drainage systems.

surface water gully see rainwater gully.

surfacing 1 see dressing.
2 in road construction and landscaping, a layer or layers of material such as tarmac, paving or concrete which form a hardwearing surface; in road construction this is made up of the base course and wearing course.
3 see roof surfacing.

surfactant see surface-acting agent.

surform tool a hand tool with a multitoothed blade for rough shaping and smoothing of wood and plastics.

surround lighting see general surround lighting.

surveillance see camera surveillance, perimeter surveillance.

surveillance camera, closed circuit television camera; one of a network of cameras installed at key points in or around a building to provide security monitoring of the movement of people.

survey the gathering of information from samples, research, measurement, photographs, etc. for a particular purpose; types included as separate entries are listed below:
*building survey; *geotechnical survey; *investigation; *land survey; *quantity survey; *property survey.

survey drawing see record drawing.
surveying the action of doing a survey; see land surveying, mapping; see also survey.
surveyor a qualified professional who carries out a survey, see building surveyor, land surveyor, quantity surveyor.

suspended base floor the lowest structural floor in a building, which transmits loading via foundations but is not constructed directly onto the ground or bedrock below.

suspended ceiling a ceiling system of hangers, runners and panels hung from the soffit of floor construction above, in which light fittings, ducting and outlets are incorporated; sometimes called a hung ceiling.

suspended floor a floor construction which spans between points of support rather than being fully supported over its whole area by the underlying ground.

suspended roof, suspension roof; a roof supported by cables.

suspended scaffold a scaffold with a working stage which is hung from a counterweighted cantilever from the ridge or eaves of a building.

suspended slab any floor or roof slab supported at intervals by columns or cross walls, which does not bear directly onto the ground.

suspended structure a structure such as a suspension bridge which relies solely on the force of tension to support loads.

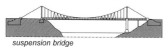
suspension bridge

suspension a liquid containing minute particles of a solid or liquid suspended in it.

suspension agent see thickening admixture.

suspension roof see suspended roof.

suspension track a proprietary profile of metal or plastics with rollers or guides for overhead mounting of blinds, signage and lighting.

Sussex bond see Flemish garden-wall bond.

swag see festoon.

swamp cypress see southern cypress.

swan-neck chisel see mortise lock chisel.

sward in landscaping, an area of tended lawn.

sway in thatched roofing, a long rod of hazel, elm or willow for fastening down a course of thatch.

sway brace see wind brace.

sweet cherry, wild cherry; [*Prunus avium*], see cherry.

sweet chestnut, Spanish chestnut; [*Castanea sativa*] a European hardwood with golden-brown, rough-textured, durable timber, whose uses are similar to that of oak.

sweetgum see gum.

swelled chamfer see oundy moulding.

Swietenia spp. see mahogany; *Swietenia macrophylla*, see Honduras mahogany.

swing door a door whose leaf is hinged so that it may open in both directions.

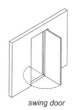
swing door

swing door hinge see double-acting hinge, double-acting spring hinge.
swing door operator a motorized lever or hinge mechanism for opening and closing an automatic swing door, operated by a signal from a detector device, remote control, etc.

swirl the irregular grain pattern that surrounds knots or crotches in a piece of sawn timber.

Swiss trowel a hand tool used for smoothing plaster in projection plastering by means of a rectangular flat blade attached to a handle.

switch a manual or automatic device for closing or opening an electric circuit.

swivel damper a smoke or flue damper which opens and closes by means of a pivot, about which it rotates; also called a pivot damper.

sycamore, harewood; [*Acer pseudoplatanus*] a hardwood with tough, light, fairly strong perishable yellowish timber, used for flooring and veneer; in North America the tree known as sycamore is the American plane [*Platanus occidentalis*].

syenite a coarse-grained, grey, bluish or reddish crystalline igneous rock containing feldspar and hornblende.

sympathetic resonance, sympathetic vibration see resonance.

synthetic man-made, as opposed to occurring naturally.
  synthetic anhydrite the mineral gypsum produced as a by-product of another process, or calcium sulphate manufactured under controlled conditions.
  synthetic fibre see artificial fibre.
  synthetic grass, astroturf, synthetic turf; a hardwearing surface covering for sports fields, a mat of raised tough plastic strands manufactured in imitation of grass.
  synthetic resin adhesive a group of adhesives whose main constituent is a synthetic phenolic or aminoplastic resin; see melamine formaldehyde glue, phenol formaldehyde glue, resorcinol formaldehyde glue, urea formaldehyde glue.
  synthetic rubber rubber produced from synthetically manufactured latex.
  synthetic rubber glue see elastomeric adhesive.

  synthetic screed see levelling compound.
  synthetic turf see synthetic grass.
Syrian arch, arcuated lintel; a major masonry arch supported on columns; often a large decorative arch in an arcade or colonnade with walling above, especially one marking an entranceway or other portal.

Syrian arch

system building a modern method of construction in which all or a certain major part of the building components for a construction project are prefabricated to save time and labour on site; see also prefabrication.
system glazing see patent glazing.
system of measurement an agreed system of unified units of measurement, such as the metric system or SI-system, by which size, quantity, mass and other physical phenomena can be quantified.
system of proportion a set of rules, principles or numbers governing the layout and relative arrangement of aesthetic forms.
system scaffolding proprietary scaffolding of specially made tubes, fixings, housings and shackles for quick and easy assembly, dismantling and storage, and automatic compliance with regulations.

T

t&g see tongue and groove.

tabernacle-work carved decorative work in a church especially for a tabernacle and its canopy, but found on other furnishings such as pulpits, screens or stalls.

table 1 the horizontal upper flat slab of a precast concrete tee beam, which takes its name from the piece of furniture with a flat horizontal working or activity surface.
2 a diagram for presenting information in a regular and clear way in columns and rows.

tabled scarf joint, hooked scarf joint; a timber lengthening joint whose halved surfaces are set back or tabled along their length for added strength.

tabled scarf joint

table formwork large-scale proprietary formwork used for casting and supporting the underside of concrete slabs in multi-storey buildings, which has its own supports so that it can be easily moved and reused in subsequent locations.

table hinge see rule joint hinge.

tablet flower an ornamental motif consisting of a series of embossed square flowers.

tablet flower

tacheometer an instrument used in surveying for measuring distances, direction and level differences.

tack 1 a flat-headed nail or pin for attaching building paper, fabric and carpets; see upholstery tack.

tack

2 the condition of a painted or glued surface which has not yet dried, and is still sticky.

tack free a stage in the drying of paint at which the painted surface is not sticky, but not fully hard.

tack hammer, brad hammer, pin hammer; a small hammer with a lightweight steel head for driving small nails, pins, brads or tacks.

tack welding, tacking; the fixing of metal pieces together or in position with temporary welds before final welding.

taenia Lat.; see tenia.

tail the lower edge of a roofing slate or tile.

talc, soapstone, steatite; natural magnesium silicate, ground and used as a filler in paints.

tallow-wood [*Eucalyptus microcorys*], see eucalyptus.

tamarack, eastern larch; [*Larix laricina*], see larch.

tambour, drum; a wall which supports a dome or cupola, cylindrical, square or polygonal in plan and often punctuated with openings.

tamping, punning, ramming, rodding, spading; the compaction of fresh concrete by the repeated manual thrusting of a sharp metal tool into it to release air voids; spading uses a spade-like tool, rodding uses a long steel rod.

tamped concrete, spaded concrete; concrete compacted by repeated tamping with a hand tool.

tamper see screed board.

t and g see tongue and groove.

tang the pointed spike at one end of a chisel blade, drill bit or file, designed to be housed into its handle or chuck.

tangentially cut see plain sawn.

tangential surface the surface of a piece of sawn timber which has been cut tangentially from the log.

tank any open or closed vessel for the storage of liquids or gases; types

included as separate entries are listed below:
*aeration tank; *cistern; *expansion tank; *gas tank; *oil storage tank; *oxidation tank, see aeration tank; *pressure tank; *reserve water tank; *sedimentation tank; *septic tank; *settlement tank, see septic tank; *settling tank, see sedimentation tank; *sewage tank, see cesspool; *storage tank; *water tank.

tanking an impervious layer of asphalt, bitumen or bituminous felt for waterproofing the outer surface of subterranean concrete or masonry structures.

tanking membrane see air-gap membrane.

tap 1 any fitting by which piped water, gas, etc. can be drawn off for use; see water tap.
2 a hard metal hand tool consisting of a threaded rod, used for cutting female or internal threads into prebored round metal holes.

tap aerator a device attached to or incorporated into the nozzle of a water tap for introducing air into the stream of water.

tape measure see measuring tape, flexible steel tape measure.

taper a conical pipe fitting for joining two pipes of different diameters.

tapered brick tapered header; see culvert stretcher, tapered stretcher; see culvert header.

tapered edge gypsum wallboard gypsum wallboard whose edges are tapered on the face side to enable butt joints to be made more easily.

tapered header see culvert stretcher.

tapered step, tapered tread; a wedge-shaped step whose front and back edges are not parallel, such as one in a spiral stair.

tapered stretcher see culvert header.

tapered tread see tapered step.

tapered tube a metal tubular product whose circumference decreases with length, used for flagpoles, masts and floodlighting poles.

tap-hole stopper a plug accessory designed to cover a tap-hole in a sink, in the case that no tap is to be installed.

taping strip, reinforcing strip; in built-up roofing, strips of material laid over joints in the underlying structure before the laying of bitumen felt.

tapping the cutting of internal screw threads in a bored hole with a tap.
tapping screw see self-tapping screw.

tar a black viscous liquid with a smoky odour, manufactured from the destructive distillation of wood or coal, traditionally used as a wood preservative.

tar epoxy paint tar-based epoxy resin paint used for waterproofing concrete or steelwork.

tar paper building paper saturated with tar, used as a moisture barrier in wall construction.

tar paving tarmacadam, tar slurry or other bituminous cements containing road tar as a binder; used for surfacing pedestrian areas and those designed for light traffic.

target cost contract a form of cost-reimbursement contract in which a nominal cost is estimated beforehand; on completion of the work, the difference in value between this target cost and the actual cost is divided between the client and contractor according to pre-agreed terms.

tarmacadam, coated macadam, tarmac; a hardwearing road surfacing made from graded aggregate coated with bitumen or road tar to bind the particles together.

tarpaulin a thin sheet of waterproof material, originally waterproofed fabric, used for the temporary protective covering of constructions and materials on site.

tarsia see intarsia.

task lighting artificial lighting designed to provide a higher level of illumination for certain localized activities such as reading, writing, drawing, etc.

tax brick a brick of larger than normal size which originated in England to avoid a brick tax levied from 1784–1850.

Taxodium distichum see southern cypress.

Taxus baccata see yew.

T-bar see T-section.

T-beam, tee beam; a flanged beam, T-shaped in cross-section to withstand greater compressive stresses.

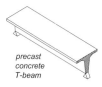

precast concrete T-beam

teagle post see principal post.

teak, Indian oak; [*Tectona grandis*] a hardwood from Burma, India and Thailand with durable, oily, dark yellow or brown timber; used for interior construction, plywood, boat-building and decorative panelling.

tear fungus see dry rot.

teazle tenon in traditional timber-framed construction, a tenon made in the top of a post, housed in a mortise in a horizontal member above.

teazle tenon

technical installation see service.

technical specification a document outlining a technical description of a product, process or service, and the requirements to be fulfilled by it.

Tectona grandis see teak.

tectonics the art of building; a pictorial composition which takes into account the structural qualities of line and surface.

tee a pipe fitting to connect one pipe to another at right angles.

tee beam see T-beam.

tee half lap joint a timber halved joint of one member meeting another at right angles, forming a tee shape.

tee hinge, strap hinge, T-hinge; a surface-mounted hinge which has one long tapered flap and one small flap, which forms a tee-shape when opened out.

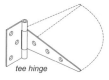

tee hinge

tee section see T-section.

Teflon trade name for polytetrafluoroethylene.

tegula, plural tegulae; 'tile' in Latin; a flat tray-shaped roofing tile used in conjunction with an imbrex or covering tile in Italian and Roman tiling.

telamon see atlas.

telecommunications the transmission of signals and messages over long distances usually by electronic means, using cables or satellites.

telecommunications network a telecommunications system comprising all outlets, exchanges, transmitters, relays, cables, satellites, antennae, etc., via which signals are transmitted.

telecommunications outlet, telecommunications socket; a plug-hole by which a telecommunications transmission device can be connected to a network or transmission system.

telephone system a digital, wireless, analogue, local, international, manual or automatic communications network using telephones.

telephone entry system, door phone; security telecommunications between an external door or gate and a restricted area, usually a send-and-receive unit connected to a monitoring centre, occupant's residence, etc.; often the same as an entry-phone.

telephone socket see telecommunications outlet.

telescopic crane, telescopic jib crane; a crane whose boom or jib is telescopic and can be easily hydraulically extended or retracted, often mounted on a vehicle.

telescopic prop a proprietary steel strut whose length can be adjusted, used for temporary propping of slabs and horizontal formwork; also called an adjustable prop.

tellurium a silvery, crystalline chemical element, **Te**, used in alloys and as a colourant in glass and ceramics.

tempera paint consisting of oils in an emulsion, used with water as a medium, which dries to form a hard, durable surface.

tempering heat treatment to increase the ductility of hardened steel by reheating it to a temperature below that of hardening, and allowing it to cool.
tempered glass see toughened glass.
tempered hardboard dense fibreboard impregnated with oil or resin for added strength, water resistance and abrasion resistance.

template any flat sheet of stiff material which has been profiled, shaped or had patterned holes cut out of it; used in marking out, draughting, lettering, and as a pattern in milling and turning on a lathe; variously called a stencil, templet, pattern or profile.

temporary works work on site which is demolished or dismantled after use and is not part of the completed construction, usually work carried out to stabilize or protect an existing building or as an aid to construction such as formwork, scaffolding, etc.

tender a written offer to carry out work or supply goods or services in given conditions at a stated price; a bid; see competitive tendering.
tender document any document which is part of a package sent out to tender; a contract document.
tendering see competitive tendering, tendering procedure, two-stage tendering.
tendering procedure the procedure for the invitation, selection and acceptance of tenders.
tender programme see outline programme.
tender sum in construction planning, the sum which a potential contractor offers as a fee for work to be undertaken, stated in his tender.

tendon, prestressing tendon; in prestressed concrete, a steel bar, wire, strand or cable stretched within the concrete to place it in compression.

tenia, taenia (Lat.); in classical architecture, a thin moulding which runs along the top of a Doric architrave, below the frieze.

tenon a rectangular protrusion cut into the end of a timber member, which fits into a recess or mortise to create a mortise and tenon joint.

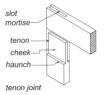

tenon joint

tenoned purlin see butt purlin.
tenoned scarf joint a timber lengthening joint in which the end of one or both pieces is fashioned with a tenon to increase the strength of the joint once assembled.
tenon joint see mortise and tenon joint for list of joints in this category.
tenon purlin see butt purlin.
tenon saw a medium-sized saw with a reinforced back, 250–350 mm in length, used for general accurate benchwork.

tensile pertaining to forces in tension.
tensile failure the failure of a structural member due to excess tensile force.
tensile force, tension; a pulling or stretching force in a structural member.
tensile reinforcement see tension reinforcement.
tensile strength in structural design, the greatest tensile stress that a member can withstand on a permanent basis.
tensile stress pulling or stretching force per unit area.

tension the state of being stretched or pulled apart by a tensile force; see tensile force.
tension brace in traditional timber frame construction, a curved convex brace running from post to sole plate for stiffening the frame, often exposed on the exterior of a half-timbered building; see tie rod.
tensioning the application of tensile stress or load to a structure, structural member, prestressing strands, etc.
tension pile, anchor pile; in foundation technology, a pile designed to resist downwards or lateral tensile forces, often a raking pile.

tension reinforcement, tensile reinforcement; reinforcing bars whose primary task is to resist forces in tension rather than shear in reinforced concrete.

tension rod see tie rod.

tension wood reaction wood from the upper surfaces of branches and leaning trunks of a hardwood tree.

tented arch see draped arch.

tent-pole capital an ancient Egyptian stone capital carved in imitation of the billowing fabric structure of a tent.

Egyptian tent-pole capital from the temple of Amun, Karnak, Thutmosis III, (Tuthmosis) c. 1450 BC

teocalli 'house of God'; an ancient Mexican or Central American temple on a truncated pyramid-shaped mound of earth and stone or brick.

teocalli, Temple of the Giant Jaguar (Temple I), Tikal, Guatemala; c. 500 AD

teopan an Aztec teocalli, a stepped pyramid temple.

teopan, Temple of the God of the Winds, Calixtlahuaca, Mexico, 15th to 16th century AD

tephra see tuff.

Teredo spp. see shipworm.

term contract a form of building contract that enables the client to order work over a prescribed period at agreed rates.

Terminalia ivorensis see idigbo; *Terminalia superba* see limba.

terminal unit see air terminal unit; supply air terminal unit.

termination 1 the end or uppermost element or component in a building or structure.
2 the point in a technical installation at which there is an interface, such as an air-conditioning outlet.

termite, white ant; [*Isoptera spp.*] a group of insect species of tropical and sub-tropical origin which cause serious damage to timber.

terms of agreement, terms of contract see conditions of contract.

terpene an oily hydrocarbon obtained from coniferous and citrus trees, used in the manufacture of solvents and germicides.

terra natural pigments such as ochre, umber and chalk made from coloured mineral earth; see earth colour for full list.

terra alba a white powdery form of the mineral gypsum.

terra di Siena see sienna.

terra merita yellow pigment made from saffron or turmeric root.

terra ombre see raw umber.

terra rossa see red oxide paint.

Terra Sienna see sienna.

terra verde see green earth.

terrace 1 a raised external level or platform in a garden, park, protruding from a building, etc. for promenading or leisure.
2 an external raised area in front of a grand building or mansion, often with ornate staircase and balustrade.
3 an urban street lined with similar buildings joined together; the row of buildings in such a street.

terraced block see stepped block.

terraced house, terrace house; one of a row of dwellings joined together by dividing walls, each having its own entrance at ground level and often a small garden; called a row house in USA. See illustration on following page.

terraced house

terracotta a fine-grained red clay from which hollow clay blocks and tiles are manufactured.

terrazzo, terrazzo concrete; a smooth concrete surface finish or thin finish facing of cement and marble or other attractive aggregate chips laid in a screed then ground and polished.

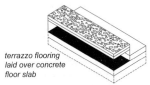

terrazzo flooring laid over concrete floor slab

terrazzo tile a concrete floor tile or wall tile with a surface of prefabricated terrazzo.

tertiary rib see lierne.

tessera Lat.; a small, thin rectangular or polygonal unit of glass, stone or ceramic material used as cladding for walls and floors; its plural is tesserae; see mosaic.

test see testing.

test core a concrete test specimen, often cylindrical, removed from an existing structure by drilling.

test cube, standard concrete cube; a specially cast and hardened sample concrete cube used to compression test a particular batch of concrete.

test cylinder, standard concrete cylinder; a specially cast and hardened sample concrete cylinder used to compression test a particular batch of concrete.

tester, sounding board; a board hung above a podium or pulpit to project the voice of a speaker forwards into the auditorium.

testing a process of defining the properties of a material or component with regard to strength, fire resistance, durability, etc. through a series of standardized controlled tests; types included as separate entries are listed below:

*air test; *compressive strength test; *concrete flow test; *concrete slump test; *cone penetration testing, deep penetration testing; *core test; *cube test; *cylinder test; *destructive testing; *dynamic penetration testing; *fire test; *flow test, see concrete flow test; *gas soundness test; *hydraulic test, see water test; *mirror test; *nondestructive testing; *penetration testing; *pipe system test; *pneumatic test, see air test; *slump test; *smoke test; *soundness test, see gas soundness test; *static penetration testing; *strength test, see compressive strength test; *vane testing;*Vebe test, see VB-consistometer test; *water test; *works cube test.

test piece, test specimen; a specially made concrete cube, cylinder or prism used in the compression testing of hardened concrete.

test pile a foundation pile sunk prior to construction to determine loading conditions, settlement characteristics, etc. in a particular location; see trial pile, preliminary pile.

test pit see trial pit.

test specimen see test piece.

Tetropium castaneum, Tetropium fuscum see spruce beetle.

textile any sheet product woven or bonded from fibres.
textile wallcovering wallcovering whose outer surface is of fabric; cloth 'wallpaper'.

texture a property relating to the smoothness, softness, coarseness, etc. of a surface, or to the structural character of a solid object or granular material.

textured finish, rustic finish, rustication; a rough face treatment for bricks achieved by scoring, blasting or other means.

textured plasterwork, patterned plasterwork; plasterwork whose surface has been rendered or tooled with a scratched, embossed or stamped pattern or texture after application, but prior to setting.

textured wallcovering a wallcovering treated with a surface layer of straw, cork or other granular material to provide a texture.

thallium a soft, bluish, metallic chemical element, **Tl**, used in alloys and as a pesticide.

thalo blue, thalo green see phthalocyanine blue, phthalocyanine green.

thatch a traditional roofing material of bunches of straw, reed or other dried plant matter.

thatch coat a layer of roofing thatch laid over a whole roof plane.

thatched roof a roof whose weatherproofing and insulating material is bundles of straw or reed (or in some cases heather or bark) held down with timber rods, wire, etc.

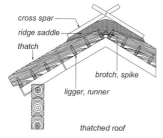

cross spar
ridge saddle
thatch
brotch, spike
ligger, runner

thatched roof

Thénard's blue see cobalt blue.

theodolite, transit (Am); an optical measuring instrument used in surveying for measuring angles in both planes by means of a sighted telescope which can be turned through both horizontal and vertical axes.

thermal break an insulated break in construction between interior and exterior to prevent the passage of heat, and thus cold bridging.

thermal-break profile, thermally broken profile; a proprietary metal window or door framing profile which is manufactured with an integrated plastics bridging piece to minimize loss of heat across its construction.

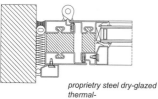

proprietry steel dry-glazed thermal-break profile system

thermal bridge see cold bridge.

thermal capacity, heat capacity, thermal inertia; a measure of the ability of a material or construction to store thermal energy and of how rapidly it warms up, given as the quantity of heat required to raise the temperature of a given construction by unit temperature.

thermal column the rising column of hot air, smoke, ash and other debris over a fire; also called a convection column.

thermal comfort the sensation of physical well-being caused by the effects of temperature, draught and humidity in a space; an empirical measure used in heating and ventilation design for an internal environment.

thermal conductance the rate of flow of thermal energy through a material or construction of given thickness, whose unit of measurement is the C-value.

thermal conduction the transfer of heat through a solid or stagnant liquid or gas by the excitation of adjacent particles within it.

thermal conductivity the rate of flow of thermal energy through a homogeneous material or construction, whose unit of measurement is the K-value.

thermal convection the transfer of heat in a liquid or gas by internal thermal currents.

thermal expansion the increase in size of a material caused by an increase in temperature.

thermal finish see flamed finish.

thermal image see thermogram.

thermal imaging see thermographic imaging.

thermal inertia see thermal capacity.

thermal insulation, heat insulation; a layer of lightweight material added to building construction, often as an interlayer in walls and roofs, etc. to restrict the flow of heat to the outside; insulation for boilers and pipes is called lagging; types included as separate entries are listed below:
*cellulose loose-fill insulation; *expanded polystyrene; *extruded polystyrene; *frost insulation; *glass wool; *loose-fill insulation; *mineral wool; *rock wool; *roof insulation.

thermally broken profile see thermal-break profile.

thermal radiation the transfer of heat in the form of electromagnetic infra-red waves.

thermal resistance a physical quantity whose basic unit is m C/W, the inverse of thermal conductance; see R-value.

thermal storage heater see storage heater.

thermal transmittance the empirical measure of a given construction to conduct heat; its basic unit of measurement is the U-value.

thermal wheel see heat recovery unit.

thermit welding, alumino-thermic welding, thermite welding; a method of fusion welding steel rails in which aluminium powder and iron oxide form a reaction which melts the steel in close proximity.

thermo-differential detector, heat differential detector; a fire detector which measures the rate of temperature rise and issues an alarm at a particular pre-specified value.

thermodynamic equilibrium see heat balance.

thermo-forming a method of forming thermoplastic mouldings by pressing sheet material against a one-sided mould and heating.

thermogram, thermal image; an image of a surface or area taken by a special camera which reacts to infrared radiation to show heat variations in a body or system.
thermographic imaging, thermal imaging; a method of creating pictures based on heat or infrared energy emitted by a viewed scene; used for checking or surveying buildings for missing or damaged insulation, air infiltration or interstitial moisture.

thermoplastics a group of plastics which always soften when heated and regain their hardness on cooling; cf. thermosetting plastics.
thermoplastic adhesive, hot-melt adhesive, hot-melt glue; glue made from a plastic which softens on heating and becomes rigid again on cooling; applied as a strip with a special electric glue gun.

thermoplastic elastomer, TPE; types of rubbery thermoplastics which remain elastic at moderate temperatures but can be easily remoulded to new forms at high temperatures.
thermoplastic glue see thermoplastic adhesive.

thermosetting plastics a group of plastics which undergo an irreversible chemical change on heating and become hard; cf. thermoplastics.
thermosetting adhesive, hot setting glue; a synthetic resin adhesive which sets into its final shape under the application of temperatures above 50°C, and cannot be reshaped by reheating once cool.

thermostat a simple control device which maintains the temperature of a system at a constant level.
thermostatic mixer, thermostatic mixing tap, thermostatic valve; a tap for sinks and showers in which hot and cold water supplies are mixed and their temperature and pressure controlled.

thick bed designating a layer of mortar over 10 mm in thickness, enabling tiling and paving to be laid onto uneven surfaces.

thickening admixture, suspension agent, thickening agent; an admixture included in a concrete mix to improve viscosity and prevent segregation and bleeding of the concrete.

thicknessing machine, thicknesser, panel planer; a milling machine for planing the rear side of a flat board or piece to the required thickness so that both faces are parallel; see surface planer.

thief-resistant lock see security lock.

thimble see wire rope thimble.

thin bed the fixing of tiling and paving in a layer of mortar less than 3 mm thick.
thin bed masonry a modern masonry practice of laying accurately sized and shaped bricks, blocks, tiles, etc. in a bed of specially developed glue mortar, with joints between blocks of less than 2 mm.

thin coat a designation of hard plasters and renders which are designed for application in very thin smooth layers of about 3 mm thick.
thin coat plaster plaster designed to be applied in very thin layers.

thin coat render render designed to be applied in very thin layers so that the texture in the substrate (brickwork, etc.) will be evident in the finish; also called thin section render.

T-hinge see tee hinge.

thinner, diluent, reducer (Am); a volatile liquid which lowers the viscosity of paint and makes it flow more easily.

thin section render see thin coat render.

thin wall plaster final coat plaster which includes a binder that hardens by drying.

thixotropy the property of a gel or viscous liquid to become fluid when shaken, brushed or otherwise agitated; useful for non-drip paints.

tholobate a cylindrical base which supports a dome.

tholos, 1 tholus, beehive tomb; 'vault' (Gk.); originally a dome-shaped corbel-vaulted masonry tomb from the Mycenaean period of ancient Greece.

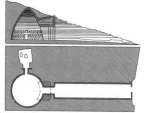

tholos tomb, Treasury of Atreus, 'Tomb of Agamemnon', Mycenae, Greece, 1325–1250 BC

2 any classical Greek building type with a circular plan, especially a round temple surrounded by a colonnade (peripteral temple).

thorium a grey, radioactive, metallic chemical element, **Th**, used in alloys and for filaments in some lamps.

thread 1 a thin cord of natural, synthetic or metal strands which have been wound together.
2 screw thread; the helical moulded windings along the shaft of a screw or bolt, or internally in a nut or cap, which provide a mechanical fixing.
thread gauge a simple device with a number of calibrated saw-toothed blades for defining the gauge of a screw thread.

threading the cutting of external screw threads on a screw.

threaded of a bolt, round bar or pipe, cast or machined with screw threads.
threaded bar see threaded rod.
threaded boss see screwed boss.
threaded pipe see screwed pipe.
threaded rod, studding, threaded bar; a length of threaded stainless or galvanized steel rod on which bolts are screwed to form joints and connections.

threaded rod

three-centred arch, anse de panier, basket arch; an arch whose intrados is composed of curves of differing radii constructed from three centres of curvature; see also pseudo three-centred arch.

three-centred arch

three coat plasterwork, render, float and set; plasterwork for rough surfaces laid in three separate layers; the first filling coat, the second coat which smooths off the surface and provides a key, and the final coat which provides a finish.

three-dimensional referring to an object or geometrical system which has length, breadth and depth.
three-dimensional coordinates a system of defining three-dimensional space on a flat plane, or as a series of numbers, using three mutually perpendicular coordinate planes, by convention referred to as horizontal or 'XY' plane, vertical or 'XZ' plane and side, profile or 'YZ' plane; also called spatial or space coordinates.

three-hinged arch, three-pinned arch; an arch which has pin joints at both its abutments and at its crown.

three-phase referring to electricity supply, usually used for providing power at 415 volts, in which there are three live conductors plus a neutral wire.

three-pinned arch see three-hinged arch.

three-pointed arch see equilateral arch.

three quarter bat, three quarter; a brick cut to three quarters of its length for use in brickwork bonding.

three quarter bat

three quarter brick see king closer.

three-quarter round an ornamental moulding which is semicircular in cross-section; see also bowtell.

three-quarter turn stair a stair which turns through 270° on its ascent.

three-quarter turn stair

threshold 1 the place in a doorway at floor level between two adjacent spaces.
2 the lowest member in a door frame; a door sill.

threshold of hearing in acoustics, the lowest sound pressure which gives rise to a sensation of sound in the human ear.

threshold of pain, pain threshold; in acoustics, the lowest sound intensity which gives rise to a sensation of pain in the human ear.

throat 1 see drip.
2 damper opening; a narrow opening between the outlet of a fireplace and a flue, over which a flue damper is often situated, to improve draught and reduce pressure in the smoke chamber.

throat restrictor an adjustable device to regulate the size of a throat in a flue system or chimney; a smoke damper.

throating see drip.

through 1 designation of a housed component or member which will penetrate right through to the other side of another.
2 a through stone, see parpend.

through and through sawing, 1 flat-sawing, plain sawing, slash sawing; the conversion of logs by sawing into planks or boards longitudinally along the grain.

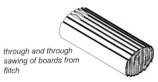

through and through sawing of boards from flitch

2 live sawing; the conversion of logs as above, but by first edging the log to provide a flat even surface on one or both sides; the flitch thus produced is sawn into sections of even dimension.

through mortise and tenon joint see through tenon joint.

through purlin, trenched purlin, laid on purlin; in timber roof construction, a purlin resting on the backs of principal rafters or notched into their upper surface.

through stone see parpend.

through tenon joint a timber mortise and tenon joint whose tenon fully penetrates the piece into which it is fitted.

through tenon joint

throw, blow; in air conditioning and mechanical ventilation, the distance that a jet of air extends out from a supply air inlet to that point at which its air speed is a specified value.

thuja, arborvitae, thuya; [*Thuja spp.*] a genus of East Asian and North American softwoods with weak, soft but durable timber; used for telephone poles, railway sleepers and exterior cladding; widely planted as hedging and as an ornamental in parks and garden and as a potted patio or balcony plant on account of its evergreen foliage; see below.

western red cedar, British Columbian cedar, giant cedar, Pacific red cedar, red cedar, giant arborvitae; [*Thuja plicata*] a North American softwood with weak but durable reddish-brown timber; used for shingles and exterior boarding.

white cedar [*Thuja occidentalis*] a North American softwood with light brown timber; used in boat-building and construction work.

thumb mould a small running mould used to make ornamental plasterwork mouldings.

thumb moulding a decorative moulding whose cross-section is that of a round edged fillet, oblique to the vertical; see also gadroon.

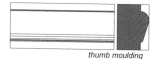

thumb moulding

thumbnail bead moulding a decorative moulding whose cross-section is that of a quadrant of a circle, its upper face convex or concave; often found at the lower join of two perpendicular planes.

thumb nut any nut which can be tightened by hand; see wing nut.

thumb screw a threaded fastener with a large round textured head, designed to be tightened by hand for applications such as removable access panels, computer casing, etc.

thumb screw

thumb slide see slide bolt; snib.

thumbtack see drawing pin.

thumb turn a small sprung handle turned to operate a latch or lock by grasping between thumb and forefinger; often used to operate a door from the inside; called a locking snib if used for locking a bathroom lock.

thunder shakes, cross shakes, lightning shakes; a timber defect caused by cross grain faults in a living tree, resulting in abrupt failure and general weakness.

thuya see thuja.

thyme oil an aromatic essential oil produced from the herb thyme [*Thymus vulgaris*], whose active component is thymol; used in painting to increase the durability of watercolours and as a fungicide and disinfectant.

tie 1 any structural bracing or stabilizing member which resists forces in tension; types included as separate entries are listed below:
*angle tie; *cavity tie, see wall tie; *diagonal tie, see angle tie; *dragon tie, see angle tie; *formwork tie, form tie; *king tie; *recoverable tie; *tie rod; *wall tie.
2 a stirrup in a vertical reinforced concrete component.
3 see clip.

tie beam 1 a beam for tying the ends of supporting posts, walls, rafters or columns together.

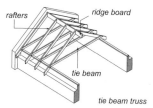

tie beam truss

2 a timber beam for connecting the upper ends of parallel side walls to prevent them from splaying outwards.
3 see ground beam.

tie beam roof in timber roof construction, a rafter roof with tie beams to prevent rafters and underlying walls and posts, etc. from splaying outwards.

tie beam truss 1 a simple roof truss with rafters tied at their lower edges by a horizontal member or tie beam.
2 a roof truss with a large tie beam as the main supporting member for the rafters, struts and other subsidiary members.

tied arch a structural arched beam, usually of steel or concrete, which is braced at its lower extremities by a horizontal tie beam, to prevent them from splaying outwards; a simple bowstring truss used in bridges, etc., often with vertical hangers between upper and lower chords.

bridge with tied arch supporting deck

tie plate a steel or wrought-iron plate bolted to either end of a tie rod to bear the outward thrust of a loaded masonry wall.

tie rod, 1 tension rod, tension brace, hanger; a steel rod by means of which any component such as a balcony or canopy is hung from overlying structure.
2 a steel or wrought-iron rod threaded at either end and often added to construction as a remedial measure; used in conjunction with tie plates to prevent parallel masonry walls and vaulting from buckling outwards under loading.

Tieghemella heckelii see makore.

tierceron in masonry vaulting, a subsidiary rib which connects a point on the ridge rib or central boss with one of the main springers or supports.

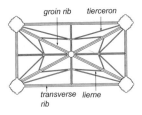

groin rib   tierceron

transverse   lierne
rib

tiering see torching.

tiger grain see wavy grain.

tightening the act of securely fastening a component or assembly with a fixing, locking screw, wedge or other device.

tight knot, adhering knot; a live or dead knot in timber held firmly in place by the surrounding wood.

tight-pin hinge see fast-pin hinge.

tight side, closed face, closed side; the outer side of a veneer sheet as peeled from a flitch, which has less checks and markings from the cutting or slicing than the loose side.

tight size, full size; in glazing, the size of the opening in the frame, measured from inner edge of rebate, in which the pane fits; larger than the sight size.

TIG welding, gas tungsten arc welding (Am), GTA welding (Am), tungsten inert-gas arc welding; a method of welding in which an arc is formed using a tungsten electrode shielded by an inert gas such as argon.

tile any thin, rectangular or polygonal product of mineral, plastics or organic material used in series to form a protective or weatherproof finish; types included as separate entries are listed below:
*brick tile; *ceramic tile; *floor tile; *ornamental tile; *parquet tile, see parquet floor square; *roof tile; *strip tiles, see strip slates; *wall tile.

tile accessory any component such as clips, spacers, special tiles, etc. designed for use in the laying or fixing of tiles.

tile cladding a weatherproof facing of tiles for an exterior wall or other surface; see tiling.

tile clip a small metal fixing for mechanically attaching a roofing or other tile in position.

tile clip

tile cutter any tool used for cutting and cropping tiles; especially a scissor-like tool for cutting or snapping ceramic tiles along prescribed cutting lines of weakness.

tiled finish see tiling.

tiled flooring see tile flooring.

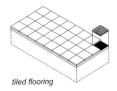

tiled flooring

tiled paving ceramic tiles laid horizontally as a hardwearing external surface.

tiled roof, tile roof; a roof whose weatherproofing is provided by roofing tiles.

tiled roofing see roof tiling.

tiled upstand see tile fillet.

tiled valley in tiled roofing, a valley formed entirely of specially formed tiles.

tile facing see tiling.

tile fillet, tile listing, tiled upstand; roofing tiles set in mortar below a parapet or abutment to act as a flashing; a tiled upstand.

tile fitting any specially shaped roofing tile.

tile flooring floor surfacing of laid tiles.

tile grout a cementitious compound applied to fill the joints between adjacent laid ceramic tiles.

tile hanging, vertical tiling, weather tiling; tiles hung vertically in overlapping courses as an external cladding for walls.

tile layer see tiler.

tile listing see tile fillet.

tiler, tile layer; a tradesman or skilled labourer who lays tiles.

tile roof see tiled roof.

Tilia spp. see lime.

tiling 1 the trade of laying tiles with butting joints as flooring, wall covering, etc.
2 the resulting surface or construction.
3 tiled finish, tile cladding, tile facing; a wall, floor or ceiling surface laid with a facing of tiles.
see roof tiling, floor tiling, wall tiling.

tiling base the wall or floor surface below which tiles are fixed; see substrate.

tiling batten one of a series of timber strips fixed across rafters or decking as a base for tiling.

tiling mortar, bedding mortar, fixing mortar; mortar used for fixing ceramic tiles to a wall.

tiling pattern the various patterns in which ceramic and other tiles can be laid.

tiling substrate see tiling base.

tilting drum mixer a concrete mixer with a rotating hinged drum in which the constituent materials are mixed, which can be tilted to enable emptying.

tilting fillet see doubling piece.

tilt-up formwork special formwork in which concrete is cast horizontally, then rotated to enable lifting to another location; used for casting prefabricated units.

timber, 1 lumber (Am); wood used for constructional purposes.
2 wood converted from sawlogs.
see list of species of tree from which softwood is obtained under softwood.
see list of species of tree from which hardwood is obtained under hardwood.

timber-based board see wood-based panel product, coreboard, particleboards, chipboard, plywoods.

timber board 1 a planed or sawn flattish section of timber used in finished flooring, external cladding, linings, etc.
2 timberboard, see bargeboard.

timber cladding cladding of sawn timber boards or joinery panels for the frames of walls, floors and roofing; also called timber facing, or, if external, weatherboarding.

timber construction building activity in which the principal framing material is wood or wood products for wall, floor or roof construction, log walls, panel products, etc.; any building or structure produced in this way, primarily of wooden parts; see timber frame.

timber defect an imperfection which lowers the quality of piece of sawn or dressed timber; see seasoning defect, sawing defect.

timber door a door whose leaf and frame are made primarily from timber; see also glazed timber door.

timber facing see timber cladding.

timber flooring any flooring material whose finish is treated wood, veneer or wood product; also generally called wood flooring or wooden flooring; types included as separate entries are listed below:
*block flooring, see end-grain wood block flooring; *board flooring; *chipboard flooring; *end-grain wood block flooring; *floorboards; *overlay flooring; *parquet flooring; *plank flooring, see wide plank flooring; *plywood flooring; *puncheon flooring; *solid timber flooring; *strip flooring, see wood strip flooring;

*timber flooring; *wide plank flooring; *wide strip flooring, see wide plank flooring; *wood block flooring, see end-grain wood block flooring; *wood board flooring; *wood flooring; *wood strip flooring.*

timber frame a structural frame for a building, partition, etc. made of timber sections fixed at their ends; see A-frame, balloon frame, platform frame.

timber-framed building, timber frame building; any building whose structural frame is of timber members clad and lined with sheet material, especially one with a frame of vertical spaced timber studs clad with sawn boards; see half-timbered building.

timber glazed door see glazed timber door.

timber joint a mechanical, glued or nailed joint formed between two or more timber members; types included as separate entries are listed below: *bridle joint; *double tenon joint; *cabinetmaker's joint, see mortise and tenon joint; *carpenter's joint, see framing joint; *corner joint; *crosslap joint, see cross half lap joint; *dado joint, see housed joint; *dovetail joint; *halved joint, halving joint, halflap joint; *housed joint, housing joint; *joinery joints, see mortise and tenon joint; *lengthening joint; *mortise and tenon joint; *scarf joint; *tenon joint, see mortise and tenon joint.*

timber lath a split timber batten fixed to a base in rows over a frame as a base for plasterwork; see lathing.

timber lathing a base for plaster made from thin strips of timber fixed to a base or structural members; see bruised lath.

timber lining any covering of boards, plywood and other wood products for the inner surface of a wall frame or structure.

timber pile a foundation pile hewn or fabricated from timber.

timber roof a roof whose structure or skeleton is of timber members.

timber scaffolding scaffolding whose structural members are timber sections.

timber seasoning see seasoning.

timber subsill the lower framing member of a window opening; a timber plate incorporated into wall construction onto which a window frame can be attached.

timber trim, joinery profile, joinery moulding; a narrow strip of machined wood used in construction as decorative edging, for covering unsightly joints, glazing beads, etc.

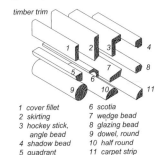

timber trim

1 *cover fillet*
2 *skirting*
3 *hockey stick, angle bead*
4 *shadow bead*
5 *quadrant*
6 *scotia*
7 *wedge bead*
8 *glazing bead*
9 *dowel, round*
10 *half round*
11 *carpet strip*

timber truss a truss whose members are wooden.

timber window a window whose frame is made primarily from treated timber; a timber-framed window; see also composite window.

timber window

timberwork the construction work of a building on site involving timber, carried out by a carpenter; see also joinery, carpentry.

time control the automatic switching on and off of lighting and other technical systems for preset periods using control gear containing a timer device.

time for completion see contract time.

time lock a lock controlled by a timer device which permits opening only at specified times.

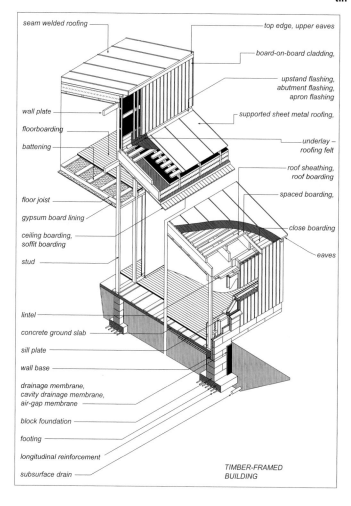

seam welded roofing

top edge, upper eaves

board-on-board cladding,

upstand flashing,
abutment flashing,
apron flashing

wall plate

supported sheet metal roofing,

floorboarding

underlay –
roofing felt

battening

roof sheathing,
roof boarding

spaced boarding,

floor joist

gypsum board lining

close boarding

ceiling boarding,
soffit boarding

eaves

stud

lintel

concrete ground slab

sill plate

wall base

drainage membrane,
cavity drainage membrane,
air-gap membrane

block foundation

footing

longitudinal reinforcement

TIMBER-FRAMED
BUILDING

subsurface drain

timer, timer switch; a switch operated by a mechanism which turns an electric current on or off after a specific duration. **2** push-button timer; a switch used for corridor lighting, etc. which, when pressed, will open a circuit for a specified duration before closing it automatically.

Timonox a trade name for antimony white pigment.

tin a chemically durable, soft, pale metal, **Sn**, with a low melting point; often used for the protective coating of other metals such as iron and copper.

tin bronze an alloy of copper with tin; true bronze.

tin plate steel sheet manufactured with a protective coating of tin, used especially to make tin cans, pots, etc.

tin plating see tinning.

tingle see clip.

tinner's hammer a hammer with a square flat face for beating and dressing sheetmetal panels.

tinning, tin plating; the coating of a metal such as copper or iron with a thin protective layer of tin; also the result of this process.

tin snips, hand shears, tin shears; a tough, scissor-like hand tool with high-leverage handles for cutting sheetmetals.

tint, shade; a colour formed when a number of pigments are mixed together; a body tint is when colour is added to the whole thickness of a material (glass, concrete) rather than just one surface.

tinted glass transparent glass coloured either with a body tint or with a coloured interlayer; see also body-tinted glass.

tinted solar control glass, heat-absorbing glass, absorbing glass; glass manufactured with a body tint to absorb heat from the sun, reduce glare, etc.

tinter see stainer.

tinting strength, staining power; the ability of a coloured pigment to modify the colour of white paint.

tip-up window see horizontal pivot window.

titanium a grey, hard, light metal, **Ti**, which is corrosion resistant and used for the toughening of steel; some compounds are used as pigments.

titanium dioxide a white, non-poisonous, chemical compound, TiO_2, used as an opaque pigment in paints (titanium white) and in plastics.

titanium oxide see titanium dioxide.

titanium pigment see titanium white.

titanium white, blanc titane, titanium pigment; a permanent and opaque white pigment whose chief component is titanium dioxide; suitable for use in oils and glues.

titano gypsum the mineral gypsum occurring as a by-product of the manufacture of titanium oxide.

Titanox a trade name for titanium white pigment.

title block an area or table of text located at the bottom right-hand corner of a design drawing, containing information about its content, scale, designer and date; also called a title panel.

toe nailing see skew nailing.

toggle see toggle bolt, hollow-wall plug, hollow-wall anchor.

toggle bolt a metal threaded fastener for fixing to drywall or hollow wall surfaces by means of a pivoted or sprung 'job' which is clamped against the reverse side of construction once the bolt has been pushed through a bored hole; see spring toggle, gravity toggle.

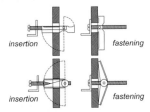

insertion   *fastening*

insertion   *fastening*

toilet 1 a room or building furnished with one or a number of water closet suites, urinals and wash basins; variously called a lavatory, convenience, cloakroom, closet or WC.

2 a receptacle for collecting human waste, a WC or water closet suite.

toilet lock see bathroom lock.

tolerance an acceptable range of variation in size or magnitude of a manufactured, supplied or constructed object to that specified; a permissible range of inaccuracy in measuring.

toluidine red an organic solvent-based vivid red pigment.

tondo a round painting, or a carving set in round space; see also medallion.

tondo

tone see colour saturation.

tongue 1 the projection along one edge of a tongue and groove board.
2 see return latch.

tongue and groove, tongued and grooved, t and g, t&g; referring to joints, boards and other sheet products whose edges are matched with tongue and groove joints.

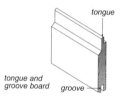

tongue

tongue and groove board   groove

tongue and groove boarding see matchboarding, open tongue and groove boarding, rough t and g board.

tongued and grooved see tongue and groove.

tongued and grooved board any building board machined with tongued and grooved edges.

tongued and grooved chipboard chipboard whose edges have been milled with a tongue and groove, used for matched flooring and sheathing.

tongue and groove joint, tongued and grooved, t and g, t&g; a joint for flush timber boarding, chipboard, etc. in which each board is milled with a flange or tongue along one long edge and a channel or groove along the other, designed to fit into one another when the boards are laid edge-on as flooring and cladding; see also barefaced tongued and grooved joint.

tongue and groove jointing, matching; the milling of the edges of building boards with a tongue and groove.

tooled finish any stonework finish in which the marks of the tools are evident.

tooling, hacking, scabbling; the working of the surface of exposed concrete or stone with a chisel, point tool or mechanical device to produce a patterned or textured finish or to roughen the surface as a key for a finish.

toothed plate connector, bulldog plate; in timber frame construction, a toothed metal plate placed between two timbers bolted together to strengthen the joint.

toothed plate connector

toothed plate fastener see nail plate.

toothed washer see tooth washer.

toothing the toothed end of a partially laid brickwork wall formed by overlapping alternate courses, used for bonding subsequent work; see also reverse toothing.

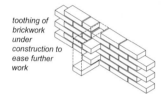

toothing of brickwork under construction to ease further work

tooth ornament see dogtooth.

tooth tool see patent claw chisel.

tooth washer, toothed washer; a circular metal washer whose inner or outer edge is stamped with crimped serrations to provide a tight bolted joint by compression; see internal tooth washer, external tooth washer.

tooth washers

top chord see upper chord.

top course tile a special roof tile which is shorter than other tiles; used for the uppermost course in roofing.

top dressing the addition of any mineral, organic or chemical material to the surface of planted and landscaped areas to improve the quality of the soil.

top edge the upper part of a sloping roof plane at a ridge or abutment.

top form formwork used for casting and supporting the upper side of concrete slabs, walls, etc.; top formwork, in full.

top hung referring to a window, casement or hatch whose opening leaf is hinged at its upper edge.

top-hung casement window, awning window a window type whose opening casement is hinged at its upper edge.

top-hung casement window

top light a narrow glazed casement at the top of a window unit, hinged at the top; any glazing above a main window, partition or door; see fanlight.

topography 1 the measuring, surveying and representation in map form of natural and artificial features in the landscape.
2 ground profile, contour; the shape of an area of land according to the changes in vertical level of its surface.

topping 1 see concrete topping, wearing course.
2 the first stage of the sharpening of a saw by levelling of the tips of its teeth with a file.

topping out the stage in a project when the structure of a building under construction has reached its full height or is completed, often marked by a small on-site ceremony.

top rail the upper framing member of a window casement or door leaf.

top raker the uppermost slanting prop in a raking shore.

top reinforcement main reinforcement for a reinforced concrete beam or slab placed near the upper surface to resist tensile forces near junctions, fixed ends and cantilevers.

topsoil soil occurring at the earth's surface, rich in root, fibrous and organic material; see also growing medium.

torch see soldering torch, blowlamp (blowtorch).

torching, rendering, tiering; a traditional practice in tiled and slate roofing whereby lime mortar is laid under the heads of roof tiles and slates as a secondary fastening and to prevent the passage of drifting snow.

tori plural of torus.

torn grain a sawing defect resulting in wood fibres frayed loose at the surface after cutting and converting timber; caused by a blunt saw or wet timber.

torque the magnitude of an axial twisting or rotating action produced by a force, equal to the actual force multiplied by the perpendicular distance from the centre of the axis about which it acts.

torque wrench a manual wrench with a gauge or meter to indicate the amount of torque transferred to the nut or bolt, and so control its final tightness.

torse see wreath.

torse grain see spiral grain.

torsion in mechanics, a twisting action on an object caused by two forces working in opposite directions perpendicular to its main axis.

torso 1 a statue of a man or beast lacking limbs and a head.
2 a spiral column in the architecture of the middle ages.

tortil see wreath.

torus pl. tori; a three-dimensional shape formed by the rotation of a circle or conic section through 360° around a point; plural is tori; a decorative convex moulding, larger than an astragal, found in classical bases; see spira.

Torx head screw a screw whose head has a patented star-shaped or serrated indentation, tightened with a special screw bit; usually used on finishing and precision work.

total cost the cost of all works, labour, construction materials and design in a construction project.

total going, run (Am), going; the horizontal dimension of a stair flight as measured on plan.

touch dry, dry to touch; in painting, a stage in drying at which finger marks will not be left on the painted surface.

touching up in painting and decorating, the covering of small missed or damaged areas with paint after the main body of painting work has been carried out.

toughened glass, tempered glass; glass that has been heated and then cooled rapidly during manufacture to produce controlled internal stresses as strengthening and to make it less dangerous on shattering; cf. annealed glass; see chemically strengthened glass, heat-soaked glass.

typical shattering of toughened glass into small pieces to avoid large and dangerous shards

toughness the property of a material to withstand repeated deformations without breaking, through ductility and tensile strength.

tourelle, touret see turret.

tourmaline a colourful boron aluminium silicate mineral used for its unusual thermoelectrical properties and as a gemstone.

tow rough fibrous material made from hemp and flax used for caulking log buildings.

tower any tall, slender structure, building or part of a building.

tower block a tall apartment block containing a number of flats on many floors.

tower bolt a large barrel bolt.

tower crane a high site crane with hoisting equipment, a control booth and a counterweighted boom or jib fixed atop a tall trussed stanchion, either static or running on rails.

town plan the layout of streets and activities in a town; a statutory document which stipulates types of use, land use restrictions, layout of areas for residential and other forms of use, etc.

town planner, planner; a person or organization responsible for designing and developing town, area and general plans.

town planning see planning.

town planning department, planning department, planning office; the administrative department of a local authority which prepares town plans for the regional area.

townscape the visual and spatial quality of streets, buildings, parks, squares and other elements in a built-up area.

Town truss a type of lattice beam patented by Ithiel Town in 1820, consisting of a series of fairly densely spaced crossing diagonals tied between an upper and lower chord.

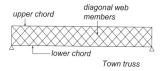

Town truss

toxicity the measure of the poisonousness of a material or substance with regard to living organisms.

toxic waste waste material or products left over from a process or use which may pose a contamination hazard to the environment and should be disposed of using special measures.

TPE thermoplastic elastomer.

trabeated describing a structural system based on the use of columns and beams; see post and beam construction.

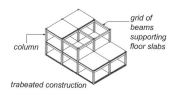

trabeated construction

trabs, trabes; Lat.; a large principal beam, often a main rafter or architrave in classical architecture, or one supporting a crucifix in a church.

tracer a large masonry chisel used for splitting rock.

tracery Gothic ornamental stone and woodwork decoration carved into an intricate vertical and interwoven framework of ribs for the upper parts of openings such as windows or perforated screens, or for the surface of vaults and walls; types included as separate entries are listed below:
*bar tracery; blind tracery, blank tracery; *branch tracery, astwerk; *decorated tracery; *fan tracery, fanwork; *flamboyant tracery; flowing, curvilinear, undulating tracery; *geometrical tracery, geometric tracery; *intersecting tracery; Kentish tracery; *loop tracery; *rectilinear, panel, perpendicular tracery; *plate tracery; *reticulated tracery; *Y-tracery.*

trachelion, necking, trachelium; the upper part of the shaft of a classical Doric column, below the shaft ring and above the hypotrachelion; sometimes also called a collarino.

trachytic tuff see trass.

track 1 a preformed steel or plastics section for guiding and supporting rollers in the operating mechanism of a sliding door, curtain, etc.; see also lighting track, suspension track.
2 a small unpaved road or route, or an assembly of rails, sleepers and fixings for a rail transport system.

trade one of the various skilled or semi-skilled technical on-site occupations, often demanding training, required in the construction of a building.
trade contractor see specialized contractor.
trade discount a reduction in prices offered by a supplier to trade customers from which the client may be entitled to benefit under terms of a building contract.
trade name the name by which a product or material is sold.
trades foreman a contractor's representative responsible for supervising construction work on site carried out by specific tradesmen.
tradesman a person skilled in a particular job of work, employed on a construction site.

trailer mixer a mobile concrete mixer designed to be towed by a vehicle.

Trametes pini see red ring rot.

trammel a compass-like device used as a guide for making an elliptical plastering moulding.

trammel rod a timber strip used in conjunction with a trammel for making an elliptical plastering moulding.

transenna a perforated screen in an early Christian church; originally referring to early forms of window with small panes made from thin sheets of translucent marble or alabaster.

transenna

transept the transverse space to either side of the crossing in a cruciform church or cathedral, the 'arms' of the cross which meet the nave and chancel.

transfer 1 in prestressed concrete, the transfer of loading from the concrete to the prestressing tendons; see also detensioning.
2 patterns, lettering, symbols or figures, vehicles and plants printed onto thin adhesive transparent plastic sheet and applied as embellishment to drawings.

transfer moulding a method of forming thermoplastics and thermosetting plastics products by heating material in a mould then applying pressure to force it through channels into its final shape; used for delicate castings.

transformer an electrical device for transmuting electrical energy to a different voltage and current level with minimal power loss.

transit see theodolite.

transitional igneous rock see hypabyssal rock.

transitional style a style in architecture which occurs during the change from one style to another, such as from Romanesque to Gothic or from Gothic to Renaissance.

transit mixer see truck mixer.

translucency, obscurance; the property of a material to allow the passage of light without being fully transparent.
translucent glass see diffuse reflection glass.

transmittance see light transmittance, thermal transmittance.

transom, transome; a horizontal framing member in a window or door frame, between two openable panels such as a door and fanlight above, or between two sashes in the same frame; also the horizontal bar in a cross.

fanlight

transom

mullion

transom light, transom window see fanlight.

transparency 1 the property of a material which permits the undiffused passage of light through it; a transparent material such as glass is also described as clear.
2 a sheet of clear acrylic or other plastic with an image or text printed on one side; used in conjunction with an overhead projector or other projecting device; a print applied to transparent or translucent material such as plastics or paper.

transparent gold ochre see Turner's yellow.

transparent mirror glass glass treated with a thin metallic foil to reflect most of the light which falls on it, rendering it transparent under certain lighting conditions and a mirror under others.

transparent oxide of chromium see viridian.

transverse arch one of a series of arches crossing the main body of a vaulted building such as a Romanesque basilica church, supported on columns on ether side of the nave; an arch in a groin, rib or fan vaulted roof which separates one vaulted bay from another; any similar or crosswise arch in a modern structure.

transverse beam see cross-beam.

transverse joint see cross joint.

transverse reinforcement see lateral reinforcement.

transverse rib, 1 a lateral protrusion in a reinforcing bar.

2 arc doubleau; a rib which runs across the space at the edge of a rib vault.
transverse ridge rib a horizontal rib which runs across the space at the ridge of a rib vault.

transverse section, cross-section; a drawing representing a cut through the shorter dimension of a site, building or object.

transverse warping see cup.

transverse wave a waveform in which displacement is perpendicular to the direction of propagation.

trap a device or construction at a drain, gully or drainage outlet, filled with water to prevent the passage of foul air from a sewer back into the building or area.

trapdoor a horizontal hinged hatch in a floor; see also access door.
trapdoor handle a device or fitting for pulling opening a trapdoor.

trapless gully a drainage gully with no trap, through which gases from the drain can freely escape.

trapped gully a gully containing a trap to prevent gases and odours escaping from the drain to which it is connected.

traprock see diabase.

trass, trachytic tuff; a variety of volcanic tuff which, by virtue of its hydraulic properties, is often used as an admixture in cement in underwater construction.

trave see bay.

travertine a variety of porous, pale-coloured limestone, tufa, deposited by springwater, often containing fossils; used in building for decorative stonework and ornament.

tray see metal tray.

tray decking see profiled sheeting.

trayle see vignette.

tread the horizontal upper surface of a step, or the shallow platform which forms a step; types listed as separate entries are listed below:
*parallel tread, see flier; *tapered tread, see tapered step; *wheel tread, see winder.
tread plate see chequerplate.

tread width in stair design, the horizontal distance from the nosing to the rear edge of a tread, often greater than the going.

treated plywood plywood whose veneers or adhesive have been treated with preservatives or resins.

treatment the application of a process, material coating, etc. to a surface, object or component in order to improve its properties; see also acoustic treatment, surface treatment, air treatment.

trefoil a decorative design consisting of three leaf motifs or lobes radiating outwards from a point; see also pointed trefoil.

trefoil motif

trefoil arch an arch composed of three lobes or foils in a cloverleaf arrangement.

trefoil arch

trefoil moulding a decorative moulding with a series of trefoil motifs joined end on end, primarily found in heraldic designs; also called a cloverleaf moulding.

trefoil moulding

trellis a loose screen with a grid or rows of jointed timber strips for supporting climbing plants.

tremie concrete underwater concrete pumped into place using a tremie, a long flexible pipe with a funnel-shaped upper end, into which concrete is poured, whose other end is located in the fresh concrete which has already been placed.

trenail a large hardwood pin, peg or nail used for fastening traditional timber joints.

trench a long, narrow excavation in earth, or similar longitudinal cut or machining in a surface such as wood.

trenched joint see notched joint.

trenched purlin see through purlin.

trench-fill foundation a rough foundation constructed by excavating a longitudinal excavation, laying reinforcing bars, and filling the excavation with concrete, without the need for formwork.

trench-fill foundation

trenching saw see grooving saw.

trench sheeting see sheet piling.

trestle see saw horse.

trial hole see trial pit.

trial pile in foundation technology, a pile sunk prior to foundation construction to determine the suitability of its functioning and design; see also test pile, preliminary pile.

trial pit, trial hole, test pit (Am); in site investigation, an excavation made on site prior to commencement of construction to ascertain the soil type, existing services, depth of bedrock, etc.

triangular arch an arch composed of two flat leaning slabs which meet at an apex to form a triangular opening; not a true arch.

triangular arch

triangular fillet see angle fillet.

triangular pediment see pediment.

triangulation 1 a method of surveying and mapping which employs trigonometry to divide an area into a grid of triangles between known fixed points.

2 in structures, the use of diagonal struts in pin-jointed frames to provide stiffening.
3 in drawing composition, the use of diagonals to define key points and assess proportions.

tribune 1 an apse in a basilica.
2 a gallery in a church above a side aisle and opening out onto a nave.
3 an important room in an Italian villa, a balcony or gallery therein.
4 a raised platform for a speaker; see tribunal.

tribunal arch an upper arch between the choir and apse of a church or basilica.

trickle ventilator a venting device incorporated into a high performance window unit to permit ventilation without draught caused by an opening.

trifoliated arch a decorative arch whose intrados is composed of three lobes or foils in a cloverleaf arrangement, and whose extrados is a round or pointed arch; especially found in Gothic architecture; see round trifoliated arch, pointed trifoliated arch.

triforium in Romanesque or Early Gothic religious architecture, an inwardly facing open wall passage, often arcaded, running above the nave arcade below clerestory level in a cathedral.

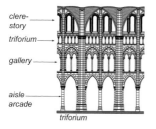

clerestory
triforium
gallery
aisle
arcade

triforium

triglyph in classical architecture, one of a series of grooved blocks or panels which line a Doric frieze and are separated by metopes; these vertical grooves, called glyphs, are arranged in groups of three.

trim a narrow strip of wood or other material used in construction as surface decoration or for covering a joint or seam, or a gap between frame and adjacent construction in a window or door opening; see architrave; a generic term for all thin sections of timber or other material attached as mouldings, beads, rails, and cover strips; see also door trim, window trim, moulding, perimeter trim, timber trim.

trimetric projection 1 'three measurements'; in general, any axonometric or oblique projection drawing in which lines parallel to all three main axes are drawn at different scales; scales and angles are chosen to produce the most realistic depictions.
2 in particular, any of a number of standardized axonometric projections in which the X and Y axes are drawn at different angles above the horizontal and the Z axis is vertical; all three axes have different scales.

trimmed beam, trimmed joist; in timber frame construction, a beam shortened to accommodate an opening or otherwise cropped, carried by a trimmer joist or beam at the edge of the opening.

trimmed rafter a rafter carried by a trimmer at the edge of an opening in roof construction.

trimmed veneer a sheet of veneer of which at least one edge has been cut straight before gluing.

trimmer, trimmer beam; in timber-framed construction, a lateral member which frames the edge of an opening in a floor or roof, and bears the ends of trimmed beams or joists; also known as a trimmer joist.

trimmer's hammer a lightweight hammer used by a flooring carpenter.

trimming 1 the removal of the ends of batches of converted timber sections to produce pieces of the same lengths for shipping and sale.
2 in timber frame construction, the cutting and framing of timbers around an opening.

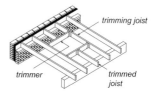

trimming joist
trimmer
trimmed joist

trimming axe see masonry axe.

trimming joist in framed floor and wall construction, a joist bounding an opening, from which trimmers are supported.

trimming rafter in timber roof construction, a rafter, from which trimmers are supported, which bounds an opening in the roof.

tringle see listel.

Trinidad bitumen a form of lake asphalt which used to be imported from Trinidad.

tripartite vault a masonry vault sprung on three points of support, triangular in plan and composed of three curved roof surfaces.

tripartite vault

tri-phosphor lamp a fluorescent lamp with good colour rendering and circuit efficacy whose colour spectrum is made up of three distinct peaks.

triple glazing glazing in which three parallel layers of glass separate the inside and outside of a building to provide thermal and acoustic insulation.

triple-glazed unit a sealed glazed unit made of three parallel sheets of glass sealed around air gaps.

triple-glazed window a window thermally insulated with three successive panes of glass, either forming a sealed unit, glazed individually or a combination of the two.

triple roof see trussed roof.

Triplochiton scleroxylon see obeche.

tripod a portable three-legged support used as an adjustable but steady mounting for an optical instrument.

trip switch see overload trip, circuit breaker.

tritium a radioactive isotope of hydrogen.

triumphal arch (Lat. arcus triumphalis); a large arched monument constructed in a public urban place to commemorate a great event, usually a victory in war; modern equivalents in urban settings.

trochilus a deeply recessed moulding, ovoid in cross-section; also called gorge; see scotia.

troughed sheeting metal and plastics profiled sheeting formed with a series of stiffening toothed protrusions in profile; steel troughed sheeting has structural strength and is often used for decking.

troughed sheeting

troughed sheet roofing thin non-structural sheetmetal or plastics troughed sheeting used as roofing material.

trough mould a formwork mould for producing an elongated recess or channel in a concrete slab.

trough roof see M-roof.

trough vault a barrel vault whose ends are closed with vaults.

trough vault

trowel a hand tool for the application, jointing, smoothing and shaping of plaster, filler, mortar, etc. by means of a flat metal blade fixed to a short handle; types included as separate entries are listed below:
*angle trowel; *bricklayer's trowel, brick trowel; *corner trowel, see angle trowel; *external angle trowel; *finishing trowel; *gauging trowel; *helicopter, see power trowel; *internal angle trowel, inside corner trowel; *jointing trowel; *laying-on trowel, see plasterer's trowel; *machine trowel, see power trowel; *margin trowel; *mason's trowel, masonry trowel, see bricklayer's trowel; *mechanical trowel,

see power trowel; *notched trowel; *outside corner trowel, see external angle trowel; *plasterer's trowel; *power trowel; *rotary trowel, see power trowel; *smoothing trowel, see finishing trowel; *spatula; *square external angle trowel; *square internal angle trowel; *Swiss trowel; *twitcher trowel, twitcher.

trowels

trowel-finished rendering rendering whose wet surface has been worked with a hand-held trowel to produce a smooth, even finish.

trowelled finish a finish for concrete produced by smoothing with a power or hand trowel.

trowelled plastering see hand-plastering.

truck mixer, transit mixer; a concrete mixer attached to a vehicle, which can mix the concrete in transit to site.

true fresco see buon fresco.

trulay rope a proprietary name for pre-formed rope.

trullisatio see roughcast.

Trumeau a masonry column, pillar or pier between two openings, often in religious buildings supporting the centre of the tympanum in an arched doorway or window.

trumeau figure a carved statuesque figure decorating a trumeau, depicting a religious person or saint.

trumpet capital a Gothic capital whose diameter increases in size towards the top; also called a bell capital.

trumpet capital

trunking, raceway (Am); openable casing for cables and wiring in an electric installation.

trunnel see gutta.

truss, lattice structure; a structural element consisting of a number of members pin-jointed at their ends to form a beam which resists loads by means of triangulation, in particular one of steel or timber used for supporting floors and roofs; types included as separate entries are listed below:

*arch braced roof truss; *arched truss, arch truss, see trussed arch; *attic truss; *base cruck truss; *Belfast truss; *Belgian truss, see Fink truss; *bowstring truss; *closed cruck truss; *collar and tie beam truss; *composite truss; *couple truss, see coupled rafters; *cruck truss; *double hammer beam truss; *fan truss; *Fink truss; *fish-bellied truss; *flat top truss, flat truss; *French truss, see Fink truss; *full cruck truss, see closed cruck truss; *half truss; *hammer-beam roof truss; *Howe truss; *joggle truss; *king post roof truss; *mansard roof truss; *open cruck truss; *plane truss; *polygonal truss; *Pratt truss; *principal roof truss; *queen post truss; *queen strut roof truss; *roof truss; *scissors truss; *secondary roof truss; *tie beam truss; *timber truss; *Town truss; *Vierendeel truss; *Warren truss; *W truss, see Fink truss.*

trussed a designation of structural components constructed of longitudinal members which are triangulated in the form of a truss.

trussed arch a truss in which both upper and lower chords are arches, with diagonal web members between; also known as an arch truss.

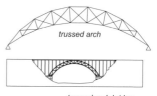

trussed arch

trussed arch bridge

trussed beam, framed beam, lattice beam; a compound beam of upper and lower chords which take compression and tension stresses respectively, and intermediate triangulated struts which hold them apart.

trussed construction any triangulated frame construction braced to form a rigid loadbearing structure.

trussed purlin a trussed beam which functions as a purlin.

trussed purlin roof a roof with purlins which are trussed beams.

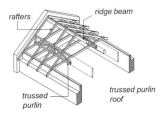

rafters
ridge beam
trussed purlin
trussed purlin roof

trussed rafters in pitched roof construction, coupled rafters with or without subsidiary supporting or bracing members.

trussed rafter roof a pitched roof with all opposite pairs of common rafters triangularly braced.

trussed roof, triple roof; a roof structure of roof trusses held together by purlins.

truss-out scaffolding scaffolding supported by and projecting from the building for which it has been erected; used where the ground cannot provide support.

truss plate construction timber frame construction in which timber members are held together by a toothed metal plate called a truss plate; see nail plate.

try and mitre square, combination square; an adjustable carpenter's tool used as a try square, mitre square, level, marking gauge, plumb, and straight edge.

trying plane see jointer plane.

try square a measuring instrument for marking lines perpendicular to a surface or checking perpendicularity, consisting of a wooden stock and straight metal blade fixed at right angles to one another.

T-section, T-bar, tee section; a structural steel section formed by rolling, whose uniform cross-section resembles a letter T with equal width of flanges.

T-square a T-shaped drawing instrument for ruling straight parallel lines, with a wooden or plastic ruler and perpendicular piece guided by hooking it over the edge of a drawing board or table.

Tsuga spp. see hemlock.

tube 1 any rigid hollow product of plastics, ceramic or metal, used for structure, framing, electrical protection, conveying liquids or gases, etc.
2 see fluorescent lamp, neon tube.

tube conveyor, pneumatic document conveyor; an in-house system for conveying light goods such as documents or money in sealed units along pipelines from one room or floor to another, driven by compressed air.

tubular pile see pipe pile.

tubular saw see hole saw.

tubular scaffolding scaffolding of steel or aluminium tubes, often with proprietary jointing and shackles, supporting scaffolding boards or grilles.

tubular section see hollow section.

tuck-in in bituminous roofing, the edge of a sheet of bitumen felt skirting tucked into a chase in an abutment.

tuck pointing in brickwork jointing, light-coloured mortar pushed into darker coloured pointing to create the illusion of thin joints between bricks.

Tudor architecture architecture in England during the reign of the Tudors (Henry VII to Elizabeth I, 1485–1603), evident principally in secular palaces and country houses, and characterized by the gradual transition from Gothic to Renaissance elements.

Tudor arch, four-centred pointed arch; a pointed arch composed of four arc segments struck from different points, sometimes with straight upper edges; see also pseudo four-centred arch.

Tudor arch

Tudor flower an English Gothic decorative motif depicting a stylized ivy leaf.

tudor flower

Tudor rose a decorative design of a red and white rose combined in a single motif; the symbol of a united England after 1485.

tudor rose

tufa a porous sedimentary rock, usually limestone, formed from the deposits of mineral-enriched springs or pools; see calcareous tufa.

tuff, volcanic tuff, tephra; volcanic rock formed by the consolidation of ash and other ejected products of volcanic action; used as building stone; see trass (trachytic tuff), ignimbrite (welded tuff).

tuffite rock consisting of volcanic tuff mixed with sedimentary rock.

tufted carpet a type of carpet with pile tufts mechanically inserted into a prewoven backing by needles.

tulipwood, American whitewood, canary wood, yellow poplar; [*Liriodendron tulipifera*] a hardwood from North America and Europe with soft greenish-brown timber; used for plywood and interior furniture.

tumbler one of a number of pivoted pins or discs which holds the bolt in a lock mechanism fast until lifted with a suitable key.

tung oil, China wood oil; a high-quality drying oil pressed from the nuts of the Chinese trees *Aleurites fordii* and *Aleurites montana*; used as a vehicle in industrial varnishes to produce tough strong coatings.

tungsten, wolfram; a heavy, grey metal, **W**, which has a high melting point; used for the filaments of electric lamps and as an alloy in steel.

tungsten carbide a very hard alloy of the metal tungsten used for tipping the edges of cutting tools.

tungsten-halogen lamp see halogen lamp.

tungsten inert-gas arc welding see TIG welding.

tungsten steel steel alloyed with tungsten and small quantities of carbon.

tunnel formwork see apartment formwork.

tunnel vault see barrel vault.

tupelo, black gum (Am); [*Nyssa spp.*] a lightweight hardwood from North America with grey sapwood and creamy yellow heartwood; used for railway sleepers, flooring, furniture and plywood.

turette see turret.

turf roof, grass roof; a roof whose weatherproofing is provided by growing turf laid over a waterproof membrane; see also green roof.

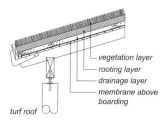

vegetation layer
rooting layer
drainage layer
membrane above boarding
turf roof

turn see thumb turn.

turnbuckle a mechanism for tensioning bracing wires, cables or rods joined end on end by means of two threaded connections housed in a sleeve, which is turned to produce a tightening force.

turnbuckle

Turnbull's blue a form of potassium ferrous ferricyanide used as a pale blue pigment.

turn button see button.

Turner's yellow, Kassler yellow, mineral yellow, Montpelier yellow, patent yellow, transparent gold ochre; an obsolete yellow lead oxychloride pigment used extensively in the past in watercolour, oil and chalk paints.

turning the shaping of wooden pieces on a lathe to create items which are predominantly circular in section.

turning chisel a woodworking chisel used for shaping wood on a lathe.

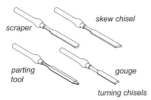

scraper

skew chisel

parting tool

gouge

turning chisels

turning gouge a turning chisel with a concave blade for removing wood, rough shaping and smoothing.

turning catch see turning latch.

turning circle in design for vehicular traffic, the minimum distance needed for the turning of a particular class of vehicle, measured variously as the outer radius or diameter of the circle it inscribes when turning through 180°.

turning latch, turning catch; a simple latch which holds a door leaf or casement in a closed position by means of a rotating piece of stiff material attached to the frame.

turning piece, camber slip, camber piece; a piece of timber with a slightly curved upper edge, used as temporary support for a flat or shallow cambered masonry arch during construction.

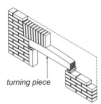

turning piece

turning saw, web saw; a workshop saw with a wooden frame constraining a blade tightened into place, which can be turned along its axis for greater flexibility in cutting curves, etc.

turning stair, winding stair; a stair whose direction of travel changes as it ascends; types included as separate entries are listed below:
*curving stair; *half turn stair; *one-turn stairs; *quarter turn stair.

turnkey contract see design and construct contract.

turn-up in bituminous roofing, the edge of a sheet of bitumen felt which acts as a skirting at an abutment.

turpentine, oil of turpentine, spirits of turpentine; volatile distillations of the resinous liquid exuded from certain pines and other coniferous trees; used in the preparation of oil paints and as a thinner; originally the resinous secretion itself; see also rosin.

turquoise, kallaite; a semi-translucent blue or blue-green mineral polished or carved as decoration and ornament.

turret a smaller defensive or decorative corner or boundary tower in a castle, fortification or palace, often with a platform and battlements; also sometimes called a tourelle, touret or turrette.

Tuscan order, Etruscan order; a simple classical Roman order, influenced by the old brick and timber temples of the Etruscans, and the Greek Doric, with smooth-shafted columns, a simple capital, base and entablature.

Tuscan capital a simple capital at the top of a column of the classical Roman Tuscan order, consisting of an echinus above an annulet, surmounted by an abacus edged with a cyma moulding.

Tuscan capital

Tuscan column a column of the Roman Tuscan order, distinguished by a gap between the shaft ring and capital.

tusk tenon joint in timber frame construction, a specially hewn tenon joint for housing the ends of joists, pinned to increase its bearing capacity.

tusk tenon joint

twining stem a decorative moulding representing the coiled stem of a climbing plant.

twining stem

twinned see coupled.

  twinned columns see coupled columns.

twin tenon joint see double tenon joint.

twin triangle tie double triangle wall tie.

twist an end-to-end rotational warping of an improperly seasoned timber board on drying, making it propeller-shaped.

twist in improperly seasoned timber board

twist drill a hardened steel drill bit with spiral cutting edges, used for boring holes in metal or wood.

twisted bar see cold twisted bar.

twisted column see spiral column.

twist gimlet see gimlet.

twisting fibres see interlocking grain.

twist tie see vertical twist tie.

twitcher trowel, twitcher, angle trowel; a hand tool for smoothing internal corners in plasterwork with a handled blade of bent steel sheet.

two-brick wall a solid bonded brick wall whose width is the sum of two brick lengths plus one intermediate joint.

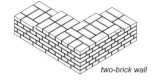

two-brick wall

two by four the traditional term for sawn timber whose cross-section is 50×100 mm; refers to dimensions in inches.

two-centred ogee arch, depressed ogee arch; an ogee arch with lower haunches constructed around two centres of curvature; lower or fatter than a normal ogee arch.

two-centred ogee arch

two coat plasterwork, render and set; plasterwork consisting of two separate layers; the first coat which smooths off the base and provides a key, and the final coat which provides a finish.

two component, two pack, two part designations of high-performance adhesives and sealants which are supplied in two separate parts which must be mixed before use for chemical hardening to occur.

two component adhesive see two-part adhesive.

two component sealant, two-part sealant; a sealant such as polyurethane products, supplied as two separate components, which must be mixed before application.

two part adhesive, two pack adhesive, two component adhesive; adhesive mixed from two separate parts before use.

two part sealant see two component sealant.

two-pipe system a central heating system in which each radiator is served by two pipe circuits: one for input hot water and the other for return water to the heating plant.

two-stage tendering in contract administration, a tendering procedure in which a contractor is selected on the basis of an approximate bill of quantities, and the price negotiated on the basis of the contractor's advice at the design stage.

two-way reinforcement concrete slab reinforcement consisting of sets or a mesh of parallel reinforcing bars laid in two perpendicular directions to provide resistance to tensile forces along two major axes.

two-way slab a reinforced concrete slab with two-way reinforcement, designed to span in two perpendicular directions.

two-way stick adhesive any adhesive applied to both surfaces to be joined.

tying wire see binding wire.

tympanum, 1 tympan; Lat.; an area of wall, panel or space enclosed within an arch and its horizontal line of springing.
2 the triangular panel or surface on the front face of a classical pediment or decorative gable.
3 see dado.

Tyrian purple, Grecian purple, ostrum, purple of the ancients; a purple pigment used by the Romans for imperial dress, originally obtained from the shellfish *Murex trunculis* and *Murex brandaris* and later manufactured synthetically; now superseded by other pigments.

Tyrolean finish a surface coating of mortar for masonry and concrete, textured after application; textured or patterned render or plasterwork.

U

UB section see I-section.

UC section see H-section.

UF urea formaldehyde.

Ulmus spp. see elm.

ultimate load the greatest load a structure or structural member can withstand before it fails.

ultimate strength, breaking strength; in the study of materials, the stress at which a material or component fails under increasing load.
ultimate compressive strength failure occurs due to compression or crushing.

ultrabasic rock a form of igneous rock whose silica content is less than 45%.

ultramarine, ultramarine blue; a greenish-blue pigment originally made from the mineral lapis lazuli until an artificial method of production was discovered in 1828; also the name given to the shade of colour of this.
ultramarine green a greenish form of ultramarine pigment.
ultramarine yellow an old name for barium yellow pigment; types of ultramarine included as separate entries are listed below:
*cobalt ultramarine; *French blue, French ultramarine, Gmellin's blue, see artifical ultramarine.

ultrasound sound with a frequency greater than that which can be heard by the human ear (greater than 15–20 kHz).
ultrasonic pertaining to ultrasound.
ultrasonic welding a method of welding stainless steels and other alloys by the application of ultrasonic vibration and light pressure.

ultraviolet radiation, UV; that part of the electromagnetic spectrum beyond the cool violet end, with wavelengths between 400–40 nm, shorter than radiation of the visible spectrum; often known as ultraviolet light when produced by lamps.
ultraviolet control glass see laminated ultraviolet light control glass, anti-fading glass.
ultraviolet lamp an electric lamp which produces light from the ultraviolet end of the spectrum.

ultraviolet light resistance the ability of a material or surface to inhibit the transmission of ultraviolet light, or to be unaffected in its presence.

umber, umbre; a general name for brown native pigments rich in oxides of iron and manganese; its colour may range from yellowish to greenish and reddish and is usually darker than sienna and ochre; umber pigments included as separate entries are listed below:
*burnt umber; *chestnut brown, raw umber; *jacaranda brown, see burnt umber; *mineral brown, see burnt umber; *raw umber; *Sicilian brown, see raw umber; *Spanish brown, see burnt umber; *terra ombre, see raw umber.

umbrella dome, melon dome, parachute dome, pumpkin dome; a domical vault which, in plan, is a polygon whose sides are arcs of a circle.

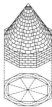

umbrella dome

uncoursed a descriprion of masonry walling which is not laid in regular horizontal courses.
uncoursed ashlar, random ashlar ashlar masonry with stones of different sizes laid in a rough bond with no or few horizontal running joints.

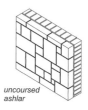

uncoursed ashlar

uncoursed rubble, random rubble masonry construction of roughly shaped stones not laid in courses.

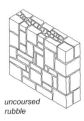

uncoursed rubble

uncoursed squared rubble masonry roughly squared pieces of stone laid as masonry with no definable coursed pattern; also called random squared rubble masonry.

uncrushed gravel coarse aggregate processed from naturally occurring gravel which has not undergone further processing of mechanical crushing.

under-and-over tile, Spanish tile, mission tile (Am); a U-shaped clay roof tile laid alternately convexly and concavely in courses to overlap one another.

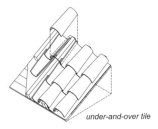

under-and-over tile

undercloak the lower overlapping part of a folded sheetmetal roofing seam or welt, covered by an overcloak.

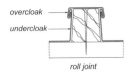

roll joint

undercoat a coat of paint or treatment applied to prepare, seal or colour a surface prior to a final or finish coat; see also plaster undercoat.

undercoat plaster plaster laid directly onto a wall or ceiling as a base onto which further coats are applied.

undercroft the vaulted cellar of a building, used for storage, or the vaulted cellar of a church, a crypt.

undercut tenon joint a timber tenon joint in which a sloping cut is made into the receiving piece to provide a greater gluing area for the tenoned end, or a ledge on which it rests.

under-deposit corrosion see deposit corrosion.

underfelt see underlay, felt underlay.

underfloor heating, floor heating; electric wires or hot water pipes laid under a floor or within floor construction as space heating and to provide a pleasantly warm floor surface in bathrooms, etc.

underground parking an area of parking located below ground, either in specially excavated structures or in the basements of buildings.

underground watering in landscaping and forestry, the provision of water directly to the roots of plants by burying perforated pipes in the soil.

undergrowth, understorey; the lowest layer of plants and shrubs that grow on a landscaped area or woodland floor.

underlay, 1 underfelt; a base layer of sheet material such as expanded polystyrene or cork sheeting laid beneath a floor covering as a vibration or noise attenuator and to provide an even base; flooring underlay.
2 in roof construction, a layer of impervious material such as polythene sheet or roofing felt laid beneath roofing such as slates, tiles, profiles sheeting, etc. as secondary protection against the penetration of water; see also base sheet, felt underlay, roofing underlay, sheathing, perforated underlay bitumen felt (vented underlay).

underpinning the addition of support beneath the foundations of an existing structure to account for an increase in loading or altered ground conditions.

underpitched vault a cross vault in which the arches at the edges of the bay are smaller than those across the bay. See illustration on facing page.

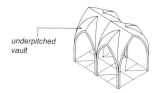

underpitched vault

under-reamed pile in foundation technology, a bored pile whose base is enlarged; also called a belled pile or pedestal pile.

undersurface see soffit.

underwater concrete concrete which is placed, and hardens, under water; see also tremie concrete.

undisturbed sample a soil sample which has been removed from the ground as a core sample and largely represents the properties in analysis of the soil from which it was taken.

undulating moulding see wave moulding.

undulating tracery see flowing tracery.

undy moulding see oundy moulding.

unedged a description of converted timber which contains wane, or has been sawn on two opposite sides but not at the edges.

unequal angle a steel angle in which the limbs are of differing lengths when viewed in cross-section.

uneven grain a pronounced visual difference between earlywood and latewood in a piece of sawn timber.

unexcavated referring to an area of a construction site which has not been dug or excavated during construction work.

unframed door 1 a rudimentary door whose leaf is made from vertical matchboarding held together with horizontal members or ledges nailed to one side, often with diagonal braces for additional stiffness.
2 see all glass door.

unheated space space in a building which contains no heating appliance and is kept at about the same temperature as external air.

uninhabitable a description of a building deemed to be unfit for occupation because of its state of disrepair, contamination, fire damage, etc.

union a pipe fitting with a loose coupling nut at its end; used for connecting a threaded pipe to an appliance; see screwed union.

union clip an accessory for joining two sections of rainwater guttering or similar component end to end.

unit, 1 unit of measurement; a value or size used by convention as a measure of a quantity (metre, second).
2 a component or group of components viewed as a whole; a module; see prefabricated unit, precast concrete unit, cladding unit, concrete paving slab, dwelling unit.
unit air-conditioner, cooler unit, room air-conditioner, self-contained air-conditioner; an independent air-treatment unit situated within the space it serves.
unit cost the price per unit (square metre, kilogram, etc.) of a commodity.
unit paver see concrete block paver.
unit price contract a standard prime contract in which a contractor agrees to carry out construction work according to a pre-determined, fixed sum for each specified unit of work performed; the final price is determined by multiplying the unit price for each unit by the measured quantity of work carried out.

universal beam see I-section.

universal column see H-section.

universal plane see combination plane.

unreinforced a description of structural concrete which does not contain steel reinforcement; unreinforced concrete is also called plain concrete.

unrolled veneer see rotary cut veneer.

unsaturated in colour science, referring to pale shades of colour which are not as intense as the same hue without white.
unsaturated polyester see polyester resin.

unskilled labourer a construction worker with little formal training, who usually works as a builder's hand.

unsound knot, decayed knot, rotten knot; a knot in timber, softer than the surrounding wood as a result of fungal attack.

untreated sewage see raw sewage.

unventilated roof roof construction which contains a vapour control layer to restrict movement of vapour above the insulation layer, and has no need for a ventilation gap within the construction.

UP polyester resin.

up-and-over door an overhead door whose single door leaf is opened by lifting it into a horizontal position above the door opening on a system of pivots, levers and springs.

up-and-over door

upholsterer's hammer a small hammer used for hammering tacks in upholstery work; it often contains a magnet in its head for holding nails.

upholstery fabric covering for furniture and fittings.
upholstery tack, upholstery nail; a small nail with a dome-shaped head, used for fastening upholstery to furniture.

upholstery tack

upholstery textile in interior design, cloth used for cladding or covering furnishings and other interior components.

U-pin see staple.

uplighting lighting designed to provide indirect light to a space by illumination of ceiling and upper wall surfaces.
uplighter a luminaire which indirectly illuminates a space or area by directing light upwards.

upper chord, top chord; the upper member in a truss.

upper glazing see top light.

upper king post see king tie.

upright see standard.

U-profile see channel.

upsetting, setting up; the making thicker of the end of a metal bar by hammering it on end while hot, as with the fixing of rivets.

upside down roof, inverted roof, protected membrane roof; a roof whose insulation is laid above the waterproofing membrane and is held in position by ballast such as shingle or concrete slabs; the insulation thus protects the waterproofing from the effects of weathering and thermal variation.

upstairs the upper floor of a building above the ground floor.

upstand an area of waterproof membrane or sheeting turned up against a wall abutment or parapet to provide a secure edge joint; see roofing upstand; slate fillet; tile fillet (tiled upstand); water check.
upstand beam a beam which protrudes from the upper face of a concrete slab, which it supports.
upstand flashing in roofing, a flashing which forms an upstand at an abutment but is not dressed into the abutting wall; it is covered by a cover flashing.

uranium yellow a permanent, expensive pigment made from uranium oxide; used in ceramics.

urban development the construction of whole areas of a town or city, controlled by planning processes to enhance or improve conditions therein.

urban fabric, urban form see urban structure.

urban planning town planning concerned with the nature, structure, and functioning of human collectives in physical space; see planning.

urban redevelopment see urban renewal, comprehensive redevelopment.

urban renewal, urban redevelopment; the reconstruction and rehabilitation of blighted or decaying urban areas and communities.

urban structure, urban fabric, urban form; the overall shape and pattern of an urban area based on its visual and material impact, density, traffic patterns and topography.

urdy moulding a crenellated moulding whose upper and lower castellations have sharpened extremities; sometimes called a vair moulding in heraldry.

urdy moulding

urea formaldehyde, UF; a clear thermosetting resin used for mouldings, WC seats, paints and stove enamels.
urea formaldehyde glue a synthetic resin glue made by chemically condensing urea with formalin.

urethane varnish see polyurethane varnish.

urinal a soil appliance for receiving urine and flushing it away into a drain; a bowl urinal or pod urinal is an individual rounded wall-mounted urinal.

use class in planning control, an official classification of proposed and existing building development according to types of use, whether residential, commercial, recreational, industrial etc.
use classes order in planning control, an official document specifying classes of use for building development, so that a change of use within the same class is not taken to involve development requiring planning consent.

U-section a metal section whose cross-section resembles the letter C or U; see channel.

user a person, animal or object for whom a building is designed and constructed.

US standard brick a standard size of brick in use in North America with regular dimensions of $8'' \times 4'' \times 2^2/_3''$ ($203.2 \times 101.6 \times 67.7$ mm); also confusingly called a modular brick.

utile, sipo; [*Entandrophragma utile*] a hardwood from West Africa with strong, heavy, rich tawny timber used for furniture, panelling and construction work.

utility 1 see service.
2 tool; auxiliary computing software for performing a simple routine task such as sorting, searching or inspecting.

utility room 1 a room adjoining a kitchen for providing additional facilities for washing, storage and other domestic activities.
2 service space; a subsidiary space or room used in conjunction with the functioning or servicing of a building or adjacent major space, largely for storage, preparation, etc.

utilization factor in lighting design, the ratio of the luminous flux received by a surface to the total luminous flux produced by individual lamps.

UV see ultraviolet radiation.

U-value, air-to-air heat transmission coefficient, coefficient of thermal transmittance, coefficient of heat transfer; a basic quantity used for heat loss calculations for external wall, roof and floor constructions, whose units are W/m^2 °C; a measure of how well the given construction will conduct heat, available from standard empirical tables of data, based on experimentation by measuring the rate of heat flow per square metre of surface for every degree of temperature difference on either side of the construction, with a surface coefficient added to allow for exposure to wind and rain.

V

V-joint a brickwork mortar joint in which the mortar is shaped with a pointed tool to form a V-shaped depression.

vacuum breaker see anti-vacuum valve.

vacuum concrete, vacuum dewatered concrete; concrete to which a vacuum is applied after placing in order to extract the excess water not needed for hydration.

vacuum concreting working with vacuum concrete.

vacuum dewatering, vacuum processing; the compaction of fresh concrete by the application of a controlled vacuum to suck out excess water.

vacuum forming a method of forming thermoplastic moulded products by sucking sheet material against a perforated one-sided mould using a vacuum.

vacuum pressure impregnated timber see pressure impregnated timber.

vacuum processing see vacuum dewatering.

vacuum sewerage a sewerage system for flat or low-lying areas in which sewage is sucked along plastic pipelines with vacuum pressure induced by a pumping station.

vacuum WC a sealed WC for use on trains, ships and aircraft in which soil is discharged into a collecting tank by means of a partial vacuum induced by a pump.

vair moulding same as urdy moulding.

valley the inside join formed by the junction of two pitched roofs meeting at an angle; a roof valley; see also tiled valley.

valley board in timber frame construction, a wide board which runs the length of a valley as a base for the valley gutter.

valley gutter in sheetmetal and other pitched roofing, a pressed sheetmetal component or other construction included in a valley for the runoff of water to a gutter or outlet.

valley rafter in timber roof construction, a diagonal rafter supporting the meeting of two sloping roofs at an inside corner or valley.

valley roof see M-roof.

valley tile a special roof tile manufactured for use in a roof valley.

value, reflectance; in colour science and painting, the relative darkness or lightness of a colour, the amount of light reflected from it.

valve a control device for closing off and regulating flow of liquids and gases in pipework.

valve box see surface box.

vanadium a metallic chemical element, V, used as an alloy to toughen steel.

vandal resistant, vandalproof; a description or property of a component, construction or finish which is designed to resist deliberate damage from vandalism by virtue of robust construction, teflon coatings, etc.

Vandyke brown, Rubens brown; a native earth pigment composed of clay and iron oxide with included organic matter; a shade of dark brown used by the Flemish painter Antonius van Dyck in the 1600s; the colour of the pigment burnt umber.

vane testing in soil investigation, the on-site testing of the stiffness of soft and silty clays by sinking a winged implement inside a tube into the soil and measuring the force required to turn it.

vanishing point in perspective drawing, one of the points at which lines converge, constructed as if at infinity.

vanity basin, counter top basin; a domestic wash basin housed in a hole cut into a worktop, usually as part of a bathroom cabinet.

vaporizing oil burner a burner in an oil heating system whose oil is vaporized and mixed with air prior to combustion.

vapour barrier, vapour check; an impervious membrane incorporated into wall construction to inhibit the passage of airborne moisture.

vapour blasting see wet blasting.

vapour check see vapour barrier.

vapour control layer a layer of impervious material or membrane included in wall, roof, floor, etc. construction to inhibit the passage of water vapour.

variable air volume system, variable volume system, VAV system; an air-conditioning system in which temperature of input air is a constant, but actual room temperature is governed by the amount of air provided to each space with the use of localized fan units.

variation, change (Am), modification (Am); a change in the nature or the extent, conditions or programming of construction work from that stipulated in a building contract, agreed and billed by a contractor extra to the contract.

variation formula see price variation formula.

variation of price contract a form of building contract in which prices may be amended to reflect changes in economic conditions; see also formula variation of price contract.

variation order in contract administration, an instruction from the client or client's representative that implements a change in the nature or extent of constructed work.

varnish a liquid coating applied to a surface as a finish, usually timberwork, joinery or furniture, forming a hardwearing transparent film.

varnish brush see flat varnish brush.

varnish size size made from varnish diluted with a solvent or thinner.

vault 1 a three-dimensional arched ceiling construction to support a floor or roof, often of masonry; types included as separate entries are listed below:
*annular vault; *barrel vault; *cambered vault, see segmental barrel vault; *cloister vault; *conical vault; *corbelled vault; *coved vault; *cradle vault, see barrel vault; *cross vault, see groin vault; *cylindrical vault, see barrel vault; *dome; *domical vault, see cloister vault; *dormer vault; *expanding vault, see conical vault; *fan vault; *Gothic vault; *groin vault, groined vault; *hexapartite vault, see sexpartite vault; *intersecting barrel vault, see groin vault; *net vault; *octopartite vault; *pointed barrel vault, pointed vault; *quadripartite vault; *rampant vault; *relieving vault; *rib vault, ribbed vault; *Roman vault; *Romanesque vault; *sail vault, see sail dome; *segmental barrel vault, segmental vault; *sexpartite vault; *stellar vault, star vault, star-ribbed vault; *surbased vault, see segmental barrel*

vault; *tripartite vault; *trough vault; *tunnel vault, see barrel vault; *underpitched vault; *wagon vault, wagonhead vault, see barrel vault.
2 an underground storage room beneath a building; a cellar; often one in which valuables are kept; a strongroom.

vaulting 1 the curved surfaces of a vault.
2 the making of masonry vaults.
3 a series of vaults.

VAV system see variable air volume system.

VB-consistometer test, VB-test, Vebe test; a test for the workability of fresh concrete, in which the time of collapse of a concrete cone on a vibrating table is measured.

vector graphics computer-aided design drawing using lines defined by their end points in space.

vegetable fibre thin fibres of plant material such as wood, hessian, sisal or jute used as reinforcement in composite materials or woven to form matting.

vegetable fibre reinforced referring to composites consisting of vegetable fibres in a binder such as clay, mud, cement or plaster; traditionally used for cast and in-situ work.

vegetable glue glue made from plant matter, especially starch glue (cassava), protein glue (soya glue), or glue from oils pressed from nuts and rape seed.

vegetable soil a thin layer of dark crumbly soil, usually topsoil, containing a large proportion of decayed vegetable matter or humus.

vehicle the main liquid body of a paint, including a thinner.

vehicle heating point, car heating point; an electrical point installed in unheated car parks and outdoor parking areas to which engine and in-car heating devices can be connected in cold weather.

vehicular ramp an inclined carriageway in a car park, roadway, etc. for vehicles to move from one level to another.

vein a linear marking or band of a different colour or material to the base matrix

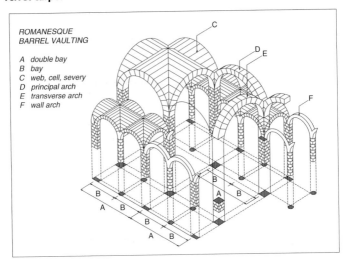

ROMANESQUE
BARREL VAULTING

A double bay
B bay
C web, cell, severy
D principal arch
E transverse arch
F wall arch

in rock and ornamental stone, especially marble and limestone.

velvet carpet a type of cut-pile carpet of a basic Wilton type.

veneer 1 sheets of wood less than 6 mm in thickness cut from a log by slicing, peeling or sawing; glued together as plywood or to cheaper boards as a decorative finish; often called wood veneer to distinguish it from brick and other veneers.
see veneering pattern for list of matches; types included as separate entries are listed below:
*back cut veneer; *burl veneer; *flat cut veneer; *half round veneer; *quarter sliced veneer; *rotary cut veneer, peeled veneer.
2 non-structural masonry cladding for the exterior of a building; see brick facing (brick veneer), stone facing (stone veneer).

veneer bolt, veneer flitch; a piece of wood or log from which veneer is peeled or sliced.

veneer cutting decorative veneer produced either by slicing or peeling.

veneer cutting   veneer peeling

veneered chipboard chipboard surfaced with a wood veneer, used for high-quality interior linings and furnishings.

veneered parquet see multilayer parquet.

veneered wall an external wall whose cladding or facing is non-structural.

veneer flitch see veneer bolt.

veneer hammer, veneering hammer; a hammer with a long thin flat face used in veneerwork for pressing down veneers during gluing.

veneering, veneerwork; **1** the process of cutting and gluing decorative glued veneers; see veneering pattern for list of matches.
2 a decorative facing of veneer on board, plywood or lower quality timber.

veneering hammer see veneer hammer.

veneering pattern the various patterns in which veneers are glued to a base; types included as separate entries are listed below:
*bookmatching, book match; *box match; *butt match; *centre match; *chevron match, see V-match; *diamond match; *herringbone pattern, herringbone match; *random match; *reverse box match; *reverse diamond match; *slip match; *sunburst matching; *vertical butt and horizontal bookmatching; *V-match.

veneer parquet see multilayer parquet.

veneer peeling decorative veneer produced by cutting the surface layer from a rotating log or flitch.

veneer pin a small round pin, 10–38 mm in length, used for temporarily fastening veneers in position until the glue has set.

veneer plywood see plywood.

veneer saw a small, fine-toothed saw for cutting veneers.

veneer slicing decorative veneer produced by straight cutting of a half log or flitch.

veneerwork see veneering.

Venetian arch 1 a decorative arch form whose intrados is formed of two adjacent semicircular arches, and whose extrados is of one, double width semicircle; the spandrel left between often contains a circular opening or panel.

Venetian arches

2 a decorative pointed arch form whose intrados and extrados are further apart at the crown than at the springing; an arch whose intrados is an elliptical arch and extrados is an ogee is also sometimes called a Venetian arch.

venetian blind, louvred blind; a raisable window-blind consisting of a number of horizontal slats of wood, metal or plastics hung by string or tape one above the other, whose angle is adjustable to allow more or less light through.

Venetian dentil moulding a dentil moulding cut with a splayed base or background.

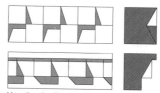

Venetian dentil mouldings

Venetian mirror glass mirror glass coated with wide strips of mirrored surface interspersed with narrower clear strips; used for providing one-way vision from surveillance and control rooms, offices, etc. to larger spaces.

Venetian motif see Palladian motif.

Venetian red see oxide red.

Venetian window, Palladian window; an ornamental window with three openings, the central portion arched.

Venice turpentine a variety of turpentine exuded from the European larch [*Larix decidua*], used as a medium in paints, varnishes and adhesives.

vent, ventilator; a grille or other device to allow the passage of fresh air to a space from the outside, or for release of stale air; an openable hatch or window to provide ventilating air; see fresh-air vent, exhaust vent, ventilation pipe.

vented underlay see perforated underlay bitumen felt.

ventilated roof roof construction with a planar gap within its thickness above the insulating layer, for the circulation of air, removal of moisture, etc.

ventilating brick see air brick.

ventilating column a vertical ventilating pipe for an underground sewer.

ventilating pipe a pipe in a drainage system for the ventilation and pressure release of a discharge pipe.

ventilating tile a special roof tile with perforations to permit ventilation.

ventilating ridge tile a special perforated ridge tile to allow for the passage of ventilating air.

ventilation 1 the maintenance of the air quality of spaces in a building by continual provision of fresh air from the outside, either by natural or mechanical means; see natural ventilation, mechanical ventilation.
2 the natural passage of air into rooms to provide fresh air, and through gaps or cavities within roof, wall and floor construction to convey excess moisture out, thus inhibiting mould and fungal attack; see also roof ventilation.

ventilation duct an air duct used in a mechanical ventilation installation, or a closed flue or other channel, through which stale air from a space can pass to the outside.

ventilation gap a space between layers in roof or wall construction allowing for the passage of circulating air to remove unwanted moisture.

ventilation installation see ventilation plant.

ventilation pipe, vent, vent pipe; a pipe connected to a drainage system which conveys foul air upwards out of a building, easing the flow of water in drains.

ventilation plant, ventilation installation; the pumps, fans, ductwork and other equipment that make up the mechanical ventilation system of a building.
ventilation plant room, air-handling plant room; a service space in a building containing intakes, mixing chambers, fans and main delivery ducts for a ventilation system.

ventilation rate see air-change rate.

ventilation riser see ventilation stack.

ventilation shaft a large vertical ventilation duct.

ventilation stack a closed flue or other vertical channel through which stale air is released to the outside, usually via natural convection; also called a vent stack or ventilation riser; if large, may be called a ventilation shaft.

ventilator see vent, trickle ventilator, eaves ventilator.

venting see fire venting.

venting layer see perforated underlay bitumen felt.

venting panel see blast venting panel.

vent pipe see stack vent, ventilation pipe.

vent soaker see pipe flashing.

vent stack see ventilation stack.

veranda, verandah; a roofed open space, terrace or porch providing shelter and shade along the sides or front of a building.

plan of holiday home,
architect N. Davies

verawood, Maracaibo lignum vitae; [*Bulnesia arborea*] an extremely heavy Venezuelan tropical hardwood.

verge 1 the join of roof and wall at a gable or sloping end of a pitched roof.
2 margin, median, reservation; a strip or area adjoining the carriageway of a road for emergency stopping, etc.
vergeboard see bargeboard.
verge tile a special roof tile for use at a verge.

vermiculation the dressing of a stonework or plaster surface with random worm-like decorative recesses or wavy lines; especially used for quoins or finer stones.

vermiculation

vermiculite any of a group of hydrous silicates of aluminium, magnesium or iron, used loose as thermal insulation and fire-retardant coatings.
vermiculite plaster, gypsum-vermiculite plaster, vermiculite-gypsum plaster, fire-retardant plaster; plaster

containing fine exfoliated vermiculite aggregate, used as a fire-retardant coating for steelwork.

vermilion, scarlet vermilion; a bright red inorganic pigment, originally manufactured from the mercury sulphide ore, cinnabar; synthetically produced since 1789.

vernacular architecture traditional rural or rustic architecture which is based on the culture of the countryside, making use of local forms and materials, building methods and craftsmanship; nowadays any architecture in mimicry of this.

vernier two adjacent sliding calibrated scales which, when read in conjunction with one another, provide a more accurate reading for measurements of linear size.

vernier callipers (also called a calliper gauge, vernier gauge); a metal or plastic instrument with sliding jaws, used for taking small-scale but accurate measurements by reading from a vernier scale.

vert emeraude see viridian.

vertical 1 a description of any line, body, etc. placed or lying perpendicular to a flat horizontal plane; see also plumb.
2 an upright member in a structural system such as a truss, or standard in a balustrade.

vertical boarding timber cladding boards laid with their long faces vertical.

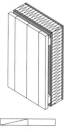

vertical boarding

vertical butt and horizontal book-matching a veneering pattern in which bookmatched veneer sheets are also matched with an array of mirrored sheets end on end; used in cases where veneers being used are not long enough to cover the whole panel heights; often simply called butt match.

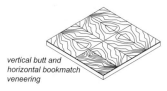

vertical butt and horizontal bookmatch veneering

vertical circulation the means of changing from one level to another within a building using stairs, lifts and ramps.

vertical folding door an overhead door with sections hinged horizontally, which fold up into an overhead space on opening; see also bi-part folding door.

vertical glazing bar an intermediate vertical glazing bar in a window; often called a mullion.

vertical grained see quartersawn.

vertical pivot window a window with an opening light hung centrally on pins at top and bottom of the frame, about which it opens.

vertical pivot window

vertical sand drain see sand drain.

vertical section a scaled drawing representing a vertical cut through a site, building or object; a horizontal section is called a plan.

vertical shore see dead shore.

vertical sliding window see sash window.

vertical tiling see tile hanging.

vertical twist tie any wall tie formed out of metal strip with a twist along its length to provide a suitable drip for gathered water; a strip tie.

vestibule a space or room directly beyond the external door of a dwelling, public building or church; also called an entrance hall, lobby or porch; an entrance hall or passage in a Roman building is called a vestibulum.

Vestorian blue a variety of Egyptian blue pigment.

viaduct a high-level masonry bridge with many arched spans, designed to carry a railway or road between two elevated points over a valley, waterway or low-lying ground.

viaduct

vibrated concrete concrete compacted by vibration.

vibrating screed board, screed; mechanical plant for levelling and compacting a concrete floor slab; a screed board with the capacity for motorized vibration.

vibrating table a machine for compacting precast concrete by means of a vibrating platform onto which the fresh concrete and formwork are placed.

vibration 1 the rapid oscillation of mechanical plant, etc. causing unwanted pressure waves to be transmitted through the air as sound, and surrounding building fabric as mechanical energy; see vibration insulation.
2 the compaction of fresh concrete by the application of mechanical vibration to release air pockets using an immersion or surface vibrator.

vibration insulation the placing of flexible material in strategic joints to attenuate vibration from mechanical plant and other sources of vibration.

vibration insulator, damper, vibration isolator (Am), isolation mount a layer of resilient material onto which mechanical equipment is placed to reduce the transmission of sound and vibration into the surrounding fabric.

vibration limit in the setting of concrete, the time after which concrete will no longer respond to vibration.

vibrator see concrete vibrator.

vibrocompaction, vibroflotation; a method of stabilization for soft ground in which a large vibrating poker is sunk into the soil using water jets from the base of the vibrator; the ground is compacted by the vibrations to form wide earth columns of compacted soil.

vibroreplacement, stone column; a method of stabilization for soft ground

similar to vibrocompaction, in which gravel is introduced into the ground during compaction to form a wide stone pile.

vice, vise (Am); a cast metal or wooden screwed device for holding and gripping objects in place while they are being worked, fixed to a workbench.

Victorian architecture architecture in England during the reign of Victoria (1837–1901), characterized by lavish ornament and eclectic styling of all types of buildings.

videoscope an endoscope with a flexible tube and a camera at the end, whose image is transmitted to a remote video monitor.

video surveillance the monitoring of internal and external space in a building using a system of fixed video cameras linked to centralized monitors; see also camera surveillance.

Vienna blue a form of the pigment cobalt blue used in glass and enamels.

Vienna lake see carmine.

Vierendeel truss a flat trussed beam with vertical web members only, connected to upper and lower chords with rigid joints; named after the Belgian engineer Arthur Vierendeel, its inventor, in 1896.

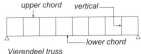

upper chord   vertical

lower chord

Vierendeel truss

viewer door viewer, see door scope.

vignette, trayle, vinette; an ornamental motif consisting of stylized vine leaves and grapes.

villa Lat.; a large classical Roman country house with an estate; originally divided into two parts, the pars urbana, or living area, and pars rustica, or working area; in more modern times, any well-to-do detached house, country house on an estate, holiday home or a so-named suburban dwelling.

vine an ornamental motif consisting of stylized leaves and stems of the vine plant, *Vitis vinifera*; see also vignette.

vine scroll ornament

vine black, grape black; a bluish black pigment consisting of carbon with impurities obtained from burnt and ground wood and other vegetable products, traditionally made from charred twigs of the vine [*Vitis vinifera*]; also known as blue black, coke black, cork black, drop black, German black, kernel black or yeast black, depending on country of origin or raw material used.

vine leaf capital a medieval capital embellished with vine leaf designs.

Gothic vine leaf capital in the chapter house of Southwell Minster, Nottinghamshire, England, 1290

vinette see vignette, vine.

vinyl the common name for polyvinyl chloride (PVC), a common plastic polymerized from vinyl chloride.

vinyl chloride a poisonous colourless gas used in the production of PVC and other polymers.

vinylidene chloride see polyvinylidene chloride.

vinyl paint an acid, alkali and weather-resistant emulsion paint based on a dispersion of vinyl or PVC in water; used on exterior masonry and plaster surfaces.

vinyl wallcovering wallcovering of a paper or fabric base with a PVC coating, available in rolls.

violation of agreement see breach of contract.

violet a general name for bluish purple colours in the visible spectrum with wavelengths between 380—430 m; named after the flower of the violet plant, *Viola spp.*; see purple for list of purple and violet pigments.

violet madder lake see alizarin.

viridian a bright, transparent, permanent green pigment consisting of hydrated chromium oxide, suitable for use in oil, watercolour and acrylic paints; variously known as Casali's green, emerald chromium oxide, emeraulde green, Guinet's green, Mittler's green, Pannetier's green, smaragd green, transparent oxide of chromium, vert emeraude.

viscose a cellulose sodium salt solution used in the manufacture of artificial silk and other plastics.

viscosity, internal friction; in hydraulics, the resistance of a liquid to flow.

vise see vice.

visible smoke detector see optical smoke detector.

visible spectrum the range of wavelengths of the electromagnetic spectrum comprising the colours in light which can be seen by the human eye.

vista in landscape design, a view along a main or grand axis; in the urban milieu lined by built form, in rural areas marked out by landmarks or bounded by natural features.

visualization the explanation or presentation of a proposal, design or idea in terms of a drawing, diagram, chart or model.

vitreous china a ceramic material with a relatively high glass content, used for sanitary fittings such as WC bowls and sinks.

vitreous enamel see enamel.

vitrification the conversion of mineral compounds into glass by fusion in high temperatures.

vitriol a traditional name given to any of a number of hydrated sulphates of metals such as iron, copper, zinc, cobalt and aluminium, or for sulphuric acid.

Vitruvian after the Roman writer, architect and engineer Vitruvius (first century BC), the author of *De architectura* (*The Ten Books on Architecture*), a work documenting Roman architecture and construction.

Vitruvian man a popular theme in theories of art and architecture from Renaissance times, depicting a man of ideal proportions with arms outstretched within a circle and square, thus proposing the proportions of the human body as a basis for aesthetic design in according with the canons of proportion suggested by Vitruvius.

Vitruvian scroll, Vitruvian wave, running dog, wave scroll; an ornamental motif consisting of a series of interconnected leaning S-shaped figures.

Vitruvian scroll

V-match, chevron match; a veneering pattern in which veneers with slanting grain are glued side by side in mirror image along a centre line, forming a series of V shapes.

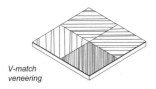

V-match veneering

vocabulary see architectural language.

void 1 an opening in floor or wall construction, such as one in a floor slab, to afford light and a visual link with the storey below.
2 space within a building or component, usually for technical installations, weight reduction, etc., which is enclosed and to which access is provided usually for maintenance only; see ceiling void, roof void.
3 air or water-filled spaces or channels within a porous solid such as concrete or wood; see air void, water void.

void box see void form.

void form, void box; a formwork mould for creating a void or opening in a cast concrete component.

voids ratio in concretework, the ratio of the volume of air to the total volume.

volatile referring to a liquid which will readily evaporate at room temperature.

volatile oil see essential oil.

volcanic glass uncrystalline vitreous rock formed when molten lava cools down very quickly.

volcanic rock, vulcanite, effusive rock, extrusive rock; types of igneous rock originally formed from rapidly solidified magma pushed to the surface of the earth's crust; these include basalt, dacite and tuff.

volcanic tuff see tuff, peperino.

volt abb. V; the SI unit of electromotive force or potential difference; one volt produces a current of one amp in a resistor with resistance one ohm.

voltage potential difference; the measure of electromotive force in an electric circuit, measured in volts.

voltage drop the loss in electrical pressure or voltage caused by resistance of cables, power lines and other transmission devices.

voltage tester a screwdriver-like device with an insulated handle containing a small lamp which lights up when a current flows through the blade.

voltaic couple see galvanic couple.

volume the physical measurement of three-dimensional space (length $\times$ width $\times$ height) whose SI unit is the cubic metre (m^3).

volume batching, proportioning by volume; the measuring out of the component parts of concrete into the desired ratio by volume as opposed to weight.

volume yield see concrete yield.

volute, helix; in classical architecture, a spiral scroll found typically as a motif in classical Ionic, Corinthian and Composite capitals; any similar ornament; see also spiral.

volute capital any capital which contains paired volutes; an Ionic, Aeolic or other capital from Asia or the Mediterranean; see Aeolic capital, Ionic capital.

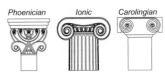

Phoenician   Ionic   Carolingian

volute capitals

voussoir a wedge-shaped stone or brick used in the construction of a true masonry arch.

vulcanite see volcanic rock, ebonite.

vulcanization the process of treating rubber with sulphur at a high temperature to increase strength and elasticity.

W

waferboard flakeboard with specially shaped flakes.

waffle floor, honeycomb floor, rectangular grid floor; a concrete floor slab constructed of a grid of downstand beams with a pattern of hollows or coffers in the soffit, both for economy of concrete and for aesthetic effect.

waffle mould, waffle form, pan form; plastic, plywood or steel reusable moulds or formwork used to cast rectangular recesses in the underside of a concrete slab to form waffle slabs and coffered ceilings.

waffle slab, coffered slab, honeycomb slab; a ribbed reinforced concrete floor or roof slab whose underside is indented with a regular arrangement of hollows; see waffle floor.

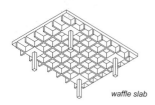

waffle slab

wagonhead vault, wagon vault see barrel vault.

wainscot, wainscoting; timber or joinery panelling, originally of oak, fixed to an interior wall below waist height.

waist 1 a thinning out in the middle of a component or element.
2 in concrete stair design, the minimum thickness of the concrete in a flight, measured between the soffit and meeting of tread and riser, perpendicular to the soffit.

wale, waler, whaler; in timber construction and formwork, a horizontal timber member which binds together vertical boards or sheet material; see waling.

waler plate a long plate which transfers loading evenly from a form tie to formwork.

waling 1 wale, waler, ranger; a horizontal beam or other structural member which holds formwork sheeting in place around cast concrete, or at the edge of an excavation.

2 in excavation work, a horizontal intermediate support for poling boards, held apart by horizontal struts across the trench.

walking line a theoretical line joining the nosings in a stair, given as the average position in plan of a person using the stair and taken by convention as 457 mm from the handrail.

walk-up apartments an apartment building less than three stories in height, with access to all flats via external stairs or a stair core.

walkway any passage or place providing a route for walking; a cloister or ambulatory in a church; a link or external gallery providing access to a building; an elevated platform or gangway on a construction site, theatre or roofspace, etc. for material conveyance, access to services and circulation, often with safety balustrades; often called a footway.

wall a vertical construction delineating and enclosing space inside a building, forming the external envelope, freestanding, etc.; it may be loadbearing or non-loadbearing.

wall anchor see toggle bolt, hollow-wall anchor.

wallboard any board product such as gypsum board, fibre board, plywood or laminates used in construction as cladding for a wall frame, as a base for a finish, or as a lining.

wallboard panel see prefabricated gypsum wallboard panel.

wall brush see flat brush.

wall cap see coping.

wall cladding weatherproofing components, sheet material, etc. for cladding the exterior wall frame and construction of a building.

wallcovering any material in thin sheet form, wallpaper, textiles, vinyl sheeting, etc., supplied in rolls and applied to interior walls as a finish or a base which can be painted.

wallcovering support the surface onto which a wallcovering is fixed; a wall or ceiling.

wall end see stopped end, return end.

wallette a model wall built for test purposes.

wall hung a description of a sanitary appliance such as a WC, basin or a bidet designed to be supported by a bracket from a wall so that there is a gap between it and the floor, its drain penetrating the rear wall.

walling the process and product of constructing walls in masonry.

wall joint in masonry construction, an internal joint which remains hidden in the thickness of a wall.

wall lining, lining paper; paper wallcovering hung as a base for a subsequent wallcovering.

wall painting see mural.

wall panel a prefabricated cladding or infill panel for walling.

wall panelling boards or joinery fixed as a timber lining for a wall, often framed.

wallpaper wallcovering of decorated or embossed sheets of sized paper, supplied in rolls.

wallpapering, paperhanging; the trade of fixing wallpaper to an internal wall surface.

wallpaper paste adhesive for fixing wallpaper, consisting of a powder such as flour or methyl cellulose mixed with water.

wall plate a longitudinal member incorporated into or placed on a wall, onto which other construction is fixed.

wall plug a plastic fixing sleeve inserted into prebored holes, enabling metal screws to be anchored to masonry and other difficult surfaces; see also legs anchor, hollow-wall plug.

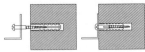

wall plug

wall tie a galvanized steel or twisted wire fixing laid at regular intervals into a masonry wall to provide stability by connecting masonrywork to a structural base, or by linking inner and outer leaves of brickwork; called a cavity tie when used in cavity walls; types included as separate entries are listed below: *butterfly wall tie; *double triangle wall tie; *fishtail wall; *strip wall tie; *twin triangle tie, double triangle wall tie; *vertical twist tie.

wall ties

wall tile any tile used for facing an internal or external wall surface.

wall tiling the laying of wall tiles, and the product of this process.

wall-to-wall carpet see fitted carpet.

wall unit see wall panel.

walnut [*Juglans spp.*] a group of hardwoods from Europe, Asia and America valued for their decorative grain figure; used for furniture and veneers; walnut trees are low and wide-spreading, planted in parks on account of their large many-stemmed exotic foliage; see below for species of walnut included in this work; see also African walnut [*Lovoa trichilioides, Lovoa klaineana*].

American walnut, black walnut; [*Juglans nigra*] a hardwood native to central and eastern United States, with rich dark brown timber, valued for its decorative figure; used for furniture, panelling and veneers.

butternut, white walnut; [*Juglans cinerea*] a hardwood native to eastern North America with pale brown timber; used for decorative veneers.

European walnut, English walnut, Persian walnut; [*Juglans regia*] a hardwood from southern Europe and China with grey streaked timber; valued for its decorative figure; used for panelling and veneers.

walnut oil a drying oil used as a vehicle in paints, pressed from the dried kernels of the common or English walnut.

wane the curved edge of a timber board cut from the edge of a log, with or without bark.

wane

waney a description of sawn timber with wane on one or both edges.

warm-air heater, fan heater; a space-heating appliance which blows out a stream of warmed air.

warm-air heating, fan heating; a heating system in which warm air is blown into spaces to maintain a certain temperature level.

warm-air unit a device which discharges a flow of warm air to provide heating and ventilation.

warm roof roof construction in which insulation is laid below the waterproofing, and a vapour barrier below the insulation.

warp 1 the distortion in shape of a piece of improperly seasoned timber due to uneven drying.
2 warp yarn; in weaving, carpetmaking and tapestry, a suspended lengthwise structural thread onto which the weft or crosswise threads are woven.

warranty see guarantee.

Warren truss a trussed beam patented by the British engineers James Warren and Willoughby Monzoni in 1848, whose web members form a series of equilateral or isosceles triangles joined by upper and lower chords; sometimes its end struts are vertical; see also Howe truss, Pratt truss, Vierendeel truss.

Warrington hammer see cross peen hammer.

wash a watery solution of material applied as a surface treatment or finish; see acid wash, whitewash; in watercolour painting, a layer or area of thin, transparent, watered-down colour often used as a base.

washable describing a coating or finish which may be washed with water and soap without causing damage.

washbasin see handrinse basin.

washboard see skirting board.

washer a perforated plate beneath a bolt-head or nut which acts as a spacer in a bolt fixing and transfers the pressure of the fixing over a wider area; types included as separate entries are listed below:

*flat washer; *lock washer; *spring lock washer; *tooth washer.

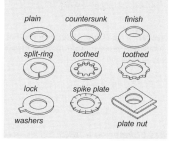

plain   countersunk   finish

split-ring   toothed   toothed

lock   spike plate

washers   plate nut

washing machine valve a water fitting for turning on or off a cold water supply to a washing machine.

waste 1 material left over from an industrial, commercial or consumer process which is relatively unusable; waste may refer to both solids and liquids, refuse is usually solid; types included as separate entries are listed below:
*biodegradable waste, see organic waste; *commercial waste; *construction waste; *domestic refuse; *garbage; *hazardous waste; *household waste, see domestic refuse; *industrial waste; *organic waste; *problem waste, see hazardous waste; *recoverable waste; *recyclable waste, see recoverable waste; *sewage; *soil water; *solid waste; *toxic waste; *trade waste, see commercial waste; *waste water.
2 the metal ring-shaped component fixed at the base of a sink, handbasin or sanitary appliance, through which waste water passes via a trap into a drain; often supplied with a fitted plug; see waste coupling, outlet, pop-up waste, slotted waste, flush grated waste.

waste chute, refuse chute; a chute within a building into which waste material can be tipped, often with a collecting vessel or rubbish room at its base.

waste coupling, waste; a pipe fitting at a plug-hole or other appliance outlet for joining it to a discharge pipe.

waste disposal unit a powered device for shredding organic household waste prior to its discharge into a drain.

> **waste mould** in ornamental plastering, a mould which has to be destroyed in order to release the casting.

waster a masonry chisel with a flat, toothed or profiled blade for producing a rough stone finish.

waster

waste water water which results from household processes, cleaning and food preparation but not from WCs or industrial processes.
waste water appliance any sanitary appliance, basin, etc. for washing, fitted with a water supply and outlet connected to a waste water drain.

water bar, water stop; a strip of metal or plastic embedded into a sill or threshold to inhibit the passage of water.

water-based, aqueous; referring to paints, varnishes, adhesives and other similar liquids which consist of a solid or liquid dissolved, suspended or dispersed in water; water-borne specifically implies to liquids which contain a suspension of polymeric particles, which fuse together once the water has evaporated.
water-based paint any paint in which the pigment is suspended or dissolved in water; often emulsion paint.

waterboard see splashboard.

water-borne see water-based for explanation.

water burnt lime slaked lime which has been incompletely mixed with water giving a coarse texture.

water/cement ratio in concretework, the ratio of water to cement in the mix, regulated to affect its compressive strength.

water check an upstand or raised fillet in a flat roof plane to convey water away from vulnerable areas.

water closet see WC.

water content the mass of water per unit volume of mix, especially in concreting, plastering and painting.

water distribution system a system of pipes, vessels and associated devices through which water is conveyed to a building or area.

water engineering in civil and ground engineering, the design and control of the flow, treatment and disposal of ground and surface water.

water fitting in hot and cold water installations, a tap, valve or other fitting connected to a water supply to control its flow or draw water off for use.

water gain see concrete bleeding.

water glass see sodium silicate.

water hammer, reverberation, pressure surge; the sudden change of velocity of water in pipework inducing pressure waves which cause a hammering noise.

water heater a device or installation for heating water in a hot water supply system; see electric water heater, pressure water heater.
water-heating plant see boiler plant.

watering the addition of water to construction processes, planting, etc. by pouring, spraying or sprinkling.

water installation see water system.

waterleaf any decorative motif based on the stylized leafs of the water lily (called lotus in antique times); found in Roman and Greek architecture, and in different form in the capitals of medieval Byzantine and Romanesque architecture; especially the stylized unribbed broad leaf motifs found adorning capitals in Norman architecture.
waterleaf and tongue, waterleaf and dart; an ornamental motif consisting of a series of stylized leaves alternating with ovoid forms; same as or similar to leaf and dart.

waterleaf capital any capital embellished with water leaf designs, especially a Norman capital with a squared block whose lower corners are carved with a leaf motif.

Byzantine waterleaf capital, cathedral at As-Suwayda, Syria, 5th–6th century

water level, 1 hydrostatic level; a simple site instrument for measuring level differences between two points on a building site, consisting of a flexible tube filled with water.
2 the level at which the upper surface of water usually rests, whether in a gauge, waterway or the water table; see also next entry.

water-line a horizontal mark indicating water level when a cistern, storage vessel, etc., is full.

water main a main water distribution pipe from a water authority, to which individual users or buildings can be connected.

water meter a device for measuring the quantity of water for consumption supplied to a building.

water of hydration in concreting and plasterwork, the water that combines chemically with a hydraulic binder.

water outlet one of the points in a building where the hot or cold water supply can be drawn off for use; usually fitted with a tap or valve.

water pipe a pipe, usually of copper, through which water is conveyed to and within a building; part of any technical installation in which water is conveyed.

water pressure the force exerted by a mass of water either to propel itself, or exerting a load on a surrounding structure.

waterproof the ability of a material or construction to resist the penetration of water; see also water-resistant.
waterproof adhesive see water-resistant adhesive.
waterproof glue see water-resistant adhesive.
waterproofing admixture see water-resisting admixture.
waterproofing membrane a layer of impervious sheet material, usually bitumen-based, incorporated into flat roof construction to prevent the passage of water downwards.
waterproof ink ink that is not soluble in water once dry.
waterproof plaster, waterproof render see damp resisting plaster.

water reducing admixture, water reducer, plasticizer; in concretework, a plasticizing admixture included in the mix to increase workability with a lower water content.

water reed [*Arundo phragmites, Phragmites australis*]; see best reed, Norfolk reed.

water-repellent cement see hydrophobic cement.

water resistant, moisture resistant; a description or specification of a material or construction which resists penetration by, and chemical reaction with, water and is otherwise physically unaffected by contact with water; see also waterproof.
water-resistant adhesive, waterproof glue; any adhesive which maintains its bond strength when in contact with water.

water-resisting admixture, waterproofing admixture; in concretework, an admixture included in the mix to inhibit the absorption or passage of water.

water seal water in the vessel of a drainage trap to prevent the passage of foul air from a drainage system.

water seasoning see ponding.

waterside plant any species of landscaping plant which usually grows near water, but not necessarily in it.

water spout see rainwater spout.

water stain a translucent colouring agent for porous surfaces such as timber, consisting of a dye suspended in water.

water stop see water bar.

water storage tank see water tank.

water supply the supply of water for a building from a main; see also water system.

water system, water installation, water supply; the piped supply of water, pipe fittings, appliances, etc., for a building; see also hot water supply system.

water tank a closed pressure vessel for storing water for use in a water supply system; see cistern, reserve water tank.

water tap, faucet (Am), tap; a water fitting, usually attached to a basin, sink or bath, from which hot or cold water can be drawn off for use.

water test, hydraulic test; a test for leaks, unwanted openings and water flow in pipework by introducing water into a closed or restricted circuit at high pressure.

watertight referring to the ability of a material or product to keep out water.

water vapour small droplets of airborne water, usually condensation from boiled or evaporated water.

water void in concretework, small spaces or voids in hardened concrete containing excess water not bound by the hydration reaction, which may render the concrete susceptible to frost damage; see capillary space.

waterway in plumbing and drainage, any pipe, channel or vessel for conveying water.

watt abb. **W**; SI basic unit of power, 1 W = 1 J/s.

wattle see flaking.

wattle and daub, rad and dab, wattle and dab; a traditional form of infill walling construction for timber frames, etc. consisting of woven horizontal twigs, often willow, covered with clay or mud; Roman wattle and daub construction was known as opus craticium.

wave 1 a series of oscillations which transfers energy through a medium without the transference of the matter itself; see sound wave.
2 see wave moulding, Vitruvian scroll (wave scroll).

wavelength the measure of a length of a physical waveform, measured as the distance between two adjacent crests.

wave moulding, undulating moulding; an ornamental motif consisting of a pattern of undulating lines; see also oundy moulding, Vitruvian scroll.

wave moulding

wave pattern a paving pattern of small stones or cobbles laid in a series of undulating and interweaving curves, resembling guilloche ornament.

wave pattern

wave scroll see Vitruvian scroll.

wavy grain, curl, sinuous grain, tiger grain; an undulating grain formation found in certain hardwoods with an irregular cell structure; used in decorative veneers.

wavy paver a specially-shaped concrete paving unit with a wavy profile, laid to create a regular pattern.

wawa see obeche.

wax a solid greasy extract from vegetable, animal and mineral sources, used in the production of paints and varnishes, as a protective finish for wooden surfaces and as a binder in wax and pastel crayons; see beeswax, carnauba wax, paraffin wax.

waxing the application of a coating of wax to a surface as a finish.

WC, 1 water closet; a room containing a water closet suite connected to a drain and water supply; see toilet.
2 see WC suite.
WC cover a hinged lid for a WC seat.
WC lock see bathroom lock.
WC pan, water closet pan; the ceramic bowl in a water closet suite where human waste is deposited.
WC seat the hinged part of a WC suite which provides a place to sit.
WC suite, water closet suite; a device with a pan, seat and flushing cistern for collection and disposal of human waste; commonly simply called a WC or toilet.

wear the mechanical degeneration of a surface, construction or appliance due to continual use, exposure to the elements, etc.

wearing course, topping, carpet; in road and external paved construction, the uppermost layer of hardwearing material in contact with traffic, usually asphalt or concrete.

weatherboarding, siding; exterior cladding of horizontal or vertical sawn timber boards for a building frame, laid side by side or overlapping; types included as separate entries are listed below:
*bead boarding; *bead edged boarding; *board and batten cladding; *board on board cladding; *butt-edged boarding, see square-edged boarding; *ceiling boarding; *clapboarding; *close boarding; *colonial siding, see clapboarding; *diagonal boarding; *exterior boarding, external boarding, see weatherboarding; *feather-jointed boarding, see spline-jointed boarding; *featheredged boarding, featherboarding; *gapped boarding, see spaced boarding; *horizontal boarding; *log cabin siding; *matchboarding; *moulded boarding, see bead boarding; *open boarding, see spaced boarding; *open tongue and groove boarding; *reeded boarding, see bead boarding; *roof boarding; *round-edged boarding, round-arris boarding; *shiplap boarding; *sound boarding, see pugging boards; *spaced boarding; *spline-jointed boarding; *square-edged boarding; *staggered siding, see board on board cladding; *tongue and groove boarding, see matchboarding; *vertical boarding.*

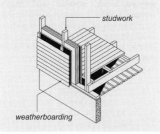

weatherboarding

weathered 1 referring to materials that have been in external conditions for some time with consequent surface deterioration such as discoloration, corrosion, exfoliation, etc.
2 referring to a sill or coping laid at a slope to allow for the runoff of rainwater.

weathered joint, weather joint, weather-struck joint, struck joint; a horizontal brickwork joint whose mortar is pressed in at the top, slanting in cross-section.

weathered pointing in brickwork, the making of weathered joints.

weather fillet see mortar fillet.

weathering the effect of rain, moisture, sun, wind and external pollutants on materials that have been in external conditions for some time; the discoloration, greying, and disintegration of untreated external wood surfaces due to the effects of the weather; see also brickwork weathering.

weathering steel steel with a high copper content, whose surface corrodes to form an oxide coating with good resistance to corrosion; marketed as Cor-Ten (see Cor-Ten entry).

weather joint see weathered joint.

weatherproof see weather resistant.
weatherproofing see roofing.

weather resistant, weatherproof; referring to a material, product or construction which is resistant to the attack of the elements.

weather seal see weatherstrip.

weather shingling timber shingles laid vertically as cladding for a wall.

weatherstrip, draught strip, draught excluder, weather seal; a strip of impervious material applied into joints between a door leaf or window casement and its frame to prevent the passage of water and air draughts, and as soundproofing.

weather-struck joint see weathered joint.

weather tiling see tile hanging.

web 1 part of a beam between the upper and lower chords or surfaces, which resists shear forces within the beam; the material, flange, etc. forming this.
2 the surface of a vault, see cell.

weber abb. **Wb;** SI unit of magnetic flux, equal to the amount of flux that produces an electromotive force of one volt as it is reduced to zero in one second; 1 Wb = 1 volt per second.

web reinforcement see shear reinforcement.

web saw see turning saw.

wedge in timber jointing, a tapered piece, used for tightening joints and fixings; see folding wedges, fox wedge.

wedge anchor, sleeve anchor, expansion bolt; a heavy-duty metal threaded fastener for fixing items to concrete or masonry, inserted in a bored hole then twisted to retract its wedged termination into a split sleeve, which expands to lock tight against the edge of the hole.

wedge anchor

wedge bead a small wedge-shaped machined timber profile used primarily as a glazing bead.

wedge bead

wedged joint any timber tenon joint using wedges driven in as tightening; see fox-wedged joint, keyed tenon joint.

wedged tenon joint

wedged scarf joint see keyed scarf joint.

weep-hole a gap for ventilation and to allow water to run out of the lower edges of cavity brickwork above a damp proof course, usually made by leaving the mortar out of vertical joints.

weevil [*Curculionidae*] a family of insects, some species of which cause great destruction to timber by boring; see eremotes weevil, wood weevil.

weft yarn in carpetmaking, weaving and tapestry, a crosswise thread woven onto the warp or structural threads, forming the main surface of the fabric.

weight batching, proportioning by weight; the measuring out of the component parts of concrete into the desired ratio by weight as opposed to volume.

weir a damming waterfall in a waterway to control the level of water upstream, often sloping downstream; in sinks and basins this type of device is often used to prevent overflowing; see following entry.

weir overflow a weir in a basin, sink or other vessel, essentially a lipped side-chute down which water can flow into a drain if the water level in the vessel rises too high.

weld 1 the act or result of welding; see welded joint.
2 a yellow vegetable pigment produced from the dyer's rocket plant [*Reseda luteola*].

welded fabric welded mesh, especially when used as concrete reinforcement; see fabric reinforcement.

welded joint, weld; a joint between metal components which has been formed by welding; see butt weld, fillet weld, lap weld.

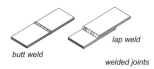

butt weld   *lap weld*

welded joints

welded mesh, welded wire mesh, welded fabric; a product manufactured from two sets of parallel steel strands or wires spot-welded at right angles to one another to form a mesh; used for fences, partitions, lathing and as concrete reinforcement; see fabric reinforcement.

welded mesh

welded plate girder see plate girder.
welded tuff see ignimbrite.
welded wire mesh see welded mesh.
welding the joining together of metal (and plastics) components by melting or pressure or a combination of both; see fusion welding, resistance welding, heat welding.

weld line the visible line along a joint, formed when two materials are welded together.

weld-on hinge a heavy-duty hinge for use with steel-framed doors and windows, of which one swivelling part is welded to the frame and one to the leaf or casement.

weld-on hinge

well 1 a traditional source of drinking and household water, a hole bored in the ground into which fresh groundwater naturally gathers.

2 shaft; a vertical void through a building to provide light and ventilation, or for a lift installation or staircase; see following examples: lift well; stairwell; light well; mat well.

well enclosure see lift well enclosure.

well module see lift shaft module.

welt, welted seam; a fastened seam or joint between two adjacent sheets of supported sheetmetal roofing; see welted edge, cross-welt, single-lock welt, double welt.

welted edge, single welt; the bent-over edge of a sheetmetal component, roofing, etc. to provide rigidity.

wenge [*Millettia laurentii*] a hardwood from Central and East African rainforests with dark brown-black, extremely tough timber; used for furniture, and exterior and interior joinery.

western framing see platform frame.

western hemlock [*Tsuga heterophylla*], see hemlock.

western larch [*Larix occidentalis*], see larch.

western red cedar, British Columbian cedar, giant cedar, Pacific red cedar, red cedar, giant arborvitae; [*Thuja plicata*], see thuja.

western white pine, soft pine; [*Pinus monticola*], see pine.

wet analysis in soil classification, the analysis of fine particular soils by allowing a sample to slowly settle in water and measuring the densities of the sediment at regular intervals.

wet and dry paper a fine abrasive paper used for sanding and smoothing; wetted with water as lubrication and to prevent the abrasive surface from clogging up.

wet area a bath, shower or other space in a building in which water can be expected to flow freely, requiring water-resistant finishes and specially located electrical fittings.

wet blasting, vapour blasting; the sandblasting of masonry with an abrasive and water, included to inhibit the spread of dust.

wet dash, dashed finish, harl, roughcast, slap dash; a rendered finish for external masonry in which mortar or plaster is thrown on a wall rough, either by hand using a trowel or by machine using an applicator.

wet-mix process a sprayed concrete process in which premixed concrete, including water, is projected through a nozzle at high velocity by a pump; see dry-mix process.

wet-pipe system a sprinkler system whose pipes are always full of water, connected to a permanent supply; see dry-pipe system.

wet removable wallcovering a wallcovering which can only be removed by scraping, having been treated by soaking in water or a stripper, or by steaming.

wet rubbing the smoothing of a surface with a fine abrasive such as sandpaper in the presence of water to clean and remove dust.

wet sieving the segregation of coarse concrete aggregate from finer particles by placing in water and sieving the mixture through a 0.075 mm mesh prior to use in concrete.

wet slaking the slaking of lime using an excess of water than is needed for hydration.

wetting the application of water to a surface or solid mass, as in curing of concrete, raising of timber grain prior to final smoothing, etc.

wettability the ability of a liquid to become immersed in a solid and make it wet.

Weymouth pine see pine.

whaler see wale.

wheelhouse a round prehistoric dwelling with a circular open central court and radiating walls defining interior space, occurring predominantly in Scotland.

wheelhouse, round house, Calf of Eday, Orkney Isles, Scotland, c. 100 BC

wheeling step, wheel step, wheel tread see winder.

wheel window see Catherine wheel window.

whetstone see hone.

whip in landscaping, a young slender-stemmed tree under two years old.

whispering gallery an acoustic space under a dome in which even a quiet noise such as a whisper may be heard all around its circumference.

white a general name for achromatic shades of colour; the lightest colour of the grey scale; white pigments included as separate entries are listed below:
*antimony white; *barium sulphate, see blanc fixe; *baryta white, see blanc fixe; *biacca; *bianco sangiovanni; *bismuth white; *blanc fixe; *blanc titane, see titanium white; *Bougival white; *ceruse; *Chinese white; *constant white, see blanc fixe; *Cremnitz white; *Dutch white; *enamel white, see blanc fixe; *English white, see whiting; *Flemish white, French white, see flake white; *Krems white, see Cremnitz white; *lime white; *lithopone; *magnesia white; *magnesium carbonate; *mineral white; *oleum white, see lithopone; *Paris white; *permanent white, see blanc fixe; *Spanish white; *St. John's white, see bianco sangiovanni; *strontium white; *terra alba; *Timonox; *titanium white; *white lead; *whiting; *zinc white.

white alder (Am); [*Alnus incana*], see alder.

white ant see termite.

white ash [*Fraxinus americana*], see ash.

white cast iron rapidly cooled cast iron, harder and more brittle than grey cast iron; used as a base for steel and malleable cast iron.

white cedar [*Thuja occidentalis*], see thuja.

white cement see white Portland cement.

white concrete a light-coloured finish concrete made with white Portland cement and a pale-coloured aggregate.

white fir [*Abies concolor*], see fir.

white lead a poisonous opaque white pigment used since ancient times in paints; composed of lead carbonates and lead sulphates.

white noise, white sound; in acoustics, unobtrusive noise of a wide range of frequencies introduced into a space to mask out unwanted background noise.

white oak [*Quercus spp.*], see oak.

white pine see pine.

white pitted rot, white pocket rot see red ring rot.

white poplar, silver poplar, abele; [*Populus alba*], see poplar.

white Portland cement, white cement; a Portland cement, made with iron-free raw materials, used to provide white cements and concretes.

white rot a general term for fungal decay which attacks both the cellulose and lignin of dead wood to leave a white stringy residue behind, causing serious decay and weakening of timber construction.

white rot fungus one of large group of fungi which cause white rot.

white spongy rot [*Antrodia serialis*] a brown rot fungus which causes decay in wooden posts and timberwork in poorly ventilated, damp underfloor spaces.

white sound see white noise.

white speck a form of white pocket rot which causes rice-sized cavities or specks in living timber; see also red ring rot.

white spirit, mineral spirit, petroleum spirit; a volatile liquid manufactured from the distillation of petroleum; used as a thinner and as a substitute for turpentine.

white spruce [*Picea glauca*]; a softwood marketed as Canadian spruce.

white walnut see walnut.

whitewash, limewash, whiting; a solution of lime or crushed chalk and water used to whiten masonry and plastered wall surfaces.

whitewashing see limewashing.

white willow, common willow; [*Salix alba*] a deciduous tree commonly planted in parks and gardens as ornament.

whiting natural calcium carbonate which is ground, washed and refined; used as an inert pigment in paints, a white pigment in water-based media, and mixed with oil to form putty; see also Paris white, whitewash.

Whitworth thread, BSW thread; a standardized range of screw threads whose dimensions are based on the number of threads per inch.

whole-brick wall see one-brick wall.

whorl decoration based on a spiral or swirling flower motif.

whorl

wicket door, 1 pass door; a small integral hinged door within a larger overhead or sliding door in factories or loading bays for the use of staff.

2 a gate to an area such as a churchyard or field.

wide plank flooring wide strip flooring; timber flooring consisting of wooden boards over 100 mm wide, or rough planks, laid parallel to one another.

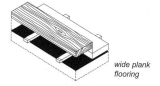

wide plank flooring

widestrip foundation a foundation type consisting of a wide rectangular concrete casting beneath a wall, requiring transverse reinforcement; used to spread the bearing of heavy loads over a larger area than with a normal strip foundation.

widestrip foundation

wiggle nail see corrugated fastener.

wild cherry the sweet cherry, see cherry.

willow [*Salix spp.*] a genus of hardwood bushes, shrubs and trees often planted as decoration and with light, resilient, pinkish white timber; its timber is used for furniture, joinery, panelling, cricket bats and artificial limbs, etc., its branches for holding down thatch and for basketwork.

Salix spp. – willow

Wilton carpet a thick and durable woven carpet which has its woven loops cut open.

wimble see gimlet.

winch, hoist; a lifting or pulling device in which a wire or cable supporting a load is wound around a drum or similar construction.

wind beam see collar beam.

wind brace 1 any structural member designed to maintain the rigidity of a structure against the forces of wind; wind bracing is a system of such braces incorporated into the structural frame of a building.

2 sway brace, purlin brace; in traditional timber frame construction, a brace at the angle of a rafter and a purlin to stiffen the roof against wind and other lateral loads.

windbreak in landscaping, a natural barrier or fabricated screen constructed to provide shelter from the wind.

winder, wheeling step, wheel tread; a tapered step in a spiral stair, whose front and back edges radiate from a single point, often attached to a newel post.

winder flight a series of winders or tapered steps which turn a corner in a turning stair.

winding stair see turning stair.

wind load the structural load on the external surfaces of a building imposed by the action of wind.

window an opening in an external wall of a building for allowing light into a space; may be a simple opening or an assembly of parts; see window assembly, window unit; types of window included as separate entries are listed below:
*access window, see access door; *aluminium-faced timber window, see composite window; *aluminium window, aluminium-framed window; *angel light; *arch window, arched window; *awning window, see top-hung casement window; *barred window; *bay window; *blank window; *blind window, see false window; *borrowed light; *bottom-hung casement window; *bow window; *casement window; *Catherine wheel window; *clerestory window, clearstory window; *composite window, compound window; *coupled light; *coupled window; *display window; *domelight; *dormer window; *double-glazed window; *double-hung sash window, see sash window; *double sash window; *double window; *factory glazed window; *false window; *fanlight; *fire window; *fixed light; *flanking window; *folding window, see sliding folding window; *French window, see casement door; *hanging sash window, see sash window; *horizontal pivot window; *horizontal sliding window, see sliding window; *Jesse window; *lancet window; *lantern light; *leper window; *light; *louvred window, louvre window; *low side window, see leper window; *marigold window, see rose window; *metal-faced window; *metal window; *offertory window, see leper window; *oriel window; *Palladian window, see Venetian window; *picture window; *pivot window; *plastic-faced window; *plastics window, see PVC-U window; *projecting window; *PVC-U window; *ribbon window, see window band; *rooflight, roof window; *rose window; *round window, roundel; *sash window; *shop window, see display window; *side-hung casement window; *side light; *sliding*

*folding window; *sliding window, sliding sash window; *steel window, steel-framed window; *strip window, see window band; *timber window, timber-framed window; *tip-up window, see horizontal pivot window; *top-hung casement window; *top light; *transom window, see fanlight; *triple-glazed window; *Venetian window; *vertical pivot window; *vertical sliding window, see sash window; *wheel window, see Catherine wheel window.*

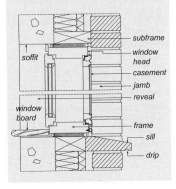

window acceptor see acceptor.

window apron that part of external wall construction beneath a window; see window back; a decorative panel or cladding beneath a window, either externally or internally.

window assembly all the parts of a window: the outer frame, sashes and glazing.

window back the internal lining between the bottom of a window and the floor; a window apron.

window band, ribbon window, strip window; a long narrow horizontal window, or windows grouped together in the same opening.

window bar see glazing bar.

window board, elbow board, sill board, window stool; a horizontal board fitted internally at the base of a window opening to form a shelf or window sill.

window box a container for decorative planting hung externally beneath a window, situated on a balcony, etc.

window buck see buck.

window casing in traditional timber window construction, the external covering surround for a window frame.

window component any part of a window, including ironmongery, frame, gasket or glazing unit.

window construction the materials, frames, glass and seals from which a window is made; the sequence in which they are assembled.

window former a formwork mould to create an opening for a window in a concrete wall.

window frame the surrounding construction for a window unit, which holds the glazing in place and in which openable parts are hung; see also casement frame.

window glass glass manufactured for use in glazing; either float glass or sheet glass.

window head the uppermost horizontal member of a window or window frame; see also window soffit.

window hinge a hinge for a window casement; a casement hinge.

window jamb a vertical side member in a window frame or window opening; see window reveal.

window lining facing for a window reveal which covers the join between frame and wall.

window louvre, grille; a construction or grille of slatted bars, profiles, etc. located externally in front of glazing to provide shade or as an external feature.

window opening an opening in the walling fabric of a building, into which a window assembly is fixed.

window pane a piece of glass fitted in a window frame.

window panel in prefabricated construction, a prefabricated wall unit which contains a fitted window.

window post in timber-framed construction, a vertical member to which the window frame is fixed at the edge of a window opening.

window reveal, window jamb; the vertical portion of wall between a window frame and the main wall surface of a building; the side wall of a window opening.

window sash see sash.

window schedule a written document listing and specifying the windows and associated accessories for a construction project.

window seat an interior window sill low and wide enough to be used as a seat, often situated in a bay window.

window shutter see shutter.

window sill 1 an external horizontal protruding construction at the base of a window for throwing off water.
2 the lowest horizontal member in a window frame.

window soffit the upper horizontal undersurface of a window opening.

window stay see casement stay.

window stile a vertical side framing member of a window casement.

window stool see window board.

window strip a draught excluder for a window.

window trim a strip of material around a window for covering joints between a window frame and surrounding wall construction.

window unit a prefabricated glazing component of glass in a frame, often containing openable casements, fittings, etc.

window wall, glazed wall; a wall, part of a wall, screen or partition made up partly or entirely of glazing; a wall which contains a window or windows.

wind shake a crack in timber, the segregating of the growth rings caused by wind strain during growth.

wind stop see draught excluder.

wing a longitudinal extension of a building, often containing additional or subsidiary spaces.

wing compass, wing dividers; in technical drawing, a compass with a lockable thumbscrew which can be tightened onto a protruding steel band to lock the arms to a set dimension.

winged knot see branched knot.

wing light see flanking window.

wing nut, butterfly nut, thumb nut; a threaded fixing for a bolt with wing-like protrusions for tightening by hand.

wing nut

winter bricklaying, cold-weather bricklaying; bricklaying in conditions where the temperature is around or below freezing point, requiring special measures to ensure good results.

winter concreting, cold-weather concreting; concreting which takes place when the average temperature is below 5°; special measures and mixes have to be used to prevent water in the fresh concrete from freezing.

winter hardy plant any species of landscaping plant which can survive outdoors during the winter months.

wire balloon a small wire basket attached over the outlets of external drainage and vent pipes, gullies, etc. to prevent blockage by fallen leaves, nesting birds, etc.; an outlet strainer.

wire brush a brush with bristles of steel wire used for roughing, scratching, cleaning up surfaces and removing scale from steel; other softer metals such as copper are sometimes used for the bristles.

wirecut brick a mass-produced brick manufactured by extruding clay through a suitably shaped die and cutting it into suitably sized pieces with a slanting wire.

wired glass, wired cast glass; glass which has been rolled with a reinforcing wire mesh in the middle.

wire drawing see cold drawing.

wire gauge a simple device for defining the gauge or diameter of wire, consisting of a plate with a number of calibrated holes or notches.

wire handle see wire pull handle.

wire lathing a galvanized wire mesh base tied at intervals to wall surfaces to provide a key for plasterwork and renderwork; wire-mesh lathing.

wire mesh any mesh product manufactured from two series of parallel metal wires woven, welded or crimped perpendicular to one another; types

included as separate entries are listed below:
*welded wire mesh, see welded mesh;
*woven wire mesh; *crimped wire mesh;
*fabric reinforcement; *conveyor belt mesh; *chain link mesh; *insect mesh, see insect screen; *hexagonal mesh, see chicken wire; *steel mesh.*

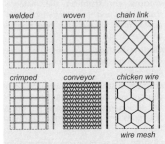

wire mesh

wire-mesh balustrade a balustrade with an infill of wire mesh in a steel or aluminium frame.
wire-mesh lathing see wire lathing.
wire-mesh reinforcement see fabric reinforcement.

wire nail a nail manufactured by mechanical stamping lengths of wire, obtainable in a range of lengths from 12–200 mm; see round wire nail (French nail), oval wire nail.

wire nail

wire pull handle a slender pull handle made from a single U-shaped metal rod.

wire rope see cable.
wire-rope balustrade see cable balustrade.
wire-rope clamp, wire-rope clip, cable clamp; a bolted metal ring fastening for clamping two lengths of wire rope together side-by-side.

wire-rope clamp

wire-rope thimble, cable thimble; a metal harness for strengthening a loop at the end of a wire rope or tensioning cable.

wire-rope thimble

wire saw a saw whose blade is a piece of wire coated with a hard abrasive material such as carborundum grit; used for cutting ceramics, metal and plastics.

wire strippers a scissor-like tool with notched jaws used for stripping the plastic insulation from electric cable.

wire wall tie any wall tie bent or twisted into shape from galvanized steel wire; also shortened to wire tie.

wire wall tie

wireway see skirting trunking.

wiring 1 the laying of cables and wires in an electric installation to form circuits; the circuits thus formed.
2 in reinforced concreting, the job of binding reinforcing bars together with wire.

withe, 1 osier; in thatched roofing, short flexible branches of willow, hazel, etc. twisted together to form a runner, with which thatch can be bound to rafters; also written as wythe; see brotch.
2 see leaf.

withe braiding see flaking.

with the grain in the milling of timber, the direction of cutting in which the grain of the piece is sloping downwards and into the milling edge.

woad a traditional blue dye made from the leaves of the woad plant [*Isatis tinctoria*].

wobble saw see drunken saw.

wolfram see tungsten.

wood an organic material made up of lignin and cellulose, obtained from the trunks of trees; called timber when used in construction; see list of species of tree from which softwood is obtained under softwood; see list of species of tree from which hardwood is obtained under hardwood.

wood adhesive, wood glue; any adhesive suitable for gluing wood.

wood-based core plywood core plywood with a core of wood.

wood-based panel product, timber-based board; a building or insulating board produced from wood products (particles, veneers, strips) pressed together with a binder or adhesive.

wood block flooring see end-grain wood block flooring, parquet.

wood board flooring, board flooring; traditional flooring of large solid timber planks laid side by side on joists.

woodcarving the working of wood with hand tools to create decorative mouldings, carvings and artifacts.
woodcarving chisel, carving chisel; a chisel used by a woodcarver for shaping, sculpting and decorative work; available in a variety of shaped blades for different uses.

wood cement chipboard, cement bonded chipboard, wood cement particleboard; chipboard whose particles are bonded together with Portland cement as opposed to resin.

wood-cement concrete, sawdust concrete; a lightweight concrete made with wood chips, wood fibres or sawdust as an aggregate.

wood cement particleboard see wood cement chipboard.

wood chipboard see chipboard.

woodchip wallpaper, ingrain wallcovering; cheap wallpaper with small chips of wood embedded in it to provide a textured finish.

wood cramp a wooden clamping device used by a joiner, tightened with a screw or folding wedges.

wood drill a hardened steel spiral-cutting drill bit, often with a positioning spur at its end, for cutting accurate holes in wood.

wooden block, wooden brick see nog.

wooden pile see timber pile.

wood-fibred plaster

wood-fibred plaster plaster containing an aggregate of wood fibres for increased strength.

wood-fired heating see solid-fuel heating.

wood float a wooden board with a handle, used for smoothing and levelling concrete and plaster surfaces; see cross-grained float, straight-grained float.

woodfloat finish a concrete surface which has been smoothed with a wood float.

wood flooring flooring such as wood-block, floorboards or parquet which form a hardwearing wooden surface; also called timber flooring.

wood glue see wood adhesive.

wood-inhabiting fungus any fungus which causes deterioration of wood.

wood joint a mechanical, glued or nailed joint between two or more wooden members; see timber joint for list of types of joints and illustrations.

wood key long round or square pegs driven into vertical pre-bored holes in log construction to tie adjacent courses together and provide lateral stability; a large dowel, peg or pin.

woodland plant in landscaping, any species of plant which usually grows in a shaded environment such as woodland or forest.

wood mastic a compound consisting of sawdust and a binder used for filling cracks and joints in timber boarding and boardwork.

wood mosaic, mosaic parquet; decorative timber flooring in wooden strips, usually less than 10 mm thick, laid in a repeated square patterned arrangement.

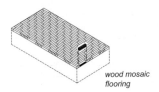

wood mosaic flooring

wood particle aggregate lightweight concrete aggregate manufactured from treated wood chips.

wood plastic composite, WPC; a wood product which has been impregnated with a plastic to restrict its moisture movement.

wood preservative see preservative.

wood primer a primer for sealing, preserving or pretreating a timber surface prior to painting.

wood roll joint see roll joint.

wood screw a screw for joining or attaching to pieces of timber, often self-tapping and with threads which are wider and steeper than those used for other purposes.

woodstain stain used on timber surfaces; see exterior woodstain.

wood strip flooring timber flooring consisting of matched wooden boards up to 100 mm wide laid parallel to one another; wood strip flooring most often refers to hardwood flooring placed on battens over a solid structural base; cf. floorboards; see solid parquet.

wood strip flooring

wood turpentine turpentine manufactured by the distillation of wood.

wood veneer see veneer.

wood wasp, horntail; [Siricidae] a family of insects whose larvae bore into softwood, causing weakening of the timber and loosening of the bark.

wood weevil, wood boring weevil; [Pentarthrum huttonii] an insect which causes damage to damp infected timber by burrowing.

woodwool slab a thick board manufactured by compressing a mixture of wood shavings and cement; used as thermal and sound insulation and cladding.

woodwork the panelling and decorative construction work of a building on site involving timber, carried out by a joiner; framing is usually referred to as timberwork; see also joinery, carpentry.

woodworking chisel a hand tool with a metal blade sharpened at one end for cutting and shaping wood; types included as separate entries are listed below:
*bench chisel; *bevelled-edge chisel, bevel edge chisel; *bruzz chisel; *butt chisel; *cant chisel, see framing chisel; *carving chisel, see woodcarving chisel; *caulking chisel, caulking iron; *corner chisel, see bruzz chisel; *dogleg chisel, see bruzz chisel; *drawer lock chisel; *firmer chisel; *floor chisel; *framing chisel; *gouge; *heading chisel, see mortise chisel; *hinge chisel; *joiner's chisel, see paring chisel; *lock chisel; *long-cornered chisel, see skew chisel; *mortise lock chisel; *mortising chisel, mortise chisel; *paring chisel; *parting chisel, parting tool; *pocket chisel, see butt chisel; *registered chisel; *ripping chisel; *sash chisel, see butt chisel; *scraping tool, scraper; *skew chisel; *swan-neck chisel, see mortise lock chisel; *turning chisel; *turning gouge; *woodcarving chisel.*

woodwork joint see wood joint, timber joint.

woodworm see furniture beetle.

woolly grain see fuzzy grain.

work 1 in mechanics, the distance through which a force operates, measured in Nm or Joules; one joule is the work required to move one newton through one metre; see energy.
2 see construction work for list of types of sitework; see also works.
3 see decorative work for list of types of ornamentation.

workability 1 the ability of a material, especially wood, stone, plastic material or metal to be easily shaped with cutting and abrasive tools; see also machinability.
2 the property of concrete that is able to be placed, pumped and vibrated with ease; see plasticity.
workability retention aid in concreting, an admixture included in the mix to increase the time during which the concrete is workable.

workbench a robust wooden bench containing in-built vices; used by a joiner in the workshop.

work face see face side.

working drawing, production drawing; a design drawing for the construction industry providing information about structure, components and materials in a project or development, from which it can be realized.

working life see pot life.

working model a rough scale model made of a design proposal at design stage to test ideas of space and massing.

working pile in foundation technology, any pile used as part of the foundation system of a building.

working plane in lighting design, a hypothetical horizontal, vertical or tilted plane for which lighting conditions are calculated; usually assumed to be 0.7 m above floor level for offices, 0.85 m for industrial applications.

working stress see permissible stress.

workmanship a required, specified or accepted standard of work on a building site, or by a craftsman.

work plan, work program see plan of work.

works 1 the body of building or construction work involved in a project; see also construction works, external works, temporary works (falsework), groundwork; see also work.
2 a manufacturing or production plant such as a brickworks or gasworks.
works contract see electrical works contract; minor works contract.
works cube test a test for concrete used for a particular development, carried out on site during the progression of work by destructive crushing of a sample cube.

worktop, work surface; the flat horizontal upper surface or component of a kitchen unit, desk, table, etc.

wormhole, borehole; a small round hole in wood caused by burrowing insects, evident as a defect in the surface.

worm's-eye referring to a view, scene or pictorial projection of an object as seen from below.

worse face see back.

woven carpet carpet manufactured by weaving crosswise threads known as weft onto suspended lengthwise structural threads; warp.

woven mesh see woven wire mesh.

woven roving see glassfibre cloth.

woven wire mesh a metal mesh product manufactured from two sets of wire strands woven together in an orthogonal arrangement, with square or polygonal openings between; used for security fencing and anti-intruder applications; see chain link mesh, conveyor belt mesh, chicken wire, hexagonal mesh.

woven wire mesh

WPC wood plastic composite.

wpm waterproofing membrane.

wrack poor quality timber, unsuitable for use in construction.

wreath ornament depicting a twisted ring of foliage, flowers, etc.

laurel wreath

wreathed column see spiral column.

wrecking strip a piece of formwork sheeting which can easily be removed to aid striking, and is destroyed in the process.

wrench see spanner.

wrinkle, riveling; a defect in a paint finish consisting of one or a number of small creases in the surface.

wrot see dressed.

wrought iron a form of ductile iron, fibrous in structure, which has little or no carbon added; easily forged and welded, and used for water pipes and rivets.

wrought nail see forged nail.

W truss see Fink truss.

wych elm [*Ulmus glabra*], see elm.

wythe see withe, leaf.

xenon a heavy, inert, gaseous chemical element, **Xe**, used in television and fluorescent tubes.

Xestobium rufovillosum see death watch beetle.

XLPE cross-linked polyethylene.

XPS see extruded polystyrene.

X-rays penetrating short wave, high-energy electromagnetic emission from naturally radioactive elements; their uses in construction include non-destructive inspection of welds and other opaque constructions.

X-ray resistant glass see lead X-ray glass.

X-ray resisting plaster, radiation-shielding mortar; plaster containing barytes, which is relatively resistant to the penetration of X-rays.

Y

Yankee screwdriver see spiral ratchet screwdriver.

yard 1 abb. **yd.**; imperial unit of length equal to 3 feet or 0.9144 m.
2 an area of land surrounded by, linked to, or belonging to a building or buildings.

yard blue, deal yard blue; blue stain occurring in timber in storage.

yarn a product manufactured of strands or fibres wound together and used in the fabrication of textiles.

Y branch a Y-shaped pipe fitting for merging pipelines in a drainage system.

yeast black a variety of vine black pigment.

yellow a colour of light from the visible spectrum which represents a range of wavelengths from 560–585 m; yellow pigments included as separate entries are listed below:
*alizarin yellow; *antimony yellow, see Naples yellow; *arsenic yellow, see king's yellow; *arylide yellow; *aureolin, see cobalt yellow; *auripigmentum, see king's yellow; *aurora yellow, see cadmium yellow; *barium yellow; *brilliant yellow, see Naples yellow; *buttercup yellow, see zinc yellow; *cadmium yellow; *Chinese yellow; *chrome yellow; *citron yellow, zinc yellow; *cobalt yellow; *gamboge; *Hansa yellow, see arylide yellow; *Indian yellow; *indanthrene; *jaune d'antimoine, jaune brilliant, see Naples yellow; *Kassler yellow, see Turner's yellow; *king's yellow; *Leipzig yellow, see chrome yellow; *massicot; *Montpelier yellow, see Turner's yellow; *Naples yellow; *Orient yellow, cadmium yellow; *Paris yellow, see chrome yellow; *patent yellow, see Turner's yellow; *permanent yellow; *puree, pwree, Indian yellow; *Royal yellow, see king's yellow; *strontium yellow; *terra merita; *transparent gold ochre, see Turner's yellow; *Turner's yellow; *ultramarine yellow; *uranium yellow; *yellow lake; *see yellow ochre; *yellow oxide of iron, see Mars colour; *yellow ultramarine, see barium yellow; *zinc yellow.

yellow birch [*Betula alleghaniensis*], see birch.

yellow cedar [*Chamaecyparis nootkatensis, Cupressus nootkatensis*] a softwood from Alaska and the west coast of North America; used in interiors, furniture and boat-building; not a true cedar (see cedar).

yellow deal commercial timber from the Scots pine tree.

yellowing the weathering of a colour, treated surface or material from white or clear to shades of yellow due to reaction with light, lack of light, heat or airborne pollution.

yellow ochre a dull yellow pigment in use since prehistoric times; yellow or yellowish-brown hydrated iron oxide produced from yellow clays.

yellow oxide of iron see Mars colour.

yellow pine, Weymouth pine, white pine; [*Pinus strobus*], see pine.

yellow poplar see tulipwood.

yellow ultramarine see barium yellow.

yew [*Taxus baccata*] the heaviest softwood in Europe with strong, resilient, reddish or purple-brown timber; used for decorative inlays and veneers, and the English longbow in the Middle Ages.

Y-form roof see butterfly roof.

yield 1 in mechanics, the permanent deformation which happens to a material, especially a metal, under stress beyond its elastic limit.
2 see concrete yield.

yield point, yield stress; in mechanics, the stress at which a body under stress suddenly deforms rapidly, shortly before failure.

yoke in traditional timber roof construction, a member joining and bracing the upper ends of rafters.

Yorkshire bond see monk bond.

Young's modulus see modulus of elasticity.

Y-tracery bar tracery found in Gothic churches of the 1300s, in which each mullion branches into a Y-shape at its upper end.

Z

zaffer, zaffre; an impure form of cobalt oxide used as a blue colourant for ceramics and glass.

Z-bar see Z-section.

ziggurat an ancient Babylonian, Mesopotamian or Assyrian tiered structure of sun-baked bricks, similar to a stepped pyramid on a rectangular or ovoid plan, with straight or spiral ramped access to a summit temple, approached by a processional way; also similar structures in early Central and South American cultures.

zigzag see chevron; indented moulding.

zinc a bluish-white, fragile metal, Zn, with good resistance to corrosion; used as a protective coating for other metals, especially steel.

zinc chromate a chemical compound, $ZnCrO_4.7H_2O$, used as a corrosion inhibitor and a yellow pigment in paints and metal primers; see also zinc yellow.

zinc chrome see zinc yellow.

zinc coated steel see galvanized steel.

zinc coating the corrosion protection of ferrous metals by application of a thin layer of zinc; the protective coating thus formed.

zinc green see cobalt green.

zinc oxide a chemical compound, ZnO, used in the manufacture of cements and glass, and as a white pigment; see zinc white.

zinc phosphate a paint used as a corrosive coating for priming steel.

zinc-rich paint a protective surface treatment for steel sheeting consisting of paint which contains 90−95% fine zinc powder; the application of this is often known as cold galvanization.

zinc silicate paint a two component paint used for priming steel.

zinc spraying, metallization, metal spraying; the application of a protective coating of atomized zinc to the surface of metals by spraying; aluminium is often also used.

zinc white, Chinese white; a harsh white pigment, often pure zinc oxide, used in paints for its properties of durability, colour retention and hardness.

zinc yellow, buttercup yellow, citron yellow, zinc chrome; a pale poisonous semi-opaque yellow pigment consisting of zinc chromate, no longer in use.

zinnober green see chrome green; zinnober is an alternative spelling of the mineral cinnabar.

zirconium a corrosion-resistant grey metal, Zr, with properties similar to those of titanium; used principally in the nuclear industry, but also in some alloys and for valve and pump components.

zirconium oxide a chemical compound, ZrO_2, used in the manufacture of ovens.

zircon white zirconium oxide used as a white pigment in ceramics.

zoisite a grey, green, pinkish or blue vitreous mineral used as a gemstone and for ornamental stone.

zoning in town planning, the division of a larger area of urban land into zones or districts, and the establishment of regulations within each zone to govern the scope of development with regard to land-use, height and volume of buildings etc. to form the basis of a local plan.

zophorus, zoophoros (Gk.); Lat.; a classical frieze with animal or human ornamentation.

Z-section a structural steel section, formed by rolling, forming or bending, whose uniform cross-section resembles the letter Z; sometimes called a Z-bar when of hot-rolled steel.